CORPORATE
FINANCIAL
ANALYSIS
—— *with* ——
MICROSOFT
EXCEL®

CORPORATE FINANCIAL ANALYSIS

— *with* —

MICROSOFT EXCEL®

FRANCIS J. CLAUSS

New York   Chicago   San Francisco   Lisbon   London   Madrid   Mexico City
Milan   New Delhi   San Juan   Seoul   Singapore   Sydney   Toronto

Contents

Preface

In today's global economies, spreadsheets have become a multinational language. They are the tools of choice for analyzing data and communicating information across the boundaries that separate nations. They have become an important management tool for developing strategies and assessing results.

Spreadsheets have also become an important tool for teaching and learning. They have been widely adopted in colleges and universities. They have the advantage of being interactive, which makes them ideal for teaching on the Internet as well as self-learning at home.

Corporate Financial Analysis with Microsoft Excel teaches *both* financial management *and* spreadsheet programming. Chapters are organized according to the essential topics of financial management, beginning with corporate financial statements. The text discusses management principles and provides clear, step-by-step instructions for using spreadsheets to apply them. It shows how to use spreadsheets for analyzing financial data and for communicating results in well-labeled tables and charts. It shows how to be better managers and decision makers, not simply skilled spreadsheet programmers.

The text assumes no more knowledge of computers and spreadsheets than how to turn a computer on, how to use a mouse, and how to perform the arithmetic operations of addition, subtraction, multiplication, and division. The first chapter begins with instructions for such basic spreadsheet actions as entering text and data, using cell references to express the relationships between items on spreadsheets and to calculate values, editing and formatting entries, and so forth. By the end of the text, the reader will have a working knowledge of a variety of financial functions available in Excel for such things as the time value of money and the payoffs of capital investments. He or she will also know how to use Excel's powerful tools for forecasting, doing sensitivity analysis, optimizing decisions, and using Monte Carlo simulation to evaluate risks. In short, anyone who studies the text will acquire a toolbox of spreadsheet skills that will help him or her understand and apply the principles of financial management—and be better prepared for a successful career in the business world.

Models Rather Than Solutions

Corporate Financial Analysis with Microsoft Excel shows how to create models that provide realistic information. Unlike pocket calculators, which are limited in their output, spreadsheet models can supply solutions over a wide range of conditions and assumptions. Models help identify what must be done to achieve desired results, determine the best strategies and tactics for maximizing profits or minimizing losses, identify conditions that must be avoided, or prepare for what might happen. Learning from models is cheaper, faster, and less hazardous than learning from real life. Spreadsheet models make this possible.

Managing Risks

Global competition puts a premium on the ability to handle risk. Although it may not appear as a separate item in a CFO's job description, risk assessment underlies all financial decisions. Risk is a high-stakes game of "What if?" analysis. *Corporate Financial Analysis with Microsoft Excel* shows how to use Monte Carlo simulation and other spreadsheet tools to gamble like a professional—without the cost. A bit of intelligent programming is the only ante needed to play the game. Spreadsheets help define the risks due to uncertain customer demands, the ups and downs of business cycles, changes by competitors, and other conditions outside a manager's control. In place of expensive experiments or learning in the school of hard knocks, you can use spreadsheet models to assess the risks and impacts of contemplated actions without actually taking them.

Teamwork

Increased worldwide competition and a market-driven economy have forced corporations to restructure their functional hierarchies in ways that promote teamwork. Rigid hierarchies that once divided finance, marketing, production, quality control, and other business functions are disappearing. In their place, functions and responsibilities are being shared in tighter alliances between areas of specialization. These changes extend outside corporate walls to subcontractors and suppliers.

The Enabling Role of IT

Information technology (IT) is the essential tool that enables a corporation to think globally and act locally. IT is the backbone of today's management information systems that corporations use to achieve higher levels of teamwork. Spreadsheets, databases, and special software are the "nuts and bolts" of ERP and other systems that link computer networks and telecommunication systems and that create extended teams.

Better Than Algebra

Most students are already familiar with spreadsheets by the time they enter college or complete their freshmen year. It is safe to say they understand the basic principles of spreadsheets better than those of algebra. Row and column labels transform the values in a spreadsheet's cells into concrete concepts rather than the abstract notations of algebraic formulas. They help one visualize the logical relationships between variables much better than equations with Xs and Ys. Spreadsheets simply provide a better way than algebra to learn any subject that involves understanding numbers.

Communicating

Spreadsheets are used to prepare tables and charts for making presentations that can be easily understood by others and that justify recommended courses of action. Spreadsheets are much more than sophisticated calculators. They are "digital storytellers" that can help you get your message across to others.

A Proven Text

Corporate Financial Analysis with Microsoft Excel is the result of the author's use of spreadsheets for teaching financial management over a four-year period. Classes have been conducted at both the graduate and undergraduate level. The text has been used for teaching in a classroom as well as for distance-learning on the Internet (via the CyberCampus system at Golden Gate University in San Francisco).

Skills Pay the Bills

Students have found that spreadsheets make learning easier and enhance their understanding of the complexities of financial management. The spreadsheet skills they have acquired have helped many of the author's students gain employment and earn raises and promotions. That is the success story related by numerous students who have studied *Corporate Financial Analysis with Microsoft Excel* and applied its teachings.

Understanding

Spreadsheets are outstanding pedagogical tools for both teaching and learning. They are akin to the popular Sudoku puzzles in having an arrangement of columns and rows. Like Sudoku puzzles, spreadsheets teach an understanding of the logical relationships between cell entries. Of course, a spreadsheet for a company's financial statements, or its month-to-month cash budget, or the projected cash inflows and outflows of expansions of corporate facilities is much larger and complex than a Sudoku grid. Students in the author's classes have repeatedly stated that financial modeling with spreadsheets helps them understand much better the inner workings of corporations and the strategies and tactics of business management for operating in worldwide markets. The interactive feature of spreadsheets, with immediate feedback for the results of their decisions in creating and using models, has provided challenges that keep students actively engaged in the process of learning. After more than half a century in the business and educational fields, the author finds spreadsheets to be a most useful pedagogical tool. Student response confirms that belief.

An Appreciation

The author has been blessed with an outstanding bunch of students in his graduate classes. Most were working full time to support themselves and their families while attending "distance-learning" classes on Golden Gate University's CyberCampus. They were mature, most with 10 to 20 years of real-life business experience. Their jobs ranged from entry level to managers and executives, with a few CFOs, CEOs, and vice presidents. They were eager to learn and invested a great deal of their time in doing the weekly homework assignments and posting their responses to my questions for discussion. They shared their experiences and how they coped with problems. Their places of business and their experience were worldwide—one of the advantages of teaching a class on the Internet. Their feedback has been invaluable in shaping and improving *Corporate Financial Analysis with Microsoft Excel*, The author is deeply indebted to them.

Francis J. Clauss
Golden Gate University
San Francisco, California

Introduction
An Overview of Financial Management

Before plunging into the creation of Excel models for financial management, it is worth a brief stop to look at the following:

- The functions and responsibilities of financial managers
- The position of financial managers and their functions in a corporate hierarchy
- The relationship of financial management to other functions, such as production and operations, marketing, sales, and quality control.
- The importance of teamwork and communications
- The role of information technology in financial management
- The role of spreadsheet models in financial management

Functional Specialization and Linkages

Today's corporations need many talents—more than any individual or business discipline can provide. Here are a just a few of the more obvious business functions that need different talents:

- Serving customers
- Manufacturing a variety of products
- Conducting research and developing new products

- Investing in facilities and equipment
- Controlling the quality of goods and services
- Ordering and receiving goods from suppliers.
- Distributing goods to worldwide markets
- Paying workers and suppliers
- Hiring workers with various types and levels of skills
- Collecting sales revenues from customers
- Managing short-term investments and borrowings

Individuals with the different talents needed to operate a business are organized in a hierarchy of departments. At the lowest levels, workers perform the specific functions and responsibilities assigned to them. At the upper levels, managers direct and coordinate the levels below them.

The concept of an organizational structure according to specific functions and responsibilities is simple. Implementing it can be difficult. At their best, business organizations are models of efficiency. At worst, they are wasteful bureaucracies. When bureaucracies run amok, the inevitable results are administrative delays, poor service, shoddy products, late deliveries, high costs, alienated customers, and eventual bankruptcy.

Think of a business as a chain consisting of links. Just as a chain is no stronger than its weakest link, so a business organization is no stronger than its weakest function. And just as a chain is a joining of many links to form a structural network, so business organizations are chains of separate functions joined together in a common enterprise.

Financial managers are an essential part of corporate networks. Their functions are inextricably linked to those of other managers, both financial and nonfinancial. Success depends on how well each does his or her job, and how well they work together as separate parts of the same corporate team.

As we develop financial models in the chapters that follow, keep in mind the concept of chains, linkages, and networks—and the need for all parts to work together.

Organizational Charts

Perhaps the quickest way to get a picture of corporate structures and the roles of financial managers is to look at an organizational chart. Figure 0-1 shows a typical organizational chart of the upper and lower levels of management for a manufacturing company. There are many variations on the chart shown, but this functional layout is generally followed.

A Board of Directors is elected by the company's stockholders to represent their interests as the company's owners. A corporate board is headed by a Chairman of the Board and typically has a number of standing committees, such as an executive committee, a finance committee, an auditing committee, a human resources and compensation committee, and others.

The president reports to the Board of Directors and is usually designated the firm's Chief Executive Officer (CEO). Immediately below the company president is the executive vice president, who may be designated the Chief Operating Officer (COO). An administrative vice president and an executive staff

Figure 0-1

A Basic Organizational Chart for a Manufacturing Company, which Shows Upper- to Middle-Management Levels of Various Functions

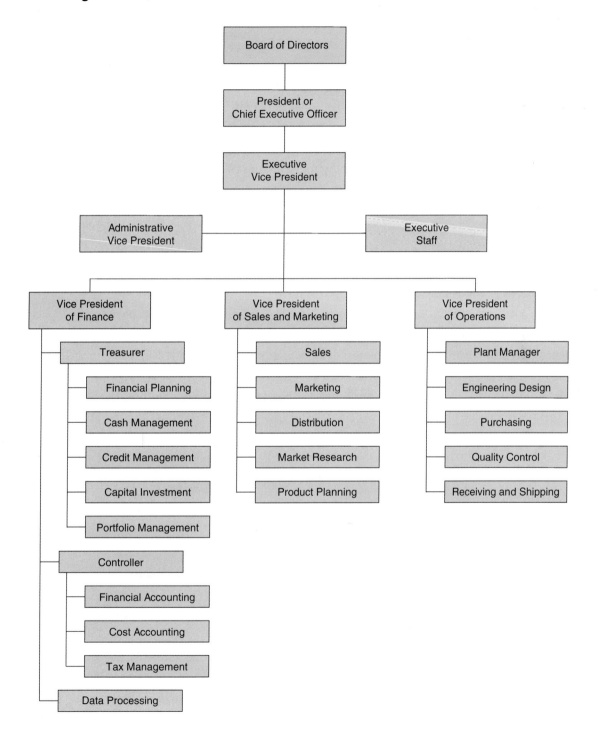

are common in large companies. A firm's legal counsel is usually part of the executive staff. Members of the staff have advisory positions rather than line or functional responsibilities.

The vice presidents of finance, sales and marketing, and operations are line positions that are responsible for actually carrying out the company's business. The vice president of finance is usually the company's chief financial officer (CFO). The essential functions of financial management are separated between those reporting to the company's treasurer and those reporting to its controller. Data processing is an important support function under the vice president for finance, although it is often a function at the vice-presidental level itself.

The details of how functions and responsibilities are organized vary from company to company and from industry to industry. Therefore, the organizational chart of any company will differ in details from Figure 0-1.

The structure shown in Figure 0-1 for financial management is common to many types of companies. The structures for sales and marketing and for operations, however, vary with the industry. For example, the vice presidents for sales or sales directors of hotels have separate functional managers under them for marketing to conference groups and to the tour industry. The sales directors of airlines have separate functional managers for passenger sales and cargo sales, as well as administrators responsible for reservations, schedules, and tariffs.

The organizations for companies in service industries also vary from that shown in Figure 0-1, which is typical for a manufacturing company. For example, the operating functions of hotels are divided between a front desk manager, executive housekeeper, chief operating engineer, materials manager, and security manager. The responsibilities of the materials manager are further divided into those for the food and beverage manager, restaurant and café manager, room services manager, and catering manager. Airline operations are divided into flight operations, ground operations, and flight equipment maintenance.

Anyone interested in managing would do well to study organizational charts. Study those of the company for which you work or would like to work. Understand the functions and responsibilities that go with each box, and how the boxes are related to each other. Do the same with the organizational charts of other firms that are available, especially those of competitors. Learn how companies are organized and how your functions and responsibilities interface with others. Companies value employees who know how to be members of their team.

A Quick Look at the F&Rs of Chief Financial Officers

Chief Financial Officers (CFOs) are responsible for their firm's financial management. Their functions and responsibilities (F&Rs) have three major components. The first is categorized as their **controllership duties**. These are **backward-looking** activities that deal with compiling and reporting historical financial information such as a company's financial statements. This information, in turn, is based on the firm's financial and cost accounting systems. Shareholders, investors, analysts, and creditors, as well as the company's upper and lower levels of managers, rely on the accuracy and timeliness of the data and reports for their actions. The second deals with **treasury duties**. These deal with the firm's **current and ongoing**

activities, such as: deciding the firm's capital structure (i.e., determining the best mix of debt, equity, and internal financing); deciding how to invest the company's money, taking into consideration risk and liquidity; and managing cash inflows and outflows. The third deals with **strategic planning**. This is **a forward-looking** activity. It includes economic forecasting of the future of the company and the impacts on it of future changes in markets, competition, and the general economy. It includes using forecasts to position the company for future profitability and long-term survival.

Teamwork

Organizational charts show the **division** of functions and responsibilities. Teamwork is what puts them back together and **combines** the parts into an effective organization. Success depends on how well the parts work as a team. Collaboration is more than just a good idea; it is the only way to survive the challenges that confront modern corporations.

As companies grow in size, the administrative levels between executives at the top and workers at the bottom grow in number. The administrative levels form a loop that routes directions and commands down to the line organizations, which actually provide service and goods to customers, and then collects information at the working level and passes it up in the form of reports to those at the top. Top-heavy structures discourage teamwork and reduce efficiency.

Entrenched ways of thinking or doing business are difficult to displace. A crisis is often needed to provide the impetus for change. World War II was such a crisis. It brought together the team that created the world's first atomic bomb, the weapon that hastened the end of World War II.

The code name for the atomic bomb's development was the Manhattan Project. It assembled a team of scientists, led by the brilliant physicist J. Robert Oppenheimer, and sequestered them in an isolated community in the Jemez Mountains of New Mexico. That community became the city of Los Alamos. The team was given the unlimited support of the U.S. government under the direction of Major General Leslie R. Groves. The incredibly complex technical details of the bomb's development need not be recited here. What is significant is that the members of the team surmounted all the problems and detonated the first man-made atomic explosion at the Trinity Site in New Mexico on July 16, 1945. The team accomplished this feat in only 28 months. To put this accomplishment in perspective, Detroit automakers still take three years or more to design a new automobile and get it into production.

The demonstration at Trinity Site was followed three weeks later, on August 6, with the dropping of the first atomic bomb on Hiroshima, Japan. On August 9, a second bomb was dropped on Nagasaki. Japan gave up the struggle five days later. On September 2, formal surrender ceremonies were held aboard the battleship USS Missouri that ended World War II.

What the Manhattan Project demonstrates so well is the power of interdisciplinary teamwork. That it took a wartime crisis to bring such a team together is also worth noting. As attempts to change peacetime private industry have since demonstrated, it often takes a corporate crisis to overcome the resistance to change administrative structures. The crisis needed to restructure an entrenched hierarchy into an efficient workforce may be a face-to-face confrontation with bankruptcy as the alternative.

Despite opposition to change, the concepts of interdisciplinary teamwork that succeeded at Los Alamos are being applied today to make corporations more effective and competitive. Their focus is on doing a job, not on maintaining an organization. The purpose of the organization is to do the work, rather than the purpose of the work is to justify an administrative hierarchy. Corporate restructuring is based on that simple concept—to determine how best to provide goods and services to customers, and then to organize the functions around the activities and processes for doing the work.

The concept of teamwork appears throughout this book. In real life, it is often disguised as a buzzword like "concurrent design" when discussing product design and the interactions between design engineers, manufacturing specialists, and procurement personnel. Financial managers use the term "activity-based costing" for accounting systems that identify the activities and organizations responsible for costs rather than collecting costs at an aggregate level, which rather defeats the purpose of cost control. (The importance of activity-based costing is discussed in Chapter 8: Cash Budgeting.) Other terms are "total quality management" or "TQM" when the focus is on product quality, and "Just-in-Time" or "JIT" when discussing inventory management. Learn the buzzwords because they are part of today's jargon. More than that, learn what they really mean, and don't let any huckster con you into a myopic view of how to apply them. Many with shortsighted understandings failed when they tried to implement buzzword concepts without recognizing their widespread consequences. The true essence of each is teamwork—truly corporate-wide teamwork that enlists personnel in the corporate enterprise regardless of their workplaces and to whom they report.

In terms of the organizational structure of Figure 0-1, teamwork means eliminating the up-and-down ladders of administrative levels that keep workers from working together. Instead of imposing vertical movements along "chains of command," the corporate structure is "flattened out" so that workers can move horizontally between organizations and work as teams.

Information Technology and Management

Computer-based management information systems (MISs) are management tools that facilitate teamwork. Their development can be traced to computer-based cost accounting systems and to the Materials Requirements Planning systems introduced into factories in the 1970s. Today's MISs are corporate-wide. They go by various names, such as Enterprise Planning Systems. In a very real sense, they replace the rungs on administrative ladders.

Figure 0-2 shows the Forecast-Plan-Implement-Control Loop that is an important part of an MIS. Each box contains a brief summary of what it should contain.

MISs collect detailed data on a variety of costs, how well services and goods satisfy quality requirements, how well customers are satisfied, and other criteria used to evaluate business operations. They accumulate the data in huge databases. Spreadsheets and special software are used to withdraw values from the databases and convert them to information, and then assemble the information in the form of reports, tables, and charts.

Figure 0-2

The Forecast-Plan-Implement-Control Loop of Management Information Systems

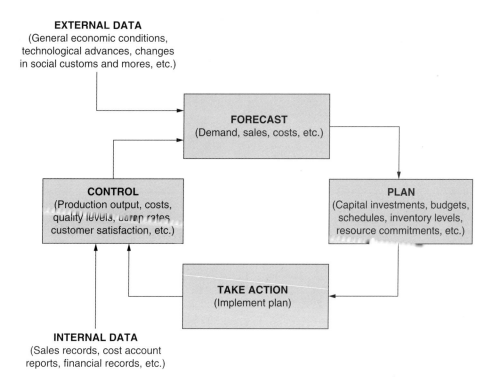

Information technology and MISs have expanded the boundaries of teamwork. It is no longer necessary or desirable to sequester team members in an isolated community that forces them to work together, as in the wartime Manhattan Project. Members of international teams now communicate in computer-based languages they all understand, draw data for analysis from common databases, and exchange information at electronic speeds.

Figure 0-3 is a simple example of the concept of using information technology to show organizational linkages and promote understanding and teamwork. It is a spreadsheet that shows the essential elements of a corporate income statement, and the results of different strategies to improve profits. (We will look at the details of income statements and other financial statements in the first and later chapters.) The spreadsheet is simply a matrix of rows and columns for organizing the information. To simplify discussion, the row numbers and column code are included in Figure 0-3.

Column B shows the base conditions. The company has annual revenues of $1 million (Cell B9). Its cost of goods sold (COGS) is 60 percent of the sales revenues, its selling and other expenses are 30 percent of the sales revenues, and its tax rate is 35 percent of its net operating income (Cells B5:B7). With these starting values, COGS is computed as $600,000 in Cell B10 (i.e., 60% of $1 million, or the product of the values in Cells B5 and B9) and the firm's gross profit is computed as $400,000 in Cell B11 (i.e., revenues of $1 million in Cell B9 minus COGS of $600,000 in Cell B10). Selling and other expenses are

Figure 0-3

Evaluation of Three Strategies for Improving After-Tax Profits

	A	B	C	D	E
1	IMPROVING THE "BOTTOM LINE" OF AN INCOME STATEMENT				
2		Base	Strategy 1	Strategy 2	Strategy 3
3			Increase Sales Revenue	Reduce Selling and Other Expenses	Reduce Cost of Goods Sold
4		Base	10%	10%	10%
5	Cost of goods sold (COGS), as percent of sales	60%	60%	60%	54%
6	Selling and other expenses, as percent of sales	30%	30%	27%	30%
7	Taxes, as percent of net income	35%	35%	35%	35%
8	Income Statement				
9	Annual sales revenues	$ 1,000,000	$ 1,100,000	$ 1,000,000	$ 1,000,000
10	Cost of goods sold	600,000	660,000	600,000	540,000
11	Gross profit	$ 400,000	$ 440,000	$ 400,000	$ 460,000
12	Selling and other expenses	300,000	330,000	270,000	300,000
13	Net operating income	$ 100,000	$ 110,000	$ 130,000	$ 160,000
14	Taxes	35,000	38,500	45,500	56,000
15	After-tax profit	$ 65,000	$ 71,500	$ 84,500	$ 104,000
16	Improvements from Base Conditions				
17	Increase in after-tax profit, dollars	na	$6,500	$19,500	$39,000
18	Increase in after-tax profit, percent	na	10%	30%	60%

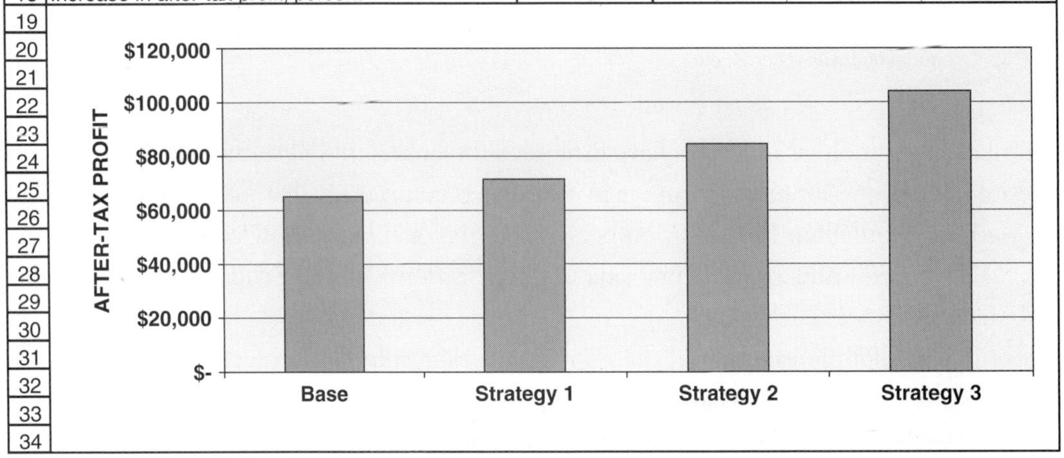

computed as $300,000 in Cell BB12 (i.e., 30% of $1 million, or the product of the values in Cells B6 and B9). Net operating income is computed as $100,000 in Cell B13 (i.e., Cell B11 minus Cell B12). Taxes of $35,000 are computed in Cell B14 (i.e., 35% of $35,000, or the product of the values in Cells B7 and B13). After-tax profit of $65,000 is computed in Cell B15 (i.e., net operating income in Cell B13 minus taxes in Cell B14).

Columns C, D, and E show the results for three different strategies the company might use to increase profit. Strategy 1 is to increase sales by 10 percent, strategy 2 is to reduce selling and other expenses by 10 percent, and strategy 3 is to reduce COGS by 10 percent. Implementing the first strategy requires actions primarily by the sales and marketing organizations, implementing the second requires actions by various organizations, and implementing the third requires actions by the operations organization (e.g., improve any or all of the functions shown in Figure 0-1 for which the vice president of operations is responsible). Note that a change of 10 percent in different functions produces significantly different changes in profits.

Although the example is intentionally simple, it illustrates some important concepts. First, financial results follow from actions in the various parts of a corporation. The results follow a path expressed by the linkages between functions on the organization chart of Figure 0-1. Second, the linkages between organizations and between actions and results can be expressed by entries in the cells of spreadsheets. Third, as a result of the first two, spreadsheets are extraordinarily powerful management tools—not merely for calculating results for given conditions, but also for analyzing the interactions between organizations and for evaluating the impacts of actions taken by different parts of a corporation. It also follows that **spreadsheets are powerful management tools** *for promoting teamwork across organizational boundaries, as well as powerful teaching tools for understanding business functions and their interrelationships.*

Communicating

Spreadsheets are much more than sophisticated calculators. Their value is as much for communicating as for calculating. They can help provide transparency into a corporation's workings. They are easily incorporated into reports and management presentations.

Successful CFOs need to communicate clearly, fully, and honestly. Failure to do that caused a number of corporate scandals in the recent past. Investors were misled by financial shenanigans at Enron, WorldCom, Global Crossing, and other major corporations that filed for bankruptcy. Between 1997 and 2000, for example, Enron reported an annual growth of 70 percent in its annual revenues and 35 percent in operating profit by moving debt off its books and other accounting tricks. Too late, lenders and other investors discovered that true revenues were lower than reported, debt levels were higher, and prospects for growth were less favorable. They began suing corporations and their executives, threatening them with large dollar penalties and prison terms. In addition to honesty, they insisted on better transparency into corporate performance.

Chief financial officers are no longer narrowly focused on the mechanics of finance. Duties that once were transaction-intensive are now knowledge-intensive.

Today's CFOs must be forward looking. They are responsible for planning that looks far into the future and across broader markets. They are strategic partners in negotiating global alliances, managing the risks of huge gambles, and organizing new corporate structures. They work closely with corporate boards, the investment community, financial markets, and government regulatory agencies.

Together with chief executive officers, CFOs are the faces of business. **They are the leaders for creating teams at the corporate and working levels**.

Spreadsheets as Tools for Financial Management

Life is complex. The famed naturalist John Muir likened the natural environment to a giant spider web. "Touch just one strand and the whole web vibrates in response," he pointed out. Corporations are also like giant spider webs of interlocking functions and responsibilities. What happens in one part affects all.

Today, the functional elements of large corporations are linked together by system of computers and software called enterprise management systems. The largest and best known of these are ORACLE and SAS. Such systems do the "heavy lifting" for managing corporate-wide operations. Yet, even in corporations with such systems, many managers have installed Excel on their office computers and use it for accessing information from corporate databases, analyzing it, and preparing reports.

Excel is entirely adequate for handling many business problems. It is more convenient, more accessible, and less costly than enterprise management systems. Indeed, using a large enterprise management system to analyze problems that spreadsheets can handle easier and faster is like using an elephant gun to shoot squirrels. Each has its proper place and use.

Excel is essentially a complete small-scale enterprise management system itself with substantial power. Unfortunately, its capabilities are largely under-appreciated and overlooked. Excel can handle much larger problems than most users recognize—including those who have used it for years. It is flexible and can solve a wide diversity of financial and other business problems.

Students in the author's classes have all, in fact, used Excel before, many for ten years or longer on their jobs. Yet none were fully aware of all that Excel offers for doing their jobs better and easier. Practically none had used it for doing Monte Carlo simulation or sensitivity analysis. Few knew how to use Excel to evaluate the impact of changes in corporate strategies or tactics. Few knew how to use Excel to calculate the risks for operating in an uncertain world. Many, in fact, had been unaware of even such simple Excel tools as sorting, conditional formatting, and regression analysis or the commands for the time value of money. You don't need an enterprise management system to do these things. What you need is to improve your Excel spreadsheet skills, which is one of this book's goals.

But sound financial management requires more than spreadsheet skills. This book is also intended to help you apply spreadsheet skills to improve your management skills.

As a financial manager, don't take a narrow view of your job. Recognize your relationship to others in the business. Understand their functions and responsibilities as well as your own, and how they're related. Understand the linkages in teamwork and how to make them. Use Excel in any financial analysis to help link the functions in corporate networks, just as enterprise management systems can do. And use Excel to **communicate** and **coordinate** as well as to **calculate**.

Chapter 1

Corporate Financial Statements

CHAPTER OBJECTIVES

Management Skills

- Identify the three key financial statements of corporations (i.e., the income statement, balance sheet, and statement of cash flows) and describe their contents and purposes.
- Follow the standard formats for organizing items on financial statements.
- Interpret the items on financial statements and recognize how they're related.
- Recognize when errors have been made in financial statements.

Spreadsheet Skills

- Create spreadsheets for financial statements.
- Organize the content of spreadsheets in logical formats.
- Label rows and columns to communicate clearly as well as to calculate correctly.
- Enter data values to show the basis for calculated values.
- Formulate and enter expressions to calculate values.
- Wrap text in rows or columns.
- Use cell references in expressions for calculated values that link the cells to other cells with data or other calculated values.
- Format values.
- Hide rows or columns of financial statements so that only selected ones are displayed.
- Link worksheets so that entries or values on one worksheet can be used for calculating values on another worksheet in the same workbook.
- Use Excel's Formula Auditing tool to examine cell linkages.
- Where possible, include tests that automatically detect errors or validate results.

Overview

A firm's financial health is summarized in three key financial reports: (1) the income statement, (2) the balance sheet, and (3) the cash flow statement. These reports summarize detailed information on a firm's financial actions during the preceding fiscal year and its financial position at the end. The Securities and Exchange Commission (SEC) requires every corporation to include these reports in its annual stockholders' report for at least the two most recent years.

Annual statements cover one-year periods ending at a specified date. For most firms, the ending date is the end of the calendar year. Many large corporations, however, operate on 12-month cycles (or fiscal years) that end at times other than December 31. In addition to annual reports to stockholders, corporations usually prepare monthly statements to guide a corporation's executives, as well as quarterly statements that must be made available to stockholders of publicly held corporations.

Financial statements are based on values from a firm's cost accounting system. The statements follow the generally accepted accounting principles (GAAP) recommended by the Financial Accounting Standards Board (FASB), which is the accounting profession's rule-setting body. In addition to the financial statements, annual stockholders' reports usually contain the president's letter and historical summaries of key operating statistics and ratios for the past five or ten years.

The information in financial statements is used in several ways. Regulators, such as federal and state security commissions, use it to enforce compliance by providing proper and accurate disclosures to stockholders and investors. Lenders or creditors use the reports to evaluate the credit rating of firms and their ability to meet scheduled payments on existing or contemplated loans. Investors base their decisions to buy, sell, or hold the corporation's stock on the information in the reports. Corporate financial managers use the information to ensure compliance with regulatory requirements, to satisfy creditors and shareholders, and to monitor the firm's performance. They also use the information to determine the value of other firms they are thinking of buying, or the value of their own firms as a basis for negotiating a selling price. Employees peruse financial statements to assess how well their firm is doing and to compare its current performance with earlier periods. Corporate executives and boards of directors often view their annual stockholders' reports as tools for marketing the company and its products and for building or improving their image.

This chapter shows how to use Excel to prepare financial statements. It defines the meanings of the financial entries and identifies the formulae for using data values of some to calculate values for others. The printouts in this chapter include column headings, row numbers, and grid lines to help identify the cells where the formulas are entered. These can be eliminated when printing the spreadsheets in reports. (Use the Sheet tab on File/Page Setup to show or hide them.)

> Notes are included below the title of many spreadsheet printouts in order to identify key cell entries and give other information. These programming notes are intended to help readers understand the modeling process, the expressions for calculating values, and the links between cells.

The three financial statements have interlocking relationships to one another. Excel makes it possible to link cell entries in one worksheet to cell entries in another so that changing data values on either worksheet changes related entries on the other.

Preparing a spreadsheet begins with understanding its purpose: who will read it, what items it will contain, and how the items are related. Values for the items will be either data values or calculated values.

> **Some Important Steps for Creating Spreadsheet Models**
> - Provide a short, descriptive title at the top.
> - Enter short, descriptive labels for the columns and rows. Include any units in which the values will be expressed (e.g., $ million, $/day, etc.).
> - Enter the known or data values. **Check the entries to ensure the data has been entered correctly.**
> - Enter expressions for calculated values. **Check the entries to ensure the expressions and calculated values are correct**. If you understand the logical relationships between items on a worksheet, you will find it easier to recognize and correct errors as they are made rather than locating errors and correcting them after a complex worksheet has been completed.

The Income Statement

Income statements provide a financial summary of a firm's operation for a specified period, such as one year ending at the date specified in the statement's title. They show the total revenues and expenses during that time. An income statement is sometimes called a "profit and loss statement," an "operating statement," or a "statement of operations." Essentially, it tells whether or not the firm is making money.

Note that the income statement does not show cash flows or reflect the company's cash position. (The cash flow statement does that.) Certain items, such as depreciation, are an expense although they do not involve a cash outlay. Some items, such as the sale of goods or services, are recognized as income even though buyers have not yet paid for them. Other items, such as purchased materials, are recognized as expenses even though the firm has not yet paid for them. Such income and expense items are recorded when they are accrued (e.g., when sold goods are shipped), not when cash actually flows.

General Format

Figure 1-1 shows the basic elements of an annual income statement. It indicates the essential information that must be provided and the standard format. Annual income statements for large corporations are organized in the same format as Figure 1-1. However, they often have a number of subdivisions with additional detail for selected items.

The income statement is organized into several sections. The upper section (Rows 4 to 15 of Figure 1-1) reports the firm's revenues and expenses from its principal operations. Below that (Rows 16 to 24) are nonoperating items, such as financing costs (e.g., interest expense) and taxes.

The so-called "bottom line" (Row 25) reports the firm's net income, or the net earnings that are available to the firm's stockholders. Holders of preferred stock are first in line to be paid from the firm's net income. They receive dividends in an amount that is fixed by the terms of the preferred stock. What is left is the "net earnings available for common stockholders" (Row 27). The last item is also expressed as the earnings per share (Row 28).

Figure 1-1

Income Statement for One Year

	A	B
1	**ABC COMPANY**	
2	**Income Statement for the Year Ended December 31, 20X2**	
3		**$ thousand (except EPS)**
4	Total Operating Revenues (or Total Sales Revenues)	2,575.0
5	Less: Cost of Goods Sold (COGS)	1,150.0
6	**Gross Profits**	**1,425.0**
7	Less: Operating Expenses	
8	Selling Expenses	275.0
9	General and Administrative Expenses (G&A)	225.0
10	Depreciation Expense	100.0
11	Fixed Expenses	75.0
12	**Total Operating Expenses**	**675.0**
13	**Net Operating Income**	**750.0**
14	Other Income	20.0
15	**Earnings before Interest and Taxes (EBIT)**	**770.0**
16	Less: Interest Expense	
17	Interest on Short-Term Notes	10.0
18	Interest on Long-Term Borrowing	50.0
19	**Total Interest Expense**	**60.0**
20	**Pretax Earnings (Earnings before Taxes, EBT)**	**710.0**
21	Less: Taxes	
22	Current Tax	160.0
23	Deferred Tax	124.0
24	Total Tax (rate = 40%)	284.0
25	**Net Income (Earnings after Taxes, EAT)**	**426.0**
26	Less: Preferred Stock Dividends	95.0
27	**Net Earnings Available for Common Stockholders**	**331.0**
28	Earnings per Share (EPS), 100,000 shares outstanding	$3.31
29	Retained Earnings	220.0
30	Dividends Paid to Holders of Common Stock	111.0

Cell entries and notes

Italicized values in Cells B4, B5, B8, B9, B10, B11, B14, B17, B18, B22, B26, and B29 are data entries. They are entered as values rounded to the nearest whole dollar (e.g., the entry in Cell B4 is 2750000) and formatted in thousands with one decimal point. Values in the other cells are calculated by the following entries:

B6: =B4-B5 "Gross Profits" equals "Total Operating Revenues" minus "COGS."
B12: =SUM(B8:B11) This command adds entries in cells B8:B11.
B13: =B6-B12 This term is also known as "Net Operating Profits."
B15: =B13+B14
B19: =B17+B18
B20: =B15-B19 Also known as "Net Profits (or Earnings) before Taxes."
B23: =B24-B22 "Deferred Tax" equals "Total Tax" minus "Current Tax."
B24: =0.40*B20 "Total Tax" equals 40% of EBT.
B25: =B20-B24 Also known as "Net Profits (or Earnings) after Taxes."
B27: =B25-B26
B28: =B27/100000 Per share value is based on 100,000 shares.
B30: =B27-B29

Firms generally divide the net earnings available for common stockholders between retained earnings and dividends paid to common stockholders (Rows 29 and 30). Retained earnings are the amount held by the company for future uses. They are the difference between the net earnings available and the amount paid to common stockholders. Retained earnings accumulate from year to year and are often used for repaying loans or financing new facilities or equipment.

Some Guides for Using Excel for Financial Modeling

Financial statements are only a few of the many reports used for communicating important information about a firm's activities. You will meet others in the chapters that follow.

Communicating as Well as Calculating

As you use Excel to create financial models, keep the importance of communicating before you. Don't think of an Excel spreadsheet as simply a sophisticated tool for calculating. Think of it also as a tool for communicating with others. As a communication tool, it must satisfy the four Cs of good communications: **Clear, Correct, Complete, and Concise**.

Spreadsheets are widely used for making presentations at business meetings and for presenting information in management reports. To be useful, they must be understandable to others—that is, to the attendees at meetings or the readers of reports. Because you may not have an opportunity to explain your work to others, your spreadsheets should be able to "stand on their own." Well-designed spreadsheets make it easy for others to understand them. Another benefit of spreadsheets is that they can help the programmer recognize and correct errors.

Titles

Add short descriptive titles at the tops of worksheets. Those shown in Figure 1-1 identify the company and the type and date of the financial statement. The first is typed in Cell A1 and the second in Cell A2. After typing, each title can be centered across Columns A and B by dragging the mouse from Column A to Column B and clicking on the "Merge and Center" button on the format toolbar. You can use the "Bold" button to emphasize the text. You can use the "Fill Color" button to add color to the cells, and the "Font Color" button to change the color of the type.

You can change the font type and size to help distinguish titles from other entries by using the "Font" and "Font Size" buttons near the left of the format toolbar.

Row and Column Labels

It is usually good practice to type row and column labels before entering data values or making calculations. Labels should be short, descriptive, and accurate. Avoid labels that can be misunderstood. Expunge ambiguities. If you don't understand something, don't cover it up with a label that could be misleading. A good rule to follow is this: "It is not enough to use labels that are so clear that others can easily understand them. Labels must be so clear that others can**NOT** easily **MIS**understand them." (Think Murphy's Law: "If anything can go wrong, it will.")

It is important that labels include not only a title but also any units. For example, the label in Cell B3 identifies the entries below as being expressed or measured in thousands of dollars, except for the value for earnings per share (Cell B28). The entry in Cell B4 is actually 2,575,000 dollars.

Excel's format toolbar contains a number of buttons and pull-down menus that are useful for formatting worksheets. Skim over the following sections on first reading, and return to them when you need help to format a worksheet.

Long Row Labels

Many row labels will be too long to fit into the default width of the columns, which is 8.43 units. There are several ways to remedy this:

1. Move the mouse's pointer to the separation line with the next column at the top of the spreadsheet, hold the left button down, and drag the line far enough to the right for the label to fit.
2. Double-click on the separation line with the next column at the top of the spreadsheet. This will change the width of the column to the minimum needed to fit the longest label in the column.
3. Hold the mouse's left button down and drag it over the column or columns whose width is to be changed. Click on Format/Column/Width and enter the value for the column width. (This assumes you know beforehand how wide you want to make the column(s) selected.)
4. Wrap the text so that it appears on more than one line. (That is more than one *line*, not more than one *row*.) To do this, click on the cell with the label to activate it, select "Alignment" from the Format menu on the format toolbar, and then click on the Wrap text button, as shown in Figure 1-2.

Figure 1-2

Alignment Dialog Box for Formatting Cells with Option for Wrapping Text Selected

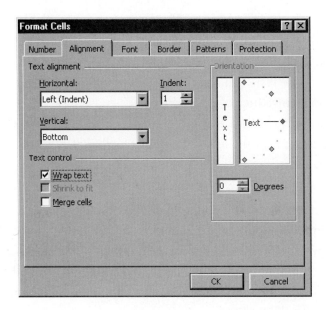

Long Column Labels

Long column headings, such as "$ thousand (except EPS)" can be shown in a single narrow column by wrapping the text so that it occupies two lines or more in a single cell. To wrap text, click on the cell and use Format/Cells/Alignment/Wrap text. Adjust row height, as necessary.

Boldfacing and Adding Color for Emphasis

To boldface information to stress its importance, click on the cells, rows, or columns with the information and then click on the **B (Bold)** button on the format toolbar or press the Ctrl/B keys. Add color or shading by selecting the cells, rows, or columns and clicking on the selection on the "Fill Color" button menu, which is also located on the format menu. *Caution:* Too much color can be distracting. Dark backgrounds make it difficult to read labels or values with black fonts.

Distinguishing between Data and Calculated Values

For discussion purposes and to distinguish them from calculated values, all data entries in Figure 1-1 have been italicized. This is done by selecting the data cell or cells and clicking the *I (Italic)* button on the format toolbar. You can also use color to distinguish between data and calculated values. (The author's use of italics for data values is a personal choice. You may wish to use a different method. If you use italics, you can always change back to a normal font for printing the final copy of the spreadsheet.)

Formatting Values

Except for earnings per share, dollar values are entered with as many significant figures as available in the data. They are then usually formatted as either thousands or millions. For example, an entry of 12,345,678 might appear as 12,346 or as 12,346.78 if the income statement is given in thousands of dollars. You can use a custom format to express entries in thousands or millions of dollars. Formatting large values to minimize the number of decimal places that are displayed makes it easier to focus on what is significant. Even though some of the significant figures are not displayed, the precise value is carried in the cell so that there is no loss of accuracy by rounding the values for display.

Custom Formatting

Open a new spreadsheet and enter the value 12,345,678 in a convenient cell. Click on the cell and then click on Format on the menu bar. Select "Custom" from the list of categories on the Format menu and type #,###,;(#,###,) in the Type box, as shown in Figure 1-3. This will cause the number 12,346 to appear in the cell, although the actual value is 12,345,678. (Note that the last digit shown has been rounded to 6 rather than 5.) If you use a minus sign so that the value in the cell is minus 12,345,678, the formatted value will appear as (12,346), with the value in parentheses. Try it.

If you wish to include one decimal place in the formatted values, change the custom format to #,###.0,;(#,###.0,). For two decimal places, change the custom format to #,###.00,;(#,###.00,). If you wish to add a dollar sign to the formatted value, with zero, one, or two decimal places, change the custom format to $#,###,;($#,###,), $#,###.0,;($#,###.0,) or $#,###.00,;($#,###.00,). Note the commas that are

Figure 1-3
_____

Dialog Box for Formatting Cell Values to Thousands
(With this format, the actual value entered in a cell will NOT be changed but it will APPEAR to have been divided by 1000.)

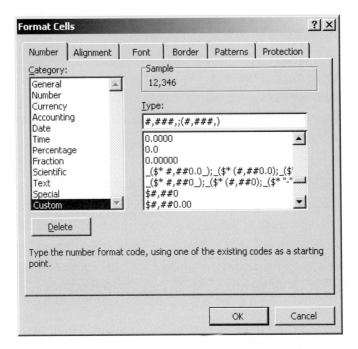

parts of the formats. Be sure to include them. You can use the "Format Painter" button on the standard toolbar to copy the format(s) of a cell (or range of cells) to another cell (or range).

You can also use the "Increase decimal" or "Decrease decimal" buttons on the formatting toolbar to increase or decrease the number of decimal places shown on the worksheet.

Indenting Subtopics in a List

Use the "Increase Indent" button on the format menu to indent selected labels or other text. You can also indent by pressing the spacebar before the text, but the indent button makes it easier.

Centering Entries

Use the "Center" button on the toolbar to center labels in the middle of a cell. Use the "Merge and Center" button to center labels in the middle of a group of cells next to one another.

Sheet Orientation

Sheet orientation can be either portrait or landscape. Portrait is preferable for spreadsheets that will be printed in reports because it avoids a reader having to twist the page in order to read it. Landscape is usually preferable for spreadsheets that will be used on projected slides.

Documenting

Documents often need to be traced back to their source. Adding your name and the date makes it easier to do this. A good place for the creator's name and date is at the bottom of the worksheet on the right side. Use =today() to add the date in the cell to the right of the cell with your name. Or use the Header/Footer dialog box in the Page Setup menu to add this information at the top or bottom of printed copies of your worksheet. Another way of documenting a worksheet is to include a formal documentation sheet as the first sheet in the folder.

Column Headings and Row Numbers

In order to refer to particular cells in the spreadsheets shown in the text, both the row numbers and the alphabetic column headings are included, as in Figure 1-1. These can be removed before printing the worksheets in corporate reports. To do this, change the settings in the File/Page Setup/Sheet tab dialog box to omit them. Figure 1-4 shows the result.

Figure 1-4

Income Statement with Column Headings, Row Numbers, and Gridlines Omitted

ABC COMPANY	
Income Statement for the Year Ended December 31, 20X2	
	$ thousand (except EPS)
Total Operating Revenues (or Total Sales Revenues)	2,575.0
Less: Cost of Goods Sold (COGS)	1,150.0
Gross Profits	**1,425.0**
Less: Operating Expenses	
Selling Expenses	275.0
General and Administrative Expenses (G&A)	225.0
Depreciation Expense	100.0
Fixed Expenses	75.0
Total Operating Expenses	**675.0**
Net Operating Income	**750.0**
Other Income	20.0
Earnings before Interest and Taxes (EBIT)	**770.0**
Less: Interest Expense	
Interest on Short-Term Notes	10.0
Interest on Long-Term Borrowing	50.0
Total Interest Expense	**60.0**
Pretax Earnings (Earnings before Taxes, EBT)	**710.0**
Less: Taxes	
Current Tax	160.0
Deferred Tax	124.0
Total Tax (rate = 40%)	284.0
Net Income (Earnings after Taxes, EAT)	**426.0**
Less: Preferred Stock Dividends	95.0
Net Earnings Available for Common Stockholders	**331.0**
Earnings per Share (EPS), 100,000 shares outstanding	$3.31
Retained Earnings	220.0
Dividends Paid to Holders of Common Stock	111.0

The Items on an Income Statement

Once you have created a skeleton of the spreadsheet with a title, column headings, and row labels, you are ready to flesh it out with data and calculated values. These are the "meat and potatoes" of what the spreadsheet is all about. You may, of course, edit the spreadsheet later to improve your first attempt at creating the skeleton.

Cell entries will include both data values and expressions for calculated values. In Figure 1-1, the entries in Cells B4, B5, B8, B9, B10, B11, B14, B17, B18, B22, B26, and B29 are data values and are italicized to distinguish them from the calculated values in other cells. *Note that the number you enter in Cell B4, for example, is NOT 2575.0, as it appears in Figure 1-1. The actual number entered is 2,575,000. It appears as 2,575.0 because it has been custom formatted that way.* Even though the number appears as 2,575.0 on the spreadsheet, the column heading makes it clear that the actual values in the column have been formatted to appear as thousands of dollars (except for earnings per share, EPS).

Large corporations usually format values on their financial statements to millions rather than thousands of dollars. (See the preceding section for details on how to custom format numbers.)

Total Operating Revenues (or *Total Sales Revenues*) is the income earned from the firm's operations during the fiscal year reported. Note that revenues are reported when they are *earned*, or *accrued*, even though no cash flow has necessarily occurred (as, for example, when goods are sold for credit or when services are rendered before being paid for).

The *Cost of Goods Sold* (COGS) for a retail firm is the amount paid to wholesalers or other suppliers for the goods that the firm resells to its customers. The cost of goods sold for a factory includes the cost of direct production labor and materials used to manufacture the goods. Direct production labor includes that used in fabricating parts and assembling them, along with purchased components, into the factory's finished goods. Material cost includes the costs of raw materials that are fabricated into parts and the costs of purchased parts and components that are assembled into products.

The cost of goods sold often involves both fixed and variable costs. In this case, the dollar value of the fixed cost remains constant from one year to the next, and only the dollar value of the variable cost would be estimated as a percentage of forecast sales.

Gross Profit is the amount left after paying for the goods that were sold. It is calculated in Figure 1-1 by the entry =B4-B5 in Cell B6.

Operating Expenses are those that are the cost of a firm's day-to-day operations rather than a direct cost for making a product. This category includes a number of items that are entered as data values. *Selling Expenses* are the costs for marketing and selling the company's products, such as advertising costs and the salaries and commissions paid to sales personnel. *General and Administrative Expenses* (G&A) include the salaries of the firm's officers and other management personnel and other costs that are included in the firm's administrative expenses (e.g., legal and accounting expenses, office supplies, travel and entertainment, insurance, telephone service, and utilities). *Fixed Expenses* include such costs as the leasing of facilities or equipment.

Depreciation Expenses are the amount by which the firm reduced the book value of its capital assets during the preceding year. Because the purposes of financial reporting are often different from those for tax legislation, the depreciation method a firm uses for *financial* reporting is not necessarily the same as what it uses for *tax* reporting. Firms are allowed to use a variety of depreciation methods for financial reporting, whereas they are required to use the Modified Accelerated Cost Recovery System (MACRS) mandated by the Internal Revenue Code for tax purposes and for reporting on the Income Statement. (Depreciation methods, including MACRS, are discussed in Chapter 11: Depreciation and Taxes. MACRS generally provides the fastest write-off and greatest reduction in taxable income. Because it usually gives the best cash flows, MACRS is the method that is most often used by financial managers for calculating *tax liability*).

Total Operating Expense is the sum of the individual expenses. It is calculated by the entry =SUM(B8:B11) in Cell B12.

Net Operating Income (also called *Net Operating Profit*) is what is left after subtracting the total operating expense from the gross profits. It is calculated by the entry =B6-B12 in Cell B13. (If the result is a negative value, it is called a *Net Operating Loss* and can be used to reduce the firm's taxes.)

Other Income is income derived from nonoperating sources. It is entered as a data value in Cell B14 of Figure 1-1.

Earnings before Interest and Taxes (EBIT, also known as *Pretax Income*) is the difference between income and the sum of the operating expenses. It is calculated by the entry =B13+B14 in Cell B15.

Interest Expense is the cost paid for borrowing funds. *Interest on Short-Term Notes* is that paid on loans from banks or commercial notes that the company issues for short terms, such as 30 days to 90 days, in order to meet payrolls and other current obligations during months when expenses exceed income. (The company may also earn interest by lending excess funds to others during periods when its income exceeds expenses.) *Interest on Long-Term Borrowing* is that paid on bonds or other multiyear debts that the company incurs in order to raise capital for capital assets, such as factories and other facilities. The Total Interest Expense is calculated by the entry =B17+B18 in Cell B19.

Subtracting nonoperating expenses, such as the total interest, from EBIT gives the *Earning before Taxes* (EBT, also known as the *Net Profits (or Earnings) before Taxes*). EBT is calculated by the entry =B15-B19 in Cell B20.

Taxes are computed by multiplying EBT by the tax rate, which is assumed in Figure 1-1 to be 40 percent. The total tax is computed by the entry =0.4*B20 in Cell B24. Note that the taxes are separated into *Current Taxes* and *Deferred Taxes*. The current tax portion (data value in Cell B22) is the amount of cash actually sent to the federal, state, and local tax authorities. The deferred tax portion (the value calculated by the entry =B24-B22 in Cell B23) is the difference between the total tax and the amount paid. This difference results from the differences between accounting income and true taxable income, which results when the firm uses the accelerated depreciation schedule for the IRS but uses straight-line depreciation, as allowed by GAAP, for reporting to its stakeholders. In theory, if the taxable income is less than the accounting income in the current year, it will be more than the accounting income later. Any taxes not paid today (i.e., the deferred taxes) must be paid in the future and are therefore a liability of the firm.

Earnings after Taxes (EAT, also known as the *Net Profits (or Earnings) after Taxes*) are what is left after subtracting taxes from EBT. For purposes of the Income Statement, the total tax is the value to be subtracted from the EBT to compute the EAT. Thus, the value of EAT is calculated by the entry =B20-B24 in Cell B25.

Preferred Stock Dividends are what is paid to holders of the firm's preferred stock, who are paid before holders of the firm's common stock. Preferred stock dividends are at a fixed rate on the preferred stock issued. They are entered as a data value in Cell B26.

Preferred stock dividends can be calculated by multiplying the number of shares of preferred stock by the dividend rate. Both of these values are unchanged from year to year unless the company issues more preferred stock to raise capital.

Net Earnings Available to Common Stockholders are what is left from the EAT after paying the holders of preferred stock first. It is calculated by the entry =B25-B26 in Cell B27.

Earnings per Share (EPS) is calculated by dividing the net earnings available to common stockholders by the weighted average number of shares of common stock outstanding during the period.[1] For 100,000 shares of common stock outstanding, it is calculated by the entry (B27/100000) in Cell B28.

Note that the format for earnings per share is different from that for the other dollar values on the income statement, as indicated by the column heading in Cell B3. EPS has been formatted in Figure 1-1 by using the currency format with two decimal places. Whereas the values in other cells in Column C appear in thousands of dollars, the value of EPS is in dollars and cents.

Retained Earnings is the portion of the net earnings available to common stockholders, if any, that is retained for investing in the company's future. It is entered as data in Cell B29. The remainder is paid to the holders of common stock; that is, the *Dividends Paid to Holders of Common Stock* are calculated by the entry =B27-B29 in Cell B30. If, on the other hand, the dividends paid to holders of common stock are a set value that is entered in Cell B30, then the retained earnings are what is left and are calculated by the entry =B27-B30 in Cell B29.)

Company policies for retaining funds versus paying dividends are the responsibility of the firm's directors. Their decisions affect corporate liquidity and stockholder morale. Company officers generally favor retaining as much income as possible in order to promote the company's growth and increase the value of its common stock. This is particularly true when there are opportunities for profitable growth through investments in capital assets or by other investment strategies (e.g., buying back stock). Thus, when profits are high, companies may retain a larger portion of their earnings and reduce the portion paid out as dividends. Companies with heavy expenditures of research and development generally favor retaining earnings. Some companies pay no regular dividends in favor of growing and increasing stock value.

Stockholders are divided between those with short-term interests who favor paying dividends and those with long-term interests who favor growth. Dividend money gets taxed twice: once at the corporate level and again at the individual level, where it is taxed at an individual's highest rate. Retained earnings are taxed only once so that a greater portion of its buying power is available for investing, which increases

---

[1] The weighted average number of shares for an annual statement is calculated as follows: Suppose there were 100,000 shares at the beginning of the fiscal year, 10,000 shares were added during the first quarter, and another 6,000 shares were added during the third quarter. The weighted average number of shares outstanding during the year would then be 109,000; that is, $100,000 \times 1/4 + 110,000 \times 1/2 + 116,000 \times 1/4 = 109,000$ shares.

shareholder equity. A company whose stock is closely held by a small number of wealthy investors tends to pay lower dividends in order to reduce the income taxes of its stockholders.

If dividends are cut to redeploy earnings that will benefit shareholders over the long run, investors should be informed of the reason for the change and how the retained funds will be used. Otherwise, cutting a stock's dividends may send a negative signal to shareholders and potential investors that a company's near-term prospects are not good.

Dividend policies are also affected by a company's financial structure. A firm with a strong cash position and liquidity is likely to pay high dividends, whereas a firm with a heavy debt load must retain more of its earnings in order to service its debt.

Changing a Worksheet's Title

The default names of worksheets in a new folder are Sheet1, Sheet2, etc. These are easily changed to names that are more descriptive and that make it easier to navigate through the sheets in a folder.

Change the sheet name of the income statement from the default name of "Sheet1" to "Income Stmnt." To do this, double-click on the Sheet tab with the left button of the mouse, type the new name, and press Enter. An alternate method is to click the right mouse button on the Sheet tab, select "Rename" from the menu, type the new name, and press Enter. (You will later change the titles of the other worksheets from Sheet2 to "Balance Sheet" and from Sheet3 to "Cash Flow Stmnt.")

Showing the Formulas in Cells

To show the formulas in cells, such as the entry in Cell B6 of Figure 1-1, click on "Options" on the Tools pull-down menu. This will open the options dialog box shown in Figure 1-5. Click on the Formulas box

Figure 1-5
___

Options Dialog Box with Formulas Box Checked

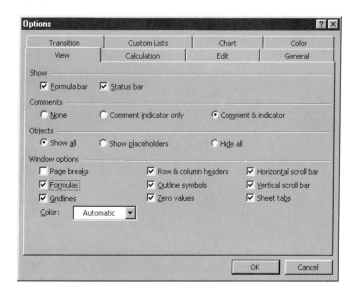

Figure 1-6

Income Statement with Formulas for Calculated Values

	A	B
1	**ABC COMPANY**	
2	**Income Statement for the Year Ended December 31, 20X2**	
3		**$ thousand (except EPS)**
4	Total Operating Revenues (or Total Sales Revenues)	2575000
5	Less: Cost of Goods Sold (COGS)	1150000
6	**Gross Profit**	**=B4-B5**
7	Less: Operating Expenses	
8	Selling Expenses	275000
9	General and Administrative Expenses (G&A)	225000
10	Depreciation Expense	100000
11	Fixed Expenses	75000
12	**Total Operating Expenses**	**=SUM(B8:B11)**
13	**Net Operating Income**	**=B6-B12**
14	Other Income	20000
15	**Earnings before Interest and Taxes (EBIT)**	**=B13+B14**
16	Less: Interest Expense	
17	Interest on Short-Term Notes	10000
18	Interest on Long-Term Borrowing	50000
19	**Total Interest Expense**	**=B17+B18**
20	**Pretax Earnings (Earnings before Taxes, EBT)**	**=B15-B19**
21	Less: Taxes	
22	Current Taxes	160000
23	Deferred Taxes	=B24-B22
24	Total Taxes (rate = 40%)	=0.4*B20
25	**Net Income (Earnings after Taxes, EAT)**	**=B20-B24**
26	Less: Preferred Stock Dividends	95000
27	**Net Earnings Available for Common Stockholders**	**=B25-B26**
28	Earnings per Share (EPS), 100,000 shares outstanding	=B27/100000
29	Retained Earnings	220000
30	Dividends Paid to Holders of Common Stock	=B27-B29

under Window options on the left side. This changes the view of the spreadsheet to that shown in Figure 1-6. Figure 1.6 shows the actual entries in each cell. Note, for example, that the entry in Cell B4 is the data value 2575000, NOT 2575.

Comparison of Last Year to Preceding Year

An important part of any analysis of how well a firm is doing is to compare results for several years. The income statements in annual reports therefore show values not only for the current year but also for at least the preceding year. Some annual reports show income statements for as many as 10 years, including the current and preceding years.

Figure 1-7 shows the income statement of Figure 1-1 with results added for the prior fiscal year.

Figure 1-7

Income Statement for Two Years

	A	B	C
1	ABC COMPANY		
2	Income Statement for the Years Ended December 31, 20X2 and 20X1		
3		$ thousand (except EPS), 20X2	$ thousand (except EPS), 20X1
4	Total Operating Revenues (or Total Sales Revenues)	2,575.0	2,050.0
5	Less: Cost of Goods Sold (COGS)	1,150.0	985.0
6	**Gross Profits**	1,425.0	1,065.0
7	Less: Operating Expenses		
8	Selling Expenses	275.0	250.0
9	General and Administrative Expenses (G&A)	225.0	205.0
10	Depreciation Expense	100.0	95.0
11	Fixed Expenses	75.0	75.0
12	**Total Operating Expenses**	675.0	625.0
13	**Net Operating Income**	750.0	440.0
14	Other Income	20.0	15.0
15	**Earnings before Interest and Taxes (EBIT)**	770.0	455.0
16	Less: Interest Expense		
17	Interest on Short-Term Notes	10.0	10.0
18	Interest on Long-Term Borrowing	50.0	55.0
19	**Total Interest Expense**	60.0	65.0
20	**Pretax Earnings (Earnings before Taxes, EBT)**	710.0	390.0
21	Less: Taxes		
22	Current Taxes	160.0	156.0
23	Deferred Taxes	124.0	.0
24	Total Taxes (rate = 40%)	284.0	156.0
25	**Net Income (Earnings after Taxes, EAT)**	426.0	234.0
26	Less: Preferred Stock Dividends	95.0	95.0
27	**Net Earnings Available for Common Stockholders**	331.0	139.0
28	Earnings per Share (EPS), 100,000 shares outstanding	$3.31	$1.39
29	Retained Earnings	220.0	50.0
30	Dividends Paid to Holders of Common Stock	111.0	89.0

Figure 1-7 is easily prepared by copying Cells B4:B30 to C4:C30 and editing only the data entries in Column C. In the process of copying Cells B4:B30 to C4:C30, the formula =B4-B5 in Cell B6 automatically changes to =C4-C5 in Cell C6, the formula =SUM (B8: B11) in Cell B12 changes to =SUM (C8: C11) in Cell C12, and so forth for the cell entries of all other calculated values. Therefore, as new *data* values are entered for the preceding year, new *calculated* values are made automatically.

The Balance Sheet

Balance sheets summarize a firm's assets, liabilities, and equity at a specific point in time. *Assets* are anything a firm owns, both tangible and intangible, that has monetary value. *Liabilities* are the firm's debts, or the claims of creditors against a firm's assets. *Equity* (also called *stockholders' equity* or *net worth*) is the difference between total assets and total liabilities. In principle, equity is what should remain for holders of common and preferred stock after a company discharges its obligations.

As every introductory course in accounting or financial management teaches, the fundamental relationship for balancing the balance sheet is

$$\text{Total Assets} = \text{Liabilities} + \text{Net Worth} \qquad (1.1)$$

A balance sheet shows what a business owns (its assets), what it owes (its liabilities), and who owns it (how ownership of its net worth or equity is divided among the holders of its preferred and common stock). In short, a firm's balance sheet is a concise statement of its financial condition.

A balance sheet has often been likened to a snapshot of a firm's financial health *at a stated time*. The picture may be quite different the day before or after, depending on the financial transactions that took place on those days.

General Format

Figure 1-8 is a balance sheet that summarizes ABC's financial status at the end of two years. (As with the spreadsheets for the income statement, data values in Figure 1-8 are italicized for instructional purposes.) Assets are grouped at the top of the balance sheet, and liabilities and net worth at the bottom. To balance, a firm's assets must equal the sum of its liabilities and net worth.

Assets

Assets are generally listed according to the length of time it would take an ongoing firm to convert them to cash.

Current Assets

Current assets include cash and other items, such as marketable securities, that the company can or expects to convert to cash in the near future—that is, in less than a year. *Cash*, as the name suggests, includes both money on-hand and in bank deposits. *Marketable securities* are short-term, interest-bearing, money-market securities that are issued by the government, businesses, and financial institutions. Firms purchase them to obtain a return on temporarily idle funds. Cash and marketable securities are often lumped together as a single item called "*Cash and Equivalents.*"

Accounts receivable is the amount of credit extended by a firm to its customers. When payments are not received within 90 days, the amounts due are generally put into a separate account for bad debt. Accounts receivable is then the amount due from others for goods and services purchased from the firm less the adjustments for potential bad debts. *Inventories* include supplies, raw materials, and components used for manufacturing products: work in-process (i.e., partially completed products): and finished products or other goods awaiting sale to a firm's customers in the near future. The value of inventories is generally reported as the lesser of cost or market value.

Figure 1-8

Balance Sheet

	A	B	C
1	**ABC COMPANY**		
2	**Balance Sheet**		
3	**as of December 31, 20X2 and December 31, 20X1**		
4		**$ thousand, 20X2**	**$ thousand, 20X1**
5	Assets		
6	**Current Assets**		
7	Cash and Equivalents	*1,565.0*	*990.0*
8	Accounts Receivable	*565.0*	*605.0*
9	Inventories	*895.0*	*1,215.0*
10	Other	*215.0*	*180.0*
11	**Total Current Assets**	**3,240.0**	**2,990.0**
12	**Fixed Assets (at cost)**		
13	Land and Buildings	*2,400.0*	*2,400.0*
14	Machinery and Equipment	*1,880.0*	*1,575.0*
15	Furniture and Fixtures	*435.0*	*390.0*
16	Vehicles	*140.0*	*115.0*
17	Less: Accumulated Depreciation	1,005.0	905.0
18	**Net Fixed Assets**	**3,850.0**	**3,575.0**
19	Other (includes certain leases)	*75.0*	*70.0*
20	**Total Fixed Assets**	**3,925.0**	**3,645.0**
21	**Total Assets**	**7,165.0**	**6,635.0**
22	Liabilities		
23	Current Liabilities		
24	Accounts Payable	*300.0*	*295.0*
25	Short-Term Notes Payable	*1,275.0*	*965.0*
26	Accruals and Other Current Liabilities	*145.0*	*295.0*
27	**Total Current Liabilities**	**1,720.0**	**1,555.0**
28	Long-Term Debt	*1,900.0*	*1,755.0*
29	**Total Liabilities**	**3,620.0**	**3,310.0**
30	Stockholder's Equity		
31	Preferred Stock	*200.0*	*200.0*
32	Common Stock ($10.00 par, 100,000 shares outstanding)	1,000.0	1,000.0
33	Paid-in capital in excess of par on common stock	*1,985.0*	*1,985.0*
34	Retained Earnings	360.0	140.0
35	**Total Stockholders' Equity**	**3,545.0**	**3,325.0**
36	**Total Liabilities and Owner's Equity**	**7,165.0**	**6,635.0**
37	**Check: Assets Equals Liabilities + Net Worth (Equity)**	**TRUE**	**TRUE**

Cell entries for calculated values

B11: =SUM(B7:B10), copy to C11
B17: =C17+'Income Stmt'!B10
B18: =SUM(B13:B16)-B17, copy to C18
B20: =B18+B19, copy to C20
B21: =B11+B20, copy to C21
B27: =SUM(B24:B26), copy to C27
B29: =B27+B28, copy to C29
B32: =10*100000, copy to C32
B34: =C34+'Income Stmt'!B29
B35: =SUM(B31:B34), copy to C35 (Cell B35 must also equal B21-B29.)
B36: =B29+B35, copy to C36 (To balance, Cell B36 must equal Cell B21.)
B37: =B21=B36, copy to C37 This uses Excel's logic test to verify balance.
    Note that the expression =IF(ABS(B21-B36)<1,"TRUE","FALSE") provides
    a test that is not subject to round-off errors.

Data values for the five types of current assets are entered in Cells B7 to B10 and Cells C7 to C10. Their sums are calculated by entering =SUM(B7:B10) in Cell B11 and copying the entry to Cell C11. Alternatively, the summation (Σ) button on the standard toolbar can used to calculate the sums.

Fixed Assets

Fixed assets are tangible and intangible items that have long lives and are not readily convertible to cash. Fixed assets include such tangible items as land, buildings, equipment, furniture, and vehicles, and such intangible items as patents, trademarks, and goodwill. They are listed at cost in Cells B13:C16. (Strictly speaking, GAAP requires assets to be carried at the lower of cost or market value. Cost is lower than market value for most assets because of inflation and other considerations.)

Although they are not shown on financial statements, other intangible assets that are part of a firm's true value are the quality of its management and, especially for companies in high-technology industries, the intellectual capital represented by its employees.

The total depreciation on fixed assets at the ends of the two years is entered in Cells B17 and C17. The depreciation at the end of 20X2 equals the depreciation at the end of 20X1 in Cell C17 plus the depreciation expense for 20X2 in Cell B10 of the Income Statement. To make this calculation, enter =C17+'Income Stmnt'!B10 in Cell B17 of the Balance Sheet (assuming that Income Stmt is the name of the worksheet for the income statement). Other ways for transferring the contents of a cell on one worksheet to a cell on another worksheet are discussed in the section *Navigating Across Worksheets in an Excel Folder* on page 23 and 24.

The net values of these four current assets are calculated by entering =SUM(B13:B16)-B17 in Cell B18 and copying the entry to C18. It is important to observe that the year-end total (or accumulated) depreciation is *subtracted* from the other values in calculating *net tangible fixed assets*.

The data values for other current assets that are not adjusted for depreciation is entered in Cells B19 and C19. The total values of fixed assets are calculated by entering =B18+B19 in Cell B20 and copying to C20.

Total Assets

Total assets are the sum of the current and fixed assets. Their values are calculated by entering =B11+B20 in Cell B21 and copying to C21.

Liabilities

Liabilities are generally listed according to the length of time in which they are due.

Current Liabilities

Current liabilities is the sum of debts owed by the firm for which payment is due in the current year. *Accounts payable* is the amount the firm owes to others for goods or services purchased from them on credit. *Short-term notes payable* are outstanding short-term loans, typically from commercial banks. This also includes commercial paper that a firm has sold to other business firms or banks. *Accruals* are liabilities for services that the firm has not yet paid and are not often billed; typical accrual items are unpaid wages and salaries due to a firm's employees and unpaid taxes due to the government.

Data values for the three types of current liabilities are entered in Cells B24:B26 and C24:C26. The firm's *Total Current Liabilities* is calculated by entering =SUM(B24:B26) in Cell B27 and copying to C27.

Long-Term Debt

Long-term debt (or *Long-Term Liabilities*) is the sum of debts owed by the firm for which repayment is not due in the current year. It generally includes various types of corporate bonds issued by the firm and long-term loans from banks that the firm has negotiated to raise funds for capital investments in facilities and other major projects. Long-term loans are usually retired by periodic repayments over their life, which is more than one year and usually less than 15 years. Long-term loans to small firms are often secured by chattel mortgages on equipment.

The role of U.S. banks in financing business has been different from that of foreign banks. The Glass-Steagall Banking Act of 1933 helped curb bank speculation by separating investment banks from commercial banks. The U.S. Congress recently repealed this act. As a result, U.S. commercial banks are now a source of both short- and long-term financing, similar to that in most other countries.

The data value for long-term debt is entered in Cells B28 and C28.

Total Liabilities

Total liabilities is the sum of the current and long-term liabilities. The repayment of this debt takes precedence over satisfying the equity of stockholders in the event the firm declares bankruptcy. Total liabilities are calculated by entering =B27+B28 in Cell B29 and copying to C29.

Stockholder's Equity

Stockholders' equity (also called *shareholders' equity* or *net worth*) represents the owners' claims on the firm. It is made up of values in four categories. The first, *preferred stock*, is a special form of stock with a fixed periodic dividend that a firm must pay before paying dividends to holders of common stock. *Common stock* represents the ownership of a corporation. Dividends on common stock are paid at the discretion of the board of directors. The *par value* of a common stock is an arbitrarily assigned per-share value used for accounting purposes. *Paid in capital in excess of par* is the amount received in the original sale of common stock in excess of the stock's par value. (The average original price received by the firm is the sum of the common stock and paid in capital in excess of par divided by the total number of shares outstanding. For the ABC Corp., this would be ($1,000,000 + $1,985,000)/100,000 shares, or $29.85/share.)

Companies that earn a profit have the option of distributing the profit to stockholders in the form of dividends or retaining it. *Retained earnings* are the cumulative total of all earnings that have been kept in the firm since its inception. To calculate, enter =C34+'Income Stmt'!B29. Most firms keep part of their profits to provide liquidity, to service debt, or to expand their capabilities without having to borrow or issue stock. When a company suffers a loss, the loss may be taken out of the retained earnings account.

If a company's stock is closely held by a limited number of high-income investors, its dividend payout is likely to be low in order to avoid the investors' paying high personal income taxes.

Total Stockholders' Equity is calculated by entering =SUM(B31:B34) in Cell B35 and copying to C35.

Verifying the Balance

Balance sheets are so called because the sum of liabilities and net worth must equal the assets. That is,

$$\text{Total Assets} = \text{Total Liabilities} + \text{Net Worth}$$

The sums on the right side of equation 1.1 are calculated by entering =B29+B35 in Cell B36 and copying to C36. The entry =B21=B36 in Cell B37 (which is copied to Cell C37) uses Excel's logical comparison operator to test whether the values in Cells B21 and B36 are equal (and the values in Cells C21 and C36 are equal). If the test is satisfied, as it is in Figure 1-8, the logical value TRUE is returned. If the test is not satisfied, FALSE would be returned. (For additional information and types of logical operators, type "logical values" in the Help/Index dialog box and click on "Display.")

The entry given in the preceding paragraph sometimes fails to return the logical value TRUE even though the balance appears satisfied. This can be due to rounding errors. Although calculations are carried out with a high level of precision, neither Excel nor any other spreadsheet provides infinite precision. For all practical purposes, the ABC's balance sheet can be judged balanced if the magnitude of the difference between the entries in Cells B21 and B36 is less than $1,000, which is precision of the data entries. The following expression can be used in Cell B37 (and copied to Cell C37) in place of the expression in the preceding paragraph:

=IF(ABS(B21-B36)<1,"TRUE", "FALSE")

Excel's ABS function is used to ensure that the difference B21-B36 is never negative, regardless of whether B21 is greater or less than B36. For example, if the difference were -$500, a "FALSE" response would result, even though the balance sheet is balanced to the precision of the data.

When all other values are given on the balance sheet, the retained earnings can be determined from the requirement that the balance sheet must balance.

The Cash Flow Statement

A Cash Flow Statement (or Statement of Cash Flows) converts accounting data, which is used for creating the income statement and balance sheet, into a picture of cash inflows and outflows. That is, the cash flow statement shows where a firm's money comes from and where it all goes. It identifies the amount generated by the firm and the amounts paid to the firm's creditors and shareholders. (Before the release of FASB Standard 95 in 1987, the "Cash Flow Statement" was known as the "Statement of Changes in Financial Position."

Another earlier version was organized differently and was called the "Sources and Uses of Funds Statement.") Cash flow statements provide useful insights into the operations and financing of firms.

A cash flow statement summarizes the inflows and outflows of funds during a specified period, typically the year just ended. The cash balance at the end of the reporting period is important information on the cash balance statement. It equals the cash balance at the beginning of the reporting period plus the cash inflows minus the cash outflows. That is,

Ending cash balance = Beginning cash balance + Cash inflows (sources) – Cash outflows (uses)   (1.2)

Components of the Cash Flow Statement

The cash flow statement generally divides cash flows into the following three components: (1) "Cash Flow from Operations," (2) "Cash Flow from Changes in Fixed Assets" (also known as "Cash Flow from Investing"), and (3) "Cash Flow from Changes in Net Working Capital" (also known as "Cash Flow from Financing").

"Cash Flow from Operations" is generally a *source* of funds, or a net cash *inflow*. This section of the cash flow statement describes the cash flows generated in the ordinary course of conducting the firm's business. It includes the revenue from selling the firm's products, depreciation expense, changes in accounts receivable, changes in inventories, changes in accounts payable, changes in short-term notes payable, and changes in other current liabilities. Note that the last five items are **changes** in their values from the beginning to the end of the reporting period.

The cash flow from a firm's operations (CF_{op}) must equal the sum of the cash flows to the firm's creditors (CF_{cred}) and its equity investors (CF_{eq}). That is,

$$CF_{op} = CF_{cred} = CF_{eq}$$ (1.3)

"Cash Flow from Changes in Fixed Assets" and "Cash Flow from Changes in Net Working Capital" are generally **uses** of funds, or cash *outflows*. The first of these two items describes the cash flows associated with **changes** in the firm's mix of long-term fixed assets. The second describes cash flows associated with **changes** in financing the firm.

Preparing the Cash Flow Statement

Figure 1-9 is the cash flow statement for the ABC Company. Two items, the firm's net income and depreciation expenses, are obtained from the income statement for the ending period. Other items represent changes in the contents of the firm's balance sheet between two periods: between 20X1 and 20X2. They are calculated as the difference between values on the balance sheet.

> The cash flow statement is the most conservative measure of a company's financial health. Short of outright fraud, cash flow is much less vulnerable to "cooking the books" and creative accounting practices intended to make a company appear more attractive to investors.

Figure 1-9

Statement of Cash Flows

	A	B
1	**ABC COMPANY**	
2	**Statement of Cash Flows for the Year Ended December 31, 20X2**	
3		**$ thousand**
4	**Cash Flows from Operations**	
5	Net Income (Earnings after Taxes, EAT)	426.0
6	Depreciation Expense	100.0
7	Deferred Taxes for Preceding Year	.0
8	Changes in Assets	
9	Change in Accounts Receivable	40.0
10	Change in Inventories	320.0
11	Change in Other Current Assets	(35.0)
12	Changes in Liabilities	
13	Change in Accounts Payable	5.0
14	Change in Short-Term Notes Payable	310.0
15	Change in Accruals and Other Current Liabilities	(150.0)
16	**Net Cash Flow from Operations**	**1,016.0**
17	**Cash Flows from Investing Activities**	
18	**Net Cash Flow from Investing Activities**	**(380.0)**
19	**Cash Flows from Financing Activities**	
20	Change in Long-Term Debt	145.0
21	Dividends Paid to Holders of Preferred and Common Stock	(206.0)
22	**Net Cash Flow from Financing Activities**	**(61.0)**
23	**Total Cash Flow from Operations, Investing, and Financing**	**575.0**
24	**Check: Total Cash Flow in 20X2 must equal the Change in Cash and Equivalents on the Balance Sheet from 20X1 to 20X2.**	**TRUE**

```
Cell entries for calculated values
     N.B. Income Stmnt is Figure 1-7, and Balance Sheet is Figure 1-8.
 B5:  ='Income Stmnt'!B25
 B6:  ='Income Stmnt'!B10
 B7:  ='Income Stmnt'C23
 B9:  =-('Balance Sheet'!B8-'Balance Sheet'!C8), copy to B10:B11
B13:  ='Balance Sheet'!B24-'Balance Sheet'!C24, copy to B14:B15
B16:  =SUM(B5:B15)
B18:  =-(('Balance Sheet'!B20+'Balance Sheet'!B17)
                    -('Balance Sheet'!C20+'Balance Sheet'!C17))
B20:  ='Balance Sheet'!B28-'Balance Sheet'!C28
B21:  =-('Income Stmnt'!B25-('Balance Sheet'!B34-'Balance Sheet'!C34))
B22:  =B20+B21
B23:  =B16+B18+B22
B24:  =IF(ABS(B23-('Balance Sheet'!B7-'Balance Sheet'!C7))>1,"FALSE","TRUE")
```

A prime stumbling point in transferring the differences between values for two periods from the balance sheet to the statement of cash flows is to recognize whether the differences should be entered as positive or negative values—that is, to recognize whether the differences represent *uses* or *sources* of funds. This determines whether the differences in value are entered on the cash flow statement as positive or negative numbers. *Increases* in asset accounts (e.g., purchases that increase the value of plant and equipment) are *uses* of funds and are cash *outflows*; they appear as *negative* values on the cash flow statement. On the other hand, *decreases* in asset accounts (e.g., the sale of plant and equipment) are *sources* of funds and are cash *inflows*; they appear as *positive* values on the cash flow statement.

Liability and equity accounts are the exact opposite. *Increases* in liability or equity accounts (e.g., accounts payable) represent *sources* of funds and are cash *inflows*; they appear as *positive* values on the cash flow statement. On the other hand, *decreases* in liability or equity accounts (e.g., accounts payable) represent *uses* of funds and are cash *outflows*; they appear as *negative* values on the cash flow statement.

To summarize, *sources* of cash that appear as *positive* values on a cash flow statement include: Decrease in any asset; increase in any liability, net profit after taxes, depreciation and other noncash charges, sale of stock, and increase in stockholder's equity. *Uses* of cash that appear as *negative* values on a cash flow statement include: Increase in any asset, decrease in any liability, net loss, dividends paid, repurchase or retirement of stock, and decrease in stockholder's equity.

Navigating Across Worksheets in an Excel Folder

There are three ways of transferring entries and cell values from one worksheet to another in the same workbook. These are illustrated for the entry in Cell B5 on the Statement of Cash Flows in Figure 1-9.

1. Type ='Income Stmt'!B25 in Cell B5 and press Enter. Pressing Enter will cause the entry in Cell B25 of the income statement to be placed in Cell B5 of the cash flow statement.
   The source sheet (in this case, Income Stmnt) is enclosed in single quotation marks and is set off from the cell column and row by the exclamation mark.
2. Type = in Cell B5 of the Cash Flow Statement, then click on the Sheet tab for the Income Statement, then click on Cell B25 of the Income Statement, and press Enter. This will place ='Income Stmt'!B25 as the entry in Cell B5 of the Cash Flow Statement.
   An alternate way to produce the same result is to select Cell B25 of the Income Statement, press Ctrl/C for copying the cell, then move to Cell B5 of the Cash Flow Statement and select "Paste Link" on the Edit drop-down menu. ("Paste Link" is in the lower left corner of the Paste Special dialog box.)
   This method is a little easier than Method 1. It avoids having to type in the name of the source worksheet, along with the quotation and exclamation marks.
3. Split the window into two horizontal sections, as in Figure 1-10, with one section exposing the worksheet for the cash flow statement and the other exposing the worksheet for the income statement (bottom).
   To split the screen, click on "New Window" on the Window pull-down menu and press Enter. Then click on "Arrange" on the Window pull-down menu, followed by clicking on "Horizontal" on the Arrange Windows dialog box. Use the worksheet tabs to select the worksheets for the statement of cash flows and balance sheet. Click on the worksheet for the cash flow statement to activate it (if it is not already active), then click on Cell B5, and type the equal sign, =. Click on the worksheet for the income statement to activate it, then click on Cell B25, and press Enter. Pressing Enter will cause the entry in Cell B25 of the income statement to be placed in Cell B5 of the cash flow statement.

Figure 1-10

Split Screen, Showing the Cash Flow Worksheet (top) and Income Statement (bottom)

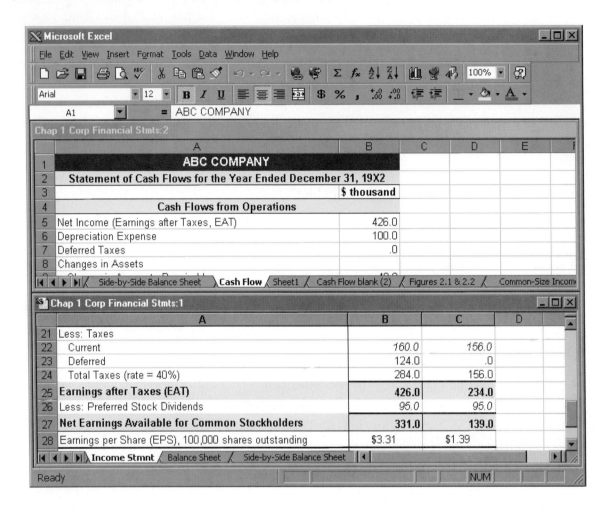

Method 3 is the easiest and quickest way when there are a number of cell entries to be transferred from one or more source sheets. After completing the transfers, remove the split by selecting "Cascade" in the Arrange Windows dialog box.

With all three methods, the entry in the value in the cash flow worksheet is the same and is linked to the value in the income statement worksheet. If the value in the income statement worksheet is changed, the same change is made automatically to the corresponding value in the cash flow worksheet.

Completing the Statement of Cash Flows

After entering the net income on the cash flow statement, use any of the methods described above to transfer the other values to the cash flow statement.

Depreciation Expense

Enter ='Income Stmnt'!B10 in Cell B6. This value was subtracted in the course of determining the net income and needs to be added back in here.

Deferred Taxes

This entry is the amount of deferred taxes from the preceding year, after adjusting for the difference between the accrued income used in calculating deferred taxes and the actual income. Since the ABC Company had no deferred taxes in 20X1, Cell B7 is zero.

Changes in Assets

Recall that an ***increase*** in the value of an asset, such as accounts receivable, inventories, and other current assets, is a *use* of funds and should appear as a *negative* value (i.e., a cash outflow) on the statement of cash flows. Enter either =-('Balance Sheet'!B8-'Balance Sheet'C8) or = 'Balance Sheet'!C8-'Balance Sheet'!B8 in Cell B9 of the cash flow statement and copy the entry to Cells B10 and B11.

Changes in Liabilities

Recall that an increase in the value of a liability, such as accounts payable, short-term notes payable, and accruals and other current liabilities, is a *source* of funds and should appear as a *positive* value (i.e., a cash inflow) on the statement of cash flows. Enter ='Balance Sheet'!B24-'Balance Sheet'!C24 in Cell B13 of the cash flow statement and copy the entry to Cells B14 and B15.

Net Cash Flow from Operations

Enter =SUM(B5:B15) in Cell B16.

Net Cash Flow from Investing Activities

This is the cash flow due to changes in fixed assets. Making an investment in a firm's fixed assets is a use of funds. Therefore, an increase in the investment in fixed assets should appear as a negative value on the cash flow statement. Enter =-(('Balance Sheet'!B20+'Balance Sheet'!B17)–('Balance Sheet'!C20+'Balance Sheet'!C17)) in Cell B18. (Because depreciation is not a cash flow, it is necessary to add the accumulated depreciation in Cells B17 and C17 to the total fixed assets in Cells B20 and C20 in order to obtain the cash flow for the investments at cost.)

Change in Long-Term Debt

An increase in long-term debt is a source of funds and is a cash inflow. Enter ='Balance Sheet'!B28-'Balance Sheet'!C28 in Cell B20.

Dividends Paid to Holders of Preferred and Common Stock

The dividends paid to shareholders in 20X2 equals the difference between the net income and retained earnings in 19X2. That is,

$$\text{Dividends Paid} = \text{Net Income} - \text{Retained Earnings} \qquad (1.4)$$

(Note that the retained earnings in 20X2 equals the difference in the accumulated retained earnings for 20X2 and 20X1.)

Enter =-('Income Stmnt'!B25-'Income Stmnt'!B29) or -('Income Stmnt'!B25 - ('Balance Sheet'!B34-'Balance Sheet'!C34)) in Cell B21. Note the minus sign because dividends paid is a cash outflow.

Net Cash Flow from Financing Activities

Enter =B20+B21 in Cell B22.

Total Cash Flow from Operations, Investing, and Financing

Enter =B16+B18+B22 in Cell B23.

Verification

The total cash flow from operations, investing, and financing must equal the change in Cash and Equivalents on the balance sheet. If it does not, there has been an error somewhere that needs correcting. The most likely type of error is confusing the positive and negative values when transferring values from the balance sheet to the cash flow statement.

To check whether or not an error has been made, enter =IF(ABS(B23-('Balance Sheet'!B7–'Balance Sheet'!C7))>1,"FALSE","TRUE") in Cell B24. (Using the absolute value of the difference avoids getting an incorrect response due to rounding errors for the reason given in the section *Verifying the Balance* on page 20.)

Insights from the Cash Flow Statement

A cash flow statement looks at values in a company's sources and uses of funds. It reveals how much of a company's cash came from its own operating activities, and how much came from investments or outside financing.

What can we learn from a company's cash flow statement? If the net cash flow is positive, it tells us how much excess cash the company generated after paying all cash expenses for the period. If negative, it tells us how much of its cash reserves from prior periods the company is using to pay its expenses. If it continues to be negative, the company will eventually run out of cash.

Concluding Remarks

Income statements, balance sheets, and cash flow statements comprise the three key financial statements. They provide coherent and visible summaries of a company's financial and credit situation. They provide a picture of what a firm is now and what it was in the recent past. We will build upon this picture as we move forward, chapter by chapter, in the text.

Creating Spreadsheet Models

Take the time up front to understand a model's purpose, the management principles involved, the relationships between the model's variables, and the difference between a model's input data and its calculated outputs. You cannot expect to be able to create a useful model unless you understand how it will be used and how its different parts are related.

Understand the difference between independent and dependent variables. Independent variables are usually entered as data values; dependent variables are entered as the expressions or formulae for calculating them.

Spreadsheet models use a combination of data values from a firm's accounting system plus expressions or formulas that calculate other values. The expressions for calculating values are simply statements of the mathematical relationships between variables. The expressions for calculating values use cell references that link calculated values to data values and other calculated values.

The design of many financial models follows more or less standard formats. Examples are the financial statements covered in this chapter. In other cases, model creators must themselves decide how to organize a spreadsheet so that it best serves its purpose. As pointed out earlier, it is usually best to start by labeling rows and columns. Then enter values and expressions or formulas in the appropriate cells. If you find out later that a better organization is possible, you can add or delete rows or columns and you can move them from one area to another. Spreadsheets are very flexible.

Whereas worksheet layouts for financial statements are fairly well standardized, in other cases modelers must strike out on their own to create layouts that fit specific cases. Here are some general guidelines for creating models:

- Understand the model's structure and purpose.
- Understand who will use the model and how often it will be used.
- Recognize that a model should be more than a one-time solution for specific set of conditions. Models go beyond one-time solutions and are a means for doing sensitivity analysis; models should be able to be "tweaked" to see how results change when input variables change.
- Recognize the input or data variables that provide the basis for the model.
- Recognize the output values and how they're related to the input values.
- Create a design or spreadsheet layout for the model. Provide clear and correct labels, including units, for all rows and columns. Critique the design and change it as necessary to make it more understandable and to eliminate unnecessary or unrelated information. For a large complex model, the original design may have to be changed several times before one that is satisfactory is achieved. Save, copy, and revise as the creative aspect of modeling proceeds.
- Enter cell expressions for calculating the final and intermediate results.
- Examine the model's performance. Check all cells to ensure that the results are reasonable and consistent. Test the model to see that it responds properly when input values are changed. Validate the model by testing it against any checks that are available.

- Save the model.
- Update the model as additional data and other information are obtained or as the model is expanded to satisfy additional purposes beyond its original purpose.

Do not focus on just getting the numbers correct. Keep in mind that computers are much more than sophisticated calculators. Recognize that spreadsheets are a means for communicating ideas and results and for justifying recommended courses of action.

As we proceed through the chapters of this text, examples will be given of what the author considers to be well-organized spreadsheets. Do not feel constrained by the examples given. Think about how you might improve them or change their format to better satisfy your own purposes.

Linking the Cells

Because of the linkage created by cell references, changing the value in a single cell causes changes in other cells. For example, changing the total operating revenue in Cell B4 of the income statement (Figure 1-1) causes changes in the earnings per share in Cell B28 of the income statement and the net income in Cell B5 of the statement of cash flows (Figure 1-11). In effect, the set of three financial

Figure 1-11

Formula Auditing Tool with "Trace Precedents" Selected

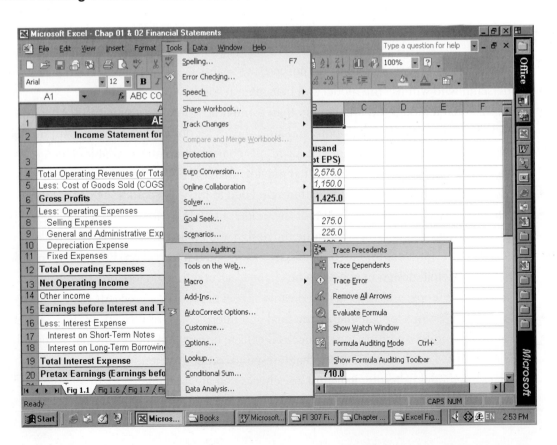

Figure 1-12

Auditing the Formula in Cell B13 to Trace Its Precedents in Cells B6 and B12

	A	B
1	ABC COMPANY	
2	Income Statement for the Year Ended December 31, 20X2	
3		$ thousand (except EPS)
4	Total Operating Revenues (or Total Sales Revenues)	2,575.0
5	Less: Cost of Goods Sold (COGS)	1,150.0
6	Gross Profits	1,425.0
7	Less: Operating Expenses	
8	Selling Expenses	275.0
9	General and Administrative Expenses (G&A)	225.0
10	Depreciation Expense	100.0
11	Fixed Expenses	75.0
12	Total Operating Expenses	675.0
13	Net Operating Income	750.0

statements is like a three-dimensional spider web. Pluck a single strand of a spider's web and the entire web vibrates in response. Similarly, changing the value in one cell causes all others linked to it to change in response.

If you wish to see the linkages displayed on your spreadsheet, use the Formula Auditing tool on the Tools drop-down menu. Figure 1-11 shows the Formula Auditing tool with the "Trace Precedents" option selection. This tool traces either the precedent cells that lead directly into a specified cell or the dependent cells that are affected by the value in the specified cell. For example, if you wish to identify the cells used to calculate the value in Cell B13, click on Cell B13 to activate it, access the Formula Auditing tool, and click on "Trace Precedents."

The result is Figure 1-12, which shows Cells B6 and B12 as the cells that are used in the entry in Cell B13 to calculate there. You can use the "Trace Dependents" option in an inverse manner to identify any cells that use the selected cell to calculate their values. For example, you should be able to show that Cell B13 is used in the formula in Cell B15. Click on "Remove All Arrows" after you're finished.

Cell linkages play an important role in using spreadsheets effectively to create models. They provide flexibility for using spreadsheets to do various types of sensitivity analysis to measure the impacts of changes. They convert spreadsheets into digital laboratories for exploring the impacts of business decisions. They make the spreadsheet a useful management tool. We will explore some of the management uses of spreadsheets in Chapter 2 and later chapters.

In this chapter, the three financial statements have been placed on separate worksheets in the same workbook. This is not essential. In Chapter 5, for example, all three financial statements are placed on the same worksheet. In still other cases, models can consist of worksheets in different workbooks. Excel makes it possible to link cells on a single worksheet, to link cells on different worksheets in a single workbook, and to link cells on different worksheets in different workbooks. Cell linkages make models extremely flexible and useful as management tools.

> ### Models vs. One-Time Solutions
>
> Models are NOT meant to be one-time solutions for a specific set of conditions. They are meant to provide a means for evaluating the impacts of changes. In order to do that, the expressions in some cells in one part of a model must contain references to cells in another part so that all parts are linked together. With proper linkage, the impacts of changes in one part of a model are automatically transmitted to other parts.
>
> The linkage in models provides managers with a low-cost means for evaluating alternate courses of action. Well-linked models make it possible to identify profitable strategies and avoid others that might not be in a company's best interests. Inserting values rather than expressions can destroy the linkage between cells and disable a model for this important use.

Management Principles

Financial statements are tools for corporate executives and managers as well as for investors. The earlier portions of the chapter have demonstrated the use of Excel to create the financial statements from data in a company's cost accounting files. The later sections tell how to obtain statements for a firm's past performance and comment on their uses for looking at a firm's past, present, and potential future performance.

Looking Backward

The SEC requires every corporation to include financial statements in its annual stockholder reports for at least the two most recent years. Corporate and outside analysts extend the time frame backward for a number of years to track a company's year-to-year and quarter-to-quarter operations. This is easily done on a spreadsheet and provides what is sometimes called "horizontal analysis." (We will use annual and quarterly data in Chapters 3 and 6 to create statistical models for projecting the trends and forecasting the future.)

Most corporations maintain Web sites on which they post their annual and quarterly financial reports for several years, as well as much other information about themselves. The sites can usually be accessed by typing "www." followed by the company name followed by ".com." Follow the directions on the initial Web page to reach the financial reports or other information you are looking for.

EDGAR (the acronym for the Electronic Data Gathering, Analysis, and Retrieval system) is a government-sponsored system that, in its own words, "performs automated collection, validation, indexing, acceptance, and forwarding of submissions by companies and others who are required by law to file forms with the U.S. Securities and Exchange Commission (SEC)." Its primary purpose is to increase the efficiency and fairness of the securities market for the benefit of investors, corporations, and the economy by accelerating the receipt, acceptance, dissemination, and analysis of time-sensitive corporate information filed with the agency. The SEC requires all public companies (except foreign companies and companies with less than $10 million in assets and 500 shareholders) to file registration statements, periodic reports, and other forms electronically through EDGAR. Anyone can access and download this information for free. At www.sec.gov/edgar.shtml you will find links to a complete list of filings available through EDGAR and instructions for searching the EDGAR database.

Companies are required to file annual reports on Form 10-K or 10-KSB on EDGAR. In addition, many companies voluntarily submit their actual annual reports. Their filings are converted to a common format that's comparable across companies. Subscribers who have paid the substantial fees can access EDGAR filings by entering www.sec.gov/edgar.shtml on their Web browser.

FreeEdgar provides unlimited, free access to EDGAR filings. Data can be downloaded directly into Excel spreadsheets. Access this service by entering www.freeedgar.com. You must register to use FreeEdgar, but registration is free.

A number of other Web sites provide free data on corporate financial statements; examples are www .yahoo.com, www.bigchart.com, www.nasdaq.com, and www.hoovers.com.

Looking Forward

Chapter 3 discusses the use of spreadsheets for forecasting a company's future annual sales. Chapter 5 discusses the use of forecasts of sales and other items to prepare income statements and balance sheets for future years. This is easily done on a spreadsheet and provides what is sometimes called "forward horizontal analysis."

Looking More Often

The rapid pace of modern business makes it increasingly difficult to live with the quarterly reporting system required by law since 1934. Investors and corporate executives find themselves captive to figures that can be six weeks or more out of date. Without timely information, they are vulnerable to unpleasant surprises, such as losses in corporate market values. Some examples of unexpected high-single-day losses of market value in 2000 were 34 percent of Procter & Gamble 42 percent of Priceline, and 52 percent of Apple Computer. Rapid changes such as these and those during the economic crises that began in late 2007 cause fear and uncertainty in the equity and financial markets. This contributes to the volatility of stocks and the cost of rising funds for day-to-day operations and invsting. To provide more current information and earlier warnings, Wall Street reporters and chief financial officers of leading companies deliver "guidance" and "pre-announcement" reports to selected analysts—a practice that favors insiders.

The accounting profession is now debating continual updating of financial reports in something approaching a 24/7 mode. This is actually being accomplished at some companies. Using information technology, executives at Cisco Systems can get the company's books closed within an hour. It is reported to have taken CEO John Chambers eight years to put this capability in place for Cisco's internal use. Other companies, piggybacking on Cisco's expertise, could probably develop similar capabilities in about half that time. (*Forbes*, 10/23/00)

Frequently updating financial reports and making them available on the Web reduces risks to investors. This should benefit a company by raising its stock price and lowering its borrowing costs.

Looking More Closely

A growing number of investors, market watchdogs, accountants, and others are convinced that traditional financial statements give incomplete and misleading information about the performance of modern knowledge-intensive companies. Technological change, globalization, and expanding information processing have been cited as three reasons why traditional financial statements have become inadequate. Alan Greenspan, Chairman of the Federal Reserve Board, noted in January of 2000 that accounting was not tracking investments in knowledge assets and warned, "There are going to be a lot of problems in the future." The problems with traditional accounting methods and financial statements, as well as the changes being considered to correct them, are discussed in an article by Thomas A. Stewart in *Fortune* for April 16, 2001.

"Cooking the books," which has been used to inflate earnings, brought down a number of major corporations in the late 1990s and early 2000s. Recognizing revenues before sales are made and capitalizing expenses are two of the more common ways to inflate net income. There are many more.

Looking at the Big Picture

You cannot become skilled at creating models without understanding what the model is supposed to do. As you proceed through this text, **think about the financial principles that each example illustrates**. Do not become completely absorbed in number-crunching, that is, don't simply transcribe numbers or expressions from the text into your worksheets without thinking about what each entry does. Recognize what each number or expression represents as you enter it on your spreadsheet. Understand the logic of the relationships between different cells on your spreadsheets. Understand how expressions in cells link different cells together so that changing one cell changes others. Learn to use spreadsheets for creating models rather than simply solving problems.

Spreadsheet models are not instant creations. They often entail a lengthy process of trying different formats for organizing information to ensure the items and cells fit together in a logical pattern. Creating a spreadsheet model will force you to be critical of your work. This will help you better understand the management principles involved.

Don't allow yourself to be frustrated when the computer does what you tell it to do rather than what you *meant* to tell it to do. Find your mistake and correct it.

Communicate as Well as Calculate

If your spreadsheets are to be useful tools for financial management, they must *communicate* as well as *calculate*. Make sure your spreadsheets are well labeled. Use Excel's charting and formatting tools to make your spreadsheets look professional and convincing.

Pro Forma Financial Statements

Pro forma income statements and balance sheets are based on assumed conditions rather than actual conditions. They do not conform to GAPP, and they are not accepted by the IRS or other taxing agencies.

Pro forma financial statements are sometimes projections of what might happen in the future rather than what actually did happen during the past quarter or year. The calculations are based on an "as if" basis for specified assumptions, which should be clearly spelled out so that the results can be understood and the risks can be assessed. In such uses, pro forma statements are important tools for planning a firm's operations – for example, for making adjustments for future increases or decreases in sales revenues, and for acquiring capital assets or reducing headcount. To prepare pro forma statements to help plan for the future, one begins with properly prepared financial statements for the preceding quarter or year and with assumptions for the future. These are then combined to estimate financial statements for the future. This important use of pro forma financial statements is discussed in Chapter 5. Excel's tools for "what if" analysis simplifies the calculations so that they can be made and summarized over a wide variety of potential future conditions.

As another example, a firm's pro forma earnings might include the income from a subsidiary that was acquired partway through the reporting period, as adjusted for what it might have been had it been acquired at the beginning of the reporting period. When properly used, this provides comparability between annual financial statements for the year of acquisition and those for subsequent years.

Unfortunately, pro forma statements are often misused. Examples of their misuse are when a firm excludes depreciation expenses and such nonrecurring expenses as restructuring costs, or when a firm omits certain expenses such as stock compensation or the amortization of goodwill and other intangible assets. Such intentional misuses are typically reported in an effort to put more positive spin on a company's earnings.

"Adjusted earnings" is a term now being used as a substitute for "pro forma earnings." Its use avoids the phrase "pro forma," which has become stigmatized because of the deliberate misuse of pro forma financial statements to mislead others. Like "pro forma earnings," "adjusted earnings" has become a much abused hideaway from the facts of life.

Chapter 2

Analysis of Financial Statements

CHAPTER OBJECTIVES

Management Skills

- Use common-size financial statements to compare the financial status of companies of different sizes—that is, perform "vertical analysis."
- Analyze year-to-year trends—that is, perform "horizontal analysis."
- Use financial ratios to gauge their financial health.
- Benchmark changes in a firm's financial ratios against other companies in the same industry.

Spreadsheet Skills

- Prepare common-size financial statements.
- Calculate and display year-to-year changes of financial statements and financial ratios.
- Transfer values from the worksheets for financial statements (e.g., those prepared in Chapter 1) to other worksheets for calculating financial ratios.
- Use IF tests and add text to identify whether or not a company's financial ratios are improving from one year to the next, and to indicate how well a company's financial ratios compare to industry averages.
- Use conditional formatting to highlight items needing management attention.

Overview

Knowing how to interpret the numbers on financial statements is the key to using them for managing a company's finances or for your own investment portfolio more effectively.

What do you see when you look at a company's financial statements? Do you see the company as healthy and robust, or as pale and sickly? Is its financial health improving or deteriorating? Are its capital assets being used efficiently? Will it be able to satisfy its creditors? Should you lend it money or buy its stock? How does the company compare with others in the same industry?

This chapter covers some methods for extracting information from financial statement. It shows how to analyze financial statements and find answers to questions such as those above. It shows how to use spreadsheets to implement the analytical techniques discussed in the following list.

1. **Common-size income statements and balance sheets:** These convert dollar values to percentages of sales and assets. Common-size financial statements are used for "vertical analysis" to see how items on financial statements are related to sales and assets. They help compare the performance of companies that vary in size.
2. **Financial ratios:** These analyze such characteristics as a firm's liquidity, its use of money, its ability to pay expenses, its profitability, and its market value. Comparing a firm's financial ratios with those for other companies in the same industry helps gauge the performance of the company's managers.
3. **Year-to-year comparisons:** These are used to identify and measure trends. This technique is often called "horizontal analysis." It can be done on a quarter-to-quarter or month-to-month basis, as well as year to year. The period-to-period trends show whether or not a company's performance is improving or deteriorating and provide an early warning of trouble spots that need management attention.

Common-Size Financial Statements

Common-size financial statements use percentages rather than dollars to express values in a firm's financial statements. They are sometimes called "percent income statements" and "percent balance statements." Common-size income statements are expressed as percentages of sales, and common-size balance statements are expressed as percentages of total assets. They simplify comparisons of a firm's performance in different years or to different companies.

Common-Size Income Statement

A common-size income statement is created by converting the dollar values to the percentages of sales revenue.

Figure 2-1

Income Statement with Values in Both Dollars (Thousands) and Percent of Sales Revenue

	A	B	C
1	ABC COMPANY		
2	Income Statement for the Year Ended December 31, 20X2		
3		$ thousand (except EPS)	Percent of Sales
4	Total Operating Revenues (or Total Sales Revenues)	2,575.0	100.00%
5	Less: Cost of Goods Sold (COGS)	1,150.0	44.66%
6	**Gross Profits**	**1,425.0**	**55.34%**
7	Less: Operating Expenses		
8	Selling Expenses	275.0	10.68%
9	General and Administrative Expenses (G&A)	225.0	8.74%
10	Depreciation Expense	100.0	3.88%
11	Fixed Expenses	75.0	2.91%
12	**Total Operating Expenses**	**675.0**	**26.21%**
13	**Net Operating Income**	**750.0**	**29.13%**
14	Other Income	20.0	0.78%
15	**Earnings before Interest and Taxes (EBIT)**	**770.0**	**29.90%**
16	Less: Interest Expense		
17	Interest on Short-Term Notes	10.0	0.39%
18	Interest on Long-Term Borrowing	50.0	1.94%
19	**Total Interest Expense**	**60.0**	**2.33%**
20	**Pretax Earnings (Earnings before Taxes, EBT)**	**710.0**	**27.57%**
21	Less: Taxes		
22	Current Tax	160.0	6.21%
23	Deferred Tax	124.0	4.82%
24	Total Tax (rate = 40%)	284.0	11.03%
25	**Net Income (Earnings after Taxes, EAT)**	**426.0**	**16.54%**
26	Less: Preferred Stock Dividends	95.0	3.69%
27	**Net Earnings Available for Common Stockholders**	**331.0**	**12.85%**
28	Earnings per Share (EPS), 100,000 shares outstanding	$3.31	
29	Retained Earnings	220.0	8.54%
30	Dividends Paid to Holders of Common Stock	111.0	4.31%

Figure 2-1 reproduces Columns A and B of the Income Statement for 20X2 for the ABC Company that was presented in Chapter 1 and adds Column C to show the percentages of sales revenue. The entry in Cell C4 is =B4/B$4 and is copied to the Range C5:C6, C8:C15, C17:C20, C22:C27, and C29:C30. Note the $ sign before 4 in the denominator of the entry. This ensures that the denominator remains in Row 4 as the entry in Cell C4 is copied down. (Dollar signs are useful for anchoring the column and/or row of a cell reference when copying an entry to other columns and rows.)

Use the "Percent Style" button on the formatting toolbar to format the ratios as percentages. To add two decimal places, click twice on the "Increase Decimal" button on the same toolbar. If you do these formatting operations in Cell C4, you can use the "Format Painter" button on the formatting toolbar to copy the format in Cell C4 to other cells with values in Column C.

Using the F4 Key to Insert $ Signs Where You Want Them

Use the F4 key as an alternative to typing $ signs. Pressing the F4 key after entering a cell reference places $ signs before both the column and the row (i.e., A1 becomes $A$1). Pressing the F4 key a second time removes the dollar sign before the column (i.e., $A$1 becomes A$1). Pressing the F4 key a third time removes the dollar sign before the row and places one before the column (i.e., A$1 becomes $A1). Pressing the F4 key a fourth time removes the last dollar sign (i.e., $A1 becomes A1).

To hide the dollar values and show only the percentage values, click on any cell in Column B and pull down the Format tab. Select "Columns" and then click Hide. Figure 2-2 shows the result, which is called a common-size income statement. To restore Column B, drag the mouse across Columns A and C of Figure 2-2 and select "Columns/Unhide" from the Format pull-down menu.

Figure 2-2

Common-Size Income Statement for the ABC Company

	A	C
1	**ABC COMPANY**	
2	**Income Statement for the Year Ended December 31, 20X2**	
3		**Percent of Sales**
4	Total Operating Revenues (or Total Sales Revenues)	100.00%
5	Less: Cost of Goods Sold (COGS)	44.66%
6	**Gross Profits**	**55.34%**
7	Less: Operating Expenses	
8	Selling Expenses	10.68%
9	General and Administrative Expenses (G&A)	8.74%
10	Depreciation Expense	3.88%
11	Fixed Expenses	2.91%
12	**Total Operating Expenses**	**26.21%**
13	**Net Operating Income**	**29.13%**
14	Other Income	0.78%
15	**Earnings before Interest and Taxes (EBIT)**	**29.90%**
16	Less: Interest Expense	
17	Interest on Short-Term Notes	0.39%
18	Interest on Long-Term Borrowing	1.94%
19	**Total Interest Expense**	**2.33%**
20	**Pretax Earnings (Earnings before Taxes, EBT)**	**27.57%**
21	Less: Taxes	
22	Current Tax	6.21%
23	Deferred Tax	4.82%
24	Total Tax (rate = 40%)	11.03%
25	**Net Income (Earnings after Taxes, EAT)**	**16.54%**
26	Less: Preferred Stock Dividends	3.69%
27	**Net Earnings Available for Common Stockholders**	**12.85%**
28	Earnings per Share (EPS), 100,000 shares outstanding	
29	Retained Earnings	8.54%
30	Dividends Paid to Holders of Common Stock	4.31%

Figure 2-3 shows the income statement for ABC Company for two years, 20X1 and 20X2, with both dollar values and percentages of total sales.

Condensed Common-Size Statements

Figure 2-4 shows a condensed common-size income statement for the two years. Figure 2-4 is produced from Figure 2-3 by hiding Columns B and D and hiding Rows 7 to 11, 16 to 18, 22 to 23, and 28 to 30 in Figure 2-3. This focuses attention on important items for analysis by hiding lower-level details.

Figure 2-3

Income Statement for the ABC Corporation for Years 20X1 and 20X2 with Values in Both Dollars (Thousands) and Percentages of Sales Revenue

	A	B	C	D	E
1	ABC COMPANY				
2	Income Statement for the Years Ended December 31, 20X2 and 20X1				
3		$ thousand (except EPS), 20X2	Percent of Sales, 20X2	$ thousand (except EPS), 20X1	Percent of Sales, 20X1
4	Total Operating Revenues (or Total Sales Revenues)	2,575.0	100.00%	2,050.0	100.00%
5	Less: Cost of Goods Sold (COGS)	1,150.0	44.66%	985.0	48.05%
6	**Gross Profits**	1,425.0	55.34%	1,065.0	51.95%
7	Less: Operating Expenses				
8	Selling Expenses	275.0	10.68%	250.0	12.20%
9	General and Administrative Expenses (G&A)	225.0	8.74%	205.0	10.00%
10	Depreciation Expense	100.0	3.88%	95.0	4.63%
11	Fixed Expenses	75.0	2.91%	75.0	3.66%
12	**Total Operating Expenses**	675.0	26.21%	625.0	30.49%
13	**Net Operating Income**	750.0	29.13%	440.0	21.46%
14	Other Income	20.0	0.78%	15.0	0.73%
15	**Earnings before Interest and Taxes (EBIT)**	770.0	29.90%	455.0	22.20%
16	Less: Interest Expense				
17	Interest on Short-Term Notes	10.0	0.39%	10.0	0.49%
18	Interest on Long-Term Borrowing	50.0	1.94%	55.0	2.68%
19	**Total Interest Expense**	60.0	2.33%	65.0	3.17%
20	**Pretax Earnings (Earnings before Taxes, EBT)**	710.0	27.57%	390.0	19.02%
21	Less: Taxes				
22	Current Taxes	160.0	6.21%	156.0	7.61%
23	Deferred Taxes	124.0	4.82%	.0	0.00%
24	Total Taxes (rate = 40%)	284.0	11.03%	156.0	7.61%
25	**Net Income (Earnings after Taxes, EAT)**	426.0	16.54%	234.0	11.41%
26	Less: Preferred Stock Dividends	95.0	3.69%	95.0	4.63%
27	**Net Earnings Available for Common Stockholders**	331.0	12.85%	139.0	6.78%
28	Earnings per Share (EPS), 100,000 shares outstanding	$3.31		$1.39	
29	Retained Earnings	220.0	8.54%	50.0	2.44%
30	Dividends Paid to Holders of Common Stock	111.0	4.31%	89.0	4.34%

Figure 2-4

Condensed Common-Size Income Statement for 20X1 and 20X2

	A	C	E
1	**ABC COMPANY**		
2	**Income Statement for the Years Ended December 31, 20X2 and 20X1**		
3		**Percent of Sales, 20X2**	**Percent of Sales, 20X1**
4	Total Operating Revenues (or Total Sales Revenues)	100.00%	100.00%
5	Less: Cost of Goods Sold (COGS)	44.66%	48.05%
6	**Gross Profits**	**55.34%**	**51.95%**
12	**Total Operating Expenses**	**26.21%**	**30.49%**
13	**Net Operating Income**	**29.13%**	**21.46%**
14	Other Income	0.78%	0.73%
15	**Earnings before Interest and Taxes (EBIT)**	**29.90%**	**22.20%**
19	**Total Interest Expense**	**2.33%**	**3.17%**
20	**Pretax Earnings (Earnings before Taxes, EBT)**	**27.57%**	**19.02%**
21	Less: Taxes		
24	Total Taxes (rate = 40%)	11.03%	7.61%
25	**Net Income (Earnings after Taxes, EAT)**	**16.54%**	**11.41%**
26	Less: Preferred Stock Dividends	3.69%	4.63%
27	**Net Earnings Available for Common Stockholders**	**12.85%**	**6.78%**

Common-Size Balance Sheets

Common-size balance sheets are prepared in the same manner as common-size income statements, except that the percentages are the *percentages of total assets* rather than total income. Figure 2-5 shows a balance sheet with values in both $ thousand and percent of total assets. To convert Figure 2-5 to a common-size balance sheet with values shown only as percentages of total assets, simply hide Columns B and D before printing.

The key cell entry is =B7/B$21 in Cell C7. Note the placement of the $ sign in the denominator of this entry. This allows the entry to be copied to other cells in Columns C and E for percentage values.

Figure 2-6 is a condensed common-size balance sheet.

Changes on Financial Statements from Preceding Year

Changes on a firm's financial statements from preceding years provide important information about a company's performance and its management. This section covers changes for the current year compared

Figure 2-5

Balance Sheet with Values in $ Thousand and Percent of Total Assets

	A	B	C	D	E
1	ABC COMPANY				
2	Balance Sheet				
3	as of December 31, 19X2 and December 31, 20X1				
4		$ thousand, 20X2	Pct. of Total Assets, 20X2	$ thousand, 20X1	Pct. of Total Assets, 20X1
5	Assets				
6	Current Assets				
7	Cash and Equivalents	1,565.0	21.84%	990.0	14.92%
8	Accounts Receivable	565.0	7.89%	605.0	9.12%
9	Inventories	895.0	12.49%	1,215.0	18.31%
10	Other	215.0	3.00%	180.0	2.71%
11	Total Current Assets	3,240.0	45.22%	2,990.0	45.06%
12	Fixed Assets (at cost)				
13	Land and Buildings	2,400.0	33.50%	2,400.0	36.17%
14	Machinery and Equipment	1,880.0	26.24%	1,575.0	23.74%
15	Furniture and Fixtures	435.0	6.07%	390.0	5.88%
16	Vehicles	140.0	1.95%	115.0	1.73%
17	Less: Accumulated Depreciation	1,005.0	14.03%	905.0	13.64%
18	Net Fixed Assets	3,850.0	53.73%	3,575.0	53.88%
19	Other (includes certain leases)	75.0	1.05%	70.0	1.06%
20	Total Fixed Assets	3,925.0	54.78%	3,645.0	54.94%
21	Total Assets	7,165.0	100.00%	6,635.0	100.00%
22	Liabilities				
23	Current Liabilities				
24	Accounts Payable	300.0	4.19%	295.0	4.45%
25	Short-Term Notes Payable	1,275.0	17.79%	965.0	14.54%
26	Accruals and Other Current Liabilities	145.0	2.02%	295.0	4.45%
27	Total Current Liabilities	1,720.0	24.01%	1,555.0	23.44%
28	Long-Term Debt	1,900.0	26.52%	1,755.0	26.45%
29	Total Liabilities	3,620.0	50.52%	3,310.0	49.89%
30	Stockholder's Equity				
31	Preferred Stock	200.0	2.79%	200.0	3.01%
32	Common Stock ($10.00 par, 100,000 shares outstanding)	1,000.0	13.96%	1,000.0	15.07%
33	Paid-in Capital in Excess of Par on Common Stock	1,985.0	27.70%	1,985.0	29.92%
34	Retained Earnings	360.0	5.02%	140.0	2.11%
35	Total Stockholders' Equity	3,545.0	49.48%	3,325.0	50.11%
36	Total Liabilities and Owner's Equity	7,165.0	100.00%	6,635.0	100.00%

to the preceding year. Long-term changes over a number of years are discussed in later sections. The year-to-year comparisons and their trends can warn of significant changes for better or worse in a firm's management. Comparisons to the industry average are important because, in the final analysis, a company's well-being is the result of the past actions and decisions relative to the economic conditions of the industry in which it operates. The comparison evaluates a company's managers relative to those of its competitors.

Figure 2-6
_____

Condensed Common-Size Balance Sheet

	A	C	E
1	**ABC COMPANY**		
2	**Balance Sheet**		
3	**as of December 31, 20X2 and December 31, 20X1**		
4		**Pct. of Total Assets, 20X2**	**Pct. of Total Assets, 20X1**
5	**Assets**		
11	**Total Current Assets**	45.22%	45.06%
20	**Total Fixed Assets**	54.78%	54.94%
21	**Total Assets**	100.00%	100.00%
22	**Liabilities**		
27	**Total Current Liabilities**	24.01%	23.44%
28	Long-Term Debt	26.52%	26.45%
29	**Total Liabilities**	50.52%	49.89%
30	**Stockholder's Equity**		
31	Preferred Stock	2.79%	3.01%
32	Common Stock ($10.00 par, 100,000 shares outstanding)	13.96%	15.07%
33	Paid-in capital in excess of par on common stock	27.70%	29.92%
34	Retained Earnings	5.02%	2.11%
35	**Total Stockholders' Equity**	49.48%	50.11%
36	**Total Liabilities and Owner's Equity**	100.00%	100.00%

Year-to-Year Changes in the Income Statement and Balance Sheet

Figure 2-7 shows the dollar and percentage changes from 20X1 to 20X2 in the Income Statement of the ABC Company, and Figure 2-8 shows similar changes in the company's Balance Sheet.

Including the percentage changes in the results helps analysts understand the reasons for changes. For example, although ABC's revenues increased only 25.6 percent, its EAT increased 82 percent, or more than three times as much. This was due to a number of things, such as the increase of only 16.8 percent in COGS, relatively small increases in operating expenses, and reductions in interest expenses.

Financial Ratios

For convenience of discussion, financial ratios are divided into the following six classes according to the types of information they provide and their uses:

1. **Liquidity ratios**, which describe a firm's short-term solvency, or its ability to meet its current obligations

Figure 2-7

Changes in the Income Statement of the ABC Company

	A	B	D	F	G
1	ABC COMPANY				
2	Income Statement for the Years Ended December 31, 20X2 and 20X1				
3		$ thousand (except EPS), 20X2	$ thousand (except EPS), 20X1	Change, $ thousand	Change, Percent
4	Total Operating Revenues (or Total Sales Revenues)	2,575.0	2,050.0	525.0	25.61%
5	Less: Cost of Goods Sold (COGS)	1,150.0	985.0	165.0	16.75%
6	**Gross Profits**	1,425.0	1,065.0	360.0	33.80%
7	Less: Operating Expenses				
8	Selling Expenses	275.0	250.0	25.0	10.00%
9	General and Administrative Expenses (G&A)	225.0	205.0	20.0	9.76%
10	Depreciation Expense	100.0	95.0	5.0	5.26%
11	Fixed Expenses	75.0	75.0	.0	0.00%
12	**Total Operating Expenses**	675.0	625.0	50.0	8.00%
13	**Net Operating Income**	750.0	440.0	310.0	70.45%
14	Other Income	20.0	15.0	5.0	33.33%
15	**Earnings before Interest and Taxes (EBIT)**	770.0	455.0	315.0	69.23%
16	Less: Interest Expense				
17	Interest on Short-Term Notes	10.0	10.0	.0	0.00%
18	Interest on Long-Term Borrowing	50.0	55.0	(5.0)	−9.09%
19	**Total Interest Expense**	60.0	65.0	(5.0)	−7.69%
20	**Pretax Earnings (Earnings before Taxes, EBT)**	710.0	390.0	320.0	82.05%
21	Less: Taxes				
22	Current Taxes	160.0	156.0	4.0	2.56%
23	Deferred Taxes	124.0	.0	124.0	
24	Total Taxes (rate = 40%)	284.0	156.0	128.0	82.05%
25	**Net Income (Earnings after Taxes, EAT)**	426.0	234.0	192.0	82.05%
26	Less: Preferred Stock Dividends	95.0	95.0	.0	0.00%
27	**Net Earnings Available for Common Stockholders**	331.0	139.0	192.0	138.13%
28	Earnings per Share (EPS), 100,000 shares outstanding	$3.31	$1.39	$1.92	138.13%
29	Retained Earnings	220.0	50.0	170.0	340.00%
30	Dividends Paid to Holders of Common Stock	111.0	89.0	22.0	24.72%

2. **Activity and efficiency ratios,** which describe how well a firm is using its investment in assets to produce sales and profits

3. **Leverage or debt ratios,** which describe to extent to which a firm relies on debt financing

4. **Coverage ratios,** which describe how well a firm is able to pay certain expenses

5. **Profitability ratios,** which describe how profitable a firm has been in relation to its assets and shareholders' equity

6. **Stockholder and market value ratios,** which describe the value of a firm in the eyes of outside investors and security markets

With some exceptions, financial ratios are based entirely on values in firms' income statements and balance sheets. The six figures that follow show portions of an Excel spreadsheet that give expressions

Figure 2-8

Changes in Balance Sheet from December 31, 20X1 to December 31, 20X2

	A	B	D	F	G
1	ABC COMPANY				
2–3	Changes in Balance Sheet from December 31, 20X1 to December 31, 20X2				
4		$ thousand, 20X2	$ thousand, 20X1	Change, $ thousand	Change, Percent
5	Assets				
6	Current Assets				
7	Cash and Equivalents	1,565.0	990.0	575.0	58.1%
8	Accounts Receivable	565.0	605.0	(40.0)	−6.6%
9	Inventories	895.0	1,215.0	(320.0)	−26.3%
10	Other	215.0	180.0	35.0	19.4%
11	Total Current Assets	3,240.0	2,990.0	250.0	8.4%
12	Fixed Assets (at cost)				
13	Land and Buildings	2,400.0	2,400.0	.0	0.0%
14	Machinery and Equipment	1,880.0	1,575.0	305.0	19.4%
15	Furniture and Fixtures	435.0	390.0	45.0	11.5%
16	Vehicles	140.0	115.0	25.0	21.7%
17	Less: Accumulated Depreciation	1,005.0	905.0	100.0	11.0%
18	Net Fixed Assets	3,850.0	3,575.0	275.0	7.7%
19	Other (includes certain leases)	75.0	70.0	5.0	7.1%
20	Total Fixed Assets	3,925.0	3,645.0	280.0	7.7%
21	Total Assets	7,165.0	6,635.0	530.0	8.0%
22	Liabilities				
23	Current Liabilities				
24	Accounts Payable	300.0	295.0	5.0	1.7%
25	Short-Term Notes Payable	1,275.0	965.0	310.0	32.1%
26	Accruals and Other Current Liabilities	145.0	295.0	(150.0)	−50.8%
27	Total Current Liabilities	1,720.0	1,555.0	165.0	10.6%
28	Long-Term Debt	1,900.0	1,755.0	145.0	8.3%
29	Total Liabilities	3,620.0	3,310.0	310.0	9.4%
30	Stockholder's Equity				
31	Preferred Stock	200.0	200.0	.0	0.0%
32	Common Stock ($10.00 par, 100,000 shares outstanding)	1,000.0	1,000.0	.0	0.0%
33	Paid-in capital in excess of par on common stock	1,985.0	1,985.0	.0	0.0%
34	Retained Earnings	360.0	140.0	220.0	157.1%
35	Total Stockholders' Equity	3,545.0	3,325.0	220.0	6.6%
36	Total Liabilities and Owner's Equity	7,165.0	6,635.0	530.0	8.0%

and cell entries for calculating the six sets of ratios and other financial measures. Values for the ABC Company, as of December 31, 20X2, are shown in Column C of the spreadsheets.

By convention, some ratios are reported as percentages. Ratios can be formatted as percentages by selecting the cell and clicking on the % button on Excel's toolbar. Thus, if the ratio of current assets to current liabilities is 1.85, the value of current assets is 185 percent of the value of current liabilities.

Figure 2-9

Liquidity Ratios

	A	B	C
1		**LIQUIDITY MEASURES**	
2	**Net Working Capital**	**Total Current Assets - Total Current Liabilities**	$1,520,000
3		='Balance Sheet'!B11 - 'Balance Sheet'!B27	
4		=$3,240,000 - $1,720,000 = $1,520,000	
5	**Ratio, Net Working Capital**	**Net Working Capital**	0.590
6	**to Sales**	**Sales**	
7		=('Balance Sheet'!B11 - 'Balance Sheet'!B27)/'Income Stmnt'!B4	
8		=($3,240,000 - $1,720,000)/$2,575,000 = $1,520,000/$2,575,000 = 0.590	
9	**Ratio, Net Working Capital**	**Net Working Capital**	0.469
10	**to Current Assets**	**Current Assets**	
11		=('Balance Sheet'!B11-'Balance Sheet'!B27)/'Balance Sheet'!B11	
12		=($3,240,000 - $1,720,000)/$3,240,000 = $1,520,000/$3,240,000 = 0.469	
13	**Current Ratio**	**Current Assets**	1.884
14		**Current Liabilities**	
15		='Balance Sheet'!B11/'Balance Sheet'!B27	
16		=$3,240,000/$1,720,000 = 1.884	
17	**Quick Ratio**	**Current Assets - Inventory**	1.363
18	**(or "Acid Test")**	**Current Liabilities**	
19		=('Balance Sheet'!B11-'Balance Sheet'!B9)/'Balance Sheet'!B27	
20		=($3,240,000 - $895,000)/$1,720,000 =$2,345,000,/$1,720,000 = 1.363	

Liquidity Measures

A firm's liquidity is a measure of its overall solvency, or its ability to satisfy short-term obligations *as they come due*. Figure 2-9 shows a set of liquidity measures (first column), the expressions for calculating them (second column), and the values for the ABC Company (third column). Values in the income and balance worksheets from Chapter 1 ("Income Stmt" and "Balance Sheet") are used for the calculations in the third column.

Net Working Capital

A firm's net working capital is its total current assets minus its current liabilities. A minimum dollar value of net working capital may be imposed as a condition for incurring long-term debt. A lending institution will require a firm to maintain sufficient working capital to protect its loan. The change in net working capital over time is useful for evaluating how well a firm's officers are operating a company on a continuing basis.

Ratio of Net Working Capital to Sales

This ratio is the net working capital divided by sales. It is often reported as the net working capital as a percent of sales. The dollar value of net working capital is useful for internal control, whereas its percentage of sales is useful for comparing a firm to other firms.

Ratio of Net Working Capital to Current Assets

This ratio is the net working capital divided by current assets. It expresses the percentage by which a firm's current assets can shrink before becoming less than the amount needed to cover current liabilities.

Current Ratio

The current ratio is the current assets divided by current liabilities. It measures a firm's ability to pay its short-term liabilities from its short-term assets. If the current ratio equals 1, its current assets equal its current liabilities and its net working capital is zero. If a firm's current ratio is 2, it means that its current assets can shrink by 50 percent and still be sufficient to cover its current liabilities.

Firms generally pay their bills from their current assets. Creditors favor a high current ratio as a sign that a firm will be able to pay its bills when due. Shareholders, on the other hand, may have a different view. Because current assets usually have lower rates of return than fixed assets, shareholders do not want too much of a firm's capital invested in current assets.

An acceptable value depends on the industry. The more predictable a firm's cash flows, the lower the value of the current ratio that is acceptable. A value of 1 would be acceptable for firms with predictable or continuous inflows of cash or other liquid assets, such as public utilities. Manufacturing firms, on the other hand, may require higher ratios because of long product development and manufacturing cycles. Values on the order of 2 are often regarded as acceptable for many industries.

A drop in the current ratio can be the first warning of financial problems. A firm in financial difficulty may be unable to pay its bills on time or may need to increase its borrowing. Current liabilities then rise faster than current assets, and the value of the current ratio falls. Plotting the month-to-month or year-to-year values of a firm's current ratio can reveal important trends in the firm's management.

Quick (or Acid-Test) Ratio

The quick (or acid-test) ratio is calculated by dividing current assets minus inventory by current liabilities. The quick ratio is similar to the current ratio except that it excludes inventory, which is generally the least liquid current asset. What is left after subtracting inventory from current assets is the sum of cash and equivalents, marketable securities, and accounts receivable—that is, so-called "quick assets" that can be liquidated on short notice. Inventories can hardly be liquidated at their book value. Therefore, for firms carrying large inventories that cannot be quickly converted into cash, the quick ratio provides a more realistic measure than does current ratio of a firm's ability to pay current obligations from current assets.

The value of the quick ratio is always less than that of the current ratio. Just as the quick and current ratios are useful measures in themselves, so also is their ratio. This is defined by the following:

$$\frac{Quick\ Ratio}{Current\ Ratio} = \frac{Current\ Assets - Inventories}{Current\ Assets}$$

A low value for the ratio (the quick ratio to the current ratio) can be a signal that inventories are higher than they should be. Inventories tie up major amounts of many firms' capital and have become a prime target for cost cutting in the last two decades. The increased attention to inventory control is reflected in what has been popularized as "Just-In-Time" inventory management.

Activity or Efficiency Ratios

Activity or efficiency ratios measure how well a firm is using its assets to generate sales. From another perspective, they measure the speed for converting various accounts into sales or cash. The most important accounts are inventories, accounts receivable, and accounts payable. Figure 2-10 is a spreadsheet for activity or efficiency ratios.

Outside analysts, who usually lack access to a firm's average values during the year, often substitute the average of year-end values reported to stockholders for the most recent and preceding years when calculating activity or efficiency ratios. This practice results in errors when sales and inventories are seasonal. For example, the average of the year-end inventories of retail stores can be much higher than the average during the entire year because of overstocking to satisfy holiday shoppers during December. In this case, the average values are better estimated by multiplying the year-end values by a factor based on experience.

The number of business days in a year varies with the company and industry. Typical values are 365, 360, and 250.

Figure 2-10
―――――――

Activity or Efficiency Ratios

	A	B	C
21		**ACTIVITY OR EFFICIENCY MEASURES**	
22		**Assumptions:** Percent of sales to customers that are on credit =	*90%*
23		Percent of company purchases that are on credit =	*95%*
24		Number of business days per year =	*365*
25	Inventory Turnover	<u>Annual Cost of Goods Sold (COGS)</u>	1.090
26	(Turnovers per year)	Average Cost of Inventory	(per year)
27		='Income Stmnt'!B5/AVERAGE('Balance Sheet'!(B9:C9))	
28		=$1,150,000/($895,000+$1,215,000)/2) = 1.090	
29	Average Collection Period	<u>Average Accounts Receivable</u> = <u>Average Accounts Receivable</u>	92.1
30	(Days)	Average Daily Credit Sales *Factor**Annual Sales Revenue/365	(days)
31		=AVERAGE('Balance Sheet'!B8:C8)/(C22*'Income Stmnt'!B4/C24)	
32		=(($565,000+$605,000)/2)/(*0.90**$2,575,000/365) = 92.1	
33	Accounts Receivable	<u>Annual Credit Sales</u>	3.962
34	Turnover Ratio	Average Accounts Receivable	(per year)
35		=C22*Income Stmnt'!B4/AVERAGE('BalanceSheet'!B8:C8)	
36		=*0.90**$2,575,000/(($565,000+$605,000)/2)= 3.962	
37	Average Payment Period	<u>Accounts Payable</u> = <u>Accounts Payable</u>	108.0
38	(Days)	Average Daily Credit Purchases Factor*Average Annual COGS/365	(days)
39		='Balance Sheet'!B24/(C23*AVERAGE(Income Stmnt'!B5:C5)/C24)	
40		=$300,000/(*0.95**(($1,150,000+$985,000)/2)/365) = 108.0	
41	Fixed Asset Turnover Ratio	<u>Annual Sales Revenue</u>	0.656
42		Fixed Assets	
43		='Income Stmnt'!B4/'Balance Sheet'!B20	
44		=$2,575,000/$3,925,000 = 0.656	
45	Total Asset Turnover Ratio	<u>Annual Sales Revenue</u>	0.359
46		Total Assets	
47		='Income Stmnt'!B4/'Balance Sheet'!B21	
48		=$2,575,000/$7,165,000 = 0.359	

Inventory Turnover

Inventories are a major expense for most firms. Funds tied up in inventories of raw material, work in-process, and finished goods are typically on the order of 20 to 50 percent of a manufacturing firm's total assets. They can equal a firm's profits for two or three years. For wholesale and retail firms, the value of inventories can be even more. Besides the cost of the goods themselves, inventories represent additional costs for purchasing, receiving, inspecting, and storing. These costs are often overlooked because they are treated as part of general and administrative (G&A) expenses rather than as separate items. Replacing traditional cost accounting systems by "*activity based costing*" (ABC) systems helps expose the causes of large expenditures on inventories that deserve closer management control.

Inventory turnover is the ratio of the cost of goods sold to the average value or cost of the goods in inventory. It measures how quickly a firm's inventory is sold. Note that the cost of the goods in inventory can vary significantly during the year so that its average during the year is different from the average of the year-end values of inventory.

Unless otherwise specified, inventory turnover is measured on an annual basis. An annual inventory turnover is the number of times a firm replaces its inventories during a year, or the number of times, on the average, items in inventory are sold to customers during the year. Ratios around 4 are common for aircraft manufacturers, whereas grocery stores have ratios of 20 or more, and bakeries selling perishable items might have ratios over 100. (For closer control, inventory turnover can be based on monthly or weekly periods rather than a full year.)

Annual ratios can be converted to the average days in inventory by dividing the ratio into the number of business days per year. For example, if the inventory turns over 7 times in a year of 365 business days, the average days in inventory would be 52.1 days (calculated as 365/7). Average days in inventory is commonly used for measuring how quickly computers and other high-tech items are moved out of factories and into the hands of customers.

Sales revenues are sometimes substituted for the cost of goods sold in calculating turnover ratios. When this is done, the turnover ratio measures the number of sales dollars generated for each dollar invested in inventories.

Average Collection Period

The average collection period is the average age of accounts receivable; in other words, it is the average time for collecting accounts receivable. It is usually expressed in days and is calculated by dividing the value of accounts receivable by the average daily sales on credit.

Because outside analysts do not have access to the actual data value, the average daily sales on credit is estimated by multiplying the annual sales by the estimated percentage of the sales on credit and then dividing by the number of business days in the year.

The average collection period evaluates how well a firm's credit and collection policies are being implemented. Its value should be less than the 30-day credit, 60-day credit, or other terms extended to customers. Many firms transfer amounts that are 90 days or more past due to a separate account for bad debts.

A low value for the average collection period is preferable, provided it is not so low that sales are lost by denying credit to credit-worthy customers because of a credit policy that is too tight.

Accounts Receivable Turnover Ratio

This is the ratio of credit sales to accounts receivable. Credit sales may be estimated as a specified percentage of the total annual sales reported to stockholders. The ratio is generally calculated on an annual basis. The accounts receivable turnover ratio expresses the dollars generated in credit sales during the year for each dollar invested in accounts receivable.

The accounts receivable turnover ratio and the average collection period are inversely related. The accounts receivable turnover ratio on an annual basis can be calculated by dividing the average collection period in days into 365.

Average Payment Period

The average payment period is the average age of accounts payable; in other words, it is the average time for paying accounts payable. This is usually expressed in days and is calculated by dividing the value of annual credit purchases by amounts payable. (The average daily credit purchases may be calculated as the annual credit sales divided by 365.) Because outside analysts do not have access to the actual data value, the value of the annual credit purchases is estimated as a percentage of the cost of goods sold.

Fixed Asset Turnover Ratio

The fixed asset turnover ratio measures how efficiently a firm is using its fixed assets (i.e., its "earning assets") to generate income from sales. It is calculated by dividing sales by net fixed assets.

Although higher ratios are generally better, acceptable values depend on the nature of the business. Firms in industries with large investments in fixed assets relative to sales, such as factories and electric utilities, will have low ratios. Firms with low investments in fixed assets relative to sales, such as wholesalers, discount chains, and management consultants, will have high ratios. Whatever the level, declines in a company's fixed asset ratio over time is a sign of impending trouble.

Total Asset Turnover Ratio

The total asset turnover ratio measures how efficiently a firm is using its total assets to generate income from sales. It is calculated by dividing sales by total assets.

Leverage or Debt Ratios

Leverage or debt ratios measure the degree to which a firm uses debt (that is, other people's money) to generate profits. The ratios described in this section measure degree of indebtedness—that is, the amount of debt relative to other balance sheet amounts. Figure 2-11 is a spreadsheet for leverage or debt ratios.

Equity, which is the term in the denominator of the last two ratios, includes: (1) The value of preferred stock, which equals its par value multiplied by the weighted number of outstanding shares; (2) the value of common stock, which equals its par value multiplied by the weighted number of

Figure 2-11

Leverage or Debt Ratios

	A	B	C
49		**LEVERAGE OR DEBT RATIOS**	
50	**Total Debt to**	<u>Total Liabilities</u>	0.505
51	**Total Assets**	**Total Assets**	
52		='Balance Sheet'!B29/'Balance Sheet'!B21	
53		=$3,620,000/$7,165,000 = 0.505	
54	**Long-Term Debt to**	<u>Long Term Debt</u>	0.265
55	**Total Assets**	**Total Assets**	
56		='Balance Sheet'!B28/'Balance Sheet'!B21	
57		=$1,900,000/$7,165,000 = 0.265	
58	**Long-Term Debt to**	<u>Long-Term Debt</u>	0.349
59	**Total Capitalization**	**Long-Term Debt + Total Stockholders' Equity**	
60		='Balance Sheet'!B28/('Balance Sheet'!B28+'Balance Sheet'!B35)	
61		=$1,900,000/($1,900,000 + $3,545,000) = 0.349	
62	**Total Debt to**	<u>Total Liabilities</u>	1.021
63	**Stockholders' Equity**	**Total Stockholders' Equity**	
64		='Balance Sheet'!B29/'Balance Sheet'!B35	
65		=$3,620,000/$3,545,000 = 1.021	
66	**Long-Term Debt to**	<u>Long-Term Debt</u>	0.536
67	**Stockholders' Equity**	**Total Stockholders' Equity**	
68		='Balance Sheet'!B28/'Balance Sheet'!B35	
69		=$1,900,000/$3,545,000 = 0.536	

outstanding shares; (3) the value of paid-in capital in excess of par on additional common stock issued; and (4) retained earnings. Their sum is the value in Cell B35 of the Balance Sheet.

Creditors become concerned when a firm carries so much debt that it has difficulty or is slow in paying bills or repaying loans. Claims of creditors must be satisfied before the distribution of earnings to shareholders. Investors are wary of large debts that make earnings volatile. On the other hand, interest on debts is a tax-deductible expense, so that debt can be a way to increase the wealth of a firm's shareholders.

Total Debt Ratio

This is the ratio of the *total* amount of debt (i.e., total liabilities, both long- and short-term) to total assets. It measures the degree to which a company's debt is supported by assets and, along with the total debt to equity ratio, is an important measure of a company's financial leverage.

Long-Term Debt Ratio

This is the ratio of only *long-term* debt to total assets. Long-term loans are of particular concern because they commit a firm to paying interest over the long term and the principal borrowed must eventually be repaid.

Ratio of Long-Term Debt to Total Capitalization

This is the ratio of long-term debt to a firm's use of long-term sources of capital, which includes long-term debt (usually in the form of bonds), preferred equity, and common equity. Common equity is the sum of common stock and retained earnings.

Total Debt to Equity Ratio

This is the ratio of total debt to total shareholders' equity. It quantifies the relationship between the funds provided by creditors to those provided by a firm's owners.

A firm with a high proportion of debt to owners' equity is highly leveraged. As the value of the ratio increases, the return to owners also increases. This means that high leverage has the advantage of accruing earnings after interest and taxes to the firm's owners rather than to its creditors. On the other hand, higher leverage increases risk when earnings drop. A highly leverage company may be forced to the point of insolvency because of the high cost of interest on its debts.

The trend in the value of the ratio with time can reveal important information about shifts in management policies for financing a firm's operations and the risks it is willing to take.

Long-Term Debt to Equity Ratio

This is the ratio of only long-term debt to total shareholders' equity.

Interest Coverage Ratios

Coverage ratios are similar to liquidity ratios but have a particular focus on a firm's ability to service its debts—that is, to pay what it owes on schedule over the lifetimes of the debts. A firm that is unable to meet its obligations is deemed to be in default. Creditors of a firm in default may seek immediate repayment, which may force a firm into bankruptcy. Figure 2-12 is a spreadsheet for interest coverage ratios.

Figure 2-12

Interest Coverage Ratios

	A	B	C
70		INTEREST COVERAGE RATIOS	
71	**Times Interest Earned**	**Earnings before Interest and Taxes (EBIT)**	12.833
72	**Ratio**	**Interest Expense**	
73		='Income Stmnt'B15/'Income Stmnt'!B19	
74		=$770,000/$60,000 = 12.833	
75	**Cash Coverage Ratio**	**Cash Available** = **EBIT + Depreciation**	14.500
76		**Interest Expense** **Interest Expense**	
77		=('Income Stmnt'!B15+'Income Stmnt'!B10)/'Income Stmnt'!B19	
78		=($770,000 + $100,000)/$60,000 = 14.500	

Times Interest Earned Ratio

This is the ratio of a firm's annual earnings before interest and taxes (EBIT) to its interest expense. It is also known as the ***interest coverage ratio***. It equals the number of times a year that interest payments are covered by current earnings. It is a measure of solvency, or a firm's ability to meet contractual interest payments. A firm that is unable to pay interest when due may suffer default on its loans. (Another interpretation is that this ratio is a test of a firm's staying power under adversity.)

An interest coverage ratio less than 1 indicates a firm is unable to generate enough cash to service its debt. A downward trend with time is an omen of oncoming difficulty. Firms with erratic and unpredictable income need higher ratios to avoid default than firms with stable rates of income.

Cash Coverage Ratio

This is the ratio of the cash available to pay interest to a firm's interest expense. The cash available to pay interest is a firm's EBIT plus its non-cash expenses, such as depreciation expense. (Recall that depreciation is a *non*-cash expense and is subtracted in the calculation of EBIT.)

Profitability Ratios

Profitability ratios provide a number of ways for examining a firm's profits in relation to factors that affect profits. High values are preferred for all of the profitability ratios. Figure 2-13 is a spreadsheet for profitability ratios.

Gross Profit Margin

This is the ratio of gross profit to sales. (Recall that gross profit is calculated by subtracting the cost of goods sold from sales revenues.) High profit margins indicate a firm is able to sell its goods or services at a low cost or high price. The gross profit margin indicates the percentage of income from sales that is available to pay a firm's expenses other than the cost of goods sold.

Operating Profit Margin

This is the ratio of the earnings before income and taxes (i.e., a firm's net operating income) to sales.

Net Profit Margin

This is the ratio of a firm's net income (i.e., its earnings after interest and taxes, EAT) to sales.

Return on Total Assets (ROA)

This is the ratio of net income (EAT) to total assets. It's also called the return on investment (ROI) or the net return on assets. Note the following relationship:

$$ROA(net) = \frac{Net\ Income}{Total\ Assets} = \frac{Net\ Income}{Sales} \times \frac{Sales}{Total\ Assets}$$

Figure 2-13

Profitability Measures

	A	B	C
80	**Gross Profit Margin**	**Gross Profit**	0.553
81		**Sales**	
82		='Income Stmnt'!B6/'Income Stmnt'!B4	
83		=$1,425,000/$2,575,000 = 0.553	
84	**Operating Profit Margin**	**Earnings before Interest and Taxes (EBIT)**	0.299
85		**Sales**	
86		='Income Smnt'!B15/'Income Stmnt'!B4	
87		=$770,000/$2,575,000 = 0.299	
88	**Net Profit Margin**	**Earnings after Interest and Taxes (EAT)**	0.165
89		**Sales**	
90		='Income Stmnt'!B25/'Income Stmnt'!B4	
91		=$426,000/$2,575,000 = 0.165	
92	**Return on Total Assets**	**Earnings after Interest and Taxes (EAT)**	0.059
93		**Total Assets**	
94		='Income Stmt'!B25/'Balance Sheet'!B21	
95		=$426,000/$7,165,000 = 0.059	
96	**Return on Equity (ROE)**	**Earnings after Interest and Taxes (EAT)**	0.120
97		**Total Stockholders' Equity**	
98		='Income Stmt'!B25/'Balance Sheet'!B35	
99		=$426,000/$3,545,000 = 0.120	
100	**Return on Common**	**Net Earnings Available to Common Stockholders**	0.099
101	**Equity**	**Common Stockholders' Equity**	
102		='Income Stmt'!B27/('Balance Sheet'!B35-'Balance Sheet'!B31)	
103		=$331,000/($3,545,000 - $200,000) = $331,000/$3,345,000 = 0.099	

That is, the net return on assets equals the product of the net profit margin times the asset turnover ratio. A high ROA is favored. However, a low value for one ratio can be offset by a high value for the other ratio.

The return on assets can also be calculated as the ratio of earnings before interest and taxes (EBIT) to assets. This is the gross return on assets. Note the following relationship:

$$ROA(gross) = \frac{EBIT}{Total\ Assets} = \frac{EBIT}{Sales} \times \frac{Sales}{Total\ Assets}$$

The gross return on assets equals the product of the operating profit margin times the total asset turnover ratio.

Firms usually face a trade-off between profit margins and turnover; it is difficult to have high values of both. Some firms have low profit margins with high turnover rates (e.g., groceries and discount retailers), while others have high profit margins with low turnover rates (e.g., jewelers and fine art galleries). Financial strategies can sometimes be expressed in terms of turnover rates and profit margins. For example, providing more liberal credit terms would decrease the asset turnover ratio because receivables would increase more than sales. Therefore, to maintain the same return on assets, the firm would have to increase its profit margin.

Return on Equity (ROE)

This is the ratio of net income (or EAT) to stockholders' equity (both preferred and common stockholders). It is a primary measure of how well a company is using the equity of its owners to achieve a high earnings rate. The year-to-year values of ROE indicate how well a company's managers are achieving a consistent rate of return.

ROE overcomes a principal disadvantage of earnings per share (EPS), which does not take into account the amount of capital needed to generate earnings. Two companies may require much different levels of capital investment to achieve the same EPS.

The following shows an algebraic construction of ROE as the product of the ratios for the net profit margin, total asset turnover, and assets to owners' equity. (This algebraic construction is known as the duPont model because of its development and use by analysts at the E. I. Du Pont de Nemours & Co. in the 1920s. (Notice that Sales and Total Assets each appear in a numerator and denominator, thereby canceling each other in the value of ROE.)

$$ROE = \frac{Net\ Income}{Owners'\ Equity} = \frac{Net\ Income}{Sales} \times \frac{Sales}{Total\ Assets} \times \frac{Total\ Assets}{Owners'\ Equity}$$

Each of the three ratios focuses attention on a different aspect of management attention.

1. The first ratio focuses on the relationship between the price and the cost of goods or services sold. It equals the net profit margin, which is the third of the profitability measures listed in Figure 2-11.
2. The second ratio focuses on how well assets are used to generate sales. It equals the total asset turnover ratio, which is the last of the activity or efficiency measures listed in Figure 2-8.
3. The third ratio focuses on the use of leverage to maximize the return to shareholders.

One should also note that the product of the first two ratios is the return on assets (ROA), which is the fourth of the profitability measures listed in Figure 2-13.

High values are generally favored for each of these three ratios in order to produce a high value for ROE. But a high value for ROE may hide a low value for one of the ratios if the other ratios are high. For example, a company with a high value for asset turnover (the second of the ratios) does not need high net profit margins (the first of the ratios) in order to show a high ROE. By looking at each ratio separately, one gets a better idea of what is driving the value of ROE and where management may need improvement.

ROE values can be inflated by a firm's excessive use of debt capital, which increases the value of the third term (the asset-to-equity ratio). This means that only a small fraction of the capital being used to conduct the business is in the form of owners' equity. To compensate for excessive debt, some analysts prefer to measure return on total capital, which includes both debt and equity in the denominator.

ROE can be viewed as a composite measure of how well management is performing in the functional areas of operations, sales, and financial management.

Return on Common Equity

This is the ratio of the net income available to holders of common stock to their equity. The net income available to common stockholders is the net income minus dividends to shareholders of preferred stock. Common equity is the difference between total equity and the equity of shareholders of preferred stock.

Stockholder and Market Value Ratios

These ratios depend on the number of shares of stock issued to holders of common and preferred stock and to their value, as established by market prices. Figure 2-14 is a spreadsheet for these ratios based on an assumed market price of $35.00 for shares of the ABC Company.

Earnings per Share (EPS)

Earnings per share is the number of dollars earned (i.e., net income or earnings after interest and taxes, EBIT) for each share of outstanding common stock.

Price-to-Earnings Ratio (P/E) and Other Per-Share Ratios

The P/E ratio is the amount buyers of a firm's common stock are willing to pay for each dollar of a firm's earnings. P/E ratios are easily found on the Web by seeking a stock price on Yahoo! or other sites and then clicking on the company of interest.

Figure 2-14

Stockholder and Market Value Ratios

	A	B	C
104		STOCKHOLDER AND MARKET VALUE RATIOS	
105		Assumptions: Number of outstanding shares of common stock =	100,000
106		Stock price, per share =	$35.00
107	Earnings per Share	Net Earnings Available to Common Stockholders	$3.31
108		Number of Outstanding Shares of Common Stock	
109		='Income Stmnt'!B28 or 'Income Stmnt'!B27/C105	
110		=$331,000/100,000 shares = $3.31	
111	Price/Earnings Ratio (P/E)	Price per Share of Common Stock	10.574
112		Earnings per Share of Common Stock	
113		=C106/'Income Stmnt'!B28	
114		=($35.00/share)/($3.31/share) = 10.574	
115	Payout Ratio	Cash Dividends Paid to Stockholders	0.484
116		Net Income (EAT)	
117		=('Income Stmnt'!B26+'Income Stmnt'!B30)/'Income Stmnt'!B25	
118		=($95,000 + $111,000)/$426,000 = $206,000/$426,000 = 0.484	
119	Retention Ratio	Retained Earnings	0.516
120		Net Income (EAT)	
121		='Income Stmnt'!B29/'Income Stmnt'!B25	
122		=$220,000/$426,000 = 0.516	
123	Market-to-Book Value	Number of Outstanding Shares of Common Stock* Price per Share	0.987
124		Total Equity of Holders of Common and Preferred Stock	
125		=C105*C106/'Balance Sheet'!B35	
126		=(100,000 shares X $35/share)/$3,545,000 = 0.987	

The P/E ratio represents the level of confidence investors have in a firm's future profitability. Their trends reflect shifts in investors' confidence. P/E ratios are widely used by investors to measure a stock's value and decide whether to buy, sell, or take other action.

Industries whose revenues and earnings are relatively insensitive to the ups-and-downs of business cycles generally have higher P/E ratios than industries whose stock values fluctuate with the economy. For example, the P/E ratios of health-care stocks are higher than those for automotive stocks. That is because when people get sick, they continue to pay for health-care products and services even when the economy is down. Auto owners, on the other hand, have more money for buying new cars when the economy is strong but hang on to their old cars and defer buying new ones when the economy falters.

The "old" rule was to be wary of stocks with P/E ratios greater than 10 or 15. Such rules "went out the window" with the soaring prices of technology stocks during the New Economy era of the 1990s. P/E ratios of 20 and more were then justified for companies with high growth rates. Recessions in biotechnology and information technology stocks that began early in the year 2000 have cut P/E ratios to a fraction of their high-flying values.

P/E ratios can be very misleading. The value of earnings in the denominator can be easily manipulated and increased to lower the ratio and make a company's stock appear more attractive. Because earnings are the net result of sales, cash flow, and debt, a company's reported earnings can be raised, for example, by adding the sale of assets into income, changing depreciation policies, cutting back on provisions for bad debt, or buying back the company's stock. ("Beyond P/E," *Fortune*, May 28, 2001, page 174) The *Fortune* article recommends that investors look at two other per-share price ratios, the price-to-sales revenue (P/SR) and price-to-cash flow (P/CF) ratios, as well as the debt-to-total capital and net income-to-total capital ratios.

Because you cannot have earnings without sales, any trouble on the top line of the income statement can point to hidden problems below. Increases in earnings without increases in sales revenue should alert you to possible accounting handiwork. The P/SR ratio is the ratio of a stock's price to the sales revenue per share. (The denominator's value is obtained by dividing the annual sales revenue by the number of outstanding shares of common stock.)

Payout Ratio

This is the ratio of the annual dividends paid to stockholders divided by the firm's net income.

Retention Ratio

This is the ratio of the retained earnings divided by the firm's net income. Note that the sum of the payout and retention ratios must equal 1.

Market-to-Book Value

This is the ratio of the value of the firm in the eyes of investors to the value of the firm on the firm's books. The numerator of this ratio is calculated as the product of the number of outstanding shares of common stock multiplied by the share price. The denominator is the total equity of stockholders. Relatively high values for the market-to-book ratio are associated with investor optimism and good returns on equity, whereas relatively low values indicate the opposite.

Comparisons of Financial Ratios

Figure 2-15 is a spreadsheet showing the comparisons for the hypothetical ABC Company and the industry in which it operates.

Values for the latest year in Column B are transferred from Figure 2-11, and values in Column C are those for 20X1. Some values for 20X1, for example inventory turnover, cannot be computed because data for the preceding year is not available to compute averages with 20X1. Industry average values for the ratios are shown in Column D. Where values are unavailable, the entries "na" are made.

Figure 2-15

Evaluation of Ratios and Their Trends

	A	B	C	D	E	F	G
1	SUMMARY OF FINANCIAL MEASURES AND EVALUATION						
2	OF 20X2 AND 20X1 RESULTS FOR ABC COMPANY						
3					Evaluation of Results		
4		ABC Company		Industry	20X2 to	20X2 to	20X2
5		20X2	20X1	Average	20X1	Industry	Overall
6	LIQUIDITY MEASURES						
7	Net Working Capital	$1,520,000	$1,435,000	na	Good	na	na
8	Ratio, Net Working Capital to Sales	0.590	0.700	0.325	Bad	Good	OK
9	Ratio, Net Working Capital to Current Assets	0.469	0.480	0.275	Bad	Good	OK
10	Current Ratio	1.884	1.923	1.400	Bad	Good	OK
11	Quick Ratio (or "Acid Test")	1.363	1.141	0.900	Good	Good	Good
12	ACTIVITY OR EFFICIENCY MEASURES						
13	Inventory Turnover (per year)	1.090	na	2.500	na	Bad	na
14	Average Collection Period (days)	92.1	na	89.5	na	Bad	na
15	Accounts Receivable Turnover Ratio (per year)	3.96	na	4.08	na	Bad	na
16	Average Payment Period (days)	108.0	na	90	na	Bad	na
17	Fixed Asset Turnover Ratio	0.656	0.562	1.500	Good	Bad	OK
18	Total Asset Turnover Ratio	0.359	0.309	0.500	Good	Bad	OK
19	LEVERAGE OR DEBT RATIOS						
20	Total Debt Ratio	0.505	0.499	0.600	Bad	Good	OK
21	Long-Term Debt Ratio	0.265	0.265	0.200	Bad	Bad	Bad
22	Ratio of Long-Term Debt to Total Capitalization	0.349	0.345	0.600	Bad	Good	OK
23	Total Debt to Equity Ratio	1.021	0.995	3.00	Bad	Good	OK
24	Long-Term Debt to Equity Ratio	0.536	0.528	2.000	Bad	Good	OK
25	INTEREST COVERAGE RATIOS						
26	Times Interest Earned Ratio	12.833	7.000	5.000	Good	Good	Good
27	Cash Coverage Ratio	14.500	8.462	6.000	Good	Good	Good
28	PROFITABILITY MEASURES						
29	Gross Profit Margin	0.553	0.520	0.300	Good	Good	Good
30	Operating Profit Margin	0.299	0.222	0.200	Good	Good	Good
31	Net Profit Margin	0.165	0.114	0.100	Good	Good	Good
32	Return on Total Assets	0.059	0.035	0.060	Good	Bad	OK
33	Return on Equity (ROE)	0.120	0.070	0.150	Good	Bad	OK
34	Return on Common Equity	0.099	0.044	0.090	Good	Good	Good

Cell entries for evaluation tests

E7: =IF(OR($B7="na",C7="na"),"na",IF($B7>C7,"Good","Bad")), copy to E8:F11, E13:F13, E15:F15, E17:F18, E26:F27, and E29:F34

E14: =IF(OR($B14="na",C14="na"),"na",IF($B14<C14,"Good","Bad")), copy to F14, E16:F16, and E20:F24

G7: =IF(OR(B7="na",C7="na",D7="na"),"na",IF(AND(B7>C7,B7>D7),"Good",IF(OR(B7>C7,B7>D7),"OK","Bad"))), copy to G8:G11,G13,G15, G17:G18, G26:G27, and G29:G34

G14: =IF(OR(B14="na",C14="na",D14="na"),"na",IF(AND(B14<C14,B14<D14),"Good",IF(OR(B14<C14,B14<D14), "OK","Bad"))), copy to G16 and G20:G24

na   Data is not available for making a comparison.

The evaluations in Column E of Figure 2-15 compare results for 20X2 and 20X1. Evaluations are "Good" or "Bad" according to whether results for 20X2 are better or worse than for 20X1. Wherever values are not available for making the comparisons, the results of the comparisons are "na."

Comparisons are programmed by using IF statements. These have the general form

IF(logical_test,result_if_test_is_true,result_if_test_is_false)

For example, an increase in net working capital in Cell B7 as compared to Cell C7 would be a "Good" result, otherwise the result would be "Bad" (otherwise the failure to increase would be "Bad"). This can be expressed by the entry =IF(B7>C7,"Good","Bad"). The quotation marks around the results indicate that the results are text entries rather than numerical values.

A comparison is not possible whenever data is missing for making the comparison. Therefore, before attempting to make a comparison, a check should be made for missing data. For example, the complete entry in Cell E7 should be

=IF(OR($B7="na",C7="na"),"na",IF($B7>C7,"Good","Bad"))

The first "IF" in this expression checks to see if data is missing in either Cell B7 or C7. If either value is missing, the result is "na." If values are available in both Cells B7 and C7, the first IF test is not satisfied, and instead of returning "na" the second IF test is made. The second IF test checks to see whether or not the value in Cell B7 is greater than that in Cell C7. If it is greater, the result is "Good"; otherwise it is "Bad."

Note carefully that, when copying the expression in Cell E7 to other cells in Column E, some of the comparisons should be reversed—that is, in some cases it is "Good" (rather than "Bad") when a value in column B is less (rather than more) than the corresponding value in Column C. For example, the entry in Cell E14 should be

=IF(OR($B14="na",C14="na"),"na",IF($B14<C14"Good","Bad"))

The reversed conditions can be handled most easily by copying the entry in Cell E7 to the other cells with comparisons in Column E and then reversing the inequality sign in Cells E14, E16, and E20:E24.

The evaluations in Column F compare results for 20X2 with the industry average values. These comparisons can be made by copying the entries in Column E to Column F. The $ signs before the two Bs in the expressions above allow the expressions in Column E to be copied to Column F so that the second IF portion of the expression works for comparisons of results for 20X2 to the average industry values.

The evaluations in Column G compare results for 20X2 with those for 20X1 **and** industry averages. As before, IF data is not available for a comparison, the comparison cannot be made. **IF** results for 20X2 are better than both those for 20X1 and the industry average, the evaluation is "Good." **IF** results for 20X2 are better for only the comparisons to 20X1 or the industry averages, but not for both, the evaluation is "OK." **IF** results for 20X2 are poorer than those for both 20X1 and industry averages, the evaluation is "Bad." For example, the entry in Cell G8 is

=IF(OR(B8="na",C8="na",D8="na"), "na",IF(AND(B8>C8,B8>D8), "Good",

IF(OR(B8>C8,B8>D8), "OK", "Bad")))

In other words, this entry says that **IF any** of the values in Cells B8, C8, or D8 is missing, the comparison cannot be made, but **IF** B8 is greater than **both** C8 **and** D8, the result is "Good"; however, IF B8 is greater than **either** C8 **or** D8 (but not both, which was tested by the first IF), the result is "OK"; and IF **neither** comparison is satisfied, the result is "Bad." Note that for each entry, there are three test conditions (i.e., three IFs) and four possible results. Also, as before, whenever the reverse conditions are better, the inequality signs should be reversed.

Values for the financial ratios of different industries are needed to determine how well a company is doing relative to other companies in the same industry. You can find such information in the following references, which are updated annually:

- *Almanac of Business and Industrial Financial Ratios.* (Prentice-Hall, Englewood Cliffs, NJ)
- *Industry Norms & Key Business Ratios.* (Dun & Bradstreet, Industry & Financial Consulting Services, Bethlehem, PA)
- *IRS Corporate Financial Ratios.* (Schonfeld & Associates, Inc., Lincolnshire, IL))
- *RMA Annual Statement Studies.* (Robert Morris Associates, The Association of Lending & Credit Risk Professionals, Philadelphia, PA)

Conditional Formatting

Some analyses compare results for large numbers of financial ratios, so that it's easy to overlook comparisons that are "Bad" and need management attention. It is therefore helpful to use some means to direct attention to the "Bad" results. Therefore, where the ratings in Figure 2-15 are "Bad," the cells have been highlighted to direct managers' attention to conditions that need improvement. This is done with Excel's conditional formatting tool.

To use conditional formatting, click on a cell to be conditionally formatted and access the "Conditional Formatting" dialog box from the Format pull-down menu. Enter the conditions in the three boxes in the top row of Figure 2-16. (Enter the word Bad in the right box. Excel will change this to ="Bad".)

Figure 2-16

Conditional Formatting Dialog Box with Condition to be Formatted

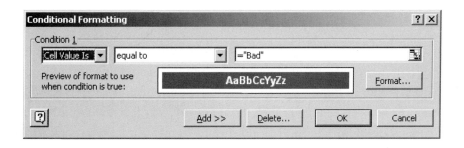

Figure 2-17

Format Cells Dialog Box for Conditional Formatting of the Font Style

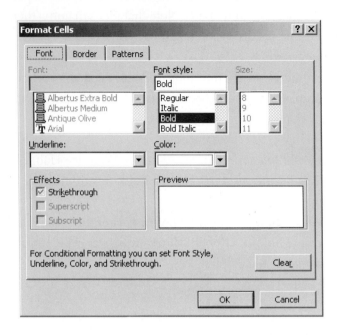

Click on the "Format" button in Figure 2-16 to access the "Format Cells" dialog box shown in Figure 2-17. Select from the options on the three sheet tabs. On the font tab, select the "Bold" style and white color, as indicated in Figure 2-17. On the patterns tab, select a deep red color for the cell shading. Press OK or the Enter key to complete formatting.

Long-Term Trends in Financial Ratios

In addition to short-term trends in financial ratios, such as those summarized in Figure 2-15, managers and investors find valuable information in how key financial ratios have remained stable, shifted, or changed abruptly up or down. Such information can indicate shifts in a firm's strategies or in the competitive markets in which it operates. The following are a few examples for real corporations and how they might be interpreted. Trend lines have been matched to past data and projected two years forward. (The material is a composite of a selection of research projects from those submitted by the authors' students.)

Nike

Founded in 1964 as Blue Ribbon Sports to import running shoes from Japan, Nike has become one of the largest sports and fitness companies in the world. Except for a slight downturn in liquidity from 2005 to 2006, the seven-year trends in Figure 2-18 shows sustained improvements in Nike's liquidity, leverage, and profitability ratios. Nike's current and quick ratios are still very favorable, but the drop in 2006 indicates potential financial problems ahead. The downward trend in Nike's leverage ratios indicates that

Figure 2-18

Selected Financial Ratios for the Nike Corporation from 2000 to 2006 and Projections

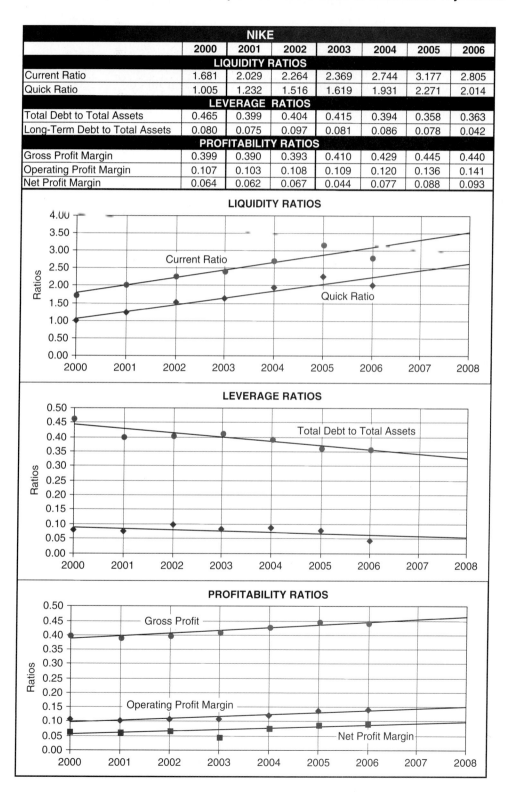

NIKE							
	2000	**2001**	**2002**	**2003**	**2004**	**2005**	**2006**
LIQUIDITY RATIOS							
Current Ratio	1.681	2.029	2.264	2.369	2.744	3.177	2.805
Quick Ratio	1.005	1.232	1.516	1.619	1.931	2.271	2.014
LEVERAGE RATIOS							
Total Debt to Total Assets	0.465	0.399	0.404	0.415	0.394	0.358	0.363
Long-Term Debt to Total Assets	0.080	0.075	0.097	0.081	0.086	0.078	0.042
PROFITABILITY RATIOS							
Gross Profit Margin	0.399	0.390	0.393	0.410	0.429	0.445	0.440
Operating Profit Margin	0.107	0.103	0.108	0.109	0.120	0.136	0.141
Net Profit Margin	0.064	0.062	0.067	0.044	0.077	0.088	0.093

Nike is reducing its use of debt to finance its operations. This change in its capital structure reduces Nike's exposure to downturns in the economy and its sales income. The upward trend of the profitability ratios indicates no problem in Nike's continuing profitability.

H. J. Heintz Company

Figure 2-19 shows the liquidity ratios of the H. J. Heintz Company from 2000 to 2006. The upswing from 2001 to 2003, following the decline from 2000 to 2001, was due to Heintz's building up cash reserves and reducing its short-term debt by selling off some of its businesses, such as Del Monte. The downward trend from 2003 can be associated with business strategies of expanding core product offerings (e.g., acquisition of HP Foods) and using cash to drive shareholder value (e.g., stock buy-backs and dividend increases). The continuing downward trend reflects business conditions (e.g., increasing costs for energy, commodities, and transportation) and competition (e.g., consolidation and narrowing profit margins). However, its current levels of liquidity are still considered financially healthy for the industry.

Figure 2-19

Liquidity Ratios for the H. J. Heintz Company from 2000 to 2006

H. J. HEINTZ COMPANY							
	2000	2001	2002	2003	2004	2005	2006
LIQUIDITY RATIOS							
Current Ratio	1.491	0.853	1.344	1.705	1.462	1.409	1.340
	1.491	0.853	1.344	1.705			
				1.705	1.462	1.409	1.340
Quick Ratio (or "Acid Test")	0.738	0.468	0.867	1.107	0.994	0.923	0.808
	0.738	0.468	0.867	1.107			
				1.107	0.994	0.923	0.808

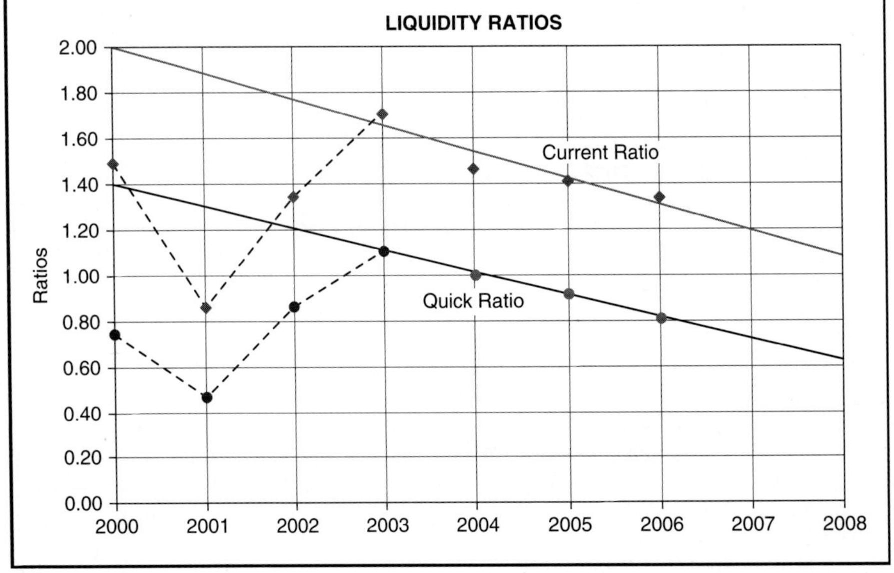

To show the behavior from 2003 to 2006 separately from the earlier behavior, values are selected from Rows 4 and 7 and copied into Rows 5, 6, 8, and 9. This gives four sets of ratios plotted in Figure 2-19. Excel's tool for inserting trend lines is used to create and project the current trend lines (i.e., from 2003 to 2006). By looking at the trend lines, investors can recognize how successful Heintz's management has been in improving the company's liquidity from 2003 to 2006 and estimate the results for the continuation of management's strategies to 2008.

Figure 2-20 is a plot of Heintz's inventory turnover. The number of turnovers per year dropped sharply from 2000 to 2001, and the overall trend since then has shown a more-or-less steady improvement from one year to the next. Both the straight line and the quadratic curve provide valid models of the past

Figure 2-20

Inventory Turnover for the H. J. Heintz Company from 2000 to 2006 with Linear and Quadratic Trend Lines Based on 2001 to 2006 Data Projected to 2008

H. J. HEINTZ COMPANY							
	2000	2001	2002	2003	2004	2005	2006
EFFICIENCY RATIOS							
Inventory Turnover (per year)	0.728	0.436	0.374	0.464	0.406	0.418	0.546
	0.728	0.436					
		0.436	0.374	0.464	0.406	0.418	0.546

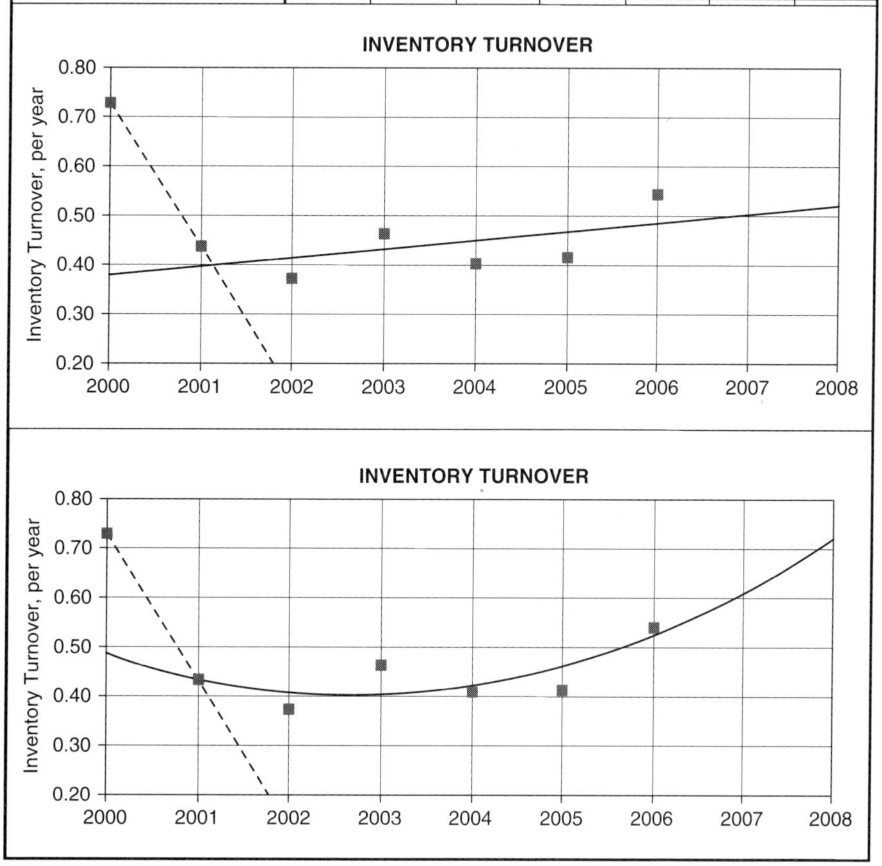

behavior, with the data scattering randomly above and below each type of trend line. The quadratic curve in the lower chart shows a more aggressive approach to improving inventory turnover than the straight line trend in the upper chart. The general rule (from statistics to choose between two regression models, both of whose errors scatter randomly about a mean error of zero), is to choose the simpler model. In this case, the choice would be the linear model, which is more conservative. However, beyond understanding just the numbers from the past, forecasting Heintz's future depends upon understanding its strategies and tactics for managing inventories.

Dell Inc.

Dell Inc. is a computer-hardware company based in Round Rock, Texas. The company sells personal computers, servers, data storage devices, network switches, personal digital assistants, computer peripherals, and other manufactured products, as well as software. It also provides technical support for its products. According to Fortune magazine, Dell ranked as the 25th-largest company in the United States in 2006 based on its annual revenue. Dell's business strategy has been based on building-to-order. This helps reduce the size of inventories and increases the number of inventory turnovers per year.

The first line of the table at the top of Figure 2-21 shows how the values for the number of turnovers per year have varied from 2001 to 2006. These values have been divided into 365 to calculate the average number of days items are held in inventory. These are shown on the second line and provide an easier concept to grasp than the turnover rate. Values for the complete trend from 2001 to 2006 follow the quadratic curve shown in Figure 2-21. As the figure shows, Dell's inventory management improved from

Figure 2-21

Dell Inc.'s Inventory Management Profile

DELL INC.						
	2001	2002	2003	2004	2005	2006
ACTIVITY EFFICIENCY MEASURES						
Inventory Turnover (turnovers per year)	64.3	75.7	99.5	107.1	102.3	88.8
Average Number of Days Held in Inventory	5.7	4.8	3.7	3.4	3.6	4.1

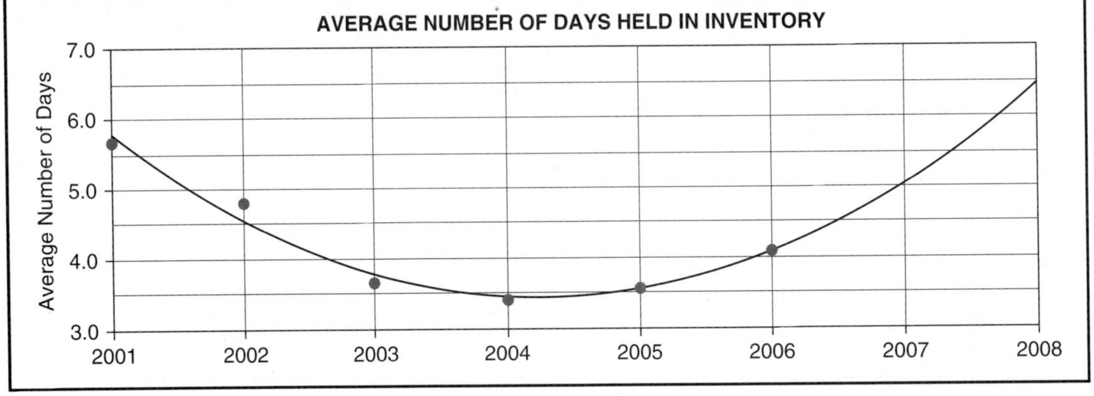

AVERAGE NUMBER OF DAYS HELD IN INVENTORY

2001 to 2004, when the "average number of days" items were held in inventory dropped from 5.7 in 2001 to 3.4 in 2004. For the last two years of data, the average time items were held in inventory increased. If this trend continues (a big IF), the average time items are held in inventory will increase to approximately 6.4 days for 2008. This represents a very significant increase in the cost of holding inventories and would adversely affect Dell's bottom line. Improving its inventory management is a significant part of Dell's management strategy.

Apple Computer, Inc.

Apple Computer, Inc. is headquartered in Cupertino, California. The company develops, sells, and supports a series of personal computers, portable media players, computer software, and computer hardware accessories. Its best known products are the the Macintosh line of personal computers, the Mac OS X operating system, the iPod portable music player, and the iTunes Store. Apple's customers are unusually devoted to the company and its products.

Figure 2-22 shows Apple's current ratio from 2000 to 2006. The values scatter randomly above and below the trend line. The drop in 2006 was largely related to the company's prepayment to secure a key component (Nand flash memory) and for its cash outflows to build a second campus and to continue the expansion of its retail outlets.

Figure 2-23 shows the turnaround in Apple's profitability ratios from 2000 to 2006 and the projection to 2008 of the trend from 2005 to 2006. The steep decline in 2001 in the returns on common equity and total assets are related to the "high-tech" bust of the time. Both ratios improved as revenues increased

Figure 2-22

Apple's Current Ratio from 2000 to 2006 and Projected Trend Line to 2008

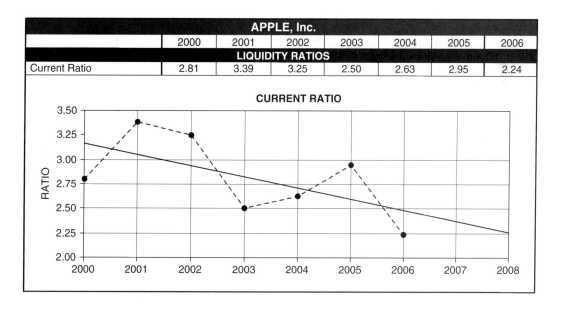

APPLE, Inc.							
	2000	2001	2002	2003	2004	2005	2006
LIQUIDITY RATIOS							
Current Ratio	2.81	3.39	3.25	2.50	2.63	2.95	2.24

Figure 2-23

Apple's Profitability Ratios for 2000 to 2006

APPLE COMPUTER							
	2000	2001	2002	2003	2004	2005	2006
PROFITABILITY MEASURES							
Return on Total Assets	0.116	−0.004	0.007	0.008	0.033	0.115	0.116
	0.116	−0.004	0.007	0.008	0.033	0.115	
						0.115	0.116
Return on Common Equity	0.195	−0.006	0.010	0.013	0.052	0.179	0.199
	0.195	−0.006	0.010	0.013	0.052	0.179	
						0.179	0.199

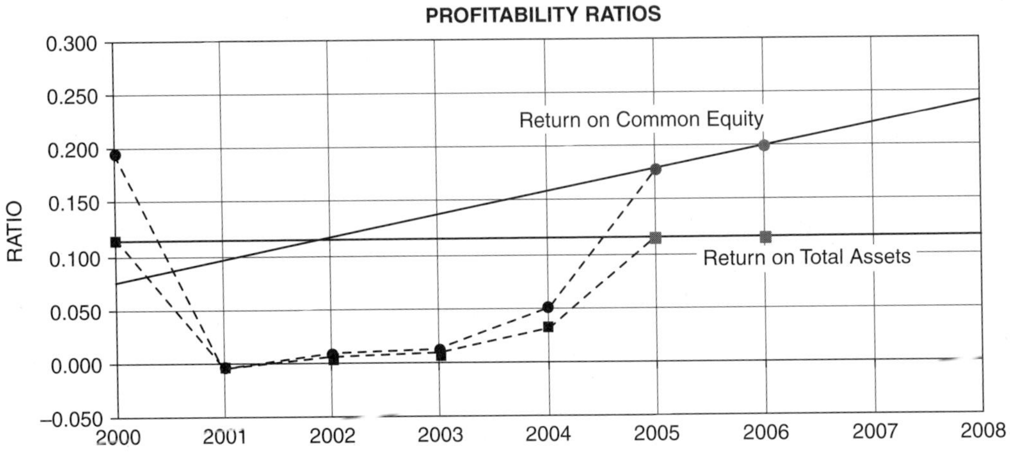

PROFITABILITY RATIOS

with the introduction of Apple's iPod and portable notebook in 2002, and later with the introduction of iTunes. Revenues from iPod sales increased to 40 percent of total sales in 2006 from 2.5 percent in 2002. (The curve for the return on total equity is not shown in Figure 2-23 because the company has had no outstanding preferred stock since 2001; the return on total equity is the same as the return on common equity since then.)

Corporate Scorecards

Corporate scorecards provide another way to measure performance. Examples include: (1) a graph of customer service that shows whether it is improving or deteriorating; (2) a tally of product defects that shows whether they are decreasing or increasing, (3) the time needed to get a new product to market, (4) the efficiency of employees, such as the worker-hours of direct labor it takes to produce a unit of factory output or serve a customer; and (5) employee satisfaction. These are only a few examples of scorecards that have been used for years. Each is tailored to a specific performance criterion that affects profits.

They measure how well a company's marketing, quality control, production, personnel management, and other functional divisions are performing. They enlarge the scope of vision provided by financial ratios alone. They are part of the growing awareness that a company's success in today's competitive environment depends on all of its divisions working together. (Shank in Fortune, February 17, 1997)

Copying and Editing

Much time can often be saved by copying worksheets that have been created to new worksheets and then editing the new worksheets for any changes. To copy an active worksheet, go to the "Edit" drop-down menu on the top toolbar and click on "Move or Copy Sheet." This will open the "Move or Copy" dialog box. Click on the "Create a Copy" box at the lower left. To place the copy in the same workbook, click on the appropriate place in the "Before sheet" box. To place the copy in a new workbook or in a different active workbook, select from the "To book" box near the top of the "Move or Copy" dialog box. After you've made your selection, click OK or press Enter.

The Need for Data That Is Accurate and Timely

Timeliness

The accounting profession is debating the need and means for continual updating of financial reports in something approaching a 24/7 mode: 24 hours each day and 7 days a week. Otherwise, the rapidity of changes holds investors and corporate executives captive to numbers and results that are several weeks or more out of date. This leaves them vulnerable to surprises, such as the losses in market value of 30 to 50 percent that have occurred in the mid to late 2000s. (Examples of this situation are Procter & Gamble lost 34 percent of its market value on the day its earnings disappointed, Priceline lost 42 percent, and Apple Computer lost 52 percent in one day.) All this fear and uncertainty contribute much to the volatility of stocks and to the cost of raising capital in the equity and financial markets. To provide more current information and warnings of unpleasant earnings, chief financial officers of leading companies deliver "guidance" and "preannouncement" reports to selected analysts—a practice that favors insiders.

Pro-Forma vs. GAAP Values

Pro-forma statements are unaudited reports that are not required to conform to the Generally Accepted Accounting Principles (GAAP)—that is, they do not need to comply with the legal requirements that satisfy tax authorities and other regulators. They use "creative accounting" practices that pump earnings and reduce costs.

Pro-forma financial statements have their roots in the markets of the 1980s for "junk bonds" (i.e., high-risk/high-yield bonds) to finance leveraged buy-outs (LBOs). (In an LBO, the assets of a target company are used as security for the loans to finance its purchase.) The use of pro-format statements increased during the great bull markets of the 1990s when companies used them to deliver overly optimistic reports to satisfy investors. Their use reached a nadir late in 2001 with the collapse of Enron, the Houston energy firm.

Concluding Remarks

The techniques described in this chapter help one better understand the company-wide efforts that go into a firm's bottom line.

Common-size financial statements assess line items on income statements as percentages of sales, and line items on balance sheets as percentages of assets. They are used for what is sometimes called "vertical analysis." This means that they help identify and assess changes in the relationships in a company's marketing, operating, investing, and financing activities. They also provide a means to compare the performance of different operating divisions of a company, as well as to assess how a company is doing relative to other companies in the same industry.

Financial ratios provide a quick look at current values for a company's liquidity, business activity, efficiency, profitability, and solvency, and how they have changed with time. For suppliers and lenders, they determine whether or not a company can meet its short-term obligations, handle additional credit, and service its debt burden. Investors use their current values and their past trends for deciding whether or not to invest in one company or another.

"Horizontal analysis" involves comparing values from one period to another. In this chapter, we have looked at the short-term trends of values on financial statements and the derived financial ratios. Trend analysis can also extend over a number of years, quarters, or even weeks.

Horizontal analysis serves as an alarm clock. When things start to go wrong, horizontal analysis sounds a wake-up call to action. It buys time for taking corrective action before minor problems grow into major crises. The combination of horizontal analysis with conditional formatting alerts CFOs and investors to dangerous trends as they develop.

Horizontal analysis helps project past behavior into the future. In the next chapter, we will analyze the trends of annual sales revenues over a number of years. The analysis will include the creation of regression equation models that can be used for forecasting future annual sales revenues.

The analytical techniques described in this chapter can also be used by a firm's executives to set performance goals for its managers. These might include improvements in year-to-year sales growth, return on equity, or inventory turnover—with executive bonuses depending on how well they satisfy the targets. The techniques can also be used by creditors to impose restrictions on a firm's actions, such as maintaining a specified ratio of current assets to current liabilities in order to qualify for loans or maintain a favorable credit rating.

Chapter 3

Forecasting Annual Revenues

CHAPTER OBJECTIVES

Management Skills

- Give examples of why forecasting is essential to good business management.
- Be able to discriminate between valid and invalid models and justify one's position.
- Define the accuracy of models and projected values.
- Understand the risks associated with projections based on past values.
- Explain why it is necessary to adjust statistical projections of past trends for future changes in trends. (This topic is discussed further in the next chapter.)
- Alert managers and investors to changes in past trends that should trigger changes in their long-term strategies and short-term tactics.

Spreadsheet Skills

- Use Excel's Chart Wizard to create a scatter plot of a set of data values.
- Select noncontiguous cell ranges for plotting.
- Insert different types of trend lines on a scatter plot to see which best fits a set of data values.
- Use Excel commands (e.g., INTERCEPT, SLOPE, and CORREL) and tools (e.g., LINEST and LOGEST) to create a statistical model that follows the trend of historical data for annual revenues.
- Insert and format text boxes on charts.
- Discriminate between random and systematic errors, validate a model, and recognize the difference between a model that is valid and one that is not.
- Evaluate the accuracy of a model and its forecasts.
- Calculate confidence limits and create downside risk curves for forecasts.
- Use $ signs and the F4 key to lock cell references so they don't change when entries are copied to other cells.
- Recognize changes in trends and the need to revise or replace a forecasting model.

Overview

A proper forecast combines a statistical projection of the past with expected changes in the future. This chapter shows how to create statistical models for projecting past behavior into the future. It also demonstrates how to recognize when past trends have changed, which is discussed further in Chapter 4.

Forecasts of both annual and seasonal revenues are essential to planning a company's future. (Forecasting seasonal revenues is discussed in Chapter 6.) Here are some of the ways in which they are used:

- Forecasts help CFOs arrange financing for capital expenditures in plants and facilities, plan month-to-month borrowing to meet payrolls and maintain inventories, and invest surplus cash in short-term securities. They help CFOs prepare financial plans and better cope with whatever the future brings.
- Forecasts help operations managers acquire manpower, equipment, and materials in time to manufacture goods or provide services when customers want them. When demands are greater than expected, companies may need to work overtime to satisfy customers, hire temporary workers to serve customers, or reorder products so as not to run out of stock and lose sales. Conversely, when demands are less than expected, inventories of finished goods can pile up, the cost of holding inventories may increase, facilities may sit idle, and workers may be sent home.
- Forecasts help sales managers keep customers happy by meeting their demands promptly. Marketing managers can better adjust prices and develop selling strategies.
- Investors decide to buy or sell stocks and other financial securities according to their expectations of a company's future success in the marketplace. These expectations are partly based on forecasts.
- Forecasts of a company's future earnings are important to the decisions of banks and other lenders to grant or to refuse to make loans for capital investments.

Regression Models

According to surveys, the top priorities of corporate managers for forecasting models are greater simplicity and better accuracy. The regression models discussed in this chapter are both simple and accurate. They are popular for making both mid- and long-range forecasts.

Regression models are equations that describe the relationship between dependent values, such as annual sales, and one or more independent variables, such as time, advertising budget, and the average personal income of buyers. They are particularly useful for making statistical projections of past behavior for several months or quarters to several years into the future. They include linear and several kinds of curvilinear equations that express the trends of historical data.

The regression models considered in this chapter employ time as the single independent variable and express annual sales as a function of time. Time is a composite proxy for such factors as population, personal income, inflation, and other demographic and economic factors that are directly related, in a causal sense, to a company's annual sales. Multivariate regression models that express annual sales as a function of a number of such variables are beyond the scope of this chapter and text. (For a more complete discussion of forecasting, including multivariate regression models, consult a text on forecasting such as those listed in the bibliography at the end of this textbook.)

A regression equation expresses the *trend* of the data. A forecast is made by extrapolating or projecting the past trend forward, into the future. **IF** an equation is a valid model of the past trend **and IF** the trend does not change in the future, the past and future values will all scatter *randomly* about the trend line. Note the **IF** conditions carefully.

Steps in Creating Regression Models

Once the data has been collected from records of the past, the steps for developing regression models to project the past trend into the future include the following:

1. Identify the type of equation that is most suitable for fitting the trend of the data.
2. Evaluate the equation's parameters--that is, determine the values of the coefficients of a regression equation for fitting the data.
3. Validate the model—that is, show that the model reproduces the data's trend.
4. Determine the model's accuracy.
5. Use the model to project future values of interest.
6. Determine the accuracy of the forecast future values.
7. Present the results in useful, management-quality formats.

Although this chapter focuses on forecasting annual revenues, the techniques are also useful for forecasting the cost of goods (COGS), net income, and other items on financial statements as well as financial ratios (as discussed in Chapters 1 and 2). Forecasting some items may be a combination of two forecasts. For example, instead of forecasting the dollar value of the cost of goods sold (COGS) directly, an analyst might make separate forecasts of annual sales and the ratio of COGS to sales, and then combine the two by multiplying the forecast sales by the forecast ratio of COGS to sales. This is a sensible way to forecast a future value that is the product of two factors that are significantly influenced by separate sets of factors: sales being affected by such factors outside a company as the general economy, and COGS being affected by internal production skills and procurement practices.

Time-series models are another way to use time as the independent variable in a forecasting model. These are autoregressive models, and they are better suited than regression models for short-term forecasts for tactical purposes. Typical applications include managing inventories of items that turn over quickly, as in supermarkets, or following the daily movement of monetary exchange rates. They can be adjusted for changes in trends and seasonality.

Forecasting is an important management tool with many applications. For service facilities, such as banks, supermarkets, hospital emergency rooms, toll bridges, and information networks, the dependent variable of forecasting models can be something as simple as the arrival of customers, which can be people, cars, or bytes of data. These vary widely during a single day.

Additional information on forecasting models can be found in many books on the subject, a few of which are listed in the bibliography.

Adjusting for Future Changes in Past Trends

The basic premise in using statistical projections of past behavior as forecasts of the future is that past trends and seasonal behavior will continue unchanged. If the projections are relatively short term (e.g., a few weeks or months) and conditions are relatively stable, the projections should be accurate enough to be useful as forecasts. For long-term forecasts, however, statistical projections of the past are best treated as the starting point for forecasting the future. They should be adjusted for changes that can be anticipated, as discussed in Chapter 4. Making adjustments for future changes in past behavior uses various types of judgmental models, such as the Delphi technique and sales force estimates, as well as large-scale economic models of national and international economies.

Spreadsheets provide many statistical and charting tools that simplify the selection and creation of forecasting models. They make it easy to create tables and charts that present results in convincing formats. For these reasons, spreadsheets have become widely used as forecasting tools.

With modern databases and software, making statistical projections of the past is relatively easy. The difficult part of forecasting is adjusting the projections for changes in past trends, especially as the time horizon increases. Globalization and other changes are upsetting many trends of the past and are making long-term forecasting especially difficult. A good understanding of economics and politics, plus a keen awareness of what is happening in the world and its significance, are important for making good long-term forecasts.

Linear Regression Models

To illustrate the development of a linear regression model for forecasting, consider the annual sales of Wal-Mart Stores, Inc. for fiscal years 1986 to 1996. (For a discussion of later changes from the 1986–1996 trend, section Case Study: *Wal-Mart Stores Revisited In 2001*, on see pages 106 to 116.) Wal-Mart Stores' annual reports give the values for annual sales shown in Cells C6:C16 of Figure 3-1. Note that these values are in millions of dollars. To simplify the regression equation, the actual years in Cells A6:A16 are replaced by the values of X (i.e., by the number of years since 1986) in Cells B6:B16.

Identifying the Type of Equation That Best Fits the Trend of Data

Identifying the trend is best done by creating a scatter plot, such as the chart in Cells F3:L24 of Figure 3-1 (upper right corner), and examining how well different types of equations fit the data. To create this chart, use the mouse to select Cells B6:C16 and then select Excel's ChartWizard. Select the "XY (Scatter)" chart type in the first dialog box, as shown in Figure 3-2. Accept the default chart sub-type to plot the data points without connecting lines. Follow the directions for steps 2, 3, and 4, as shown in Figures 3-3 to 3-5.

Figure 3-4 provides for a number of options. **These can be exercised at this point or later.** Figure 3-4, for example, shows entries for the titles of the chart and the two axes. You can add major

Figure 3-1

Spreadsheet for Linear Regression Model

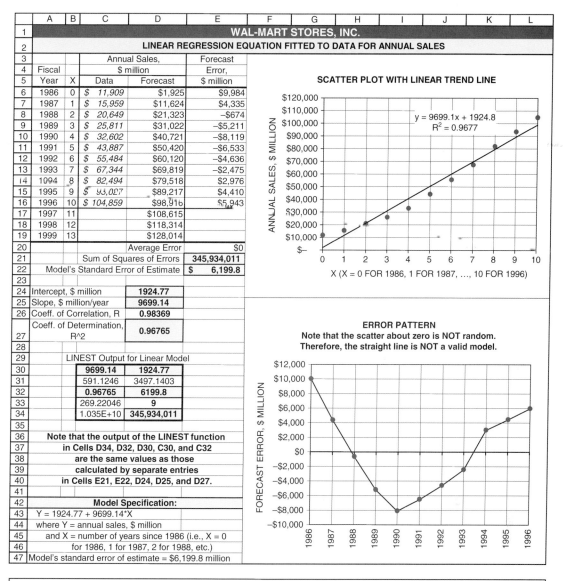

	A	B	C	D	E	F–L
1				WAL-MART STORES, INC.		
2			LINEAR REGRESSION EQUATION FITTED TO DATA FOR ANNUAL SALES			
3			Annual Sales,		Forecast	
4	Fiscal		$ million		Error,	
5	Year	X	Data	Forecast	$ million	
6	1986	0	$ 11,909	$1,925	$9,984	
7	1987	1	$ 15,959	$11,624	$4,335	
8	1988	2	$ 20,649	$21,323	–$674	
9	1989	3	$ 25,811	$31,022	–$5,211	
10	1990	4	$ 32,602	$40,721	–$8,119	
11	1991	5	$ 43,887	$50,420	–$6,533	
12	1992	6	$ 55,484	$60,120	–$4,636	
13	1993	7	$ 67,344	$69,819	–$2,475	
14	1994	8	$ 82,494	$79,518	$2,976	
15	1995	9	$ 93,027	$89,217	$4,410	
16	1996	10	$ 104,859	$98,916	$5,943	
17	1997	11		$108,615		
18	1998	12		$118,314		
19	1999	13		$128,014		
20				Average Error	$0	
21			Sum of Squares of Errors		345,934,011	
22			Model's Standard Error of Estimate		$ 6,199.8	
23						
24	Intercept, $ million			1924.77		
25	Slope, $ million/year			9699.14		
26	Coeff. of Correlation, R			0.98369		
27	Coeff. of Determination, R^2			0.96765		
28						
29			LINEST Output for Linear Model			
30			9699.14	1924.77		
31			591.1246	3497.1403		
32			0.96765	6199.8		
33			269.22046	9		
34			1.035E+10	345,934,011		
35						
36		Note that the output of the LINEST function				
37		in Cells D34, D32, D30, C30, and C32				
38		are the same values as those				
39		calculated by separate entries				
40		in Cells E21, E22, D24, D25, and D27.				
41						
42		Model Specification:				
43	Y = 1924.77 + 9699.14*X					
44	where Y = annual sales, $ million					
45	and X = number of years since 1986 (i.e., X = 0					
46	for 1986, 1 for 1987, 2 for 1988, etc.)					
47	Model's standard error of estimate = $6,199.8 million					

SCATTER PLOT WITH LINEAR TREND LINE

$y = 9699.1x + 1924.8$
$R^2 = 0.9677$

ANNUAL SALES, $ MILLION

X (X = 0 FOR 1986, 1 FOR 1987, …, 10 FOR 1996)

ERROR PATTERN
Note that the scatter about zero is NOT random.
Therefore, the straight line is NOT a valid model.

FORECAST ERROR, $ MILLION

Key Cell Entries

D24:	=INTERCEPT(C6:C16,B6:B16)	Calculates intercept of straight-line fitted to data's trend
D25:	=SLOPE(C6:C16,B6:B16)	Calculates slope of straight-line fitted to data's trend
D6:	=$D$24+$D$25*B6, copy to D7:D19	Uses intercept and slope values to calculate forecast values for year value
E6:	=C6-D6, copy to E7:E16	Calculates error as data value minus forecast value
E20:	=AVERAGE(E6:E16)	Calculates average error over range of data (must be zero)
E21:	=SUMSQ(E6:E16)	Calculates sum of the squares of the errors
E22:	=SQRT(E21/(11-2))	Calculates the model's standard error of estimate
D26:	=CORREL(C6:C16,B6:B16)	Calculates degree of linear correlation between data values and year number
D27:	=D26^2	Calculates coefficient of determination
C30:D34:	=LINEST(C6:C16,B6:B16,1,1)	Generates output for LINEST function

N.B. Data values have been inserted in Cells C6:C16 as 11909, 15959, etc. and should be read as millions of dollars. For example, the value in Cell C6 should be read as $11,909,000,000, $11,909 million, or $11.909 billion.

  Wal-Mart's fiscal year begins on February 1st of the calendar year and ends on January 31 of the following calendar year. For example, fiscal 1986 runs from February 1, 1986 to January 31, 1987.

Figure 3-2

Dialog Box for Step 1 to Create the Scatter Plot

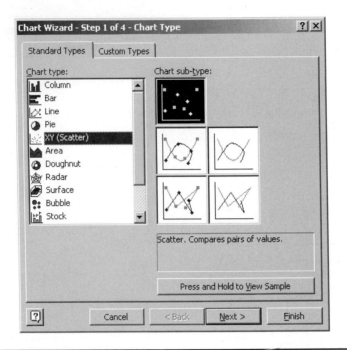

Important: Note the chart type and sub-type that have been selected.

and minor gridlines at this point. By default, major gridlines are provided for the vertical axis only; major gridlines have been added to the scatter diagram in Figure 3-1. You can also delete the legend box at the right, which reads "Series 1." The legend has been deleted from the scatter diagram in Figure 3-1 because it is unnecessary, since there is only one series. These and other formatting options can be deferred until later, after the chart has been created.

After plotting the data points in the scatter diagram in the upper right corner of Figure 3-1, you need to decide the kind of line or curve that best fits the data's trend. For help, click on the chart to put it into the edit mode. Next, click on one of the data points and select "Add Trendline" from the chart pull-down menu. This will open the dialog box shown in Figure 3-6. The default is a straight line, shown in the upper left corner of the dialog box. We will accept the linear trend line for evaluation only.

Choose the XY (Scatter) Chart Type

The "XY (Scatter)" chart type is used for almost all charts in the text. It is usually a better choice than the "Line" chart type, which is often the default type and can cause problems in formatting.

Figure 3-3

Dialog Box for Step 2 to Create the Scatter Chart

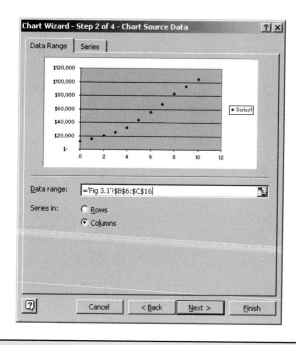

Make sure that the data range is correct and the series of data are in columns.

Figure 3-4

Dialog Box for Step 3 to Create the Scatter Chart

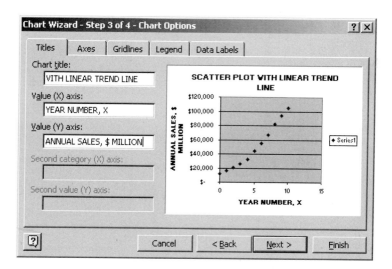

Take time to examine the contents of the Axes, Gridlines, Legend, and Data Labels sheet tabs. They provide options for improving the formats of charts.

Figure 3-5

Dialog Box for Step 4 to Create the Scatter Chart

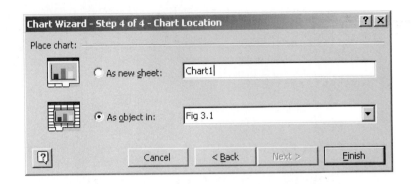

Note that the default setting is to place the chart on the active worksheet.

BEFORE clicking on the OK button to accept the entry in Figure 3-6, click on the Options tab of the Add Trendline dialog box. This accesses the Options dialog box shown in Figure 3-7. Click on the boxes to select "Display equation on chart" and "Display R-squared value on chart." Then click on

Figure 3-6

Dialog Box for Inserting a Trend Line

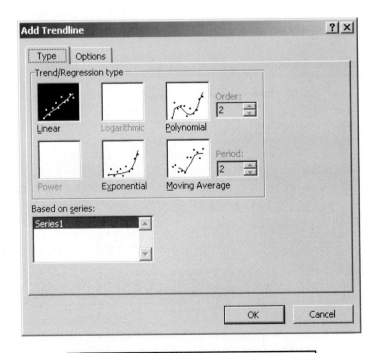

Default setting shown is a linear trend line.

Figure 3-7

Options Box for Adding a Trend Line

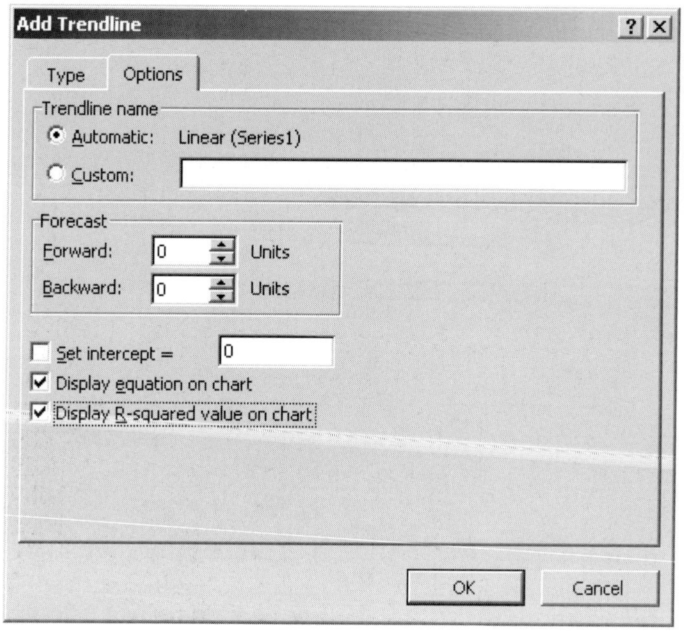

Note that the trend line can be projected forward or backward.

the OK button or press Enter. The results are shown in the scatter diagram in the upper right corner of Figure 3-1. Although the straight line shows that the annual sales increase with each successive year, the data scatters systematically about the trend line, with the extreme points lying above the trend line and the intermediate points lying below. We will return shortly to examine this scatter more critically and discuss its significance.

To format the trend line, double-click on it to open the "Format Trendline" dialog box shown in Figure 3-8. Select an appropriate type, color, and weight for the line.

To format a single point on the trend line, click on the trend line to activate it, then click a second time on the point to be formatted. On the Format drop-down menu, click on "Selected Data Point" to open the "Format Data Point" dialog box. Select an appropriate type, color, and size for the point.

The scales for the horizontal and vertical (i.e., X and Y) axes in the scatter diagram of Figure 3-1 have been changed from the default values shown in Figure 3-3. To change the Y scale, for example, double-click on one of the values in the scatter diagram to open the "Format Axis" dialog box shown in Figure 3-9. Select the "Scale" tab and enter the values shown in Figure 3-9. The settings shown indicate that the scale of the Y-axis runs from 0 to 120,000 with major increments of 10,000. (If you wish to include minor gridlines on the chart, you can also add a value for the minor unit.)

Figure 3-8

"Format Trendline" Dialog Box

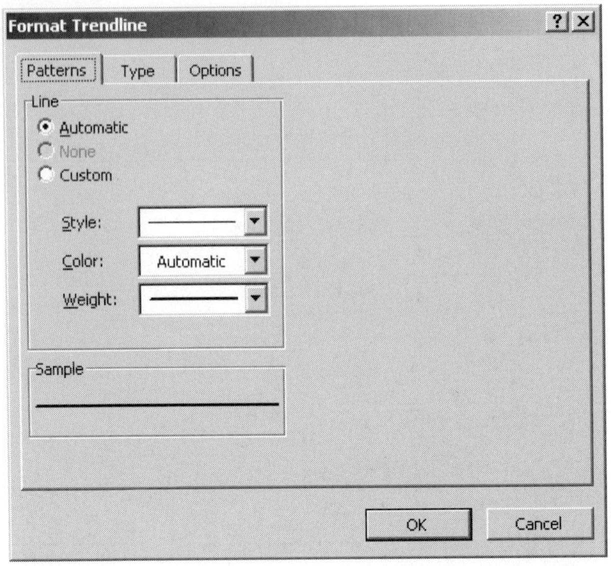

Select the style, color, and weight for the trend line.

Figure 3-9

"Format Axis" Dialog Box with Settings for the Scale of the Y-Axis in the Scatter Diagram at the Upper Right of Figure 3-1

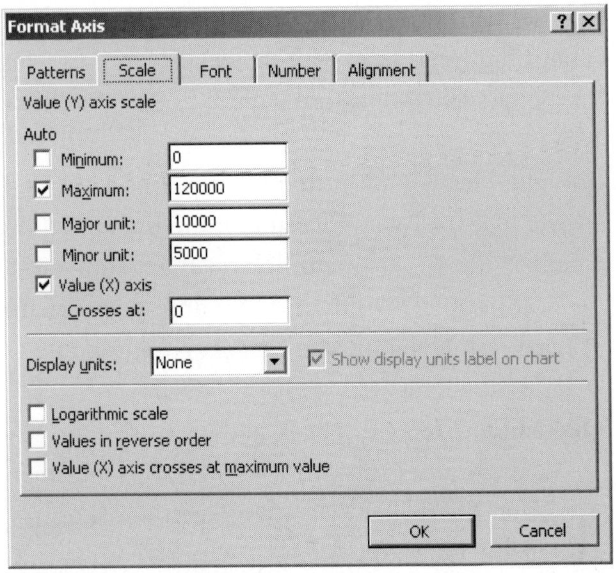

Take time to examine the options provided on each of the five sheet tabs.

Figure 3-10

Using the "Patterns" Tab on the "Format Axis" Dialog Box to Move the Tick Mark Labels for the X-Axis to the Bottom of the Chart

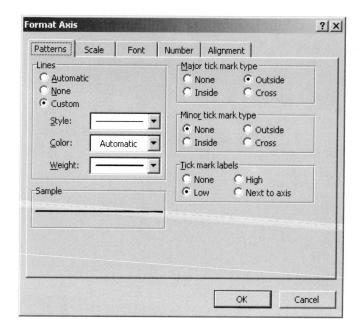

To move the calendar years to the bottom of the error pattern chart of Figure 3-1, double-click on one of the values to open the "Format Axis" dialog box. Select the "Patterns" tab and click the "Low" button for "Tick mark labels," as shown in Figure 3-10.

To align the values for the calendar years at 90 degrees to the axis, go to the "Alignment" tab of the "Format Axis" dialog box and enter "90" for the value of "Degrees" or use the mouse cursor to rotate the "Text" arm to the upright position, as shown in Figure 3-11. (The default position is zero degrees.)

Evaluating the Parameters of the Linear Regression Model

The **general** equation for a straight-line or linear relationship between two variables is

$$Y = a + bX \qquad (3.1)$$

where Y = the dependent variable (here Wal-Mart's annual sales)

X = the independent variable (here the year number)

a = the value of Y when $X = 0$ (called the Y-intercept)

and b = the rate of change of Y with respect to X (i.e., the slope of the line)

The equation for a linear trend line to fit the data for Wal-Mart's annual sales from 1986 to 1996 is included on the scatter diagram. It is (after putting it in the form of equation 3.1),

$$Y = 1924.8 + 9699.1X \qquad (3.2)$$

Figure 3-11

Aligning Values at Right Angles to the X-Axis of a Chart

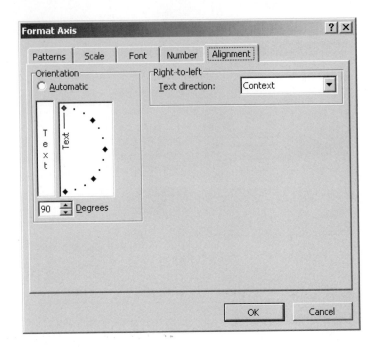

where Y is Wal-Mart's annual sales in millions of dollars and X is the number of years since 1986 (i.e., X = 0 for 1986, 1 for 1987, ..., 13 for 1999). Equation 3.2 and the definition of the variables X and Y constitute a **specification** for the model of Wal-Mart's annual sales as a linear function of the year. (Note the model specification given in Rows 42 to 47 of Figure 3-1.)

Excel's INTERCEPT and SLOPE Commands

Excel's INTERCEPT and SLOPE commands provide another way to evaluate the intercept and slope of the straight line that best fits the data. The syntax for these commands is

INTERCEPT(*range of dependent variable, range of independent variable*)

and

SLOPE(*range of dependent variable, range of independent variable*).

Enter =INTERCEPT(C6:C16,B6:B16) and SLOPE(C6:C16,B6:B16) in Cells D24 and D25 of Figure 3-1 to give the values 1924.77 and 9699.14. These are the same values (within the round-off) as shown in the scatter diagram. Cells D24 and D25 can be referenced for using the values to make calculations.

Using the Model's Parameters to Forecast

To use the model to forecast or "fit" values of Y to values of X, enter =$D$24+$D$25*B6 in Cell D6 and copy the entry to Cells D7:D19. Note the $ signs on Cells D24 and D25 in this entry. The $ signs are included to keep the entries for the intercept and slope constant as the entry in D6 is copied to Cells D7:D19.

Calculate the Errors

The next step is to calculate the errors. Errors are the differences between the data values of the dependent variable Y and the values of Y forecast by the model. Statisticians also call them deviations or residuals. By convention, errors are calculated by subtracting the forecast values from the data values rather than vice versa. Therefore, the errors are calculated by entering =C6-D6 in Cell E6 and copying the entry to E7:E16. Note that individual errors can be either positive or negative and their average in cell E20 is exactly zero.

Validate the Model

Model validation is an important step that is often overlooked. Recall that the basic assumption of using past data to forecast the future is that the past trend will continue. Therefore, a valid model for projecting the past trend forward must be a valid model of the past. If a model does not follow the trend of the data for the past, it is not a valid model of the past—that is, it is an invalid model because it does not satisfy the basic idea of using past data to forecast the future by projecting the past trend forward. Invalid models lead to invalid projections and should be rejected.

Even valid models lead to erroneous projections if the past trend changes and projected values are not adjusted for the change. Using past history to forecast the future therefore consists of two essential steps: (1) Creating a statistical model of the past that can be projected forward and (2) adjusting projected values for any changes in the past trend that can be anticipated. Both steps are essential for making forecasts.

Understanding how to validate a model of the past is important. Unfortunately, most students leave their statistics courses without having been instructed on how to validate regression models. Worse, many leave with an incorrect understanding that leads them to accept invalid models. For example, many mistakenly believe that a correlation coefficient close to one ensures that a regression model is valid. The result is many erroneous business forecasts, as the author has observed in his professional career.

In order for a model to be valid, the data values must scatter **randomly** above and below the trend line on a scatter diagram, such as the one shown in the upper right corner of Figure 3-1, and the average error must be zero. The key word here is "*randomly*." Unfortunately, it is often difficult to distinguish between a **systematic** and a **random** scattering about the trend line. Many students, for example, don't recognize the systematic way in which the data values are displaced about the trend line in the scatter plot of Figure 3-1; they believe the scatter is random because there are about the same number of points above the line as below it. Until it is pointed out to them, they fail to recognize that the scatter is systematic rather than random and that *the trend of the data is actually a curve rather than a straight line*.

Analyzing the errors provides a more sensitive and useful test of randomness and model validity than simply looking at a scatter diagram. Errors are the differences between the data and fitted values, such as those given in Column E of Figure 3-1. On the scatter diagram, they are the displacements of the data values above and below the trend line.

In terms of the forecast errors, a valid model must satisfy **each** of two conditions: (1) The average error is zero and (2) the errors scatter randomly rather than systematically about the average of zero (or, in the case of exponential models, as explained later, about a geometric mean of one). The first condition is automatically satisfied for the linear regression model if the spreadsheet entries are correct. The second condition may or may not be satisfied. *Therefore, you need to check the error pattern to see if its scatter is random or systematic.*

Scanning the column of Cells from E6 to E16 in Figure 3-1 is one way to examine whether or not the errors are random or systematic. Note that the errors starts out largely positive (Cell E6), get successively smaller and take on negative values as one moves down the column until a minimum value is reached near the center (Cell E10), and then get successively larger as one continues to move down the column to a maximum at the end (Cell E16). This is systematic behavior, not random, and the model is therefore not valid.

Because a picture can be worth a thousand words, the error pattern is plotted in the lower right chart of Figure 3-1. This chart is created by plotting Cells B6:B16 and E6:E16. Figure 3-12 shows the settings

Figure 3-12

Format Axis Dialog Box with Selections for Weight of Major Gridlines and Placement of Units for the X-Axis at the Bottom of the Chart

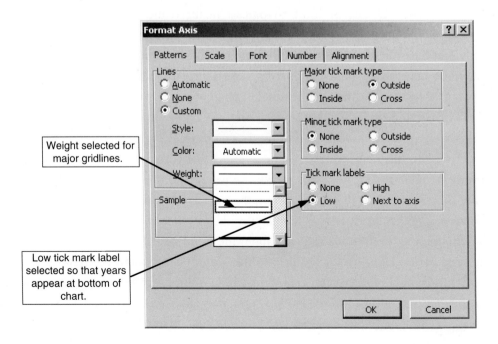

for formatting the weight of the major gridlines and for moving the years for the units of the X-axis to the bottom of the chart.

Examine the column of error values and their pattern in Figure 3-1. It should be clear that the errors are positive at both extremes and decrease monotonically to a minimum near the midpoint. In other words, the error pattern is *systematic* rather than *random,* and you should conclude that, therefore, the linear model is **not** valid. That is the same conclusion we drew from examining the values in Cells E6:E16. However, the chart for the error pattern may provide an easier way to distinguish between random and systematic scatter, and it makes the conclusion that the linear model is not valid more convincing.

Because the errors behave in a systematic rather than random manner, you can anticipate that annual sales forecast by the linear model for the next few years (e.g., 1997 to 1999) would be consistently less than actual values, with the error increasing as you forecast farther and farther into the future.

It is important to be able to prove that the model you choose is valid. Conversely, it is important to be able to prove that someone else's model is not valid when it unfairly projects values that are not in your own best interests. Model validity is an important issue in contract negotiations or settlements based on future values. The best way to destroy the opposite side's position is to prove that it is based on a false model of the data. **Destroying the model destroys the logic for reaching unfavorable conclusions.** It destroys an opponent's position. Learn to use numbers to your advantage.

Although we reject the linear model at this point, we continue our discussion with several additional considerations before proceeding to curvilinear models that represent the data better than the linear model.

Measure the Model's Accuracy

A model's accuracy or precision is limited by the *random* scatter in the data, and a future value might be more than or less than what the model predicts. In fact, *with a valid model,* there is a 50 percent chance a future value will be more than projected by the model and a 50 percent chance it will be less. Determining how far off the mark our forecasts might be is important for determining how much safety stock or how much extra service capacity we should provide to ensure that we are able to satisfy our customers promptly, for example, or to estimate the risk for breaking even on an investment.

To evaluate a model's accuracy, we calculate its **standard error of estimate**. This is abbreviated SEE and is defined by the following equation:

$$SEE = \sqrt{\frac{\sum (Y_{data} - Y_{fcst})^2}{df}} \qquad (3.3)$$

In words, a model's standard error of estimate is equal to the square root of the sum of the squares of the errors divided by the degrees of freedom. The number of degrees of freedom equals the number of sets (here, the number of pairs) of data values minus the number of model parameters we've estimated in the model. We have 11 pairs of data values for annual sales and year number, and we have estimated values for two parameters, the model's intercept and slope, therefore, $df = 11 - 2 = 9$.

As described earlier, some of our model's errors will be negative and others positive. However, if you square a negative number, the result is positive. The sum of the squares of the errors is calculated by entering the command =SUMSQ(E6:E16) in cell E21. The result is a very large number (345,934,011). (You may recall from statistics that the values of a and b in the model are those that minimize the sum of the squares of the errors. You can find a detailed discussion of the procedure in a statistics text. However, it is not necessary to understand the procedure to use Excel's commands.)

Substituting values for the sum of the squares of the errors and the number of degrees of freedom into the equation for the model's SEE, we obtain

$$SEE = \sqrt{345,934,011/(11-2)} = 6199.8 \text{ (millions of dollars)}$$

This value is calculated by the entry =SQRT(E21/(11-2)) in cell E22 of the spreadsheet. (We could also calculate SEE by the entry =SQRT(SUMSQ(E6:E16)/(11-2)) and omit a separate calculation of the sum of the squares of the errors.)

Excel's CORREL Command and Coefficients of Correlation and Determination

The coefficient of correlation (R) is calculated by the entry =CORREL(C6:C16,B6:B16) in Cell D26. This value for R (0.98369) is converted to the coefficient of determination (R^2) by the entry =D26^2 in Cell D27. Note that the value 0.96765 for the value of R^2 is the same (within the round-off) as that shown below the equation on the scatter diagram.

You can understand the significance of the coefficients better if you recall the use of sample statistics as estimates of population statistics. **In the absence of any consistent pattern in a set of sample values,** statistics teaches that **the sample's average value is the best estimate** we can make of a future value of the population from which the sample was taken. The variability of sample values about the sample's average value is expressed by the sample's standard deviation, which is defined in the same way as equation 3.3 except that the sample's mean or average value replaces the forecast values.

On the other hand, if there *is* a consistent trend in the values of the sample, we can use that trend to develop a model (e.g., a regression equation) that gives a *better* estimate of a future value than simply the average of the past. The better values are, of course, the values forecast with the model. We can now compare the standard deviation of the data values about their forecast values with the standard deviation of the data values about their average. Or, more conveniently, we can use variance in place of standard deviation in the comparison. (Recall that variance is simply the square of the standard deviation.)

In the following expression, the numerator is the variance of the data values about their **forecast** values, and the denominator is the variance of the data values about their **mean** value. If the data follows a trend so that the forecasting model provides a better forecast of the future than the average of the past, the numerator will be less than the denominator. We can interpret the ratio as the ratio of the unexplained variance (i.e., the errors in the numerator that result from the data's scatter about the trend) to the total variance of the data values about their mean (i.e., the differences between the data values and their mean).

A good forecasting model should account for (or "explain") a good deal of the total variance and leave only a small "unexplained" variance.

$$\frac{\dfrac{\sum (Y_{data} - Y_{fcst})^2}{n}}{\dfrac{\sum (Y_{data} - Y_{mean})^2}{n}} = \text{ratio of unexplained variance to total variance}$$

The ratio of the unexplained variance to the total variance is known as the coefficient of **non**determination. The coefficient of **determination** equals 1 minus the coefficient of **non**determination. For the linear regression model for Wal-Mart Stores, the coefficient of determination is 0.96765. You can verify this value by entering =1-(STDEV(E6:E16)/STDEV(C6/C16))^2 in a convenient place on the spreadsheet of Figure 3-1. The resulting value will be 0.96765, the same as that shown in Cells D27 and C32. (This value can also be obtained with the entry =(STDEV(D6:D16)/STDEV(C6:C16))^2.)

Note that the different coefficients respond only to the **magnitudes** of the differences between the data values and the forecast values or the mean value. There is absolutely nothing in the coefficients that recognizes the pattern of the differences—the coefficients are completely blind to whether the forecast errors scatter randomly or systematically. Because of this blindness, they **cannot** be used to validate a model. (We emphasize this point because many students, even very good ones, have been misled on this matter in their courses in statistics.)

Excel's LINEST Command

Much of the information provided above by using separate command functions can be obtained more easily by using Excel's LINEST command, which provides additional statistical information (some of which the reader can safely ignore or refer to later). The command's syntax is

LINEST(*range of known y values, range of known x values, const, stats*)

The entry for *const* is either TRUE or FALSE, depending upon whether the intercept *a* is to be calculated normally, as we have done in the preceding, or is to be set equal to zero, with the value of *b* adjusted to fit the equation *y = bx*. The value 1 can be substituted for TRUE, and if an entry for *const* is omitted, *b* is calculated normally. The entry for *stats* is TRUE (or 1) if the additional regression statistics described below are desired. If the entry for *stats* is FALSE (or is omitted), only values for the intercept and slope are returned.

To use the LINEST command, first select a block of 2 columns by 5 rows (e.g., cells C30:D34 of Figure 3-1) by dragging the mouse over them. Then, type =LINEST(C6:C16,B6:B16,1,1) and enter by pressing the three keys "Ctrl," "Shift," and "Enter." The result is the set of values shown in Cells C30:D34.

Table 3-1

Format for Output of Excel's LINEST Command for Linear Regression with a Single Dependent Variable

Slope	Intercept
Standard error for slope	Standard error for intercept
Coefficient of determination	**Standard error of estimate**
F statistic	**Degrees of freedom**
Regression sum of squares	**Residual sum of squares**

Table 3-1 shows how the output of the LINEST command in cells C30:D34 of Figure 3-1 is organized. We have already encountered some of these values. The two values in the top row of the LINEST output are the **intercept** (Cell D30) and **slope** (Cell C30). Note that the values are exactly the same as those calculated earlier with the INTERCEPT and SLOPE commands. The model's **standard error of estimate** (Cell D32, third row of second column) matches that calculated in Cell E22. The **coefficient of determination** (Cell C32, third row of first column) matches that in Cell D27. The model's **degrees of freedom** (Cell D33, fourth row of second column) is 9 (i.e., 11 pairs of data values less 2 degrees of freedom lost for the estimates of the intercept and slope). The **residual sum of squares** (Cell D34, fifth row of second column) is the sum of the squares of the errors in Cell E21.

Other values, which are of little interest to the present discussion, are as follows. The **regression sum of squares** (Cell C34) is the difference between the sum of the squares of the differences between data values and their mean. The **standard errors for the slope and intercept** are given in Cells C31 and D31. The **F statistic** in Cell C33 is a measure of correlation, or its lack. (For details, consult a statistics text.)

Excel's Regression Routine

Excel has a regression routine that provides additional statistical information. The regression routine is not as convenient as the LINEST command and is not discussed in these notes. (If you are interested in exploring the regression routine, you can access it by clicking on Data Analysis on the Tools pull-down menu and selecting Regression from the Data Analysis dialog box.)

Quadratic Regression Models

Quadratic regression models are similar to linear regression models but include the square of the independent variable as a third term in the equations. Depending on one's choice of symbols for the parameters, the general form of the equation for a quadratic regression model can be written as either

$$Y = a + bX + cX^2 \tag{3.4}$$

or

$$Y = b_0 + b_1X + b_2X^2 \tag{3.5}$$

where the subscripts on the coefficients in equation 3.5 indicate the power of the independent variable X associated with it. A mathematician would say that a quadratic equation expresses the dependence of the variable Y on a single independent variable, X. A spreadsheet, however, treats the squared value of independent variable as a second independent variable. It is the squared value, of course, that deflects the trend line from a straight-line path. If its coefficient is positive, the deflection is upward to higher values of Y; if negative, the deflection is downward to lower values.

To create a new spreadsheet for the quadratic model, first save the spreadsheet for Figure 3-1 and make a copy of it. (Use Edit/Move or Copy Sheet.) To change the trend line on the scatter diagram of the new sheet, first delete the linear trend line. (Click on the linear trend line to activate it and press the Delete key.) Click on the data and repeat the steps for adding a linear trend line, but choose a second-order polynomial as shown in the Add Trendline dialog box of Figure 3-13. Use the option tab to display the equation and R-squared value on the chart. The result is shown in the upper right corner of Figure 3-14.

Using LINEST to Develop a Quadratic Regression Model

Figure 3-14 shows results with a quadratic regression model used to analyze the annual sales data for Wal-Mart Stores, Inc. (To prepare this spreadsheet, first copy Figure 3-1 to a new spreadsheet, as directed above, and clear the entries in Cells A21:D40.) Then insert a new Column C (between the values for X and the data) for values of X^2. Enter =B6^2 in Cell C6 and copy the entry to C7:C19.

Figure 3-13

Add Trendline Dialog Box with Quadratic Trendline Chosen

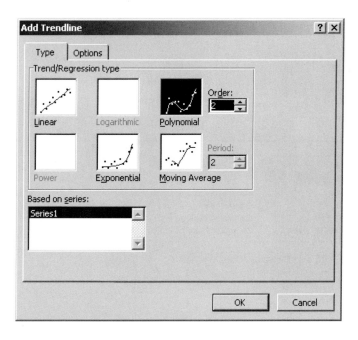

Figure 3-14

Spreadsheet for Quadratic Regression Model

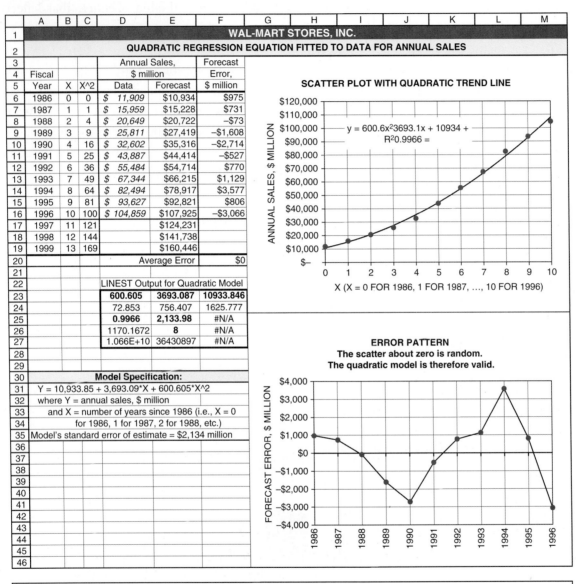

	A	B	C	D	E	F
1				WAL-MART STORES, INC.		
2				QUADRATIC REGRESSION EQUATION FITTED TO DATA FOR ANNUAL SALES		
3				Annual Sales,		Forecast
4	Fiscal			\$ million		Error,
5	Year	X	X^2	Data	Forecast	\$ million
6	1986	0	0	\$ 11,909	\$10,934	\$975
7	1987	1	1	\$ 15,959	\$15,228	\$731
8	1988	2	4	\$ 20,649	\$20,722	−\$73
9	1989	3	9	\$ 25,811	\$27,419	−\$1,608
10	1990	4	16	\$ 32,602	\$35,316	−\$2,714
11	1991	5	25	\$ 43,887	\$44,414	−\$527
12	1992	6	36	\$ 55,484	\$54,714	\$770
13	1993	7	49	\$ 67,344	\$66,215	\$1,129
14	1994	8	64	\$ 82,494	\$78,917	\$3,577
15	1995	9	81	\$ 93,627	\$92,821	\$806
16	1996	10	100	\$ 104,859	\$107,925	−\$3,066
17	1997	11	121		\$124,231	
18	1998	12	144		\$141,738	
19	1999	13	169		\$160,446	
20				Average Error		\$0
21						
22				LINEST Output for Quadratic Model		
23				600.605	3693.087	10933.846
24				72.853	756.407	1625.777
25				0.9966	2,133.98	#N/A
26				1170.1672	8	#N/A
27				1.066E+10	36430897	#N/A
28						
29						
30				Model Specification:		
31		Y = 10,933.85 + 3,693.09*X + 600.605*X^2				
32		where Y = annual sales, \$ million				
33		and X = number of years since 1986 (i.e., X = 0				
34		for 1986, 1 for 1987, 2 for 1988, etc.)				
35	Model's standard error of estimate = \$2,134 million					
36						
37						
38						
39						
40						
41						
42						
43						
44						
45						
46						

SCATTER PLOT WITH QUADRATIC TREND LINE

$y = 600.6x^2 3693.1x + 10934 +$
$R^2 0.9966 =$

ANNUAL SALES, \$ MILLION

X (X = 0 FOR 1986, 1 FOR 1987, ..., 10 FOR 1996)

ERROR PATTERN
The scatter about zero is random.
The quadratic model is therefore valid.

FORECAST ERROR, \$ MILLION

Key Cell Entries

E6: =$F$23+$E$23*B6+$D$23*B6^2,
copy to E7:E19 — Uses model's parameters to calculate forecast values for year values

F6: =D6-E6, copy to F7:F16 — Calculates error as data value minus forecast value

F20: =AVERAGE(F6:F16) — Calculates average error over range of data (must be zero)

D23:F27: =LINEST(D6:D16,B6:C16,1,1) — Generates output for LINEST function

With the mouse, select Cells D23:F27, type =LINEST(D6:D16,B6:C16,1,1), and press Ctrl/Shift/Enter. The result is shown in the 3-column/5-row matrix labeled "LINEST Output for Quadratic Model." The values in Cells D23:G23 are the values of c, b, and a, respectively, in equation 3.4. That is, the equation for the quadratic model for Wal-Mart's annual sales is

$$Y = 10,933.846 + 3693.087\, X + 600.605\, X^2 \tag{3.6}$$

where the variables Y and X are as defined before. Note that the values for the three coefficients are the same as those for the quadratic trend line on the scatter diagram (within the round-off error, of course).

To use the model's parameters to make forecasts, enter =$F$23+$E$23*B6+$D$23*C6 in Cell E6 and copy the entry to E7:E19. To calculate the errors, enter =D6-E6 in Cell F6 and copy it to F7:F19. To validate the model, first show that the average error is zero (enter =SUM(F6:F16) in Cell F20), then show that the errors scatter randomly rather than systematically (error pattern at lower right).

Comparing the quadratic to the linear model, you should note, first of all, that the systematic behavior of the errors with the linear model has been eliminated and the errors scatter more or less randomly about the mean value of zero. The error pattern shown in Figure 3-12 is not consistent enough so that we can say with reasonable assurance what the next error would be if the past behavior continued. Based on the error pattern for XYR = 0 to 10, there is no statistical basis for saying that the error when XYR = 11 will be either positive or negative, or by how much over the previous range of values. In other words, there is no statistical basis for saying that the model is not valid (as there was for the linear regression model of the data).

Although we cannot reject the quadratic regression model as invalid, we have some hesitancy about accepting it for forecasting annual sales for the next few years. The error pattern follows a downward trend for four years, from XYR = 0 to 4 (i.e., 1986 to 1990), then an upward trend for the next four years, from XYR 4 to 8 (i.e., 1990 to 1994), and then another downward trend for the last three years, from XYR 8 to 10 (i.e., 1994 to 1996). Something must be going on at Wal-Mart to account for this unusual behavior. We shall return to an examination of this behavior later in this chapter and provide a more general discussion of changes in past trends in Chapter 4.

To complete the comparison of the quadratic to the linear regression model, we should note that the standard error of estimate for the quadratic model ($2,133.98 million) is significantly less than for the linear model ($6,199.8 million), and the coefficient of determination for the quadratic model (0.9966) is greater than for the linear model (0.9677).

Exponential Regression Model

A common business example of a curvilinear trend is the exponential curve for the increase in the value of money with time when the principal and interest are reinvested at a compound rate of interest. Curves for such behavior are concave upwards; the increase in value from one year to the next gets greater each year because of the increasing size of the accumulated funds on which interest is paid. The general equation for such behavior is

$$F = P(1 + i)^n \qquad (3.7)$$

where F = future value, after n periods from the start

P = present value of deposit or investment (i.e., the value of F when $n = 0$)

i = periodic rate of interest (e.g., the annual rate of interest, compounded annually)

and n = number of interest-bearing periods (e.g., the number of years in the future)

Equation 3.7 is used in financial analyses to project present values to the future or, by using its inverse, to find the present value of a stream of future cash flows. Besides its use for calculating future financial values, equation 3.7 is also useful for projecting many other business trends where the rate of change is a percentage of the base value.

For forecasting, we can rewrite equation 3.7 in the form

$$Y = AB^X \qquad (3.8)$$

Note the similarity of equations 3.7 and 3.8. In equation 3.8, Y is the dependent variable (such as the annual sales revenue) whose value depends on X (where X is the year or year number). For comparison, Y corresponds to the future value of money in equation 3.7, and X to the number of interest-bearing periods. If we set X equal to zero in equation 3.8, we obtain Y = A, corresponding to the present value (i.e., the value at year number zero). The parameter B in equation 3.8 corresponds to one plus the rate of increase per unit change of X—that is, to 1+i in equation 3.7.

Copy the spreadsheet for the linear model a second time for analyzing the use of an exponential model to fit the data for Wal-Mart's annual sales. To change the trend line on the scatter diagram of the new sheet, first delete the linear trend line. (Click on the linear trend line to activate it and press the Delete key.) Click on the data and repeat the steps for adding a linear trend line, but choose the exponential model, as shown in the Add Trendline dialog box of Figure 3-15. Use the option tab to display the equation and R-squared value on the chart. The result is shown in the upper right corner of Figure 3-16.

Using LOGEST to Evaluate an Exponential Model's Parameters

To fit a set of data values to an exponential regression equation, we need to evaluate the two parameters A and B of Equation 3.8. Once we've determined the value of B in equation 3.8, we can subtract one from it to find the relative rate of change (e.g., the percentage rate of increase or decrease).

Excel provides the LOGEST function for evaluating the parameters A and B in the exponential regression model. Its syntax is

=LOGEST(*range of known y values, range of known x values, 1, 1*)

Figure 3-16 shows the development of an exponential regression model for the annual revenues of Wal-Mart based on the company's annual sales for 1986 to 1996. The parameters of the exponential model

Figure 3-15

Dialog Box for Inserting an Exponential Trend Line

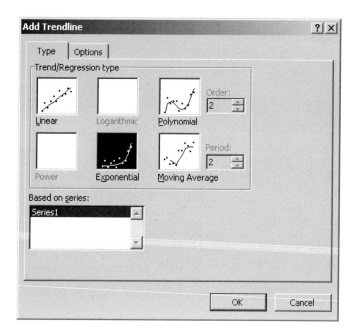

are evaluated by selecting Cells C23:D27 and entering =LOGEST(C6:C16,B6:B16,1,1). (Remember to use Control/Shift/Enter to enter an array.) The results give the following equation for an exponential model of Wal-Mart's annual sales:

$$Y = 13,152.81 \times 1.2501^{XYR} \tag{3.9}$$

where Y = the annual sales revenue, in \$ million
and XYR = the number of years since 1986 (i.e., $XYR = 0$ for 1986, 1 for 1987, etc.)

Equation 3.9 indicates that the average rate of increase in Wal-Mart's annual sales from 1986 to 1996 was 25.01 percent. This value is based on fitting the exponential curve to all 11 data values. It can also be obtained by considering only the extreme values (although this will be only an approximation if there is considerable random scatter in the data). Thus,

$$\sqrt[10]{\frac{104,859}{11,909}} - 1 = 1.2501 - 1 = 0.2501 = 25.01\%$$

The form of the exponential regression given in the scatter plot is different from that shown by equation 3.9, which was determined by using Excel's LOGEST function. However, the two are mathematically the same. For some reason of its own, Excel uses different conventions when it determines the equation for the regression line as an option to inserting the trend line and when it evaluates results

Figure 3-16

Spreadsheet for Exponential Regression Model

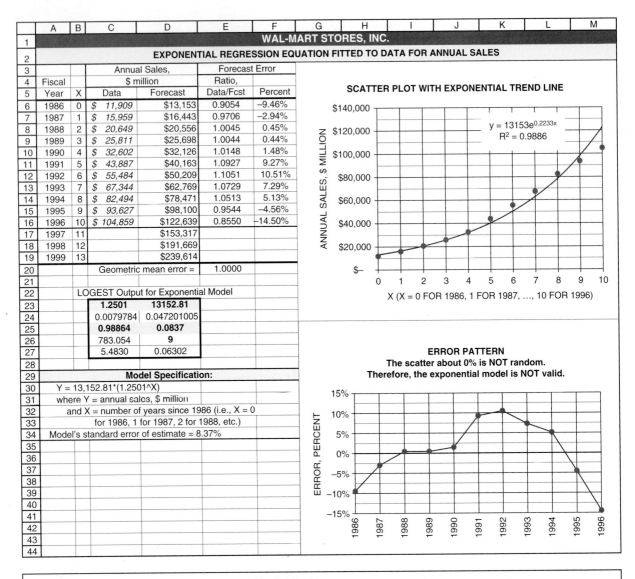

Key Cell Entries

D6: =$D$23*($C$23^B6), copy to D7:D19   Uses LOGEST output to forecast values

E6: =C6/D6, copy to E7:E16   Computes errors as the ratio of data values to forecast values.

E20: =GEOMEAN(E6:E16)   Computes geometric mean of error ratios. (must equal one)

F6: =E6-1 or (C6-D6)/D6, copy to F7:F16   Computes percent error with the LOGEST function. When inserting an exponential trend line, it uses natural logarithms with a base e, which equals 2.71828. When evaluating results with the LOGEST function, it uses common logarithms with a base 10. To place the equation given in the scatter plot in the same form as equation 3.9, note that

$$e^{0.2233} = 1.250 \text{ (correct to 4 significant figures)}$$

which is the value shown in Cell C23 of the LOGEST output in Figure 3-16. That is,

$$13,153e^{0.2233XYR} = 13,153 \times 1.250^{XYR}$$

Because 10 is the base of our decimal numbering system, we shall use the exponential forecasting equation in the form of equation 3.9. Equation 3.9 has the additional advantage of showing that the annual rate of increase of Wal-Mart's sales revenues is 0.2501, or 25.01 percent.

To use the exponential model to forecast Wal-Mart's annual sales, enter =$D$23*$C$23^B6 in Cell D6 and copy the entry to D7:D19.

The exponential model minimizes the sum of the squares of the RELATIVE errors; the exponential model looks at the *ratios* of the data to forecast values rather than their *differences*. The error ratios are calculated by entering =C6/D6 in Cell E6 and copying the entry to Cells E7:E16.

For an exponential model to be valid, the geometric mean of its error ratios must equal 1. The geometric mean is calculated by entering =GEOMEAN(E6:E16) in Cell E20.

Error ratios can be converted to percent errors by subtracting 1 from the error ratios or by dividing the difference between the data and forecast values by the forecast values. Thus, the entry in Cell F6 of Figure 3-16 can be either =E6-1 or =(C6-D6)/D6. The entry in F6 is copied down over the range F7:F16.

The error pattern is plotted in the lower chart of Figure 3-16. The error pattern is systematic. The errors rise from a ratio below zero for the first year to a maximum ratio near the middle of the data range, and then decrease to a negative value at the last year. In other words, the errors follow a fairly consistent path, increasing from an initial low negative value to a maximum positive value and then turning down to a final low negative value. Because the error pattern is systematic rather than random, we cannot reasonably conclude that the exponential model is valid. We therefore conclude that the exponential model is not valid, and we reject it.

Forecast Errors and Confidence Limits

Single-point forecasts are always wrong. At best, future values are less than the single-point forecasts 50 percent of the time and more the other 50 percent of the time. It is important, therefore, to treat forecasts not as single values, but rather as probability distributions. Knowing how widely future values might vary about the mean values of the distributions is important for assessing financial risks and for devising strategies and tactics to cope with the unexpected.

Standard Forecast Error

Although the standard error of estimate expresses the **model's** accuracy, it does **not** measure a **forecast's** accuracy. You might intuitively expect that forecast errors should increase as we project a past trend farther and farther into the future, beyond the range of the data. This behavior is expressed by the following equation for calculating the **standard forecast error** (SFE) for a forecast:

$$SFE = SEE \sqrt{1 + \frac{1}{n} + \frac{(X_i - \overline{X})^2}{\sum_{i=1}^{n}(X_i - \overline{X})^2}} \tag{3.10}$$

where X_i = the value of the independent variable for which the forecast is made

$\overline{X}$ = the mean or average value of the data for the independent variable. (Because spreadsheets cannot show superscripts, we have used XM to label the mean on the spreadsheets in the text.)

and n = the number of pairs of data values

The expression $X_i - \overline{X}$ in equation 3.10 measures the distance of a value of X_i from the data's midpoint, $\overline{X}$. Note that X_i can be any value either within or beyond the range of data, **but that the summation in the denominator of the third term of the radical is only over the range of data values.**

Figures 3-17, 3-18, and 3-19 show the linear, quadratic, and exponential models previously created for Wal-Mart with the addition of the standard forecast errors described in this section and the confidence limits described in the next section of this chapter. In Figure 3-17, values of $X_i - \overline{X}$ are calculated by entering =B6-AVERAGE($B$6:$B$16) in Cell F6 and copying to F7:F19. Standard forecast errors are then calculated by entering =$D$24*SQRT(1+1/11+ F6^2/ SUMSQ($F$6:$F$16)) in Cell G6 and copying it to G7:G19. **It is important to recognize that the range of cells for the SUMSQ function is only over the range of data values—from Rows 6 to 16, and NOT from Rows 6 to 19.** With 11 data values and X values running from 0 to 10, the mean or average value of X is 5. This is the midpoint of the *data*. Note the $ signs in the entries to fix cell references. You can type in the $ signs or press the F4 key after entering the cell references to place a $ sign before both the column and row. (Pressing the F4 key a second time deletes the $ sign before the column and retains the one before the row. Pressing the F4 key a third time deletes the $ sign before the row and puts one before the column. Pressing the F4 key a fourth time deletes the $ sign before the column so that the cell reference appears with no $ signs.)

Note that the SFEs are a minimum at the data's midpoint, where the value is slightly greater than the model's SEE. Note also that the SFEs increase as we move in either direction from the midpoint, and they have the same value when the distances from the midpoint are equal (e.g., the values $7,118 million in Cells G6 and G16, which are five years before and five years after the midpoint at 1992). **If these conditions are not satisfied, an error has been made in the entries.** Find the error and correct it!

Standard forecast errors for the quadratic and exponential regression models are calculated in the same way as for the linear model. However, the interpretation is different for the SFEs of the exponential model. The SFEs of exponential models are *relative* errors. Therefore, the SFEs in Cells F6:F19 of Figure 3-19 are labeled as percentages rather than dollar differences.

Figure 3-17

Linear Model with Standard Forecast Errors and Confidence Limits Added

	A	B	C	D	E	F	G	H	I
1				WAL-MART STORES, INC.					
2				LINEAR REGRESSION EQUATION FITTED TO DATA FOR ANNUAL SALES					
3			Annual Sales,		Forecast		Std. Fcst.	80% Confidence Limits	
4	Fiscal		$ million		Error,	X-XM,	Error, SFE	Minimum	Maximum
5	Year	X	Data	Forecast	$ million	years	$ million	$ million	$ million
6	1986	0	$ 11,909	$1,925	$9,984	–5.0	$7,118	–$7,920	$11,769
7	1987	1	$ 15,959	$11,624	$4,335	–4.0	$6,894	$2,090	$21,158
8	1988	2	$ 20,649	$21,323	–$674	–3.0	$6,714	$12,038	$30,609
9	1989	3	$ 25,811	$31,022	–$5,211	–2.0	$6,582	$21,918	$40,126
10	1990	4	$ 32,602	$40,721	–$8,119	–1.0	$6,502	$31,728	$49,714
11	1991	5	$ 43,887	$50,420	–$6,533	0.0	$6,475	$41,465	$59,376
12	1992	6	$ 55,484	$60,120	–$4,636	1.0	$6,502	$51,127	$69,113
13	1993	7	$ 67,344	$69,819	–$2,475	2.0	$6,582	$60,715	$78,922
14	1994	8	$ 82,494	$79,518	$2,976	3.0	$6,714	$70,232	$88,803
15	1995	9	$ 93,627	$89,217	$4,410	4.0	$6,894	$79,683	$98,751
16	1996	10	$ 104,859	$98,916	$5,943	5.0	$7,118	$89,072	$108,761
17	1997	11		$108,615		6.0	$7,383	$98,404	$118,826
18	1998	12		$118,314		7.0	$7,685	$107,686	$128,942
19	1999	13		$128,014		8.0	$8,018	$116,924	$139,103
20				Average Error	$0			Student's t =	1.3830
21			LINEST Output for Linear Model						
22			9699.14	1924.77		Note: The confidence limits are calculated only			
23			591.1246	3497.1403		to demonstrate the procedure. Because the			
24			0.96765	6199.8		model is not valid, we can have no confidence in			
25			269.22046	9		the limits shown above in Columns H and I.			
26			1.035E+10	345,934,011					
27				Key Cell Entries					
28			D6:	=$D$22+$C$22*B6, copy to D7:D19					
29			F6:	=B6-AVERAGE($B$6:$B$16), copy to F7:F19					
30			G6:	=$D$24*SQRT(1+1/11+F6^2/SUMSQ($F$6:$F$16)), copy to G7:G19					
31			H6:	=D6-$I$20*G6, copy to H7:H19					
32			I6:	=D6+$I$20*G6, copy to I7:I19					
33			I20:	=TINV(0.20,D25)					

DATA VALUES, LINEAR REGRESSION LINE,
AND MINIMUM AND MAXIMUM CONFIDENCE LIMITS

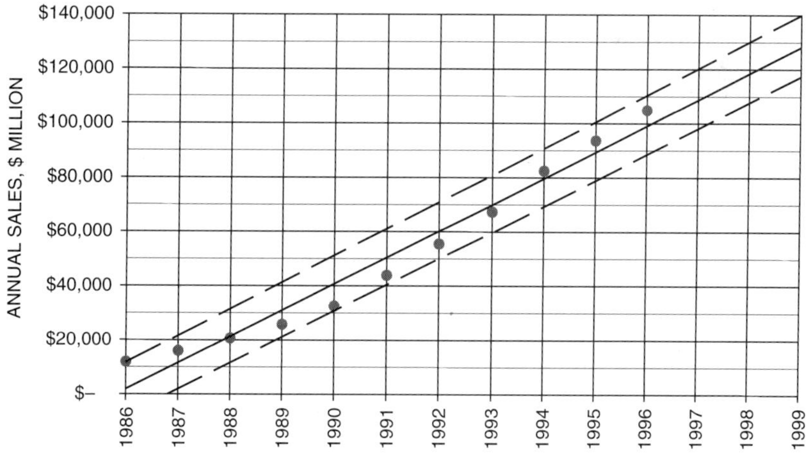

Figure 3-18

Quadratic Model with Standard Forecast Errors and Confidence Limits Added

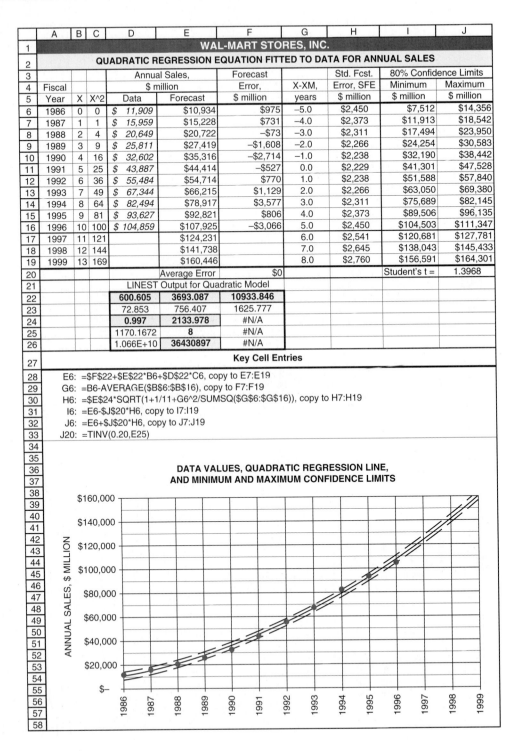

	A	B	C	D	E	F	G	H	I	J
1					WAL-MART STORES, INC.					
2				QUADRATIC REGRESSION EQUATION FITTED TO DATA FOR ANNUAL SALES						
3				Annual Sales,		Forecast		Std. Fcst.	80% Confidence Limits	
4	Fiscal			$ million		Error,	X-XM,	Error, SFE	Minimum	Maximum
5	Year	X	X^2	Data	Forecast	$ million	years	$ million	$ million	$ million
6	1986	0	0	$ 11,909	$10,934	$975	−5.0	$2,450	$7,512	$14,356
7	1987	1	1	$ 15,959	$15,228	$731	−4.0	$2,373	$11,913	$18,542
8	1988	2	4	$ 20,649	$20,722	−$73	−3.0	$2,311	$17,494	$23,950
9	1989	3	9	$ 25,811	$27,419	−$1,608	−2.0	$2,266	$24,254	$30,583
10	1990	4	16	$ 32,602	$35,316	−$2,714	−1.0	$2,238	$32,190	$38,442
11	1991	5	25	$ 43,887	$44,414	−$527	0.0	$2,229	$41,301	$47,528
12	1992	6	36	$ 55,484	$54,714	$770	1.0	$2,238	$51,588	$57,840
13	1993	7	49	$ 67,344	$66,215	$1,129	2.0	$2,266	$63,050	$69,380
14	1994	8	64	$ 82,494	$78,917	$3,577	3.0	$2,311	$75,689	$82,145
15	1995	9	81	$ 93,627	$92,821	$806	4.0	$2,373	$89,506	$96,135
16	1996	10	100	$ 104,859	$107,925	−$3,066	5.0	$2,450	$104,503	$111,347
17	1997	11	121		$124,231		6.0	$2,541	$120,681	$127,781
18	1998	12	144		$141,738		7.0	$2,645	$138,043	$145,433
19	1999	13	169		$160,446		8.0	$2,760	$156,591	$164,301
20					Average Error	$0			Student's t =	1.3968
21				LINEST Output for Quadratic Model						
22				600.605	3693.087	10933.846				
23				72.853	756.407	1625.777				
24				0.997	2133.978	#N/A				
25				1170.1672	8	#N/A				
26				1.066E+10	36430897	#N/A				
27					Key Cell Entries					
28	E6: =$F$22+$E$22*B6+$D$22*C6, copy to E7:E19									
29	G6: =B6−AVERAGE($B$6:$B$16), copy to F7:F19									
30	H6: =$E$24*SQRT(1+1/11+G6^2/SUMSQ($G$6:$G$16)), copy to H7:H19									
31	I6: =E6−$J$20*H6, copy to I7:I19									
32	J6: =E6+$J$20*H6, copy to J7:J19									
33	J20: =TINV(0.20,E25)									
34										
35										
36				DATA VALUES, QUADRATIC REGRESSION LINE,						
37				AND MINIMUM AND MAXIMUM CONFIDENCE LIMITS						

Figure 3-19

Exponential Model with Standard Forecast Errors and Confidence Limits Added

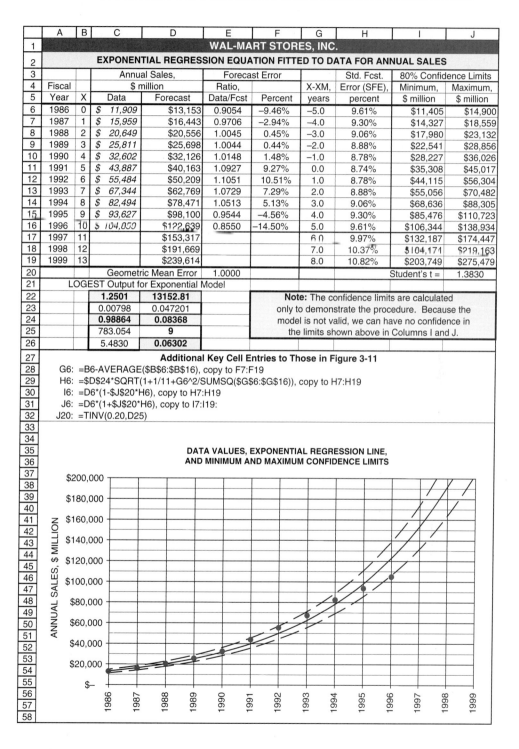

	A	B	C	D	E	F	G	H	I	J
1					**WAL-MART STORES, INC.**					
2				**EXPONENTIAL REGRESSION EQUATION FITTED TO DATA FOR ANNUAL SALES**						
3			Annual Sales,		Forecast Error			Std. Fcst.	80% Confidence Limits	
4	Fiscal		$ million		Ratio,		X-XM,	Error (SFE),	Minimum,	Maximum,
5	Year	X	Data	Forecast	Data/Fcst	Percent	years	percent	$ million	$ million
6	1986	0	$ 11,909	$13,153	0.9054	−9.46%	−5.0	9.61%	$11,405	$14,900
7	1987	1	$ 15,959	$16,443	0.9706	−2.94%	−4.0	9.30%	$14,327	$18,559
8	1988	2	$ 20,649	$20,556	1.0045	0.45%	−3.0	9.06%	$17,980	$23,132
9	1989	3	$ 25,811	$25,698	1.0044	0.44%	−2.0	8.88%	$22,541	$28,856
10	1990	4	$ 32,602	$32,126	1.0148	1.48%	−1.0	8.78%	$28,227	$36,026
11	1991	5	$ 43,887	$40,163	1.0927	9.27%	0.0	8.74%	$35,308	$45,017
12	1992	6	$ 55,484	$50,209	1.1051	10.51%	1.0	8.78%	$44,115	$56,304
13	1993	7	$ 67,344	$62,769	1.0729	7.29%	2.0	8.88%	$55,056	$70,482
14	1994	8	$ 82,494	$78,471	1.0513	5.13%	3.0	9.06%	$68,636	$88,305
15	1995	9	$ 93,627	$98,100	0.9544	−4.56%	4.0	9.30%	$85,476	$110,723
16	1996	10	$ 104,859	$122,639	0.8550	−14.50%	5.0	9.61%	$106,344	$138,934
17	1997	11		$153,317			6.0	9.97%	$132,187	$174,447
18	1998	12		$191,669			7.0	10.37%	$104,171	$219,163
19	1999	13		$239,614			8.0	10.82%	$203,749	$275,479
20			Geometric Mean Error		1.0000				Student's t =	1.3830
21			LOGEST Output for Exponential Model							
22			**1.2501**	**13152.81**			Note: The confidence limits are calculated			
23			0.00798	0.047201			only to demonstrate the procedure. Because the			
24			**0.98864**	**0.08368**			model is not valid, we can have no confidence in			
25			783.054	**9**			the limits shown above in Columns I and J.			
26			5.4830	**0.06302**						
27				**Additional Key Cell Entries to Those in Figure 3-11**						
28			G6:	=B6-AVERAGE($B$6:$B$16), copy to F7:F19						
29			H6:	=$D$24*SQRT(1+1/11+G6^2/SUMSQ($G$6:$G$16)), copy to H7:H19						
30			I6:	=D6*(1-$J$20*H6), copy to H7:H19						
31			J6:	=D6*(1+$J$20*H6), copy to I7:I19:						
32			J20:	=TINV(0.20,D25)						

DATA VALUES, EXPONENTIAL REGRESSION LINE,
AND MINIMUM AND MAXIMUM CONFIDENCE LIMITS

Standard forecast errors are essentially like standard deviations. However, their meaning is seldom clear to those without knowledge of statistics. Therefore, in the next section we use the standard forecast errors and the properties of normal distribution curves to express confidence ranges in terms of the range of values within which there is a known probability that future values will occur.

Confidence Range

The random scatter of actual values about a trend line follows a normal distribution. This makes it possible to use the properties of the normal distribution to calculate a confidence range for forecast values—that is, to calculate the minimum and maximum values for which there is a specified probability that an actual value will fall in the future.

For models in which the forecast error is measured by the difference between data and forecast values, such as the linear and quadratic models, the minimum and maximum values are defined by the equations:

$$\text{Minimum} = \text{Fitted value} - t^*\text{SFE} \tag{3.11}$$

$$\text{Maximum} = \text{Fitted value} + t^*\text{SFE} \tag{3.12}$$

where t is the value of Student's t for a specific level of confidence. (For large samples of data, with 30 or more sets of values, we could use Z values for the normal distribution.)

For models in which the forecast error is measured by the ratio of the data to forecast values, such as the exponential model, the minimum and maximum values are defined by the equations:

$$\text{Minimum} = \text{Fitted value}^*(1 - t^*\text{SFE}) \tag{3.13}$$

$$\text{Maximum} = \text{Fitted value}^*(1 + t^*\text{SFE}) \tag{3.14}$$

As an example, suppose you wish to know the minimum value for which there is only a 10 percent chance a future value will be less, and the maximum for which there is only a 10 percent chance a future value will be more. In other words, you are interested in the range for which you can be 80 percent sure the future value will lie. The choice of 80 percent is arbitrary. You might, for example, prefer to define a larger range in which you could be 90 percent sure of finding a future value, or a smaller range in which you're only 75 percent sure of finding a future value. The value of t in equations 3.11 to 3.14 depends on how much confidence you wish to have in using the results to make decisions, or, conversely, on how much risk you are willing to take.

Excel's TINV(*probability, degrees_freedom*) function command returns the value of the Student's t statistic for the probability of a two-tailed Student's t distribution and the specified degrees of freedom. You must note that the TINV command is for **a two-tailed test**; therefore, if you wish to obtain the boundaries for the middle 80 percent of the probability distribution, you should enter 0.20 for the probability value. (That is, the middle 80 percent leaves 10 percent in **each** of the **two** tails of the probability distribution for a total of 20 percent in the two tails.) The value of Student's t for the linear model is calculated in cell I20 of Figure 3-17 by the entry =TINV(0.20,D25). Note that Cell D25 in this entry is the number of degrees of freedom. For the linear model with 11 pairs of data values and 2 parameters in the regression equation, the number of degrees of freedom is 9 (i.e., 11 − 2). Student's *t* value for the linear model is 1.383. As the number of degrees of freedom becomes less, the value of Student's *t* increases. Thus, for 7 degrees of freedom, the Student *t* value is 1.415 for the middle 80 percent of the probability distribution.

Figure 3-20 shows the position of the confidence limits on the bell-shaped normal probability distribution. The SFEs are multiplied by the value of Student's *t* and their products are then subtracted or added to the fitted values to give the minimum and maximum values for the confidence range. (If you wish to create a chart such as Figure 3-20, first set up a series of values for the X-axis. Then use Excel's NORMDIST command to generate values for the Y-axis corresponding to the x values. Use a mean of zero and a standard deviation of one in the NORMDIST command. Enter FALSE to get the probability mass function. For additional information, use the HELP menu.)

Equations 3.11 and 3.12 are used to calculate the confidence limits for the linear and quadratic models shown in Figures 3-17 and 3-18. To compute the lower and upper confidence limits for the linear model, enter =D6-$I$20*G6 in cell H6 and =D6+$I$20*G6 in Cell I6 and copy the entries to H7;I19. Thus, for example, the forecast annual sales for 1997 is $108,615 million; there is a 10 percent chance the annual sales will be as low as $98,404 million, or less; and there is a 10 percent chance the annual sales will be as high as $118,826 million, or higher.

Figure 3-20

Normal Distribution of Values about the Forecast

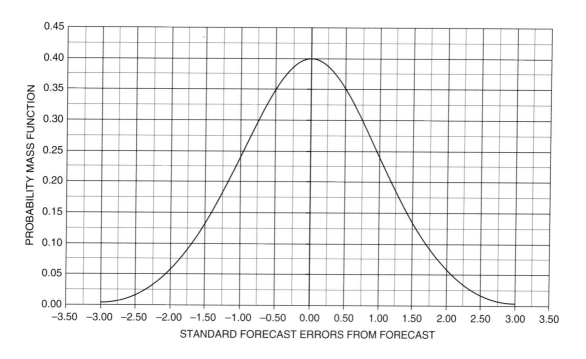

Equations 3.13 and 3.14 are used to calculate the confidence limits for the exponential model in Figure 3-19. Enter =D6*(1-$J$20*H6) in Cell I6 and =D6*(1+$J$20*H6) in Cell J6 and copy the entries to I7:J19.

Note the charts at the bottoms of Figures 3-17, 3-18, and 3-19. For the linear and quadratic models, the confidence limits diverge or splay out like dog bones, with the narrowest ranges at the midpoints of the data. For the exponential model, for which the forecast errors are *relative* errors, the confidence limits on an arithmetic scale become wider and wider apart as annual sales increases.

Analysis of Change in Trend

Life is a process of change. The concluding sections of this chapter reexamine the quadratic model that was developed for Wal-Mart Stores to recognize when the trend changes and to develop a new model for the new trend. (Chapter 4 provides additional instructions for recognizing when trends change and for changing or modifying a forecasting model to respond to the change.) Recall that there was no systematic behavior in the error pattern that would justify rejecting the quadratic model developed in Figure 3-14. Nevertheless, the pattern during the last three years indicated something was changing at Wal-Mart. Thus, the error for 1994 was much larger in a positive sense than for any previous year, and that for 1996 was much larger in a negative sense. We need a model that recognizes the change in trend that starts in 1994.

One way to investigate the statistics of what is happening is to derive a quadratic model for the data from 1986 to only 1993 and analyze how well the model predicts the data for 1994 to 1996. Figure 3-21 shows the analysis. You should note the following:

1. The error pattern at the lower left of Figure 3-21 is random from 1986 to 1994. However, there is a large, abrupt drop in the values of the errors for 1995 and 1996.
2. Consistent with the error pattern, the data values for 1995 and 1996 are seen to lie below the curve for the model in the chart at the lower right of Figure 3-18.
3. The data values for 1995 and 1996 are well below the lower confidence limits for the forecasting model based on the 1986–1993 data.

The messages in Column K alert the user whenever a data value is outside the confidence limits. To provide this message, enter =IF(OR(D6<I6,D6>J6),"YES", "NO") in Cell K6 and copy the entry to Cells K7:K16. This entry provides the message "YES" whenever a data value is less than the corresponding lower confidence limit or more than the upper confidence limit and "NO" otherwise. The cells are conditionally formatted to draw attention to "YES" messages. Figure 3-22 shows the "Conditional Formatting" dialog box with the entries for formatting cells with "YES." (This dialog box is accessed from the "Format" drop-down menu.)

What is important is to recognize that the past trend from 1986 to 1993 has changed. From the standpoint of making better projections of the past trend, it means modifying or changing the model.

Figure 3-21

Quadratic Model Based on Data for 1986 to 1993

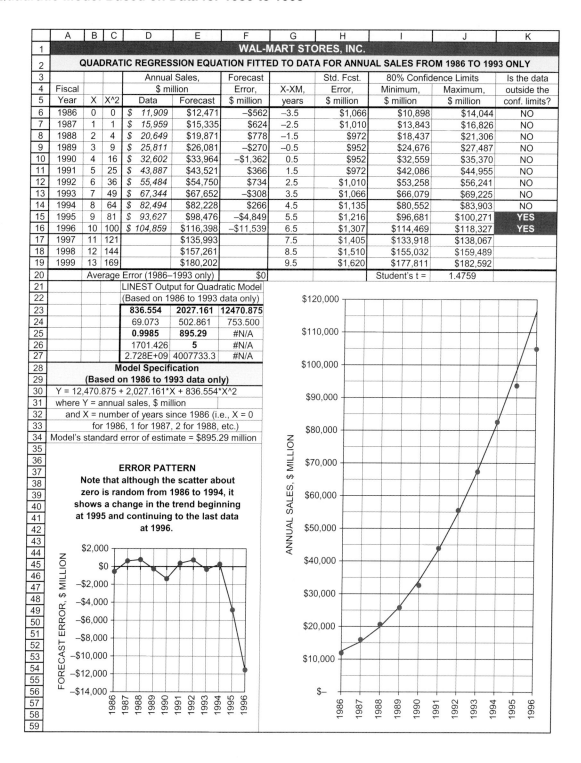

	A	B	C	D	E	F	G	H	I	J	K
1						WAL-MART STORES, INC.					
2				QUADRATIC REGRESSION EQUATION FITTED TO DATA FOR ANNUAL SALES FROM 1986 TO 1993 ONLY							
3				Annual Sales,		Forecast		Std. Fcst.	80% Confidence Limits		Is the data
4	Fiscal			$ million		Error,	X-XM,	Error,	Minimum,	Maximum,	outside the
5	Year	X	X^2	Data	Forecast	$ million	years	$ million	$ million	$ million	conf. limits?
6	1986	0	0	$ 11,909	$12,471	−$562	−3.5	$1,066	$10,898	$14,044	NO
7	1987	1	1	$ 15,959	$15,335	$624	−2.5	$1,010	$13,843	$16,826	NO
8	1988	2	4	$ 20,649	$19,871	$778	−1.5	$972	$18,437	$21,306	NO
9	1989	3	9	$ 25,811	$26,081	−$270	−0.5	$952	$24,676	$27,487	NO
10	1990	4	16	$ 32,602	$33,964	−$1,362	0.5	$952	$32,559	$35,370	NO
11	1991	5	25	$ 43,887	$43,521	$366	1.5	$972	$42,086	$44,955	NO
12	1992	6	36	$ 55,484	$54,750	$734	2.5	$1,010	$53,258	$56,241	NO
13	1993	7	49	$ 67,344	$67,652	−$308	3.5	$1,066	$66,079	$69,225	NO
14	1994	8	64	$ 82,494	$82,228	$266	4.5	$1,135	$80,552	$83,903	NO
15	1995	9	81	$ 93,627	$98,476	−$4,849	5.5	$1,216	$96,681	$100,271	YES
16	1996	10	100	$ 104,859	$116,398	−$11,539	6.5	$1,307	$114,469	$118,327	YES
17	1997	11	121		$135,993		7.5	$1,405	$133,918	$138,067	
18	1998	12	144		$157,261		8.5	$1,510	$155,032	$159,489	
19	1999	13	169		$180,202		9.5	$1,620	$177,811	$182,592	
20		Average Error (1986–1993 only)				$0			Student's t =	1.4759	
21				LINEST Output for Quadratic Model							
22				(Based on 1986 to 1993 data only)							
23				836.554	2027.161	12470.875					
24				69.073	502.861	753.500					
25				0.9985	895.29	#N/A					
26				1701.426	5	#N/A					
27				2.728E+09	4007733.3	#N/A					
28				Model Specification							
29				(Based on 1986 to 1993 data only)							
30		Y = 12,470.875 + 2,027.161*X + 836.554*X^2									
31		where Y = annual sales, $ million									
32		and X = number of years since 1986 (i.e., X = 0									
33		for 1986, 1 for 1987, 2 for 1988, etc.)									
34		Model's standard error of estimate = $895.29 million									

Figure 3-22

"Conditional Formatting" Dialog Box with Formatting Entries When Cell Value in "YES"

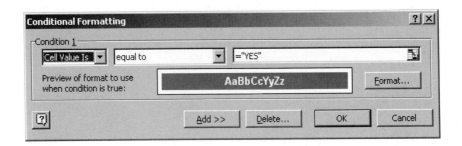

From the standpoint of company management or outside investors, **it means that something has changed that has triggered a change in the past trend.** The cause may be something external to the company (e.g., changes in the general economic conditions or competition) or internal (e.g., changes in corporate strategies or upheavals in corporate management). Learning the cause requires delving beneath the numbers and taking into account what is going on in the world, in the industry, and in the company. In short, whether using regression equations to project future values or to improve managing or investing activities, it is important to be alert for changes in past trends and to take corrective action as quickly as possible.

Cubic Regression Equation

There are several ways to create a model that recognizes the downturn in Wal-Mart's annual sales from the trend for a quadratic model. One of these is to use a cubic regression equation.

Cubic regression models are similar to linear and quadratic models but include the cube of the independent variable as a fourth term in the regression equation. Depending on one's choice of symbols for the parameters, the general form of the equation for a cubic regression model can be written as either

$$Y = a + bX + cX^2 + dX^3 \tag{3.15}$$

or

$$Y = b_0 + b_1X + b_2X^2 + b_3X^3 \tag{3.16}$$

where the subscripts of the coefficients in equation 3.16 indicate the power of the independent variable X associated with it.

Figure 3-23 shows results with a cubic regression model used to analyze the annual sales data for Wal-Mart Stores, Inc. To prepare this spreadsheet, edit a copy of Figure 3-21. Insert a column for values of X^3 between the values for X^2 and the data. Enter =B6^3 in Cell D6 and copy the entry to D7:C19.

With the mouse, select Cells D23:G27, type =LINEST(E6:E16,B6:D16,1,1), and press Ctrl/Shift/Enter. The result is shown in the fourth column by the 5-row matrix labeled "LINEST Output for Cubic Model."

Figure 3-23

Spreadsheet for Cubic Regression Model

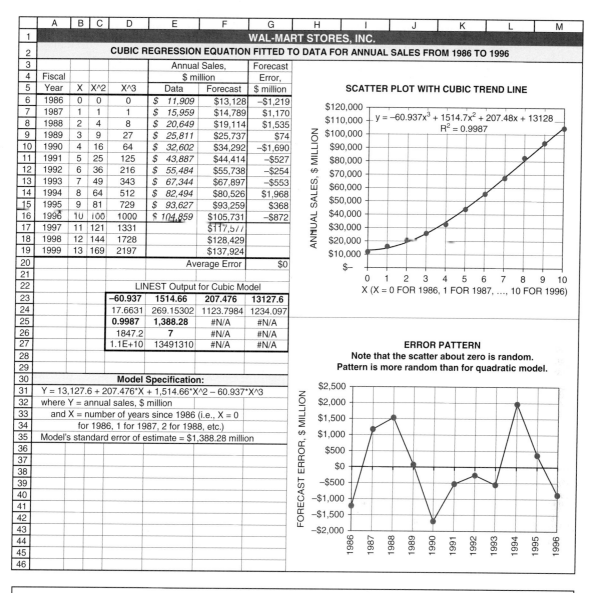

	A	B	C	D	E	F	G	H	I	J	K	L	M
1							WAL-MART STORES, INC.						
2						CUBIC REGRESSION EQUATION FITTED TO DATA FOR ANNUAL SALES FROM 1986 TO 1996							
3					Annual Sales,		Forecast						
4	Fiscal				$ million		Error,						
5	Year	X	X^2	X^3	Data	Forecast	$ million						
6	1986	0	0	0	$ 11,909	$13,128	−$1,219						
7	1987	1	1	1	$ 15,959	$14,789	$1,170						
8	1988	2	4	8	$ 20,649	$19,114	$1,535						
9	1989	3	9	27	$ 25,811	$25,737	$74						
10	1990	4	16	64	$ 32,602	$34,292	−$1,690						
11	1991	5	25	125	$ 43,887	$44,414	−$527						
12	1992	6	36	216	$ 55,484	$55,738	−$254						
13	1993	7	49	343	$ 67,344	$67,897	−$553						
14	1994	8	64	512	$ 82,494	$80,526	$1,968						
15	1995	9	81	729	$ 93,627	$93,259	$368						
16	1996	10	100	1000	$ 104,859	$105,731	−$872						
17	1997	11	121	1331		$117,577							
18	1998	12	144	1728		$128,429							
19	1999	13	169	2197		$137,924							
20						Average Error	$0						
21													
22					LINEST Output for Cubic Model								
23				−60.937	1514.66	207.476	13127.6						
24				17.6631	269.15302	1123.7984	1234.097						
25				0.9987	1,388.28	#N/A	#N/A						
26				1847.2	7	#N/A	#N/A						
27				1.1E+10	13491310	#N/A	#N/A						
28													
29													
30				Model Specification:									
31	Y = 13,127.6 + 207.476*X + 1,514.66*X^2 − 60.937*X^3												
32	where Y = annual sales, $ million												
33	and X = number of years since 1986 (i.e., X = 0												
34	for 1986, 1 for 1987, 2 for 1988, etc.)												
35	Model's standard error of estimate = $1,388.28 million												
36													
37													
38													
39													
40													
41													
42													
43													
44													
45													
46													

SCATTER PLOT WITH CUBIC TREND LINE

$y = -60.937x^3 + 1514.7x^2 + 207.48x + 13128$
$R^2 = 0.9987$

X (X = 0 FOR 1986, 1 FOR 1987, ..., 10 FOR 1996)

ERROR PATTERN
Note that the scatter about zero is random.
Pattern is more random than for quadratic model.

Key Cell Entries

F6: =$G$23+$F$23*B6+$E$23*B6^2+$D$23*B6^3,	
copy to F7:F19	Uses model's parameters to calculate forecast values for year values
G6: =E6-F6, copy to G7:G16	Calculates error as data value minus forecast value
G20: =AVERAGE(G6:G16)	Calculates average error over range of data (must be zero)
D23:G27: =LINEST (E6:E16,B6:D16,1,1)	Generates output for LINEST function.

The values in Cells D23:G23 are the values of *d*, *c*, *b*, and *a*, respectively, in equation 3.15. The equation for the cubic model for Wal-Mart's annual sales is

$$Y = 13{,}127.6 + 207.476X + 1{,}514.66X^2 - 60.937X^3 \qquad (3.17)$$

where the variables Y and X are as defined before. Note that the values for the four coefficients are the same as those for the cubic trend line on the scatter diagram (within the round-off, of course). Also note that the coefficient of X^3 is negative, which expresses the downturn in the trend that becomes more important as the values of X increase.

To use the model's parameters to make forecasts, enter =$G$23+$F$23*B6+$E$23*C6 +$D$23*D6 in Cell F6 and copy the entry to F7:F19. To calculate the errors, enter =E6-F6 in Cell G6 and copy it to G7:G19. To validate the model, first show that the average error is zero (enter =SUM(G6:G16) in Cell G20), then show that the errors scatter randomly rather than systematically (error pattern at lower right).

Figure 3-24 shows the standard forecast errors and confidence limits for the cubic model. The chart at the bottom compares the linear, quadratic, and cubic models. Note that the forecasts for 1997 to 1999 with the cubic model lie between those for the linear and quadratic models and are significantly different. Wal-Mart's actual sales revenues for 1997 were $117,958 million. This compares very favorably with the $117,577 million forecast by the cubic model we accepted (Cell F17 of Figures 3-23 and 3-24).

Text Boxes

To insert the text boxes that identify the trend lines in Figure 3-24, click on the "Text Box" icon on the drawing toolbar. (The drawing toolbar is usually at the bottom of the screen. If the drawing toolbar is not visible, go to the "View" drop-down menu, select "Toolbars," and click on "Drawing.") This will change the shape of the cursor to a crosshair. Drag the crosshair over a portion of the chart to create a rectangle in which the label will be placed. Type the label in the text box. Change the shape and size of the text box so that it is approximately what is needed to accommodate the text. Drag the text box to a suitable position on the chart by clicking on its border and moving the mouse cursor.

Format the text box by double-clicking on its border to open the "Format Text Box" dialog box shown as Figure 3-25. This provides many options, as indicated by the tabs. To provide the text boxes shown in Figure 3-24, use the "Color and Lines" tab to change the fill color to the background color of the chart and change the color of the line to "No line," as shown in Figure 3-25. The "Font" tab allows one to change the type of font, its style, its size, its color, etc. Use the different sheet tabs of the "Format Text Box" dialog box to format text boxes as desired. After you have completed the first text box, you can copy and edit the text for the other two. To make two copies, click on the border of the first text box and press the Ctrl/C keys, move the cursor to a suitable position and press the Ctrl/V keys, move to another position and press the Ctrl/V keys again. To delete a text box, click on its border and then on the Delete key.

Use the mouse cursor to move a text box to an appropriate position on the chart. Start by grabbing the text box by clicking on the border around it. Then, while holding the mouse button down, drag the text box to the desired location and release the mouse button.

Figure 3-24

Cubic Regression Model with 80% Confidence Ranges and Chart Comparing Linear, Quadratic, and Cubic Models

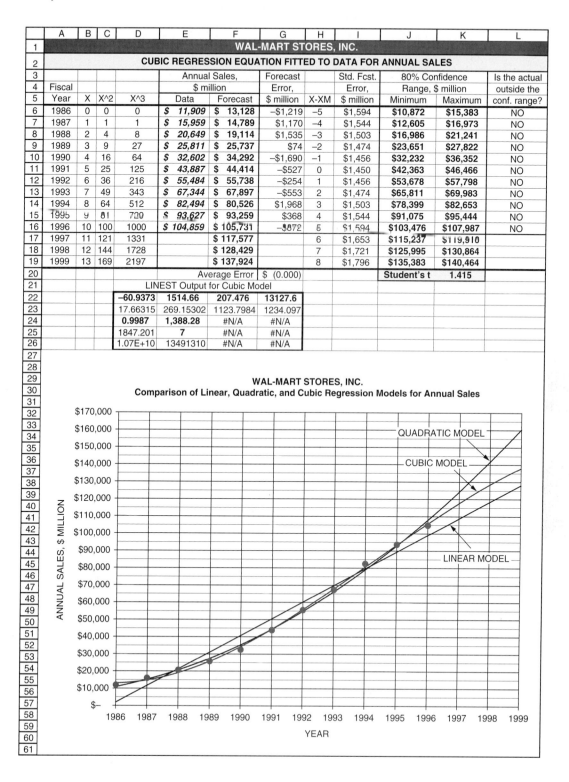

	A	B	C	D	E	F	G	H	I	J	K	L
1						WAL-MART STORES, INC.						
2						CUBIC REGRESSION EQUATION FITTED TO DATA FOR ANNUAL SALES						
3					Annual Sales,		Forecast		Std. Fcst.	80% Confidence		Is the actual
4	Fiscal				$ million		Error,		Error,	Range, $ million		outside the
5	Year	X	X^2	X^3	Data	Forecast	$ million	X-XM	$ million	Minimum	Maximum	conf. range?
6	1986	0	0	0	$ 11,909	$ 13,128	−$1,219	−5	$1,594	$10,872	$15,383	NO
7	1987	1	1	1	$ 15,959	$ 14,789	$1,170	−4	$1,544	$12,605	$16,973	NO
8	1988	2	4	8	$ 20,649	$ 19,114	$1,535	−3	$1,503	$16,986	$21,241	NO
9	1989	3	9	27	$ 25,811	$ 25,737	$74	−2	$1,474	$23,651	$27,822	NO
10	1990	4	16	64	$ 32,602	$ 34,292	−$1,690	−1	$1,456	$32,232	$36,352	NO
11	1991	5	25	125	$ 43,887	$ 44,414	−$527	0	$1,450	$42,363	$46,466	NO
12	1992	6	36	216	$ 55,484	$ 55,738	−$254	1	$1,456	$53,678	$57,798	NO
13	1993	7	49	343	$ 67,344	$ 67,897	−$553	2	$1,474	$65,811	$69,983	NO
14	1994	8	64	512	$ 82,494	$ 80,526	$1,968	3	$1,503	$78,399	$82,653	NO
15	1995	9	81	729	$ 93,627	$ 93,259	$368	4	$1,544	$91,075	$95,444	NO
16	1996	10	100	1000	$ 104,859	$ 105,731	−$872	5	$1,594	$103,476	$107,987	NO
17	1997	11	121	1331		$ 117,577		6	$1,653	$115,237	$119,910	
18	1998	12	144	1728		$ 128,429		7	$1,721	$125,995	$130,864	
19	1999	13	169	2197		$ 137,924		8	$1,796	$135,383	$140,464	
20					Average Error		$ (0.000)			Student's t	1.415	
21				LINEST Output for Cubic Model								
22				−60.9373	1514.66	207.476	13127.6					
23				17.66315	269.15302	1123.7984	1234.097					
24				0.9987	1,388.28	#N/A	#N/A					
25				1847.201	7	#N/A	#N/A					
26				1.07E+10	13491310	#N/A	#N/A					
27												
28												
29						WAL-MART STORES, INC.						
30					Comparison of Linear, Quadratic, and Cubic Regression Models for Annual Sales							

WAL-MART STORES, INC.
Comparison of Linear, Quadratic, and Cubic Regression Models for Annual Sales

QUADRATIC MODEL
CUBIC MODEL
LINEAR MODEL

ANNUAL SALES, $ MILLION

$170,000
$160,000
$150,000
$140,000
$130,000
$120,000
$110,000
$100,000
$90,000
$80,000
$70,000
$60,000
$50,000
$40,000
$30,000
$20,000
$10,000
$–

1986 1987 1988 1989 1990 1991 1992 1993 1994 1995 1996 1997 1998 1999

YEAR

Figure 3-25

"Format Text Box" Dialog Box

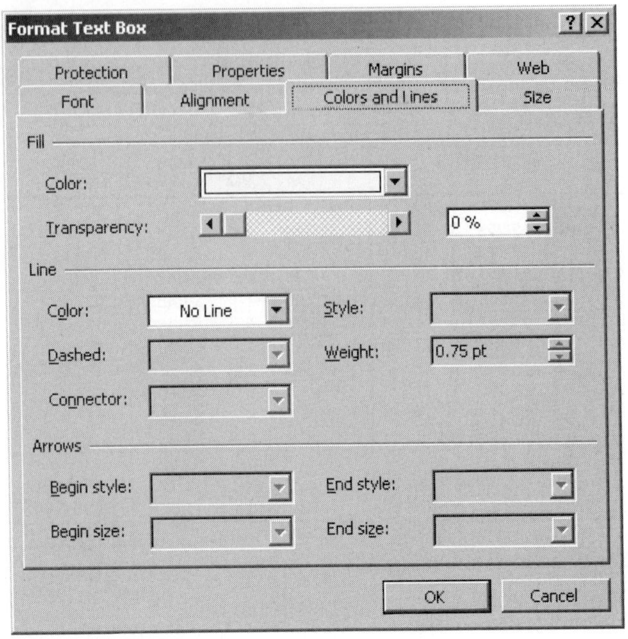

Figure 3-26 shows the results when the 1997 data is added to that for 1986 to 1996 and a new cubic forecasting model is created. By running your eye down the errors in Column I of Figure 3-26, you should be able to recognize that the errors scatter randomly. The average error in Cell G20 is zero. We conclude this is a valid model. The values of the parameters in its regression equation are only slightly different from the earlier model without the 1997 data (Figure 3-24).

Case Study: Wal-Mart Stores Revisited in 2001

We revisited Wal-Mart to see how well its performance beyond 1997 matched the projections in Figure 3-26 with a cubic model based on the 1986–1997 data. We were particularly interested in understanding the downturn after 1994 and its cause, and to see whether or not the downturn continued.

An article in *Business Week* in February of 1998 noted that Wal-Mart was putting its house in order to recover from the slide in its rate of growth that began several years earlier, and was finally starting to benefit from a series of investments it began making in 1994 to enter the European market. The article concluded that the changes should result in an 11% climb in annual revenues to $131 billion. That is only slightly higher than the sales of $128,938 million projected by the cubic model based on the data between 1986 and 1997. In fact, Wal-Mart's sales for fiscal 1998 were $137,634 million, which is significantly higher than forecast by the cubic model based on the 1986–1997 data.

Figure 3-26

Cubic Regression Model Based on 1986 to 1997 Data

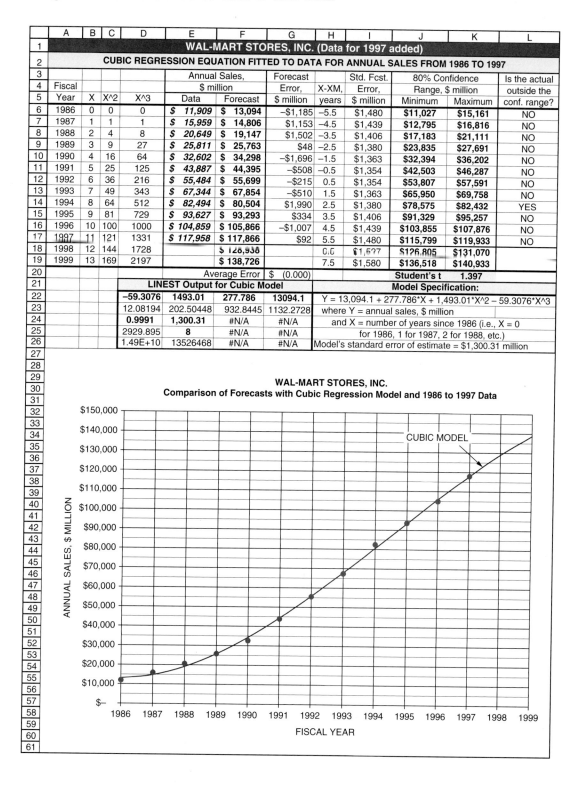

	A	B	C	D	E	F	G	H	I	J	K	L
1	WAL-MART STORES, INC. (Data for 1997 added)											
2	CUBIC REGRESSION EQUATION FITTED TO DATA FOR ANNUAL SALES FROM 1986 TO 1997											
3					Annual Sales,		Forecast		Std. Fcst.	80% Confidence		Is the actual
4	Fiscal				$ million		Error,	X-XM,	Error,	Range, $ million		outside the
5	Year	X	X^2	X^3	Data	Forecast	$ million	years	$ million	Minimum	Maximum	conf. range?
6	1986	0	0	0	$ 11,909	$ 13,094	–$1,185	–5.5	$1,480	$11,027	$15,161	NO
7	1987	1	1	1	$ 15,959	$ 14,806	$1,153	–4.5	$1,439	$12,795	$16,816	NO
8	1988	2	4	8	$ 20,649	$ 19,147	$1,502	–3.5	$1,406	$17,183	$21,111	NO
9	1989	3	9	27	$ 25,811	$ 25,763	$48	–2.5	$1,380	$23,835	$27,691	NO
10	1990	4	16	64	$ 32,602	$ 34,298	–$1,696	–1.5	$1,363	$32,394	$36,202	NO
11	1991	5	25	125	$ 43,887	$ 44,395	–$508	–0.5	$1,354	$42,503	$46,287	NO
12	1992	6	36	216	$ 55,484	$ 55,699	–$215	0.5	$1,354	$53,807	$57,591	NO
13	1993	7	49	343	$ 67,344	$ 67,854	–$510	1.5	$1,363	$65,950	$69,758	NO
14	1994	8	64	512	$ 82,494	$ 80,504	$1,990	2.5	$1,380	$78,575	$82,432	YES
15	1995	9	81	729	$ 93,627	$ 93,293	$334	3.5	$1,406	$91,329	$95,257	NO
16	1996	10	100	1000	$ 104,859	$ 105,866	–$1,007	4.5	$1,439	$103,855	$107,876	NO
17	1997	11	121	1331	$ 117,958	$ 117,866	$92	5.5	$1,480	$115,799	$119,933	NO
18	1998	12	144	1728		$ 128,938		6.5	$1,527	$126,805	$131,070	
19	1999	13	169	2197		$ 138,726		7.5	$1,580	$136,518	$140,933	
20					Average Error	$ (0.000)				Student's t	1.397	
21				LINEST Output for Cubic Model				Model Specification:				
22				–59.3076	1493.01	277.786	13094.1	Y = 13,094.1 + 277.786*X + 1,493.01*X^2 – 59.3076*X^3				
23				12.08194	202.50448	932.8445	1132.2728	where Y = annual sales, $ million				
24				0.9991	1,300.31	#N/A	#N/A	and X = number of years since 1986 (i.e., X = 0				
25				2929.895	8	#N/A	#N/A	for 1986, 1 for 1987, 2 for 1988, etc.)				
26				1.49E+10	13526468	#N/A	#N/A	Model's standard error of estimate = $1,300.31 million				

WAL-MART STORES, INC.
Comparison of Forecasts with Cubic Regression Model and 1986 to 1997 Data

CUBIC MODEL

Figure 3-27

Evaluation of the Cubic Model based on 1986 to 1997 Data for the Subsequent Three Years

	A	B	C	D	E	F	G	H	I	J	K	L
1							WAL-MART STORES, INC.					
2					CUBIC REGRESSION EQUATION FITTED TO DATA FOR ANNUAL SALES FROM 1986 TO 1997							
3					Annual Sales,		Forecast		Std. Fcst.	80% Confidence		Is the actual
4	Fiscal				$ million		Error,	X-XM,	Error,	Range, $ million		outside the
5	Year	X	X^2	X^3	Data	Forecast	$ million	years	$ million	Minimum	Maximum	conf. range?
6	1986	0	0	0	$ 11,909	$ 13,094	–$1,185	–5.5	$1,480	$11,027	$15,161	NO
7	1987	1	1	1	$ 15,959	$ 14,806	$1,153	–4.5	$1,439	$12,795	$16,816	NO
8	1988	2	4	8	$ 20,649	$ 19,147	$1,502	–3.5	$1,406	$17,183	$21,111	NO
9	1989	3	9	27	$ 25,811	$ 25,763	$48	–2.5	$1,380	$23,835	$27,691	NO
10	1990	4	16	64	$ 32,602	$ 34,298	–$1,696	–1.5	$1,363	$32,394	$36,202	NO
11	1991	5	25	125	$ 43,887	$ 44,395	–$508	–0.5	$1,354	$42,503	$46,287	NO
12	1992	6	36	216	$ 55,484	$ 55,699	–$215	0.5	$1,354	$53,807	$57,591	NO
13	1993	7	49	343	$ 67,344	$ 67,854	–$510	1.5	$1,363	$65,950	$69,758	NO
14	1994	8	64	512	$ 82,494	$ 80,504	$1,990	2.5	$1,380	$78,575	$82,432	YES
15	1995	9	81	729	$ 93,627	$ 93,293	$334	3.5	$1,406	$91,329	$95,257	NO
16	1996	10	100	1000	$ 104,859	$ 105,866	–$1,007	4.5	$1,439	$103,855	$107,876	NO
17	1997	11	121	1331	$ 117,958	$ 117,866	$92	5.5	$1,480	$115,799	$119,933	NO
18	1998	12	144	1728	$ 137,634	$ 128,938	$8,696	6.5	$1,527	$126,805	$131,070	YES
19	1999	13	169	2197	$ 165,013	$ 138,726	$26,287	7.5	$1,580	$136,518	$140,933	YES
20	2000	14	196	2744	$ 191,329	$ 146,873	$44,456	8.5	$1,639	$144,584	$149,163	YES
21				Average Error (1986 to 1997)			$ (0.000)			Student's t	1.397	
22				LINEST Output (1876–1886 data)						Model Specification:		
23				–59.3076	1493.01	277.786	13094.1	Y = 13,094.1 + 277.786*X + 1,493.01*X^2 – 59.3076*X^3				
24				12.08194	202.50448	932.8445	1132.2728	where Y = annual sales, $ million				
25				0.9991	1,300.31	#N/A	#N/A	and X = number of years since 1986 (i.e., X = 0				
26				2929.895	8	#N/A	#N/A	for 1986, 1 for 1987, 2 for 1988, etc.)				
27				1.49E+10	13526468	#N/A	#N/A	Model's standard error of estimate = $1,300.31 million				

Figure 3-27 adds the data for 1998, 1999, and 2000 and compares the data values over the complete range with the forecasts made with the cubic model based on the 1986–1997 data. The comparison demonstrates convincingly that the Wal-Mart has dramatically reversed the slowdown in the rate of increase of its annual sales projected by the cubic model based on the 1986–1997 data. Although the cubic model accurately followed the downturn up to 1997, it was not a valid model for projecting later behavior.

A new model was necessary to represent the trend from 1994 onward. Figure 3.28 shows the results for a quadratic model based on the data from 1994 to 2000. The data and the quadratic model recapture the earlier upward curvature of the trend line from 1986 to 1994. Compare the results in Figures 3.27 and 3.28, and notice how handsomely the changes that Wal-Mart's management made earlier have paid off!

IF the upward trend from 1994 to 2000 continues, the new model shown in Figure 3-28 projects annual sales of $223,539 million for Wal-Mart's 2001 fiscal year, and $259,662 million for 2002. That is a big **IF** in view of the current downturn in the worldwide economy. Once more, the statistical projections should be adjusted downward to account for the latest economic and other conditions.

Figure 3-28

Quadratic Model Fitted to Data for 1994 to 2000

	A	B	C	D	E	F	G	H	I	J	K
1	WAL-MART STORES, INC.										
2	QUADRATIC REGRESSION EQUATION FITTED TO DATA FOR ANNUAL SALES FROM 1994 TO 2000										
3				Annual Sales,		Forecast		Std. Fcst.	80% Confidence		Is the actual
4	Fiscal			$ million		Error,	X-XM,	Error,	Range, $ million		outside the
5	Year	X	X^2	Data	Forecast	$ million	years	$ million	Minimum	Maximum	conf. range?
6	1994	8	64	$ 82,494	$ 83,875	–$1,381	–3.0	$2,371	$80,239	$87,511	NO
7	1995	9	81	$ 93,627	$ 91,698	$1,929	–2.0	$2,222	$88,291	$95,105	NO
8	1996	10	100	$ 104,859	$ 103,564	$1,295	–1.0	$2,128	$100,302	$106,826	NO
9	1997	11	121	$ 117,958	$ 119,473	–$1,515	0.0	$2,095	$116,261	$122,685	NO
10	1998	12	144	$ 137,634	$ 139,425	–$1,791	1.0	$2,128	$136,163	$142,687	NO
11	1999	13	169	$ 165,013	$ 163,420	$1,593	2.0	$2,222	$160,013	$166,827	NO
12	2000	14	196	$ 191,329	$ 191,458	–$129	3.0	$2,371	$187,822	$195,094	NO
13	2001	15	225		$ 223,539		4.0	$2,566	$219,605	$227,473	
14	2002	16	256		$ 259,662		5.0	$2,796	$255,375	$263,949	
15				Average Error (1994 to 2000)		$ (0.000)			Student's t	1.533	
16				LINEST Output (1994–2000 data)			Model Specification:				
17				2,021.48	–26,542.05	166,837.1	Y = 166,837.1 – 26,542.05*X + 2,012.48*X^2				
18				213.83	4,718.73	25,357.98	where Y = annual sales, $ million				
19				0.9984	1959.75	#N/A	and X = number of years since 1986 (i.e., X = 0				
20				1216.6391	4	#N/A	for 1986, 1 for 1987, 2 for 1988, etc.)				
21				9.345E+09	15362423	#N/A	Model's standard error of estimate = $1,959.75 million				

Case Study: Wal-Mart Stores Revisited 2005 and 2006

Wal-Mart Stores Annual Report for 2004 (page 18) restated the financial information for all years to reflect the sale of McLane Company, Inc. that occurred in fiscal 2004. As a result, annual sales revenues reported earlier have been reduced. Figure 3-29 shows the revised values for the seven years from 1998 to 2004, along with a quadratic model based on the 1998 to 2004 revised data and forecasts for 2005 and 2006 made with the new model.

The trend of the new values from 1998 to 2004 follows a quadratic model with only a slight curvature. Errors scatter randomly about a mean value of zero, the coefficient of determination (R-squared) is very close to one, and the model's standard error of estimate is $1,959.75 million.

Wal-Mart Stores Annual Report for 2006, which was obtained after the above analysis, showed that the company's sales for 2005 and 2006 were $285,222 million and $312,427 million. These are in excellent agreement with the values projected by the quadratic model based on the data from 1996 to 2004 (Cells E13:E14 of Figure 3-29).

Can Wal-Mart Stores sustain its revenue growth indefinitely? The year-to-year change in dollars increased from 2000 to 2001 by $24,583 million. This increased from 2005 to 2006 by $27,205 million. Because of the higher base used in each calculation, however, the percentage change decreased. Thus, the percentage increase from 2000 to 2001 was 15.7 percent and dropped to only 9.5 percent from 2005 to 2006.

Figure 3-29

Quadratic Model Fitted to Revised Data for 1998 to 2004

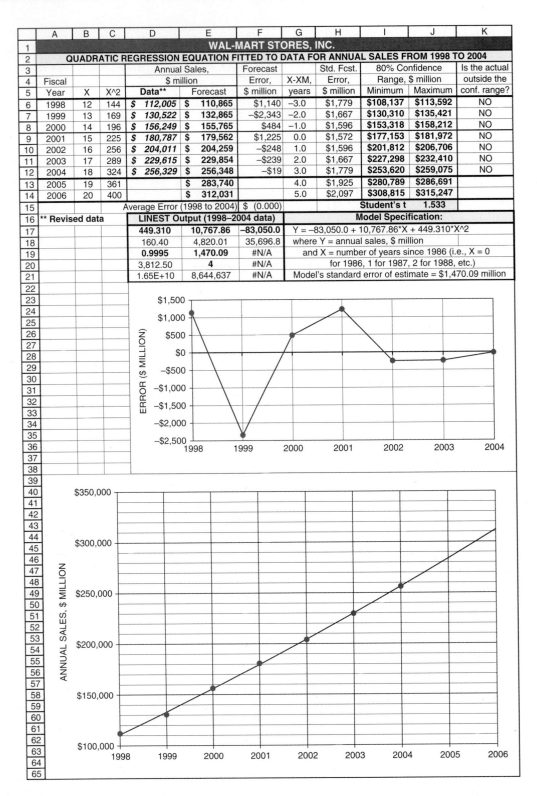

	A	B	C	D	E	F	G	H	I	J	K
1					WAL-MART STORES, INC.						
2				QUADRATIC REGRESSION EQUATION FITTED TO DATA FOR ANNUAL SALES FROM 1998 TO 2004							
3				Annual Sales,		Forecast		Std. Fcst.	80% Confidence		Is the actual
4	Fiscal			$ million		Error,	X-XM,	Error,	Range, $ million		outside the
5	Year	X	X^2	Data**	Forecast	$ million	years	$ million	Minimum	Maximum	conf. range?
6	1998	12	144	$ 112,005	$ 110,865	$1,140	−3.0	$1,779	$108,137	$113,592	NO
7	1999	13	169	$ 130,522	$ 132,865	−$2,343	−2.0	$1,667	$130,310	$135,421	NO
8	2000	14	196	$ 156,249	$ 155,765	$484	−1.0	$1,596	$153,318	$158,212	NO
9	2001	15	225	$ 180,787	$ 179,562	$1,225	0.0	$1,572	$177,153	$181,972	NO
10	2002	16	256	$ 204,011	$ 204,259	−$248	1.0	$1,596	$201,812	$206,706	NO
11	2003	17	289	$ 229,615	$ 229,854	−$239	2.0	$1,667	$227,298	$232,410	NO
12	2004	18	324	$ 256,329	$ 256,348	−$19	3.0	$1,779	$253,620	$259,075	NO
13	2005	19	361		$ 283,740		4.0	$1,925	$280,789	$286,691	
14	2006	20	400		$ 312,031		5.0	$2,097	$308,815	$315,247	
15				Average Error (1998 to 2004)		$ (0.000)			Student's t	1.533	
16	** Revised data			LINEST Output (1998–2004 data)					Model Specification:		
17				449.310	10,767.86	−83,050.0			Y = −83,050.0 + 10,767.86*X + 449.310*X^2		
18				160.40	4,820.01	35,696.8			where Y = annual sales, $ million		
19				0.9995	1,470.09	#N/A			and X = number of years since 1986 (i.e., X = 0		
20				3,812.50	4	#N/A			for 1986, 1 for 1987, 2 for 1988, etc.)		
21				1.65E+10	8,644,637	#N/A			Model's standard error of estimate = $1,470.09 million		

Downside Risk Curves

Figure 3-30 is a "downside risk" curve that illustrates another way for describing a forecast's uncertainty—in this case, the uncertainty for the forecast of Wal-Mart's annual sales for 2005 based on the quadratic model for the revised 1998 to 2004 data.

Figure 3-30

Downside Risk Curve for 2005 Annual Sales

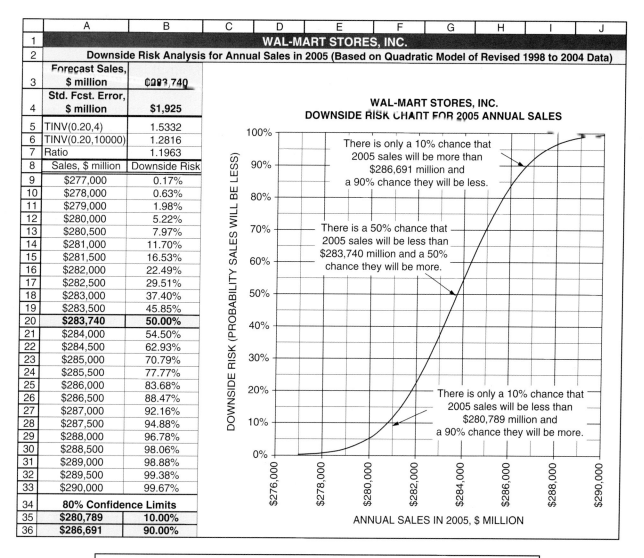

	A	B
1	**WAL-MART STORES, INC.**	
2	**Downside Risk Analysis for Annual Sales in 2005 (Based on Quadratic Model of Revised 1998 to 2004 Data)**	
3	**Forecast Sales, $ million**	**$283,740**
4	**Std. Fcst. Error, $ million**	**$1,925**
5	TINV(0.20,4)	1.5332
6	TINV(0.20,10000)	1.2816
7	Ratio	1.1963
8	**Sales, $ million**	**Downside Risk**
9	$277,000	0.17%
10	$278,000	0.63%
11	$279,000	1.98%
12	$280,000	5.22%
13	$280,500	7.97%
14	$281,000	11.70%
15	$281,500	16.53%
16	$282,000	22.49%
17	$282,500	29.51%
18	$283,000	37.40%
19	$283,500	45.85%
20	**$283,740**	**50.00%**
21	$284,000	54.50%
22	$284,500	62.93%
23	$285,000	70.79%
24	$285,500	77.77%
25	$286,000	83.68%
26	$286,500	88.47%
27	$287,000	92.16%
28	$287,500	94.88%
29	$288,000	96.78%
30	$288,500	98.06%
31	$289,000	98.88%
32	$289,500	99.38%
33	$290,000	99.67%
34	**80% Confidence Limits**	
35	**$280,789**	**10.00%**
36	**$286,691**	**90.00%**

WAL-MART STORES, INC.
DOWNSIDE RISK CHART FOR 2005 ANNUAL SALES

There is only a 10% chance that 2005 sales will be more than $286,691 million and a 90% chance they will be less.

There is a 50% chance that 2005 sales will be less than $283,740 million and a 50% chance they will be more.

There is only a 10% chance that 2005 sales will be less than $280,789 million and a 90% chance they will be more.

Y-axis: DOWNSIDE RISK (PROBABILITY SALES WILL BE LESS)
X-axis: ANNUAL SALES IN 2005, $ MILLION

Key Cell Entries

A20: =B3   B5: =TINV(0.20,4)
B3: ='Fig 3.31'!E13   B6: =TINV(0).20,10,000
B4: ='Fig 3.31'!H13   B7: =B5/B6
B9: =NORMDIST(A9,$B$3,$B$7*$B$4,TRUE), copy to B10:B33 and to B35:B36
Solver settings for conf. limits: Set Cell B35 equal to 0.10 by changing Cell A35.
                                            Set Cell B36 equal to 0.90 by changing Cell A36.

To create the chart shown in Figure 3-29, first enter the values of the forecast and its standard forecast error in Cells B3 and B4. In Cells A9:A33 enter a series of values that runs from below the forecast to above it. Then use Excel's NORMDIST function to generate the cumulative probabilities for these values. The syntax for this function is

$$NORMDIST(x, mean, standard\ deviation, const)$$

To use the NORMDIST command to generate a Student's t distribution, multiply the standard deviation by the ratio of Student's t for a two-tail probability with the given degrees of freedom to the value of Student's t for a two-tail probability with infinite degrees of freedom. Thus, the entry =TINV(0.20,4) in Cell B5 gives 1.5332, the entry =TINV(0.20,10000) in Cell B6 gives 1.2816, and the entry =B5/B6 in Cell B7 gives 1.1963 for the ratio.

Enter =NORMDIST(A9,$B$3,$B$7*$B$4,TRUE) in Cell B9 and copy it to B10:B33. This generates the series of values for cumulative probability in Cells B10:B33, which is plotted in the chart at the right. The entry in Cell B9 is also copied to Cells B35 and B36 and the Solver tool is used to determine the values in Cells A35 and A36 to set the values in Cells B35 and B36 equal to 10 percent and 90 percent, respectively.

The downside risk curve can be used to evaluate the risk for achieving different net present values or rates of return from investments that depend on how well future markets or customer demands agree with their forecast values.

Values on a downside risk curve depend on the values of the forecast and standard forecast error. These may be the values calculated by the forecasting model based on the past trend, as in Figure 3-29, or they may be values obtained by adjustments based on anticipated changes from the values calculated by the forecasting model.

Higher-Order Polynomials

The linear, quadratic, and cubic models examined in this chapter use equations that are classed as first-, second-, and third-order polynomials, according to the highest-value exponent on the independent variable. We have seen that increasing the order of the regression equation seems to improve the model in terms of reducing the standard error of estimate and increasing the coefficient of determination or correlation. A reasonable question might be, "Why not use quartic, quintic, or higher-order models (i.e., fourth-, fifth-, and higher-order polynomials)?" One can readily demonstrate, for example, that if six pairs of data values are available, a fifth-order polynomial will provide a perfect correlation, with all values calculated for the independent variable exactly matching the corresponding data values. Similarly, a seventh-order polynomial will match all of six pairs of data values, and so forth. A "perfect" fit to the data can always be obtained by using a polynomial of an order that is one higher than the number of data values. However, what one wants is *not* a fit to the values of the data but a fit to the trend of the data because it is the trend that is projected.

The problem with higher-order polynomials that match data points exactly is that their curves become unstable and bounce up and down in response to the data's **random scatter** instead of following the data's **overall trend**. In general, one should use the **lowest**-order polynomial that matches the data's **trend**. This is sometimes cited as the "rule of parsimony," or being frugal and not using more terms in the regression equation than needed for a valid model that follows the trend.

Also note that although the coefficients of determination and correlation will improve as more and more terms are added to the regression equation, the standard error of estimate may get worse. This is because the number of degrees of freedom decreases as more and more terms are added. Each additional term in the equation reduces the number of degrees of freedom in the denominator of equation 3.3. Beyond a certain point, reducing the sum of the squares of the errors in the numerator is offset by reducing the number of degrees of freedom in the denominator, with the result that standard errors of estimate increase.

Be very skeptical of forecasts made with fourth- or higher-order regression equations. To repeat, the purpose of the regression equation is to match the *trend* of the data, not simply to reproduce the *values* of the data. It is the trend of the past that is to be projected to the future.

A Critique of Correlation Coefficients

A myth persists that when a regression model's coefficient of correlation or determination is close to one, the model must be a valid representation of the trend of the data on which it is based. Figures 3-31 and 3-32 provide a further demonstration of the fallacy of this myth.

The two figures show results for linear and quadratic models based on Wal-Mart's annual sales from 2000 to 2006. The diagram at the bottom of Figure 3-31 combined with the coefficient of determination of 0.99867 would convince the unwary that the linear model is valid and its projections to 2007 and 2008 are consistent with the data's trend from 2000 to 2006. Note, that there is a very slight curvature in the data's trend, which is barely visible in the chart and is easily overlooked. The chart of the error diagram, however, shows that the sequence is systematic rather than random. It is systematic because if the error trend continues, the next error will be greater than the last. This systematic scatter of the error pattern indicates the model is **not** valid. It also means that the model's projections to 2007 and 2008 are, in fact, **not** consistent with the past trend.

Now compare the results in Figure 3-31 for the linear model with those in Figure 3-32 for the quadratic model. The scatter in the error pattern for the quadratic model is random. It is not possible to say, for example, whether the next error will be negative or positive if the trend continues. This indicates the quadratic model *is* valid. Most important for a manager basing decisions on a statistical model is the past behavior; **the projections for 2007 and 2008 are significantly higher for the quadratic model than for the linear model**. In fact, the projection for 2008 with the quadratic model is greater than the upper confidence limit for the linear model.

Don't be misled by the value of coefficient of correlation or determination. Plot the errors and note whether their scatter about a mean value of zero is random (valid model) or systematic (invalid model).

Figure 3-31

Analysis of Wal-Mart Data from 2000 to 2006 with a Linear Model

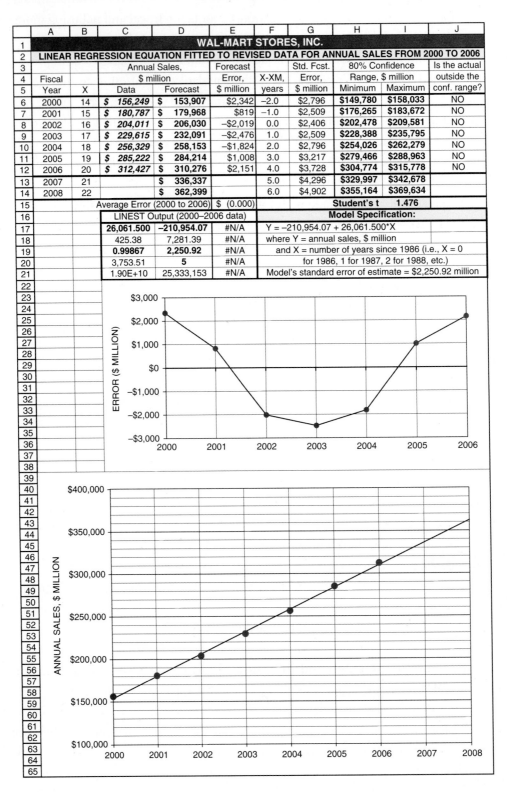

	A	B	C	D	E	F	G	H	I	J
1				WAL-MART STORES, INC.						
2		LINEAR REGRESSION EQUATION FITTED TO REVISED DATA FOR ANNUAL SALES FROM 2000 TO 2006								
3			Annual Sales,		Forecast		Std. Fcst.	80% Confidence		Is the actual
4	Fiscal		$ million		Error,	X-XM,	Error,	Range, $ million		outside the
5	Year	X	Data	Forecast	$ million	years	$ million	Minimum	Maximum	conf. range?
6	2000	14	$ 156,249	$ 153,907	$2,342	–2.0	$2,796	$149,780	$158,033	NO
7	2001	15	$ 180,787	$ 179,968	$819	–1.0	$2,509	$176,265	$183,672	NO
8	2002	16	$ 204,011	$ 206,030	–$2,019	0.0	$2,406	$202,478	$209,581	NO
9	2003	17	$ 229,615	$ 232,091	–$2,476	1.0	$2,509	$228,388	$235,795	NO
10	2004	18	$ 256,329	$ 258,153	–$1,824	2.0	$2,796	$254,026	$262,279	NO
11	2005	19	$ 285,222	$ 284,214	$1,008	3.0	$3,217	$279,466	$288,963	NO
12	2006	20	$ 312,427	$ 310,276	$2,151	4.0	$3,728	$304,774	$315,778	NO
13	2007	21		$ 336,337		5.0	$4,296	$329,997	$342,678	
14	2008	22		$ 362,399		6.0	$4,902	$355,164	$369,634	
15			Average Error (2000 to 2006)		$ (0.000)			Student's t	1.476	
16			LINEST Output (2000–2006 data)					Model Specification:		
17			26,061.500	–210,954.07	#N/A			Y = –210,954.07 + 26,061.500*X		
18			425.38	7,281.39	#N/A			where Y = annual sales, $ million		
19			0.99867	2,250.92	#N/A			and X = number of years since 1986 (i.e., X = 0		
20			3,753.51	5	#N/A			for 1986, 1 for 1987, 2 for 1988, etc.)		
21			1.90E+10	25,333,153	#N/A			Model's standard error of estimate = $2,250.92 million		

Figure 3-32

Analysis of Wal-Mart Data from 2000 to 2006 with Quadratic Model

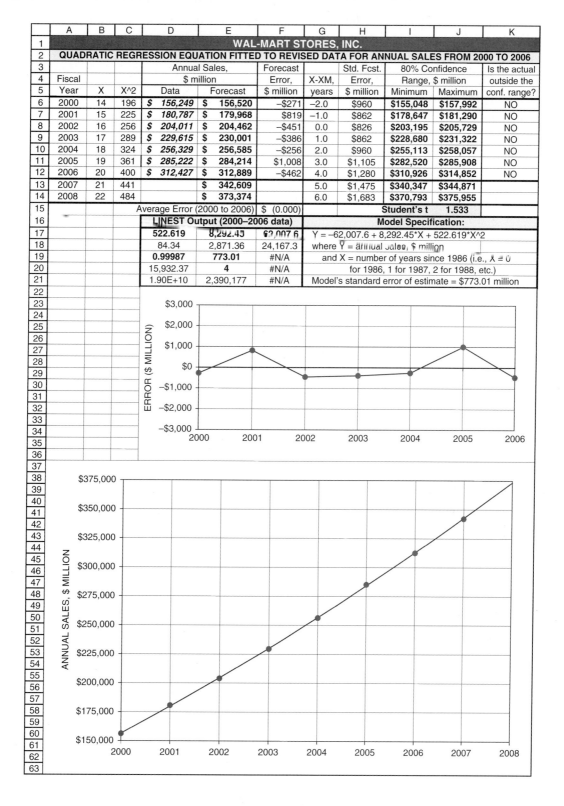

An exercise that is left for the reader is to derive the quadratic equation for the systematic error pattern with the linear model and then add that equation's parameters (or coefficients) to those for the linear model of the data. If done correctly, the result will be the quadratic model of the data. This may help convince one that the error pattern of the linear model is systematic rather than random and the linear model of the data is invalid whereas the quadratic model is valid.

Concluding Remarks

You need to know where you have been to understand where you are going. Statistical projections of the past, when they are adjusted for changes the future may portend, help one understand the future.

What can we learn from the analysis in this chapter of Wal-Mart's annual sales? Above all, we must recognize that statistical projections of the past are only the starting points for making forecasts. As changes occur in a company's strategies or in economic conditions, the statistical projections need to be adjusted upward or downward. Statistical models based on past behavior should be revised and updated as new data is obtained.

Confidence limits are useful tools for recognizing when a forecasting model is no longer valid. They are similar to the quality control limits that have been used for many years for controlling factory processes and that have more recently been extended to controlling the quality of services. When new data values fall outside the confidence limits, it is a warning that:

- The old model may need to be revised,
- Management strategies may need to be changed, and
- Investors may want to change their portfolios.

Forecasting models and confidence limits are also useful for detecting the impacts of changes in management policies, general economic conditions, or other factors that affect sales. They can be used to verify the beneficial effects of management strategies undertaken to improve sales. Note, for example, how the long-term benefits of the strategies taken by Wal-Mart in 1994 produced large long-term benefits, even though they temporarily slowed down the company's sales growth in the short term.

Time as the Independent Variable

When records of a company's past revenues are available in a company's database, a regression model of the past is a good starting point for forecasting a firm's annual revenues. Developing and using the models should be essentially a computer-based operation that, once set up, can be updated automatically and used repeatedly. Intervention is required when actual future values depart significantly from the model's predictions.

The regression models covered in this chapter use time as the single independent variable. Time is a composite variable that aggregates the effects of such factors as population growth, inflation, increase in personal disposable income, and other economic factors that change with time. These factors, rather than time itself, are the causes for such effects as the increase in corporate sales revenues described in this chapter.

When economic and other conditions are fairly stable, they are closely related to time so that time can serve as a useful proxy in the regression equation for the underlying factors causing change. However, when economic and other conditions are volatile (i.e., they are chaotic and poorly related to time), time is no longer a useful proxy for the factors causing changes in trends.

When conditions are unstable, forecasts can often be improved by using multivariate regression equations. Instead of using time as a single independent variable, multivariate regression equations use various demographic and economic factors that have a more direct, causal relationship to sales revenues. Multivariate regression equations are one of the types of equations taught in statistics classes. They are used in large, macroeconomic models of the national and international economy (e.g., Wharton, Chase-Manhattan, and DRI). Such models consist of large databases and thousands of multivariate regression equations and numerous input and output variables. Number crunching past data, however, is only one half of the forecasting process. In addition to the database and analytical software, companies in this business have specialists in various industries and observers in many nations who are constantly monitoring developments. After crunching all the numbers, the results are adjusted based on information from the specialists. Even with the largest macroeconomic models, statistical projections of the past must be adjusted for changes that can be anticipated in the future.

Scatter Diagrams

Scatter diagrams help one understand the behavior of a set of data values. Excel's Chart Wizard makes it easy to create them. Excel also makes it easy to insert different types of trend lines (e.g., linear, quadratic, cubic, or exponential) on scatter diagrams. Scatter diagrams and trend lines help answer such questions as: Do the data values follow a trend? Do they scatter about a selected trend line randomly or systematically? If the answer to the last question is not clear because of the scale, one can prepare a scatter diagram for forecast errors to see whether or not the errors scatter randomly or systematically about a mean value of zero.

It is also easy to include on a scatter diagram both the equation for the trend line and its coefficient of determination (i.e., its *R*-square value). You can use the equation later to verify the parameters of the model you subsequently determine with Excel's LINEST or LOGEST functions before using the model to examine the data scatter critically, to project future values, and to calculate confidence limits.

Scatter diagrams are a good place to start when creating a model and validating it. They can help you understand what is going on. They can help you "get the picture." Use them!

Misconceptions about Model Validity

It is important to know whether a forecasting model is valid or not. Yet model validation appears to be one of the least understood and most frequently ignored aspects of forecasting.

One cannot have much confidence in the statistical projections of a model that does not accurately represent the past trend. Unfortunately, statistics classes often fail to show how to validate models. In fact, many of them completely overlook the matter of model validation and suggest it is not important. Look for "validation" in the index of your statistics textbook and you probably won't find it.

Many students are left with the false impression that a high coefficient of determination or correlation validates a model. In fact, a model can have a high coefficient of correlation and be invalid. This has been demonstrated by the linear and exponential models of the Wal-Mart data, which are invalid even though their coefficients of correlation are greater than 0.98. Conversely, a model can have a low coefficient of correlation and nevertheless be valid. This happens when the data values scatter widely but randomly about the trend of the data. In such a case, the model's accuracy, as measured by its standard error of estimate, will be poor and limited by the random scatter of the data about its trend. Though random scatter limits a model's accuracy, the model can still be a valid model of the data's behavior.

Error Analysis and Model Validity

The test of model validity is simply stated: The *data values* must scatter randomly about the model's trend line with an average or mean error of zero or, equivalently; the *errors* must scatter randomly rather than systematically about an arithmetic or mean error of zero (or, about a geometric mean of one for an exponential model). Errors are simply the difference between data and forecast values (or the differences between the logarithms of the data and forecast values for an exponential model). They show up on scatter plots as the differences between the data points and the model's trend line. But because the differences are often small compared to the data values, it may be difficult to spot the differences on scatter plots of the data values and to recognize whether or not they scatter randomly about the model's trend line. It is wise, therefore, to calculate and plot the errors themselves.

If the errors scatter randomly about a mean value of zero, there is no consistent trend that can be used to estimate the next error. Conversely, if the errors scatter systematically about their mean, they follow a consistent trend that can be used to estimate the next error. The error patterns of the linear and exponential models of Wal-Mart's annual revenues for 1986 to 1996 (Figures 3-1 and 3-16) are good examples of systematic scatter about a mean error of zero.

Model Validity and Accuracy

Don't confuse validity with accuracy. They are not the same. Be very clear about the requirements for model validity—that data values scatter randomly rather than systematically about the trend line (or, equivalently, that errors scatter randomly about an average of zero or, for exponential models, a geometric mean of one). Understand that a model's accuracy is expressed by its standard error of estimate, and the accuracy of forecasts is expressed by their standard forecast errors and confidence limits.

Model Validity and Business Negotiations

Financial managers engage in many negotiations. Their success requires certain personal skills as well as understanding numbers. As the section *Keeping Your Cool at the Bargaining Table* on page 119 points out, a negotiator who doesn't understand models and numbers is at the mercy of others who do. You should learn not to surrender to any number crunching that looks impressive but is wrong. Skilled negotiators are able to propose their positions forcefully and defend them. They can recognize unfavorable and invalid positions presented from the other side of the bargaining table.

Understand how to validate a model and how to recognize one that is not valid. Understand invalid statistical arguments that may be advanced to defend invalid models and how to refute them. Understand what statistical parameters do measure and what they do not.

Keeping Your Cool at the Bargaining Table

As each party at a bargaining table advances its position and argues against the other, negotiations often become heated and issues become personal. One of the most beneficial aspects of numbers is that they are completely impersonal. However unhappy you may be with them or their significance, you can't get angry at the numbers themselves. Because they are impersonal, numbers avoid personal disagreements and force adversaries to focus on the real issues rather than personal differences. Make sure your data are correct and complete, and that your models are valid. Valid data and analyses promote good-faith negotiations and help reach agreements that are fair to both sides.

Updating and Adjusting Spreadsheet Models

Creating a forecasting model is not a one-time job. An advantage of spreadsheets is that they are flexible and easily modified. You can copy and edit them whenever conditions change. Creating a new model to replace one that is no longer valid is not difficult. This has been demonstrated by the continued analysis of the data for Wal-Mart for many pages after the first acceptance of the quadratic model.

Unfortunately, the past seldom repeats itself exactly. Take advantage of other means for anticipating changes. For example, have sales personnel provide estimates of future sales based on their first-hand knowledge of customers in their territories. Collect and combine the individual estimates. Adjust the figures on the basis of your knowledge of markets or experience with past forecasts from sales personnel. Have the corporation's planning staff make adjustments on the basis of decisions on new products, expanding or contracting facilities, or other internal decisions. Make further adjustments on the basis of external information, such as competition, key economic indicators (e.g., the gross domestic product, disposable personal income, new housing starts, birth rates, and various demographic data), and global markets, and how they might be affected by international relations. Use the Internet and other resources to sharpen your vision of future changes. In short, look both ways before you leap.

View forecasting as a combination of "bottom-up" and "top-down" techniques. Quantitative techniques that provide statistical projections of the past are a "bottom-up" technique. The qualitative or semi-quantitative techniques used by planning staffs based on corporate objectives, competition, economic factors, and so forth are "top-down" techniques. The outputs of the two techniques should be combined and any differences reconciled to arrive at a consensus forecast.

Survey of Forecasting Practices in U.S. Corporations

Several surveys between 1975 and 1994 have shown that U.S. corporations relied more heavily on judgmental methods for forecasting sales than on statistical or quantitative methods. Sales forecasts were used typically for strategic planning (e.g., capital investments in facilities and equipment) and for production and scheduling. The job of forecasting sales was generally assigned to a high-level executive such as the vice president of sales and marketing, the director of marketing, or the director of corporate planning. The major obstacles cited by these forecasters to using quantitative methods were the lack of relevant data, low organizational support, and little familiarity with quantitative techniques. When quantitative methods were used, the results were frequently adjusted to account for perceived changes in economic conditions, competition, and corporate strategies or tactics, as they should be whenever the forces responsible for past trends change.

Of the statistical techniques, regression analysis was most favored for long-term applications such as capital budgeting, and time-series methods (e.g., exponential smoothing or moving averages) for short-term scheduling. Both methods were used for seasonal cash budgeting.

A major reason for favoring judgmental techniques in the past has been the lack of accuracy of statistical projections. In many cases, poor accuracy is due to improper use of statistical methods by forecasters who have received poor and misleading educations in statistics, rather than to shortcomings of the statistical techniques. It is disheartening, for example, to see a persistent use of linear models for projecting trends that follow curved paths rather than straight lines, or persistent failures to recognize when a model is not valid and should not be used to make statistical projections of past trends. The author's students, most of them full-time workers employed in industry, have unanimously reflected being taught that a high coefficient of correlation or determination validated a model—even when the model should be recognized as obviously invalid. As the examples in the text illustrate, annual sales generally follow curves that are concave upward with time, with the result that using linear models routinely *under*estimates future sales.

Another part of the reason for favoring linear models may be a decided preference to underestimate future demand for a company's products rather than to overestimate it. The most prevalent reason for favoring under-estimating is that there is less top-management displeasure when actual future demands surpass expectations than when they fall short—that is, job security is favored by doing better rather than doing worse. On the other hand, some managers prefer to over-forecast as a ploy for getting more staff and budget to "build their empires." Sales managers often favor overestimating future demand to ensure that there will be enough inventory on hand to satisfy their customers' demands. This strategy is favored when shortages are very costly and low-cost storage is available. On the other hand, overestimating can result in high costs for holding excess inventory when demand is lower than forecast. One way to control a sales manager's overestimating demand is to charge a part of the cost of holding excess inventories to the operating budget of his or her organization.

Even the best forecast can be politically dangerous, especially if the forecaster's boss doesn't like it. Some years ago at the Ford Motor Company, a forecaster's projections were not as optimistic as the chairman of the board wanted to hear. What eventually happened was that the forecaster was fired, even though his forecast turned out to be correct. One of the other Ford executives remarked, "I have observed that the people who get ahead in this company are those who understand what the top man wants to hear, and then figure out a way to support his view" (or words to that effect). In an earlier case at Litton Industries in 1973, an executive compelled a forecaster to provide a higher sales projection for microwave ovens several times before he would accept the result, even though the final forecast was much higher than the data justified. The final forecast was used to justify the capital investment in a new plant in order to provide the additional capacity needed to satisfy the upward-revised forecast the executive had insisted on having. The new plant turned out to be a "white elephant" when the future demand turned out more in line with the original forecast and much less than the forced revision upward. (Marshall, et al., 1975)

Will forecasting improve? Information technology has certainly made it possible to collect and store large masses of historical sales data and to access it for statistical analysis. But whether or not forecasting improves depends on two groups: (1) business managers who are willing to support forecasting efforts by investing in management information systems that collect the relevant data that is needed and by hiring specialists with the requisite talents and then understanding their analyses and (2) educators who have a better understanding of the capabilities and limitations of the statistical techniques they teach and can go beyond simple number crunching.

Summary

Aside from using Excel to do the number crunching, here is a summary of the important lessons you should learn from Chapter 3:

- Life does not always follow a straight line. Its path is usually curved. As the movie *Out of Africa* quipped, "God made the world round so you can't see too far down the road ahead of you."
- Life is not always certain. Knowing the range of outcomes and their probabilities is as important as knowing what is most likely to happen. You need some idea of the range of outcomes in order to prepare yourself for whatever might happen. Confidence limits are for real. (We will discuss more about confidence limits and risks in later chapters.)
- Statistics is not a dirty word. It is actually a very useful tool. Learn to use it.
- Regression analysis is not a terrible monster. With spreadsheets, you can experiment with different models to find the one that is best for taming the beast.
- Knowledge is power. Knowing when an opponent's position is based on a model that is not valid improves your position at the bargaining table. Knowing whether or not your own position is justified is important for defending yourself. It is to your advantage to learn how to recognize the difference between what is true and what is false, between models that are valid and those that are not. Not knowing can be deadly.
- Forecasting is a "heads up" game. You cannot forecast with your eyes glued on the past, regardless of how good you are at crunching numbers. You must perceive any twists and turns in the path ahead to avoid accidents. You may need to adjust your statistical projections of the past to make sound forecasts of the future.
- Sometimes the most valuable forecast is one that turns out wrong. This can alert managers and investors that they need to make changes to whatever they are doing.

The primary focus in this chapter has been on the statistical techniques to project past trends and their programming on spreadsheets. In the following chapter, we will expand on using company, industry, and general economic knowledge to adjust statistical *projections of the past* to provide better *forecasts of the future*. Throughout both chapters, we will exploit the flexibility of Excel for analyzing alternate models and adding company and general economic knowledge to historical data.

A good forecaster is like Janus, the god of Roman mythology who was the guardian of the portals and the patron of beginnings and endings. Janus is shown with two faces, one in front and the other at the back of his head, symbolizing his power to look in both directions at once. Read Chapter 4 for a few techniques that can penetrate the fog that beclouds the road ahead and obscures the scenery you are passing through.

Reference

Zellner, Wendy, "A Grand Reopening for Wal-Mart" (Business Week, Feb. 9, 1998, pp. 86 and 88)

Chapter 4

Turning Points in Financial Trends

CHAPTER OBJECTIVES

Management Skills

- Perform close, critical examinations to determine how well statistical models fit data trends and recognize departures from past trends.
- Use sound judgment, experience, and semiquantitative protocols to adjust statistical projections of the past for anticipated changes in trends in order to provide more accurate forecasts of the future.
- Provide real-life examples that illustrate techniques for recognizing turning points and periodically revising forecasts and management strategies.
- Keep abreast of changes in a company's strategies and recognize the need for "insider information" to forecast its financial health.

Spreadsheet Skills

- Create charts that consist of different trend lines for different periods.
- Use dummy variables to splice curves that consist of two or more different trend lines into a single, continuous curve.

Overview

"Go with the flow" is nice advice. But navigating in a stream with ever-changing currents and unexpected riptides is a challenge. Unwary pilots can be sucked under. So it is in the real world of business.

The basic premise for using statistical projections of the past as forecasts of the future is that the past trends will continue, or, to state it more usefully, that the forces that shaped behavior in the past will persist unchanged. Unfortunately, "the future ain't always what it used to be." The following are a few reasons why it is seldom safe to assume that the future is going to be a clone of the past:

1. Corporate strategies change.
2. Technological advances create new products and make old ones obsolete.
3. Competitors reduce the price or improve the quality of their products.
4. New competitors enter the market or old ones leave.
5. Upheavals in political forces and the social environment change what consumers want or can afford.
6. Periods of economic expansion are followed by recessions.

Blind reliance on statistical projections of the past is like driving down a highway while staring in the rear view mirror. Or, to put it more bluntly: "Anyone who simply extrapolates past trends, however elegant the algebra, is an educated fool." (Robert Kuttner, *Business Week*, September 6, 1999)

It would be wrong, however, to conclude that projections of the past are worthless. To ignore them because of their shortcomings is to deprive oneself of the lessons of history. Viewing life as completely chaotic and incomprehensible is as foolish as blind faith that the past will continue unchanged. What is needed is a **combination** of what we **know** about the past and what we can **anticipate** for the future.

Long-range forecasting is best viewed as a two-step process that begins with statistical projections of the past and adds the best judgment of how past trends might change. Many corporations employ long-range planning staffs to prepare the statistical projections and present them, along with pertinent economic, political, and social information, to top management. Executive committees then adjust the statistical projections up or down to reflect their own knowledge and experience and to coordinate the projections with the business strategies they intend to follow in the future.

To simplify the forecasting procedure, it is helpful to separate a sales forecast into two parts: (1) The overall markets for the types of products or services being forecast and (2) the company's shares of the overall markets. Each part is adjusted differently. A company's sales is the product of the total market for its products multiplied by its market shares.

General economic conditions, political forces, and demographic factors that are outside a company's control affect the overall market. A company can respond to the external forces but has little or no control over them. A company's market shares, however, are largely determined by its strategies and the strategies of competitors, such as the prices charged for products, the quality of products, advertising, and customer relations. Changes in strategies should certainly cause changes that would not otherwise happen. Being close to customers is important to shaping strategies that best satisfy their needs and wants.

Case Study: ABB Electric

ABB Electric was incorporated in Wisconsin in 1970 to design and manufacture a line of medium-power transformers. Its initial capital was provided by ASEA-AB Sweden and RTE Corporation. Its mission was to penetrate the North American market, which was then dominated by General Electric, Westinghouse, and McGraw-Edison. ABB Electric's share of the market over 18 years, from 1971 to 1988, varied as shown in Table 4-1. (Gensch, Aversa, and Moore, 1990)

Table 4-1
___

Market Share of ABB Electric

Year	Market Share	Year	Market Share
1971	2%	1980	16%
1972	4%	1981	18%
1973	6%	1082	24%
1974	6%	1983	25%
1975	8%	1984	24%
1976	15%	1985	28%
1977	17%	1986	30%
1978	17%	1987	34%
1979	18%	1988	40%

Use the data in Table 4-1 to project market shares for 1989 and 1990. Discuss the results.

Linear Regression Model: Figure 4-2 is a spreadsheet for fitting a linear regression equation to the data and projecting the results to 1990. The equation for the linear forecasting model is

$$Y = -0.18 + 1.96*X$$

where Y is the market share, in percent, and X is the number of years since the company's founding in 1970.

At first glance, the linear model appears acceptable. Errors appear to scatter randomly about a mean value of zero, and the coefficient of determination is 0.9521, which is close to one. Using this model, the projected market shares for 1989 and 1990 are 37.1% and 39.0%, respectively.

Model Adjustment: The linear regression model should **not** be accepted for forecasting the future. Although market share has grown strongly in each of the four years since 1984, the projected sales for both 1989 and 1990 are lower than for 1988.

(Continued)

Figure 4-2

Analysis of ABB Electric's Market Share with a Linear Regression Model based on 1971 to 1988 Data

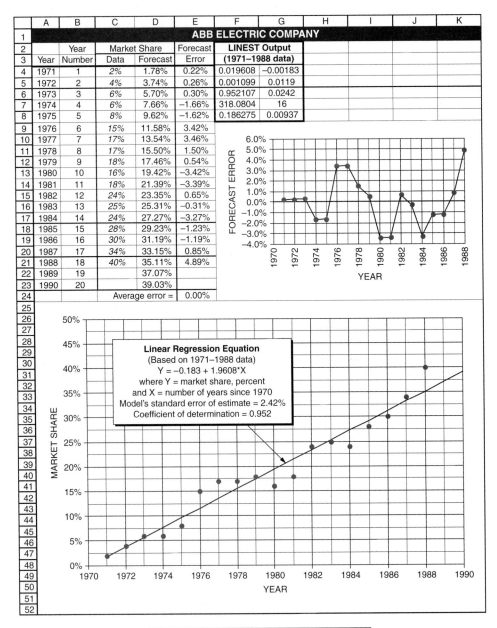

	A	B	C	D	E	F	G
1				ABB ELECTRIC COMPANY			
2		Year	Market Share		Forecast	LINEST Output	
3	Year	Number	Data	Forecast	Error	(1971–1988 data)	
4	1971	1	2%	1.78%	0.22%	0.019608	−0.00183
5	1972	2	4%	3.74%	0.26%	0.001099	0.0119
6	1973	3	6%	5.70%	0.30%	0.952107	0.0242
7	1974	4	6%	7.66%	−1.66%	318.0804	16
8	1975	5	8%	9.62%	−1.62%	0.186275	0.00937
9	1976	6	15%	11.58%	3.42%		
10	1977	7	17%	13.54%	3.46%		
11	1978	8	17%	15.50%	1.50%		
12	1979	9	18%	17.46%	0.54%		
13	1980	10	16%	19.42%	−3.42%		
14	1981	11	18%	21.39%	−3.39%		
15	1982	12	24%	23.35%	0.65%		
16	1983	13	25%	25.31%	−0.31%		
17	1984	14	24%	27.27%	−3.27%		
18	1985	15	28%	29.23%	−1.23%		
19	1986	16	30%	31.19%	−1.19%		
20	1987	17	34%	33.15%	0.85%		
21	1988	18	40%	35.11%	4.89%		
22	1989	19		37.07%			
23	1990	20		39.03%			
24				Average error =	0.00%		

Linear Regression Equation
(Based on 1971–1988 data)
Y = −0.183 + 1.9608*X
where Y = market share, percent
and X = number of years since 1970
Model's standard error of estimate = 2.42%
Coefficient of determination = 0.952

Key Cell Entries
F3:G7: = LINEST(C4:C21,B4:B21,1,1)
D4: = $G$4+$F$4*B4, copy to D5:D23
E4: = C4−D4, copy to E5:E21
E24: = AVERAGE(E4:E21)

(Continued)

The underlying reasons for the year-to-year behavior and the deviations between the actual and forecast market shares between 1971 and 1988 can be found in the company's history and changes in its strategies. The company lost money during its first three years of operation, and it was further impacted by an industry-wide change in 1974 that cut industry sales in half. To turn itself around, the company brought in a consultant who used management science models to develop a new marketing strategy and improve other areas of operation, particularly quality control. In 1975, the company offered a full five-year warranty on all its products compared to the standard one-year warranty offered by its competitors as late as 1989. This was a dramatic statement of quality assurance.

The emphasis on quality in the company's marketing strategy paid off. ABB Electric achieved an extremely high level of quality in its design, manufacturing, and process control operations. These improvements repositioned ABB Electric as the low-cost, as well as the high-quality, producer in the industry. The effect of the change in the company's strategy in 1975 can be noted in the market shares for the years 1976 and 1977.

From 1977 to 1981, however, market share stagnated at around 17 to 18 percent. The company reacted with a further change in its marketing strategy in 1981. The essence of the new strategy (details are given in the reference) was to identify customers with a greater potential for buying ABB products. This strategy increased market share in 1982, after which market share leveled off around 24 to 25 percent. In 1983 the company launched a new product, a completely integrated and self-contained substation called a power delivery system (PDS), which offered substantial improvements in safety, maintenance, and ease of installation while requiring less space than existing stations. The new product resulted in a sharp increase in market share, beginning in 1985 and continuing through the end of the last period for which data were available in the reference.

Figure 4-3 shows the revised spreadsheet, with a new linear regression equation based on the data for **only 1984 to 1988**. The rate of increase in market share growth can be seen by comparing the coefficients of X in the two linear regression equations—1.96 percent per year from 1971 to 1988, and 3.80 percent per year from 1984 to 1988.

From the forecaster's standpoint, the moral of the story is that statistical projections of past trends must be examined critically and adjusted for whatever changes a company makes in its strategies. From the standpoint of a company's managers, the moral is to react promptly whenever actual sales or profits drop below forecast values, analyze the situation, and change strategies to ensure continued growth and survival. Trend lines for many companies (as well as the Dow-Jones Average) are, in fact, a series of plateaus connected by rising or falling values. Plateaus and the changes between them are significant indicators of a company's management and the general economy, and their causes are worth investigating.

(Continued)

Figure 4-3

Analysis of ABB Electric's Market Share with a Linear Regression Model based on 1984 to 1988 Data Only

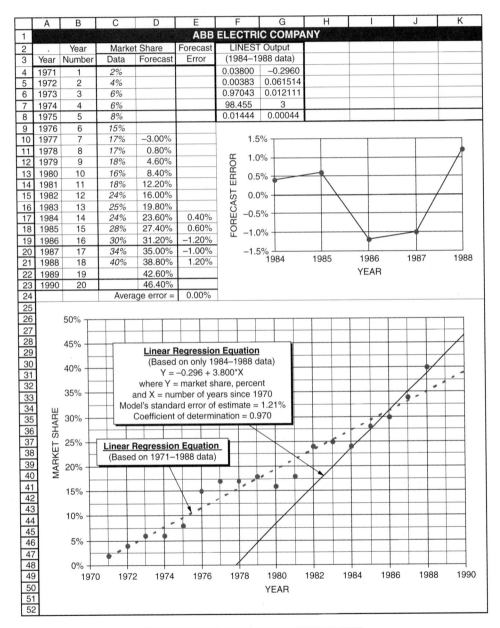

	A	B	C	D	E	F	G
1						ABB ELECTRIC COMPANY	
2	.	Year	Market Share		Forecast	LINEST Output	
3	Year	Number	Data	Forecast	Error	(1984–1988 data)	
4	1971	1	2%			0.03800	−0.2960
5	1972	2	4%			0.00383	0.061514
6	1973	3	6%			0.97043	0.012111
7	1974	4	6%			98.455	3
8	1975	5	8%			0.01444	0.00044
9	1976	6	15%				
10	1977	7	17%	−3.00%			
11	1978	8	17%	0.80%			
12	1979	9	18%	4.60%			
13	1980	10	16%	8.40%			
14	1981	11	18%	12.20%			
15	1982	12	24%	16.00%			
16	1983	13	25%	19.80%			
17	1984	14	24%	23.60%	0.40%		
18	1985	15	28%	27.40%	0.60%		
19	1986	16	30%	31.20%	−1.20%		
20	1987	17	34%	35.00%	−1.00%		
21	1988	18	40%	38.80%	1.20%		
22	1989	19		42.60%			
23	1990	20		46.40%			
24				Average error =	0.00%		

Linear Regression Equation
(Based on only 1984–1988 data)
Y = −0.296 + 3.800*X
where Y = market share, percent
and X = number of years since 1970
Model's standard error of estimate = 1.21%
Coefficient of determination = 0.970

Linear Regression Equation
(Based on 1971–1988 data)

Key Cell Entries
F3:G7: = LINEST(C17:C21,B17:B21,1,1)
D10: = $G$4+$F$4*B10, copy to D11:D23
E17: = C17−D17, copy to E18:E21
'E24: = AVERAGE(E17:E21)

Technology and Product Lifetimes

The lifetime curves for many of today's high-tech products begin with a short incubation period, during which sales are generated slowly with customer acceptance. This is followed by a steep rise in revenues that might last for a few years, after which the increase in sales slows down as still newer products are introduced and begin to displace the old. Eventually, sales decline over a short period and drop to zero. All this may happen with a span of three to five years.

High-tech companies are particularly vulnerable to changes in past trends. Product lifetimes in the information technology industry can be as short as several years. The following is an example of one of the leading companies in California's Silicon Valley.

Case Study: Sun Microsystems, Inc.

Sun Microsystems, Inc. (Sun) is the world's leading producer of computer workstations. Founded in 1982 in Mountain View, California, Sun by 1990 had grown into a multibillion dollar giant by selling fast, inexpensive workstations for engineers, publishers, and brokers, whose jobs require more power than ordinary desktop computers. Table 4-2 shows the growth in SUN's annual revenues, starting with a modest $9 million in its first full year of operation and ending in 1993, which was the latest year for which data were available when this analysis was first made. (Data through the end of Sun's fiscal year 1999 are presented and discussed later.)

Table 4-2

Annual Revenues of Sun Microsystems, Inc.

Fiscal Year (ends July 31)	1983	1984	1985	1986	1987	1988	1989	1990	1991	1992	1993
Annual Revenues, $ million	9	39	115	210	538	1,052	1,765	2,466	3,221	3,589	4,309

Analyze the 1983 to 1993 data, explain what has been going on, and estimate the 1994 revenue.

Solution: Figure 4-4 is a spreadsheet for fitting both a quadratic and a cubic regression equation to the data. The two regression models were based on the values for the 11 years from 1983 to 1993, which were the only data available at the time of the author's first analysis. Figure 4-4 includes data for the next six years, from 1994 to 1999. This allowed the models based on the first 11 years to be tested for their ability to forecast the last six. The resulting equations for the quadratic and cubic models are, respectively,

$$Y = -105.622 + 43.02401X + 41.84033X^2$$

and

$$Y = 102.0559 - 286.954X + 128.373X^2 + 5.76884X^3$$

where Y = annual revenues, in $ million, and X = number of years since 1983 (i.e., $X = 0$ for 1983, $X = 1$ for 1984, etc.). Cells F8:F21 and H8:H21 show values projected with these two equations for annual revenues from 1983 to 1999. Cells J8:J21 show averages of the values projected by the two equations.

(Continued)

Figure 4-4

Analysis of Annual Sales Revenue for Sun Microsystems, Inc.

	A	B	C	D	E	F	G	H	I	J	K
1						SUN MICROSYSTEMS, INC.					
2								Quadratic Equation		Cubic Equation	
3			Annual Revenues,					Projected		Projected	
4		Data	Change from					Annual	Forecast	Annual	Forecast
5		Values	Year Before					Revenues,	Error,	Revenues,	Error,
6	Year	$ million	$ million	percent	X	X^2	X^3	$ million	$ million	$ million	$ million
7	1983	9			0	0	0	−105.6	114.6	102.1	−93.1
8	1984	39	30	333.33%	1	1	1	−20.8	59.8	−62.3	101.3
9	1985	115	76	194.87%	2	4	8	147.8	−32.8	−4.5	119.5
10	1986	210	95	82.61%	3	9	27	400.0	−190.0	240.8	−30.8
11	1987	538	328	156.19%	4	16	64	735.9	−197.9	639.0	−101.0
12	1988	1,052	514	95.54%	5	25	125	1,155.5	−103.5	1,155.5	−103.5
13	1989	1,765	713	67.78%	6	36	216	1,658.8	106.2	1,755.7	9.3
14	1990	2,466	701	39.72%	7	49	343	2,245.7	220.3	2,404.9	61.1
15	1991	3,221	755	30.62%	8	64	512	2,916.4	304.6	3,068.6	152.4
16	1992	3,589	368	11.43%	9	81	729	3,670.7	−81.7	3,712.2	−123.2
17	1993	4,309	720	20.06%	10	100	1000	4,508.7	−199.7	4,301.0	8.0
18	1994	4,670	361	8.38%	11	121	1331	5,430.3	−760.3	4,800.4	−130.4
19	1995	5,902	1,232	26.38%	12	144	1728	6,435.7	−533.7	5,175.8	726.2
20	1996	7,095	1,193	20.21%	13	169	2197	7,524.7	−429.7	5,392.5	1,702.5
21	1997	8,598	1,503	21.18%	14	196	2744	8,697.4	−99.4	5,416.1	3,181.9
22	1998	9,791	1,193	13.88%	15	225	3375	9,953.8	−162.8	5,211.8	4,579.2
23	1999	11,806			16	256	4096	11,293.9	512.1	4,745.1	7,060.9
24	2000				17	289	4913	12,717.6		3,981.3	
25	Following values are based on the model developed from the data for only 1983 to 1993.										
26				Average error for 1983 to 1993 =					0.00000		0.00000
27								LINEST Output for Quadratic			
28								(Based on 1983–1993 data)			
29								41.84033	43.02401	−105.6224	
30								6.64318	68.974	148.2486	
31								0.9880	194.590	#N/A	
32								329.0983	8	#N/A	
33								24922690	302921	#N/A	
34								LINEST Output for Cubic			
35								(Based on 1983–1993 data)			
36								−5.768842	128.373	−286.9538	102.0559
37								1.500278	22.8614	95.45353	104.8221
38								0.996141	117.9184	#N/A	#N/A
39								602.3907	7	#N/A	#N/A
40								25128278	97333.26	#N/A	#N/A

Figure 4-5 is a chart of the data and a trend line for the quadratic and cubic regression models. Data points are included for the years from 1983 to 1999. When the quadratic model was first fit to the 1983 to 1993 data, the departure of the data for 1990 to 1993 from the quadratic curve was first noted. The initial upward curvature from 1983 to 1990 appeared to be followed by a slowing down and heeling over. This behavior could be represented by the cubic regression curve shown in the plot. It suggested that something had been going on at Sun that needed fixing.

(Continued)

Figure 4-5

Data and Curves for Quadratic and Cubic Regression Models for Sun Microsystems, Inc.

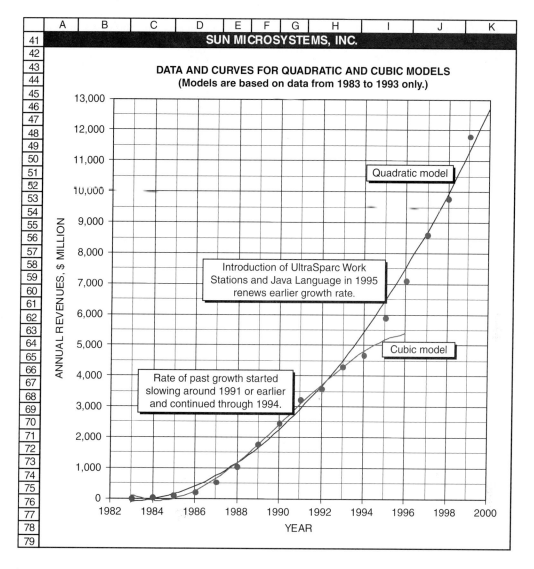

In fact, by 1993 Sun's Sparc Workstations, which had been the major source of the company's income, were being surpassed by workstations produced by Sun's competitors, such as Silicon Graphics and Hewlett-Packard. Sun's market share was eroding. As early as 1993, a critical examination of the data revealed that Sun's revenues were no longer following the initial upward curvature of the quadratic model. You should be able to recognize that the rate of increase had begun to taper off in 1992. As a result, a forecast of 1994 sales based on a quadratic model of the data from 1983 to 1993 would be too high, which it was. The actual revenue for 1994 was only $4,670 million as compared to the value of $5,430 million projected by the quadratic model, a difference of $760.3 million.

(Continued)

The cubic regression equation was able to show the gradual tapering off of the annual rate of growth. It provided better forecasts than the quadratic model for almost every year from 1987 to 1994. After that, things changed again and the growth rate started increasing.

Sun's management recognized that a new and more powerful workstation was needed to stop the erosion of the company's market share and get back on the earlier growth curve. Sun completed development of the new workstation, the UltraSparc, in 1995 and "sales took off." Sun's success with the new workstation meant it needed another new forecasting model. The cubic model developed at the end of 1993 to predict 1994 sales was not useful for forecasting 1995 sales. We can throw the cubic model out at this point. It did a good job predicting 1994 sales, but it was no longer a good model for forecasting beyond 1994 because of the action Sun had taken to reverse the drop in its market share for workstations.

You can see in the chart of Figure 4-5 how successful the new workstation was in recapturing sales. Between 1995 and 1998, Sun's sales gradually moved back toward the quadratic regression line they had followed earlier. However, the errors from 1993 to 1998 were all negative; the actual sales for each of those six years were less than the values projected by the quadratic model based on the 1983 to 1993 data. Then, in 1999, the actual sales were greater than the projected value.

Sun Update, 1999

An alternate approach to correcting the quadratic model based on the 1983 to 1998 data is to discard the older data and base the model on only the newer data. For example, the analysis in Figure 4-6 deletes the pre-1994 data and fits a quadratic regression equation to the data for the five years from 1994 to 1998. Although the errors for 1994 to 1998 are small, the projected value for 1999 falls short by $597.4 million. Note that compared to the year-to-year changes in sales revenue from 1994 to 1997, the change from 1997 to 1998 was relatively small. Sun's revenue increase from 1998 to 1999 was more in line with its earlier increases. The combinations caused the model's projection for 1999 to be 5 percent less than actual sales proved to be.

A second alternative is shown in Figures 4-7 and 4-8. This approach uses a quadratic regression equation and all 16 data values from 1983 to 1998. In order to create a single equation that fits the trends before and after the introduction of Sun's new workstation, a dummy variable has been introduced. Values of the dummy variable are 0 for years prior to 1992 and 1 for years after 1994. In between, for the years 1992, 1993, and 1994, the dummy variable has values of 1/4, 1/2, and 3/4. The gradual change in the values of the dummy variable allows the two sections of the curve to be spliced together smoothly. (The dashed curve shows the extension of the quadratic model without the dummy correction.)

The quadratic equation for this model has four parameters—the usual three for a quadratic model plus a fourth for the coefficient of the dummy variable. Excel's LINEST function is used as before, with four columns and five rows for the output. The result for the regression equation is

$$Y = -56.512 - 26.156 \times X + 53.010 \times X^2 - 1512.883 \times DV$$

where Y is the annual sales (in $ million), X is the number of years since 1983, and DV is the dummy variable, which has the values 0 for 1983 to 1991, 1/4 for 1992, 1/2 for 1993, 3/4 for 1994, and 1 for 1995 and the years thereafter. The model's forecast of $11,582.7 million for 1999 is $143.3 million, or 1.2 percent, less than the actual revenues of $11,726 million. This is somewhat better than the forecast made with the quadratic model based on only the 1994 to 1998 data (Figure 4-6).

The coefficient of the dummy variable measures the offset between the early and late parts of the curve. With the proper units here, it has a value of $1,512.883 million, or approximately $1.5 billion of annual sales. The offset between the early and late parts of a trend line, such as shown in the regression equation and Figure 4-7, is a measure the "penalty" the company paid for not responding quickly to competition and replacing its old workstations with new and more competitive models.

(Continued)

Figure 4-6

Results with Quadratic Regression Model Based on 1994 to 1998 Data

	A	B	C	D	E	F	G	H
1				SUN MICROSYSTEMS, INC.				
2							Quadratic Equation	
3			Annual Revenues,				Projected	
4		Data	Change from				Annual	Forecast
5		Values	Year Before				Revenues,	Error,
6	Year	$ million	$ million	percent	X	X^2	$ million	$ million
7	1994	4,670			11	121	4,656.7	13.3
8	1995	5,902	1,232	26.38%	12	144	5,900.8	1.2
9	1996	7,095	1,193	20.21%	13	169	7,178.1	−83.1
10	1997	8,598	1,503	21.18%	14	196	8,488.4	109.6
11	1998	9,791	1,193	13.88%	15	225	9,831.9	−40.9
12	1999	11,806	2,015	20.58%	16	256	11,208.6	597.4
13	2000				17	289	12,618.4	
14						Average error for 1994–1998 =		0.000
15	**LINEST Output for Quadratic**							
16	**(Based on 1994–1998 data)**							
17	1.657E+01	862.9429	−6840.771					
18	27.2278	708.654	4566.510					
19	0.99876	101.877	#N/A					
20	806.5887	2	#N/A					
21	16743029	20757.83	#N/A					

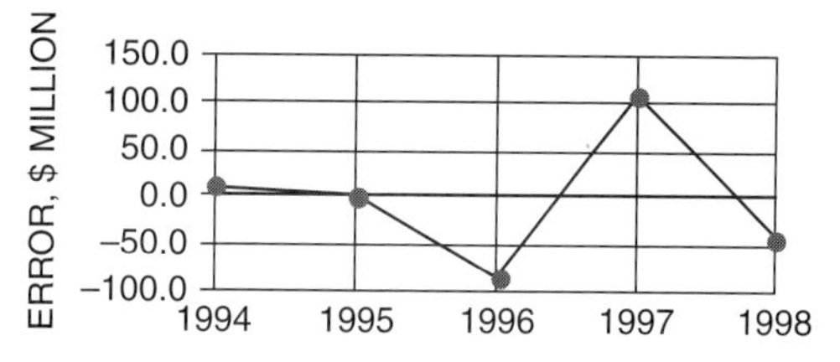

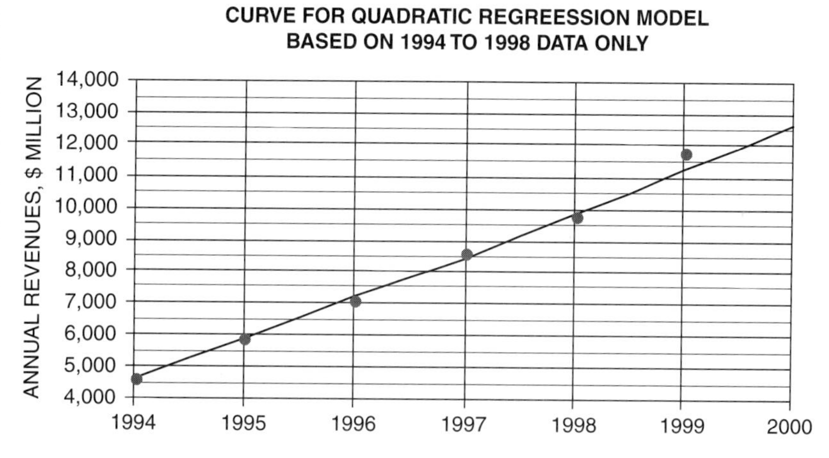

CURVE FOR QUADRATIC REGREESSION MODEL
BASED ON 1994 TO 1998 DATA ONLY

(Continued)

Figure 4-7

Results with Quadratic Regression Model with Dummy Variable Based on 1983 to 1998 Data

SUN MICROSYSTEMS, INC.

Year	Annual Revenues, Data Values $ million	Change from Year Before $ million	percent	X	X^2	Dummy	Quadratic Regression Model with Dummy Variable — Projected Annual Revenues, $ million	Forecast Error, $ million	X-XM	Standard Forecast Error, $ million	80% Confidence Limits Lower	Upper	Is data outside conf. limits?
1983	9			0	0	0	−56.5	65.5	−7.5	155.5	−267.4	154.4	NO
1984	39	30	333.33%	1	1	0	−29.7	68.7	−6.5	152.9	−237.0	177.7	NO
1985	115	76	194.87%	2	4	0	103.2	11.8	−5.5	150.6	−101.0	307.4	NO
1986	210	95	82.61%	3	9	0	342.1	−132.1	−4.5	148.6	140.5	543.7	NO
1987	538	328	156.19%	4	16	0	687.0	−149.0	−3.5	147.1	487.6	886.5	NO
1988	1,052	514	95.54%	5	25	0	1,138.0	−86.0	−2.5	145.9	940.1	1,335.8	NO
1989	1,765	713	67.78%	6	36	0	1,694.9	70.1	−1.5	145.1	1,498.1	1,891.7	NO
1990	2,466	701	39.72%	7	49	0	2,357.9	108.1	−0.5	144.7	2,161.7	2,554.1	NO
1991	3,221	755	30.62%	8	64	0	3,126.9	94.1	0.5	144.7	2,930.7	3,323.1	NO
1992	3,589	368	11.43%	9	81	0.25	3,623.7	−34.7	1.5	145.1	3,426.9	3,820.5	NO
1993	4,309	720	20.06%	10	100	0.50	4,226.5	82.5	2.5	145.9	4,028.7	4,424.4	NO
1994	4,670	361	8.38%	11	121	0.75	4,935.4	−265.4	3.5	147.1	4,735.9	5,134.8	YES
1995	5,902	1,232	26.38%	12	144	1	5,750.2	151.8	4.5	148.6	5,548.6	5,951.8	NO
1996	7,095	1,193	20.21%	13	169	1	7,049.3	45.7	5.5	150.6	6,845.1	7,253.5	NO
1997	8,598	1,503	21.18%	14	196	1	8,454.4	143.6	6.5	152.9	8,247.1	8,661.8	NO
1998	9,791	1,193	13.88%	15	225	1	9,965.6	−174.6	7.5	155.5	9,754.7	10,176.5	NO
1999	11,726	1,935	19.76%	16	256	1	11,582.7	143.3	8.5	158.4	11,367.9	11,797.6	NO
2000				17	289	1	13,305.9		9.5	161.7	13,086.6	13,525.2	
average (1991-2001) =			19.10%				Average error =	0.0000		Student's t =	1.3562		

LINEST Output for Quadratic Model with Dummy Variable (Based on 1983–1998 data)

−1512.88	53.010	−26.1559	−56.512
263.954	2.788	30.320	93.338
0.9984	140.322	#N/A	#N/A
2556.135	12	#N/A	#N/A
1.5E+08	236284.2	#N/A	#N/A

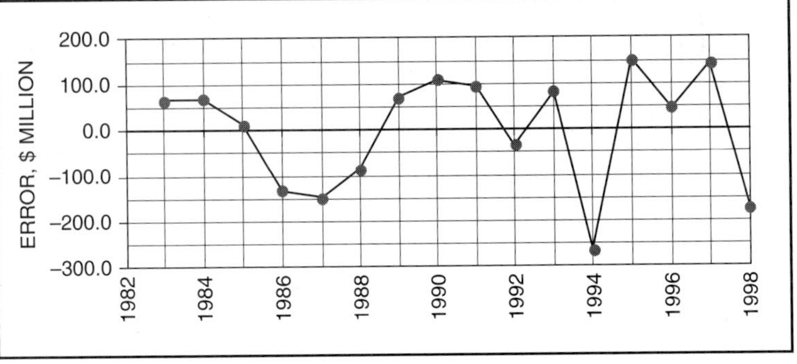

(Continued)

Figure 4-8
_____

Chart of Results with Quadratic Regression with Dummy Variable Based on 1983 to 1998 Data

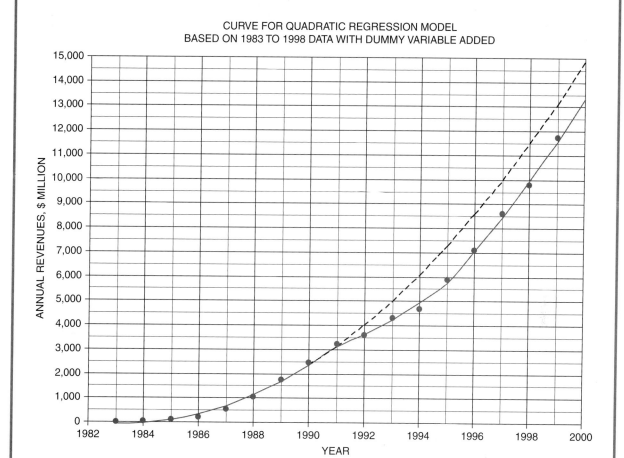

CURVE FOR QUADRATIC REGRESSION MODEL
BASED ON 1983 TO 1998 DATA WITH DUMMY VARIABLE ADDED

Sun Update, 2002

Figures 4-9 and 4-10 show an update of the quadratic model with dummy variable. (Note that the annual sales for 1997, 1998, and 1999 have been restated and are slightly different from those used in Figures 4-4 to 4-8. The model remains based on the 1983 to 1998 data.)

After slowdowns in the percentage rate of growth in 1998 and 1999, Sun had a "banner" year in 2000. Its reported annual sales revenue for 2000 was $15,721 million, an increase of 33.16 percent over that for 1999. This growth rate dropped to 16 percent between 2000 and 2001.

The new model projects annual revenue of $22,093 million for 2002, which is a 21 percent increase from the actual value of $18,250 million for 2001. In view of the downturn in the global economy, it is likely that the actual annual revenue for 2002 will be significantly less than the projected value of $22,093 million—possibly around $20,000 million, which would be an increase of approximately 10 percent over that for 2001, with a range of plus-or-minus $600 thousand. Stay tuned.

(Continued)

Figure 4-9

Results with Quadratic Regression Model with Dummy Variable Based on 1983 to 1998 Data with Data Added for 1999 to 2001

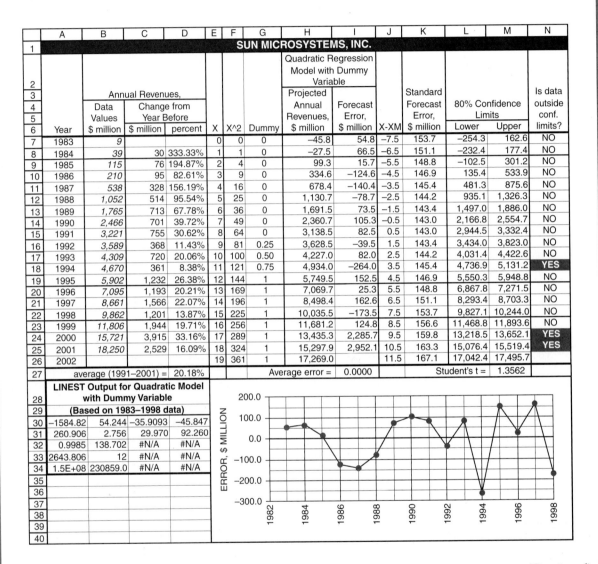

	A	B	C	D	E	F	G	H	I	J	K	L	M	N
1								SUN MICROSYSTEMS, INC.						
2								Quadratic Regression Model with Dummy Variable						Is data outside conf. limits?
3		Annual Revenues,						Projected			Standard	80% Confidence Limits		
4		Data	Change from					Annual	Forecast		Forecast			
5		Values	Year Before					Revenues,	Error,		Error,			
6	Year	$ million	$ million	percent	X	X^2	Dummy	$ million	$ million	X-XM	$ million	Lower	Upper	
7	1983	9			0	0	0	−45.8	54.8	−7.5	153.7	−254.3	162.6	NO
8	1984	39	30	333.33%	1	1	0	−27.5	66.5	−6.5	151.1	−232.4	177.4	NO
9	1985	115	76	194.87%	2	4	0	99.3	15.7	−5.5	148.8	−102.5	301.2	NO
10	1986	210	95	82.61%	3	9	0	334.6	−124.6	−4.5	146.9	135.4	533.9	NO
11	1987	538	328	156.19%	4	16	0	678.4	−140.4	−3.5	145.4	481.3	875.6	NO
12	1988	1,052	514	95.54%	5	25	0	1,130.7	−78.7	−2.5	144.2	935.1	1,326.3	NO
13	1989	1,765	713	67.78%	6	36	0	1,691.5	73.5	−1.5	143.4	1,497.0	1,886.0	NO
14	1990	2,466	701	39.72%	7	49	0	2,360.7	105.3	−0.5	143.0	2,166.8	2,554.7	NO
15	1991	3,221	755	30.62%	8	64	0	3,138.5	82.5	0.5	143.0	2,944.5	3,332.4	NO
16	1992	3,589	368	11.43%	9	81	0.25	3,628.5	−39.5	1.5	143.4	3,434.0	3,823.0	NO
17	1993	4,309	720	20.06%	10	100	0.50	4,227.0	82.0	2.5	144.2	4,031.4	4,422.6	NO
18	1994	4,670	361	8.38%	11	121	0.75	4,934.0	−264.0	3.5	145.4	4,736.9	5,131.2	YES
19	1995	5,902	1,232	26.38%	12	144	1	5,749.5	152.5	4.5	146.9	5,550.3	5,948.8	NO
20	1996	7,095	1,193	20.21%	13	169	1	7,069.7	25.3	5.5	148.8	6,867.8	7,271.5	NO
21	1997	8,661	1,566	22.07%	14	196	1	8,498.4	162.6	6.5	151.1	8,293.4	8,703.3	NO
22	1998	9,862	1,201	13.87%	15	225	1	10,035.5	−173.5	7.5	153.7	9,827.1	10,244.0	NO
23	1999	11,806	1,944	19.71%	16	256	1	11,681.2	124.8	8.5	156.6	11,468.8	11,893.6	NO
24	2000	15,721	3,915	33.16%	17	289	1	13,435.3	2,285.7	9.5	159.8	13,218.5	13,652.1	YES
25	2001	18,250	2,529	16.09%	18	324	1	15,297.9	2,952.1	10.5	163.3	15,076.4	15,519.4	YES
26	2002				19	361	1	17,269.0		11.5	167.1	17,042.3	17,495.7	
27	average (1991–2001) =			20.18%				Average error =	0.0000			Student's t =	1.3562	

	A	B	C	D
28	LINEST Output for Quadratic Model with Dummy Variable			
29	(Based on 1983–1998 data)			
30	−1584.82	54.244	−35.9093	−45.847
31	260.906	2.756	29.970	92.260
32	0.9985	138.702	#N/A	#N/A
33	2643.806	12	#N/A	#N/A
34	1.5E+08	230859.0	#N/A	#N/A
35				
36				
37				
38				
39				
40				

(Continued)

Figure 4-10

Results with Quadratic Regression Model with Dummy Variable Based on 1983 to 1998 Data with Data Added for 1999 to 2001

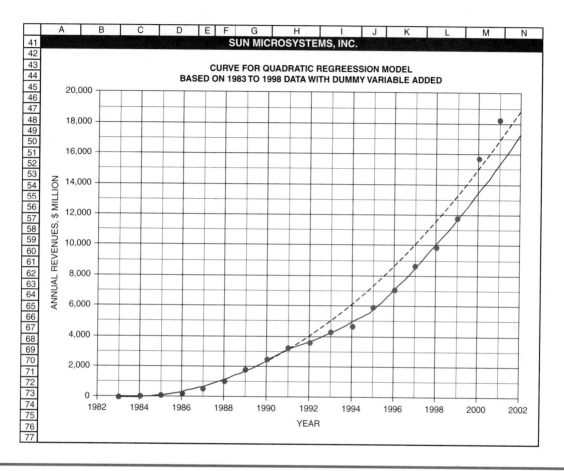

New Products That Are "Blockbusters"

New products that are substantial improvements over old ones can cause sales revenues to skyrocket overnight.

Case Study: Microsoft Corporation

Figure 4-11 shows data for the annual revenues of Microsoft Corporation fitted with a quadratic model based on the data from 1986 to 1995. The model is expressed by the following equation:

$$Y = 272.295 - 56.3326 \times XYR + 77.6955 \times XYR^2$$

where Y = the annual sales revenue in $ million
and XYR = the number of years since 1986 (i.e., $XYR = 0$ for 1986, 1 for 1987,..., 14 for 2000)

(Continued)

Figure 4-11

Quadratic Regression Model for Microsoft Corporation

	A	B	C	D	E	F	G	H
1				MICROSOFT				
2		Annual Revenues,					Projected	
3		Data	Change from				Annual	Forecast
4		Values	Year Before				Revenues,	Error,
5	Year	$ million	$ million	percent	X	X^2	$ million	$ million
6	1986	198			0	0	272.3	−74.8
7	1987	346	148	75.13%	1	1	293.7	52.2
8	1988	591	245	70.81%	2	4	470.4	120.4
9	1989	804	213	36.00%	3	9	802.6	1.0
10	1990	1,183	380	47.28%	4	16	1,290.1	−106.6
11	1991	1,850	667	56.32%	5	25	1,933.0	-83.0
12	1992	2,780	930	50.27%	6	36	2,731.3	48.7
13	1993	3,790	1,010	36.33%	7	49	3,685.0	105.0
14	1994	4,710	920	24.27%	8	64	4,794.1	-84.1
15	1995	6,080	1,370	29.09%	9	81	6,058.6	21.4
16	1996	9,050	2,970	48.85%	10	100	7,478.5	1,571.5
17	1997	11,940	2,890	31.93%	11	121	9,053.8	2,886.2
18	1998	15,260	3,320	27.81%	12	144	10,784.5	4,475.5
19	1999	19,750	4,490	29.42%	13	169	12,670.5	7,079.5
20	2000				14	196	14,712.0	
21					Average error (1986–1995) =			0.0
22	LINEST Output for Quadratic Model							
23	(Based on 1986–1995 data)							
24	77.6955	−56.3326	272.295					
25	4.09597	38.2924	74					
26	0.99834	94.1182	#N/A					
27	2104.77	7	#N/A					
28	3.7E+07	62007.6	#N/A					

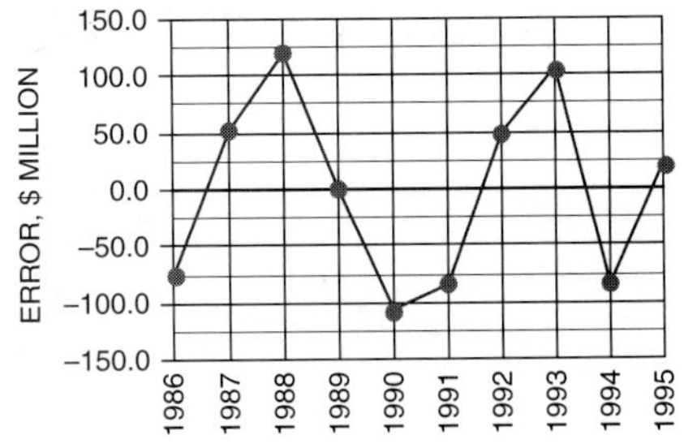

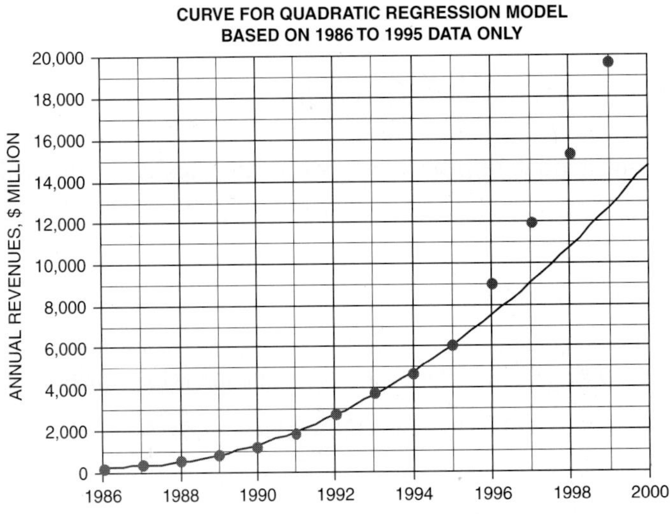

CURVE FOR QUADRATIC REGRESSION MODEL
BASED ON 1986 TO 1995 DATA ONLY

(Continued)

The quadratic regression equation appears to model the data's trend very well from 1986 to 1995, with the forecast errors scattering randomly about a mean value of zero and a standard error of estimate equal to $94.1 million. Yet the forecast for 1996, just one year from the last value on which the model was based, is very far off the mark. Actual sales for 1996 were $9,050 million, which is $1,571.5 million more than the forecast of only $7,478.5 million. What happened?

What happened was the introduction in late 1995 of Windows 95—a major improvement over Microsoft's previous operating system used by the majority of personal computers. Windows 95 was a blockbuster product that reversed the downward trend of Microsoft's year-to-year percentage growth in sales revenues. It was as though the forecasting model based on the trend for the previous 10 years was for a different company.

Microsoft Update, 2002

Figure 4-12 shows an analysis of the data from 1994 to 2001 for the "new" Microsoft. A cubic regression equation is used in Figure 4-12 to capture the initial upswing from 1994 to 1998/1999 followed by a downturn in 2000 and 2001 from the earlier trend.

Figure 4-12

Results for Microsoft with Data for 1994 to 2001

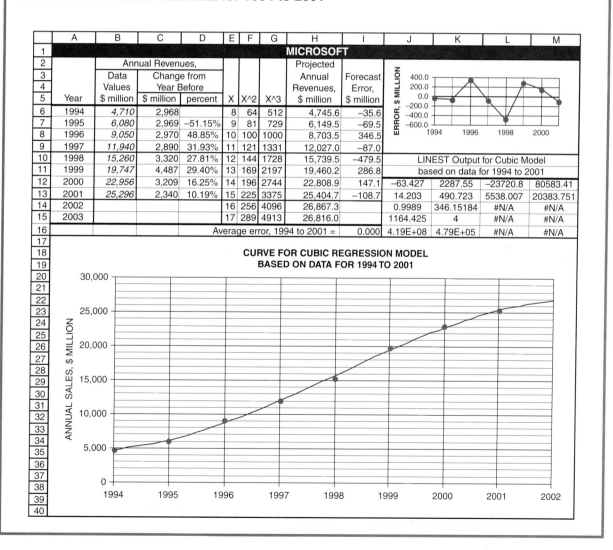

New Top Management

Figure 4-13 shows results for IBM Corporation based on sales revenue from 1992 to 1998. Annual revenues were fairly flat from 1992 to 1994 at around $64 billion. There was a big jump from 1994 to 1995, and then a steady climb from 1995 to 1998. What happened?

Figure 4-13

Annual Revenues for the IBM Corporation

	A	B	C	D	E	F	G	H
1					IBM CORPORATION			
2					Linear Model		Quadratic Model	
3				Data,	Forecast,	Error,	Forecast,	Error,
4	Year	X	XSQ	$ million	$ million	$ million	$ million	$ million
5	1992			64,523				
6	1993			62,716				
7	1994			64,052				
8	1995	0	0	71,940	72,254	–314	72,042	–102
9	1996	1	1	75,947	75,428	519	75,640	307
10	1997	2	4	78,508	78,603	–95	78,815	–307
11	1998	3	9	81,667	81,777	–110	81,565	102
12	1999	4	16		84,951		83,891	
13	2000	5	25		88,125		85,793	
14					LINEST Outputs			
15				Linear Model		Quadratic Model		
16				3174.20	72254.20	–212.00	3810.20	72042.20
17				197.148	368.830	228.526	715.4	445.479
18				0.9923	440.836	0.9959	457.052	#N/A
19				259.230	2	121.011	1	#N/A
20				50377728	388672.8	50557504	208896.8	#N/A

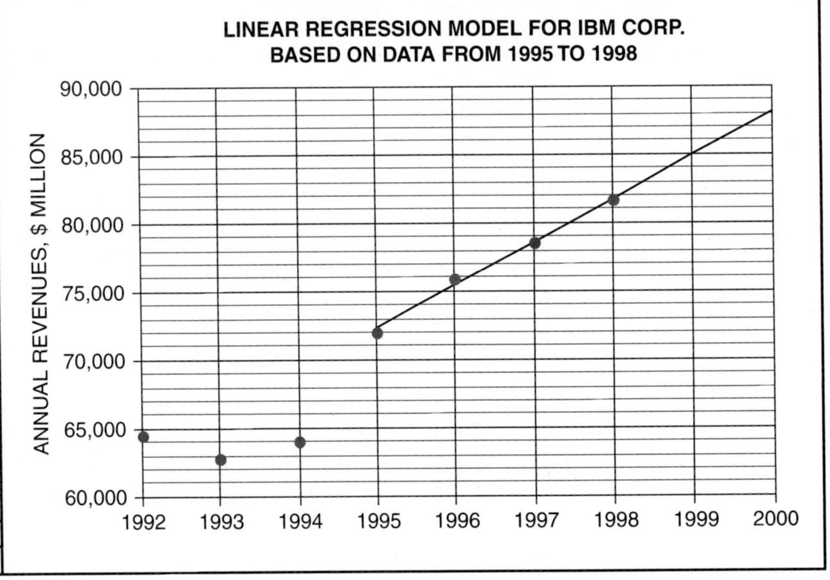

LINEAR REGRESSION MODEL FOR IBM CORP. BASED ON DATA FROM 1995 TO 1998

What happened was that Lou Gerstner became IBM's new chief executive officer in April of 1993 and shook things up. IBM effectively became a new company. The trend line for annual sales shows a distinct break from the past and a slope upward that reflected new corporate strategies.

The trend line for the "new IBM" shown in Figure 4-13 is based on the data only from 1995 to 1998. The earlier data are no longer useful for forecasting IBM's future sales because it is no longer relevant to what is currently going on at IBM. Based on a linear model for projecting IBM's annual sales from 1995 to 1998, sales for 1999 are expected to be on the order of $84,951 million. This is certainly a questionable forecast, since it is based on a projection of only three data values.

IBM Update, 2002

Figure 4-14 shows results from 1993 to 2001. IBM's total revenues have been "disaggregated" into five product segments, and trend lines have been inserted on the chart for the annual revenues in the three product segments responsible for the majority of IBM's sales. The significant changes during Gerstner's reign can be seen by comparing the revenue streams from hardware and global services. Note that global services, which accounted for only $10,953 million or 17.5 percent of IBM's revenues in 1993, had approximately tripled by 1999 to $32,172 million and 36.7 percent. Hardware sales, which had been IBM's principal revenue source, fluctuated between $35,419 and $36,630 between 1995 and 1998 had a modest rise to $37,041 million in 1999. In 2001, revenues from global services exceed those from hardware sales.

Note that the sales achieved by IBM in 1999 reached $87,548 million, which is 3 percent more than the projected value of $84,951 in Figure 4-13. Figure 4-13 helps explain what was happening at Big Blue that, together with the surging economy of 1999 and increases in e-business and business-to-business networks, was responsible for the better-than-projected revenues for 1999.

As part of the general economic downturn, total annual revenues shrank to $85,866 million in 2001 from $88,396 in 2000. In contrast, IBM's annual revenues from global services increased to $34,956 million in 2001 from $33,152 million in 2000.

Using projected values picked off Figure 4-14 for 2002, the projections for the annual revenue for 2002 from IBM's three most important products are:

Global Services	$35,000 million
Hardware	$30,500 million
Software	$12,000 million
Subtotal	$77,500 million

Because these three products account for 94.7 percent of the total, IBM's total annual revenue for 2002 is projected to be $81,840 million (calculated as $77,500 million/0.957). The decrease from the annual revenue of $85,866 million in 2001 is primarily due to the projected decrease in revenue from software.

Figure 4-14

Breakdown of IBM's Annual Revenues by Product and Year

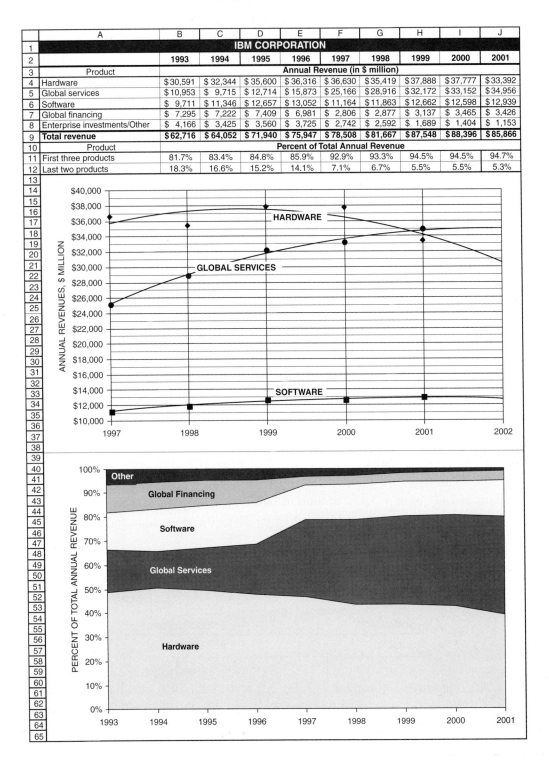

	A	B	C	D	E	F	G	H	I	J
1					IBM CORPORATION					
2		1993	1994	1995	1996	1997	1998	1999	2000	2001
3	Product	Annual Revenue (in $ million)								
4	Hardware	$30,591	$32,344	$35,600	$36,316	$36,630	$35,419	$37,888	$37,777	$33,392
5	Global services	$10,953	$ 9,715	$12,714	$15,873	$25,166	$28,916	$32,172	$33,152	$34,956
6	Software	$ 9,711	$11,346	$12,657	$13,052	$11,164	$11,863	$12,662	$12,598	$12,939
7	Global financing	$ 7,295	$ 7,222	$ 7,409	$ 6,981	$ 2,806	$ 2,877	$ 3,137	$ 3,465	$ 3,426
8	Enterprise investments/Other	$ 4,166	$ 3,425	$ 3,560	$ 3,725	$ 2,742	$ 2,592	$ 1,689	$ 1,404	$ 1,153
9	Total revenue	$62,716	$64,052	$71,940	$75,947	$78,508	$81,667	$87,548	$88,396	$85,866
10	Product	Percent of Total Annual Revenue								
11	First three products	81.7%	83.4%	84.8%	85.9%	92.9%	93.3%	94.5%	94.5%	94.7%
12	Last two products	18.3%	16.6%	15.2%	14.1%	7.1%	6.7%	5.5%	5.5%	5.3%

Risk Management and Anticipating the Future

In this section we consider some of the techniques for adjusting the statistical projections of the past for changes that can be anticipated in the future. The techniques are a mix of experience, qualitative judgments, and semiquantitative analysis. Because of the amount of personal judgment involved, they are often termed "judgmental." The remainder of this chapter covers the following judgmental methods:

1. Sales force composites
2. Jury of executive opinion
3. Consumer surveys
4. Professional "trend spotters"
5. Delphi technique
6. Analog models
7. Scenario analysis
8. Intelligence gathering and industrial espionage

Sales Force Composites

This is one of the most common of the subjective methods for forecasting. Details vary from company to company, but generally the method starts with periodic (e.g., monthly or quarterly) estimates by salesmen of future customer demands in their territories.

Standard forms or worksheets that contain statistics on past demands give salesmen a perspective from which to work forward and make it easier to compile results. Sales managers may also discuss the business outlook and provide other direction to their sales personnel prior to the latter's making their estimates. Estimates based on customers' acceptance of the firm's products and other firsthand information are usually broken down by product, customer, and territory or marketing area.

District sales managers collect and review the individual estimates and forward them, with their own comments, to corporate headquarters. Here, further compilation and revision are made to include the effects of planned advertising campaigns, price reductions, model changes, new or expanded product lines, competition, and other factors affecting a company's marketing strategy. The final revision becomes the firm's sales forecast.

Conceptually, this technique is simple and straightforward. Unlike the statistical techniques described in the preceding chapters, it requires no special technical skills. It uses information from sources closest to the market. It reduces sampling error by including estimates from a number of individuals spread over a large sales area. It provides a breakdown by products or product lines that is needed to plan production. Aside from these advantages, a sales force composite shares responsibility for forecasting with the sales force, thereby building morale and helping motivate individual performance.

Forecasts by sales personnel can be very subjective. Success depends very much on how well they "know their territory." Estimates may also be affected by lack of time or interest on the part of sales personnel, by personal levels of optimism or pessimism, and by what the sales force perceives their bosses want to hear. Turning estimates into sales quotas or "bogies" can result in unduly low estimates so that sales personnel can more easily meet the goals set for them.

Jury of Executive Opinion

This method brings together senior executives and managers to discuss sales for the next year or more. Members come to the meeting with relevant statistics on sales and industry trends as well as their own knowledge of a particular branch of the business and the local, national, and international conditions that affect it. The statistical projections previously prepared by the planning staff are discussed, along with the effects of new forces that can change past trends. The group may reconsider the basic assumptions about the economy and the firm's markets that were used in making the statistical projections. Differing opinions are argued and reconciled to arrive at an average or consensus estimate. The jury's deliberations produce an approved sales forecast for the following year or more that becomes the basis for the company's production and marketing plans. The executive juries may also approve long-range plans for acquiring new plant facilities and equipment or for directing research and development to provide new or improved products. These go to financial planning committees for preparing the company's annual budgets.

Factors for Consideration

Although often criticized for being based on personal feelings, the method brings to the forecast the perspective of seasoned executives who are responsible for implementing their decisions. They add to the mathematical models a consideration of factors that cannot be quantified. They look for turning points in trends and assess their impacts on the company's future.

In predicting future trends, the executives might consider such business indicators as the following, and how they may have been used or overlooked in making the statistical projections:

- **General economic trends**. These might be evaluated by such indicators as Gross Domestic Product (GDP), personal income, bank deposits, personal savings, industrial inventories, automobile production, consumer price index, wholesale commodity prices, stock market level, employment and unemployment rates, interest rates, and inflation rates. Values for these are published by federal agencies and various trade and business associations.

    The Conference Board, an industry-supported organization founded in 1916 by a group of concerned business leaders, is another important source of business information. Its Leading Economic Indicators evaluates economic activity and signals peaks and troughs ahead in the business cycle. Its Consumer Confidence Index reports monthly on consumers' level of optimism about the short-term outlook and their buying intentions. (See the section below on Consumer Surveys.) The Conference Board's Web site is www.conference-board.org.

- **Lifestyles.** Changes in consumers' living habits and social mores are related to shifts in demand for certain goods and services. For example, consider such changes and their effects on demand as the following: Drinking habits (increase in wine consumption and decrease in hard liquor consumption), attitudes toward sex (hospitals provide more abortions, sex change operations, and treatment of venereal diseases), psychological stress (more psychiatric services and social workers), shorter work week (more travel and leisure services), and tax law complexity (more jobs for preparing tax returns).

- **Demographic data.** Examples include birth rate, marriage rate, and population; these can be total values or values separated by age, geographic area, cities vs. rural, sex, ethnic type, etc.). Changes in these indicators signal shifts in future demands for housing, schools, clothing, toys, insurance, health care, etc.

- **Government actions.** These include monetary and fiscal policies, as well as any other actions that affect the general economy, consumer borrowing and spending, and so on. Examples of specific actions include: changes in tax laws (e.g., tax rates and depreciation of capital assets); interest rates (consider effects of high interest rates on the automotive and home construction industries); federal budgets in the defense industry; farm support; budgets for health, education, and welfare; import-export regulations; ecological and environmental protection; and legislation that enlarges or restricts international competition.

- **Labor/Workforce climate.** Examples include labor union activity; schedules for contract negotiations; and the likelihood of strikes and their impacts on markets, suppliers, and the distribution of goods.

- **Shifts in international political scene.** Examples include: war and political upheavals (effects of foreign markets and the availability of raw materials); rates of exchange for foreign currency (effects of market demands and foreign competition); and the development of emerging, third-world nations.

- **Natural events.** These include general weather patterns and natural disasters, such as droughts, floods, hurricanes, and earthquakes. These may disrupt markets and supplies of raw materials and commodities.

- **Major scientific discoveries and technological advances.** Recent examples include advances in microelectronics, computers, telecommunications, biotechnology, laser applications, and microsurgery.

- **Energy sources and costs.** Products that consume large amounts of energy in their production are at a disadvantage as energy costs rise; new sources of energy affect the design and location of homes and factories.

Monitoring all the various sources of information is time-consuming. The effort can be shared by assigning areas to different executives and their staffs, who then report periodically to the executive committee. Alternatively, a corporation can hire the services of consultants specializing in particular areas.

Improving Deliberations and Results

The method considers "the big picture." It does not break down forecasts by individual product, customer, type of sale, etc. It can be very costly in its use of the time of high-priced executives. Much of the method's success depends on the skill of the chairman in soliciting opinions and encouraging an open discussion of differing opinions. Otherwise, the jury's deliberations can degenerate into a "guessing game" or a "rubber stamping" of what has already been decided by the chief.

The very strength of a jury of executive opinion can cause problems. Major objections leveled at this method by critics are:

- It is based on personal opinions that are not always as objective as they should be. Although most opinions may be well formed, others may be based on inadequate information, misunderstandings, or a parochial self-interest rather than a true, company-wide viewpoint.
- Although the method provides a broad perspective and more complete recognition of factors that influence forecasts, it is difficult to reduce the varied opinions to a common denominator and coordinate the inputs from executives in different product or functional areas of management.
- Executives' time is valuable. The method uses the time of high-priced people whose talents are needed elsewhere in the company's activities.
- It addresses only "the big picture" without getting involved in the details needed for a company's day-to-day operations.
- In evaluating statistical projections of the past, executives may not fully understand the assumptions made or the limits of the mathematical models or other methods used.

Formalized procedures help overcome these shortcomings and improve the method's objectivity and accuracy. However the procedures are used, they must be convenient and provide a consistent format for assembling inputs from different points of view into a composite.

Formalized techniques begin by listing the various factors that might change past trends. These can be organized into classes and subclasses, as suggested in the left column of Figure 4-15. Figure 4-15 is in the form of a spreadsheet, which simplifies evaluations and their consolidation. Separate evaluation sheets are prepared for each product or corporate division. Each evaluator is asked to check the appropriate columns to indicate his or her opinion as to whether each factor would tend to increase, decrease, or have no effect on the sales forecast. Evaluations are prepared prior to the sales forecasting meeting and are consolidated by staff assistants. Where there is common agreement, a sales forecast can be quickly finalized according to the group's consensus. This leaves more time to discuss and resolve issues where there is disagreement.

Protocol Analysis and Expert Systems

The rationale used by executives to reach their decisions one year can be used the following year. Corrections can be made from one year to the next to improve the procedure and its forecasts. This aspect of judgmental forecasting has been named *protocol analysis*. In order to use it, executive forecasters must

Figure 4-15

Opinion Survey Spreadsheet for "Jury of Executives" Method for Collecting Opinions and Adjusting Statistical Projections of Past Sales or Demands

	A	B	C	D	E	F
1		Effect on Past Sales Trends				
2		Increase		No	Decrease	
3		Strong	Weak	Effect	Weak	Strong
4	**Factor**	*2*	*1*	*0*	*−1*	*−2*
5	**GENERAL ECONOMIC TRENDS**					
6	International		1			
7	National	1				
8	Local	1				
9	**GOVERNMENT ACTION**					
10	Federal monetary policy (e.g., money supply)				1	
11	Federal fiscal policy (e.g., taxation)		1			
12	Social welfare programs				1	
13	Defense spending/Military procurement				1	
14	Environmental policies			1		
15	**CONDITIONS SPECIFIC TO THE INDUSTRY**					
16	International (e.g., foreign markets, tariffs)		1			
17	National			1		
18	Local			1		
19	Labor/Workforce climate		1			
20	Energy sources and costs					1
21	**CONDITIONS SPECIFIC TO THE FIRM**					
22	Changes in market share		1			
23	Advertising campaigns		1			
24	New products planned for introduction		1			
25	**CONDITIONS SPECIFIC TO THE TYPE OF PRODUCT**					
26	Demogrphic shifts in the market		1			
27	"Life style" shifts in the market			1		
28	Impacts of new technology				1	
29	Impacts of changes in laws			1		
30	Introduction of new products by competitors				1	
31	**OTHER FACTORS, AS IDENTIFIED**					
32	List other factors					
33						
34	**COLUMN SCORES**	4	8	0	−5	−2
35			**FINAL SCORE**			5
36	**Key Cell Entries**					
37	B34: =B4*SUM(B6:B33), copy to C34:F34					
38	F35: =SUM(B34:F34)					

describe the rationale by which their value judgments are determined, however arbitrary the rationale might appear. Staffs can record and condense the remarks at meetings into rationale statements. In other instances, a facilitator or staff person can interview each executive and ask him or her to "think aloud" while forecasting. The protocol (i.e., the forecasting rationale) used one year, together with its record of successes and failures and the reasons for any differences, can be used to improve and expedite forecasting the next year.

Protocol analysis makes the forecasting rationale of executives explicit. It helps communicate one expert's knowledge and reasons to others. Its payoffs are saving executives' time in making forecasts and improving their accuracy. It allows for making the forecasting procedure more comprehensive and accurate in using knowledge and experience. The protocols can be programmed on computers to create *expert systems.*

Consumer Surveys

Consumer surveys determine what consumers want by asking them. They treat consumers as the final judges or experts for determining demand. For new products, consumer surveys may be the only way to estimate the potential market.

Using consumer surveys to forecast sales begins with defining precisely what is to be forecast. Is it the national market for consumer electronics? Is it the industrial market for original equipment components? Or is it the local market for cable television service?

Consumer surveys are of two types: (1) **Attitude surveys**, which measure shifts in consumer attitudes and expectations, or their willingness to buy and (2) **Intent-to-Buy surveys**, which measure whether or not consumers will buy a specific product or type of product during a specified future time period. Typical of *attitude surveys* are the Consumer Confidence Index and the Buying Plans Index, both of which are prepared by National Family Opinions, Inc. for the Conference Board. The Business Confidence Index provided by the Conference Board is based on responses from 1000 executives from all types of business. Attitude surveys are made by asking questions such as how well consumers like or dislike certain products or types of products, how optimistic or pessimistic they regard their own conditions in the near future, whether or not they expect to be better or worse off next year or the same, and how well they perceive or expect the national economy to be next year or five years from now.

An example of an *intent-to-buy* type of consumer survey is that provided by the University of Michigan, which regularly surveys consumers and forecasts the sale of consumer durable goods (e.g., appliances and furniture). McGraw-Hill surveys selected corporations and forecasts investments in machine tools and equipment. Many industries, such as the electronics, have associations that forecast demand for their products.

Consumer Spending

Consumer spending accounts for nearly two-thirds of the gross domestic product. As a result, consumers are the ones who are said to lead the way to a healthy economy.

Consumer spending is a good barometer to follow. The impetus for most business recoveries is provided by consumer spending and housing starts. Sustained buying of such consumer items as automobiles, household furnishing, refrigerators, appliances, and other durable goods eventually leads to major increases in capital investment by manufacturers. On the other hand, declines in consumer spending are causes for concern over chances for a recession in the economy. Consumer spending decreases sharply before and during recessions.

Consumer spending is stimulated by higher personal income and lower interest and tax rates. Consumers increase their spending level when their debt-to-income ratio is low and when their liquid assets, such as their bank accounts, are large. An increase in the money supply means that consumers are accumulating larger cash balances. This triggers their shifting any balance in excess of what they desire to hold in savings accounts into income-earning assets, so that stock prices rise and interest rates fall. As financial yields decline, consumers step up their consumption of housing and durable goods.

Personal consumption expenditures are an overall measure of consumer spending that goes directly into the gross domestic product. These expenditures include both goods and services. Services make up about one-half of all consumer outlays but are not included in retail sales.

Retail spending includes food and beverages, clothing, furniture, home furnishings, automobiles, general merchandise, and so forth. It does not include services. Retail sales fluctuate seasonally and are published on a monthly basis. Several months of data are needed to pinpoint a trend. Strong consumer demand for cars, high-definition televisions, and similar durable goods coincident with high levels of personal savings and high levels of building permits and starts signals a strong economy. There is typically a six- to nine-month lag from the start of a housing boom before the retail sector shows significant benefits from increased sales of various types of household goods and furnishings.

Industry Spending

One of the most useful surveys is that of the National Association of Purchasing Managers (NAPM). Begun in 1930, the NAPM business survey is made by a committee of about 250 purchasing managers from various U.S. manufacturing industries, of which 95 represent manufacturers of nondurable goods (e.g., food, textiles, apparel, tobacco, paper, printing, chemicals, petroleum, rubber, and plastics), and the other 155 represent manufacturers of durable goods (e.g., transportation equipment, furniture, lumber, stone, glass, primary metals, fabricated metals, and machinery). Members are surveyed each month on their company's production, new orders, prices paid for raw materials, employment, inventories, and vendor deliveries. The Department of Commerce uses the survey to compile a composite index, which has been used as a leading indicator of U.S. business conditions.

Procedure for Making Consumer Surveys

Though simple in principle, consumer surveys are expensive. Care is needed in wording questions and training interviewers so as not to bias responses. The subjective opinions of buyers on what they expect to buy are analyzed by statistical means to project levels of demand and the confidence for bracketing forecasts between specific levels. For statistically valid conclusions, samples must be large and truly representative of the population.

Consumer surveys can be made by mail, by telephone, and by face-to-face interview. The mailed questionnaire is the most popular method for reaching a broad spectrum of consumers because it is generally cheaper than the others. **Mail surveys** can also be done in a way that protects the respondent's identity. This sometimes makes it possible to obtain information that would otherwise be withheld. Questions on mail surveys should be designed to be understood easily and answered quickly, such as by the respondent's checking his or her choice of several possible answers. The number of questions should be kept to a minimum. A survey with more than ten questions may prompt a potential respondent to discard it. A stamped, self-addressed envelope should be provided for returning the survey form, and a time limit should be set so that respondents do not pigeon-hole the questionnaires. The principal disadvantage of mail surveys is that the response rate is very low.

Telephone surveys can be made at reasonable cost. Results are obtained quickly at a few central locations and can be quickly tabulated. Their main disadvantage is being limited to a few short, straight-to-the-point questions.

Face-to-face interviews are preferred when there are few buyers involved, when comprehensive information is needed, or when the product is new and potential buyers would not otherwise know its advantages. The main disadvantage is that interviews are the most expensive way to contact potential customers. Having salesmen do the interviewing by asking informal questions as part of their sales contacts reduces the cost of this method but can distort the results, either as a result of bias by salesmen or reticence of customers.

Focus groups are a special form of face-to-face interviews introduced in the 1960s. They are an outgrowth of what psychologists call "group dynamics." A typical focus group is a gathering of eight to fifteen strangers who meet for an hour or two and describe their feelings about tires, health insurance, frozen dinners, or other types of products. Participants are typically paid $25 to $50 a session, unless they represent a hard-to-reach audience such as physicians or business executives, for which the pay may be several hundred dollars. Sessions are held in a "living room setting" in conference rooms in local hotels, motels, or homes. The cost to a client is upward of $3000 a session. Market researchers find that "talk is cheap" and that focus groups are an inexpensive way to gather opinions. For clients, the output is an in-depth perspective on the matter of interest that often reveals viewpoints previously overlooked.

Professional "Trend Spotters"

Professional "trend spotters" are business seers who sell their services to corporations and institutional investors for spotting emerging trends. This type of management consultant has proliferated since the late 1970s. Trend-spotting firms typically charge clients annual fees of upward of $25,000. In return, they provide monthly trend reports, telephone bulletins, and quarterly visits to discuss the impacts of trends. Among the better-known trend spotters are: (1) Naisbitt Group, Washington, DC; (2) Business Intelligence Program of SRI International, California; (3) Inferential Focus, New York; (4) Perception International, Connecticut; (5) Weiner Eldrich Brown, New York; (6) Williams Inference Service, Massachusetts; and (7) Yankelovich Skelly & White, New York.

Trend-spotters offer a more detached view of the world than corporate forecasters. They claim to be more receptive to spotting changes than those who are conditioned to seeing what they expect to see rather than what actually is. Most trend-spotters look for incipient trends by reading newspapers and magazines. They look for unusual events and try to identify their ramifications on current trends. They are attuned to such things as social changes, women's rights movements, working women, divorce rates, single-parent families, moral issues, rejection of authority, reactions of society to ecology, political pressures and shifts, public crazes (e.g., health food and fitness), consumer advocacy groups, lobbies, and leisure activities. The trends are translated into their impacts on business, such as: more eating out, more fast-food and take-out services, less salt in food, lower cholesterol foods, more child-care services, more home maintenance services, types of home-care products that are quicker rather than more thorough in cleaning, and so forth.

Delphi Technique

"Delphi Technique" is an impressive name for a simple concept—using the consensus of a panel of experts to forecast the future. It is a variation on an ancient approach whereby Greeks traveled to the city of Delphi to ask the oracle there to foretell their future. The opinions of wise men, who are in touch with the world, are used in similar fashion today by many companies. Their opinions may have to substitute for hard data when no historical data exists, as with many new products and technologies. Opinions are also important for evaluating factors that cannot be quantified, such as the direction government policies might take in the future or the reactions of the public to new technology. Using a panel of experts rather than a single one is simply acknowledging that "two heads are better than one." What one expert might overlook, others will hopefully catch. Individual biases should cancel out in the process of reaching a consensus.

In its full-blown form for technological forecasting, the Delphi technique is a formalized procedure for soliciting and organizing expert opinion anonymously under the direction of a coordinator. The procedure is designed to overcome some of the disadvantages of face-to-face committee meetings. Because the names of those expressing different opinions are unknown to anyone but the coordinator, a member of a Delphi panel is under no pressure to agree with the majority even though he or she feels the majority is wrong. The technique also overcomes the undue influence of a strong vocal minority that pushes its views, the vulnerability to being dominated by strong individuals, and the face-saving situations that often develop when positions are taken too early and panelists thereafter feel compelled to defend themselves rather than their positions. Although the procedure outlined below refers specifically to forecasting technological advances and their impacts, Delphi panels can be assembled for other purposes where a consensus of informed opinion is helpful.

The Delphi technique differs from conventional face-to-face group interactions by providing anonymity to participants. A coordinator is used as a neutral interface. The coordinator's job is to initiate responses and to control the feedback of information through a series of "rounds," which are usually conducted by mail. A participant does not know the identity of the others and is free to change his or her position during the series of rounds without admitting it to the others. Each idea or opinion can be judged on its own merits, without influence by the position of its originator. The Delphi technique thus focuses on topics and minimizes personal issues. It avoids the pitfalls of committee action and ending up with a compromise that no one really wants, as expressed by the saying "The camel is a horse designed by a committee."

On the first round of a Delphi forecasting panel, the experts are asked to forecast events or trends in a selected subject area for which the panel has been organized. Sometimes an initial list of events is provided, but more often, the panelists "start with a blank sheet of paper" and are asked to identify any significant events or trends themselves. The questionnaires are returned to the coordinator, who consolidates the forecasts into a single set by combining like items. Items deemed of lesser importance may be dropped, especially if the list would otherwise be very long and cumbersome.

On round two, the panelists receive the consolidated list and are asked to estimate each event's time of occurrence. In most cases, panelists are asked to estimate only what they consider the most likely date for an event. In other cases, they are asked to provide three dates: a barely possible early date, the most likely date, and a later date by which the event is virtually certain to occur. These may be quantified as the dates for 10, 50, and 90 percent probability of the event's happening. The coordinator collects the forecasts and prepares a statistical summary of the events, which usually contains the median date and the upper and lower quartile dates.

On round three, the panelists receive the statistical summary and are asked to reconsider their forecasts. Panelists may stick with the previous forecasts or make new ones for each event. If their forecasts fall outside the upper or lower quartile dates, they must present reasons why they feel they are correct and the others are wrong. Their reasons may be specific factors that other panelists have overlooked or different interpretations of factors than given by others. When the coordinator receives the written responses, he or she revises the statistical summary of the forecasts and prepares a summary of the reasons given for advancing or delaying forecasts.

On round four, the panelists receive the revised statistical summary and the reasons given for any revisions. They are asked to take the reasons into account and make new forecasts. They may also be asked to justify their positions if their forecasts remain outside the upper or lower quartiles and to comment upon the arguments advanced during the third round. The coordinator again computes the medians and quartiles of the forecast dates, and these results are generally final. The coordinator also consolidates and summarizes the arguments and comments presented by the panelists. This provides a record of what the panelists believe to be important for affecting the forecasts.

Four rounds are usually sufficient. A fifth may be added if deemed useful. Three and sometimes two rounds are enough if the panel starts with a well-defined list of events for forecasting and there is general agreement.

The Delphi technique is designed to reach a consensus. It displays disagreements where they exist and searches for their causes. The rounds are judged a success if they reach stability and the reasons for any divergences are clearly enunciated. Panelists can stick with their original views, if they wish. However, the opportunity to consider alternatives and reconsider their original positions in an anonymous setting removes the problem of "saving face" if they wish to change their positions. When convincing arguments are presented by one panelist, the arguments themselves are considered without influence by that panelist's reputation or position. Although panelists often have widely different forecasts on early rounds, the transfer of information and the anonymous interaction generally causes the forecasts to converge to fairly well-defined dates for each event.

The subjects addressed by Delphi panels vary. One panel might be concerned with forecasting how soon scientific discoveries might emerge from research laboratories into commercial practice. Another might be concerned with the time for transferring advances in spacecraft and weapons technology to consumer products. Another might be concerned with forecasting public acceptance or resistance to implementing certain technologies in different areas. All of these concerns can be expected to affect future markets for products and services.

Delphi panelists are chosen to represent expert knowledge in a variety of areas—political, military, social, demographic, ecological, and economic as well as purely technical. They may all be employees of a company making a forecast that requires intimate knowledge of their company's policies, organization, technical, and other internal matters. A company panel might, for example, include members from the financial, marketing, engineering, legal, research and development, production, and quality control organizations. On the other hand, if the forecast does not depend on knowledge of a specific company but more on a general familiarity with areas that bear on the subject, some or all of the experts might come from outside the company. Management consultants, university professors, former legislators or political figures, and other professionals outside a company bring a fresh point of view that is not inhibited by company inbreeding. A Delphi panel for forecasting trends in an industry might include panelists representing different disciplines and different companies in the industry, plus a few nonindustry members with general knowledge of related political, social, economic, and other factors.

Delphi panelists selected should be able to respond thoughtfully and completely on each round. Because experts are generally busy people, the mechanics of answering questionnaires should be as simple as possible. The number of questions should be kept to a reasonable limit—perhaps no more than 25 or, at most, 50. Where possible, answers should be given by checking one's choice from a list of alternatives or by filling in blanks. Arguments from earlier rounds should be summarized and presented concisely and completely. Questionnaires should be designed for the convenience of the panelists rather than the coordinator. Panelists should understand that serving on a Delphi panel is not like responding to a one-time opinion poll. They must commit themselves to continuing with the interplay among members on successive rounds that is an essential feature of the Delphi technique.

The success of a Delphi panel depends on the skill of the coordinator as well as each panelist. The coordinator must be a good communicator. When a response is wordy, the coordinator's job is to identify what is essential and provide a summary without altering the panelist's position. When responses overlap, the coordinator must combine them into a single statement without losing the essence of any single sentence. Occasionally a coordinator may find it necessary or helpful either to restate or to clarify an event being forecast, to divide an event into two or more separate events, or to combine several events into a single one.

The Delphi technique has been expedited in recent times by using electronic mail, with panelists working at terminals from which they can receive and transmit information to the coordinator.

Analog Models

Analog models for forecasting are useful for forecasting a new variable for which no hard data are available based on the behavior of a similar variable for which hard data are available. Examples include:

- Forecasting sales of a new product based on past sales for a similar product
- Forecasting widespread sales of a new product based on a consumer survey or a sample of consumer reaction to the new product in one or several limited marketing areas

- Forecasting sales of an established product in a new marketing area based on sales in established marketing areas (e.g., forecasting foreign sales based on sales in local markets, with adjustments for differences in social and economic factors)

Using an analog model to forecast sales of a new product or an existing product in a new market begins with defining the characteristics of the new product or market and proceeds according to the following steps:

1. Identify an analog model and its markets and obtain data on its characteristics and past sales.
2. Determine how well the analog model matches the characteristics and market of the new product. Identify the ways in which the parameters of the analog model are the same as or are different from those that define the conditions under which the forecast is to be made. These might be comparison of cost or selling price, physical size, types of advertising and advertising budgets, consumer characteristics (e.g., number of households, personal income, social characteristics, etc.), location of sales outlets, public transportation, availability of parking, and so forth.
3. Use the results from step 2 to convert the parameters of the model to their corresponding values for the new product or market.
4. Estimate the extent to which forecast performance is expected to match the analog model. Are forecast sales, for example, expected to be the same as, less than, or greater than those of the analog model? This might be stated as probabilities; for example, a 10 percent chance that forecast sales will be less than half the sales of the analog, a 50 percent chance they will be approximately the same, and a 40 percent chance that they will be more than half again as much as the analog.
5. Make the forecast.

Scenario Analysis

Writing scenarios of the future was popularized in the writings of Kahn and Weiner, particularly in the book *The Year 2000*. They defined scenarios as "hypothetical sequences of events constructed for the purpose of focusing attention on causal processes and decision-points." Scenarios help managers recognize how some hypothetical situation might come about, step by step, and what alternatives exist for each actor, at each step, for preventing, diverting, or helping the process. The technique might be viewed as an extension of "brainstorming."

Preparing scenarios for the future differs from the Delphi technique described earlier. Scenario writers are not asked to extrapolate from the present to the future. Nor are they asked to forecast the most *probable* future. Instead, they are asked to identify *possible* futures. The concept is similar to that of contingency or disaster planning. Scenario writers deal with possible future technological, economic, political, environmental, and social aspects of the world of the future. By studying a number of possible future scenarios, a company seeks to identify any future events significant enough to call for a major shift in its strategies. An electronics company, for example, might consider scenarios that include major technological breakthroughs, political barriers that restrict trade among nations, and economic and social changes among emerging third-world nations.

Scenario analysis analyzes alternative futures and how business strategies might best cope with them. Scenarios ask what might happen if:

- Competitors introduce (or do not introduce) new and better products.
- Laws change to allow new types of products or services to be marketed or to restrict old ones.
- Technological breakthroughs occur in new materials or new sources of energy.
- The economy improves (or does not improve) next year.
- The U.S. government restricts (or liberalizes) the importation of competitive products.

Scenarios analysis can be useful for forecasting short-term markets for new products or for adjusting statistical projections of long-range markets for existing products. It proceeds by the following series of steps.

1. Define exactly what is to be forecast.
2. Identify the key variables that affect the value of what is to be forecast.
3. Describe possible future scenarios. The key word here is "possible."
4. Identify which elements of the scenarios are certain and which are uncertain.
5. Estimate the probabilities for the scenario elements that are uncertain.
6. Prepare forecasts based on the possible scenarios.

Scenarios can be used in several ways to make forecasts. One method is to make forecasts for the best-on-best combination of future outcomes, the worst-on-worst, the most probable, and the mean. This approach yields a "middle ground" base value and defines the values at the extremes. Another method is to discount future outcomes by their probabilities of occurring to give expected values. This information can be assembled in payoff tables or decision trees. A third is to use Monte Carlo simulation to evaluate the probabilities and risks of different future values.

Spreadsheets help analyze and quantify the results of scenarios. The scenario might be presented in a financial spreadsheet that shows the potential future worth and rate of return from an investment in a new product or production technology. "What if?" analyses can be carried out to show the consequences of expansions or contractions in markets, different marketing strategies, faster product development, reduced product lifetimes, and so forth. Spreadsheets facilitate making the calculations and then preparing the results in tabular or chart formats that make effective management presentations.

Scenario writing is often part of a company's contingency planning. Scenarios help prevent surprises and their consequences. By identifying possible future situations, companies can prepare effective courses of action to cope with situations that might otherwise unexpectedly when they are least prepared.

Scenario analysis often reveals that "unthinkable" situations might truly happen, and that future dangers cannot be ignored because their likelihood is small. It helps executives and upper-level managers see future problems and opportunities more clearly. Although uncertainty cannot be planned away, the enhanced knowledge generated by scenario analysis leads to better judgments of the future and how to cope with it.

Thinking the Unthinkable

September 11, 2001 was the day the unthinkable happened—when terrorists destroyed the World Trade Center in the city of New York as well as parts of the Pentagon building in Washington, DC. Fortunately, although the exact nature of the attack was not foreseen, major banks and other financial organizations had prepared beforehand for a disaster and had backup copies of critical information in files at other locations.

Rather than working forward from the past, scenario writers can work backward from possible futures. They might speculate on future wants or needs, and then identify the technology and other factors that are needed to reach the future. As applied to business forecasting, this type of scenario analysis follows the procedures of systems analysis that are used during the planning and scheduling stages for managing large-scale research and development projects. Systems analysis procedures are used in developing work breakdown structures for the development of new weapons systems that require technological breakthroughs. A work breakdown structure is a formalized system that identifies the various developments that must be made in order to reach a desired overall end. (Work breakdown structures and their variations are sometimes called "relevance trees" and "mission flow diagrams.") A work breakdown structure becomes the basis of detailed work plans for accomplishing each element of the work breakdown structure. Management techniques are described in texts on project management.

Several additional procedures have been proposed to examine the interactions among several future trends and scenarios and to consolidate them into a single forecast. Some are more formalized and quantitative than others. They help check the consistency of future scenarios developed by specialists in different disciplines. Among the techniques mentioned in the literature for doing this are the following:

- **Iteration through synopses.** This method consists in developing independent scenarios for each of a number of disciplines (e.g., economic, political, social, and technical), and then modifying them through an iterative process to make them compatible with one another. The method is intended to secure a final scenario that is as consistent as possible with the initial scenarios based on single disciplines. Like the Delphi method, it offers the advantage of an interdisciplinary approach by specialists in several fields and seeks to reconcile differences through an iterative process of successive modifications.
- **Cross-impact matrices.** This is described as a "method of analysis which permits an orderly investigation of the potential interactions among items in a forecasted set of occurrences. It requires a methodical questioning about the potential impact of one item, should it occur, on the others of the set in terms of mode of linkage, and the time when the effect of the first

on the second might be expected. Having collected the judgments or data linking all possible combinations of items in terms of mode, strength and time, it is possible to perform an analysis which revises the initial estimates of probability of the items in the set." Although the method involves a quantitative assessment, the values for the probabilities and measures of effect are the subjective judgments of the analysts.

Intelligence Gathering and Industrial Espionage

Realistically, any firm's business strategies must recognize what its competitors might be doing. In effect, a firm must make battle plans for winning victory over its competitors.

Some simple (and ethical) methods for gathering information on how well competitors (and the economy) are doing are:

- **Factory-watching.** Counting the number of workers or customers entering and leaving a competitor's factory or service facility during its hours of operation.
- **Parking space assessment.** Counting or measuring the parking area available to and used by a competitor's employees and its customers.
- **Truck shipments.** Counting the number of trucks that enter and leave a competitor's facilities and noting their size.
- **Shopping centers.** Noting the availability of parking spaces at shopping centers. More empty spaces follow a reduction in local employment.

More sophisticated means are used to gain important knowledge of competitors' current and future positions in such areas as product design, manufacturing technology and costs, inspection methods and quality control, plant capacity, sources of supply, customers, marketing strategies, and pricing policies. Not too many years ago, when markets were robust and competition slim, many firms planned their business strategies with little regard for competitors. That situation has largely disappeared. One security consultant summarized the present trend as follows: "There is a great deal more attention being paid to all phases of competitor analysis than I have seen before. Understanding your competitors' positions and how they might evolve is the essence of the strategic game."

American companies were once notably backward in knowing about their competitors. The Soviet government and Japanese companies, on the other hand, were acknowledged experts in business intelligence. The Japanese "have been legendary for deploying armies of engineers and marketing specialists to gather information on American manufacturing techniques, product design and technology. And by using that information to pinpoint American companies' weaknesses, they have been able to carve out formidable positions in industries ranging from steel and automobiles to semiconductors and consumer electronics." (*San Francisco Chronicle*, November 11, 1985)

In addition to traditional spying techniques, according to an FBI representative, Soviet intelligence officers used personal computers and modems to gain access into the data banks of companies in California's Silicon Valley that were working on sensitive military projects. Soviet agents were well known to target employees and worked on them to become sources of information. Their special targets were employees with ego problems, who were envious of others, who had a grudge against their company because of how they had been treated, or who resented some aspect of U.S. policy. Technology transfer, aided by such sources, greatly helped the Soviets advance their military capabilities in the 1970s to early 1990s, before the collapse of the Soviet Union.

American companies have become more aggressive in industrial intelligence. Many have either established formal intelligence units or designated specialists to oversee their intelligence efforts. Many hire outside firms or consultants, which are frequently former agents of the Central Intelligence Agency.

American businessmen now tour competitors' factories. Competitors' products are dissected to identify design features and manufacturing methods. Competitors' customers, suppliers, and former employees are pumped for information.

Companies disclose information in their annual reports that can be useful in assessing their competitive positions and strategies. Annual reports give extensive financial data and often describe efforts to develop new products, improve manufacturing facilities, cut costs, and improve quality. Speeches by company executives, especially those given to stockbroker groups to help a company's financial position, can contain valuable information for analyzing a company's competitive position. Speeches and interviews of company executives are often given in the interest of public relations. They are reported in newspapers, magazines, and trade journals, or aired on television and radio. Many contain business intelligence that is helpful to competitors.

Other information is obtained by tracking patents. Patent applications force companies to reveal information that might otherwise be held secret in exchange for the legal protection of a patent.

Former employees who are disgruntled and have left because of disagreements with their former managers are fertile sources of information on competitors. One company that consults on industrial intelligence maintains a huge database of former employees, who might be good sources of information. The company reports that although they never pay for information, "Half of the former employees we call don't care to discuss it. About 20 percent can't because of confidentiality agreements. The other 30 percent, you can't get off the phone." (as quoted in *San Francisco Chronicle*, November 11, 1985)

Sometimes, of course, companies step across the legal limits for obtaining information. Stealing a company's documents on its product plans or proprietary technology, for example, has possible civil and criminal penalties.

Macroeconomic Models

With the advent of computer-based systems for accumulating and analyzing large databases of information for national and worldwide economies, economists began to construct quantitative models to describe and extrapolate the information and to use the results to guide business strategies. The following have been among the best known of these companies, which now provide (or did in the past) consulting services to worldwide clients in industry and government. Their information is based not only on their massive computer programs and databases for analyzing worldwide economic data, but also upon professionals who monitor government and industrial activities and use their knowledge and judgment to adjust the statistical analyses to current conditions.

1. **Wharton Econometric Forecasting Associates** (WEFA): WEFA was a spin-off of the Wharton School at the University of Pennsylvania. It began in 1961 as a corporate-funded research project in the Economic Research Unit (ERU) of the university's economics department. ERU was responsible for maintaining and using what became known as the Wharton Quarterly Model (WQM) and the Wharton Index of Capacity Utilization. In 1963, the organization of ERU was incorporated and launched by the university trustees as WEFA, a "not-for-profit" organization. In the ensuing years, WEFA was acquired and passed through the hands of a number of buyers. In 2001, WEFA and DRI (see below) were purchased by Global Insights, Inc. to provide business executives, investors, and public officials with economic information.

2. **Data Resources, Inc.** (DRI): DRI was cofounded in 1969 by a Harvard economics professor, an economic consultant, and a member of the Council of Economic Advisors. DRI was purchased by McGraw-Hill in 1979, and merged with WEFA in 2001 to form Global Insight, Inc.

3. **Chase Econometrics:** Chase Econometrics was an independent subsidiary of Chase Manhattan Bank. Chase Econometrics' research covered the world, with in-depth analysis of the U.S. national and regional economy, including key industries such as steel, nonferrous metals, automobiles, and energy. The firm merged with FEMA in 1987 and became part of Global Insights, Inc. in 2001.

4. **IHS Inc.** (IHS): HIS is a publicly traded (NYSE: *IHS*) business information services company headquartered in Englewood, Colorado. It acquired Global Insights, Inc. in 2008. IHS, Inc. includes a number of other economic consulting companies in addition to the three listed above. IHS serves international clients in four major areas: energy, product lifecycle, environment, and security.

Detailed information about these firms can be found on the Internet.

Business Cycles

From our nation's founding in 1776, its long-term trend of economic activity has been a gradually rising one. Superimposed over the trend have been many cycles of change from prosperity to depression, from depression to recovery, repeatedly.

The National Bureau of Economic Research (NBER) is the prime source of information on business cycles. NBER is a private, nonprofit research organization founded in 1920. Its purpose is "to ascertain and to present to the public important economic facts and their interpretation in a scientific and impartial manner." By common consent, NBER identifies and establishes the "official" or generally accepted dates of the turning points of business cycles.

Figure 4-16 lists the 32 complete cycles in the United States that NBER has identified from 1854 to mid-2008. Each cycle rises from an **initial trough**, passes through a **peak** or **crest**, and drops to a **terminal trough**. The terminal trough of one cycle becomes the initial trough of the next. The duration of time from the initial trough to the peak is termed the cycle's **expansion duration**, and that from the peak to the terminal trough is the cycle's **contraction duration**.

Figure 4-16
_____

United States Business Cycles

	BUSINESS CYCLES IN THE UNITED STATES						
	Source: National Bureau of Economic Research						
	Business Cycle			Duration, Months			Ratio Expansion to Contraction
	Initial Trough	Peak	Terminal Trough	Expan-sion	Contrac-tion	Full Cycle	
1	Dec 1854	Jun 1857	Dec 1858	30	18	48	1.67
2	Dec 1858	Oct 1860	Jun 1861	22	8	30	2.75
3	Jun 1861	Apr 1865	Dec 1867	46	32	78	1.44
4	Dec 1867	Jun 1869	Dec 1870	18	18	36	1.00
5	Dec 1870	Oct 1873	Mar 1879	34	65	99	0.52
6	Mar 1879	Mar 1881	May 1885	36	38	74	0.95
7	May 1885	Mar 1887	Apr 1888	22	13	35	1.69
8	Apr 1888	Jul 1890	May 1891	27	10	37	2.70
9	May 1891	Jan 1893	Jun 1894	20	17	37	1.18
10	Jun 1894	Dec 1895	Jun 1897	18	18	36	1.00
11	Jun 1897	Jun 1899	Dec 1900	24	18	42	1.33
12	Dec 1900	Sep 1902	Aug 1904	21	23	44	0.91
13	Aug 1904	May 1907	Jun 1908	33	13	46	2.54
14	Jun 1908	Jan 1910	Jan 1912	19	24	43	0.79
15	Jan 1912	Jan 1913	Dec 1914	12	23	35	0.52
16	Dec 1914	Aug 1918	Mar 1919	44	7	51	6.29
17	Mar 1919	Jan 1920	Jul 1921	10	18	28	0.56
18	Jul 1921	May 1923	Jul 1924	22	14	36	1.57
19	Jul 1924	Oct 1926	Nov 1927	27	13	40	2.08
20	Nov 1927	Aug 1929	Mar 1933	21	43	64	0.49
21	Mar 1933	May 1937	Jun 1938	50	13	63	3.85
22	Jun 1938	Feb 1945	Oct 1945	80	8	88	10.00
23	Oct 1945	Nov 1948	Oct 1949	37	11	48	3.36
24	Oct 1949	Jul 1953	May 1954	45	10	55	4.50
25	May 1954	Aug 1957	Apr 1958	39	8	47	4.88
26	Apr 1958	Apr 1960	Feb 1961	24	10	34	2.40
27	Feb 1961	Dec 1969	Nov 1970	106	11	117	9.64
28	Nov 1970	Nov 1973	Mar 1975	36	16	52	2.25
29	Mar 1975	Jan 1980	Jul 1980	58	6	64	9.67
30	Jul 1980	Jul 1981	Nov 1982	12	16	28	0.75
31	Nov 1982	Jul 1990	Mar 1991	92	8	100	11.50
32	Mar 1991	Mar 2001	Nov 2001	120	8	128	15.00
33	Nov 2001	Dec 2007					
			Average =	37.66	17.44	55.09	3.43
			Median =	28.50	13.50	46.50	1.88
			Minimum =	10	6	28	0.49
			Maximum =	120	65	128	15.00

For all 32 cycles, expansion generally lasted about twice as long as contractions. There were several notable exceptions to this. The contraction phase of the cycle from November 1927 to March 1933 lasted slightly more than twice as long as that cycle's expansion phase and slightly less than the expansion phase of the cycle that followed. The expansion phases for the two cycles from June 1938 to October 1945 and from February 1961 to November 1970 were about ten times as long as the contraction phases of the two cycles. Both of these cycles were longer than average (80 and 106 months, respectively) and involved wartime activities.

The cyclic variations superimposed over the general upward trend have been associated with wartime booms and postwar depressions; with the births of new industries, such as the railroads, and their overexpansion; and with investments and stock speculations. The general upswing is related to increasing population and many other factors, such as increasing capital investment, increasing production efficiency, and technological progress. Upswings in business cycles are characterized by high rates of investment, rapidly rising productivity, and full use of productive capacity. Conversely, the downswings are associated with low investment, declining output, and idle capacity. Such changes may be related to changes in worldwide economic conditions, changes in federal legislation and tax laws, changes in the federal government's fiscal or monetary policies, changes in federal spending, wars and lesser international incidents, and so forth. They are caused by changes in the forces that have affected activity in the past or by the emergence of new forces. To a great extent, business cycles are caused by the penchant of markets to overreact. "Euphoria on the upside and panic on the downside prevent real-world markets from being as perfectly self-correcting as they are in textbooks. Businesses over invest, expecting that booms will last forever. When overbuilding and excess capacity lead to disappointing returns and even bankruptcies, businesses pull back sharply. This cycle of misperception and excess intensifies the minute swings of normal economic equilibrium." (Kuttner, 1997)

The cycles of change are recurrent but not periodic; they do not recur regularly with time. Some cycles have been as short as a year, others as long as ten years or more. The magnitudes of their up and down swings are unequal. Some cycles are more severe than others, with greater percentages of unemployment during the depression part of the cycle and greater percentages of inflation during the recovery portion.

Cycles for specific industries or businesses do not necessarily coincide exactly with the cycles for the national economy, although there is a general tendency for industry trends to be influenced by national trends.

Figure 4-17 shows the durations for the expansion and contraction periods for the 31 U.S. business cycles from 1854 to mid-2008. The general trends are for expansions to last longer and for contractions to become shorter. Governments have had only mixed success in using fiscal and monetary policies to temper periods of boom and bust. Industry, on the other hand, has made changes that may help ameliorate economic ups and downs. "Just-in-time" practices and other changes in business strategies should help. Mass production methods in huge plants designed to manufacture a single product and operate efficiently over narrow rates of output are giving way to more flexible systems that can produce different products and operate efficiently over wider rates of output. Inventories are leaner. Service industries have become a greater portion of the total economy than manufacturing. Wages are no longer as rigidly fixed.

Figure 4-17

United States Business Cycle Expansions and Contractions Since 1854

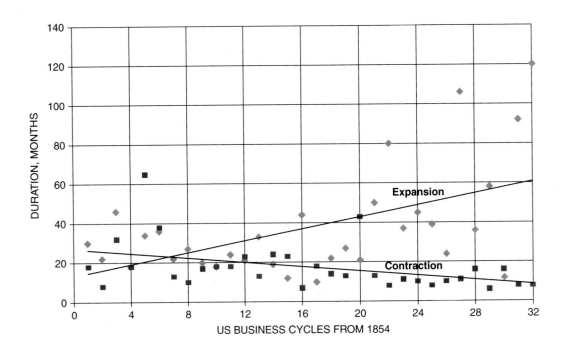

These factors make the economy more resilient and, when guided by astute management in business and government, better able to adjust to changes.

Economic Indicators

As the brief overview of business cycles illustrates, there are many factors that influence where the economy is heading at any time. Economists have focused on a few of these that appear to give the best early indications of the turns.

Table 4-3 is a list of business cycle indicators compiled by the National Bureau of Economic Research (NBER). The **leading indicators** are those that historically tend to reach their cyclical peaks and troughs earlier than the corresponding points in the aggregate economic activity. Leading indicators therefore have the potential for signaling turning points, either upturns or downturns, before they occur. **Lagging indicators** reach their turning points after the turns in the general economic activity and are not satisfactory as predictors. However, they can help verify any trends thought to have been indicated by the leading indicators and to distinguish them from what are termed "statistical aberrations." **Coincident indicators** are those that reach their turning points at the same time as the general economic activity. They can give an early verification of trends indicated by leading indicators.

Table 4-3

Business Cycle Indicators

Leading Indicators

Average manufacturing workweek, hours

Average weekly initial claims for unemployment insurance, thousands

New orders for consumer goods and materials, billions

Vendor performance, slower deliveries diffusion index, percent

Contracts and orders for plant and equipment, billions

Index of new building permits for private housing, 1967 = 100

Change in manufacturers' unfilled orders for durable goods, percent

Index of price of 500 common stocks (1941-1943 = 10)

M2 Money Supply, billions

Index of Consumer Expectations by Univ. of Michigan (1961 = 100)

Coincident Indicators

Employees on nonagricultural payrolls, thousands

Personal income less transfer payments, billions

Index of industrial production (1987 = 100)

Manufacturing and trade sales, millions

Lagging Indicators

Average duration of unemployment, weeks

Ratio of manufacturing and trade inventories to sales in 1987

Change in labor cost per unit of manufacturing output, percent

Average prime rate charged by banks, percent

Commercial and industrial loans outstanding, millions

Ratio of outstanding consumer installment credit to personal income, percent

Change in Consumer Price Index for services, percent

Concluding Remarks

To repeat the admonition at the beginning of this chapter, "Anyone who simply extrapolates past trends, *however elegant the algebra,* is an educated fool." Or, in the words of Shakespeare's Macbeth, "And all our yesterdays have lighted fools the way to dusty death. … It is a tale told by an idiot, full of sound and fury, signifying nothing."

Statistical projections are but one way to learn and apply the lessons of the past. They are a start for heeding Winston Churchill's oft-quoted admonition, "Those who ignore the lessons of history are doomed to repeat the mistakes of the past."

Statistical projections of the past help reveal the past and guide the future. *But they need to be examined critically*, in the light of how the world is changing, *to understand their message and its significance.* And they need to be changed when the past changes.

What can we learn from the examples in this chapter? Certainly there is considerable value in using knowledge of the past to forecast the future. To knowledge of the past we need to add our best knowledge and expectations for the future. Several examples in Chapters 3 and 4 recognized new trends as they appeared and illustrated management actions to cope with them. Other examples looked back only after trends had changed. In both cases, analyses were made to explain why later values departed from the projections of earlier trends. Forecasts should be more than number-crunching exercises to extrapolate past data. They should include a critical analysis of shifting global forces that shape future markets.

Forecasting a company's performance is difficult to do without "insider information" of changes in company strategies as well as information on the global economy. The importance of such information to anyone involved in making forecasts is well illustrated by the examples in Chapters 3 and 4. A critical post-analysis can also be important for identifying what went wrong that needs to be corrected before it is too late. The sooner this is done when trends change unexpectedly, the better.

Sometimes the most valuable forecast is one that doesn't come true. For example, when actual sales or net income falls below the projected trend of the past, it can be a *warning* that more than the forecasting model needs to be changed. *It can also indicate that management needs to change.* Deviations from past trends should alert managers to take action promptly to avert a crisis and ensure a better future. Start with a good model of the past and recognize when a change occurs. Then, instead of saying the model is no good, be a detective and search out the reason for the change. Revise the model *and management strategies* accordingly.

References

Gensch, Denni., Nicola Versa and Steven Moore. "A Choice-Modeling Market Information System that Enabled ABB Electric to Expand Its Market Share". Interfaces, 20(1), Jan-Feb 1990, pp. 16–25

Kuttner, Robert. 1997. "The Nails Aren't in the Coffin of the Business Cycle Yet," Business Week, Feb. 3, 1997, pg. 26

Chapter 5

Forecasting Financial Statements

CHAPTER OBJECTIVES

Management Skills

- Use forecasts of annual sales and other considerations to forecast financial statements as part of a firm's long-range plans.
- Analyze the impacts of potential changes in future growth and other factors on gross profits, earnings after taxes, and other financial results.

Spreadsheet Skills

- Incorporate forecasts of future annual revenues and other items into future Income Statements and Balance Sheets.
- Use Excel's Scenario Manager tool to perform sensitivity analysis.

Overview

This chapter shows how to prepare financial statements for the future, whereas Chapter 1 showed how to prepare them for the past.

Financial statements are sales driven, and their values for the future are no better than the forecast values of sales on which they are based. That is why forecasting annual sales, the subject of Chapters 3 and 4, is so important.

Forecasting financial statements is not a simple activity. In large firms, planning committees that report to corporate executives direct and coordinate planning activities. Along with projected sales, forecasts are needed for many other items on financial statements. These are provided by a company's various functional and operating divisions. Once input data have been collected, spreadsheets help organize the information and do the calculations.

The accuracy of forecast financial statements depends, of course, on the thoroughness and care taken in forecasting individual items on the statements. Since forecasts are never precisely correct, Chapter 5 also shows how to analyze the sensitivity of forecast results to variations in the input values.

Evaluating Future Values on Financial Statements

Forecasting financial statements begins with forecasting individual items on the financial statements. Some items have a constant relationship to sales. This broad statement, of course, is never exactly the case, although the "percentage of sales" method may be close enough to approximate some items once the level of sales has been forecast. Other items do not change as a result of sales but are determined by company policies, by changes that the company cannot control, or by the long-range planning process.

Items on the Income Statement

Sales Income or Revenues

Forecasts of future sales are the single most important input to future plans. Forecasting sales is generally a function of a firm's marketing division. The preceding chapter showed how to use regression analysis to make statistical projections of past sales trends. It also discussed the need to adjust statistical projections for anticipated changes in past trends.

Unfortunately, even the best forecasts are never precisely correct. At best, there is a 50 percent probability that future sales will be higher than their forecast values, and a 50 percent probability they will be lower. Financial planners should know the accuracy of the forecasts as well as their most probable values. Accuracy can be expressed in statistical terms, such as the standard error of forecast or the upper and lower limits of the range within which there is a specified probability actual future values will range.

Cost of Goods Sold (COGS)

COGS is the only income variable that is clearly proportional to sales. For example, if COGS averages 60 percent of the revenue generated by selling goods during the last few years, we assume that COGS will continue to equal 60 percent of annual sales for the next few years, unless there is some clear justification for a different percentage.

Productivity generally improves with time, largely due to improved technology for manufacturing goods and providing services. This is offset, more or less, by increases in the costs of labor and materials due to inflation. Depending on the level of competition, changes in cost are passed on to customers in the form of reductions or increases in selling price. As a result, although the **dollar** value of COGS changes with time, it remains at a fairly constant **percentage** of sales.

Selling Expenses

Selling expenses depend on the level of competition as well as the level of sales. As competition increases, advertising and promotion costs can increase from year to year at a faster percentage rate than sales.

General and Administrative Expenses (G&A)

General and administrative expenses (G&A) includes a variety of costs, such as the salaries of managers and executives, electric power and other utilities, and other costs associated with the firm's administration that are not directly tied to the level of operation. Some of these may increase faster than sales and others slower. In the absence of better information, expressing G&A as a constant percentage of sales may provide a reasonable approximation.

Fixed Expenses

These are not fixed in an absolute sense. They include the cost of such items as leases, which are often renegotiated at higher prices at the end of each contract period. When fixed expenses are known to change, their correct values should be used rather than a single fixed value over the entire period for which financial statements are being prepared.

Depreciation Expense

Depreciation expense depends on the amount and age of the firm's assets, the firm's method of depreciation, the remaining lifetimes of assets, and the salvage values of assets. Future depreciation expenses depend on both the continuing depreciation of past investments in capital assets as well as the depreciation of future investments in capital assets. (Depreciation is covered in Chapter 11.)

Interest Expense

Interest expense depends on the short-term borrowings, on the long-term debt in the firm's capital structure, and on the rates of interest paid on each. Interest rates vary from year to year.

Taxes

Taxes are calculated from the firm's EBIT and the tax rate.

Items Listed as Assets on the Balance Sheet

Cash and Equivalents

Although firms need some ready cash to operate, the amount is not necessarily in proportion to sales. When sales increase, for example, a firm may choose to invest and earn interest on some or all of the increase rather than simply accumulating it. Although the amount of cash and equivalents may change with sales level, it will probably change at a lower rate. For example, an increase of 10 percent in sales revenue may result in an increase of only 1 or 2 percent in cash and equivalents.

Accounts Receivable

Accounts receivable should vary approximately in proportion to sales. However, if a firm's average collection period exceeds the industry norm (see Chapter 2), the company may institute tactics to shorten it. In that case, accounts receivable, as a percent of sales, should decrease.

Inventory

Inventory should generally vary approximately in proportion to sales. However, as a result of "Just-in-Time" inventory management systems and better forecasting, many companies have found it profitable to reduce inventories and safety stocks. (Note the comments on inventory management in Chapter 8: Cash Budgeting.)

Fixed Assets

The value of this item is the purchase price the firm paid for its fixed assets—that is, for the land, buildings, machinery, equipment, furniture, fixtures, and vehicles it owns. Although a firm will likely buy or sell fixed assets during the years covered by the forecasts, its purchases and sales of fixed assets are not likely to change in proportion to the changes in sales. The values of this item on the balance sheet will therefore depend on upper management's plans for the future capital investments.

Accumulated Depreciation

Accumulated depreciation at the end of a year is the sum of that accumulated at the end of the preceding year plus the annual depreciation for the year. The annual depreciation for the year is calculated on the income statement. (Depreciation is discussed in Chapter 11.)

Net Fixed Assets

This is the difference between the value of fixed assets and accumulated depreciation. It is a calculated value on the income statement.

Total Assets

This is a calculated value on the income statement.

Items Listed as Liabilities on the Balance Sheet

Accounts Payable

Accounts payable should vary approximately in proportion to sales.

Short-Term Notes Payable

This item depends on management's decisions about the level of short-term debt.

Accruals and Other Current Liabilities

This amount can be left unchanged unless there is specific information as to its future values.

Long-Term Debt

This item is left unchanged from the last completed year. We will find later that in order to balance the balance sheet, we will calculate the amount of discretionary funds (long-term debt and common stock) needed to support the forecast changes.

Common Stock

This item is left unchanged from the last completed year. We will find later that in order to balance the balance sheet, we will calculate the amount of discretionary funds (long-term debt and common stock) needed to support the forecast changes.

Retained Earnings

This account accumulates earnings that are retained from one year to the next. The retained earnings at the end of the current year equals the sum of the retained earnings at the end of the previous year plus the retained earnings for the current year.

An Example

The following example illustrates how to forecast a company's income statement and balance sheet for the next few years based on its financial statements for the past year, its forecasts for future sales, and pertinent assumptions and changes in its corporate strategy. To provide transparency and promote understanding, all assumptions and changes in corporate strategy are listed at the bottom of each statement.

Example 5.1: ABC's income statement and balance sheet for the years 20X1 and 20X2 are given in Chapter 1. Using the financial statements for 20X2 as a starting point and the assumptions given below, forecast ABC's income statement and balance sheet for the next three years—from 20X3 to 20X5.

Assumptions for the Income Statement

The marketing organization has reviewed its annual sales for the last five years and made a statistical projection of their trend to the next year. Following this, the firm's planning staff reviewed the growth of worldwide competition and markets, as well as changes in other socioeconomic conditions, and analyzed how they might affect the statistical projections of past trends. As a result of their analyses, they concluded that the firm's annual sales revenues will increase 11.5 percent each year from its value of $2,575,000 for the year just completed.

Discussions between the marketing and manufacturing organizations indicate that, although production costs are expected to drop, selling prices will also drop in parallel. As a result, the cost of goods sold will remain at the same percentage of sales as in 20X2.

The marketing organization expects that because of increasing competition, selling expenses, as a percentage of sales, will increase 0.20 percent each year for the next three. This means, for example, that if the selling expenses were 15.00 percent of sales the first year, the selling expenses would be 15.20 percent of sales the second year, 15.40 percent of sales the third year, and so forth.

Discussions between the CFO's office and the managers of the various divisions indicate that in order to improve the company's financial well-being, general and administrative expenses will be held to an increase of only 8 percent each year from the value $225,000 in 20X2.

The annual depreciation on the firm's existing capital assets is expected to decline 10 percent each year. The annual depreciation on new capital assets is expected to average 15 percent in the year of their purchase and then decline 10 percent each year thereafter.

The annual fixed expenses, which are currently $75,000, are expected to increase 5 percent for the next two years. They will jump to $115,000 for the third year, when the company's current building lease expires and a new one will be negotiated for a larger building.

Income from other sources will increase at one-half the rate of increase for sales.

Interest paid on short-term and long-term borrowing will increase 6 percent each year from their current values of $10,000 and $50,000.

The tax rate will remain at 40 percent, and the ratio of current taxes to deferred taxes will remain the same for the next three years.

There will be no change in the dividends paid to holders of preferred stock. The number of outstanding shares of common stock will remain at 100,000, and the dividends paid to holders of common stock will increase 10 percent each year for the next three.

Assumptions for the Balance Sheet

Cash and equivalents will increase 3 percent per year—approximately at the rate of inflation.

Accounts receivable and accounts payable are expected to keep pace with sales. That is, the year-to-year percentage increases in accounts receivable and accounts payable will be the same as the corresponding year-to-year percentage increases in sales.

The value of inventories will increase at the same percentage rate as sales. The value of other current assets will increase 5 percent per year.

In order to handle the increased customer demand and sales for the next three years, the company will need to invest in additional capital assets, such as buildings, machinery, equipment, furniture, fixtures, and vehicles. The company expects that its total investment in new fixed assets each year will equal 5 percent of its net fixed assets (i.e., assets at purchase price less accumulated depreciation) at the end of the preceding year and that its mix of assets (i.e., the ratio of the cost of each type of asset to the total cost) will remain constant. (Accumulated depreciation will increase each year by the amounts on the income statement.)

(Continued)

Other fixed assets, including certain leases, will remain constant.

Short-term notes payable and accruals and other current liabilities will increase 3 percent per year.

There will be no change during the next three years in the company's long-term debt, preferred stock, common stock, or paid-in capital in excess of par on common stock.

Solution: Figure 5-1 is the solution for the **income statement**. The lower portion of this figure shows the basis for the forecasts. Most values in this section, though not all, are annual percentage growth. Among the exceptions are: (1) the data value of $115,000 for the fixed expenses in 20X5 on the income statement, (2) the calculated values for the ratio of COGS to sales, and (3) the calculated values for the ratio of selling expenses to sales. The entries provide visibility (i.e., "transparency") for the assumptions on which the forecasts are based. They also provide flexibility for examining the impacts of any changes in these assumptions (which we will do later). If desired, Rows 32 to 49 can be hidden when the financial statements are printed.

Total Sales Revenues: The percent increase each year is given as 11.5%. This value is entered in Cell C35. Because the percent increase will be the same each year, enter =C35 in D35 and copy the entry to E35. The entry is Cell C5 is =B5*(1+C35), which is copied to D5:E5.

Cost of Goods Sold (COGS): The ratio of COGS to sales is evaluated by entering =B6/B5 in Cell C47. Because the ratio will be the same each year, enter =C47 in Cell D47 and copy the entry to E47. The values for COGS each year are calculated by entering =C5*C47 in Cell C6 and copying it to D6:E6.

Gross Profits: Copy the entry =B5-B6 in Cell B7 to C7:E7.

Selling Expenses: The increase in the ratio of selling expenses to sales in 19X3 as compared to 20X2 is entered as 0.0020 (i.e., 0.20%) in Cell C48. Because this year-to-year increase is the same from 20X3 to 20X4 and from 20X4 to 20X5, enter =C48 in D48 and copy it to E48.

To calculate the ratio of selling expenses to sales in 20X2, enter =B9/B5 in Cell B49. (If a column is included on the worksheet with values for 20X1 as well as for 20X2, the ratio can be calculated as the average of the ratios for the last two years—that is, for 20X1 and 20X2.) The ratios in 20X3 to 20X5 are calculated by entering =B49+C48 in Cell C49 and copying to D49:E49.

The selling expenses for 20X3 to 20X5 are calculated by entering =C5*C49 in Cell C9 and copying the entry to D9:E9.

General and Administrative Expenses: Enter =B10*(1+C36) in Cell C10 and copy the entry to D10:E10.

Depreciation Expense: Note that the annual depreciation expense includes that for existing assets and that for assets purchased in the future. The decrease of 10% per year in the depreciation expense for previously purchased equipment is entered in Cell C38. Since this decrease is the same for 20X4 and 20X5, enter =C38 in D38 and copy it to E38. The value of 15 percent for the depreciation expense for newly purchased equipment in the year of its purchase is entered in Cell C39. Since this percentage is the same for investments in capital assets in 20X4 and 20X5, enter =C39 in D39 and copy it to E39.

To calculate the depreciation expenses for 20X3 to 20X5, enter =B11*(1+C38)+(SUM(C63:C66)-SUM(B63:B66))*C39 in Cell C11 and copy the entry to Cells D11:E11. The first part of this entry computes the depreciation on assets purchased in prior years, and the second part adds the depreciation for new assets. (The values of fixed assets are in Rows 63 to 66 of the balance sheet.)

Fixed Expenses: Enter the assumed value of 5% increase for 20X3 and 20X4 in Cell C40. The entry in Cell D40 is =C40, and the entry for 20X5 in Cell E41 is the value $115,000. The values for 20X3 and 20X4 are calculated by entering =B12*(1+C40) in Cell C12 in copying it to D12. For the value for 20X5, enter =E41 in Cell E12. (Another way is to enter =IF(C41>0,C41,B12*(1+C40)) in Cell C12 and copy the entry to D12:E12.)

Total Operating Expenses: Copy the entry =SUM(B9:B12) in Cell B13 to C13:E13.

(Continued)

Figure 5-1

Income Statement for 20X2 and Forecasts for 20X3, 20X4, and 20X5

	A	B	C	D	E
1	ABC COMPANY				
2-3	Income Statement for Year Ended December 31, 20X2 and Forecast for Next 3 Years — Values in $ thousand, except EPS				
4		20X2	20X3	20X4	20X5
5	Total Operating Revenues (or Total Sales Revenues)	$2,575.0	$2,871.1	$3,201.3	$3,569.5
6	Less: Cost of Goods Sold (COGS)	$1,150.0	$1,282.3	$1,429.7	$1,594.1
7	Gross Profits	$1,425.0	$1,588.9	$1,771.6	$1,975.3
8	Less: Operating Expenses				
9	Selling Expenses	$275.0	$312.4	$354.7	$402.6
10	General and Administrative Expenses (G&A)	$225.0	$243.0	$262.4	$283.4
11	Depreciation Expense	$100.0	$118.9	$136.4	$152.6
12	Fixed Expenses	$75.0	$78.8	$82.7	$115.0
13	Total Operating Expenses	$675.0	$753.0	$836.2	$953.7
14	Net Operating Income	$750.0	$835.9	$935.4	$1,021.6
15	Other Income	$20.0	$21.2	$22.4	$23.7
16	Earnings before Interest and Taxes (EBIT)	$770.0	$857.0	$957.7	$1,045.3
17	Less: Interest Expense				
18	Interest on Short-Term Notes	$10.0	$10.6	$11.2	$11.9
19	Interest on Long-Term Borrowing	$50.0	$53.0	$56.2	$59.6
20	Total Interest Expense	$60.0	$63.6	$67.4	$71.5
21	Earnings before Taxes (EBT)	$710.0	$793.4	$890.3	$973.8
22	Less: Taxes (rate = 40%)				
23	Current	$160.0	$178.8	$200.6	$219.5
24	Deferred	$124.0	$138.6	$155.5	$170.1
25	Total taxes (rate = 40%)	$284.0	$317.4	$356.1	$389.5
26	Earnings after Taxes (EAT)	$426.0	$476.1	$534.2	$584.3
27	Less: Preferred Stock Dividends	$95.0	$95.0	$95.0	$95.0
28	Net Earnings Available for Common Stockholders	$331.0	$381.1	$439.2	$489.3
29	Earnings per Share (EPS), 100,000 shares outstanding	$ 3.31	$ 3.81	$ 4.39	$ 4.89
30	Retained Earnings	$220.0	$259.0	$304.9	$341.5
31	Dividends Paid to Holders of Common Stock	$111.0	$122.1	$134.3	$147.7
32	Assumptions for 3-Year Projections on Income Statement				
33		20X2	20X3	20X4	20X5
34	Projected Annual Growth from Year Before				
35	Total Sales Revenues		11.50%	11.50%	11.50%
36	General and Administrative Expenses		8.00%	8.00%	8.00%
37	Depreciation Expense				
38	Existing Capital Assets		−10.00%	−10.00%	−10.00%
39	New Capital Assets in Year of Purchase		15.00%	15.00%	15.00%
40	Fixed Expenses		5.00%	5.00%	
41	Fixed Expenses, value for 20X5 ($ thousand)				$115.0
42	Other Income		5.75%	5.75%	5.75%
43	Interest on Short-Term Notes		6.00%	6.00%	6.00%
44	Interest on Long-Term Borrowing		6.00%	6.00%	6.00%
45	Dividends Paid to Holders of Common Stock		10.00%	10.00%	10.00%
46	Projected Ratios				
47	COGS to Sales		44.66%	44.66%	44.66%
48	Annual Increase in Ratio of Selling Expenses to Sales		0.20%	0.20%	0.20%
49	Selling Expenses to Sales	10.68%	10.88%	11.08%	11.28%
50	Projected Tax Rate	40%	40%	40%	40%

(Continued)

Net Operating Income: Copy the entry =B7-B13 in Cell B14 to C14:E14.

Other Income: The percentage increase in Other Income is assumed to be one-half the percentage increase in Sales Revenue. Therefore, enter =C35/2 in Cell C42 and copy it to D42:E42. The values of other income for 20X3 to 20X5 are calculated by entering =B15*(1+C42) in Cell C15 in copy it to D15:E15.)

Earnings before Interest and Taxes (EBIT): Copy the entry =B14+B15 in Cell B16 to C16:E16.

Interest on Short-Term Notes: Enter the annual percentage increase of 6% in Cell C43. Enter =C43 in Cell D43 and copy the entry to E43. To compute the interest on short-term notes in 20X3 to 20X5, enter =B18*(1+C43) in Cell C18 and copy the entry to D18:E18.

Interest on Long-Term Borrowing: Enter the annual percentage increase of 6% in Cell C44. Enter =C44 in Cell D44 and copy the entry to E44. To compute the interest on long-term borrowing in 20X3 to 20X5, enter =B19*(1+C44) in Cell C19 and copy the entry to D19:E19. (Alternatively, you can copy the entry in Cell C18 to C19:E19.)

Total Interest Expense: Copy the entry =B18+B19 in Cell B20 to C20:E20.

Earnings before Taxes (EBT): Copy the entry =B16-B20 in Cell B21 to C21:E21.

Taxes: Enter the tax rate of 40% in Cell C50. Enter =C50 in Cell D50 and copy to E50. The **total** taxes for 20X3 to 20X5 are calculated by entering =C50*C21 in Cell C25 and copying the entry to Cells D25:E25. From the problem statement, the ratios of current and deferred taxes to total taxes remain constant. Therefore, to calculate **current** taxes for 20X3 to 20X5, enter =($B$23/$B$25)*C25 in Cell C23 and copy it to D23:E23. To calculate **deferred** taxes, enter = C25-C23 in Cell C24 and copy the entry to D24:E24. (Alternatively, calculate the deferred taxes by entering =($B$24/$B$25)*C25 in Cell C24 and copying it to D24:E24.)

Earnings after Taxes (EAT): Copy the entry =B21-B25 in Cell B26 to C26:E26.

Preferred Stock Dividends: Because preferred stock dividends are constant, the values for 20X3 to 20X5 are repeats of the value in 20X2. Enter =B27 in Cell C27 and copy it to Cells D27:E27.

Net Earnings Available for Common Stockholders: Copy the entry =B26-B27 in Cell B28 to Cells C28:E28.

Earnings per Share (EPS): Copy the entry =B28/100000 in Cell B29 to Cells C29:E29.

Retained Earnings: Enter =C28-C31 in Cell C30 and copy it to Cells C30:E30.

Dividends Paid to Holders of Common Stock: Enter the annual percentage increase of 10% in Cell C45. Enter =C45 in Cell D45 and copy the entry to E45. To calculate values for 20X3 to 20X5, enter =B31*(1+C45) in Cell C31 and copy it to Cells D31:E31.

Balance Sheet: Figure 5-2 shows the **balance sheet**. To facilitate using Excel's scenario analysis tool, the balance sheet has been placed below the income statement on the same worksheet rather than on a separate worksheet. Cell entries for the forecast values for 20X3, 20X4, and 20X5 are shown in the lower section of Figure 5-2.

Current Assets

Cash and Equivalents: The percent increase each year is given as 3.0%. Enter this value in Cell C92, then enter =C92 in Cell D92 and copy the entry to E92. To calculate the values for 20X3 to 20X5, enter =B57*(1+C92) in Cell C57 and copy to D57:E57.

Accounts Receivable: The percent increase each year is assumed to be the same as for sales revenue. Enter =C35 in Cell C93 and copy to D93:E93. Enter =B58*(1+C93) in Cell C58 and copy to D58:E58. (Alternatively, copy the entry in Cell C57 to C58:E58.)

(Continued)

Figure 5-2

Balance Sheet for 20X2 and Forecasts for 20X3, 20X4, and 20X5

	A	B	C	D	E
51	ABC COMPANY				
52	Balance Sheet as of December 31, 20X2 and Forecast for Next 3 Years				
53	Values in $ thousand				
54		20X2	20X3	20X4	20X5
55	Assets				
56	**Current Assets**				
57	Cash and Equivalents	$1,565.0	$1,612.0	$1,660.3	$1,710.1
58	Accounts Receivable	$565.0	$630.0	$702.4	$783.2
59	Inventories	$895.0	$997.9	$1,112.7	$1,240.6
60	Other Current Assets	$215.0	$225.8	$237.0	$248.9
61	Total Current Assets	$3,240.0	$3,465.6	$3,712.5	$3,982.9
62	Fixed Assets (at cost)				
63	Land and Buildings	$2,400.0	$2,495.2	$2,592.1	$2,690.6
64	Machinery and Equipment	$1,880.0	$1,954.5	$2,030.5	$2,107.6
65	Furniture and Fixtures	$435.0	$452.2	$469.8	$487.7
66	Vehicles	$140.0	$145.6	$151.2	$157.0
67	Less: Accumulated Depreciation	$1,005.0	$1,123.9	$1,260.3	$1,412.9
68	Net Fixed Assets	$3,850.0	$3,923.6	$3,983.4	$4,029.9
69	Other Fixed Assets (includes certain leases)	$75.0	$75.0	$75.0	$75.0
70	Total Fixed Assets	$3,925.0	$3,998.6	$4,058.4	$4,104.9
71	Total Assets	$7,165.0	$7,464.2	$7,770.8	$8,087.8
72	Liabilities				
73	Current Liabilities				
74	Accounts Payable	$300.0	$334.5	$373.0	$415.9
75	Short-Term Notes Payable	$1,275.0	$1,313.3	$1,352.6	$1,393.2
76	Accruals and Other Current Liabilities	$145.0	$149.4	$153.8	$158.4
77	Total Current Liabilities	$1,720.0	$1,797.1	$1,879.4	$1,967.5
78	Long-Term Debt	$1,900.0	$1,900.0	$1,900.0	$1,900.0
79	Total Liabilities	$3,620.0	$3,697.1	$3,779.4	$3,867.5
80	Stockholders' Equity				
81	Preferred Stock	$200.0	$200.0	$200.0	$200.0
82	Common Stock ($10.00 par, 100,000 shares outstanding)	$1,000.0	$1,000.0	$1,000.0	$1,000.0
83	Paid-In Capital in Excess of Par on Common Stock	$1,985.0	$1,985.0	$1,985.0	$1,985.0
84	Retained Earnings	$360.0	$619.0	$923.8	$1,265.4
85	Total Stockholders' Equity	$3,545.0	$3,804.0	$4,108.8	$4,450.4
86	Total Liabilities and Owner's Equity	$7,165.0	$7,501.1	$7,888.3	$8,317.9
87	Discretionary Financing Needed		($36.8)	($117.4)	($230.2)
88			Surplus	Surplus	Surplus
89	Assumptions for 5-Year Projections on Balance Sheet				
90			20X3	20X4	20X5
91	**Projected Annual Growth Rates from Year Before**				
92	Cash and Equivalents		3.0%	3.0%	3.0%
93	Accounts Receivable		11.5%	11.5%	11.5%
94	Inventories		11.5%	11.5%	11.5%
95	Other Current Assets		5.0%	5.0%	5.0%
96	Sum of New Fixed Assets/Preceding Net Value of Fixed Assets		5.0%	5.0%	5.0%
97	Other Fixed Assets (including certain leases)		0.0%	0.0%	0.0%
98	Accounts Payable		11.5%	11.5%	11.5%
99	Short-Term Notes Payable		3.0%	3.0%	3.0%
100	Accruals and Other Current Liabilities		3.0%	3.0%	3.0%
101	Long-Term Debt		0.0%	0.0%	0.0%
102	Preferred Stock		0.0%	0.0%	0.0%
103	Common Stock		0.0%	0.0%	0.0%
104	Paid-In Capital in Excess of Par on Common Stock		0.0%	0.0%	0.0%

(Continued)

Inventories: The percent increase each year is assumed to be the same as the percentage increase in sales revenue. Therefore, enter =C35 in C94 and copy it to D94:E94. Enter =B59*(1+C94) in Cell C59 and copy it to D59:E59. (Alternatively, copy the entry in Cell C57 to C58:E59.)

Other Current Assets: The percent increase is given as 5.0% and is assumed to be the same each year. Therefore, enter 5% in Cell C95, then enter =C95 in Cell D95 and copy the entry to E95. Enter =B60*(1+C95) in Cell C60 and copy it to D60:E60. (Alternatively, copy the entry in Cell C57 to C58:E60.)

Total Current Assets: Copy the entry =SUM(B57:B60) in Cell B61 to C61:E61.

Fixed Assets

Land and Buildings, Machinery and Equipment, Furniture and Fixtures, and Vehicles): The sum of the firm's new investments each year in these four fixed assets is given as 5% of the net fixed assets at the end of the preceding year. It is also given that the mix of the assets (i.e., the percentage of each of the four types of fixed assets in the mix) is constant.

The value 5% is entered in Cell C96. Enter =C96 in Cell D96 and copy it to E96.

To calculate the total investment in an asset, enter =B63+B$68*C$96*$B63/SUM($B$63:$B$66) in Cell C63 and copy the entry to C63:E66. (Study the second term of this entry carefully to understand its logic. The second term is the new investment in an asset during a given year. This is added to the investment at the end of the preceding year to give the total investment in the asset at the end of the given year. The expression B$68*C$96 in the second term is the total new investment. The ratio $B63/SUM($B$63:$B$66) is the percentage of the total new investment that is in buildings. As the entry is copied down, the ratio changes to the percentages of the total new investment that is in the other assets. Note the $ signs in the entry.)

Accumulated Depreciation: Enter =B67+C11 in Cell C67 and copy it to D67:E67.

Net Fixed Assets: Copy the entry =SUM(B63:B66)-B67 in Cell B68 to C68:E68.

Other Fixed Assets: The percent increase each year is given as zero. This value is entered in Cell C97, and the entry =C97 in Cell D97 is copied to E97. Enter =B69*(1+C97) in Cell C69 and copy it to D69:E69.

Total Fixed Assets: Copy the entry =B68+B69 in Cell B70 to C70:E70.

Liabilities

Accounts Payable: The percent increase each year is the same as for sales revenue. Enter =C35 in Cell C98 and copy to D98:E98. Enter =B74*(1+C98) Cell C74 and copy to D74:E74.

Short-Term Notes Payable: The percentage increase of 3% is entered in Cell C99. Enter =C99 in Cell D99 and copy to D99:E99. Enter =B75*(1+C99) in Cell C75 and copy to D75:E75.

Accruals and Other Current Liabilities: The percentage increase of 3% is entered in Cell C100. Enter =C100 in Cell D100 and copy to D100:E100. Enter =B76*(1+C100) in Cell C76 and copy to D76:E76.

Total Current Liabilities: Copy the entry =SUM(B74:B76) in Cell B77 to C77:E77.

Long-Term Debt: Enter the percentage increase of zero in Cell C101. Enter =C101 in Cell D101 and copy it to E101. Enter =B78*(1+C101) in Cell C78 and copy it to D78:E78.

Total Liabilities: Copy the entry =B77+B78 in Cell B79 to C79:E79.

(Continued)

Stockholders' Equity

Preferred Stock, Common Stock, and Paid-In Capital in Excess of Par on Common Stock: Enter the percentage increases of zero in Cells C102:C104. Enter =C102 in Cell D102 and copy the entry to D102:E104. Enter =B81*(1+C102) in Cell C81 and copy to Cells C81:E83.

Retained Earnings: Enter =B84+C30 in Cell C84 and copy to D84:E84.

Total Stockholder's Equity: Copy the entry =SUM(B81:B84) in Cell B85 to C85:E85.

Total Liabilities and Owner's Equity: Copy the entry =B79+B85 in Cell B86 to C86:E86.

Discretionary Financing Needed: Note that the balance sheet does not appear to balance for 20X3 to 20X5. The difference between total assets and total liabilities plus owner's equity is the amount of Discretionary Financing Needed. It is calculated by entering =C71-C86 in Cell C87 and copying to Cell D87:E87.

    If the total for the Discretionary Financing Needed is positive, it indicates that the company will need to borrow money. On the other hand, if it is negative, the company will have a surplus. To indicate which, enter =IF(C87>0,"Deficit", "Surplus") in Cell C88 and copy to D88:E88. (Alternatively, you can enter =IF(C71>C86,"Deficit","Surplus") in Cell C88 and copy it to D88:E88.) The resulting negative value in Cell C87 of Figure 5-2 (-36,800) indicates that the ABC company can expect to have more in discretionary funds than needed to support the forecast acquisition of fixed assets in 20X3.

Sensitivity Analysis

Forecast financial statements are sensitive to the assumptions about the future. This creates uncertainties and risks in the forecast financial statements. Several methods are used to analyze the impacts of the assumptions, such as What if? analysis, scenario analysis, and one- and two-variable input tables. The following example illustrates the use of Excel's Scenario Manager tool to do sensitivity analysis. It examines the effects of different rates of growth for sales revenues and annual investments in new fixed assets.

Example 5.2:   ABC's CFO feels uncomfortable because the increases in sales revenues and investments in fixed assets are both uncertain. (The current values for these increases are 11.5 percent for sales revenues and 5 percent for investments in fixed assets.)

    To help understand the range of possibilities, analyze the impacts of the following scenarios on the total operating revenues, gross profits, earnings after taxes (EAT), and the need for discretionary financing in 20X3, 20X4, and 20X5.

Scenario	1	2	3	4	5	6
Increase in annual sales revenues	10%	10%	10%	12%	12%	12%
Annual investment in new fixed assets	4%	6%	8%	4%	6%	8%

(Continued)

Figure 5-3

Effects of Changes in Annual Growth of Sales Revenues and Investments in Fixed Assets (Edited Results from Scenario Analysis)

	A	B	C	D	E	F	G	H	I	J
1				ABC COMPANY						
2			Sensitivity of Results to Growth of Annual Sales Revenue and Investment in Fixed Assets							
3	Sales Revenue Growth			10.00%	10.00%	10.00%		12.00%	12.00%	12.00%
4	Investment in New Assets			4.0%	6.0%	8.0%		4.0%	6.0%	8.0%
5	Item	Year		Values in $ thousand				Values in $ thousand		
6	Total Sales Revenues	20X3		$2,832.5	$2,832.5	$2,832.5		$2,884.0	$2,884.0	$2,884.0
7		20X4		$3,115.8	$3,115.8	$3,115.8		$3,230.1	$3,230.1	$3,230.1
8		20X5		$3,427.3	$3,427.3	$3,427.3		$3,617.7	$3,617.7	$3,617.7
9	Gross Profits	20X3		$1,567.5	$1,567.5	$1,567.5		$1,596.0	$1,596.0	$1,596.0
10		20X4		$1,724.3	$1,724.3	$1,724.3		$1,787.5	$1,787.5	$1,787.5
11		20X5		$1,896.7	$1,896.7	$1,896.7		$2,002.0	$2,002.0	$2,002.0
12	Earnings after Tax (EAT)	20X3		$469.1	$462.2	$455.3		$483.0	$476.1	$469.1
13		20X4		$518.0	$504.5	$490.6		$548.7	$535.1	$521.2
14		20X5		$556.3	$536.3	$515.7		$607.0	$587.1	$566.4
15	Discretionary Funding Needed (surplus)	20X3		($80.0)	($7.7)	$64.7		($70.7)	$1.7	$74.1
16		20X4		($194.9)	($49.8)	$97.7		($187.9)	($42.8)	$104.7
17		20X5		($330.9)	($113.3)	$111.5		($340.4)	($122.7)	$102.1

As before, the CFO assumes that the increases in the annual investments in fixed asset items will be the same each year for each of the four categories of fixed assets listed in Rows 63 to 66 of the Balance Sheet.

Solution: Figure 5-3 shows the solution (after editing the results shown later in Figure 5-10).

The steps to using Excel's Scenario Manager tool to produce Figure 5-3 are as follows:

1. On the spreadsheet of Figures 5-1 and 5-2, access the Scenario Manager tool, click on "Scenarios" on the "Tools" drop-down menu, as shown in Figure 5-4. This will open the "Scenario Manager" dialog box shown in Figure 5-5.
2. Click the "Add" button to open the "Add Scenario" dialog box shown in Figure 5-6. Enter a title such as "Scenario 1" in the first box, and enter C35,C96 for the two input cells whose values will be changed for each scenario.
3. Click "OK" or press "Enter" to open the "Scenario Values" dialog box shown in Figure 5-7. Replace the default values of the input variables (i.e., the current spreadsheet values in Cells C35 and C96) to the values for Scenario 1, as shown in Figure 5-7.
4. Click on the "Add" button to return to the "Add Scenario" dialog box and repeat steps 3 and 4 to complete the conditions for the six scenarios. After completing the "Scenario Values" dialog box with the values of the input variables for the last scenario, click the "OK" button or press "Enter" to return to the "Scenario Manager" dialog box shown in Figure 5-8.

(Continued)

Figure 5-4

"Scenarios" Selected on "Tools" Drop-Down Menu

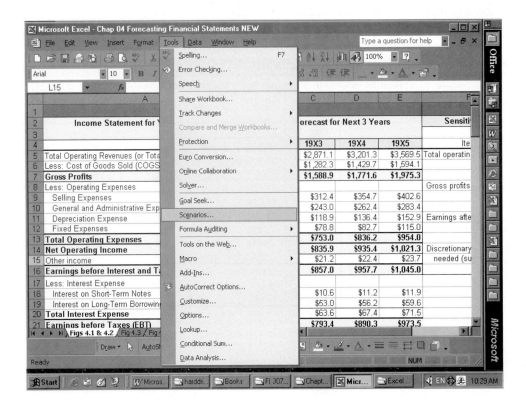

Figure 5-5

"Scenario Manager" Dialog Box

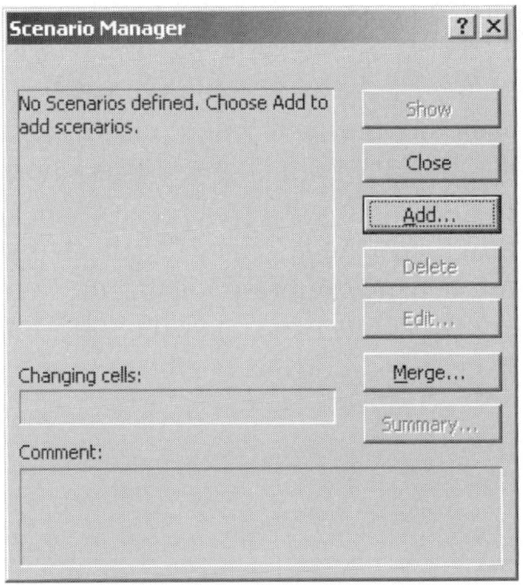

(Continued)

Figure 5-6
___

"Add Scenario" Dialog Box with Entries for Scenario 1

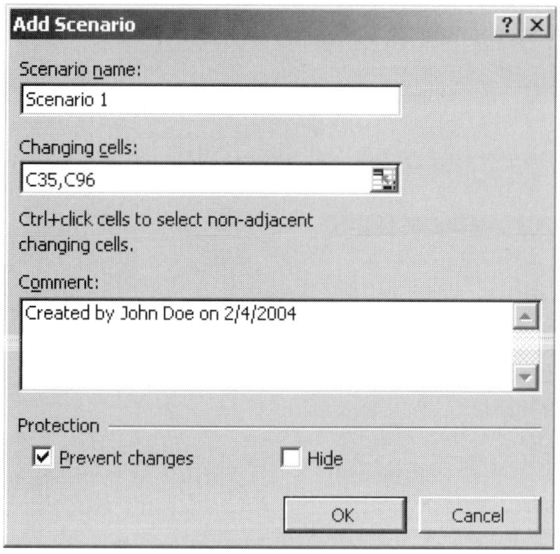

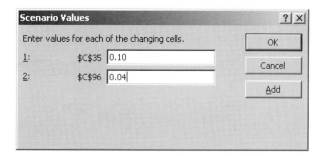

Figure 5-7
___

"Scenario Values" Dialog Box with Input Values for Scenario 1

5. Click on the "Summary" button of the "Scenario Manager" dialog box shown in Figure 5-8 to open the "Scenario Summary" dialog box shown in Figure 5-9. Enter the cell references for the output variables. These are Cells C5:E5 for the annual revenues, Cells C7:E7 for the gross profits, Cells C26:E26 for the earnings after taxes, and Cells C87:E87 for the discretionary income or surplus for the three years.
6. Click on the "OK" button or press "Enter" to produce the unedited results shown in Figure 5-10.
7. Edit the results in Figure 5-10 to provide a well-identified, management-quality output that can be easily read and understood, as in Figure 5-3.

(Continued)

Figure 5-8

"Scenario Manager" Dialog Box with Six Scenarios Created

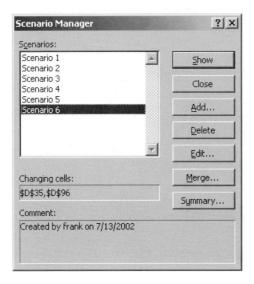

Figure 5-9

"Scenario Summary" Dialog Box with Result Cells Identified

Figure 5-11 shows how the values for the discretionary funds needed (or surplus) vary with annual investments in new fixed assets from 4 to 8 percent of the net fixed assets at the end of the preceding year. It indicates that for a 12 percent annual growth in sales, the company will need to raise funds in 20X3 only if the investment in new fixed assets is greater than 6.0 percent. It also indicates there will be a cumulative surplus of discretionary funds at the end of 20X5 so long as the annual investments in fixed assets remain below 7.1 percent. If greater investments in new fixed assets are necessary, the company will need to raise funds to cover their cost.

(Continued)

Figure 5-10

Results from Scenario Analysis before Editing

	A	B	C	D	E	F	G	H	I	J
1										
2						Scenario Summary				
3				Current Values	Scenario 1	Scenario 2	Scenario 3	Scenario 4	Scenario 5	Scenario 6
5		Changing Cells:								
6			$C$35	11.50%	10.00%	10.00%	10.00%	12.00%	12.00%	12.00%
7			$C$96	5.0%	4.0%	6.0%	8.0%	4.0%	6.0%	8.0%
8		Result Cells:								
9			$C$5	$2,871.1	$2,832.5	$2,832.5	$2,832.5	$2,884.0	$2,884.0	$2,884.0
10			$D$5	$3,201.3	$3,115.8	$3,115.8	$3,115.8	$3,230.1	$3,230.1	$3,230.1
11			$E$5	$3,569.5	$3,427.3	$3,427.3	$3,427.3	$3,617.7	$3,617.7	$3,617.7
12			$C$7	$1,588.9	$1,567.5	$1,567.5	$1,567.5	$1,596.0	$1,596.0	$1,596.0
13			$D$7	$1,771.6	$1,724.3	$1,724.3	$1,724.3	$1,787.5	$1,787.5	$1,787.5
14			$E$7	$1,975.3	$1,896.7	$1,896.7	$1,896.7	$2,002.0	$2,002.0	$2,002.0
15			$C$26	$476.1	$469.1	$462.2	$455.3	$483.0	$476.1	$469.1
16			$D$26	$534.2	$518.0	$504.5	$490.6	$548.7	$535.1	$521.2
17			$E$26	$584.3	$556.3	$536.3	$515.7	$607.0	$587.1	$566.4
18			$C$87	($36.8)	($80.0)	($7.7)	$64.7	($70.7)	$1.7	$74.1
19			$D$87	($117.4)	($194.9)	($49.8)	$97.7	($187.9)	($42.8)	$104.7
20			$E$87	($230.2)	($330.9)	($113.3)	$111.5	($340.4)	($122.7)	$102.1
21		Notes: Current Values column represents values of changing cells at								
22		time Scenario Summary Report was created. Changing cells for each								
23		scenario are highlighted in gray.								

Figure 5-11

Sensitivity of the Discretionary Funds Needed or Surplus to Changes in the Annual Investment in Fixed Assets at a 12% Growth in Annual Sales Revenues

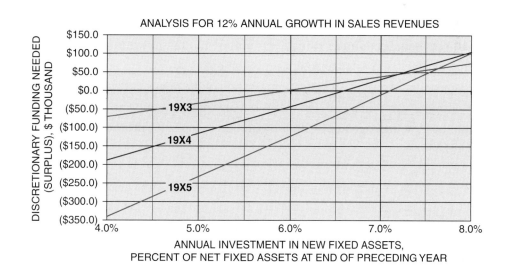

Concluding Remarks

Forecasting financial statements is an essential part of financial planning. Such forecasts integrate the expectations of different corporate divisions as well as the expectations of the marketing, sales, production, finance, and other functional organizations within each division. **Spreadsheet models consolidate data** and other detailed information from various sources and then show their impacts on a firm's financial statements.

Forecasting financial statements is based on forecasts of future sales and various assumptions related to a firm's short- and long-term strategies. These should be well understood by the managers of the different divisions and departments who will base their operating strategies and day-to-day tactics on them. To ensure their visibility, the assumptions should be shown on the worksheets, for example, at the bottom of each financial statement, as in the text, or in some other convenient area. **Spreadsheet models provide transparency**. They make the assumptions visible to anyone who needs to know the basis of the forecasts.

Spreadsheet models are flexible. The assumptions can be edited for changes. For example, the managers of marketing and production might cooperate to reduce the size of inventories needed to satisfy sales so that the annual increase in inventories might be only 90 percent of the annual increase in sales revenues rather than 100 percent. In this case, the entry in Cell C94 of Figure 5-2 would be =0.90*C35. This would result in the value 10.35 percent in Cells C94:E94 (which would appear as 10.4 percent for formatting to one decimal place), as well as changes in other values on the financial statements. Reducing inventories can, in fact, increase net operating income and profits substantially—a benefit we will examine in Chapter 8 on cash budgeting.

Spreadsheet models can be used for sensitivity analysis. Linking the assumptions to calculated values in the income statement and balance sheet sections provides the flexibility for evaluating the impacts of changes in the assumptions. This type of sensitivity analysis is easily done for different scenarios. Spreadsheets can easily show the impacts of changes in input values or assumptions on results.

Spreadsheet models communicate. Their output can be shown in the form of well-labeled tables and charts that make effective management presentations.

This chapter should give you a better appreciation of the power and value of spreadsheet models, not only for forecasting a firm's financial statements but also for integrating and coordinating the functions of various segments of the management hierarchy, in other words, for **promoting teamwork**.

Chapter 6

Forecasting Seasonal Revenues

CHAPTER OBJECTIVES

Management Skills

- Recognize seasonal variations in a firm's income and their importance to financial, sales, marketing, personnel, and operational management.
- Explain what is meant by "seasonally adjusted annual rates" and how to calculate them.

Spreadsheet Skills

- Create a seasonally-adjusted model by joining seasonal adjustments to the model for an annual trend line.
- Create a seasonally-adjusted model by joining seasonal adjustments to a model for a moving-average trend line.
- Use error feedback to correct a forecasting model so that the average error is zero.
- Create an automatic feedback system for using future values to revise a forecasting model and improve forecasts of the future.

Overview

Seasonal variations are those that recur regularly with time. They are quite common. They appear, for example, as monthly, quarterly, or semiannual "peaks and valleys" on sales charts.

Department stores provide a well-known example of seasonal behavior. Because of holiday shopping, sales are very strong in December, when a store may do more than a third of its annual business. December peaks are followed by the slow months of January and February, during which store managers discount prices and hold storewide sales to attract customers. The *month-to-month* "ups-and-downs" of store sales are superimposed on the overall, *year-to-year* trend for sales to increase, decrease, or remain stationary from one year to the next.

During months when cash flows are on the downside, chief financial officers resort to short-term borrowing in order to meet payrolls and pay bills. On the other hand, during periods when cash inflows exceed cash outflows, they invest excess cash in short-term commercial paper. Seasonal behavior is also important in adjusting inventories and the scheduling of work forces. For these reasons, forecasting seasonal revenues is important to cash budgeting, which is discussed in Chapter 8. It is also important to satisfying customer demands promptly and to minimizing the costs of operating a business.

> ### The Two Components of Seasonal Forecasting
>
> Seasonally-adjusted forecasting models have two components: One part projects the overall trend with time, and the second adjusts the trend for periodic variations above and below it.

Developing a regression equation for a seasonally-adjusted forecasting model takes three separate steps: (1) Remove the seasonality from the raw data, (2) develop a model for the trend line for the deseasonalized data—that is, for the overall trend with time, and (3) put the seasonality back into the model by multiplying or adding seasonal corrections to the deseasonalized trend line. For example, monthly or quarterly data can be deseasonalized either by calculating annual values or by using 12-month or 4-quarter moving averages. Regression analysis can then be used to calculate the parameters for the **deseasonalized trend line**, which can be either straight or curved. Multiplicative seasonal corrections can be determined from the ratios of period data values to deseasonalized trend values, and additive corrections can be determined from the differences between period data values and deseasonalized trend values. These corrections adjust for the amounts by which period values (e.g., quarterly or monthly values) are greater or less than the amounts on the deseasonalized trend line.

The seasonal corrections are called **specific seasonal indices** (SSIs). If the trend line projects annual values, the SSIs can be the fractions or percentages of the annual values for specific periods. Thus, once we have projected annual values, as in Chapter 3, the amounts for specific periods are calculated by multiplying the projected annual values by the SSIs. For example, if 30 percent of a company's annual sales occur in December and the projected *annual* sales is $10 million, the forecast sales for December would be $3 million (i.e., 30 percent of $10 million). The sum of the multiplicative SSIs for all periods in one complete year (whether, for example, for the 12 months or 4 quarters in a year) should equal one, or 100 percent.

If the deseasonalized trend line is for a moving average (either a 4-quarter or 12-month moving average, for example), the SSIs can be either additive or multiplicative. If the SSI is additive, it adds a positive value to the moving-average value to forecast the value for a peak period when actual values are above the moving average; if negative, it adds a negative amount to forecast the value for a period when actual values are below the moving average. If the SSI is multiplicative, it multiplies the moving-average value by a number greater than one for peak periods and by a number less than one for valleys. Although both additive and multiplicative SSIs might be used with moving-average trend lines, multiplicative SSIs are more common.

Seasonality is a recognized factor in reporting economic data and forecasting future behavior. Statistics for business sectors with pronounced peaks and valleys during the year are commonly reported in terms of **seasonally-adjusted annual rates** (SAARs). Government statistics on rates of housing construction, gross domestic product, and unemployment are examples of economic activity that is reported on a seasonally adjusted basis. Economists use SAARs for reporting data on retail sales, consumer spending, and many other measures of economic activity. CFOs use SAARs to project experience in the first part of a year to estimate equivalent annual values for the entire year and to adjust their plans for hiring and inventory levels in subsequent quarters and months.

Annual Trend Line with Multiplicative Corrections

In Chapter 3 we developed a cubic regression model for the annual trend of the sales of Wal-Mart Stores, Inc. In this section of Chapter 6, we will modify that model for annual sales to forecast quarterly sales.

Column E of Figure 6-1 shows the values from the first quarter of fiscal 1991 to the second quarter of fiscal 1997. Although Wal-Mart's annual sales increase from one year to the next, the quarterly sales go up or down as we move from one quarter to the next. Moreover, the "up-down" pattern is consistent from one year to the next. In each year, Wal-Mart's sales for the second quarter are higher than for the first, those for the third quarter are slightly higher than for the second, and sales for the fourth quarter are substantially higher than for the third. From the fourth quarter of one year to the first quarter of the next, the quarterly sales drop. Our model for projecting quarterly sales must incorporate both the year-to-year trend of annual sales and the quarter-to-quarter variations in the quarterly values.

Deseasonalized Trend Line

In Chapter 3, we developed a cubic model for the *annual* sales for Wal-Mart based on data from 1986 to 1996 (equation 3.17). This **part** (and it is only a part) of our seasonally-adjusted model for forecasting quarterly sales is

$$Y_{Year} = 13,127.6 + 207.476X_{Year} + 1,514.66X_{Year}^2 - 60.9373X_{Year}^3 \qquad (6.1)$$

where Y_{Year} = annual sales, \$ million
and X_{Year} = number of years since 1986 (i.e., $X_{Year} = 0$ for 1986, 1 for 1987,..., 5 for 1991, etc.)

We will use equation 6.1 for *annual* sales as the first part (i.e., the deseasonalized trend line) of our model for the firm's *quarterly* sales. (Later in the chapter we will update the model with more recent data.)

Figure 6-1

Seasonally-Adjusted Annual Trend Line Model (Trial Model)

	A	B	C	D	E	F	G	H	I	J	K	L	M	N	O
1								WAL-MART STORES, INC.							
2					Seasonally-Adjusted Cubic Annual Trend Line for Quarterly Sales (Based on Quarters 1 to 26)										
3					Actual	Forecast	Ratio,	SSI,	Forecast			Standard	Quarterly Sales		Actual
4					Quarterly	Annual	Quarterly	Avg. Ratio	Quarterly	Forecast		Forecast	80% Confidence		Outside
5	Fiscal				Sales,	Sales,	to Fcast	for Like	Sales,	Error,		Error,	Range, $ million		Conf.
6	Year	XYR	Quarter	X	$ million	$ million	Annual	Quarters	$ million	$ million	X-XM	$ million	Minimum	Maximum	Range?
7	1991	5	1st	1	9,280	44,414	0.20894	0.21332	9,474	−194	−12.5	463.8	8,861	10,088	---
8	1991	5	2nd	2	10,340	44,414	0.23281	0.24006	10,662	−322	−11.5	460.5	10,053	11,271	---
9	1991	5	3rd	3	10,627	44,414	0.23927	0.24573	10,914	−287	−10.5	457.4	10,309	11,519	---
10	1991	5	4th	4	13,640	44,414	0.30711	0.30084	13,362	278	−9.5	454.6	12,760	13,963	---
11	1992	6	1st	5	11,649	55,738	0.20900	0.21332	11,890	−241	−8.5	452.0	11,292	12,488	---
12	1992	6	2nd	6	13,028	55,738	0.23374	0.24006	13,380	−352	−7.5	449.8	12,785	13,976	---
13	1992	6	3rd	7	13,683	55,738	0.24549	0.24573	13,696	−13	−6.5	447.8	13,104	14,289	---
14	1992	6	4th	8	17,124	55,738	0.30722	0.30084	16,768	356	−5.5	446.0	16,178	17,359	---
15	1993	7	1st	9	13,920	67,897	0.20502	0.21332	14,484	−564	−4.5	444.6	13,895	15,072	---
16	1993	7	2nd	10	16,237	67,897	0.23914	0.24006	16,299	−62	−3.5	443.4	15,713	16,886	---
17	1993	7	3rd	11	16,827	67,897	0.24783	0.24573	16,684	143	−2.5	442.6	16,099	17,270	---
18	1993	7	4th	12	20,360	67,897	0.29987	0.30084	20,426	−66	−1.5	442.0	19,841	21,011	---
19	1994	8	1st	13	17,686	80,526	0.21963	0.21332	17,178	508	−0.5	441.7	16,593	17,762	---
20	1994	8	2nd	14	19,942	80,526	0.24765	0.24006	19,331	611	0.5	441.7	18,747	19,915	YES
21	1994	8	3rd	15	20,418	80,526	0.25356	0.24573	19,788	630	1.5	442.0	19,203	20,372	YES
22	1994	8	4th	16	24,448	80,526	0.30360	0.30084	24,226	222	2.5	442.6	23,640	24,811	---
23	1995	9	1st	17	20,440	93,259	0.21917	0.21332	19,894	546	3.5	443.4	19,307	20,481	---
24	1995	9	2nd	18	22,723	93,259	0.24365	0.24006	22,388	335	4.5	444.6	21,799	22,976	---
25	1995	9	3rd	19	22,913	93,259	0.24569	0.24573	22,917	−4	5.5	446.0	22,326	23,507	---
26	1995	9	4th	20	27,551	93,259	0.29542	0.30084	28,056	−505	6.5	447.8	27,464	28,649	---
27	1996	10	1st	21	22,772	105,731	0.21538	0.21332	22,555	217	7.5	449.8	21,960	23,150	---
28	1996	10	2nd	22	25,587	105,731	0.24200	0.24006	25,382	205	8.5	452.0	24,784	25,980	---
29	1996	10	3rd	23	25,644	105,731	0.24254	0.24573	25,981	−337	9.5	454.6	25,380	26,583	---
30	1996	10	4th	24	30,856	105,731	0.29183	0.30084	31,809	−953	10.5	457.4	31,203	32,414	YES
31	1997	11	1st	25	25,409	117,577	0.21611	0.21332	25,081	328	11.5	460.5	24,472	25,691	---
32	1997	11	2nd	26	28,386	117,577	0.24143	0.24006	28,225	161	12.5	463.8	27,612	28,839	---
33	1997	11	3rd	27		117,577		0.24573	28,892		13.5	467.4	28,274	29,511	
34	1997	11	4th	28		117,577		0.30084	35,372		14.5	471.2	34,749	35,996	
35	1998	12	1st	29		128,429		0.21332	27,397		15.5	475.3	26,768	28,025	
36	1998	12	2nd	30		128,429		0.24006	30,831		16.5	479.6	30,196	31,465	
37	1998	12	3rd	31		128,429		0.24573	31,559		17.5	484.2	30,918	32,199	
38	1998	12	4th	32		128,429		0.30084	38,637		18.5	488.9	37,990	39,284	
39	1999	13	1st	33		137,924		0.21332	29,422		19.5	493.9	28,768	30,075	
40	1999	13	2nd	34		137,924		0.24006	33,110		20.5	499.0	32,449	33,770	
41	1999	13	3rd	35		137,924		0.24573	33,892		21.5	504.4	33,225	34,559	
42	1999	13	4th	36		137,924		0.30084	41,493		22.5	510.0	40,819	42,168	
43								Average Error, $ million		24.573		Student's t value		1.323	
44								Sum of Squares of Errors		3,944,687		Sum of qrtrly fcsts for 1997		117,571	
45							Model's Standard Error of Estimate, $ million			433.41			1998	128,423	
46							Model's Coefficient of Correlation			0.997903			1999	137,917	
47					Sum of Average Seasonal Ratios			0.99995							

Key Cell Entries

F7: ='Figure 3.25'!$G$23+'Figure 3.25'!$F$23*'Figure 5.1'!B7+'Figure 3.25'!$E$23*'Figure 5.1'!B7^2+
    'Figure 3.25'!$D$23*'Figure 5.1'!B7^3, copy to F8:F42. (This entry uses the cubic model for annual values from Chapter 3.)

G7: =E7/F7, copy to G8:G32

H7: =AVERAGE(G7,G11,G15,G19,G23,G27,G31), copy to H10

H11: =H7, copy to H12:H42

I7: =F7*H7, copy to I8:I42

J7: =E7-I7, copy to J8:32

K7: =D7-AVERAGE($D$7:$D$32), copy to K8:K42

L7: =$J$45*SQRT(1+1/$D$32+K7^2/SUMSQ($K$7:$K$32)), copy to L8:L42

M7: =I7-$N$43*L7, copy to M8:M42

N7: =I7+$N$43*L7, copy to N8:N42

O7: =IF(OR(E7<M7,E7>N7), "YES","---"), copy to O8:O32

J43: =AVERAGE(J7:J32)

J44: =SUMSQ(J7:J32)

J45: =SQRT(J44/(26-5))

J46: =CORREL(E7:E32,I7:I32)

H47: =SUM(H7:H10)

N43: =TINV(0.2,26-5)

N44: =SUM(I31:I34)

N45: =SUM(I35:I38)

N46: =SUM(I39:I42)

The parameters for the model of annual sales are in Cells D23:G23 of Figure 3-25. We use these values for making the entry in Cell F7 of Figure 6-1. Although the cell entry shown at the bottom of Figure 6-1 can be typed in, it is easier to make the entry by moving back and forth between the worksheets for Figure 3-25 and Figure 6-1. (The following assumes that both worksheets are in the same file or, if they are in different files, both files are open.) To do this, proceed by the following steps:

- Start by clicking on Cell F7 of Figure 6-1 and entering the = sign.
- Click on the sheet tab for Figure 3-25 and click on Cell G23. Press the F4 key to place the $ signs on Cell G23 so that it becomes $G$23. Then enter the + sign.
- Click on Cell F23 on Figure 3-25. Press the F4 key to place the $ signs on Cell F23 so that it becomes $F$23. Then enter the * sign for multiplication, click on Cell B7 on Figure 6-1, and enter the + sign
- Click on Cell E23 on Figure 3-25. Press the F4 key to place the $ signs on Cell E23 so that it becomes $E$23. Then enter the * sign for multiplication, click on Cell B7 on Figure 6-1, enter the ^ sign for exponentiation, enter 2, and enter the + sign.
- Click on Cell D23 on Figure 3-25. Press the F4 key to place the $ signs on Cell D23 so that it becomes $D$23. Then enter the * sign for multiplication, click on Cell B7 on Figure 6-1, enter the ^ sign for exponentiation, and enter 3.
- Press Enter to enter the formula in Cell F7 of Figure 6-1.

Once you have correctly entered the formula in Cell F7 to forecast annual sales for the year in Cell B7, copy the formula to Cells F8:F42 to forecast annual sales for all of the years on the spreadsheet.

Note that the values for XYR in Column 2 of Figure 6-1 begin with XYR = 5 for 1991, corresponding to the numbering system we used before on Figure 3-20 for the annual sales model. (Because we lacked quarterly sales values for earlier years when this analysis was made, we based the seasonal corrections for the forecasting model only on the quarterly sales from the first quarter of 1991 to the second quarter of 1997, which was the last quarter for which data were available. The parameters of the portion of the model for the annual trend, however, are based on the annual sales from 1986 to 1996.)

Seasonal Corrections

The quarterly SSIs are evaluated in two steps: (1) The ratios of **actual quarterly** sales to **forecast annual** sales in the same year are calculated in Cells G7:G32, and (2) the SSIs for specific quarters are calculated as the averages of the ratios for all quarters of the same type in Cells H7:H32.

For the first step, the entry in Cell G7 is =E7/F7, which is copied to G8:G32. For the second step, the entry in Cell H7 is =AVERAGE(G7,G11,G15,G19,G23,G27,G31), which computes the average of the seven ratios for the first quarters of the years 1991 to 1997. The entry in Cell H7 can be copied to the Range H8:H10 to compute the average ratios (or SSIs) for the seven 2nd quarters and six 3rd and 4th quarters for 1991 to 1997. (Note that since there are no entries in Cells G33 and G34, those entries are ignored so that the averages in Cells H9 and H10 are calculated correctly.)

The four averages are used as the SSIs for discounting annual sales values for all years to their quarterly components. We have copied them in Figure 6-1 for the years 1992 to 1999 by entering =H7 in Cell H11 and copying the entry to the Range H12:H42. Note how the same quarterly SSIs are repeated for each year.

We have now completed the derivation of our model (which has yet to be validated before being accepted). It can be specified by the following equation and definitions of the variables:

$$Y_{Qtr} = (13{,}127.6 + 207.476X_{Year} + 1{,}514.66X^2_{Year} - 60.9373X^3_{Year}) \times SSI_{Qtr} \qquad (6.2)$$

where Y_{Qtr} = quarterly sales, $ million

X_{Year} = number of years since 1986 (i.e., X_{Year} = 0 for 1986, 1 for 1987, ..., 5 for 1991, etc.)

and SSI_{Qtr} = 0.21332 for 1st quarters, 0.24006 for 2nd quarters, 0.24573 for 3rd quarters, and 0.30084 for 4th quarters. That is, an average of 21.332 percent of the annual sales in any year is in the first quarter, 24.006 percent in the second quarter, 24.573 perceny in the third quarter, and 30.084 percent in the fourth quarter. (The value in Cell H47 shows that adding the ratios for the four quarters gives a total of 0.99995, or not quite exactly one.)

Using the Model to Calculate Quarterly Sales and Errors

To forecast quarterly sales from the first quarter of 1991 to the end of 1999, enter =F7*H7 in Cell I7 and copy the entry to I8:I42.

To calculate forecast errors, enter =E7-I7 in Cell J7 and copy it to J8:J32. To calculate the average error, enter =AVERAGE(J7:J32) in Cell J43. Note that the average error is $24.573 million rather than zero.

Refining the Model

Unlike the regression models discussed in Chapter 3, for which either the mean arithmetic error is automatically zero or the geometric mean error is automatically one (provided, of course, the calculations are done correctly), the mean error for the seasonal model is **not** automatically zero. Nor is the sum of the average ratios for the seasons automatically one, as shown by the result calculated in Cell H47 in Figure 6-1. The latter condition is necessary so that the sum of the sales for all four quarters of any year equals the annual sales for the same year.

In this section, we show how to refine the model so that (1) the sum of the SSIs for the four quarters equals one and (2) the average forecast error is zero. The results are shown in Figure 6-2.

Figure 6-2 is a copy of Figure 6-1 with three new columns inserted. One column is inserted between Columns H and I of Figure 6-1 to create the new Column I in Figure 6-2, and two columns are inserted between Columns J and K of Figure 6-1 to create the new Columns L and M in Figure 6-2. (Note that to fit Figure 6-2 on the page, Columns F and G have been hidden in Figure 6-2. These two columns are the same as Columns F and G in Figure 6-1.)

Figure 6-2

Seasonally Adjusted Model with Average Error Equal to Zero and the Sum of the Four Quarterly SSIs Equal to One

	A	B	C	D	E	H	I	J	K	L	M	N	O	P	Q	R
1									WAL-MART STORES, INC.							
2								Seasonally-Adjusted Cubic Annual Trend Line for Quarterly Sales (Based on Quarters 1 to 26)								
3					Actual	Prelim SSI,	Refined	Prelim.	Prelim.	Refined	Refined		Standard	Quarterly Sales		Actual
4					Quarterly	Avg. Ratio	SSI	Forecast	Forecast	Forecast	Forecast		Forecast	80% Confidence		Outside
5	Fiscal				Sales,	for Like	for Like	Sales,	Error,	Sales,	Error,		Error,	Range, $ million		Conf.
6	Year	XYR	Quarter	X	$ million	Quarters	Quarters	$ million	$ million	$ million	$ million	X-XM	$ million	Minimum	Maximum	Range?
7	1991	5	1st	1	9,280	0.21332	0.21333	9,475	−195	9,499	−219	−12.5	474.34	8,870	10,127	---
8	1991	5	2nd	2	10,340	0.24006	0.24007	10,663	−323	10,686	−346	−11.5	470.93	10,062	11,310	---
9	1991	5	3rd	3	10,627	0.24573	0.24574	10,914	−287	10,938	−311	−10.5	467.78	10,318	11,558	---
10	1991	5	4th	4	13,640	0.30084	0.30086	13,362	278	13,386	254	9.5	464.90	12,770	14,002	---
11	1992	6	1st	5	11,649	0.21332	0.21333	11,091	−242	11,914	−265	−8.5	462.29	11,302	12,527	---
12	1992	6	2nd	6	13,028	0.24006	0.24007	13,381	−353	13,405	−377	−7.5	459.96	12,795	14,014	---
13	1992	6	3rd	7	13,683	0.24573	0.24574	13,697	−14	13,721	−38	−6.5	457.91	13,114	14,328	---
14	1992	6	4th	8	17,124	0.30084	0.30086	16,769	355	16,793	331	−5.5	456.15	16,188	17,397	---
15	1993	7	1st	9	13,920	0.21332	0.21333	14,484	−564	14,508	−588	−4.5	454.67	13,906	15,111	---
16	1993	7	2nd	10	16,237	0.24006	0.24007	16,300	−63	16,324	−87	−3.5	453.49	15,723	16,925	---
17	1993	7	3rd	11	16,827	0.24573	0.24574	16,685	142	16,709	118	−2.5	452.60	16,109	17,309	---
18	1993	7	4th	12	20,360	0.30084	0.30086	20,427	−67	20,451	−91	−1.5	452.01	19,852	21,050	---
19	1994	8	1st	13	17,686	0.21332	0.21333	17,179	507	17,202	484	−0.5	451.71	16,604	17,801	---
20	1994	8	2nd	14	19,942	0.24006	0.24007	19,332	610	19,356	586	0.5	451.71	18,757	19,954	---
21	1994	8	3rd	15	20,418	0.24573	0.24574	19,789	629	19,812	606	1.5	452.01	19,213	20,411	YES
22	1994	8	4th	16	24,448	0.30084	0.30086	24,227	221	24,251	197	2.5	452.60	23,651	24,850	---
23	1995	9	1st	17	20,440	0.21332	0.21333	19,895	545	19,919	521	3.5	453.49	19,318	20,520	---
24	1995	9	2nd	18	22,723	0.24006	0.24007	22,389	334	22,412	311	4.5	454.67	21,810	23,015	---
25	1995	9	3rd	19	22,913	0.24573	0.24574	22,918	−5	22,941	−28	5.5	456.15	22,337	23,546	---
26	1995	9	4th	20	27,551	0.30084	0.30086	28,058	−507	28,081	−530	6.5	457.91	27,475	28,688	---
27	1996	10	1st	21	22,772	0.21332	0.21333	22,556	216	22,579	193	7.5	459.96	21,970	23,189	---
28	1996	10	2nd	22	25,587	0.24006	0.24007	25,383	204	25,407	180	8.5	462.29	24,794	26,019	---
29	1996	10	3rd	23	25,644	0.24573	0.24574	25,983	−339	26,006	−362	9.5	464.90	25,390	26,622	---
30	1996	10	4th	24	30,856	0.30084	0.30086	31,810	−954	31,834	−978	10.5	467.78	31,214	32,454	YES
31	1997	11	1st	25	25,409	0.21332	0.21333	25,083	326	25,106	303	11.5	470.93	24,482	25,730	---
32	1997	11	2nd	26	28,386	0.24006	0.24007	28,227	159	28,250	136	12.5	474.34	27,622	28,879	---
33	1997	11	3rd	27		0.24573	0.24574	28,893		28,917		13.5	478.01	28,284	29,551	
34	1997	11	4th	28		0.30084	0.30086	35,374		35,397		14.5	481.92	34,759	36,036	
35	1998	12	1st	29		0.21332	0.21333	27,398		27,422		15.5	486.09	26,777	28,066	
36	1998	12	2nd	30		0.24006	0.24007	30,832		30,856		16.5	490.49	30,206	31,506	
37	1998	12	3rd	31		0.24573	0.24574	31,560		31,584		17.5	495.12	30,928	32,240	
38	1998	12	4th	32		0.30084	0.30086	38,639		38,663		18.5	499.98	38,000	39,325	
39	1999	13	1st	33		0.21332	0.21333	29,423		29,447		19.5	505.06	28,778	30,116	
40	1999	13	2nd	34		0.24006	0.24007	33,111		33,135		20.5	510.35	32,459	33,811	
41	1999	13	3rd	35		0.24573	0.24574	33,894		33,917		21.5	515.85	33,234	34,601	
42	1999	13	4th	36		0.30084	0.30086	41,495		41,519		22.5	521.55	40,828	42,210	
43							Average Error, $ million	23.636		0.000			Student's t value	1.325		
44							Sum of Squares of Errors	3,943,577		3,929,053			Sum of qrtrly fcsts for 1997	117,671		
45						Model's Standard Error of Estimate, $ million		433.35		443.23			1998	128,524		
46						Model's Coefficient of Correlation		0.997903		0.997903			1999	138,018		
47			Sum of ratios and SSIs =			0.99995	1.00000									

(Note: Columns F and G have been hidden. They are the same as in Figure 6-1.)

Key Cell Entries Added or Changed for Editing a Copy of Figure 6-1 to Create Figure 6-2

I7: =H7/$H$47, copy to I8:I42

I47: =SUM(I7:I10)

J7: =F7*I7, copy to J8:J42 (Column F contains forecast annual sales. See Figure 6-1.)

L7: =J7+$K$43, copy to L8:L42 (This entry adds the average error in Cell K43 to each of the preliminary forecasts in Cells J7:J42)

M7: =E7-L7, copy to M8:M32

M43: =AVERAGE(M7:M32)

M44: =SUMSQ(M7:M32)

M45: =SQRT(M44/(26-6))

M46: =CORREL(E7:E32,L7:L32)

O7: =$M$45*SQRT(1+1/26+N7^2/SUMSQ($N$7:$N$32)), copy to O8:O42

P7: =L7-$Q$43*O7, copy to P8:P42

Q7: =L7+$Q$43*O7, copy to Q8:Q42

Q43: =TINV(0.20,(26-6))

Q44: =SUM(L31:L34)

Q45: =SUM(L35:L38)

Q46: =SUM(L39:L42)

Refining the SSIs

To refine the SSIs so that their sum is exactly one, enter =H7/$H$47 in Cell I7 and copy to I8:I42. The sum of the adjusted SSIs is calculated by entering =SUM(I7:I10) in Cell I47. Because the sum 0.99995 in Cell H47 is close to one to begin with, the refined values of the SSIs are very close to their preliminary values. In fact, the differences between the preliminary and refined SSI values in Columns H and I is only 1 or 2 in the fifth decimal place (i.e., a difference of less than 0.01%).

Using the Refined SSIs to Make Preliminary Forecasts

The preliminary forecasts in Column J are made by changing the entry in Cell J7 to =F7*I7 and copying to the Range J8:J42.

Calculating Errors of the Preliminary Forecasts

The errors should be automatically updated by the entries made in Column K back in Figure 6-1. Unlike the regression models in Chapter 3, the average error for the seasonally-adjusted model is not automatically zero (Cell K43).

Making the Average Error Equal to Zero

To make the average error exactly equal to zero, refine the preliminary values of the forecasts in Column J of Figure 6-2 by adding back the average error in Cell K43. Thus, the forecasts in the Column L of Figure 6-2 have been made by entering =J7+$K$43 in Cell L7 and copying it to L8:L42.

The Refined Model

The equation for the refined model is derived by adding the average error of 23.636 in Cell K43 to Equation 5.2. Thus,

$$Y_{Qtr} = (13{,}127.6 + 207.476X_{Year} + 1{,}514.66X^2_{Year} - 60.9373X^3_{Year}) \times SSI_{Qtr} + 23.636 \qquad (6.3)$$

where the variables are as defined for equation 6.2 and the values for the seasonal adjustments are 0.21333 for 1st quarters, 0.24007 for 2nd quarters, 0.24574 for 3rd quarters, and 0.30086 for 4th quarters.

　　Note that there are six parameters in this model whose values have been estimated: four for the portion that projects annual values, one for changing the annual values to quarterly values, and one for adjusting the seasonal values so that the average error is zero.

Errors and Average Error

To calculate the errors, enter =E7-L7 in Cell M7 and copy it to M8:M32. To calculate the average error, enter =AVERAGE(M7:M32) in Cell M43. Note that the average error has now been forced to equal zero exactly.

　　Note that in calculating the standard forecast errors in Cells K45 and M45, the number of degrees of freedom lost changes from 5 in Cell J45 (one for each of the four parameters of the cubic regression equation for annual sales plus one for the set of SSIs) to 6 in Cell M45 (one additional degree of freedom lost for the average error feedback).

Validating the Refined Model

Figure 6-3 shows the error pattern for the refined model. (To match quarters on the horizontal axis, the major increments are 4 and the minor ones are 1.) Note that the errors scatter fairly randomly over most of the range. However, there is a run of six positive values from quarters 13 to 18 (i.e., the first quarter of 1994 to the second quarter of 1995), which was the period when Wal-Mart was introducing a new expansion strategy.

Figure 6-3

Error Pattern for the Refined Model

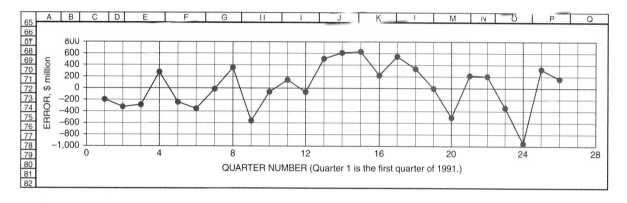

Determining the Model's Accuracy

The model's standard error of estimate is calculated by the entry =SQRT(M44/(26-6)) in Cell M45. The number of degrees of freedom in the denominator is calculated as the difference between the number of pairs of data values (26) and the degrees of freedom lost by estimating values for the model's parameters (6). (That is, the degrees of freedom lost is the sum of the four parameters in the annual trend model plus one parameter to adjust an annual value to a quarterly value and one parameter to make the average error equal zero.)

Note that although the sum of the squares of the errors is less in Cell M44 than in Cell K44, the value for the refined model's standard error of estimate ($443.23 million, Cell M45) is slightly more than that for the preliminary model ($433.35 million, Cell K45). This is because the number of degrees of freedom in the denominator of the expression for calculating the model's standard error of estimate is less in Cell M45 than in Cell K45.

Model's Coefficient of Correlation

The refined model's coefficient of correlation, 0.997903, is calculated in Cell M46 by the entry =CORREL(E7:E32,L7:L32). The value is the same (to six decimal places) as for the trial model.

Standard Forecast Errors

Standard forecast errors are calculated by copying the entry =$M$45*SQRT(1+1/26+N7^2/ SUMSQ($N$7:$N$32)) in Cell O7 to the Range O8:O42.

Note that the standard forecast error is a minimum ($451.71 million) at quarters 13 and 14 (i.e., the quarters next to the midpoint) and splays out symmetrically, like a "dog bone," on both sides of the midpoint. As a check on the reasonableness of the values for the standard forecast errors, note that the minimum is only slightly (i.e., less than 1 percent) larger than the model's standard error of estimate ($443.23 million, Cell M45). If the minimum standard forecast error was negative or substantially larger than the model's standard error of estimate, an error has likely been made that should be corrected.

Confidence Limits

The value for Student's t is calculated by the entry =TINV(0.20,(26-6)) in Cell Q43. The minimum or lower limits of the 80 percent confidence range are calculated by entering =L7-$Q$43*O7 in Cell P7 and copying it to the Range P8:P42. The maximum or upper limits are calculated by entering =L7+$Q$43*O7 in Cell Q7 and copying it to the Range Q8:Q42.

Comparison of Trial and Refined Models

Although the forecasts and confidence limits for quarters 27 to 36 with the refined model in Figure 6-2 are different from those for the trial model in Figure 6-1, the differences are relatively small (less than 0.2 percent) compared to the values being forecast. Therefore, even though the trial model's average error is not exactly zero and it fails to satisfy the strict requirement for a valid model, the trial model nevertheless provides useful estimates of future quarterly sales and confidence limits.

One might reasonably argue that the refinements have not made the results more useful, in a practical sense, and that making the refinements is an unnecessary exercise. On the other hand, making the refinements and providing a valid model is not difficult with spreadsheets.

Centered-Moving-Average Trend Model with Multiplicative Corrections

The general equation for a seasonally-adjusted forecasting model based on multiplicative seasonal corrections to a centered-moving-average (CMA) that follows a linear trend is

$$Y_{Period} = (a + bX_{Period}) \times SSI_{Period} \tag{6.4}$$

where Y_{Period} = period value (e.g., the value for a specific month or quarter)

a = intercept of the **centered-moving-average** trend line

b = slope of the **centered-moving-average** trend line

X_{Period} = number of periods (e.g., months or quarters) from a specified base period

and SSI_{Period} = a set of seasonal corrections, called "specific seasonal indices," one for each period in the year

Figure 6-4 illustrates the development of a seasonally-adjusted forecasting model based on multiplicative seasonal corrections to a linear model of the centered-moving-average trend line. (If the CMA trend line is curved, a curvilinear model is used for the trend line rather than a linear model.)

Figure 6-4

Linear Centered-Moving-Average Model with Multiplicative Quarterly SSIs

	A	B	C	D	E	F	G	H	I	J	K	L	M	N	O	P
1								WAL-MART STORES, INC.								
2							Seasonally-Adjusted Centered-Moving-Average Model (Linear CMA Model, Based on Quarters 1 to 26)									
3					Actual			Ratio,		Forecast			Standard	Quarterly Sales		Actual
4					Quarterly	Centered Moving		Sales to		Quarterly	Forecast		Forecast	80% Confidence		Outside
5	Fiscal				Sales,	Average, $ million		Projected		Sales,	Error,		Error,	Range, $ million		Conf.
6	Year	XYR	Qrtr.	X	$ mill.	Calculated	Projected	CMA	SSI	$ mill.	$ mill.	X-XM	$ million	Minimum	Maximum	Range?
7	1991	5	1st	1	9,280		9,610	0.96569	0.91704	8,813	467	−12.5	340.9	8,363	9,262	YES
8	1991	5	2nd	2	10,340		10,389	0.99528	0.98596	10,243	97	−11.5	338.5	9,797	10,690	---
9	1991	5	3rd	3	10,627	11,268	11,168	0.95153	0.96653	10,794	−167	−10.5	336.2	10,351	11,238	---
10	1991	5	4th	4	13,640	11,900	11,948	1.14165	1.13250	13,531	109	−9.5	334.1	13,090	13,972	---
11	1992	6	1st	5	11,649	12,618	12,727	0.91530	0.91704	11,671	−22	−8.5	332.3	11,233	12,110	---
12	1992	6	2nd	6	13,028	13,436	13,506	0.96459	0.98596	13,317	−289	−7.5	330.6	12,880	13,753	---
13	1992	6	3rd	7	13,603	14,155	14,286	0.95782	0.96653	13,807	−124	−6.5	329.1	13,373	14,242	---
14	1992	6	4th	8	17,124	14,840	15,065	1.13669	1.13250	17,061	63	−5.5	327.8	16,628	17,493	---
15	1993	7	1st	9	13,920	15,634	15,844	0.87856	0.91704	14,530	−610	−4.5	326.8	14,099	14,961	YES
16	1993	7	2nd	10	16,237	16,432	16,623	0.97675	0.98596	16,390	−153	−3.5	325.9	15,960	16,820	---
17	1993	7	3rd	11	16,827	17,307	17,403	0.96692	0.96653	16,820	7	−2.5	325.3	16,391	17,249	---
18	1993	7	4th	12	20,360	18,241	18,182	1.11978	1.13250	20,591	−231	−1.5	324.9	20,163	21,020	---
19	1994	8	1st	13	17,686	19,153	18,961	0.93274	0.91704	17,388	298	−0.5	324.6	16,960	17,817	---
20	1994	8	2nd	14	19,942	20,113	19,741	1.01020	0.98596	19,463	479	0.5	324.6	19,035	19,892	YES
21	1994	8	3rd	15	20,418	20,968	20,520	0.99503	0.96653	19,833	585	1.5	324.9	19,404	20,262	YES
22	1994	8	4th	16	24,448	21,660	21,299	1.14783	1.13250	24,121	327	2.5	325.3	23,692	24,551	---
23	1995	9	1st	17	20,440	22,319	22,079	0.92578	0.91704	20,247	193	3.5	325.9	19,817	20,677	---
24	1995	9	2nd	18	22,723	23,019	22,858	0.99410	0.98596	22,537	186	4.5	326.8	22,106	22,968	---
25	1995	9	3rd	19	22,913	23,698	23,637	0.96936	0.96653	22,846	67	5.5	327.8	22,413	23,279	---
26	1995	9	4th	20	27,551	24,348	24,416	1.12838	1.13250	27,652	−101	6.5	329.1	27,217	28,086	---
27	1996	10	1st	21	22,772	25,047	25,196	0.90380	0.91704	23,106	−334	7.5	330.6	22,669	23,542	---
28	1996	10	2nd	22	25,587	25,802	25,975	0.98506	0.98596	25,610	−23	8.5	332.3	25,172	26,049	---
29	1996	10	3rd	23	25,644	26,544	26,754	0.95850	0.96653	25,859	−215	9.5	334.1	25,418	26,300	---
30	1996	10	4th	24	30,856	27,224	27,534	1.12066	1.13250	31,182	−326	10.5	336.2	30,738	31,625	---
31	1997	11	1st	25	25,409		28,313	0.89743	0.91704	25,964	−555	11.5	338.5	25,518	26,411	YES
32	1997	11	2nd	26	28,386		29,092	0.97572	0.98596	28,684	−298	12.5	340.9	28,234	29,134	---
33	1997	11	3rd	27			29,872		0.96653	28,872		13.5	343.5	28,418	29,325	
34	1997	11	4th	28			30,651		1.13250	34,712		14.5	346.4	34,255	35,169	
35	1998	12	1st	29			31,430		0.91704	28,823		15.5	349.4	28,362	29,284	
36	1998	12	2nd	30			32,210		0.98596	31,757		16.5	352.5	31,292	32,222	
37	1998	12	3rd	31			32,989		0.96653	31,885		17.5	355.8	31,415	32,354	
38	1998	12	4th	32			33,768		1.13250	38,242		18.5	359.3	37,768	38,717	
39	1999	13	1st	33			34,547		0.91704	31,682		19.5	363.0	31,203	32,160	
40	1999	13	2nd	34			35,327		0.98596	34,831		20.5	366.8	34,347	35,315	
41	1999	13	3rd	35			36,106		0.96653	34,897		21.5	370.7	34,408	35,387	
42	1999	13	4th	36			36,885		1.13250	41,773		22.5	374.8	41,278	42,267	
43			Parameters for					Average Error, $ million			−21.95			Student's t value	1.319	
44			Linear CMA Model					Sum of Squares of Errors			2,333,911					
45			Intercept		8830.4178			Model's Std. Err. of Est., $ million			318.55					
46			Slope		779.30407			Model's Coefficient of Correlation			0.9988					

Key Cell Entries

E45: =INTERCEPT(F9:F30,D9:D30)

E46: =SLOPE(F9:F30,D9:D30)

F9: =(AVERAGE(E7:E10)+AVERAGE(E8:E11))/2, copy to F10:F30

G7: =$E$45+$E$46*D7, copy to G8:G42

H7: =E7/G7, copy to H8:H32

I7: =AVERAGE(H7,H11,H15,H19,H23,H27,H31), copy to I8:I10

I11: =I7, copy to I12:I42

J7: =G7*I7, copy to J8:J42

K7: =E7-J7, copy to K8:K32

K43: =AVERAGE(K7:K32)

K44: =SUMSQ(K7:K32)

K45: =SQRT(K44/(26-3))

K46: =CORREL(J7:J32,E7:E32)

The Deseasonalized Trend Line

Since a period in the model is one quarter and there are four quarters in the season of one full year, we use a 4-quarter moving average for the deseasonalized trend line. Regardless of whether we start with the first or any other quarter, the average of four successive quarters will always be based on values from a 1st, 2nd, 3rd, and 4th quarter. The quarters may be in two different years, but there will always be exactly one of each type. It is convenient and makes the results easier to understand, although not mathematically essential, to center the values on the trend line so that they are opposite data values in time.

If we take the average of the first four quarters of data, the result is centered in time midway between the 2nd and 3rd quarters. Similarly, if we take the average of data values for quarters 2, 3, 4, and 5, the result is centered midway between the 3rd and 4th quarters. To get an average that is centered opposite the data for the 3rd quarter, we take the average of the averages for quarters 1, 2, 3, and 4 and quarters 2, 3, 4, and 5. Thus, to get a moving average that is centered opposite the data value for quarter 3, we enter in cell F9 of the spreadsheet =(AVERAGE(E7:E10)+AVERAGE(E8:E11))/2. This entry is copied to the range F10:F30. The result is a sequence of 4-quarter centered-moving-averages (CMAs) from quarters 3 to 24. Note that we cannot compute moving averages from the data for either the first two or the last two quarters of the data range.

To help select a model for the centered-moving-averages, we have plotted a scatter diagram in Figure 6-5 and inserted a linear trend line, along with the trend line's equation and coefficient of determination, which is 0.9982.

The intercept and slope of the CMA trend line are evaluated in cells E45 and E46 of Figure 6-4 by the entries =INTERCEPT(F9:F30,D9:D30) and =SLOPE(F9:F30,D9:D30). This gives an intercept of $8830.42 million and a slope of $779.304 million per quarter. These agree within the round-off of the values in Figure 6-5.

Projecting the Centered-Moving-Average Trend Line

The intercept and slope are used to project the CMA trend line from quarters 1 to 36 by entering =$E$45+$E$46*D7 in G7 and copying it to G8:G42.

The Seasonal Corrections

The SSIs represent the ratios of the quarterly data values to the corresponding values of the **projected CMA**. (In the preceding *annual* trend model, they were the ratios of quarterly data values to the corresponding *annual* values.)

The ratios in Column H are calculated by entering =E7/G7 in Cell H7 and copying to H8:H32. The SSIs in Column I are calculated by entering =AVERAGE(H7,H11,H15,H19,H23,H27,H31) in Cell I7 and copying to I8:I10, followed by entering =I7 in Cell I11 and copying to I12:I42.

We have now completed the derivation of our model. It can be expressed by the equation

$$Y_{Qtr} = (8{,}830.4 + 779.3X_{Qtr}) \times SSI_{Qtr} \tag{6.5}$$

Figure 6-5

Scatter Plot for Centered-Moving-Averages with Linear Trend Line Inserted

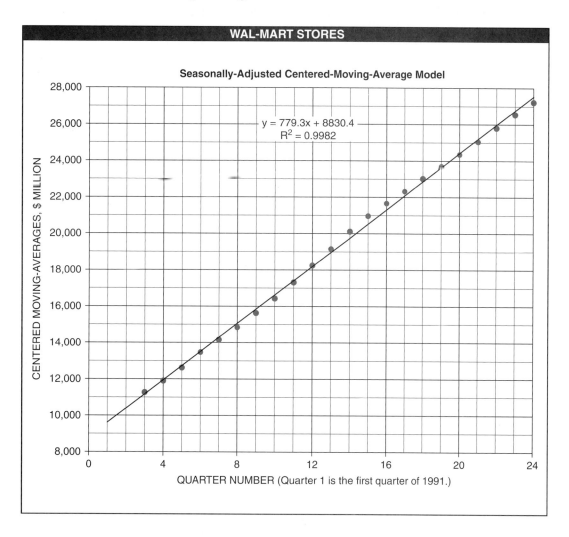

where Y_{Qtr} = quarterly sales, \$ million

X_{Qtr} = number of quarters since the last quarter of 1990 (i.e., X_{Qtr} = 1 for the 1st quarter of 1992, X_{Qtr} = 2 for the 2nd quarter of 1992,…,X_{Qtr} = 36 for the 4th quarter of 2000)

SSI_{Qtr} = 0.91704 for 1st quarters, 0.98596 for 2nd quarters, 0.96653 for 3rd quarters, and 1.13250 for 4th quarters.

Using the Model to Forecast

Forecasts of quarterly sales are made by entering =G7*I7 in Cell J7 and copying it to J8:J42.

Validating the Model

Errors are calculated by entering =E7-J7 in Cell K7 and copying it to the range K8:K32. Figure 6-6 is a plot of the error pattern. There is rather persistent downward trend of the errors beyond quarter 15. Because the errors do not scatter randomly, we reject the model as not valid.

The behavior of the errors in Figure 6-6 matches the deviations of the data points above and below the linear trend line in Figure 6-5. As in Chapter 3, we conclude from the data that something has been changing at Wal-Mart Stores during the last few years from what had been happening earlier. (Refer to the discussions in Chapters 3 for the problems Wal-Mart was facing in those years that might explain the behavior.)

Revising the Model

Several attempts were made without success to obtain a random error pattern over the range of data from the first quarter of 1991 to the second quarter of 1997. These attempts included using quadratic and cubic regression models instead of a linear regression model for the CMA trend line.

Because the problems arose after quarter 16, we decided to base a model on only the more recent values—that is, on values for only quarters 17 to 26. Figure 6-7 shows the results. To prepare this worksheet, copy Figure 6-4 to a new worksheet. Save the values for the calculated centered

Figure 6-6
___

Error Pattern for Linear Model of Centered-Moving-Averages with Quarterly Corrections

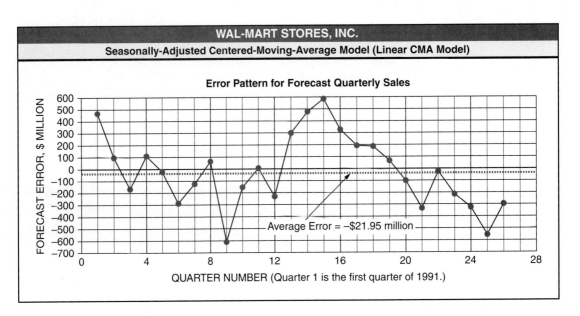

(The line for the average error has been inserted with the drawing toolbar.)

Figure 6-7

Results for Seasonally-Adjusted Centered-Moving-Average Model with a Linear Model for the Centered-Moving-Average Trend Line Based on Quarters 17 to 26

	A	B	C	D	E	F	G	H	I	J	K	L	M	N	O	P
1								WAL-MART STORES, INC.								
2					Seasonally-Adjusted Centered-Moving-Average Model (Linear CMA Model Based on Quarters 17 to 26 Only)											
3					Actual			Ratio,		Fcst.			Std.	Quarterly Sales		Actual
4					Qrtrly	Centered Moving		Sales to	Avg.	Qrtrly	Fcst.		Fcst.	80% Confidence		Outside
5	Fiscal				Sales,	Average, $ million		Proj.	Ratio,	Sales,	Error,		Error,	Range, $ mill.		Conf.
6	Year	XYR	Qrtr.	X	$ mill.	Calculated	Projected	CMA	SSI	$ mill.	$ mill.	X-XM	$ mill.	Min	Max	Range?
7	1995	9	1st	17	20,440	22,319	22,293	0.9169	0.9115	20,320	120	-4.5	88.6	20,195	20,445	NO
8	1995	9	2nd	18	22,723	23,019	22,995	0.9882	0.9906	22,780	-57	-3.5	85.3	22,659	22,901	NO
9	1995	9	3rd	19	22,913	23,698	23,697	0.9669	0.9672	22,920	-7	-2.5	82.8	22,803	23,037	NO
10	1995	9	4th	20	27,551	24,348	24,399	1.1292	1.1316	27,611	60	-1.5	81.1	27,496	27,726	NO
11	1996	10	1st	21	22,772	25,047	25,101	0.9072	0.9115	22,880	-108	-0.5	80.2	22,766	22,993	NO
12	1996	10	2nd	22	25,587	25,802	25,803	0.9916	0.9906	25,562	25	0.5	80.2	25,448	25,675	NO
13	1996	10	3rd	23	25,644	26,544	26,505	0.9675	0.9672	25,636	8	1.5	81.1	25,521	25,751	NO
14	1996	10	4th	24	30,856	27,224	27,207	1.1341	1.1316	30,789	67	2.5	82.8	30,672	30,906	NO
15	1997	11	1st	25	25,409		27,909	0.9104	0.9115	25,439	-30	3.5	85.3	25,319	25,560	NO
16	1997	11	2nd	26	28,386		28,611	0.9921	0.9906	28,343	43	4.5	88.6	28,218	28,469	NO
17	1997	11	3rd	27			29,313		0.9672	28,352		5.5	92.5	28,221	28,483	na
18	1997	11	4th	28			30,015		1.1316	33,967		6.5	96.9	33,830	34,104	na
19	1998	12	1st	29			30,717		0.9115	27,999		7.5	101.9	27,855	28,143	na
20	1998	12	2nd	30			31,419		0.9906	31,125		8.5	107.3	30,973	31,277	na
21	1998	12	3rd	31			32,121		0.9672	31,068		9.5	113.1	30,908	31,228	na
22	1998	12	4th	32			32,823		1.1316	37,144		10.5	119.2	36,976	37,313	na
23	1999	13	1st	33			33,525		0.9115	30,558		11.5	125.5	30,381	30,736	na
24	1999	13	2nd	34			34,227		0.9906	33,907		12.5	132.1	33,720	34,094	na
25	1999	13	3rd	35			34,930		0.9672	33,784		13.5	138.9	33,588	33,981	na
26	1999	13	4th	36			35,632		1.1316	40,322		14.5	145.8	40,116	40,529	na
27			Parameters for					Average Error, $ million			0.072		Student's t value		1.4149	
28			Linear CMA Model					Sum of Squares of Errors			40,802		Sum of qrtrly fcsts for 1997			116,102
29			Intercept	10,358.58				Model's Std. Err. of Est., $ million			76.35				1998	127,337
30			Slope	702.027				Model's Coefficient of Correlation			0.99977				1999	138,572

moving averages for quarters 17 and 18. (Use Copy/Edit/Paste Special/Values.) Then delete the rows for 1991 to 1994.

We chose a linear model for the trend line represented by the 4-quarter centered-moving-averages. The equation for the complete model, with multiplicative corrections to the trend line, is:

$$Y_{Qtr} = (10{,}358.58 + 702.027X_{Qtr}) \times SSI_{Qtr} \qquad (6.6)$$

where the variables have the same definitions as for equation 6.6 and the values for the SSIs for the 1st, 2nd, 3rd, and 4th quarters are 0.9115, 0.9906, 0.9672, and 1.1316, respectively.

A major change in equation 6.6 from that for the earlier model (equation 6.5) is that the value of the intercept for the projected CMA trend line is higher and the slope is less. The smaller slope means that the dollar value of Wal-Mart's sales has not increased from quarter to quarter as rapidly in recent years as in earlier years (i.e., before 1995).

Validating the Revised Model

The errors are calculated in the same manner as before and plotted in Figure 6-8.

Figure 6-8

Error Pattern for Seasonally-Adjusted Centered-Moving-Average Model with Linear Model for Centered-Moving-Average Trend Line Based on Quarters 17 to 26 Only

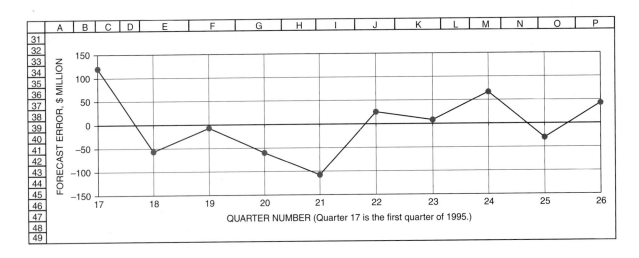

The average error for this model is $0.072 million (Cell K27). The error could be driven to zero by the same technique used earlier—that is, by adding the error to the model expressed by equation 6.6. However, because the average error is so small, the results would not change significantly. For all practical purposes, the average error of $0.072 million can be regarded as essentially zero.

The error pattern shown in Figure 6-8 appears random. We conclude that the revised model is a valid representation of the quarterly sales from the first quarter of 1995 to the second quarter of 1997.

Figure 6-9 provides a comparison of the data and forecast values for Wal-Mart's quarterly sales and the revised model (i.e., the centered-moving-average trend line based on data for quarters 17 to 26).

Determining the Model's Accuracy

The sum of the squares of the errors in cell K28 of Figure 6-7 is calculated by the entry =SUMSQ(K7:K16). The model's standard error of estimate in cell K29 is calculated by the entry =SQRT(K28/(10-3)), where 10 is the number of quarterly data values and 3 is the number of parameters in the model for forecasting a quarterly value. Results show that the model's standard error of estimate is $76.35 million.

Standard Forecast Errors

The standard forecast errors are computed by two steps. The first step is to compute the values in Column L, which express the number of quarters a period is from the midpoint of the data values used to derive the model represented by equation 6.6. For the 10 quarters of data used to derive the model, the midpoint of the data is midway between quarters 21 and 22—at quarter "21.5." The distances "X - XM" in Column L are calculated by entering =D7-AVERAGE($D$7:$D$16) in Cell L7 and copying it to the Range L8:L26.

Figure 6-9
___

Comparison of Data Values, Forecast Values, and Centered-Moving-Average Trend Line

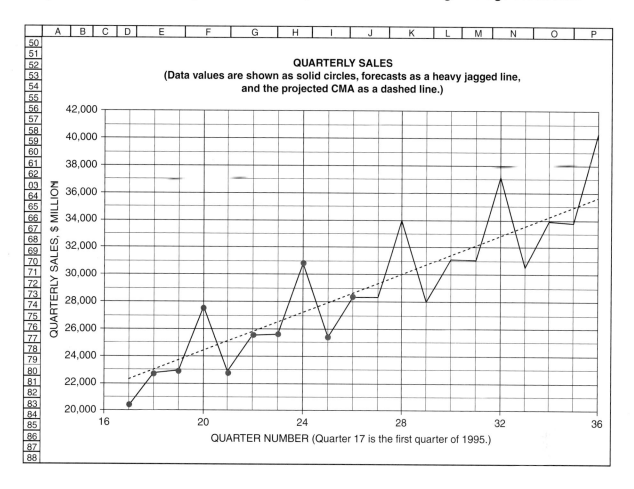

To calculate the standard forecast errors, enter =$K$29*SQRT(1+1/10 +L7^2/SUMSQ($L$7:$L$16)) in Cell M7 and copy it to the Range M8:M26. Note that there are only 10 data values in this formula. The standard forecast error is a minimum for quarters 21 and 22 (i.e., the quarters next to the midpoint) and splays out like a dog bone on both sides of the midpoint. Note also that the minimum standard forecast error ($80.2 million, Cells M11 and M12) is slightly larger (about 6 percent) than the model's standard error of estimate ($76.35 million, Cell K29), which is reasonable.

Confidence Limits

For the range in which there is an 80 percent probability that a future value will lie, we first need to determine the value of Student's *t*. This is done by the entry =TINV(0.20,10-3) in Cell O27, where 10 is the number of sets of data values used to derive the model and three is the number of degrees of freedom lost by estimating the two parameters of the linear model for the centered-moving-average trend line and one quarterly correction for a forecast value.

The minimum or lower limits of the 80 percent confidence range are calculated by entering =J7-$O$27*M7 in Cell N7 and copying it to the Range N8:N26. The maximum or upper limits are calculated by entering =J7+$O$27*M7 in Cell O7 and copying it to the Range O8:O26.

Monitoring the Forecasting Process

To monitor how well the forecasting model has performed and will perform in the future, enter =IF(E7=0,"na",IF(E7<N7, "Lower",IF(E7>O7, "Upper","NO"))) in Cell P7 and copy the entry to the Range P8:P26. As future values for the actual quarterly cells are added for the third quarter of 1998 and later, the entries in P17:P26 will alert the user whenever an actual value falls outside the confidence limits, and, if so, which limit. If this happens, the user should be aware that there is a high probability that the future is no longer following the past behavior and the forecasting model needs correcting.

Comparing the Models and Making a Selection

Figure 6-10 compares results for the two models—that is, for the seasonally-adjusted annual trend line model expressed by equation 6.3 (Figure 6-2) and the seasonally-adjusted centered-moving-average trend line expressed by equation 6.6 (Figure 6-7). Figure 6-10 also gives average values for the two models, which might be accepted as a reasonable compromise for forecasting the future.

Figure 6-10

Comparisons of the Forecasts from the Third Quarter of 1997 to the Fourth Quarter of 1999 for the Two Seasonally-Adjusted Models

	A	B	C	D	E	F	G	H	I	J	K	L
1	WAL-MART STORES, INC.											
2				Forecast Quarterly Sales, $ million			Minimum 80% Confidence Level, $ million			Maximum 80% Confidence Level, $ million		
3				Cubic	Linear		Cubic	Linear		Cubic	Linear	
4				Annual	CMA		Annual	CMA		Annual	CMA	
5	Fiscal			Model	Model		Model	Model		Model	Model	
6	Year	Qrtr.	X	(Eq. 5.3)	(Eq. 5.6)	Average	(Eq. 5.3)	(Eq. 5.6)	Average	(Eq. 5.3)	(Eq. 5.6)	Average
7	1997	3rd	27	28,917	28,352	28,635	28,284	28,221	28,252	29,551	28,483	29,017
8	1997	4th	28	35,397	33,967	34,682	34,759	33,830	34,294	36,036	34,104	35,070
9	1998	1st	29	27,422	27,999	27,710	26,777	27,855	27,316	28,066	28,143	28,104
10	1998	2nd	30	30,856	31,125	30,990	30,206	30,973	30,590	31,506	31,277	31,391
11	1998	3rd	31	31,584	31,068	31,326	30,928	30,908	30,918	32,240	31,228	31,734
12	1998	4th	32	38,663	37,144	37,904	38,000	36,976	37,488	39,325	37,313	38,319
13	1999	1st	33	29,447	30,558	30,003	28,778	30,381	29,579	30,116	30,736	30,426
14	1999	2nd	34	33,135	33,907	33,521	32,459	33,720	33,089	33,811	34,094	33,953
15	1999	3rd	35	33,917	33,784	33,851	33,234	33,588	33,411	34,601	33,981	34,291
16	1999	4th	36	41,519	40,322	40,921	40,828	40,116	40,472	42,210	40,529	41,369
17	Std. Error of Est.			443.23	76.35							
18	NB. Seasonally-Adjusted Cubic Annual Model is based on data for quarters 1 to 26.											
19	Seasonally-Adjusted Linear CMA Model is based on data for quarters 17 to 26 only.											

Case Study: Wal-Mart Stores, Inc. Revisited

As trends change, forecasting models need to be revised. Periodic values of sales (e.g., quarterly, monthly, or weekly) can provide early warnings of when revision is needed. This section demonstrates the techniques for recognizing the warnings and revising models. We will demonstrate the steps beginning with the cubic annual model with quarterly corrections developed in Figure 6-2, which was based on a cubic regression model for annual sales from 1986 to 1996 (Figure 3-25) and quarterly SSIs from the first quarter of 1991 to the second quarter of 1997.

Figure 6-11 is an updated version of Figure 6-2 with the addition of Wal-Mart's actual quarterly sales for the third and fourth quarters of 1997 and all four quarters of 1998 and 1999 in Column E. (The forecast annual sales and the refined SSIs are based on the model developed in Figure 6-2.)

Figure 6-11

Copy of Figure 6-2 with Additions of Sales Values for Quarters 27 to 36 and 95% Confidence Limits

	A	B	C	D	E	F	I	J	L	M	P	Q	R
1								WAL-MART STORES, INC.					
2							Seasonally-Adjusted Cubic Annual Trend Line for Quarterly Sales (Based on Quarters 1 to 26)						
3					Actual	Forecast	Refined	Prelim.	Refined	Refined	Quarterly Sales		Quarterly
4					Quarterly	Annual	SSI	Forecast	Forecast	Forecast	95% Confidence		Sales
5	Fiscal				Sales,	Sales,	for Like	Sales,	Sales,	Error,	Range, $ million		Outside
6	Year	XYR	Quarter	X	$ million	$ million	Quarters	$ million	$ million	$ million	Minimum	Maximum	Limits?
7	1991	5	1st	1	*9,280*	44,414	0.21333	9,475	9,499	−219	8,509	10,488	---
8	1991	5	2nd	2	*10,340*	44,414	0.24007	10,663	10,686	−346	9,704	11,669	---
9	1991	5	3rd	3	*10,627*	44,414	0.24574	10,914	10,938	−311	9,962	11,914	---
10	1991	5	4th	4	*13,640*	44,414	0.30086	13,362	13,386	254	12,416	14,356	---
11	1992	6	1st	5	*11,649*	55,738	0.21333	11,891	11,914	−265	10,950	12,879	---
12	1992	6	2nd	6	*13,028*	55,738	0.24007	13,381	13,405	−377	12,445	14,364	---
13	1992	6	3rd	7	*13,683*	55,738	0.24574	13,697	13,721	−38	12,766	14,676	---
14	1992	6	4th	8	*17,124*	55,738	0.30086	16,769	16,793	331	15,841	17,744	---
15	1993	7	1st	9	*13,920*	67,897	0.21333	14,484	14,508	−588	13,560	15,457	---
16	1993	7	2nd	10	*16,237*	67,897	0.24007	16,300	16,324	−87	15,378	17,270	---
17	1993	7	3rd	11	*16,827*	67,897	0.24574	16,685	16,709	118	15,765	17,653	---
18	1993	7	4th	12	*20,360*	67,897	0.30086	20,427	20,451	−91	19,508	21,394	---
19	1994	8	1st	13	*17,686*	80,526	0.21333	17,179	17,202	484	16,260	18,145	---
20	1994	8	2nd	14	*19,942*	80,526	0.24007	19,332	19,356	586	18,413	20,298	---
21	1994	8	3rd	15	*20,418*	80,526	0.24574	19,789	19,812	606	18,869	20,755	---
22	1994	8	4th	16	*24,448*	80,526	0.30086	24,227	24,251	197	23,306	25,195	---
23	1995	9	1st	17	*20,440*	93,259	0.21333	19,895	19,919	521	18,973	20,865	---
24	1995	9	2nd	18	*22,723*	93,259	0.24007	22,389	22,412	311	21,464	23,361	---
25	1995	9	3rd	19	*22,913*	93,259	0.24574	22,918	22,941	−28	21,990	23,893	---
26	1995	9	4th	20	*27,551*	93,259	0.30086	28,058	28,081	−530	27,126	29,037	---
27	1996	10	1st	21	*22,772*	105,731	0.21333	22,556	22,579	193	21,620	23,539	---
28	1996	10	2nd	22	*25,587*	105,731	0.24007	25,383	25,407	180	24,442	26,371	---
29	1996	10	3rd	23	*25,644*	105,731	0.24574	25,983	26,006	−362	25,036	26,976	---
30	1996	10	4th	24	*30,856*	105,731	0.30086	31,810	31,834	−978	30,858	32,810	YES
31	1997	11	1st	25	*25,409*	117,577	0.21333	25,083	25,106	303	24,124	26,089	---
32	1997	11	2nd	26	*28,386*	117,577	0.24007	28,227	28,250	136	27,261	29,240	---
33	1997	11	3rd	27	*28,777*	117,577	0.24574	28,893	28,917	−140	27,920	29,914	---
34	1997	11	4th	28	*35,386*	117,577	0.30086	35,374	35,397	−11	34,392	36,403	---
35	1998	12	1st	29	*29,819*	128,429	0.21333	27,398	27,422	2,397	26,408	28,435	YES
36	1998	12	2nd	30	*33,521*	128,429	0.24007	30,832	30,856	2,665	29,833	31,879	YES
37	1998	12	3rd	31	*33,509*	128,429	0.24574	31,560	31,584	1,925	30,551	32,617	YES
38	1998	12	4th	32	*40,785*	128,429	0.30086	38,639	38,663	2,122	37,620	39,706	YES
39	1999	13	1st	33	*34,717*	137,924	0.21333	29,423	29,447	5,270	28,393	30,501	YES
40	1999	13	2nd	34	*38,470*	137,924	0.24007	33,111	33,135	5,335	32,070	34,200	YES
41	1999	13	3rd	35	*40,432*	137,924	0.24574	33,894	33,917	6,515	32,841	34,993	YES
42	1999	13	4th	36	*51,394*	137,924	0.30086	41,495	41,519	9,875	40,431	42,607	YES
43				Average Error for Quarters 1 to 26, $ million						0.000	Student's t	2.086	
44				Sum of Squares of Errors for Quarters 1 to 26						3,929,053			
45				Model's Standard Error of Estimate, $ million						443.23			
46				Model's Coefficient of Correlation						0.997903			
47			Sum of ratios and SSIs =			1.00000							

(Columns G and H and the sum of the ratios and SSIs in Columns G and H have been hidden.)

(Continued)

The first step in deciding when to intervene and revise the model is to recognize when revision is needed. To do this, we have tightened the upper and lower limits to a 95 percent confidence range rather than 80 percent. This is done by changing the entry in Cell Q43 to =TINV(0.05,26-6). (Note that six degrees of freedom have been lost—four for the coefficients of the cubic model, one for the SSI, and one for adjusting the average error to zero.) The value 0.05 for the first argument of the TINV function sets the limits at slightly more than two standard forecast errors from the forecast values, which is the normal range used for industrial process control. Setting control limits too narrowly (e.g., 80 percent) runs the risk of overreacting to differences that might reasonably occur from random scatter and cause corrective action that was not necessary. On the other hand, setting control limits too widely runs the risk of underreacting to real differences and failing to take corrective action that was necessary. Industrial process control sets the limits at either two or three standard deviations from the process mean, with two being common practice in the manufacture of semiconductor devices.

The first quarter for which sales falls outside the 95 percent control limits is the fourth quarter of 1996. The result in Cell R30 provides an alert. However, the actual sales ($30,856 million, Cell E30) are only slightly less than the lower confidence limit ($30,863 million, Cell P30) so the only action needed at this time is to watch the results for the first quarter of 1997 closely to see if a real drift has started. Because the actual sales revenue was within the confidence limits for the first quarter of 1997, as well as the three following quarters for 1997, no action was needed to change the model at this time.

The alert in Cell R35 for the first quarter of 1998 is a strong alert, with actual sales well above the upper control limit. We can be better than 95 percent sure that the forecasting model needs to be changed. Therefore, **at this point the forecasts for the remaining three quarters of 1998 should be revised.** If action is not taken to revise the forecasts and the change in trend persists, actual quarterly revenues will be well above the forecast quarterly sales for the rest of 1998 and will be even more above the forecast quarterly sales for 1999. This is demonstrated by the results in Rows 35 to 42 of Figure 6-11, as pointed out by the warnings in Cells R35:R42. The paragraphs that follow describe how to take advantage of the early warning in Cell R35 and to revise or correct the model to adjust for the changing trend and to make projections more accurate.

Figure 6-12 shows how the model can be corrected beginning immediately after the quarterly sales value has been obtained for the first quarter of 1998. (Note that Rows 7 to 30 have been hidden.)

Figure 6-12

Revised Forecasts for Second, Third, and Fourth Quarter Sales of 1998

	A	C	E	F	I	L	M	P	Q	R	S	T	U	V
1							WAL-MART STORES, INC.							
2							Seasonally-Adjusted Cubic Annual Trend Line for Quarterly Sales							
3			Actual	Forecast	Refined	**Refined**	Refined	Quarterly Sales		Quarterly	Quarterly	Revised Projections		
4			**Quarterly**	Annual	SSI	**Forecast**	Forecast	95% Confidence		Sales	Divided by	Annual	Quarter	
5	Fiscal		**Sales,**	Sales,	for Like	**Sales,**	Error,	Range, $ million		Outside	Refined SSI,	Sales	Sales	Error
6	Year	Quarter	$ million	$ million	Quarters	$ million	$ million	Minimum	Maximum	Limits?	$ million	$ million	$ million	$ million
31	1997	1st	25,409	117,577	0.21333	25,106	303	24,124	26,089	---				
32	1997	2nd	28,386	117,577	0.24007	28,250	136	27,261	29,240	---				
33	1997	3rd	28,777	117,577	0.24574	28,917	−140	27,920	29,914	---				
34	1997	4th	35,386	117,577	0.30086	35,397	−11	34,392	36,403	---				
35	1998	1st	29,819	128,429	0.21333	27,422	2,397	26,408	28,435	YES	139,778			
36	1998	2nd	33,521	128,429	0.24007	30,856	2,665	29,833	31,879	YES	139,630	139,778	33,557	−36
37	1998	3rd	33,509	128,429	0.24574	31,584	1,925	30,551	32,617	YES	136,359	139,704	34,331	−822
38	1998	4th	40,785	128,429	0.30086	38,663	2,122	37,620	39,706	YES	135,562	138,589	41,696	−911
39			Average Error for Quarters 1 to 26, $ million				0.000	Student's t	2.086					
40			Sum of Squares of Errors for Quarters 1 to 26				3,929,053							
41			Model's Standard Error of Estimate, $ million				443.23							
42			Model's Coefficient of Correlation				0.997903							
43	Sum of ratios and SSIs =			1.00000										

Key Cell Entries for Revised Projections
Cell S35: =E35/I35, copy to S36:S38
Cell T36: =AVERAGE(S$35:S35), copy to T37:T38
Cell U36: =T36*I36, copy to U37:U38
Cell V36: =E36-U36, copy to V37:V38

(Continued)

The essence of the model is to provide a new estimate of the annual sales for 1998 based on the actual sales for the first quarter of 1998 and the SSI for the first quarter. The new estimate for the annual sales for 1998 is calculated in Cell S35 as the value of the quarterly sales in Cell E35 divided by the SSI for the first quarter in Cell I35; thus,

$$\$29,833 \text{ million}/0.21333 = \$139,778 \text{ million}$$

Multiplying this value for the annual sales by the SSI for the second quarter in Cell I36 gives the revised forecast for the sales for the second quarter of 1998 in Cell U36; thus,

$$\$139,778 \text{ million} \times 0.24007 = \$33,557 \text{ million}$$

The error is calculated by the entry =E36-U36 in Cell V36 to give –$36 million; thus,

$$\$33,521 \text{ million} - \$33,557 \text{ million} = -\$36 \text{ million}$$

We can continue in this manner through the last quarter of 1998, calculating new estimates of the annual sales for 1998 in the manner indicated in Figure 6-12 as additional quarterly sales data are obtained. Once data for the fourth quarter of 1998 have been obtained, we can add the quarterly sales for 1998 to determine the annual sales for 1998. With the annual sales for 1998, we can next update the annual sales portion of the model.

The new model for the annual sales portion must reflect the upward trend of annual sales that we can observe by comparing the actual quarterly sales for 1998 in Cells E35:E38 with the values obtained with the old model in Cells L35:L38 (or by comparing the revised values in Cells T36:T38 with the old values in Cells F36:F38. The downward curvature with the cubic model for annual sales must be replaced with a model for annual sales that has an upward curvature and is based on the most recent data.

Figure 6-13 creates a quadratic model for annual sales based on the data from 1997 to 1999—that is, for quarters 25 to 36. (Because the three parameters of the quadratic model are based on only three years of annual sales, the coefficient of determination in Cell F31 is exactly one.) The values for the quarterly SSIs are revised based on the quarterly sales from the first quarter of 1997 to the fourth quarter of 1999, and the model's forecasts are projected to the four quarters of 2000 (Cells M19:M22). Although the forecasts for the first and second quarters of 2000 are within the 95 percent confidence limits, those for the third and fourth quarters of 2000 are outside. There is also an indication as early as the second quarter of 2000 that the projections of annual sales are too high and may need to be reduced. Cells U21 and U22 provide revised forecasts for the third and fourth quarters of 2000 that are closer to what the actual sales proved to be.

Figure 6-14 shows the next revision based on the quarterly and annual sales from 1997 to 2000. Again, a quadratic regression model is developed for the annual sales, and the values of the quarterly SSIs are revised. The model was used to project the quarterly sales for 2001 (Cells L23:L26). The forecasts of quarterly sales for the first, second, and third quarters of 2001 (which were the last quarters for which data values were available at the time of writing) are all within the model's confidence limits.

When data are obtained for the fourth quarter of 2001, the model will again be revised and used to forecast sales for each of the four quarters of 2002.

Periodic updating to take advantage of the latest information and data can be done as often as periodic values are obtained. Instead of quarterly, the technique demonstrated in this section can be used with monthly or weekly data. (Wal-Mart's weekly sales are available on the company's Web site.)

(Continued)

Figure 6-13

Quadratic Regression Model of Annual Sales with Quarterly SSIs Based on 1997 to 1999 Values

	A	B	C	D	E	F	G	H	I	J	K	L	M	N	O	P	Q	R	S	T
1										WAL-MART STORES, INC.										
2							Seasonally-Adjusted Quadratic Annual Trend Line for Quarterly Sales (based on 1997 to 1999 data)													
3–6	Fiscal Year	XYR	Quarter	X	**Actual Quarterly Sales, $ million**	Forecast Annual Sales, $ million	Ratio, Quarterly to Annual	Average Ratio for Like Quarters	Refined SSI for Like Quarters	**Forecast Sales, $ million**	Forecast Error, $ million	X-XM	Standard Forecast Error, $ million	Quarterly Sales 95% Confidence Range, $ million Minimum	Maximum	Quarterly Sales Outside Limits?	Quarterly Divided by SSI $ million	Revised Projections Annual Sales $ million	Quarter Sales $ million	Error $ million
7	1997	11	1st	25	***25,409***	117,958	0.21541	0.21415	0.21415	**25,261**	148	−5.5	892	**23,205**	**27,317**	NO				
8	1997	11	2nd	26	***28,386***	117,958	0.24064	0.23911	0.23911	**28,205**	181	−4.5	867	**26,205**	**30,205**	NO				
9	1997	11	3rd	27	***28,777***	117,958	0.24396	0.24415	0.24415	**28,799**	−22	−3.5	847	**26,846**	**30,753**	NO				
10	1997	11	4th	28	***35,386***	117,958	0.29999	0.30259	0.30259	**35,693**	−307	−2.5	832	**33,775**	**37,611**	NO				
11	1998	12	1st	29	***29,819***	137,634	0.21665	0.21415	0.21415	**29,474**	345	−1.5	821	**27,580**	**31,369**	NO				
12	1998	12	2nd	30	***33,521***	137,634	0.24355	0.23911	0.23911	**32,910**	611	−0.5	816	**31,028**	**34,792**	NO				
13	1998	12	3rd	31	***33,509***	137,634	0.24346	0.24415	0.24415	**33,603**	−94	0.5	816	**31,721**	**35,485**	NO				
14	1998	12	4th	32	***40,785***	137,634	0.29633	0.30259	0.30259	**41,647**	−862	1.5	821	**39,753**	**43,541**	NO				
15	1999	13	1st	33	***34,717***	165,013	0.21039	0.21415	0.21415	**35,338**	−621	2.5	832	**33,419**	**37,256**	NO				
16	1999	13	2nd	34	***38,470***	165,013	0.23313	0.23911	0.23911	**39,456**	−986	3.5	847	**37,503**	**41,410**	NO				
17	1999	13	3rd	35	***40,432***	165,013	0.24502	0.24415	0.24415	**40,288**	144	4.5	867	**38,288**	**42,288**	NO				
18	1999	13	4th	36	***51,394***	165,013	0.31145	0.30259	0.30259	**49,931**	1,463	5.5	892	**47,875**	**51,987**	NO				
19	2000	14	1st	37	***42,985***	200,095			0.21415	**42,850**	135	6.5	920	**40,729**	**44,972**	NO	200,723			
20	2000	14	2nd	38	***46,112***	200,095			0.23911	**47,845**	−1,733	7.5	952	**45,649**	**50,040**	NO	192,849	200,723	47,995	−1,883
21	2000	14	3rd	39	***45,676***	200,095			0.24415	**48,853**	−3,177	8.5	988	**46,576**	**51,130**	YES	187,082	196,786	48,045	−2,369
22	2000	14	4th	40	***56,556***	200,095			0.30259	**60,547**	−3,991	9.5	1,026	**58,181**	**62,913**	YES	186,906	193,551	58,567	−2,011
23									Average Error for Quarters 25 to 36, $ million		**0.000**			Student's t value	2.306					
24									Sum of Squares of Errors for Quarters 25 to 36		4,911,381									
25									Model's Standard Error of Estimate, $ million		783.53									
26									Model's Coefficient of Correlation		0.995594									
27							Sum of SSIs	1.00000	1.00000											
28		XYR	XYR^2		Annual Sales, $ million	LINEST Output (1997–1999)														
29	1997	11	*121*		117,958	**3,851.50**	**−68,908**	**409,920**												
30	1998	12	*144*		137,634	0.00	0.00	0.00												
31	1999	13	*169*		165,013	**1.00**	**0**	#N/A												
32	2000	14	*196*			0.00	0.00	#N/A												
33						1.12E+09	7.7E−15	#N/A												

Key Cell Entries

Cell E29: =SUM(E7:E10)
Cell E30: =SUM(E11:E14)
Cell E31: =SUM(E15:E18)
Cell K25: =SQRT(K24/(12-4))
Cell O23: =TINV(0.05,12-4)
Cell Q19: =E19/I19, copy to Q20:Q22
Cell R20: =AVERAGE(Q$19:Q19), copy to R21:R22
Cell S20: =R20*I20, copy to S21:S22
Cell T20: =E20-S20, copy to T21:T22

Figure 6-14

Quadratic Regression Model of Annual Sales with Quarterly SSIs Based on 1997 to 2000 Values

	A	B	C	D	E	F	G	H	I	J	K	L	M	N	O	P
1										WAL-MART STORES, INC.						
2							Seasonally-Adjusted Quadratic Annual Trend Line for Quarterly Sales									
3–6	Fiscal Year	XYR	Quarter	XQ	Actual Quarterly Sales, $ million	Forecast Annual Sales, $ million	Ratio, Quarterly to Annual	Average Ratio for Like Quarters	Refined SSI for Like Quarters	**Prelim. Forecast Sales, $ million**	Forecast Error, $ million	X-XM	Standard Forecast Error, $ million	Quarterly Sales 95% Confidence Range, $ million Minimum	Maximum	Quarterly Sales Outside Limits?
7	1997	11	1st	25	*25,409*	117,520	0.21621	0.21676	0.21676	25,474	−65	−7.5	1,093	23,091	27,856	NO
8	1997	11	2nd	26	*28,386*	117,520	0.24154	0.23956	0.23956	28,153	233	−6.5	1,075	25,811	30,495	NO
9	1997	11	3rd	27	*28,777*	117,520	0.24487	0.24280	0.24280	28,534	243	−5.5	1,059	26,227	30,841	NO
10	1997	11	4th	28	*35,386*	117,520	0.30111	0.30088	0.30088	35,359	27	−4.5	1,045	33,082	37,636	NO
11	1998	12	1st	29	*29,819*	138,949	0.21460	0.21676	0.21676	30,119	−300	−3.5	1,034	27,865	32,372	NO
12	1998	12	2nd	30	*33,521*	138,949	0.24125	0.23956	0.23956	33,287	234	−2.5	1,026	31,052	35,522	NO
13	1998	12	3rd	31	*33,509*	138,949	0.24116	0.24280	0.24280	33,737	−228	−1.5	1,020	31,514	35,960	NO
14	1998	12	4th	32	*40,785*	138,949	0.29353	0.30088	0.30088	41,806	−1,021	−0.5	1,017	39,590	44,023	NO
15	1999	13	1st	33	*34,717*	163,698	0.21208	0.21676	0.21676	35,483	−766	0.5	1,017	33,267	37,700	NO
16	1999	13	2nd	34	*38,470*	163,698	0.23501	0.23956	0.23956	39,216	−746	1.5	1,020	36,993	41,439	NO
17	1999	13	3rd	35	*40,432*	163,698	0.24699	0.24280	0.24280	39,746	686	2.5	1,026	37,511	41,981	NO
18	1999	13	4th	36	*51,394*	163,698	0.31396	0.30088	0.30088	49,253	2,141	3.5	1,034	47,000	51,506	NO
19	2000	14	1st	37	*42,985*	191,767	0.22415	0.21676	0.21676	41,568	1,417	4.5	1,045	39,290	43,845	NO
20	2000	14	2nd	38	*46,112*	191,767	0.24046	0.23956	0.23956	45,940	172	5.5	1,059	43,633	48,247	NO
21	2000	14	3rd	39	*45,676*	191,767	0.23818	0.24280	0.24280	46,561	−885	6.5	1,075	44,219	48,903	NO
22	2000	14	4th	40	*56,556*	191,767	0.29492	0.30088	0.30088	57,698	−1,142	7.5	1,093	55,316	60,081	NO
23	2001	15	1st	41	*48,052*	223,157			0.21676	48,372	−320	8.5	1,114	45,944	50,799	NO
24	2001	15	2nd	42	***52,799***	223,157			0.23956	**53,460**	−661	9.5	1,137	50,982	55,937	NO
25	2001	15	3rd	43	***52,738***	223,157			0.24280	**54,183**	−1,445	10.5	1,162	51,651	56,714	NO
26	2001	15	4th	44	***na***	223,157			0.30088	**67,142**		11.5	1,189	64,552	69,733	
27									Average Error for Quarters 25 to 40, $ million		**0.000**			Student's t value	2.179	
28									Sum of Squares of Errors for Quarters 25 to 40		11,683,433					
29									Model's Standard Error of Estimate, $ million		986.72					
30									Model's Coefficient of Correlation		0.994897					
31							Sum of SSIs	1.00000	1.00000							
32		XYR	XYR^2		Annual Sales, $ million	LINEST Output (1997–2000)										
33	1997	11	*121*		117,958	1660.00	−16750.8	100918.5								
34	1998	12	*144*		137,634	980.07	24517.4	152308.5								
35	1999	13	*169*		165,013	0.9988	1960.14	#N/A								
36	2000	14	*196*		191,329	399.99046	1	#N/A								
37						3.074E+09	3842138	#N/A								

Concluding Remarks

Seasonality is an important consideration in many financial plans and decisions. For example, cash budgets are usually based on forecasts of the month-to-month variations in customer demands. The ups and downs of seasonal demands and sales revenues present a timing problem for CFOs. At some times they need to borrow money, while at other times they have excess cash on hand to invest in short-term securities. Solving the timing problem must also recognize the time lags between when sales are made and customers pay for them, as well as the time lags between when goods are received and suppliers must be paid. We will pursue the timing problem further in Chapter 8 on cash budgeting.

Seasonality is especially important in inventory management. To satisfy customers promptly, firms must maintain adequate safety stocks of goods. However, inventories and safety stocks entail additional expenses for providing and operating storage facilities and for tying up funds that might otherwise be invested more profitably. As a result, a firm's monthly cost for holding inventories and safety stocks is typically 2 to 2.5 percent of the cost of the average amount that is held during the month. In other words, for an item that costs $100, it also costs between $2.00 and $2.50 each month the item sits on a shelf, waiting to be used to satisfy a customer's demand.

Seasonality is important in personnel staffing. Employees of service facilities, for example, must be available to serve customers promptly. Most firms provide steady employment and must pay their employees whether customers come or not. Frequent hiring and firing of employees to match the size of the workforce to variations in customer demands is generally a self-defeating strategy for several reasons. Just as annual trends in revenues are important for long-range financial planning (e.g., capital budgeting, the subject of Chapters 12 to 15), so are seasonal variations important for planning short-term financial tactics (e.g., cash budgeting, the subject of Chapter 8).

The pages that follow present selected comments from students in the author's classes in financial modeling. They illustrate a variety of seasonal behaviors and methods for coping.

Students' Experiences with Seasonality

Here are a few of the comments, slightly edited, that the author has received from students regarding seasonality at companies where they worked. Note the problems and some solutions.

* * *

I formerly owned and operated a 48-seat pizza parlor on the Monterey Peninsula, which is heavily dependent on tourism. Our peak season was Memorial Day to Labor Day, and it was not unusual to do 50% of our yearly business in that time span. Things got hectic during that period and presented two major challenges: labor and inventory.

We had to double our staff every summer, which meant we had to hire in late April to early May and get people up to speed for the craziness of the summer rush. Unfortunately, new employees are a drag on earnings as they are not very productive at first. It really takes a while for them to figure out what is going on. That meant having a veteran "baby sit" with a rookie until the rookie got up to speed.

The inventory of "raw materials" was also a constant challenge because of spoilage. We used only fresh vegetables and, as most of you know, they don't have a long shelf life—usually three to four days—so you really had

(Continued)

to monitor inventory levels. Too much inventory and you threw money into the dumpster; not enough inventory and you've got unhappy customers! You really had to stay on top of inventory or spoilage will kill you.

I kept detailed records of each day's business including number, size, and type of pizza sold so I could figure out what I would need for labor and inventory. By the time I sold the shop, I had records for six years and could accurately predict within 10% of how much business we would do on any given day or night.

* * *

I used to work for a company in Taiwan that sells computer peripherals. Our business was impacted by customer shopping patterns, particularly those of students. February and September sales were the highest. Each of those two months contributed 20% of annual sales. Chinese New Year usually began in February, and meanwhile workers received their annual bonuses and students received money given to children as a Spring Festival gift. In September the new school year begansand students had full pockets after working part-time during summer vacations. Students had a high motivation to purchase new stuff with their money. During the months of February and September, the company's management recruited more part-time employees as sales personnel and to answer inquiries from customers.

* * *

The greatest variation for our petrochemical company is the switch from gasoline for summer driving to fuel oil for winter heating. … If gas prices are low, people will drive more for their summer vacations, and this increases demand and strains our entire production and storage network. Likewise, if winter is early or severe, demand for fuel oil increases and strains our production and storage network. These variations are so great and important that we hire outside consultants to help us develop our production schedules.

* * *

I work for a food company, and we are not just dealing with seasonal consumer demands but also with seasonal crops. Sales are usually up during the holiday seasons, while our fruit and vegetable raw materials are usually harvested during one half of the year. At the peak of harvest, our processing plants operates 24 hours a day/7 days a week for at least three months. While most of the 12 facilities operate year-round with slower production rates, some are shut down within a short period of time for inspection and maintenance. Once in great while, we also experience a shortage of supply in the United States. Therefore, we must purchase products overseas in order to have a continuing supply to offer our consumers. In this case, we have to state on the label where these products were packed.

* * *

I used to work for a chocolate company. Sales revenue spiked sharply in the months before major winter and spring holidays (e.g., Christmas and Easter). In the summertime, sales were less than 1/10th of those in peak season (after all, consumers do not want to buy a product that will melt on the way home, and so demand from our customers, the retailers, was very low).

Seasonal variations in sales created several problems. … One of the most difficult was the great swings in the need for operating capital. After a long summer season of slow sales and low cash flow we had to build inventory. Furthermore, once the inventory was sold, we had to wait 30 to 45 days for the receivable to turn into cash. This often stretched our revolving credit line to the limit. Generally, we tried to keep an adequate level of equity to cope with this. In one dire year, however, all other options were exhausted, so we paid vendors on a "squeaky wheel gets the grease" basis, opportunistically taking advantage of vendors who weren't monitoring their own receivables closely. If a vendor called, we placed the check in the mail immediately. In hindsight, this was not the best approach to the problem, but it did get us out of a tight spot without any real damage to our credit.

* * *

I used to work in the consumer retail industry, and seasonal variations were definitely a primary concern for management. It was not uncommon to have over 40% of annual sales volume concentrated in the months of November and December.

(Continued)

Availability of merchandise for the year-end rush was the biggest problem. Orders with suppliers usually had to be placed by March, long before management was able to gauge in a meaningful manner what the demand situation would be like by November. This meant the tying up of precious working capital and potential losses due to overstocking of goods. Another big headache for retail merchants is ensuring proper staffing levels during various phases of their business cycle. Generally, most retailers tend to hire temporary personnel during busy times, while maintaining a regular crew during the rest of year. This practice usually leads to everybody going after the same pool of available workers at the same time, thus driving up cost and sometimes giving poor customer service.

I work at Pacific Gas & Electric (PG&E). We have three main seasonal effects: summer electric, winter gas, and power line maintenance. California uses a lot of electrical energy for air conditioning during the summer, using as much during summer as the other nine months combined. In winter California uses a lot of gas for heating, and that can be a significant amount of energy. Power line maintenance is a constant activity but weather can cause major problems. Hot summers can cause fires that affect power lines. The company needs to do major tree trimming prior to the summer. Wet winter weather causes many problems that require maintenance teams to be on constant high alert.

Since we don't produce all our power, we need to buy it from the market. The timing of these purchases can have a huge effect in the price we pay. ... Long-term fixed-rate contracts are a way to control market price fluctuations. However, if the future has lower rates (than your contracts) it can be very costly to the company. State regulators (CPUC) try to limit the use of these types of arrangements. The other thing we have employed in the last few years is price hedging.

* * *

I used to work for an international travel agency in China. Our clients were tour groups, individual travelers and commercial people from different countries. The tour peak season starts from end of March to October each year, with highs in the months of June, July, and August. About 80% of annual sales occur during this period. Like our competitors, we did our best to negotiate discount rate with vendors like hotels, restaurants, cruise, ground transportation companies and airlines. Most vendors offer most favorable prices in travel off-season. We promoted "Super saver winter tour package" during Chinese New Year in January and February. There was a shortage of foreign language speaking tour guides in high season, and we hired college students from campus to work for us the whole summer. We offered training programs to them in low season and hired them to work in the summer peak season.

* * *

Currently, I have my own floral business that especially caters for weddings and special events. About 25% of wedding events take place in the spring, 50% in the summer, 15% in the fall and 10% in the winter. Brides choose a florist around 6–9 months before their wedding. Hence, there is a big lag time from when the actual sales take place to when the balances are paid off, which is two months before the wedding. As result, accounts receivable as a percentage of sales is very low during fall and winter.

One of the management problems is trying to have sufficient budget during the fall and winter to cover selling expenses and G&A expenses since these expenses are the highest during fall and winter to capture customers who are looking for florists. To cope with this problem, I have to decide on my budget for each quarter six months in advance. For example, I make sure that a portion of sales revenues received, mostly during spring and summer, are saved to cover for selling expenses and G&A expenses for that fall and winter.

Another problem is extending business hours to include Sunday during fall and winter when it is peak season for consultations. Wholesale flowers cost more during fall and winter, therefore, retail prices have to be adjusted to reflect the increase in cost of goods sold.

Developing Seasonally-Adjusted Models

Developing a seasonally-adjusted forecasting model takes three separate steps: (1) Remove the seasonality from the raw data, (2) develop a model for the trend line for the deseasonalized data, and (3) put the seasonality back into the model by multiplying or adding seasonal corrections to the deseasonalized trend line. The purpose of the first step (i.e., deseasonalizing the raw data) is to remove the periodic ups and downs and produce a smooth trend line to which a regression equation can be fit in the second step. The third step completes the model by putting the period-to-period variations about the deseasonalized trend line.

The development of accurate models for projecting past trends into the future does not always proceed in a straightforward manner. It often involves trying first one type of model, and then another, and another until a satisfactory model is produced. It requires examining results carefully and recognizing discrepancies, however minor, between the trends of the data and forecast values. Above all, it requires a willingness to be critical of one's work, to repeat analyses with changes in the type of model and range of data, and not to be satisfied with anything less than a thorough analysis. Excel contributes tools that simplify copying and editing models so that a forecaster can easily experiment with different models.

Recognizing and Adjusting Statistical Models for Changes in Past Trend

We again emphasize that even the best statistical projections of past trends should be adjusted for changes that can be anticipated in management policies, the actions of competitors, general economic conditions, and consumer preferences. It helps to have good knowledge of a company's management plus reliable information about its competitors and its markets.

Confidence limits provide a means for monitoring a model's continued ability to forecast the future. Future data values that are outside the confidence limits indicate that past trends have likely changed and that the statistical model of the past may need revision.

This chapter demonstrated techniques for recognizing when a statistical model based on past trends is no longer valid and for correcting models. The more frequent the periodic values (e.g., monthly or weekly instead of quarterly), the sooner will changes in past trends be recognized—and the sooner the model can be improved to give more accurate forecasts of the future, as well as the sooner appropriate corrective action can be taken to handle any management problems that arise from poor forecasts. Many companies are investing in management control systems that are quick to recognize changes in past trends and alert managers that they need to react.

Taking Appropriate Management Action When a Past Trend Changes

Don't look to forecasting models only as tools for forecasting the future. Use them also to recognize and examine turning points in a company's performance. These may be related to changes in such outside influences as the general economy, competition, and technology. The models can help evaluate how effectively a company's management is coping or capitalizing on such changes. They can help spot problems a company's management may be having.

At the time of this writing, Wal-Mart had reportedly resolved the management difficulties caused by its expanding several years ago into new market areas. Unless beset by new problems, Wal-Mart sales should benefit from this change from the immediate past and the statistical projections based on the past data should be increased.

Coping with Seasonality

Developing off-season products is one of the strategies companies use to cope with the difficulties of seasonality. For example, a sports equipment manufacturer might produce snow skis for winter demands to offset the decline in summertime demands for water skis. A clothing manufacturer might add cold-weather parkas as an off-season product to swimsuits. Companies providing financial services might offer estate planning and payroll services along with the preparation of quarterly financial reports and income tax returns. Additional solutions are described in the students' comments on seasonality.

Chapter 7

The Time Value of Money

CHAPTER OBJECTIVES

Management Skills

- Understand and be able to apply the concepts of the time value of money.
- Recognize the sensitivity of financial payoffs to changes in interest rates and other conditions that business managers must cope with.
- Tailor a series of future cash inflows or outflows necessary to satisfy present or future business objectives.

Spreadsheet Skills

- Use Excel's financial commands to convert future values to their equivalent present values, and vice versa.
- Use Excel's financial commands to determine the net present value of a series of future cash flows.
- Calculate periodic payments for mortgages and other loans to identify how much of each payment goes to paying off the principal and how much goes to paying interest.
- Use Excel's Goal Seek and Solver tools to achieve an objective.
- Create one- and two-variable input tables to do sensitivity analysis.

Overview

Given a choice between $50,000 now or 10 years from now, which would you take? A wise person would take the money now, knowing that "A dollar today is worth more than a dollar tomorrow." The value of money increases with time because one can invest money today in a bank account, bond, certificate of deposit, or other financial instrument that bears interest and watch it grow to more than its original amount.

Of course, because of inflation, the *buying* power of a dollar can decline with time. The rate of inflation expresses the rate of decrease of money's buying power. Even though you may have more dollars in the future, they will buy less than before whenever the rate of inflation exceeds the rate of appreciation.

One must pay interest to borrow money to purchase factories or homes. Money borrowed today must be repaid in the future with an *equivalent value* that is equal to the amount borrowed plus interest.

One speaks of the rate at which money increases while it is invested or deposited in a bank as the rate at which it appreciates in value, or the **rate of interest** it earns. Financial analysts speak of the time value of money as the **discount rate**, and they use it to discount future amounts of money back to their present equivalent values. When applied to capital budgeting, the term **cost of capital** is used to describe the rate a firm must pay to raise funds through borrowing and issuing stock—and which it must earn back in order to break even on a capital investment. The time value of money is an important concept that is used in cash budgeting, determining the cost of capital, and evaluating capital investments. These topics are covered in later chapters.

This chapter discusses the time value of money and shows how to move monetary values forward and backward in time. Its focus is on Excel's financial commands for calculating equivalent values of money at different times and at different discount rates. The commands allow one to move a present value forward to an equivalent value in the future, or to move a future value backward to its present equivalent. The commands also cover *annuities*, or series of fixed amounts that are paid or received at certain, regular intervals. Annuities also can be moved back and forth in time to a single equivalent present value or to a single equivalent future value.

This chapter provides examples that show how to use a number of Excel's financial commands that deal with the time value of money. Excel provides almost 200 financial functions to choose from. In this chapter, we will describe the selection and use of only those listed in Table 7-1.

The complete set of almost 200 financial functions is included in Excel's Analysis ToolPak. The functions can be accessed by clicking on the "Insert Function" button on the upper toolbar. This opens the dialog box shown in Figure 7-1. Select "Financial" in Figure 7-1 and press Enter or click OK.

Scroll down the list on the right side and click on the particular financial function you want. Figure 7-2 shows the dialog box with the function "FV," for "future value," selected. The line near the bottom shows the function's syntax, and below that is a brief explanation of what the function does.

Click on the "Help on this function" text in Figure 7-2 to open the dialog box shown in Figure 7-3. Enter the cell references for the interest rate, number of periods, periodic payment, and present value. The entries shown in Figure 7-3 are for Example 7.1, which is presented on page 221.

Table 7-1

Financial Functions Covered in This Chapter

FV(*rate, number of periods, payment, present value, type*)

> Computes the **future value** of a series of equal *payments* and/or a *present value* after a specified *number of periods* at a specified *rate* of interest. Payments can be made at either the beginning or end of each period, as specified by the value for *type* (0 for end, 1 for beginning).

PV(*rate, number of periods, payment, future value, type*)

> Computes the **present value** of a series of equal *payments* and/or a *future value* after a specified *number of periods* at a specified *rate* of interest. Payments can be made at either the beginning or end of each period, as specified by the value for *type*.

NPV(*rate, value1, value2,...*)

> Computes the **present value** of a series of future cash flows (*value1, value2, ...*) at a specified *rate* of interest. Cash flows are at the ends of successive periods, beginning with the first, and do not have to be equal to each other.

PMT(*rate, number of periods, present value, future value, type*)

> Computes the value of a series of equal **payments** equivalent to a given *present value* or *future present value* for a specified *number of periods* at a specified *rate* of interest. Payments can be made at either the beginning or end of each period, as specified by the value for *type*. The PMT function is useful for computing monthly mortgage payments to repay the *present value* of a loan or the periodic investments in sinking funds to accumulate a given *future value*.

PPMT(*rate, period, number of periods, present value, future value, type*)

IPMT(*rate, period, number of periods, present value, future value, type*)

> These two functions compute the amounts of a payment to principal (PPMT) and to interest (IPMT) during a given *period*. The second argument, *period*, is the number of the period for which the value of the interest or principal is computed. The other five arguments are the same as for the PMT command. Payments can be made at either the beginning or end of each period, as specified by the value for *type*.

CUMPRINC(*rate, number of periods, present value, start_period, end_period, type*)

CUMIPMT(*rate, number of periods, present value, start_period, end_period, type*)

> These two functions compute the sums or **cumulative** amounts of the payments to **principal** (CUMPRINC) and the payments to **interest** (CUMIPMT) from a given *start period* to a given *end period*. Payments can be made at either the beginning or end of each period, as specified by the value for *type*.

NPER(*rate, payment, present value, future value, type*)

> Computes the number **of periods** for repaying the *present value* of a loan, for example, or to accumulate a given *future value* for a given series of *payments* at a specified *rate* of interest.

RATE(*number of periods, payment, present value, future value, type, guess*)

> Computes the **rate of return** from a series of equal *payments*, a *present value*, and/or a *future value* after a given *number of periods*. The *guess* argument provides a starting point for Excel's iterative procedure for calculating the rate. Like the *type* argument, *guess* is optional. If omitted, Excel begins with a default *guess* of 0.10 (i.e., 10%) to calculate the net present value. If the #NUM! error message results, try another guess. Payments can be made at either the beginning or end of each period, as specified by the value for *type*.

Figure 7-1

"Insert Function" Dialog Box with "Financial" Selected

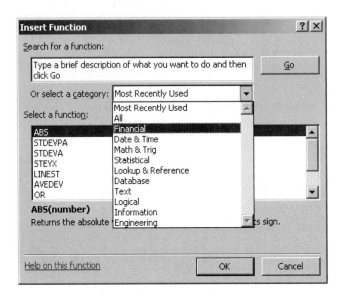

How to Add Excel Tools

If only a partial set of the financial functions can be accessed from Excel's "Insert Function," you will need to install the full set. To do this, click on "Add-Ins" on the "Tools" drop-down menu on the top toolbar and select "Analysis ToolPak" at the top of the "Add-Ins" menu.

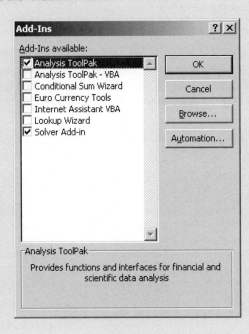

Figure 7-2
___

Insert Function Dialog Box with Function for Future Value (FV) Selected

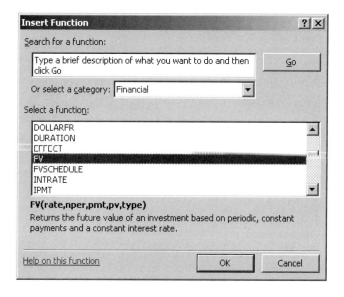

Figure 7-3
___

**Dialog Box for the FV Function
(Entries are the rate, number of periods, periodic payment, and present value for Example 7.1 on page 221.)**

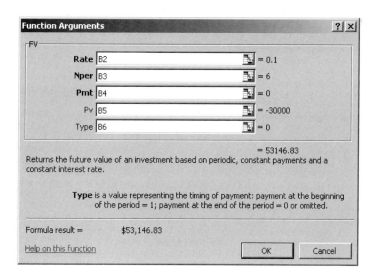

  This chapter shows the algebraic equations that define many of the basic relationships used in evaluating the time value of money. Excel's functional commands simplify calculations so that it is not necessary to program the equations themselves.

Moving from the Present to the Future

In order to convert from present to future values (or the reverse), we must know what the time value of money is. This is specified by the rate of appreciation or the interest rate, which is also referred to as the discount rate. If a bank charges an annual interest rate of 10 percent on loans it makes, any money borrowed from the bank is said to have a time value of 10%/year.

The effect of interest is a compound one. If we invest a principal sum at some rate of interest and keep reinvesting the original sum plus any earned interest, the amount of interest earned each year will increase with time. The annual interest increases each year because the amount on which interest is calculated (i.e., the original investment plus accumulated interest) increases each year. For example, a principal of $100 invested at a rate of interest of 10%/year, compounded annually, will increase at the end of the first year to a total of

$$\$100(1 + 0.10) = \$100 + \$10 = \$110$$

If the original principal and the first year's interest are reinvested at 10 percent for a second year, the total at the end of the second year will be

$$\$110(1 + 0.10) = \$110 + \$11 = \$121$$

This is the same result from using the relation

$$\$100(1 + 0.10)^2 = \$121$$

In like manner, by the end of three years, investing and reinvesting both the original principal and accumulated interest at a 10 percent rate of interest, compounded annually, will provide a total of

$$\$121(1 + 0.10) = \$133.10$$

This result can also be calculated as

$$\$100(1 + 0.10)^3 = \$133.10$$

If the original principal of $100 and the accumulated interest continue to earn 10%/year, compounded annually, for n years, the total at the end of n years will be

$$\$100(1 + 0.10)^n$$

Or, in general, the future value (F) of the present value (P) of a principal amount after a specified number of periods (n) with compound interest at a specified rate of interest per period (i) is given by the equation

$$F = P(1 + i)^n \tag{7.1}$$

The FV Function

Among the most useful financial functions that Excel provides is the future value function, FV. It can be used to find the future value of a single present value, a series of equal values made at the end of each period (i.e., annuities), or a combination of the two. Its syntax is as follows:

= FV(rate, number of periods, payment, present value, type)

where   *rate* = the interest rate per period (i.e., per year, month, etc.), which remains constant throughout the total number of periods

number of periods = total number of periods (i.e., number of years, months, etc.)

payment = the payment made each period (periodic payments, if any, remain constant throughout the total number of periods)

present values = the present value of an investment, or, if periodic payments are made, the lump-sum amount that the series of future payments is worth right now

and   *type* = 0 if periodic payments are made at the end of each period, 1 if periodic payments are made at the beginning of each period

Simple, Compound, and Continuous Interest

At the top of Figure 7-4 is a comparison of the future values of $100 at a 10 percent annual rate of interest calculated with simple, compound, and continuous rates. Values are shown for compounding annually, compounding monthly, and compounding continuously.

Cell entries for calculating year-end values of a deposit of $100 at 10 percent annual interest are as follows:

Simple Annual Interest	Cell D6	=$D$5*(1+$F$2*C6)	Copy to D7:D25
Compounded Annually	Cell E6	=$E$5*(1+$F$2)^(C6)	Copy to E7:E25
Compounded Monthly	Cell F6	=$F$5*(1+$F$2/12)^(C6*12)	Copy to F7:F25
Compounded Continuously	Cell G6	=$G$5*EXP($F$2*C6)	Copy to G7:G25

Note that when an annual rate of interest is compounded monthly, the monthly rate is 1/12th the annual rate and the number of months is 12 times the number of years. When using Excel's PV and other commands for the time value of money, it is important to convert an annual rate of interest with periodic compounding to a periodic rate (e.g., quarterly, monthly, or weekly, as appropriate) and the number of periods to the number of periods in a year (e.g., 4, 12, or 52). Most business investments or loans are calculated at nominal annual rates compounded monthly.

The **actual periodic** rate equals the *annual* rate with periodic compounding divided by the number of interest-bearing periods per year. Thus, if the annual rate is 18 percent, compounded monthly, the actual monthly rate is 18%/12, or 1.5 percent. In this case, the **actual annual** rate would be

$$\text{Actual annual rate} = (1 + 0.015)^{12} - 1 = 1.1956182 - 1 = 0.1956182 = 19.56182\%$$

To restate this result, a **nominal annual** rate of 18 percent that is compounded monthly equals both an **actual monthly** rate of 1.5 percent and an **actual annual** rate of 19.56182 percent.

As the period for compounding is made shorter and shorter, the results approach those for continuous compounding as a limit.

The chart at the bottom of Figure 7-4 shows curves for the future year-end values of $100 with simple interest at 10 percent, interest compounded annually at an annual rate of 10 percent, and interest

Figure 7-4

Comparison of Future Year-End Values of $100 with Simple and Compound Interest Rates

	A	B	C	D	E	F	G	H	I
1			YEAR-END VALUES OF A DEPOSIT OF $100						
2					Annual Rate =	10%			
3					Compound Interest				
4			Year	Simple Annual Interest	Compounded Annually	Compounded Monthly	Compounded Continuously		
5			0	$100.00	$100.00	$100.00	$100.00		
6			1	$110.00	$110.00	$110.47	$110.52		
7			2	$120.00	$121.00	$122.04	$122.14		
8			3	$130.00	$133.10	$134.82	$134.99		
9			4	$140.00	$146.41	$148.94	$149.18		
10			5	$150.00	$161.05	$164.53	$164.87		
11			6	$160.00	$177.16	$181.76	$182.21		
12			7	$170.00	$194.87	$200.79	$201.38		
13			8	$180.00	$214.36	$221.82	$222.55		
14			9	$190.00	$235.79	$245.04	$245.96		
15			10	$200.00	$259.37	$270.70	$271.83		
16			11	$210.00	$285.31	$299.05	$300.42		
17			12	$220.00	$313.84	$330.36	$332.01		
18			13	$230.00	$345.23	$364.96	$366.93		
19			14	$240.00	$379.75	$403.17	$405.52		
20			15	$250.00	$417.72	$445.39	$448.17		
21			16	$260.00	$459.50	$492.03	$495.30		
22			17	$270.00	$505.45	$543.55	$547.39		
23			18	$280.00	$555.99	$600.47	$604.96		
24			19	$290.00	$611.59	$663.35	$668.59		
25			20	$300.00	$672.75	$732.81	$738.91		

26
27
28
29
30
31
32
33
34
35
36
37
38
39
40
41
42
43
44
45
46
47
48
49
50
51
52
53
54

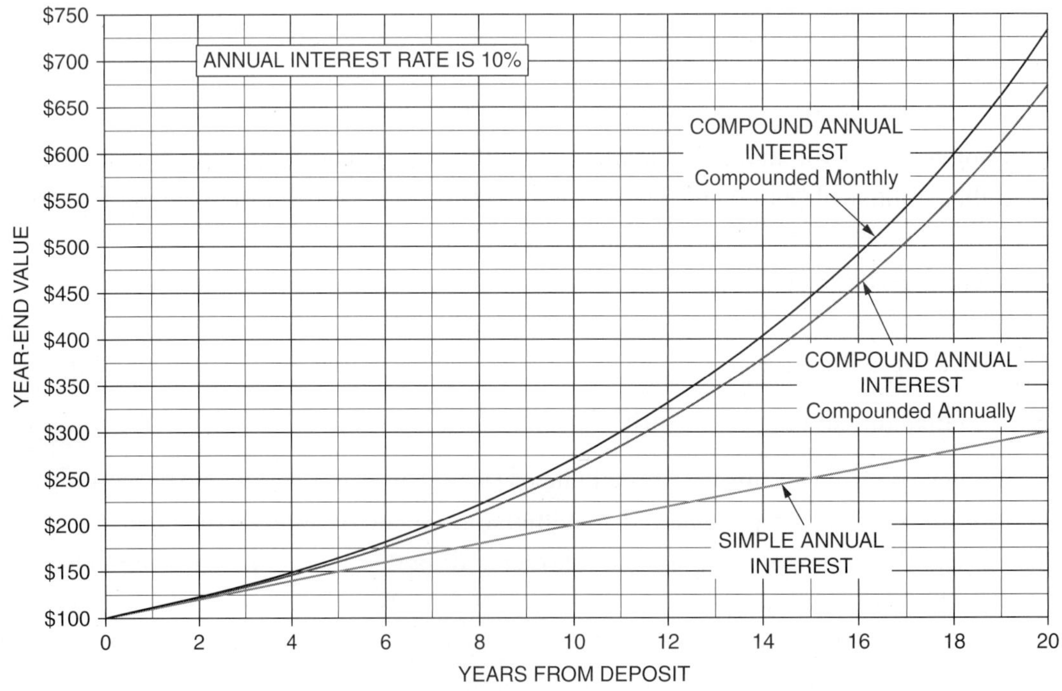

compounded monthly at a nominal annual rate of 10 percent. (A curve for continuous compounding is not shown. It would be only slightly above that for monthly compounding.)

Converting a Present Value to Its Future Equivalent

The following example illustrates the use of equation 7.1 and Excel's FV function to calculate the future value of an investment.

Example 7.1:   A sum of $30,000 is invested at an annual rate of interest of 10 percent, compounded annually. What is the value of the investment at the end of six years—that is, six years after making the investment?

Solution: Substituting values into Equation 6.1 gives

$$F = \$30,000(1 + 0.10)^6 = \$30,000(1.771561) = \$53,146.83$$

Figure 7-5 shows the spreadsheet solution obtained with Excel's FV function. Cells B2:B6 contain the data values for the problem. The entry in Cell B7 is =FV(B2,B3,B4,B5,B6). If the final argument B6 is omitted, the function's default value of zero is assumed.

Figure 7-5

Future Value of a One-Time Investment

	A	B
1	**Example 7.1: FUTURE VALUE OF AN INVESTMENT**	
2	Annual rate of interest, compounded yearly	10%
3	Number of years	6
4	Periodic payment	0
5	Present value of investment	($30,000)
6	Periodic payments at beginning (1) or end (0) of periods	0
7	**Future value**	**$53,146.83**

Key Cell Entry: B7: =FV(B2,B3,B4,B5,B6)

The entry in Cell B7 can either be typed in or can be made with the help of the dialog box for the FV function shown in Figure 7-3, which is accessed by clicking on "Help on this function" at the lower left of Figure 7-2. As the cell references are inserted, the data values appear on the right side of the entry boxes. When the final cell reference is entered, the value for FV also appears at the bottom of the column of data values, as shown in Figure 7-3.

Note the sign convention used with the spreadsheet and FV function. Because the investment of $30,000 in Cell B5 is an outflow of money, it is written as a negative value by enclosing it in parentheses. Alternatively, it could be written with a minus sign. The future value of $53,146.83 at the end of six years is an inflow and is therefore written as a positive value.

The future value of $53,146.83 could also be calculated by entering the values directly in the function—that is, by entering =FV(10%,6,0,-30000,0). This is undesirable when creating models because it hides the values used for the calculation and shows only the result and because it makes it impossible to use the entry for sensitivity analysis.

Calculating the Future Value of a Series of Equal Future Payments

Equation 7.2 is the formula for calculating the future value of a series of equal future payments.

$$F = A \times \left[\frac{(1+i)^n - 1}{i} \right] \tag{7.2}$$

where F = future value

A = periodic payment

i = interest rate per interest period

and n = number of interest-bearing periods

The following example illustrates the use of Excel's FV function to calculate the future value of a series of equal future payments.

Example 7.2:   The CFO of the Baker Company invests $10,000 at the end of each month into a sinking fund to accumulate capital for new equipment that will be purchased at the end of two years. The money invested will earn interest at a 5 percent annual rate, compounded monthly. How much will be available in the sinking fund at the end of two years?

Solution: Figure 7-6 is a spreadsheet solution. Note that in the key entry in Cell B7, the annual interest rate of 5 percent is converted to a monthly rate by **dividing** the annual rate in Cell B2 by 12, and the total number of monthly periods is calculated by **multiplying** the entry for the number of years in Cell B3 by 12. Also note that the final value in the FV function is 0 (from Cell B6), which indicates that the CFO makes the monthly investments at the **end** of each month rather than the beginning.

At the end of two years, the sinking fund will amount to $251,859.21, of which $240,000 is the sum of the 24 monthly payments of $10,000 each, and $11,859.21 is the total amount of interest accumulated.

If the last two arguments in the FV function are omitted, it is assumed that the calculation is for the future value of a series of equal periodic payments and there is no present value. That is, the same result is obtained if the entry in Cell B7 is =FV(B2/12,B3*12,B4).To use equation 7.2 to verify the solution with Excel's FV function, note that

$$F = \$10,000 \times \left[\frac{(1+0.05/12)^{24} - 1}{0.05/12} \right] = \$10,000 \times \frac{0.104941}{0.004166} = \$251,859.21$$

Figure 7-6

Future Value of a Series of Payments

	A	B
1	**Example 7.2: FUTURE VALUE OF A SERIES OF PAYMENTS**	
2	Annual rate of interest, compounded monthly	5%
3	Number of years	2
4	Monthly investment	($10,000)
5	Present value	0
6	Periodic payments at beginning (1) or end (0) of periods	0
7	**Future value**	**$251,859.21**

Key Cell Entry: B7: =FV(B2/12,B3*12,B4,B5,B6)

Example 7.3: Suppose the monthly payments of $10,000 (see preceding example) are made at the **beginning** of each month instead of at the end. How would this affect the answer to Example 7.2?

Answer: $252,908.62 (The solution is left to the reader.)

Calculating the Future Value of a Present Value and a Series of Periodic Values

The following example illustrates the use of Excel's FV function to calculate the future value of an initial investment followed by a series of constant periodic investments.

Example 7.4: Suppose that in addition to depositing $10,000 at the end of each month into a sinking fund (see Example 7.2), the CFO of the Baker Company begins with an initial deposit of $200,000 at the beginning of the first month. How would this affect the answer to Example 7.2?

Solution: Figure 7-7 shows the solution. The key entry in Cell B6 is =FV(B2/12,B3*12,B4,B5,B6). The future value of the sinking fund is $472,847.47. Of this amount, $440,000 is the sum of the initial and periodic deposits, and $32,847.47 is the total amount of interest earned during the two years.

Note that this example differs from the preceding example in having an initial investment in addition to the series of equal future monthly payments. The future value of the $200,000 at the end of two years is readily calculated as

$$F = \$200,000 \times (1+0.05/12)^{24} = \$200,000 \times 1.104941 = \$220,988.27$$

Adding this amount to the future value of the series of $10,000 monthly payments gives

$$F = \$251,859.21 + \$220,988.27 = \$472,847.48$$

which is the same as obtained by using Excel's FV function.

Figure 7-7

Future Value of a Sinking Fund with Initial and Periodic Deposits

	A	B
1	Example 7.4: FUTURE VALUE OF A SINKING FUND	
2	Annual rate of interest, compounded monthly	5%
3	Number of years	2
4	Monthly investment	($10,000)
5	Initial investment	($200,000)
6	Periodic payments at beginning (1) or end (0) of periods	0
7	**Future value**	$472,847.47

Key Cell Entry: B7: =FV(B2/12,B3*12,B4,B5,B6)

The PV Function

Excel's PV function is used to calculate the present value of a single future amount, a series of equal future amounts, or a combination of the two.

Moving from the Future to the Present

Equation 7.1 can be inverted to express the present value of a future amount; thus,

$$P = \frac{F}{(1+i)^n} \tag{7.3}$$

Equation 7.3 can be used to calculate the amount of money that must be invested at the present time (P) in order to grow to a given future value (F) in a certain number of interest-bearing periods (n) when invested at a specified rate of return per interest-bearing period (i).

The PV Function

Excel provides the PV function for finding the present value of a single future value, or a series of equal values made at the end of each period (i.e., annuities), or a combination of the two. Its syntax is

= PV(*rate, number of periods, payment, future value, type*)

where *rate* = the interest rate per period (i.e., per year, month, etc.), which remains constant throughout the total number of periods

number of periods = total number of periods (i.e., number of years, months, etc.)

payment = the payment made each period. (Periodic payments, if any, remain constant throughout the total number of periods.)

future value = the future value, or the cash balance you want to attain after the last payment is made. If *future value* is omitted, it is assumed to be zero (e.g., the future value of a loan is zero).

and *type* = 0 if periodic payments are made at the end of each period, 1 if periodic payments are made at the beginning of each period.

Converting a Future Value to Its Present Equivalent

The following example illustrates the use of Excel's PV function to discount a future value to its present value.

Example 7.5: How large a lump sum of money would an individual need to invest at an annual rate of interest of 10 percent, compounded annually, in order to have $30,000 at the end of six years?

Solution: Substituting values into equation 7.2 gives

$$P = \frac{\$30,000}{(1+0.10)^6} = \frac{\$30,000}{1.771561} = \$16,934.22$$

(Continued)

Figure 7-8 shows the same result with Excel's PV function. The key entry is =PV(B2,B3,B4,B5) in Cell B7. Note that the present value in Cell B7 is negative, which indicates a cash outflow from the individual, and the future value in Cell B5 is positive, which indicates a cash inflow to the individual.

The result shows that the present value of $30,000 received six years from the present at a discount rate of 10 percent per year, compounded annually, is $16,934.22. One can interpret this result to mean that if one can earn an annual rate of interest of 10 percent, compounded annually, he or she must invest $16,934.22 in order to have $30,000 after six years.

Figure 7-8

Present Value Needed to Generate a Given Future Value

	A	B
1	**Example 7.5: MOVING FROM FUTURE TO PRESENT**	
2	Annual rate of interest, compounded yearly	10%
3	Number of years	6
4	Periodic payments	0
5	Future value	$30,000
6	Periodic payments at beginning (1) or end (0) of periods	0
7	**Present value**	**($16,934.22)**

Key Cell Entry: B7: =PV(B2,B3,B4,B5,B6)

Present Value of a Series of Equal Periodic Payments

The present value of a series of **equal** periodic payments made at the **ends** of the periods can be computed by the formula

$$P = A \times \left[\frac{(1+i)^n - 1}{i(1+i)^n} \right] \tag{7.4}$$

where P = present value

A = periodic payment (**N.B. Periodic payments must all be equal and must be made at the end of each period.**)

i = periodic rate of compound interest

and n = number of interest-bearing periods

Example 7.6: What is the present value of a series of monthly payments of $200 made at the end of each month for the next five years? Assume that the discount rate is 5 percent per year, compounded monthly.

Solution: Substituting values into equation 7.4 gives the following for the present value of the payments made at the **end** of each month.

$$P_{end} = \$200 \times \left[\frac{(1+0.05/12)^{5 \times 12} - 1}{(0.05/12)(1+0.05/12)^{5 \times 12}} \right] = \$10,598.14$$

(Continued)

Figure 7-9 is a spreadsheet solution. The key entry in Cell B7 is =PV(B2/12,B3*12,B4,B5,B6).

Figure 7-9

Present Value of a Series of Equal Future Payments Made at the Ends of the Periods

	A	B
1	**Example 7.6: PRESENT VALUE OF A SERIES OF EQUAL FUTURE PAYMENTS MADE AT THE END OF EACH PERIOD**	
2	Annual rate of interest, compounded monthly	5%
3	Number of years	5
4	Monthly payments (beginning of month)	($200)
5	Future value	0
6	Monthly payments made at beginning (1) or end (0) of month	0
7	**Present value**	**$10,598.14**

Key Cell Entry: B7: =PV(B2/12,B3*12,B4,B5,B6)

Example 7.7: What would be the present value of the monthly payments in Example 7.6 if the payments were made at the beginning of each month rather than the end?

Solution: If the payments are made at the beginning of each period rather than the end, the value obtained by equation 7.3 must be adjusted to the present value one period earlier. Thus, if the payments for Example 7.6 are made at the **beginning** rather than the **end** of each month, the present value calculated by Equation 6.3 would be adjusted as follows:

$$P_{begin} = \$10,598.14 \times (1 + 0.05/12) = \$10,642.30$$

Excel's PV function simplifies the calculation by using *type* (i.e., the last argument in the function) to specify whether the periodic payments are made at the period beginnings or ends. Figure 7-10 shows the result by simply changing the entry in Cell B6 to 1 from 0.

Figure 7-10

Present Value of a Series of Equal Future Payments Made at the Beginnings of the Periods Rather Than at the Ends

	A	B
1	**Example 7.7: PRESENT VALUE OF A SERIES OF EQUAL FUTURE PAYMENTS MADE AT THE BEGINNING OF EACH PERIOD**	
2	Annual rate of interest, compounded monthly	5%
3	Number of years	5
4	Monthly payments (beginning of month)	($200)
5	Future value	0
6	Monthly payments made at beginning (1) or end (0) of month	1
7	**Present value**	**$10,642.30**

Key Cell Entry: B7: =PV(B2/12,B3*12,B4,B5,B6)

Using Present Values to Choose Best Alternative

The following example uses the PV function to compute the present values of the future cash flows of three alternatives at a given discount rate in order to identify the most attractive alternative.

Example 7.8: Suppose you are given the following three cash inflows from which to choose.

Alternative A: Year-end receipts of $7,000 for each of the next four years
Alternative B: A single, lump-sum receipt of $31,000 at the end of four years
Alternative C: Year-end receipts of $2,600 for each of the next four years plus a lump-sum receipt of $20,000 at the end of four years

Which alternative would you choose if the discount rate of money was 6 percent, and why?

Solution: Figure 7-11 shows the solution. The basis for choosing between the alternatives is the present value of the future cash flows. To compute these, enter =-PV(B6,B7,B4,B5) in Cell B8 and copy the entry to Cells C8:D8. To identify the alternative with the highest present value of the future cash flows, enter =IF(B8=MAX(B8:D8),B3, IF(C8=MAX(B8,D8),C3,D3)) in Cell D9. The best alternative to choose is Alternative C.

Figure 7-11

Present Values for Future Cash Inflows

	A	B	C	D
1	Example 7.8: PRESENT VALUES OF FUTURE CASH INFLOWS			
2			Alternative	
3		A	B	C
4	Periodic payment for next four years	$7,000	$0	$2,600
5	Lump-sum payment at end of four years	$0	$31,000	$20,000
6	Discount rate, percent per year	6.0%	6.0%	6.0%
7	Number of years	4	4	4
8	Present value of future cash inflows	$24,255.74	$24,554.90	$24,851.15
9			Best alternative	C

> **Key Cell Entries**
> B8: = –PV(B6,B7,B4,B5) and copy to C8:D8
> D9: =IF(B8=MAX(B8:D8),B3,IF(C8=MAX(B8:D8),C3,D3))

Using Goal Seek to Determine the Discount Rate for Equal Present Values

The following example shows how to use Excel's Goal Seek tool to determine the discount rate that produces equal present values for two alternatives.

Example 7.9: At what discount rate are the present values of the future cash flows of Alternatives A and C equal? What is the present value of the future cash flows of Alternative B at the same discount rate?

Solution: Figure 7-12 shows the solution obtained with Excel's Goal Seek tool. To use this tool, we need to make two changes to the spreadsheet for the preceding example. We need to link the discount rates for all three alternatives. To do this, enter =B6 in Cell C6 and copy the entry to Cell D6. In Cell D9, calculate the difference between the present values of Alternatives A and C by the entry =B8-D8.

Figure 7-12

Discount Rate for the Present Values of Alternatives A and C to be Equal

	A	B	C	D
1	Example 7.9: DISCOUNT RATE FOR EQUAL PRESENT VALUES OF A AND C			
2			Alternative	
3		A	B	C
4	Periodic payment for next four years	$7,000	$0	$2,600
5	Lump-sum payment at end of four years	$0	$31,000	$20,000
6	Discount rate, percent per year	8.59%	8.59%	8.59%
7	Number of years	4	4	4
8	Present value of future cash inflows	$22,884.35	$22,295.90	$22,884.35
9	Difference of PVs between Alternatives A and C			($0.00)

```
Key Cell Entries Added to Preceding Spreadsheet
        C6: =B6, copy to D6
        D9: =B8-D8
```

Access the Goal Seek dialog box shown in Figure 7-13 on the Tools drop-down menu and make the settings shown. The strategy is to use Goal Seek to find the value in Cell B6 that makes the difference in Cell D9 between the present values of Alternatives A and C equal. Clicking OK or pressing Enter causes the Goal Seek Status box shown in Figure 7-14 to appear.

Clicking OK or pressing Enter produces the results shown in Figure 7-12.

Figure 7-13

Goal Seek Dialog Box with Settings for Example 7.9

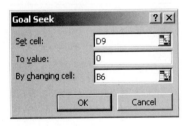

(Continued)

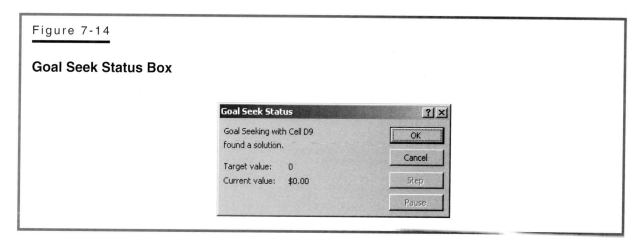

Figure 7-14

Goal Seek Status Box

Effect of Discount Rate on Present Value

The following example examines the effect of the discount rate of money on the present values of the future cash inflows of Example 7.9.

Example 7.10: Evaluate the effect of changes in the discount rate of money from 0 percent to 12 percent on the present values of the three future cash inflows of Example 7.9. Use increments of 1 percent in the discount rate, and indicate which alternative is the best choice at each discount rate.

Solution: Figure 7-15 is the solution. To compute the present values, enter =−PV($B13,C$7,C$4,C$5) in Cell C13 and copy the entry to C13:E25. To identify the best choice at each discount rate, enter =IF(C13=MAX(C13:E13),C$3,IF(D13=MAX(C13:E13),D$3,E$3)) in Cell F13 and copy the entry to F14:F25.

Note that the best choice depends on the time value of money, as expressed by the discount rate. If money has no time value, its value is the same regardless of when it is received. Therefore, Alternative B is the best choice since it returns a total of $31,000, whereas Alternatives A and C return smaller total amounts of $28,000 and $28,400.

As the time value of money increases, it is better to receive it sooner than later. Thus, as the results in Figure 7-15 demonstrate, the best choice passes from Alternative B to Alternative C to Alternative A as the discount rate increases from 0 to 12 percent. This is important to an investor who borrows money to make an investment intended to provide a set of future cash flows. As the discount rate (i.e., the interest rate the investor pays to borrow money) increases, it becomes increasingly important to the investor to be repaid as soon as possible. This is because the present value of income received further and further into the future becomes less and less as the rate of interest increases.

The NPV Function

An important limitation on Excel's PV and FV functions is that future periodic cash flows must be equal in amount and equally spaced. This section describes the use of the NPV function for calculating present values of a series of future periodic cash flows that are unequal.

Figure 7-15
___

Sensitivity of Present Values of Future Cash Inflows to Discount Rate

	A	B	C	D	E	F
1	Example 7.10: SENSITIVITY OF PRESENT VALUES TO DISCOUNT RATE					
2				Alternative		
3			A	B	C	
4	Periodic payment for next four years		$7,000	$0	$2,600	
5	Lump-sum payment at end of four years		$0	$31,000	$20,000	
6	Discount rate, percent per year		6.0%	6.0%	6.0%	
7	Number of years		4	4	4	
8	Present value of future cash inflows		$24,255.74	$24,554.90	$24,851.15	
9				Best choice	C	
10			Sensitivity Analysis			
11		Discount Rate,		Alternative		Best
12		percent per year	A	B	C	Choice
13		0.0%	$28,000.00	$31,000.00	$30,400.00	B
14		1.0%	$27,313.76	$29,790.39	$29,364.72	B
15		2.0%	$26,654.10	$28,639.21	$28,377.00	B
16		3.0%	$26,019.69	$27,543.10	$27,434.20	B
17		4.0%	$25,409.27	$26,498.93	$26,533.81	C
18		5.0%	$24,821.65	$25,503.78	$25,673.52	C
19		6.0%	$24,255.74	$24,554.90	$24,851.15	C
20		7.0%	$23,710.48	$23,649.75	$24,064.65	C
21		8.0%	$23,184.89	$22,785.93	$23,312.13	C
22		9.0%	$22,678.04	$21,961.18	$22,591.78	A
23		10.0%	$22,189.06	$21,173.42	$21,901.92	A
24		11.0%	$21,717.12	$20,420.66	$21,240.98	A
25		12.0%	$21,261.45	$19,701.06	$20,607.47	A

Key Cell Entries
C13: =−PV($B13,C$7,C$4,C$5), copy to C13:E25
F13: =IF(C13=MAX(C13:E13),C$3,IF(D13=MAX(C13:E13),D$3,E$3)), copy to F14:F25

Present Value of a Series of Unequal Future Values

Suppose an investment generates a series of future cash flows. The present value of the series is the sum of the present values of each of the future cash flows. If the future cash flows are realized at the **ends** of the periods and there are n periods, their net present value is given by the equation

$$P = \frac{F_1}{(1+i)} + \frac{F_2}{(1+i)^2} + \frac{F_3}{(1+i)^3} + \ldots + \frac{F_n}{(1+i)^n} = \sum_{k=1}^{n} \frac{F_k}{(1+i)^k} \qquad (7.5)$$

Example 7.11: Find the present value of the following cash flows, each of which is received at year end for the next five years:

Year	1	2	3	4	5
Future cash flow	$4,500	$8,000	$10,000	$5,000	$2,000

If the discount rate of money is 10 percent per year, what is the present value of the stream of future cash flows?

(Continued)

Solution: Inserting values into equation 7.5 gives

$$P = \frac{\$4,500}{(1+0.10)} + \frac{\$8,000}{(1+0.10)^2} + \frac{\$10,000}{(1+0.10)^3} + \frac{\$5,000}{(1+0.10)^4} + \frac{\$2,000}{(1+0.10)^5}$$

$$= \$4,090.91 + \$6,611.57 + \$7,513.15 + \$3,415.07 + \$1,241.84 = \$22,872.54$$

Figure 7-16 is a spreadsheet solution that shows this method of solution and an alternate method based on using Excel's NPV (for net present value) function.

> *Method 1:* Row 6 shows present values for each of the year-end cash flows, and Row 7 shows cumulative values. The future end-of-year values are discounted to their present values by entering =B3/(1+$B$4)^B2 in Cell B6 and copying to C6:F6. The sums of the present values are calculated by entering =SUM($B$6:B6) in Cell B7 and copying to C7:F7. At the end of five years, the total present value of the year-end cash flows is $22,872.54.
>
> *Method 2:* Row 9 shows the cumulative values calculated with Excel's NPV function. The syntax for this function is

$$NPV(rate, value1, value2, \ldots)$$

where *rate* is the discount rate (or rate of interest) over the length of one period, and *value1, value2,…* are 1 to 29 arguments representing the cash flows. Note that the range of values can also be expressed by entering the cell IDs for the first and last cells of the range separated by a colon. Dollar signs are used on the cell ID for *rate* and *value1* if the entry is to be copied to other cells. Enter =NPV($B$4,$B$3:B3) in Cell B9 and copy to C9:F9. The net present value of the future cash flows is $22,872.54, the same as by Method 1.

Note that the NPV function differs from the PV function in two important respects: (1) The PV function is limited to periodic cash flows in the future that are **equal** and occur in **successive** periods, whereas the NPV function can be used for a variable series of periodic cash flows, either negative, positive, or zero in amount. (2) The PV function allows the periodic cash flows to take place at either the beginning or the end of each period, whereas the NPV function assumes that **all** future cash flows occur at the ends of the periods and the periods are equally spaced (e.g., at the ends of successive years).

One of the most common uses of the NPV function is the evaluation of capital investments. This important use is discussed in Chapters 10 to 15.

Figure 7-16

Present Value of a Series of Unequal Future Cash Flows

	A	B	C	D	E	F
1	Example 7.11: PRESENT VALUE OF UNEQUAL FUTURE CASH FLOWS					
2	Year	1	2	3	4	5
3	Year-end cash flow	*$4,500.00*	$8,000.00	$10,000.00	$5,000.00	$2,000.00
4	Annual discount rate	*10%*				
5	Method 1: Discount future values to the present by using Equation 6.5					
6	Present value	$4,090.91	$6,611.57	$7,513.15	$3,415.07	$1,241.84
7	Sum of present values	$4,090.91	$10,702.48	$18,215.63	$21,630.69	**$22,872.54**
8	Method 2: Use Excel's NPV function					
9	Net present value	$4,090.91	$10,702.48	$18,215.63	$21,630.69	**$22,872.54**

> **Key Cell Entries**
>
> B6: =B3/(1+$B$4)^B2, copy to C6:F6
> B7: =SUM($B$6:B6), copy to C7:F7
> B9: =NPV($B$4,$B$3:B3), copy to C9:F9

Periodic Payments and Receipts

Many business and personal situations involve *periodic* payments or receipts that are equal from one period to the next. Examples include:

- Monthly payments on **home mortgages** or **automobile loans**
- Monthly receipts from **retirement systems**
- Monthly or biweekly **deductions** from pay checks into company credit unions
- Annual **payments** for home and life insurance
- Annual investments into **sinking funds** to accumulate cash to replace equipment or make other future capital investments.

Case Study: An Investment Decision

An investor has the choice of two alternatives for investing $10,000. Alternative A returns a single lump sum of $30,000 at the end of the fourth year—that is, four years after making the investment. Alternative B returns a cash inflow of $5,800 at the end of each year for the next four.

   a. If the discount rate of money is 10 percent, compounded annually, which investment has the higher net present value?
   b. If the discount rate of money is 20 percent, compounded annually, which investment has the higher net present value?
   c. What is the discount rate at which the two alternatives are equally attractive?
   d. Prepare a one-variable input table to show the sensitivity of the net present values of the two alternatives to discount rates from 10 to 20 percent.
   e. Prepare a chart of the results from part e.

Solution: Figure 7-17 shows the results, with the key cell entries below. The original investment of $10,000 is shown at year 0, which corresponds to the beginning of the first year. The NPV function is used to calculate the net present values in Cells B11:C11, B15:C15, and B19:C19 for the year-end cash flows in Cells B5:C8 and the discount rates in Cells B10, B14, and B18. (An arbitrary value for the discount rate is entered in Cell B18 and is later changed by using the Solver tool to obtain the value for part c.) Note the $ signs on the entry in Cell B11 so that it can be copied to Cells C11, B15:C15, and B19:C19.

   To determine the discount rate that makes the two alternatives equally attractive, we determine the discount rate in Cell B18 that makes the difference in Cell C20 between the NPVs in Cells B19 and C19 equal. To do this, use the Solver tool with the settings shown in Figure 7-18, which change the value of the discount rate in Cell B18 to make the difference between the two NPVs in Cell C20 equal to zero. (Although the logic may seem strange, another way to determine the discount rate with Solver is to maximize or minimize the value in Cell B19 or C19 by changing Cell B18 subject to the constraint that B19=C19. This method eliminates the need for using the difference in Cell C20.)

   Choose a suitable portion of the worksheet for the sensitivity analysis, such as Cells E2:G15. Enter values for the discount rate in Cells E5:E15. Enter =B14 in Cell D4, =B15 in Cell E4, and =C15 in Cell F4. Custom format Cells D4:F4 to label the results in the cells below. Then drag the mouse to highlight Cells E4:G15, select "Table" from the "Data" drop-down menu to open the "Table" dialog box shown in Figure 7-19, enter B14 for the column input cell, and click OK or press the Enter key. Format the results as shown in Figure 7-17.

(Continued)

Figure 7-17

Evaluation of Two Investments

	A	B	C	D	E	F	G
1			Case Study: INVESTMENT DECISION				
2		\multicolumn{2}{c}{Year-End Cash Flows}			Part d		
3	Year	Alternative A	Alternative B		\multicolumn{3}{c}{NPV of Alternative}	
4	0	$ (10,000)	$ (10,000)		Discount Rate	Alternative A	Alternative B
5	1	$ -	$ 5,800		10.0%	$ 10,490.40	$ 8,385.22
6	2	$ -	$ 5,800		11.0%	$ 9,761.93	$ 7,994.18
7	3	$ -	$ 5,800		12.0%	$ 9,065.54	$ 7,616.63
8	4	$ 30,000	$ 5,800		13.0%	$ 8,399.56	$ 7,251.93
9		\multicolumn{2}{c}{Part a}			14.0%	$ 7,762.41	$ 6,899.53
10	Discount rate	10.0%			15.0%	$ 7,152.60	$ 6,558.87
11	NPV of Alternative	$ 10,490.40	$ 8,385.22		16.0%	$ 6,568.73	$ 6,229.45
12	Best choice	Alternative A	---		17.0%	$ 6,009.50	$ 5,910.76
13		\multicolumn{2}{c}{Part b}			18.0%	$ 5,473.67	$ 5,602.36
14	Discount rate	20.0%			19.0%	$ 4,960.06	$ 5,303.80
15	NPV of Alternative	$ 4,467.59	$ 5,014.66		20.0%	$ 4,467.59	$ 5,014.66
16	Best choice	---	Alternative B				
17		\multicolumn{2}{c}{Part c}					
18	Discount rate	17.43%					
19	NPV of Alternative	$ 5,777.76	$ 5,777.76				
20		Difference =	$ (0.00)				
21		\multicolumn{6}{c}{Part e}					

Part e: Net Present Value vs. Discount Rate chart showing Alternative A and Alternative B lines from 10% to 20%.

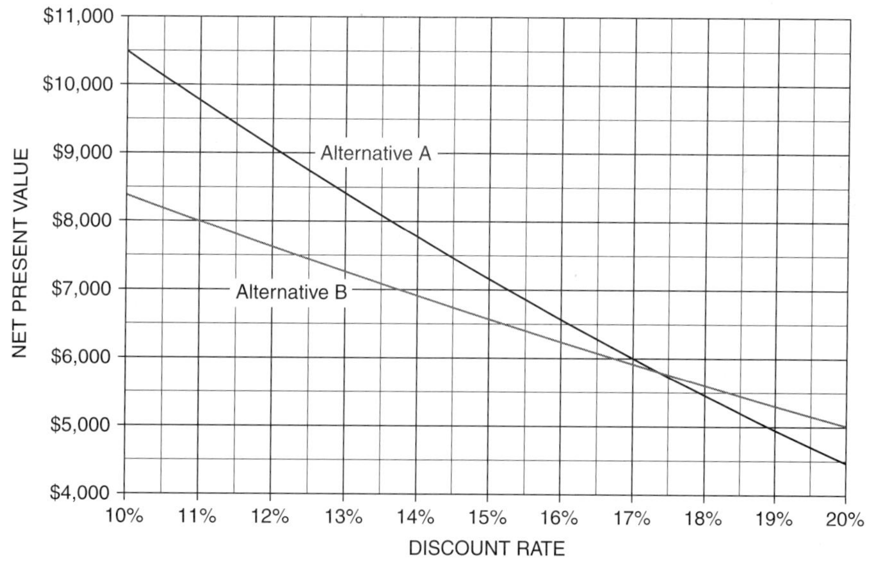

Key Cell Entries

B11: =NPV($B10,B$5:B$8)+B$4, copy to C11, B15:C15, and B19:C19
B12: =IF(B11>C11,$B$3,"---"), copy to B16
C12: =IF(C11>B11,$C$3,"---"), copy to C16
C20: =B19-C19
 E4: =B14 (Custom format Cell E4 with text.)
 F4: =B15, copy to G4 (Custom format Cells F4 and G4 with text.)

(Continued)

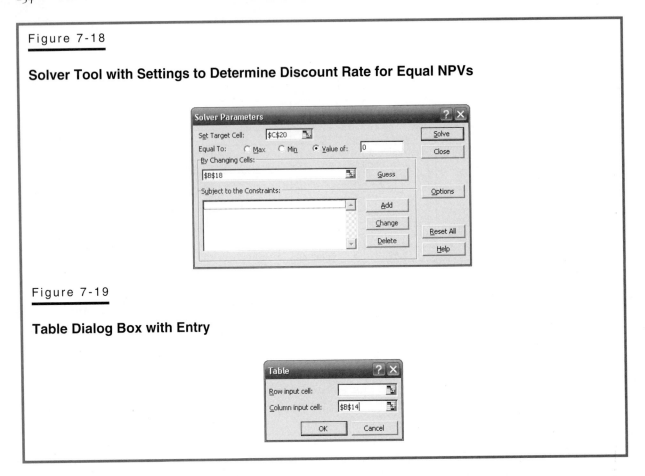

Figure 7-18

Solver Tool with Settings to Determine Discount Rate for Equal NPVs

Figure 7-19

Table Dialog Box with Entry

The technical term *annuity* is used for a fixed amount of money that is paid or received at regular intervals, such as annually, quarterly, or monthly. Moving a single annuity payment or receipt back and forth in time to find its equivalent present or future value, and vice versa, is an important operation in financial analysis. This section discusses Excel's special functions for analyzing such situations to determine, for example, (1) the amount of periodic payments needed to pay off a loan at a specified rate of interest and loan life, (2) the amount of periodic payments needed to provide a certain future amount after a fixed time and at a specified rate of interest, (3) the amount of the outstanding principal of a loan after a given number of payments at a specified interest rate, and so forth.

The PMT Function

Excel's PMT function calculates the value of a periodic payment for paying back (i.e., amortizing) a loan in a specified number of periods and at a specified interest rate. It is also used to calculate the value of a periodic amount or deposit that should be set aside to accumulate a future amount. Its form is

$$=PMT(rate, number\ of\ periods, present\ value, future\ value, type)$$

where *rate* is the periodic rate of interest, *number of periods* is the number of periods for completely paying back the loan or accumulating a future amount, *present value* is the amount loaned, and *future value* is the future amount to be accumulated. Either *present value* or *future value* must be zero, depending on whether one wishes to calculate the periodic amount for a specified present value (e.g., a loan) or for a specified amount to be accumulated in the future.

The PMT function allows for periodic payments or receipts at either the ends or the beginnings of periods. This is done with the *type* argument, which can either be 0 (the default setting) if the periodic payments or receipts are at the end of each period or changed to 1 if they are at the beginning. When the PMT function is used with a present value and payments or receipts are at the ends of the periods, the last two arguments can be omitted.

Example 7.12:   The Morgan Company plans to borrow money to purchase an office building for its headquarters. The building it has selected has a price tag of $10 million. The company will make a down payment of $2 million and take a first mortgage on the balance of $8 million. The lender agrees to provide a 30-year mortgage on the principal of $8 million at an annual interest rate of 10 percent, compounded monthly, with monthly payments at the end of each month. How much will Morgan pay monthly on their mortgage?

Solution: Figure 7-20 is a spreadsheet solution.

The Morgan Company's monthly payment is calculated by the entry

$$=PMT(B2/12,B3*12,B4,B5,B6)$$

in cell B7, which results in the value ($70,205.73). The parentheses indicate this is a cash outflow or expense.

Figure 7-20

Monthly Mortgage Payments

	A	B
1	Example 7:12: MONTHLY MORTGAGE PAYMENTS	
2	Nominal annual rate of interest, compounded monthly	10.00%
3	Loan life, years	30
4	Amount of loan	$8,000,000
5	Future value	0
6	Payments at beginning (1) or end (0) of month	0
7	**Monthly payment**	**($70,205.73)**

Key Cell Entry: B7: =PMT(B2/12,B3*12,B4,B5,B6)

Example 7.13:   To save for a new computer system that will be purchased two years from the present, the financial manager of Argosy Services wants to put aside monthly amounts into a bank account that pays a nominal annual rate of interest of 6 percent, compounded monthly. The deposits will be made at the beginning of each month, and the new computer system will cost $20,000 when it is purchased two years from the present. What should be the amount of the monthly deposits?

Solution: Figure 7-21 is a spreadsheet solution. The monthly deposits are calculated by the entry

$$=PMT(B2/12,B3*12,B4,B5,B6)$$

in cell B6, which returns the value ($786.41).

(Continued)

Figure 7-21

Monthly Payments to a Sinking Fund

	A	B
1	Example 7.13: ARGOSY SERVICES	
2	Nominal annual rate of interest, compounded monthly	6.00%
3	Loan life, years	2
4	Present value	0
5	Future value	$20,000
6	Payments at beginning (1) or end (0) of month	1
7	**Monthly payment**	**($782.50)**

Key Cell Entry: B6: =PMT(B2/12,B3*12,B4,B5,B6)

Example 7.14: In the preceding example, suppose that instead of making deposits at the beginning of each month, the finance manager of Argosy Services makes them at the end of each month. What would be the amount of the monthly payments?

Solution: The solution is left to the reader. The answer is $786.41.

Calculating Periodic Payments for a Given Future Value and a Given Present Value

The following example illustrates the use of Excel's FV function and its Solver tool to determine the periodic payments needed to accumulate a specified future value in a specified period of time and at a specified rate of interest.

Example 7.15: Refer to the conditions for Example 7.4. How much would the CFO of the Baker Company have to deposit at the end of each month for two years (in addition to the initial deposit of $200,000) for the sinking fund to have a future value of $500,000?

Solution: Figure 7-22 shows a spreadsheet solution. It shows that the CFO must deposit $11,078.08 at the end of each month in order for the fund's future value to equal $500,000.

Figure 7-22

Periodic Payments to Achieve a Given Future Value

	A	B
1	Example 7.15: PERIODIC PAYMENTS FOR GIVEN FUTURE VALUE	
2	Annual rate of interest, compounded monthly	5%
3	Number of years	2
4	Initial investment	($200,000)
5	Periodic payments at beginning (1) or end (0) of periods	0
6	Future value	$500,000
7	**Monthly investment**	**($11,078.08)**

Key Cell Entry: B7: =PMT(B2/12,B3*12,B4,B6,B5)

The IPMT and PPMT Commands

The IPMT and PPMT functions calculate the interest and principal portions of the periodic payments or receipts. They have the following forms:

$$=IPMT(rate,\ period,\ number\ of\ periods,\ present\ value,\ future\ value,\ type)$$
$$=PPMT(rate,\ period,\ number\ of\ periods,\ present\ value,\ future\ value,\ type)$$

The second argument, *period*, is the number of the period for which the value of the interest or principal is computed. The other five arguments are the same as for the PMT command.

Example 7.16: If the Morgan Company pays off its $8 million mortgage by monthly payments of $70,205.73 (see Example 7.12) at the end of each month for 30 years, how much interest will the company pay for the first and last months of the mortgage?

Solution: Figure 7-23 is a spreadsheet solution.

The amounts of interest and principal paid in the first month are calculated by entering

$$=IPMT(\$B\$2/12,B\$8,\$B\$3*12,\$B\$4,\$B\$5,\$B\$6)$$

and

$$=PPMT(\$B\$2/12,B\$8,\$B\$3*12,\$B\$4,\$B\$5,\$B\$6)$$

in cells B9 and B10. (By writing the entry for IPMT in Cell B9 with the $ signs as shown, it can be copied to Cell B10 and edited by merely changing the first letter of the function from I to P.)

The entries in Cell B9 and B10 are copied to Cells C9 and C10 for the 360th month. The first monthly payment of $70,205.73 is divided between $66,666.67 to interest and a reduction of $3,539.06 in outstanding principal. The 360th and last payment of $70,205.73 is divided $580.21 to interest and $69,625.51 as the final amount to principal that completes paying off the mortgage.

Figure 7-23

Payments to Interest and to Principal for the First and Last Months of a 30-Year Mortgage

	A	B	C
1	Example 7.16: MORGAN COMPANY'S MORTGAGE		
2	Nominal annual rate of interest, compounded monthly	10.00%	
3	Loan life, years	30	
4	Amount of loan	$8,000,000	
5	Future value	0	
6	Payments at beginning (1) or end (0) of month	0	
7	Monthly payment	($70,205.73)	
8	Period of interest, months from start	1	360
9	Payment to interest for the period	($66,666.67)	($580.21)
10	Payment to principal for the period	($3,539.06)	($69,625.51)

Key Cell Entries

B7: =PMT(B2/12,B3*12,B4,B5,B6)
B9: =IPMT($B$2/12,B$8,$B$3*12,$B$4,$B$5,$B$6), copy to C9
B10: =PPMT($B$2/12,B$8,$B$3*12,$B$4,$B$5,$B$6), copy to C10

The CUMPRINC and CUMIPMT Functions

The cumulative amounts paid to principal and to interest between two specified periods are important values. For example, the outstanding principal owed on a loan is the difference between the amount of the original loan minus the cumulative payments to principal from the beginning of the loan to the specified period. For many loans, the cumulative payment to interest during a calendar or fiscal year is a deductible expense that reduces taxable income.

The CUMPRINC and CUMIPMT functions calculate the sum of the payments to principal and to interest between two specified periods. They have the following forms:

=CUMPRINC(*rate, nper, pv, start_period, end_period, type*)
=CUMIPMT(*rate, nper, pv, start_period, end_period, type*)

Example 7.17: The CFO of the Morgan Company (see Example 7.16) wants to know how much interest the company will pay on its $8 million mortgage during the first year of the mortgage, and how much the company will pay toward reducing the principal during the first year.

Solution: Figure 7-24 is a spreadsheet solution.

The entry in Cell B8 is CUMIPMT($B$2/12,$B$3*12,$B$4,1,12,$B$6). The dollar signs are included so that the entry can be copied to Cell B9 and edited by changing the function name to CUMPRINC. Note that the sum of the cumulative payments to interest and to principal equals the total payments during the year, or $842,468.71 (computed as the sum of cells B8 and B9, or as 12 X $70,205.73).

Figure 7-24

Payments to Interest and Principalfor the First Year of a 30-Year Mortgage

	A	B
1	Example 7.17: MORGAN COMPANY'S MORTGAGE	
2	Nominal annual rate of interest, compounded monthly	10.00%
3	Loan life, years	30
4	Amount of loan	$8,000,000
5	Future value	0
6	Payments at beginning (1) or end (0) of month	0
7	Monthly payment	($70,205.73)
8	**Cumulative payments to interest for first year**	$ (797,998.42)
9	**Cumulative payments to principal for first year**	$ (44,470.29)

Key Cell Entries

B8: =CUMIPMT($B$2/12,$B$3*12,$B$4,1,12,$B$6)
B9: =CUMPRINC($B$2/12,$B$3*12,$B$4,1,12,$B$6)

(Continued)

Example 7.18: For planning purposes, the CFO of the Morgan Company (see preceding example) needs a table and chart that show how the annual payments to interest and to principal change during each of the 30 years of the mortgage.

Solution: Figure 7-25 is a spreadsheet solution.

Figure 7-25

Amortization Schedule

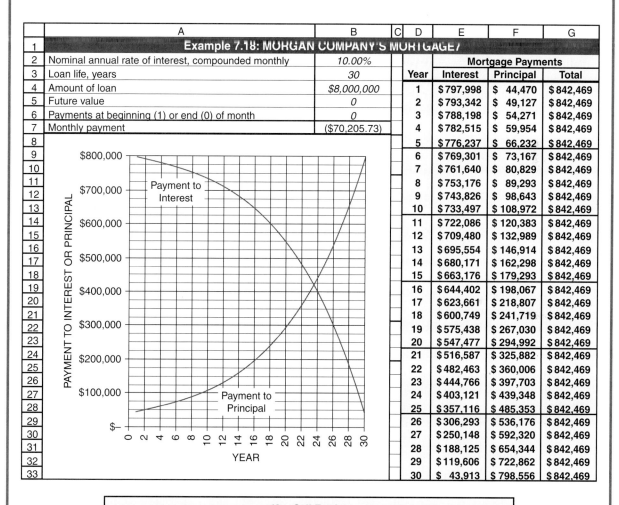

	A	B	C	D	E	F	G
1	Example 7.18: MORGAN COMPANY'S MORTGAGE						
2	Nominal annual rate of interest, compounded monthly	10.00%			Mortgage Payments		
3	Loan life, years	30		Year	Interest	Principal	Total
4	Amount of loan	$8,000,000		1	$797,998	$ 44,470	$842,469
5	Future value	0		2	$793,342	$ 49,127	$842,469
6	Payments at beginning (1) or end (0) of month	0		3	$788,198	$ 54,271	$842,469
7	Monthly payment	($70,205.73)		4	$782,515	$ 59,954	$842,469
8				5	$776,237	$ 66,232	$842,469
9				6	$769,301	$ 73,167	$842,469
10				7	$761,640	$ 80,829	$842,469
11				8	$753,176	$ 89,293	$842,469
12				9	$743,826	$ 98,643	$842,469
13				10	$733,497	$108,972	$842,469
14				11	$722,086	$120,383	$842,469
15				12	$709,480	$132,989	$842,469
16				13	$695,554	$146,914	$842,469
17				14	$680,171	$162,298	$842,469
18				15	$663,176	$179,293	$842,469
19				16	$644,402	$198,067	$842,469
20				17	$623,661	$218,807	$842,469
21				18	$600,749	$241,719	$842,469
22				19	$575,438	$267,030	$842,469
23				20	$547,477	$294,992	$842,469
24				21	$516,587	$325,882	$842,469
25				22	$482,463	$360,006	$842,469
26				23	$444,766	$397,703	$842,469
27				24	$403,121	$439,348	$842,469
28				25	$357,116	$485,353	$842,469
29				26	$306,293	$536,176	$842,469
30				27	$250,148	$592,320	$842,469
31				28	$188,125	$654,344	$842,469
32				29	$119,606	$722,862	$842,469
33				30	$ 43,913	$798,556	$842,469

Key Cell Entries

E4: =−CUMIPMT($B$2/12,$B$3*12,$B$4,$D4*12-11,$D4*12,$B$6), copy to E5:E33
F4: =−CUMPRINC($B$2/12,$B$3*12,$B$4,$D4*12-11,$D4*12,$B$6), copy to F5:F33
G4: =−12*$B$7, copy to G5:G33
Note the minus sign immediately after the equal sign in these entries. This converts the interest, principal, and total payments to positive values in the table and chart.

(Continued)

The annual amounts paid each year to interest is calculated by entering the following in Cell E4 and copying it to the range E5:E33.

$$=CUMIPMT(\$B\$2/12,\$B\$3*12,\$B\$4,\$D4*12\text{-}11,\$D4*12,\$B\$6)$$

This entry is copied to F4 and the function name is changed to CUMPRINC. The entry in Cell F4 is then copied to the range F5:F33.

Note that the first month of the first year is calculated by the term $D4*12-11, and the last month is calculated by the term $D4*12, where D4 is the year number, beginning with the year the mortgage becomes effective. This assumes that the mortgage became effective in January, so that there were 12 monthly payments in the first year.

When mortgage payments start later than the first month of the year, the terms for the start and end periods in CUMIPMT and CUMPRINC must be changed from those given above. For example, if the company's fiscal year is the same as the calendar year and the first mortgage payment is made at the end of May, the fifth month, there would be only eight payments that year. The numbers for the first and last of the eight payments for the first year would be expressed either by the numbers 1 and 8 or by the terms $D4*12-11 and $D4*12-4, where D4 = 1. The numbers for the first and last payments for the second year (payment numbers 9 to 20) would be $D5*12-15 and $D5*12-4. Because D5 equals 2, executing these terms gives the values 2*12 – 15 = 9 and 2*12 – 4 = 20. The entries for the second year could then be copied for the remaining years. The final year in which payments are made would be year 31, and the term for the final end period would be 360.

Case Study: Iverson's Home Mortgage

Mr. and Mrs. Iverson have applied for a mortgage loan on a new home. The new home has a price of $250,000. The Iversons will make a down payment of $50,000 and take a 30-year mortgage on the balance. The mortgage company will charge a nominal annual interest rate of 9 percent, compounded monthly.

a. What will be the month-end mortgage payments the Iversons will pay?
b. The loan is made July 1, and the Iversons will make their first month-end payment at the end of July. When computing their taxable income, the Iversons can deduct the interest they paid on their mortgage during the **calendar** year for which they file their income tax. If the Iversons continue to make their monthly payments by the end of each month, how much interest will be a deductible expense on their income tax for the calendar year in which they took out their home mortgage? (Note that the first calendar year of the mortgage is from July to December; that is, from months one to six of the mortgage.) How much interest will be a deductible expense for the next year after that? How much interest will they be able to deduct as an allowable expense for the second calendar year.
c. What would be the total amount of interest the Iversons would pay if their mortgage continued in effect for the entire 30 years?
d. Suppose that at the end of three years (i.e., 36 months) from the time they took out the mortgage, the financial conditions of the Iversons have improved and interest rates have declined. The Iversons then wish to consider paying off the remaining balance due on their mortgage with a new mortgage having a life of 20 years. The new 20-year mortgage the Iversons will take out to replace their original mortgage has a nominal annual interest rate of 8 percent, compounded monthly. What will be the principal of the new mortgage and the Iversons' monthly payments on it?

(Continued)

e. At the end of an additional five years after taking out the new mortgage (i.e., a total of eight years from their original home mortgage), the Iversons have added to their family and need a larger home. As part of the transactions for buying the new home, they need to pay off the balance due on the mortgage for their old home. How much will be the unpaid balance of their mortgage on their old home at this point?

f. What will be the market value of the home at the time of sale (i.e., eight years from its purchase) if its market value appreciates at a rate of 3.5 percent per year over the eight years that the Iversons have owned the home? Assuming that the Iverson's pay a fee of 6 percent of the selling price, and the selling price is the same as the market value at the time of sale, how much will the Iversons receive from the sale of their home after paying the selling expenses and paying off the balance due on the mortgage?

g. Create a one-variable input table that shows the effect of the rate of appreciation for the market value of the Iversons' home on the net proceeds they will receive from the sale of their home after paying the 6 percent sellers fee and the unpaid balance of their mortgage. Use appreciation rates of 2, 3, 4, and 5 percent.

h. Create a two-variable input table that shows the effect of changes in the rate of appreciation for the market value of the Iversons' home and the rate of interest for their 20-year mortgage on the net proceeds they will receive from the sale of their home. Use appreciation rates of 2, 3, 4, and 5 percent and mortgage rates of interest of 6, 7, 8, 9, and 10 percent.

Solution: Figure 7-26 is a solution for parts a to f of the case study, Figure 7-27 is a solution for part g, and Figure 7-30 is a solution for part h.

To create the one-variable input table shown in Figure 7-27, first enter the series of annual rates of appreciation in a convenient part of the worksheet, such as Cells E6:E9. Then, to link the table to the net receipts from selling the house on the main part of the spreadsheet, enter =B30 in Cell F5. Custom format Cell F5 as the text "from Sales." Drag the mouse cursor to highlight Cells E5:F9, click on "Table" on the "Data" drop-down menu to access the "Table" dialog box, and enter B25 for the column input cell, as shown in Figure 7-28. This entry completes the linkage to the main part of the spreadsheet. Finally, click OK or press Enter to produce the results shown in Figure 7-27.

To produce the two-variable input table shown in Figure 7-29, first enter the series of values for the mortgage's annual rates of interest in Cells F14:J14 and the series of values for the annual rates of appreciation in Cells E15:E18. Then, to link the table to the net receipts from selling the house on the main part of the spreadsheet, enter =B30 in Cell E14. Hide the value in Cell E14 by custom formatting the cell with the text "Appreciation." Drag the mouse cursor to highlight Cells E14:J18, click on "Table" on the "Data" drop-down menu to access the "Table" dialog box, and enter B18 for the row input cell and B25 for the column input cell, as shown in Figure 7-30. These entries complete the linkage to the main part of the spreadsheet Finally, click OK or press Enter to produce the results shown in Figure 7-26.

(Continued)

Figure 7-26

Solution for Parts a to f of Iversons' Home Mortgage

	A	B	C
1	**IVERSONS' HOME MORTGAGE**		
2	**Initial mortgage**		
3	Home price	$250,000.00	
4	Down payment	$50,000.00	
5	Mortgage principal	$200,000.00	
6	Annual interest rate	9.00%	
7	Term, years	30	
8	Monthly payment	$1,609.25	a
9	Interest, months 1 to 6	$8,987.59	b1
10	Interest, months 7 to 18	$17,881.90	b2
11	Cumulative payments to principal at month 36	$4,495.74	
12	Mortgage principal at month 36	$195,504.26	
13	Interest, months 1 to 360	$379,328.28	c
14	Total payments after 360 months	$579,328.28	
15	Interest, months 1 to 360 (alternate calculation)	$379,328.28	c
16	**New mortgage at end of 3 years of mortgage**		
17	Mortgage principal	$195,504.26	
18	Annual interest rate	8.00%	
19	Term, years	20	
20	Monthly payment	$1,635.28	d
21	**Pay off new mortgage after 5 more years (8 years from start)**		
22	Cumulative payments to principal at month 60 of new mortgage	$24,388.01	
23	Unpaid balance at end of month 60 of new mortgage	$171,116.25	e
24	**Gain on investment**		
25	Annual rate of appreciation of home value	3.50%	
26	Selling price = Market value of home at end of 8 years	$329,202.26	f1
27	Selling expenses, as percent of selling price	6.00%	
28	Selling expenses	$19,752.14	
29	Unpaid mortgage balance at time of sale	$171,116.25	
30	Net receipts from sale	$138,333.88	
31	Dollar gain (net receipts minus down payment)	$88,333.88	f2
32	Annual compound rate of appreciation of down payment	13.57%	f3

Key Cell Entries

B8: =−PMT(B6/12,B7*12,B5)
B9: =−CUMIPMT(B6/12,B7*12,B5,1,6,0)
B10: =−CUMIPMT(B6/12,B7*12,B5,7,18,0)
B11: =−CUMPRINC(B6/12,B7*12,B5,1,36,0)
B12: =B5−B11
B13: =−CUMIPMT(B6/12,B7*12,B5,1,360,0)
B14: =360*B8
B15: =B14−B5
B17: =B5−B11 or =B12

B20: =−PMT(B18/12,B19*12,B17)
B22: =−CUMPRINC(B18/12,B19*12,B17,1,60,0)
B23: =B17−B22
B26: =FV(B25,8,,−B3)
B28: =B26*B27
B29: =B23
B30: =B26−B28−B29
B31: =B30−B4
B32: =(B30/B4)^(1/8)−1 or RATE(8,0,−B4,B30,0)

(Continued)

Figure 7-27

One-Variable Input Table for Part g

	E	F
2	One-Variable Input Table	
3	Annual Rate	Net
4	of	Receipts
5	Appreciation	from Sale
6	2.0%	$104,223.71
7	3.0%	$126,574.72
8	4.0%	$150,497.48
9	5.0%	$170,005.70

Key Cell Entry
F5: =B30

Figure 7-28

Table Dialog Box with Entry for One-Variable Input Table

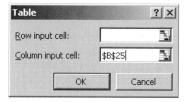

Figure 7-29

Two-Variable Input Table for Part h

	E	F	G	H	I	J
11	Two-Variable Input Table					
12	Annual Rate	Annual Rate of Interest of Mortgage				
13	of					
14	Appreciation	6.0%	7.0%	8.0%	9.0%	10.0%
15	2.0%	$109,357.62	$106,704.58	$104,223.71	$101,913.89	$99,772.35
16	3.0%	$131,708.64	$129,055.59	$126,574.72	$124,264.91	$122,123.37
17	4.0%	$155,631.39	$152,978.35	$150,497.48	$148,187.67	$146,046.12
18	5.0%	$181,219.70	$178,566.65	$176,085.78	$173,775.97	$171,634.43

Key Cell Entry   E14: =B30

(Continued)

Figure 7-30

Table Dialog Box with Entry for Two-Variable Input Table

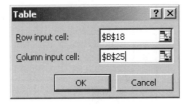

The NPER Command

The NPER command calculates the number of periods needed at a given interest rate to pay off a loan of specified amount or to accumulate a specified future amount. Its form is

$$NPER(rate, payment, present value, future value, type)$$

Example 7.19: Refer to Example 7.17. Suppose the CFO for the Morgan Company plans to make monthly payments of $100,000 rather than $70,250.73. How long would it then take to repay the $8 million mortgage at 10 percent annual interest, compounded monthly?

Solution: Figure 7-31 is a spreadsheet solution. The number of months is calculated by entering

$$=NPER(B2/12,B8,B4,B5,B6)$$

in cell B9, which returns the value 132.38 months, or a fraction of a month longer than 11 years.

Figure 7-31

Number of Months to Pay Off Mortgage with Given Monthly Payment

	A	B
1	**Example 7.19: MORGAN COMPANY'S MORTGAGE**	
2	Nominal annual rate of interest, compounded monthly	10.00%
3	Loan life, years	30
4	Amount of loan	$8,000,000
5	Future value	0
6	Payments at beginning (1) or end (0) of month	0
7	Monthly payment	($70,205.73)
8	New value of monthly payment	($100,000)
9	**New number of months to pay off mortgage**	**132.38**
10	**New loan life, years**	**11.03**

Key Cell Entries

B9: =NPER(B2/12,B8,B4,B5,B6)
B10: =B9/12

Example 7.20: The CFO of the Morgan Company notes that the solution to Example 7.19 is a non-integer number of months that is slightly longer than 11 years. To what amount would she have to increase the monthly payments in order to pay off the loan at the end of 11 years—that is, in exactly 132 months?

Solution: Figure 7-32 is a spreadsheet solution. The entry in Cell B8 for the new monthly payment is =PMT(B2/12,B9,B4,B5,B6), which returns the answer $100,159.02. The negative sign indicates it is a cash outflow).

Figure 7-32

Monthly Payments to Pay Off Mortgage in a Given Number of Years

	A	B
1	Example 7.20: MORGAN COMPANY'S MORTGAGE	
2	Nominal annual rate of interest, compounded monthly	10.00%
3	Loan life, years	30
4	Amount of loan	$8,000,000
5	Future value	0
6	Payments at beginning (1) or end (0) of month	0
7	Monthly payment	($70,205.73)
8	**New value of monthly payment**	**($100,159.02)**
9	New number of months to pay off mortgage	132.00
10	New loan life, years	11.00

> **Key Cell Entry** B8: =PMT(B2/12,B9,B4,B5,B6)

The RATE Function

The RATE function calculates the rate of return for an investment that generates a series of **equal** periodic payments in **successive** periods or a single lump-sum payment. Its form is

$$=\text{RATE}(\textit{number of periods, payment, present value, future value, type, guess})$$

Use the *payment* argument for computing the rate of return from a series of equal payments and the *future value* argument for the rate of return from a single future amount. (Note that unlike IRR, the RATE function can be used only for *equal* periodic payments.) The *guess* argument provides a starting point for Excel's iterative procedure for calculating the rate. Like the *type* argument, *guess* is optional. If omitted, Excel begins with a default *guess* of 0.10 (i.e., 10 percent) to calculate the net present value. If the calculated net present value is not zero, Excel repeats with a second trial value for *guess*, which is lower if the calculated net present value with the first guess is less than zero, and higher if it is greater. This process continues until Excel either arrives at the correct rate or completes 20 iterations. If the #NUM! error message results, try another guess.

Example 7.21: As a result of spending $25,000 to purchase special equipment to produce its products, a company estimates that its after-tax cash flow will increase by $12,000 for each of the next three years. What rate of return is expected for the investment?

Solution: Figure 7-33 is a spreadsheet solution. The annual rate of return is calculated in Cell B5 by the entry =RATE(B4,B3,B2)), which returns the value 20.71 percent.

Figure 7-33

Rate of Return on an Investment in New Equipment

	A	B
1	Example 7.21: RETURN ON INVESTMENT	
2	Equipment cost	($25,000)
3	Year-end after-tax cash inflows	$12,000
4	Number of years of cash inflows	3
5	After-tax annual rate of return	20.71%

Key Cell Entry B5: =RATE(B4,B3,B2)

Case Study: Foremost Mortgage Company

Doris Eppley is a branch manager of the Foremost Mortgage Company. Carlos and Maria Hernandez have come to the company to arrange a mortgage for the purchase of a new house.

The purchase price of the new house is $200,000. Mr. and Mrs. Hernandez propose to make a down payment of $20,000 and take out a 30-year first mortgage on the remainder.

Ms. Eppley advises them that the current nominal annual rate of interest for 30-year first mortgages on homes is 10.25 percent, compounded monthly. The loan is to be repaid in monthly installments beginning at the end of the loan's first month.

a. What are the monthly payments to pay back the loan fully at the end of 30 years? What is the total amount of interest that Mr. and Mrs. Hernandez will pay during that time?

b. If Mr. and Mrs. Hernandez increase their monthly payments by $10, how soon will their loan be paid off, and how much interest will they have paid? How much interest will they have saved by paying their loan off early as a result of increasing their monthly payments by $10?

c. Determine the number of months for paying off their mortgage and the total interest Mr. and Mrs. Hernandez will have paid during that time if they increase their monthly payments by $10, $20, $30, or $40. **Do not round-off the fractional portions of months**; show the number of months to 2 decimal places (e.g., 292.45). Save the answers on your spreadsheet. (You can solve this and the next part by programming them as part of your spreadsheet or you can use Scenario Analysis.)

d. Add a new section to your spreadsheet. Begin by showing the number of months for paying off the Hernandez's mortgage with the values from part c rounded to the nearest whole number. (For example, if adding $20 to the monthly payment results in the answer 292.45 months in part c, round the number of periods to 292 months in part d.) Use these new values for the number of months (or periods) to recompute the amount of the monthly payments. (If done correctly, you will find that the new monthly payments should be within 20 cents, more or less, of the values of $10, $20, $30, or $40.) Determine how much interest Mr. and Mrs. Hernandez will have paid by the time they have completely paid off their mortgage at the new monthly payments. Also determine how much interest the couple will pay over the lifetime of the mortgage.

(Continued)

Solution: Figure 7-34 shows the results.

Note that increasing the monthly payments by exactly $10, $20, $30, and $40 results in non-integer values for the number of months to maturity in Cells C11:F11. The total interest payments over the life of the mortgage are calculated by entering =B10*B11-$B$5 in Cell C14 and copying to D14:F14. (Although a non-integer number of months is unrealistic, we can think of the last payment as being a fraction of the monthly payment.)

Be aware of the problem if you use the CUMIPMT function in Cells C15:F15 with *non-integer* values for the number of months to maturity. Excel rounds down the values to an integer number of months (i.e., to 346, 333, 322, and 312) for calculating the total interest paid over the mortgage's term. **This results in values in Cells C15:F15 that are lower than the correct values in Cells C14:F14.** (See the note in the upper right corner of Figure 7-35.)

In practice, we can round off the non-integer number of months for making payments to the nearest integer and recalculate the monthly payments, total payments to interest, and interest saved. To do this, begin by entering =ROUND(C11,0) in Cell C18 and copying it to D18:F18. Use the values in C18:F18 to recalculate the monthly payments, increase in monthly payment, total interest paid, and total interest saved, as shown in the lower section of Figure 7-34.

Effects of Inflation and Taxes on Interest Rate

Taxes and inflation are part of real life. Realistically, their effects must be included in any calculations of the future buying power of money.

Effect of Taxes

If a person invests $10,000 at a nominal 10 percent annual interest, he will have $11,000 at the end of one year. That is a dollar gain of $1,000 over his initial investment. However, if his income tax rate is 30 percent, he must pay $300 tax on the gain of $1,000. That leaves him with an after-tax dollar gain of $700, or an after-tax rate of return of only 7 percent.

In general, the after-tax rate of return is given by the formula

$$i_{after} = (1 - i_{tax}) \times i_{before} \qquad (7.6)$$

where i_{after} = after-tax rate
i_{before} = before-tax rate
and i_{tax} = tax rate

Thus, for the conditions stated,

$$i_{after} = (1 - 0.30) \times 0.10 = 0.70 \times 0.10 = 0.070 = 7.0\%$$

Effect of Inflation

Inflation robs money of its buying power. It is said to be the cruelest form of taxation, for it reduces the buying power of older people and others on a fixed income.

Figure 7-34

Analysis of Benefits for Increasing Monthly Mortgage Payments

	A	B	C	D	E	F
1	FOREMOST MORTGAGE COMPANY					
2	Purchase price of new home	$200,000	Note that the total interest payments over the mortgage term in Cells C15:F15 by using the CUMINT function do not match the results calculated in Cells C14:F14 by multiplying the number of months by the monthly payment and subtracting the mortgage principal.			
3	Down payment	$20,000				
4	Mortgage data					
5	Principal	$180,000				
6	Term or duration, years	30				
7	Nominal annual rate, compounded monthly	10.25%				
8	Calculated values		Results for given increases of $10, $20, $30, and $40 to monthly payments			
9	Increase in monthly payment	$0.00	$10.00	$20.00	$30.00	$40.00
10	Monthly payment	$1,612.98	$1,622.98	$1,632.98	$1,642.98	$1,652.98
11	Number of months to maturity	360	346.10	333.81	322.82	312.89
12	Number of years to maturity	30	28.84	27.82	26.90	26.07
13	Total interest paid over mortgage term					
14	Calculated as B10*B11-B5, C10*C11-B5, etc.	$400,673.64	$381,713.12	$365,112.90	$350,390.24	$337,195.12
15	Calculated with CUMIPMT function	$400,673.64	$381,578.28	$364,017.93	$349,294.97	$336,023.69
16	Interest saved by increasing monthly payment	$0.00	$18,960.52	$35,560.74	$50,283.40	$63,478.52
17	Calculated values		Revision for rounding months to nearest whole numbers and recalculating monthly payment (optional)			
18	Number of months to maturity	360	346	334	323	313
19	Number of years to maturity	30	28.83	27.83	26.92	26.08
20	Monthly payment	$1,612.98	$1,623.06	$1,632.82	$1,642.81	$1,652.86
21	Increase in monthly payment	$0.00	$10.08	$19.84	$29.83	$39.88
22	Total interest paid over mortgage term					
23	Calculated as B18*B20-$B5, C18*C20-$B5, etc.	$400,673.64	$381,578.28	$365,362.66	$350,628.11	$337,345.83
24	Calculated with CUMIPMT function	($B$7/12,B18,$	$381,578.28	$365,362.66	$350,628.11	$337,345.83
25	Interest saved by increasing monthly payment	$0.00	$19,095.36	$35,310.98	$50,045.53	$63,327.81

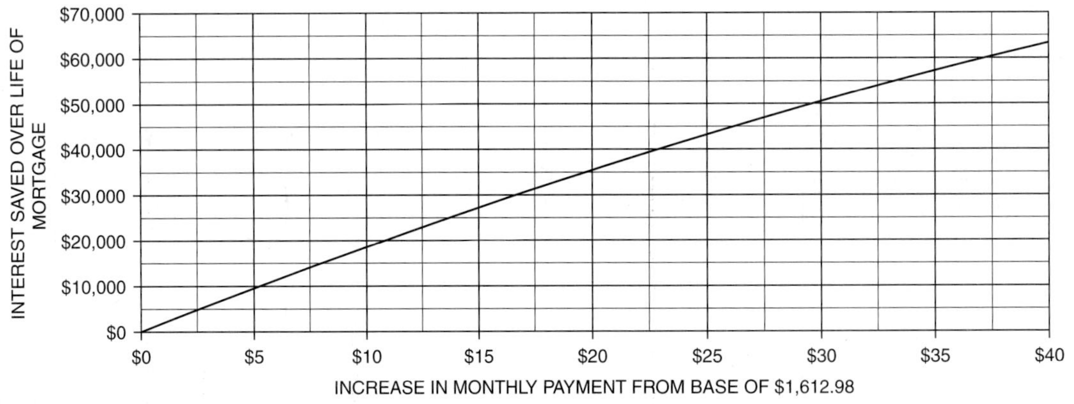

Chart: INTEREST SAVED OVER LIFE OF MORTGAGE vs INCREASE IN MONTHLY PAYMENT FROM BASE OF $1,612.98

Key Cell Entries

C11: =NPER($B$7/12,-C10,$B$5), copy to D11:F11
C12: =C11/12
C18: =ROUND(C11,0), copy to D18:F18
B15: =–CUMIPMT($B$7/12,B11,$B$5,1,B11,0), copy to C15:F15 (But note the values in C15:F15 are incorrect. See text.)
B24: =–CUMIPMT($B$7/12,B18,$B$5,1,B18,0), copy to C24:F24

B14: =B10*B11–$B$5, copy to C14:F14
B16: =$B$14–B14, copy to C16:F16
B23: =B18*B20–$B5, copy to C23:F23

If a person invests $10,000 at a nominal 10 percent annual interest, he will have $11,000 at the end of one year. That is a dollar gain of $1,000 over his initial investment. However, if the inflation rate is 4 percent per year, it will cost $10,400 to purchase the same goods that could have been purchased a year earlier for only $10,000. To put it another way, the purchasing power of $11,000 after one year would have required an initial investment of $11,000/(1+0.04) = $10,576.92 a year earlier in order to keep up with the reduction in buying power due to inflation. This represents a gain in real buying power of $576.92. In other words, the effective rate of return is $576.92/$10,000 = 0.0577 = 5.77%.

In general, the effective rate of interest after correcting for inflation is given by the formula

$$i_{eff} = \frac{i_{nom} - i_{inf}}{1 + i_{inf}} \tag{7.7}$$

where i_{eff} = effective rate of interest (after correcting for inflation)
 i_{nom} = nominal rate of interest (before correcting for inflation)
and i_{inf} = rate of inflation

Thus, for the conditions stated,

$$i_{eff} = \frac{0.10 - 0.04}{1 + 0.04} = \frac{0.06}{1.04} = 0.0577 = 5.77\%$$

Inflation creates a moving target for calculating payments to sinking funds if the goal is to accumulate a fund in dollars rather than buying power.

Combined Effect of Inflation and Taxes

From the preceding solution for the effect of taxes, the investor of $10,000 receives an after-tax cash inflow of $10,700 after a year for his investment of $10,000 at 10 percent interest. The effect of 4 percent inflation is to reduce the buying power of the $10,700 to $10,700/(1+0.04) = $10,288.46. The net gain after inflation and taxes is therefore only $288.46, or a 2.88 percent gain in buying power. This result can also be obtained by combining equations 7.6 and 7.7 in the form:

$$i_{ati} = \frac{(1 - i_{tax}) \times i_{before} - i_{inf}}{1 + i_{inf}} \tag{7.8}$$

where i_{ati} = the interest after taxes and inflation and the other variables are as defined before. Thus, substituting values into equation 6.8, the investment of $10,000 at a nominal interest rate of 10 percent, a tax rate of 30 percent, and an inflation rate of 4 percent has a rate of interest after taxes and inflation (i.e., an increase in buying power) of

$$i_{ati} = \frac{(1 - 0.30) \times 0.10 - 0.04}{1 + 0.04} = \frac{0.07 - 0.04}{1.04} = \frac{0.03}{1.04} = 0.028846 = 2.88\%$$

as before.

Of course, if the investor had done nothing, the buying power of his $10,000 would be only $10,000/1.04 = $9,615.38 at the end of one year due to inflation. This would have been a loss of $384.62

in buying power, or a return of −3.85 percent for not investing. Thus, by investing rather than not investing, the investor has increased his buying power after taxes and inflation by 6.73 percent (calculated as 2.88% minus a loss of 3.85%).

Concluding Remarks

The time value of money is one of the most important concepts in managing one's personal finances or those of a global corporation. It is important in saving for future needs or borrowing to meet present needs.

The time value of money is measured by the interest rate at which future values are discounted to their present equivalent values, or the rate at which present values will increase with time. Interest rates are usually quoted on an annual basis. Interest can be compounded annually, monthly, or continuously.

Excel provides almost 200 financial functions. These simplify many financial calculations, such as loan and mortgage payments, future values of sinking funds, net present values of capital investments, and the values of bonds or coupons. Some of these calculations have been illustrated in this chapter. Others will be demonstrated in future chapters.

Common arguments used in the financial functions are the periodic interest rate, the number of periods, the amount of periodic payments, present and future values, and whether payments are made at the beginnings or ends of periods. These must be entered in the proper sequence. Use the Help menu to remind you of the arguments and the sequence in which they must be entered.

Excel's Goal Seek tool is useful for determining action that must be taken to reach a desired goal. For example, it can be used to determine the periodic payments needed to accumulate a fund sufficient to satisfy future needs. It uses an iterative procedure to find the value of a variable that is necessary for a related variable to have a specific value.

Chapter 8

Cash Budgeting

CHAPTER OBJECTIVES

Management Skills

- Understand the purpose of cash budgeting and its role in a company's financial and operating plans.
- Recognize the inputs required for cash budgeting and identify the organizations that are responsible for providing them.
- Edit cash budgets for changes in corporate policies and operating strategies.
- Evaluate alternate strategies to satisfy fluctuating or seasonal customer demands at minimum cost.

Spreadsheet Skills

- Consolidate inputs from various parts of a business organization into a worksheet.
- Evaluate a firm's cash collections, disbursements, and ending cash balance for successive periods.
- Forecast the short-term borrowing and investing that a CFO must plan for.
- Create one-variable input tables to evaluate the impacts of changes in interest rates, safety stocks, and other variables on a firm's operations and costs.
- Include the cost of holding inventories in a cash budget.
- Include the cost of working overtime in a cash budget.

Overview

A *cash budget* is a plan for managing the flow of cash in the short term. (A capital budget, as discussed in later chapters, is a long-term plan for managing the flow of cash associated with acquiring a capital asset.) A cash budget answers questions such as, "How much will the operating division—that is, manufacturing or service operations—need to pay its workers and suppliers over the next 12 months or four quarters? How much income does a firm expect each period from selling its products? What shall be done with excess funds during periods when cash inflows exceed cash outflows? How much borrowing will be needed to pay current operating expenses during periods when cash outflows exceed cash inflows?"

The last questions are particularly important to financial officers who must maintain a firm's liquidity and invest excess funds. Excess funds can be invested in short-term commercial paper, for example, and borrowed funds can be obtained from banks and other sources. In order to operate efficiently, chief financial officers need to know beforehand when they will have excess funds to invest and when they will need to borrow, and how much. Cash budgets provide CFOs with the following types of useful information:

1. They measure the financial impacts of sales forecasts on a company's cash inflows and outflows.
2. They provide time for the chief financial officer to arrange for borrowing when needed to maintain adequate cash balances and for investing when the company has excess funds.
3. When compared to a firm's monthly or quarterly performance, they provide timely warnings of whether or not a firm's operations are satisfactory and what corrective action, if any, might need to be taken.

Cash budgets typically cover a one-year period, with the year divided into weeks, months, or quarters. Firms with seasonal variations and uncertain cash flows generally use weekly or monthly divisions, whereas firms with stable patterns of cash flow may prepare cash budgets on a quarterly basis.

A cash budget identifies any mismatch between cash inflow and cash outflow. Any mismatch in the short term—that is, from month to month or quarter to quarter—is solved by short-term financing. This involves investing in short-term money markets when inflow exceeds outflow and borrowing when outflow exceeds inflow.

Capital Budgeting and the Balance Sheet

In terms of the financial statements described in Chapter 1, **cash budgeting**, the focus of this chapter, is related to the current assets and liabilities portions of a firm's balance sheet. **Capital budgeting**, which is the subject of later chapters, is related to the fixed assets, long-term debt, and stockholder's equity sections of a balance sheet.

Cash budgets contain inputs from several divisions in a firm. To develop a spreadsheet model for the firm's cash budget, it is helpful to separate the budget into its components, model the components, and then assemble the results from the components into the firm's cash budget. In other words, the spreadsheet for developing a cash budget has three distinctly different areas:

1. A **work area**, usually at the top, which computes revenues and costs. For large organizations, this may include information from different functional organizations of a firm. For example, one section of the work area might provide marketing and sales information on actual past sales and projected future sales and selling prices. This type of information is used to calculate cash inflows. Another area might include information on product output, wages for manufacturing items or providing services, material costs, and inventory levels. This type of information is used to calculate cash outflows.
2. The **cash budget** proper, which includes a listing of each of the cash inflows (e.g., receipts from sales and interest earned on investments) and cash outflows (e.g., labor and material costs, salaries, and sales commissions), and their values for each period. This area of the worksheet integrates the cash flows from the work area.
3. The cash flows associated with **financing activities**. This section is usually at the bottom. It includes calculations of the ending balances for each period and the amounts of money that must either be borrowed to maintain a minimum balance or invested when the ending balance would otherwise be more than needed to maintain liquidity.

Cash Receipts or Inflows

The most common components of cash receipts or inflows during a given period are (1) cash sales, (2) collections of accounts receivable, and (3) other cash receipts (e.g., dividends received, interest received, proceeds from sale of equipment, stock and bond sale proceeds, and lease receipts). The collection of accounts receivable may be lagged one or more months from the time sales are made.

The first two items in the preceding paragraph comprise a firm's operating income or revenues, and its total for the year is reported at the top of the annual income statement. The third item is a result of financial operations and is reported in the lower sections of the annual income statement.

Monthly or quarterly sales are generally not spread evenly across the year. For example, because of strong holiday shopping, retail stores enjoy their biggest sales in December or during the fourth quarter. January and February are months when retail sales are at their lowest. Spring is the time for highest sales of new automobiles. Seasonal variations have significant effects on cash flows.

Example 8.1: Gloriana Stores had sales of $600,000 in November and $800,000 in December. It expects sales to be as follows during the first six months of the next year:

Month	January	February	March	April	May	June
Sales	$500,000	$450,000	$550,000	$600,000	$625,000	$600,000

(Continued)

In the past, 20 percent of Gloriana's sales are paid in cash at the time of the sale, 50 percent are paid the following month, and 30 percent are paid in the second month following the sale. Prepare a spreadsheet showing the expected inflow of operating revenues for the first six months of next year.

Solution: Figure 8-1 shows the solution. Values in Row 4 for the actual sales in November and December and the forecast sales in the first six months of next year are used to calculate the cash inflows in Rows 6, 7, and 8. Note the lags between when sales are made and revenues are received. Cell entries for calculating monthly receipts are =$B$6*D4 in Cell D6, =$B$7*C4 in Cell D7, and =$B$8*B4 in Cell D8. These entries are copied to E6:I6, E7:I7, and E8:I8, respectively.

Figure 8-1

Monthly Operating Revenues

	A	B	C	D	E	F	G	H	I
1	Example 8.1: GLORIANA STORES								
2	Expected Monthly Operating Revenues for First Six Months of Next Year								
3		November	December	January	February	March	April	May	June
4	Sales (Actuals and Forecasts)	$600,000	$800,000	$500,000	$450,000	$550,000	$600,000	$625,000	$600,000
5	Sales Revenues	Pct. Rec'd							
6	Same month as sale	20%		$100,000	$90,000	$110,000	$120,000	$125,000	$120,000
7	Lagged 1 month	50%		$400,000	$250,000	$225,000	$275,000	$300,000	$312,500
8	Lagged 2 months	30%		$180,000	$240,000	$150,000	$135,000	$165,000	$180,000
9	Cash Inflow from Operating Revenues			$680,000	$580,000	$485,000	$530,000	$590,000	$612,500

Key Cell Entries

D6: =$B$6*D4, copy to E6:I6 — Cash sales are 20% of current sales.
D7: =$B$7*C4, copy to E7:I7 — Current revenue includes 50% from sales the previous month.
D8: =$B$8*B4, copy to D8:I8 — Current revenue includes 30% from sales made two months earlier.
D9: = SUM(D6:D8), copy to E9:I9 — Total revenue is sum of revenues from sales for three months.

Cash Disbursements for Direct Operating Costs

One of a firm's major cash disbursements is its payments for the goods it sells to its customers. For retailers, this is the cost of the goods sold. For factories, it is the cost of direct production labor plus raw materials and components that are used to manufacture the goods sold.

The cost of goods sold by retailers can be closely approximated by multiplying the dollar value of sales by a percentage based on past records. Payments may be made at the time of purchasing the goods or their delivery, or one or more periods later.

Example 8.2: An analysis of the records of Gloriana Stores (see preceding example) shows that the cost of goods they sell has averaged 70 percent of the dollar value of sales. To save inventory holding costs, Gloriana schedules its receipts of goods for the beginning of the month in which the goods are expected to be sold. (Note that this is an oversimplification to demonstrate a programming method. In practice, stores cannot operate without inventories, and inventory holding costs are a major expense of doing business. Inventory holding costs are included in a later example.)

Gloriana pays for 10 percent of its purchased goods in the same month that the suppliers deliver the goods. The store pays for 40 percent of its purchased goods in the month following delivery and for 50 percent of its purchased goods two months after delivery. Sales during November and December of last year and forecast sales for the first six months of next year are as given in Example 8.1. What are the cash outflows to pay for purchased goods for each of the first six months of next year?

Solution: Figure 8-2 shows a spreadsheet solution. The dollar values for actual sales in November and December and the forecast sales for the first six months of next year are shown in Cells B4:I4. The monthly costs of purchased goods are evaluated by entering =$B$5*B4 in Cell B6 and copying the entry to C6:I6. The entries for calculating the monthly cash outflows to pay for them are =$B$8*D6 in Cell D8, =$B$9*C6 in Cell D9, and =$B$10*B6 in Cell D10. These entries are copied to E8:I8, E9:I9 and E10:I10, respectively.

Figure 8-2

Cash Outflows to Pay for Goods Purchased

	A	B	C	D	E	F	G	H	I
1		Example 8.2: GLORIANA STORES							
2		Expected Monthly Payments for Goods Purchased during the First Six Months of Next Year							
3		November	December	January	February	March	April	May	June
4	Sales	$600,000	$800,000	$500,000	$450,000	$550,000	$600,000	$625,000	$600,000
5	Cost of Purchased Goods, Percent of Sales	70%							
6	Cost of Purchased Goods, Dollars	$420,000	$560,000	$350,000	$315,000	$385,000	$420,000	$437,500	$420,000
7	Payments for Purchased Goods	Pct. Paid							
8	Same month as purchase	10%		$35,000	$31,500	$38,500	$42,000	$43,750	$42,000
9	Lagged 1 month	40%		$224,000	$140,000	$126,000	$154,000	$168,000	$175,000
10	Lagged 2 months	50%		$210,000	$280,000	$175,000	$157,500	$192,500	$210,000
11	Cash Outflow to Pay for Goods Sold			$469,000	$451,500	$339,500	$353,500	$404,250	$427,000

Key Cell Entries

B6: =$B$5*B4, copy to C6:I6	Cost for goods is 70% of sales.
D8: =$B$8*D6, copy to E8:I8	Payments for goods purchased in current month.
D9: =$B$9*C6, copy to E9:I9	Payments for goods purchased last month.
D10: =$B$10*B6, copy to E10:I10	Payments for goods purchased two months ago.
D11: =SUM(D8:D10), copy to E11:I11	Sum of current cash outflow for goods purchased.

Short-Term Borrowing and Investing

A cash budget helps a firm plan its short-term cash flows. During periods when cash outflows exceed operating inflows, firms borrow against their lines of credit at banks or issue short-term commercial paper. This consists of promissory notes that are sold to other firms, insurance companies, banks, and pension funds. When cash inflows exceed outflows, firms deposit money in their bank accounts or purchase commercial paper or other marketable securities.

Case Study: Keystone Department Store

Sales last year at the Keystone Department Store were $600,000 in November and $950,000 in December. Forecast sales for the first six months of the current year are as follows:

January	February	March	April	May	June
$300,000	$375,000	$450,000	$600,000	$550,000	$600,000

Twenty percent (20%) of all sales are cash sales, 50 percent of all sales are paid for the following month, and the remainder of all sales are paid for two months after the sale.

The cost of goods that Keystone buys from wholesalers for resale at its store is 70 percent of the selling price. Keystone pays cash for 10 percent of the goods it purchases for retailing, it pays for 40 percent of its purchases the following month, and it pays for the remainder two months after purchase.

Wages and salaries depend on the level of sales. Keystone maintains a base cadre of managers, supervisors, and clerks for which it pays $60,000 each month, including benefits. This cadre is the minimum needed to operate the store efficiently during January, which is the month of lowest sales. For other months, when there are more customers than in January, Keystone hires part-time clerks to augment its workforce. The amount it pays for part-time clerks during months other than January is 20 percent of the amount by which the monthly sales exceed the January sales. For example, the cost of part-time clerks in February is $15,000 (calculated as 20 percent of the difference between $375,000 and $300,000).

Other monthly operating expenses are constant at the following amounts:

Monthly mortgage payment	$20,000
Utilities	3,000
Interest on long-term loans	10,000

Keystone expects to pay taxes of $6,000 in January and $7,000 in April. It also expects to pay quarterly dividends of $20,000 to its shareholders in January and April.

Keystone ended the past year with a cash balance of $20,000 and with short-term (30-day) borrowing of $65,000.

Keystone's chief financial officer (CFO) has set $15,000 as the minimum month-end cash balance and $40,000 as the maximum. Short-term investing and borrowing are for 30 days. At the end of 30 days, borrowed money must be repaid with interest at an annual rate of 8 percent. Each month, the company receives back the principal of any loans it made the previous month, plus interest at an annual rate of 6 percent.

Among the things the CFO wants to know are the estimates for how much cash will need to be borrowed each month, if any, in order to keep the month-end cash balance from dropping below $15,000. The CFO

(Continued)

also wants to know how much cash will be needed to invest each month, if any, to keep the month-end cash balance from exceeding $40,000.

* * *

a. Provide a cash budget for the six months from January to June of the current year.
b. Copy your spreadsheet from part a and edit it to analyze the effects of making the following changes:
   Ten percent of sales are cash sales, 70 percent of the sales are paid for the following month, and the remainder is paid for two months after sale.
   Keystone pays cash for 10 percent of the goods it purchases for retailing, it pays for 75 percent of its purchases the following month, and it pays the remainder two months after purchase.
c. Which situation, a or b, is more favorable to Keystone? Give a justification for your response.
d. If the situation in part b were to prevail in the future, what changes might Keystone's CFO reasonably make to the values for the minimum and maximum cash balances? Give justification for your response.

Solution:

a. Figure 8-3 is a cash budget for the first six months of the current year.
   Data values in Figure 8-3 are italicized. Cell entries for calculating monthly sales receipts (cash inflows) are as follows:

D8	=$B$8*D4	Copy to E8:I8	Cash sales are 20% of current sales.
D9	=$B$9*C4	Copy to E9:I9	Current revenue includes 50% from sales previous month.
D10	=$B$10*B4	Copy to E10:I10	Current revenue includes 30% from sales two months earlier.
D11	=SUM(D8:D10)	Copy to E11:I11	Total revenues are the sum of cash sales and revenues from sales made one and two months earlier.

The six-month sums are calculated by entering =SUM(D8:I8) in Cell J8 and copying to J9:J11. The dollar values of the cost of goods sold each month are computed by entering =$B$14*B4 in Cell B15 and copying the entry to C15:I15. The six-month total is calculated in Cell J15 by the entry =SUM(D15:I15).
The payments for purchased goods are calculated by the following entries:

D18	=$B$18*D15	Copy to E18:I18	Payments made in the month of purchase
D19	=$B$19*C15	Copy to E19:I19	Payments made in the month following purchase
D20	=$B$20*B15	Copy to E20:I20	Payments made two months after purchase
D21	=SUM(D18:D20)	Copy to E21:I21	Monthly cash outflow to pay for goods purchased

The six-month sums for payments are calculated by entering =SUM(D18:I18) in Cell J18 and copying to J19:J21.
The monthly increments for wages and salaries when sales are above the January level are calculated by entering =IF(D4>$D$4,$B$25*(D4-$D$4),0) in Cell D26 and copying it to E26:I26. This IF statement first checks to see if the monthly sales are above the January level. If they are, it enters 20 percent of the incremental difference. Otherwise, if the monthly sales are not above the January level, it enters 0.
The total monthly payments for wages and salaries are the sums of the payments of $60,000 for the base cadre of workers plus the increments. These are calculated by entering =D24+D26 in Cell D27 and copying to E27:I27.
The monthly cash outflows for operating and other expenses are calculated by entering =SUM(D27:D32) in D33 and copying to E33:I33. The six-month totals in Column J (both here and all sections below) are calculated in the same manner as before for receipts and payments for goods—that is, by adding the entries in columns D to I.

(Continued)

Figure 8-3

Cash Budget for Keystone Department Store

	A	B	C	D	E	F	G	H	I	J
1	KEYSTONE DEPARTMENT STORE: Part a									
2	Cash Budget for First Six Months of Next Year									
3		Nov	Dec	Jan	Feb	March	April	May	June	6-month Total
4	Sales (Actuals and Forecasts)	$ 600,000	$ 950,000	$ 300,000	$ 375,000	$ 450,000	$ 600,000	$ 550,000	$ 600,000	$ 2,875,000
5	Sale of Goods									
6	Sales Revenues or Income									
7		Percent								
8	Same month as sale	20%		$ 60,000	$ 75,000	$ 90,000	$ 120,000	$ 110,000	$ 120,000	$ 575,000
9	Lagged 1 month	50%		$ 475,000	$ 150,000	$ 187,500	$ 225,000	$ 300,000	$ 275,000	1,612,500
10	Lagged 2 months	30%		$ 180,000	$ 285,000	$ 90,000	$ 112,500	$ 135,000	$ 180,000	982,500
11	Cash Inflow from Operating Revenues			$ 715,000	$ 510,000	$ 367,500	$ 457,500	$ 545,000	$ 575,000	$ 3,170,000
12	Cost of Goods Purchased for Sale									
13	Cost of Purchased Goods									
14	As Percent of Sales	70%								
15	Dollar Value	$ 420,000	$ 665,000	$ 210,000	$ 262,500	$ 315,000	$ 420,000	$ 385,000	$ 420,000	$ 2,012,500
16	Payments for Purchased Goods									
17		Percent								
18	Same month as purchase	10%		$ 21,000	$ 26,250	$ 31,500	$ 42,000	$ 38,500	$ 42,000	$ 201,250
19	Lagged 1 month	40%		$ 266,000	$ 84,000	$ 105,000	$ 126,000	$ 168,000	$ 154,000	903,000
20	Lagged 2 months	50%		$ 210,000	$ 332,500	$ 105,000	$ 131,250	$ 157,500	$ 210,000	1,146,250
21	Cash Outflow to Pay for Goods Sold			$ 497,000	$ 442,750	$ 241,500	$ 299,250	$ 364,000	$ 406,000	$ 2,250,500
22	Operating and Other Expenses									
23	Wages and Salaries									
24	Base			$60,000	$60,000	$60,000	$60,000	$60,000	$60,000	$ 360,000
25	Increment, as Percent of Sales above January Sales	20%								
26	Increment, Dollar Value			$ -	$ 15,000	$ 30,000	$ 60,000	$50,000	$ 60,000	215,000
27	Total Wages and Salaries			$60,000	$75,000	$90,000	$120,000	$110,000	$120,000	$ 575,000
28	Monthly Mortgage Payment			20,000	20,000	20,000	20,000	20,000	20,000	120,000
29	Utilities			3,000	3,000	3,000	3,000	3,000	3,000	18,000
30	Interest on Long-Term Loans			10,000	10,000	10,000	10,000	10,000	10,000	60,000
31	Dividends to Shareholders			20,000	0	0	20,000	0	0	40,000
32	Taxes			6,000	0	0	7,000	0	0	13,000
33	Cash Outflow for Operating and Other Expenses			$119,000	$108,000	$123,000	$180,000	$143,000	$153,000	$ 826,000
34	Summary of Cash Balances and Cash Flows									
35	Beginning Cash Balance			$ 20,000	$ 40,000	$ 15,000	$ 15,870	$ 15,000	$ 31,981	$ 40,000
36	Cash Inflows (Outflows) from Operations									
37	Cash Flow from Sales (Inflow)			715,000	510,000	367,500	457,500	545,000	575,000	3,170,000
38	Cash Flow to Purchase Goods Sold (Outflow)			(497,000)	(442,750)	(241,500)	(299,250)	(364,000)	(406,000)	(2,250,500)
39	Cash Flow for Operating and Other Expenses (Outflow)			(119,000)	(108,000)	(123,000)	(180,000)	(143,000)	(153,000)	(826,000)
40	Total Cash Flow from Operations			$ 99,000	$ (40,750)	$ 3,000	$ (21,750)	$ 38,000	$ 16,000	$ 93,500
41	Cash Flow from Previous Month's Investing (Inflow)									
42	Return of Principal Invested			0	13,567	0	0	0	0	
43	Interest Earned			0	68	0	0	0	0	68
44	Cash Flow from Previous Month Borrowing (Outflow)									
45	Loan Payoff			(65,000)	0	(2,115)	0	(20,880)	0	
46	Interest Paid			(433)	0	(14)	0	(139)	0	(587)
47	Unadjusted Cash Balance before New Borrowing or Investing			$ 53,567	$ 12,885	$ 15,870	$ (5,880)	$ 31,981	$ 47,981	
48	New Borrowing or Investing									
49	Amount Invested		$ -	$ 13,567	$ -	$ -	$ -	$ -	$ 7,981	
50	Amount Borrowed		65,000	0	2,115	0	20,880	0	0	
51	Ending Cash Balance			$ 20,000	$ 40,000	$ 15,000	$ 15,870	$ 15,000	$ 31,981	$ 40,000
52	Basis for Calculations of Short-Term Borrowing and Investing									
53				Minimum Cash Balance		$15,000				
54				Maximum Cash Balance		$40,000				
55				Annual Rate for Investing		6.0%				
56				Annual Rate for Borrowing		8.0%				

(Conditions for part a)

(Continued)

The beginning cash balance in January is the ending cash balance in December. December's ending cash balance is the data value in Cell C51. The beginning cash balances are set by the entry =C51 in Cell D35, which is copied to E35:I35.

The cash flows from operations are calculated in Rows 37:40. The monthly cash inflows from sales are transferred from the upper section of the spreadsheet by entering =D11 in D37 and copying to E37:I37. The monthly cash outflows to pay for purchased goods are transferred from the upper section by entering =-D21 in D38 and copying to E38:I38. The monthly cash outflows to pay for operating and other expenses are transferred from the upper section by entering =-D33 in D39 and copying to E39:I39. The total monthly cash flows from operations are calculated by entering =SUM(D37:D39) in Cell D40 and copying to E40:I40.

The cash flows from the preceding month's investing and borrowing are calculated in Rows 41:46. The returns of the sums invested in the preceding months are transferred by entering =C49 in Cell D42 and copying to E42:I42. The interest earned on the sums invested in the preceding months is calculated entering =C49*$F$55/12 in Cell D43 and copying to E43:I43. These are cash inflows and therefore positive.

The payments of the sums borrowed in the preceding months are transferred by entering =-C50 in Cell D45 and copying to E45:I45. The interest paid on the sums borrowed in the preceding months is calculated by entering =-C50*$F$56/12 in Cell D46 and copying to E46:I46. These are cash outflows and therefore negative.

The unadjusted cash balances before new investing or borrowing are calculated by entering =D35+D40+SUM(D42:D46) in Cell D47 and copying to E47:I47.

The monthly amounts of new investments are calculated by entering =IF(D47>$F$54,D47-$F$54,0) in Cell D49 and copying to E49:I49. The monthly amounts of new borrowings are calculated by entering =IF(D47<$F$53,$F$53-D47,0) in Cell D50 and copying to E50:I50.

The monthly ending cash balances are calculated by entering D47-D49+D50 in Cell D51 and copying to E51:I51.

Figure 8-4 is a reconciliation of the cash inflows and the cash outflows from the beginning of the first month to the end of the last month. The item labeled "Capital Outlays" is included to show any outflows of cash to pay for purchases of capital assets. (The value of capital outlays is zero for Keystone.)

Figure 8-4

Reconciliation of Cash Flows

	A	B	C	D	E	F	G
57	Reconciliation of Cash Flows for January 1 to June 30						
58	Cash Inflows			Cash Outflows			
59	Beginning Balance	$ 20,000		Repay Beginning Short-Term Loan			$ 65,000
60	Total Collections	$ 3,170,000		Inventory Payments			$ 2,250,500
61	Short-Term Interest Income	$ 68		Wages and Salaries			$ 575,000
62		$ 3,190,068		Mortgage Payments			$ 120,000
63				Utilities			$ 18,000
64				Interest on Long-Term Loans			$ 60,000
65				Dividends to Shareholders			$ 40,000
66				Taxes			$ 13,000
67				Capital Outlays			$ -
68				Interest on Short-Term Loans			$ 587
69				Ending Cash Balance			$ 40,000
70				Current Investing			$ 7,981
71							$ 3,190,068

(Continued)

Figure 8-5

Cash Budget for Keystone Department Store

	A	B	C	D	E	F	G	H	I	J
1	KEYSTONE DEPARTMENT STORE: Part b									
2	Cash Budget for First Six Months of Next Year									
3		Nov	Dec	Jan	Feb	March	April	May	June	6-month Total
4	Sales (Actuals and Forecasts)	$ 600,000	$ 950,000	$ 300,000	$ 375,000	$ 450,000	$ 600,000	$ 550,000	$ 600,000	$ 2,875,000
5				Sale of Goods						
6	Sales Revenues or Income									
7		Percent								
8	Same month as sale	10%		$ 30,000	$ 37,500	$ 45,000	$ 60,000	$ 55,000	$ 60,000	$ 287,500
9	Lagged 1 month	70%		$ 665,000	$ 210,000	$ 262,500	$ 315,000	$ 420,000	$ 385,000	2,257,500
10	Lagged 2 months	20%		$ 120,000	$ 190,000	$ 60,000	$ 75,000	$ 90,000	$ 120,000	655,000
11	Cash Inflow from Operating Revenues			$ 815,000	$ 437,500	$ 367,500	$ 450,000	$ 565,000	$ 565,000	$ 3,200,000
12				Cost of Goods Purchased for Sale						
13	Cost of Purchased Goods									
14	As Percent of Sales	70%								
15	Dollar Value	$ 420,000	$ 665,000	$ 210,000	$ 262,500	$ 315,000	$ 420,000	$ 385,000	$ 420,000	$ 2,012,500
16	Payments for Purchased Goods									
17		Percent								
18	Same month as purchase	10%		$ 21,000	$ 26,250	$ 31,500	$ 42,000	$ 38,500	$ 42,000	$ 201,250
19	Lagged 1 month	75%		$ 498,750	$ 157,500	$ 196,875	$ 236,250	$ 315,000	$ 288,750	1,693,125
20	Lagged 2 months	15%		$ 63,000	$ 99,750	$ 31,500	$ 39,375	$ 47,250	$ 63,000	343,875
21	Cash Outflow to Pay for Goods Sold			$ 582,750	$ 283,500	$ 259,875	$ 317,625	$ 400,750	$ 393,750	$ 2,238,250
22				Operating and Other Expenses						
23	Wages and Salaries									
24	Base			$60,000	$60,000	$60,000	$60,000	$60,000	$60,000	$ 360,000
25	Increment, as Percent of Sales above January Sales	20%								
26	Increment, Dollar Value			$ -	$ 15,000	$ 30,000	$ 60,000	$ 50,000	$ 60,000	215,000
27	Total Wages and Salaries			$60,000	$75,000	$90,000	$120,000	$110,000	$120,000	$ 575,000
28	Monthly Mortgage Payment			20,000	20,000	20,000	20,000	20,000	20,000	120,000
29	Utilities			3,000	3,000	3,000	3,000	3,000	3,000	18,000
30	Interest on Long-Term Loans			10,000	10,000	10,000	10,000	10,000	10,000	60,000
31	Dividends to Shareholders			20,000	0	0	20,000	0	0	40,000
32	Taxes			6,000	0	0	7,000	0	0	13,000
33	Cash Outflow for Operating and Other Expenses			$119,000	$108,000	$123,000	$180,000	$143,000	$153,000	$ 826,000
34				Summary of Cash Balances and Cash Flows						
35	Beginning Cash Balance			$ 20,000	$ 40,000	$ 40,000	$ 40,000	$ 40,000	$ 40,000	$ 40,000
36	Cash Inflows (Outflows) from Operations									
37	Cash Flow from Sales (Inflow)			815,000	437,500	367,500	450,000	565,000	565,000	3,200,000
38	Cash Flow to Purchase Goods Sold (Outflow)			(582,750)	(283,500)	(259,875)	(317,625)	(400,750)	(393,750)	(2,238,250)
39	Cash Flow for Operating and Other Expenses (Outflow)			(119,000)	(108,000)	(123,000)	(180,000)	(143,000)	(153,000)	(826,000)
40	Total Cash Flow from Operations			$ 113,250	$ 46,000	$ (15,375)	$ (47,625)	$ 21,250	$ 18,250	$ 135,750
41	Cash Flow from Previous Month's Investing (Inflow)									
42	Return of Principal Invested			0	27,817	73,956	58,951	11,620	32,928	
43	Interest Earned			0	139	370	295	58	165	1,026
44	Cash Flow from Previous Month Borrowing (Outflow)									
45	Loan Payoff			(65,000)	0	0	0	0	0	
46	Interest Paid			(433)	0	0	0	0	0	(433)
47	Unadjusted Cash Balance before New Borrowing or Investing			$ 67,817	$ 113,956	$ 98,951	$ 51,620	$ 72,928	$ 91,343	
48	New Borrowing or Investing									
49	Amount Invested		$ -	$ 27,817	$ 73,956	$ 58,951	$ 11,620	$ 32,928	$ 51,343	
50	Amount Borrowed		65,000	0	0	0	0	0	0	
51	Ending Cash Balance			$ 20,000	$ 40,000	$ 40,000	$ 40,000	$ 40,000	$ 40,000	$ 40,000
52				Basis for Calculations of Short-Term Borrowing and Investing						
53				Minimum Cash Balance		$15,000				
54				Maximum Cash Balance		$40,000				
55				Annual Rate for Investing		6.0%				
56				Annual Rate for Borrowing		8.0%				

(Conditions for part b, with new values in Cells B8:B10 and B18:B20)

(Continued)

b. Figure 8-5 is the spreadsheet solution for part b. This spreadsheet is prepared by copying Figure 8-3 and changing the values in Cells B8:B10 and B18:B20.

Figure 8-6 is a reconciliation of the cash flows. Note that compared to the original conditions of part a, the new conditions of part b result in a larger cash inflow from collections and interest from short-term lending, as well as a larger amount of current investing at the end of the six-month period.

c. Situation b is more favorable to Keystone than situation a. On the positive side, situation b results in more interest earned on short-term investing, less interest paid for short-term borrowing, and a greater amount of short-term investing in June. On the negative side, situation b has more money owed for goods purchased at the end of the six months and less receipts still to be paid.

d. If the situation in part b continues, Keystone has less need to borrow and more opportunity to invest. It should lower the minimum cash balance to a value less than $15,000 and lower the maximum cash balance to a value less than $40,000. This might be done, for example, by reducing the minimum cash balance to $10,000 and the maximum cash balance to $30,000, which will increase the short-term interest income by $253.

Figure 8-6

Reconciliation of Cash Flow from January 1 to June 30

	A	B	C	D	E	F	G
57	Reconciliation of Cash Flows for January 1 to June 30						
58	**Cash Inflows**			**Cash Outflows**			
59	Beginning Balance	$ 20,000		Repay Beginning Short-Term Loan			$ 65,000
60	Total Collections	$ 3,200,000		Inventory Payments			$ 2,238,250
61	Short-Term Interest Income	$ 1,026		Wages and Salaries			$ 575,000
62		$ 3,221,026		Mortgage Payments			$ 120,000
63				Utilities			$ 18,000
64				Interest on Long-Term Loans			$ 60,000
65				Dividends to Shareholders			$ 40,000
66				Taxes			$ 13,000
67				Capital Outlays			$ -
68				Interest on Short-Term Loans			$ 433
69				Ending Cash Balance			$ 40,000
70				Current Investing			$ 51,343
71							$ 3,221,026

(Conditions of part b)

Factory Production

The following sections discuss cash budgeting for factory production. Cash budgeting for factory production introduces some complexities not present for retail stores.

Seasonality

For factories, cash flows to pay for direct production costs are not directly proportional to sales. This is because customer demands are seasonal, with sales varying significantly from one period to the next,

whereas factory output is proportional to the number of workdays during the period. Varying factory output to match demand would require frequent changes in the size of the workforce by hiring when demand is up and firing when demand is down. This alternative is costly for several reasons, not the least of which are the cost for hiring and training newly hired workers and the cost of unemployment compensation for fired workers.

Instead of frequent hiring and firing to match production capacity to consumer demand, factories use inventories to cope with seasonal variations in demand—that is, with the seasonal disparities between production rates and demand rates. Excess production is held in storage when demand is less than factory output, and stored units are used to supply demand when demand exceeds output.

Besides inventories, factories often use overtime to cope with periods of peak demand. They maintain a workforce size slightly below that based on the annual demand, and they work overtime during seasons of above-average demand. This is particularly true when products are high priced, such as automobiles. Customer demand and production rates of automobiles are low in late fall and winter and peak in the spring and summer. Assembly-line workers expect to work heavy overtime during the peak periods, when 53-hour weeks may be worked, and somewhat less than 40 hours per week during the off-seasons. Plant capacity may be designed to provide 75 to 80 percent of the peak demand based on a 53-hour week. This means that all orders during the peak season cannot be satisfied promptly. Most customers during the peak-demand period must wait for delivery. By operating below demand during the peak season, even with overtime, the factories can operate near normal capacity for the rest of the year.

Inventories

Consultants hired to improve a firm's profitability often begin by looking at the firm's inventory management. The reason is simple: Inventories are a major cost of doing business. Reducing inventories provides a large, immediate saving that is repeated over and over throughout each year. Throughout the world, companies are exerting special efforts to manage inventories more efficiently.

Funds tied up in inventories are often the major part of a company's invested capital. The total value of a factory's inventories is usually between 20 and 50 percent of a firm's total assets and may equal the profits earned over two or three years. In wholesale and retail firms, the value of inventories may be even more. For many corporations, the 1990s have been a period of improving inventory management. Slashing bloated inventories has been a major part of the effort to be competitive.

Don't Overlook the Cost of Holding Inventories

Typically, the cost of holding an item in inventory for one year is between 25 and 35 percent of the item's cost, or approximately 2 to 3 percent of the item's cost per month. About half of the cost of holding goods in inventory is interest on the cost of the goods themselves, and the other half consists of the costs of operating warehouses or other storage facilities, insurance, pilferage, etc.

Reducing inventories can provide huge cost saving. Large corporations have reported annual savings on the order of $1 billion or more by reducing inventories!

Inventories are often a company's major capital asset. A portion of the value of inventories is often used as collateral for borrowing funds to maintain them.

Traditional cost accounting systems treat inventory holding costs as overhead rather than as a direct production cost. This causes these costs, which can be very substantial, to be overlooked. Companies that have converted from traditional cost accounting practices to "activity-based costing" (so-called ABC cost accounting) may treat inventory holding costs as a direct cost of sales operations rather than as overhead.)

Case Study: Ashley Manufacturing

We shall use this case study demonstrate how copying and editing spreadsheets can be used to evaluate different management operational strategies.

Strategy 1: Annual Capacity Equals Annual Demand with Large Safety Stock

Rod Morgan, the chief financial officer (CFO) of Ashley Manufacturing, is in the process of planning budgets and cash flows for the coming year. He needs a cash budget statement that provides a month-by-month summary of what is expected for the firm's cash inflows and outflows for the coming year, beginning in January, as well as the totals for the entire year.

Ashley manufactures only one product, which it currently sells to wholesalers at a price of $920 each. The price will be raised to $960/unit at the beginning of June of the coming year. On the average, one-third of the purchases are paid for by the wholesalers during the month of purchase, and the other two-thirds of the purchases are paid for during the following month.

The company's marketing division has forecast total customer demands of 32,000 units for next year. Demand is seasonal and varies from month to month. The following values show the monthly sales forecast, as percentages of the annual sales:

Month	Jan	Feb	March	April	May	June	July	Aug	Sept	Oct	Nov	Dec
Sales	5%	7%	9%	11%	14%	12%	11%	9%	7%	6%	5%	4%

Sales completed during December of the current year will be 1,200 units.

The starting value for the direct labor cost is $145/unit, and the cost of raw materials and components is $460/unit. The contract with the factory workers' union is due to be renegotiated in February. The CFO expects that the new contract will call for a 5 percent increase in direct labor cost starting July 1 of the coming year and will remain constant thereafter for the next two years. You may assume that the amount paid each month to workers equals the number of units produced during the month multiplied by the unit cost for direct labor.

Material costs are expected to increase *each month* at a nominal *annual* rate of inflation of 3.0 percent next year. In other words, beginning with a material cost of $460/unit for units manufactured in January of the coming year, the cost of materials will be 0.25 percent higher in February and will continue to climb 0.25 percent for each month thereafter to the end of the year.

Ashley works closely with its suppliers to provide an efficient just-in-time system for managing materials. Materials are delivered in the same month that they are used in production. In return, Ashley pays its suppliers promptly after delivery.

Monthly salaries for indirect labor are currently $80,000. A raise of 5 percent for salaried workers will become effective on August 1 of the coming year.

The company's salesmen receive a 4 percent commission on all sales. The commissions are paid in the same month that the sales take place.

(Continued)

Ashley's advertising expenses each month are set at 2.5 percent of the sales that were made (i.e., the sales "booked") in the preceding month.

Payroll taxes, social security taxes, health insurance, and other fringe benefits amount to 41 percent of all labor costs—that is, 41 percent of the total cost of salaries and the wages paid to factory workers.

The cost of leasing Ashley's factory and warehouse is $85,000/month. The current lease ends on September 30 of next year. A renewal has been negotiated at $100,000/month, beginning the month of October and continuing for the next two years.

The CFO expects to start the new year with an on-hand inventory of 3400 units. The company regards this as an ample safety stock to satisfy its customers during months of peak demand, when demand exceeds capacity. Any units that are unsold one month are added to inventory for the following month. The value of the beginning inventory, at cost, is $2,035,000. The company uses an "average cost" policy for determining the cost of goods sold each month. The average cost is calculated as the value of the inventory at the beginning of the month plus the cost of production that month divided by the sum of the number of units in inventory at the beginning of the month plus the number of units produced that month.

Monthly inventory holding costs are 2 percent of the value of the average inventory for the month. The average inventory value for a month is one-half the sum of the values of the inventory at the beginning and end of the month.

Interest on *long-term* notes is $12,000/month.

Ashley's production capacity, based on a 40-hour workweek with no overtime, is 32,000 units/year. Ashley has a policy of maintaining its workforce at a constant level. The annual output of 32,000 units on regular time is therefore spread over the months in proportion to the number of workdays in each month. Ashley shuts down for two weeks during the Christmas–New Years holiday season and observes the usual national holidays. The number of workdays each month of the coming year varies as follows:

Month	Jan	Feb	March	April	May	June	July	Aug	Sept	Oct	Nov	Dec
Workdays	19	19	21	22	21	21	22	21	21	23	19	15

All production is on regular time; the company does not work overtime.

Cash on-hand at the end of the December is $45,000. Ashley's CFO wants a minimum of $30,000 on-hand at the end of each month and a maximum of $50,000. If necessary, the CFO will make short-term borrowings at an annual rate of interest of 7 percent to bring the cash on-hand up to the minimum. The CFO will also use any excess over the maximum cash on-hand each month to invest in short-term commercial paper at an average annual rate of interest of 5 percent. You may assume that "short-term" means 30 days (i.e., one month). Therefore, any short-term borrowing is paid back with interest during the following month, and any short-term investments are collected with interest during the following month.

Ashley's CFO expects to pay income taxes of $100,000 in March, $120,000 in June and September, and $130,000 in December. The company will pay dividends of $50,000 to its shareholders in January, April, July, and October.

* * *

a. Prepare a cash budget statement, with a breakdown of cash flows for each month and totals for the entire year.
b. Provide a summary of cash inflows and outflows for the year. Make sure the total cash inflow equals the total cash outflow. How well does it appear the company is doing? What do you see as the CFO's principal concerns for handling the month-to-month cash inflows and outflows next year?
c. How often should Ashley's cash budget plan be updated in order to satisfy the needs of the company's CFO? What inputs are required from Ashley's financial, marketing, and production organizations to update the plan?

(Continued)

Solution:

a. Figures 8-7 and 8-8 show Ashley's cash budget for the first and last six months of the year.

Figure 8-7

First Six Months of Cash Budget for Ashley Manufacturing

	A	B	C	D	E	F	G	H
1		ASHLEY MANUFACTURING: Strategy #1						
2		Dec-96	Jan-97	Feb-97	Mar-97	Apr-97	May-97	Jun-97
3	SALES							
4	Percent of annual		5%	7%	9%	11%	14%	12%
5	Forecast demand, units	1,200	1,600	2,240	2,880	3,520	4,480	3,840
6	Sales completed, units	1,200	1,600	2,240	2,880	3,520	4,480	3,840
7	Unit selling price	$920.00	$920.00	$920.00	$920.00	$920.00	$920.00	$960.00
8	Sales completed, dollars	$ 1,104,000	$ 1,472,000	$ 2,060,800	$ 2,649,600	$ 3,238,400	$ 4,121,600	$ 3,686,400
9	MANUFACTURING: Strategy #1							
10	Workdays		19	19	21	22	21	21
11	Units output		2,492	2,492	2,754	2,885	2,754	2,754
12	Direct labor cost, $/unit *increase in July*	5.0%	$145.00	$145.00	$145.00	$145.00	$145.00	$145.00
13	Material cost, $/unit *annual increase*	3.0%	$460.00	$461.15	$462.30	$463.46	$464.62	$465.78
14	Direct labor cost, total		$ 361,311	$ 361,311	$ 399,344	$ 418,361	$ 399,344	$ 399,344
15	Material cost, total		$ 1,146,230	$ 1,149,095	$ 1,273,228	$ 1,337,192	$ 1,279,602	$ 1,282,801
16	Total manufacturing cost		$ 1,507,541	$ 1,510,407	$ 1,672,572	$ 1,755,553	$ 1,678,946	$ 1,682,145
17	INVENTORY LEVEL							
18	Start of month, units		3,400	4,292	4,544	4,418	3,783	2,057
19	End of month, units	3,400	4,292	4,544	4,418	3,783	2,057	971
20	Average, units		3,846	4,418	4,481	4,100	2,920	1,514
21	INVENTORY VALUE, AT COST							
22	Start of month		$ 2,035,000	$ 2,580,515	$ 2,740,067	$ 2,671,215	$ 2,293,079	$ 1,249,899
23	Added		$ 1,507,541	$ 1,510,407	$ 1,672,572	$ 1,755,553	$ 1,678,946	$ 1,682,145
24	Total before sales		$ 3,542,541	$ 4,090,922	$ 4,412,639	$ 4,426,768	$ 3,972,025	$ 2,932,044
25	Average unit cost of those sold		$601.27	$603.06	$604.66	$606.16	$607.62	$609.43
26	End of month (total after sales)	$2,035,000	$ 2,580,515	$ 2,740,067	$ 2,671,215	$ 2,293,079	$ 1,249,899	$ 591,844
27	Average value of inventory		$ 2,307,758	$ 2,660,291	$ 2,705,641	$ 2,482,147	$ 1,771,489	$ 920,871
28	CASH INFLOWS FROM SALES							
29	Cash from sales last month	66.67%	$ 736,000	$ 981,333	$ 1,373,867	$ 1,766,400	$ 2,158,933	$ 2,747,733
30	Cash from sales this month	33.33%	$ 490,667	$ 686,933	$ 883,200	$ 1,079,467	$ 1,373,867	$ 1,228,800
31	Total sales receipts (cash inflow)		$ 1,226,667	$ 1,668,267	$ 2,257,067	$ 2,845,867	$ 3,532,800	$ 3,976,533
32	MISCELLANEOUS EXPENSES							
33	Salaries *increase in August*	5.0%	$ 80,000	$ 80,000	$ 80,000	$ 80,000	$ 80,000	$ 80,000
34	Advertising *pct of preceding sales*	2.5%	$ 27,600	$ 36,800	$ 51,520	$ 66,240	$ 80,960	$ 103,040
35	Commissions *pct of sales*	4.0%	$ 58,880	$ 82,432	$ 105,984	$ 129,536	$ 164,864	$ 147,456
36	Fringe benefits *pct of wages and salaries*	41.0%	$ 180,938	$ 180,938	$ 196,531	$ 204,328	$ 196,531	$ 196,531
37	Interest on long-term notes		$ 12,000	$ 12,000	$ 12,000	$ 12,000	$ 12,000	$ 12,000
38	Inventory holding cost *pct of avg inventory*	2.0%	$ 46,155	$ 53,206	$ 54,113	$ 49,643	$ 35,430	$ 18,417
39	Long-term leases		$ 85,000	$ 85,000	$ 85,000	$ 85,000	$ 85,000	$ 85,000
40	Income tax				$ 100,000			$ 120,000
41	Dividends to shareholders		$ 50,000			$ 50,000		
42	Total miscellaneous expenses		$ 540,573	$ 530,376	$ 685,148	$ 676,747	$ 654,785	$ 762,445
43	Cost of manufacturing labor and materials		$ 1,507,541	$ 1,510,407	$ 1,672,572	$ 1,755,553	$ 1,678,946	$ 1,682,145
44	CASH OUTFLOW FROM OPERATIONS		$ 2,048,114	$ 2,040,782	$ 2,357,720	$ 2,432,300	$ 2,333,731	$ 2,444,590
45	NET CASH FLOW FROM OPERATIONS		$ (821,447)	$ (372,515)	$ (100,653)	$ 413,567	$ 1,199,069	$ 1,531,944
46	CASH FLOWS FOR FINANCIAL ACTIVITIES							
47	Opening cash balance		$ 45,000	$ 30,000	$ 30,000	$ 30,000	$ 30,000	$ 50,000
48	Return of previous invested principal		$ -	$ -	$ -	$ -	$ -	$ 288,716
49	Interest inflow from previous investing		$ -	$ -	$ -	$ -	$ -	$ 1,203
50	Payoff of previous borrowed principal		$ -	$ (806,447)	$ (1,183,667)	$ (1,291,225)	$ (885,190)	$ -
51	Interest outflow for previous borrowing		$ -	$ (4,704)	$ (6,905)	$ (7,532)	$ (5,164)	$ -
52	Cash balance before new short-term investing or borrowing		$ (776,447)	$ (1,153,667)	$ (1,261,225)	$ (855,190)	$ 338,716	$ 1,871,862
53	New short-term investing		$ -	$ -	$ -	$ -	$ 288,716	$ 1,821,862
54	New short-term borrowing		$ 806,447	$ 1,183,667	$ 1,291,225	$ 885,190	$ -	$ -
55	Ending cash balance	$ 45,000	$ 30,000	$ 30,000	$ 30,000	$ 30,000	$ 50,000	$ 50,000
56			Cash balance policy					
57			Minimum month-end balance			$30,000		
58			Maximum month-end balance			$50,000		
59			Annual interest rate for borrowing			7.0%		
60			Annual interest rate for investing			5.0%		

(Strategy 1: Annual capacity of 32,000 units equals annual demand.)

(Continued)

Figure 8-8

Final Six Months of Cash Budget for Ashley Manufacturing

	A	I	J	K	L	M	N	O
1		ASHLEY MANUFACTURING: Strategy #1						
2		Jul-97	Aug-97	Sep-97	Oct-97	Nov-97	Dec-97	All 1997
3	SALES							
4	Percent of annual	11%	9%	7%	6%	5%	4%	
5	Forecast demand, units	3,520	2,880	2,240	1,920	1,600	1,280	32,000
6	Sales completed, units	3,520	2,880	2,240	1,920	1,600	1,280	32,000
7	Unit selling price	$960.00	$960.00	$960.00	$960.00	$960.00	$960.00	
8	Sales completed, dollars	$ 3,379,200	$ 2,764,800	$ 2,150,400	$ 1,843,200	$ 1,536,000	$ 1,228,800	$ 30,131,200
9	MANUFACTURING: Strategy #1							
10	Workdays	22	21	21	23	19	15	244
11	Units output	2,885	2,754	2,754	3,016	2,492	1,967	32,000
12	Direct labor cost, $/unit *increase in July*	$152.25	$152.25	$152.25	$152.25	$152.25	$152.25	
13	Material cost, $/unit *annual increase*	$466.94	$468.11	$469.28	$470.45	$471.63	$472.81	
14	Direct labor cost, total	$ 439,279	$ 419,311	$ 419,311	$ 459,246	$ 379,377	$ 299,508	$ 4,755,049
15	Material cost, total	$ 1,347,246	$ 1,289,223	$ 1,292,446	$ 1,419,075	$ 1,175,210	$ 930,117	$ 14,921,462
16	Total manufacturing cost	$ 1,786,525	$ 1,708,534	$ 1,711,757	$ 1,878,321	$ 1,554,587	$ 1,229,625	$ 19,676,512
17	INVENTORY LEVEL							
18	Start of month, units	971	336	210	725	1,821	2,713	
19	End of month, units	336	210	725	1,821	2,713	3,400	
20	Average, units	654	273	468	1,273	2,267	3,056	
21	INVENTORY VALUE, AT COST							
22	Start of month	$ 591,844	$ 207,465	$ 130,498	$ 450,275	$ 1,133,481	$ 1,690,822	
23	Added	$ 1,786,525	$ 1,708,534	$ 1,711,757	$ 1,878,321	$ 1,554,587	$ 1,229,625	
24	Total before sales	$ 2,378,369	$ 1,915,999	$ 1,842,255	$ 2,328,595	$ 2,688,068	$ 2,920,447	
25	Average unit cost of those sold	$616.73	$619.97	$621.42	$622.46	$623.28	$624.03	
26	End of month (total after sales)	$ 207,465	$ 130,498	$ 450,275	$ 1,133,481	$ 1,690,822	$ 2,121,692	
27	Average value of inventory	$ 399,654	$ 168,981	$ 290,386	$ 791,878	$ 1,412,152	$ 1,906,257	
28	CASH INFLOWS FROM SALES							
29	Cash from sales last month	$ 2,457,600	$ 2,252,800	$ 1,843,200	$ 1,433,600	$ 1,228,800	$ 1,024,000	
30	Cash from sales this month	$ 1,126,400	$ 921,600	$ 716,800	$ 614,400	$ 512,000	$ 409,600	
31	Total sales receipts (cash inflow)	$ 3,584,000	$ 3,174,400	$ 2,560,000	$ 2,048,000	$ 1,740,800	$ 1,433,600	$ 30,048,000
32	MISCELLANEOUS EXPENSES							
33	Salaries *increase in August*	$ 80,000	$ 84,000	$ 84,000	$ 84,000	$ 84,000	$ 84,000	$ 980,000
34	Advertising *pct of preceding sales*	$ 92,160	$ 84,480	$ 69,120	$ 53,760	$ 46,080	$ 38,400	$ 750,160
35	Commissions *pct of sales*	$ 135,168	$ 110,592	$ 86,016	$ 73,728	$ 61,440	$ 49,152	$ 1,205,248
36	Fringe benefits *pct of wages and salaries*	$ 212,904	$ 206,358	$ 206,358	$ 222,731	$ 189,985	$ 157,238	$ 2,351,370
37	Interest on long-term notes	$ 12,000	$ 12,000	$ 12,000	$ 12,000	$ 12,000	$ 12,000	$ 144,000
38	Inventory holding cost *pct of avg inventory*	$ 7,993	$ 3,380	$ 5,808	$ 15,838	$ 28,243	$ 38,125	$ 356,350
39	Long-term leases	$ 85,000	$ 85,000	$ 85,000	$ 100,000	$ 100,000	$ 100,000	$ 1,065,000
40	Income tax			$ 120,000			$ 130,000	$ 470,000
41	Dividends to shareholders	$ 50,000			$ 50,000			$ 200,000
42	Total miscellaneous expenses	$ 675,225	$ 585,809	$ 668,301	$ 612,056	$ 521,748	$ 608,916	$ 7,522,128
43	Cost of manufacturing labor and materials	$ 1,786,525	$ 1,708,534	$ 1,711,757	$ 1,878,321	$ 1,554,587	$ 1,229,625	$ 19,676,512
44	CASH OUTFLOW FROM OPERATIONS	$ 2,461,750	$ 2,294,344	$ 2,380,059	$ 2,490,377	$ 2,076,334	$ 1,838,540	$ 27,198,640
45	NET CASH FLOW FROM OPERATIONS	$ 1,122,250	$ 880,056	$ 179,941	$ (442,377)	$ (335,534)	$ (404,940)	$ 2,849,360
46	CASH FLOWS FOR FINANCIAL ACTIVITIES							
47	Opening cash balance	$ 50,000	$ 50,000	$ 50,000	$ 50,000	$ 50,000	$ 50,000	
48	Return of previous invested principal	$ 1,821,862	$ 2,951,703	$ 3,844,059	$ 4,040,017	$ 3,614,473	$ 3,293,999	
49	Interest inflow from previous investing	$ 7,591	$ 12,299	$ 16,017	$ 16,833	$ 15,060	$ 13,725	$ 82,728
50	Payoff of previous borrowed principal	$ -	$ -	$ -	$ -	$ -	$ -	$ -
51	Interest outflow for previous borrowing	$ -	$ -	$ -	$ -	$ -	$ -	$ (24,305)
52	Cash balance before new short-term investing or borrowing	$ 3,001,703	$ 3,894,059	$ 4,090,017	$ 3,664,473	$ 3,343,999	$ 2,952,784	
53	New short-term investing	$ 2,951,703	$ 3,844,059	$ 4,040,017	$ 3,614,473	$ 3,293,999	$ 2,902,784	
54	New short-term borrowing	$ -	$ -	$ -	$ -	$ -	$ -	
55	Ending cash balance	$ 50,000	$ 50,000	$ 50,000	$ 50,000	$ 50,000	$ 50,000	

(Strategy 1: Annual capacity of 32,000 units equals annual demand.)

Sales: The seasonal percentages of the annual units sold each month are entered as data values in Cells C4:N4. The number of units of forecast annual demand is entered as a data value in Cell O5. The units of monthly forecast demand are calculated by entering =C4*$O$5 in Cell C5 and copying to D5:N5.

(Continued)

The actual number of units sold each month depends on the demand and the number available to satisfy demand. The completed sales will equal the forecast demand unless there are not enough units available to satisfy all of the forecast demand. In that case, only the number of units available can be sold, and some demand will be unsatisfied. The number of units available for sale in any month is the sum of the number of units in inventory at the start of the month plus the number of units produced that month. The inventory at the start of the month (Row 18) equals the inventory carryover from the end of the preceding month (Row 19). The number of units produced each month is calculated in Row 11. The entries for Rows 11, 18, and 19 are described later.

We can use an IF statement to calculate the completed sales each month. The IF statement first checks whether or not enough units are available to satisfy all forecast demand and then calculates the actual number of units that can be sold. To do this, enter =IF(C18+C11>C5,C5,C18+C11) in Cell C6 and copy to D6:N6. The logic for the statement is represented by the following:

If (start inventory + production) > demand, then sold = demand, else sold = start inventory + production

The unit selling prices each month are entered as data in Cells B7:N7. The dollar values of the sales completed each month are calculated by entering =B6*B7 in Cell B8 and copying to C8:N8.

Manufacturing: The numbers of workdays each month are entered as data values in Cells C10:N10. The total number of workdays in the year is calculated by entering =SUM(C10:N10) in Cell O10.

For this scenario, the annual production capacity equals the annual demand of 32,000 units. The value 32,000 is therefore entered as a data value in Cell O11. The number of units produced each month equals the total production for the year multiplied by the ratio of the number of workdays in a month to the total number of workdays for the entire year. The numbers of units produced each month are therefore calculated by entering =$O$11*C10/$O$10 in Cell C11 and copying the entry to D11:N11.

The direct labor cost per unit is entered as data in Cells C12:H12 for the months of January to June. This cost increases in July by 5 percent, the data value in Cell B12. The new value in July is calculated in Cell I12 by the entry =H12*(1+B12). The entry in Cell J12 for the cost in August is either =I12 or $I$12 and is copied to K12:N12.

The material cost per unit in January is entered as a data value in Cell C13. This cost increases each month at a nominal annual rate of 3 percent, the data value in Cell B13, compounded monthly. The materials costs for February and later months are calculated by entering =C13*(1+$B$13/12) in Cell D13 and copying to E13:N13. The monthly costs for labor and materials are the products of the number of units produced multiplied by the unit costs for labor and materials. These costs are calculated by entering =C$11*C12 in Cell C14 and copying to C14:N15. (Note the $ sign to lock the number of units in Row 11 when the entry is copied down from Row 14 to Row 15.) The total monthly manufacturing costs are calculated by entering =C14+C15 in Cell C16 and copying to D16:N16. The total annual manufacturing costs are calculated by entering =SUM(C14:N14) in Cell O14 and copying to O15:O16.

Inventory Level: The number of units in inventory at the end of the preceding year (i.e., the month preceding the first month of the planned cash budget) is entered as a data value in Cell B19. The month-end inventories are transferred to the start-of-month inventories for the following month by entering =B19 in Cell C18 and copying to D18:N18. The month-end inventories equal the start-of-the month inventories plus the units made during the month minus the units sold during the month. Enter =C18+C11-C6 in C19 and copy to D19:N19. The average numbers of units in inventory each month are calculated by entering =(C18+C19)/2 or =AVERAGE(C18:C19) in Cell C20 and copying to D20:N20. (In later calculations, we will use the average numbers of units in inventory each month to calculate the average inventory values and the monthly costs for holding inventory.)

Inventory Value, at Cost: The value of the units in inventory at the end of the preceding month of the planned cash budget is entered as a data value in Cell B26. The month-end values are transferred to the start-of-month inventories by entering =B26 in Cell C22 and copying to D22:N22. The value of inventory added each month is the total manufacturing cost. These are copied from Row 16 by entering =C16 in Cell C23 and copying to D23:N23.

(Continued)

The total value of inventory before sales each month (i.e., the value of the units available for sale each month) is calculated by entering =C22+C23 in Cell C24 and copying to D24:N24. The average unit costs of the units sold are calculated by entering =C24/(C11+C18) in Cell C25 and copying to D25:N25.

The month-end values of inventory are the differences between the values before sales minus the costs of the sales completed each month. The month-end values of inventory are therefore calculated by entering =C24-C6*C25 in Cell C26 and copying to D26:N26. The average monthly values of the inventory are calculated by entering =(C22+C26)/2 in Cell C27 and copying to D27:N27.

Cash Inflows from Sales: The data value for the percentage of monthly sales made one month that are paid for during the following month is entered as =2/3 in Cell B29 and formatted as a percent with two decimal places. (To avoid round-off, it is important to enter this value as =2/3 rather than 66.67%. This gives the actual value in Cell B29 as 0.666666666 … .) The data value for the percentage of monthly sales made one month that are paid for during the same month is entered as =1/3 in Cell B30 and formatted as a percent with two decimal places.

The cash inflows from sales last month and the current month are calculated by entering =$B$29*B8 in Cell C29 and =$B$30*C8 in Cell C30 and copying the pair of entries to D29:N30. The total monthly cash receipts or cash inflow from sales are calculated by entering =C29+C30 in Cell C31 and copying to D31:N31. The total annual cash inflow from sales is calculated by entering =SUM(C31:N31) in Cell O31.

Miscellaneous Expenses: The expense for salaries in January is entered as a data value in Cell C33. Since the monthly salary expense remains constant until August, the entries for the months of February to July are made by entering =C33 in D33 and copying to E33:I33. In August, salaries are increased by 5 percent (the data value in Cell B33) and remain at the new value throughout the rest of the year. The monthly salary expense for August is calculated by the entry =I33*(1+B33) in Cell J33. Entries for the monthly salary expenses for September to December are made by entering =J33 in Cell K33 and copying to L33:N33.

The data value entered in Cell B34 is the advertising cost as a percent of sales completed the preceding month. The monthly costs for advertising are calculated by entering =$B$34*B8 in Cell C34 and copying to D34:N34.

The data value in Cell B35 is the commissions as a percent of sales during the month. The monthly costs for commissions are calculated by entering =$B$35*C8 in Cell C35 and copying to D35:N35.

The data value in Cell B36 is the sum of the fringe benefits as a percent of the total of wages and salaries during the month. The monthly fringe expenses are calculated by entering =$B$36*(C14+C33) in Cell C36 and copying to D36:N36. (Note that fringe benefits are based on wages paid for work done on regular time only; that is, overtime is not included in the calculation of the cost of fringe benefits such as holidays and health benefits. This will become important later when work on overtime is included in the development of the cash budget.)

The data value in Cell C37 is the interest on long-term notes. The value is copied to D37:N37.

The monthly costs for holding inventory, as a percent of the average value of the inventory, is entered as a data value in Cell B38. The monthly inventory holding costs are calculated by entering =$B$38*C27 in Cell C38 and copying to D38:N38.

The monthly expense for long-term leases for the months of January to September is entered as data in Cell C39 and copied to D39:K39. The monthly expense for long-term leases for the months of October to December is entered as a data value in Cell L39 and copied to M39:N39.

Quarterly income tax payments are entered as data in Cells E40, H40, K40, and N40. Quarterly dividend payments are entered as data in Cells C41, F41, I41, and L41.

The monthly totals of the miscellaneous expenses are calculated by entering =SUM(C33:C41) in Cell C42 and copying to D42:N42.

The total monthly costs of manufacturing labor and material are copied to Row 43 from Row 16 by entering =C16 in Cell C43 and copying to D43:N43.

Totals for the year are calculated by entering =SUM(C33:N33) in Cell O33 and copying to O34:O43.

(Continued)

Cash Outflow for Operating Cost: The monthly totals of the cash outflow for operating costs are calculated by entering =C42+C43 in Cell C44 and copying to D44:N44. The total for the year is calculated by entering =SUM(C44:N44) in Cell O44.

Net Cash Flow from Operations: Monthly values for the net cash flow from operations are calculated by entering =C31-C44 in Cell C45 and copying to D45:N45. The total for the year is calculated by entering =SUM(C45:N45) in Cell O45.

Cash Flow from Financial Activities: The ending cash balance for the month preceding the first month of the cash budget is entered as a data value in Cell B55.

The opening cash balances each month equal the ending cash balances from the preceding month. These are transferred to Row 47 by entering =B55 in Cell C47 and copying to D47:N47.

Each month, there is a cash inflow from any investing the preceding month. This inflow equals the amount invested in short-term (i.e., 30-day) commercial notes the preceding month plus the interest earned on it. These are calculated by entering =B53 in Cell C48, entering =B53*$F$60/12 in Cell C49, and copying the pair of entries to D48:N49.

Each month, there is a cash outflow from any borrowing the preceding month. This outflow equals the amount borrowed the preceding month that must be repaid plus interest. These are calculated by entering =-B54 in Cell C50, entering =-B54*$F$59/12 in Cell C51, and copying the pair of entries to D50:N51. Note the minus signs in these entries because they are cash **out**flows.

The month-end values for the cash balance before new short-term investing or borrowing (which is often called the "unadjusted cash balance") are calculated by entering =SUM(C45:C51) in Cell C52 and copying to D52:N52.

Values for the minimum and maximum month-end cash balances are entered as data in Cells F57 and F58. New short-term investing is made in any month for which the unadjusted cash balance in Cells C52:N52 is more than the value in Cell F58, and new short-term borrowing is made in any month for which the unadjusted cash balance is less than the value in Cell F57. These determinations are made by entering =IF(C52>$F$58,C52-$F$58,0) in Cell C53, entering =IF(C52<$F$57,$F$57-C52,0) in Cell C54, and copying the pair of entries to D53:N53.

To calculate month-end cash balances, enter =C52-C53+C54 in Cell C55 and copy to D55:N55.

Cash Flow Reconciliation and Other Information: The upper portion of Figure 8-9 is a cash flow reconciliation for the year. This is made by transferring the indicated inflows and outflows from the main body of the spreadsheet and calculating their sums.

Figure 8-9

Cash Flow Reconciliation and Other Information for Ashley Manufacturing (Strategy #1)

	A	B	C	D	E	F	G
61	ASHLEY MANUFACTURING: Strategy #1						
62	Cash Inflow-Outflow Reconciliation for the Year						
63	Inflows			Outflows			
64	Starting cash balance	$ 45,000		Manufacturing labor and material			$ 19,676,512
65	Sales receipts	$ 30,048,000		Other operating expenses			$ 7,522,128
66	Interest earned on short-term investing	$ 82,728		Interest paid on short-term borrowing			$ 24,305
67	Total	$ 30,175,728		End of-year short-term investments			$ 2,902,784
68				Ending cash balance			$ 50,000
69						Total	$ 30,175,728
70	Other Information for Comparison of Strategies						
71	Inventory holding cost for the year	$ 356,350		End-of-Year Numbers			
72	Net cash flow from operations for the year	$ 2,849,360		Inventory, units			3,400
73				Inventory, value at cost			$ 2,121,692
74				Inventory + short-term investments			$ 5,024,476

(Continued)

The lower section of Figure 8-9 provides additional information that can be useful to financial managers. It shows the total cost for holding inventories for the 12-month period (Cell B71). This is a significantly larger value than the interest earned and paid as a result of short-term borrowing and lending. It also shows the number of units in inventory at the end of the 12-month period and its value (Cells G72 and G73). Note that the value of inventory at the end of the year (Cell G73) is of the same order of magnitude as the end-of-year short-term investments (Cell G67).

Overall, the company appears to be doing well. It should revise its cash budget plan monthly with updated information from its sales and marketing organizations on the actual number of units sold the past month, new forecasts of monthly demands for the next 12 months, any revisions to manufacturing capacity and costs, any changes in labor and material costs, any changes in interest rates for short-term borrowing and investing, and so forth. The key to continuing to operate profitably is to stay on top of what is happening and to take action promptly to correct any negative trends before they become serious problems or disasters.

Sensitivity Analysis

Ashley's CFO is concerned about the impacts of changes in the rates of interest for borrowing and investing money. To study the impacts, prepare a one-variable input table to show how changes in the annual interest rate for borrowing would affect the end-of-year short-term investment and the net interest earned as a result of borrowing and lending activity. Analyze variations from 6 to 12 percent for the rate of interest for borrowing in increments of 2 percent. Assume that the spread between the rates for borrowing and lending is 2 percent—that is, assume that the annual rate for investing will be 2 percent less than the rate for borrowing—and that the rates will persist throughout the entire year. Plot the results.

Solution: Figure 8-10 shows the results.

To link the rate of interest for investing to that for the rate for borrowing, change the entry in Cell F60 from a data value to the expression =F59-0.02.

To create the table of values shown in Cells Q5:U8 in Figure 8-10, begin by entering the values for the annual rates of interest for borrowing in Cells Q5:Q8. Then make the following entries in Cells Q4:T4:

Q4: =F59	This transfers the values from Cells Q5:Q8 to Cell F58.
R4: =N53	This transfers the calculated values in Cell N53 to R5:R8.
S4: =O49	This transfers the calculated values in Cell O49 to S5:S8.
T4: =O51	This transfers the calculated values in Cell O51 to T5:T8.

As these entries are made, Cells Q4:T4 will show the values in Cells F59, N53, O49, and O51. To hide these values, we have formatted the cells with the following custom formats:

Q4: "for Borrowing"   R4: "Invested"   S4: "Investing"   T4: "Borrowing"

The next step is to drag the mouse to select the Range Q4:T8. With this range highlighted, click on Table on the Data menu to access the dialog box shown in Figure 8-11. Enter F59 as the column input cell and click OK or press Enter. This results in the values shown in Cells Q5:T8.

For the entries in Cells U5:U8, enter =S5+T5 in Cell U5 and copy the entry to U6:U8.

Figure 8-10

Effect of Annual Interest Rate for Borrowing on Amounts of Interest Earned, Paid, and Net for the Year

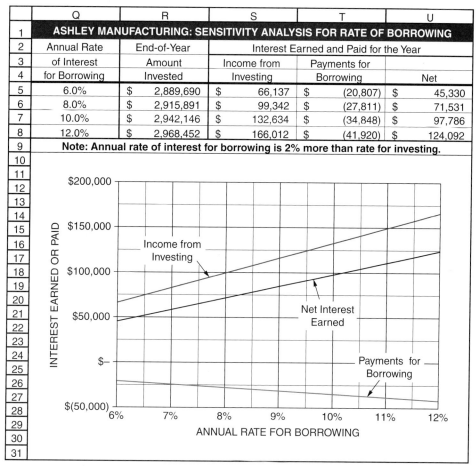

	Q	R	S	T	U
1	ASHLEY MANUFACTURING: SENSITIVITY ANALYSIS FOR RATE OF BORROWING				
2	Annual Rate	End-of-Year	Interest Earned and Paid for the Year		
3	of Interest	Amount	Income from	Payments for	
4	for Borrowing	Invested	Investing	Borrowing	Net
5	6.0%	$ 2,889,690	$ 66,137	$ (20,807)	$ 45,330
6	8.0%	$ 2,915,891	$ 99,342	$ (27,811)	$ 71,531
7	10.0%	$ 2,942,146	$ 132,634	$ (34,848)	$ 97,786
8	12.0%	$ 2,968,452	$ 166,012	$ (41,920)	$ 124,092
9	Note: Annual rate of interest for borrowing is 2% more than rate for investing.				

(Cell entries in Row 4 have been hidden by custom formatting as text.)

Figure 8-11

Table Dialog Box with Entry for Column Input Cell

Case Study: Ashley Manufacturing (continued)

Strategy 2: Reduced Annual Capacity

To avoid the high inventory holding costs of the first strategy, Ashley might choose to reduce its annual capacity to somewhat less than the annual demand. If customers are not satisfied unless their demands are met promptly, the results of such a strategy will be lost sales. This is shown in Figures 8-12, 8-13, and 8-14. (Figures 8-12 and 8-13 show only the first 10 rows of the complete spreadsheets. Note that Rows 9 and 10 have been inserted in a copy of the worksheet for Strategy 1 in order to account for lost sales. The preparation of the complete spreadsheet for this strategy is left to the reader.)

Figure 8-12

First Six Months of Sales Results with Annual Capacity Reduced to 30,000 Units

	A	B	C	D	E	F	G	H
1	ASHLEY MANUFACTURING: Strategy #2							
2		Dec-96	Jan-97	Feb-97	Mar-97	Apr-97	May-97	Jun-97
3	SALES							
4	Percent of annual		5%	7%	9%	11%	14%	12%
5	Forecast demand, units	1,200	1,600	2,240	2,880	3,520	4,480	3,840
6	Sales completed, units	1,200	1,600	2,240	2,880	3,520	4,480	3,803
7	Unit selling price	$920.00	$920.00	$920.00	$920.00	$920.00	$920.00	$960.00
8	Sales completed, dollars	$ 1,104,000	$ 1,472,000	$ 2,060,800	$ 2,649,600	$ 3,238,400	$ 4,121,600	$ 3,650,833
9	Lost sales, units		0	0	0	0	0	37
10	Lost sales, dollars		$ -	$ -	$ -	$ -	$ -	$ 35,567

Figure 8-13

Second Six Months of Sales Results with Annual Capacity Reduced to 30,000 Units

	A	I	J	K	L	M	N	O
1	ASHLEY MANUFACTURING: Strategy #2							
2		Jul-97	Aug-97	Sep-97	Oct-97	Nov-97	Dec-97	All 1997
3	SALES							
4	Percent of annual	11%	9%	7%	6%	5%	4%	
5	Forecast demand, units	3,520	2,880	2,240	1,920	1,600	1,280	32,000
6	Sales completed, units	2,705	2,582	2,240	1,920	1,600	1,280	30,850
7	Unit selling price	$960.00	$960.00	$960.00	$960.00	$960.00	$960.00	
8	Sales completed, dollars	$ 2,596,721	$ 2,478,689	$ 2,150,400	$ 1,843,200	$ 1,536,000	$ 1,228,800	$ 29,027,043
9	Lost sales, units	815	298	0	0	0	0	1,150
10	Lost sales, dollars	$ 782,479	$ 286,111	$ -	$ -	$ -	$ -	$ 1,104,157

Figures 8-9 and 8-14 provide some interesting comparisons between Strategies 1 and 2. Even though the reduced capacity results in losing some sales, Strategy 2 provides a larger net cash flow from operations and a larger value for short-term investing at the end of the year. If this seems strange, note that the labor and material costs and other operating expenses are less, as is also the value of the year-end inventory and the annual holding costs of inventory. Liquidity has improved, as shown by the increase in the end-of-year short-term investments and the reduction in the value of the inventory.

Losing sales, however, is not a good strategy. We therefore move on to other strategies that avoid losing sales and provide better profits.

(Continued)

Figure 8-14

Cash Flow Reconciliation and Other Information with Annual Capacity Reduced to 30,000 Units

	A	B	C	D	E	F	G
63	ASHLEY MANUFACTURING: Strategy #2						
64	Cash Inflow-Outflow Reconciliation for the Year						
65	Inflows			Outflows			
66	Starting cash balance	$ 45,000		Manufacturing labor and material			$ 18,446,730
67	Sales receipts	$ 28,943,843		Other operating expenses			$ 7,253,994
68	Interest earned on short-term investing	$ 93,516		Interest paid on short-term borrowing			$ 17,830
69	Total	$ 29,082,359		End-of-year short-term investments			$ 3,313,805
70				Ending cash balance			$ 50,000
71						Total	$ 29,082,359
72	Other Information for Comparison of Strategies						
73	Inventory holding cost for the year	$ 281,835		End-of-year numbers			
74	Net cash flow from operations for the year	$ 3,243,119		Inventory, units			2,550
75	Lost sales, units	1,150		Inventory, value at cost			$ 1,591,844
76	Lost sales, dollars	$ 1,104,157		Inventory + short-term investments			$ 4,905,649

Case Study: Ashley Manufacturing (continued)

Strategy 3: Overtime Used with Annual Capacity Less Than Annual Demand

The first strategy for Ashley Manufacturing was based on an annual production capacity equal to the annual demand. This strategy required stockpiling large inventories in months when demand was less than the units available and using the inventory to satisfy demand in months when demand was greater than the units available. Although this satisfied all demands and avoided losing any sales, it resulted in large inventory holding costs. For example, note the large costs for holding inventories in January to May.

Companies use different strategies to avoid large inventory holding costs. The first of the alternate strategies we evaluate is to set the workforce at a level somewhat below that needed to satisfy the average monthly demand and use overtime during months when demand is high. This minimizes the cost to hold inventory but adds the premium cost of working overtime.

Let us begin by considering what would happen if Ashley's normal production capacity was reduced to 30,000 units/year while the forecast demand remained at 32,000 units/year. Overtime needs to be worked in any month when demand exceeds the sum of what is available from the inventory at the beginning of the month and the units produced on **regular time** during the month.

The company also recognizes that the actual demands of customers will not be the same as the forecast demands. Demands will be less than forecast some months, and other months will be more. To guard against losing sales when actual demand is greater than forecast demand, the company will use overtime production whenever it is necessary to provide a safety stock as well as to satisfy forecast demand. The amount of the safety stock will depend on the company's policies for satisfying customers and on the accuracy of its forecasts. For the purpose of illustration, assume that the planned safety stock left in inventory at the end of a month should not be less than 10 percent of the forecast demand for the month.

Figures 8-15 to 8-17 give the results. To perform the analysis, copy the spreadsheet for Figures 8-7 and 8-8 to a new worksheet and change the value for the annual production capacity in Cell O11 of the copy to 30,000. (Row 11 of the copy becomes Row 12 in Figures 8-15 and 8-16 after further editing, as described below.)

Because all forecast demands are met, the entry in Cell C6 can be changed to =C5, and the entry can be copied to D6:N6. (Alternatively, after the changes in the next two paragraphs have been made, the entry in Cell C6 can be edited to =IF(C23+C14>C5,C5,C23+C14) and copied to D6:N6.)

Insert a new row after Row 10 of the copied spreadsheet. The new row is Row 11 in Figure 8-15. Enter the label "Safety stock, percent of forecast demand" in Cell A11 and the value 10% in Cell B11.

(Continued)

Figure 8-15

First Six Months with Overtime to Provide 10% Safety Stock (Strategy #3)

	A	B	C	D	E	F	G	H
1	ASHLEY MANUFACTURING: Strategy #3							
2		Dec-96	Jan-97	Feb-97	Mar-97	Apr-97	May-97	Jun-97
3	**SALES**							
4	Percent of annual		5%	7%	9%	11%	14%	12%
5	Forecast demand, units	1,200	1,600	2,240	2,880	3,520	4,480	3,840
6	Sales completed, units	1,200	1,600	2,240	2,880	3,520	4,480	3,840
7	Unit selling price	$920.00	$920.00	$920.00	$920.00	$920.00	$920.00	$960.00
8	Sales completed, dollars	$ 1,104,000	$ 1,472,000	$ 2,060,800	$ 2,649,600	$ 3,238,400	$ 4,121,600	$ 3,686,400
9	**MANUFACTURING**							
10	Workdays		19	19	21	22	21	21
11	Safety stock, percent of forecast demand	10%						
12	Units produced on regular time		2,336	2,336	2,582	2,705	2,582	2,582
13	Units produced on overtime		0	0	0	0	0	421
14	Total units produced		2,336	2,336	2,582	2,705	2,582	3,003
15	Direct labor cost, $/unit *increase in July*	5.0%	$145.00	$145.00	$145.00	$145.00	$145.00	$145.00
16	Material cost, $/unit *annual increase*	3.0%	$460.00	$461.15	$462.30	$463.46	$464.62	$465.78
17	Direct labor cost, regular time		$ 338,730	$ 338,730	$ 374,385	$ 392,213	$ 374,385	$ 374,385
18	Direct labor cost, overtime		$ -	$ -	$ -	$ -	$ -	$ 91,578
19	Direct labor cost, total		$ 338,730	$ 338,730	$ 374,385	$ 392,213	$ 374,385	$ 465,963
20	Material cost, total		$ 1,074,590	$ 1,077,277	$ 1,193,651	$ 1,253,618	$ 1,199,627	$ 1,398,741
21	Total manufacturing cost		$ 1,413,320	$ 1,416,006	$ 1,568,036	$ 1,645,831	$ 1,574,012	$ 1,864,705
22	**INVENTORY LEVEL**							
23	Start of month, units		3,400	4,136	4,232	3,934	3,119	1,221
24	End of month, units	3,400	4,136	4,232	3,934	3,119	1,221	384
25	Average, units		3,768	4,184	4,083	3,527	2,170	802
26	**INVENTORY VALUE, AT COST**							
27	Start of month		$ 2,035,000	$ 2,486,456	$ 2,551,823	$ 2,378,588	$ 1,890,676	$ 742,035
28	Added		$ 1,413,320	$ 1,416,006	$ 1,568,036	$ 1,645,831	$ 1,574,012	$ 1,864,705
29	Total before sales		$ 3,448,320	$ 3,902,462	$ 4,119,859	$ 4,024,418	$ 3,464,688	$ 2,606,739
30	Average unit cost of those sold		$601.16	$602.96	$604.61	$606.18	$607.74	$617.13
31	End of month (total after sales)	$2,035,000	$ 2,486,456	$ 2,551,823	$ 2,378,588	$ 1,890,676	$ 742,035	$ 236,976
32	Average value of inventory		$ 2,260,728	$ 2,519,140	$ 2,465,205	$ 2,134,632	$ 1,316,355	$ 489,505
33	**CASH INFLOWS FROM SALES**							
34	Cash from sales last month	66.67%	$ 736,000	$ 981,333	$ 1,373,867	$ 1,766,400	$ 2,158,933	$ 2,747,733
35	Cash from sales this month	33.33%	$ 490,667	$ 686,933	$ 883,200	$ 1,079,467	$ 1,373,867	$ 1,228,800
36	Total sales receipts (cash inflow)		$ 1,226,667	$ 1,668,267	$ 2,257,067	$ 2,845,867	$ 3,532,800	$ 3,976,533
37	**MISCELLANEOUS EXPENSES**							
38	Salaries *increase in August*	5.0%	$ 80,000	$ 80,000	$ 80,000	$ 80,000	$ 80,000	$ 80,000
39	Advertising *pct of preceding sales*	2.5%	$ 27,600	$ 36,800	$ 51,520	$ 66,240	$ 80,960	$ 103,040
40	Commissions *pct of sales*	4.0%	$ 58,880	$ 82,432	$ 105,984	$ 129,536	$ 164,864	$ 147,456
41	Fringe benefits *pct of wages and salaries*	41.0%	$ 171,679	$ 171,679	$ 186,298	$ 193,607	$ 186,298	$ 186,298
42	Interest on long-term notes		$ 12,000	$ 12,000	$ 12,000	$ 12,000	$ 12,000	$ 12,000
43	Inventory holding cost *pct of avg inventory*	2.0%	$ 45,215	$ 50,383	$ 49,304	$ 42,693	$ 26,327	$ 9,790
44	Long-term leases		$ 85,000	$ 85,000	$ 85,000	$ 85,000	$ 85,000	$ 85,000
45	Income tax				$ 100,000			$ 120,000
46	Dividends to shareholders		$ 50,000			$ 50,000		
47	Total miscellaneous expenses		$ 530,374	$ 518,294	$ 670,106	$ 659,076	$ 635,449	$ 743,584
48	Cost of manufacturing labor and materials		$ 1,413,320	$ 1,416,006	$ 1,568,036	$ 1,645,831	$ 1,574,012	$ 1,864,705
49	**CASH OUTFLOW FROM OPERATIONS**		$ 1,943,693	$ 1,934,300	$ 2,238,142	$ 2,304,907	$ 2,209,461	$ 2,608,289
50	**NET CASH FLOW FROM OPERATIONS**		$ (717,027)	$ (266,033)	$ 18,924	$ 540,960	$ 1,323,339	$ 1,368,244
51	**CASH FLOWS FOR FINANCIAL ACTIVITIES**							
52	Opening cash balance		$ 45,000	$ 30,000	$ 30,000	$ 30,000	$ 30,000	$ 50,000
53	Return of previous invested principal		$ -	$ -	$ -	$ -	$ -	$ 877,333
54	Interest inflow from previous investing		$ -	$ -	$ -	$ -	$ -	$ 3,656
55	Payoff of previous borrowed principal		$ -	$ (702,027)	$ (972,155)	$ (958,902)	$ (423,535)	$ -
56	Interest outflow for previous borrowing		$ -	$ (4,095)	$ (5,671)	$ (5,594)	$ (2,471)	$ -
57	Cash balance before new short-term investing or borrowing		$ (672,027)	$ (942,155)	$ (928,902)	$ (393,535)	$ 927,333	$ 2,299,233
58	New short-term investing		$ -	$ -	$ -	$ -	$ 877,333	$ 2,249,233
59	New short-term borrowing		$ 702,027	$ 972,155	$ 958,902	$ 423,535	$ -	$ -
60	**Ending cash balance**	$ 45,000	$ 30,000	$ 30,000	$ 30,000	$ 30,000	$ 50,000	$ 50,000
61			Cash balance policy					
62			Minimum month-end balance			$30,000		
63			Maximum month-end balance			$50,000		
64			Annual interest rate for borrowing			7.0%		
65			Annual interest rate for investing			5.0%		

(Continued)

Figure 8-16

Last Six Months with Overtime to Provide 10% Safety Stock

	A	I	J	K	L	M	N	O
1	ASHLEY MANUFACTURING: Strategy #3							
2		Jul-97	Aug-97	Sep-97	Oct-97	Nov-97	Dec-97	All 1997
3	**SALES**							
4	Percent of annual	11%	9%	7%	6%	5%	4%	
5	Forecast demand, units	3,520	2,880	2,240	1,920	1,600	1,280	32,000
6	Sales completed, units	3,520	2,880	2,240	1,920	1,600	1,280	32,000
7	Unit selling price	$960.00	$960.00	$960.00	$960.00	$960.00	$960.00	
8	Sales completed, dollars	$ 3,379,200	$ 2,764,800	$ 2,150,400	$ 1,843,200	$ 1,536,000	$ 1,228,800	$ 30,131,200
9	**MANUFACTURING**							
10	Workdays	22	21	21	23	19	15	244
11	Safety stock, percent of forecast demand							
12	Units produced on regular time	2,705	2,582	2,582	2,828	2,336	1,844	30,000
13	Units produced on overtime	783	234	0	0	0	0	1,438
14	Total units produced	3,488	2,816	2,582	2,828	2,336	1,844	31,438
15	Direct labor cost, $/unit *increase in July*	$152.25	$152.25	$152.25	$152.25	$152.25	$152.25	
16	Material cost, $/unit *annual increase*	$466.94	$468.11	$469.28	$470.45	$471.63	$472.81	
17	Direct labor cost, regular time	$ 411,824	$ 393,105	$ 393,105	$ 430,543	$ 355,666	$ 280,789	$ 4,457,859
18	Direct labor cost, overtime	$ 178,836	$ 53,447	$ -	$ -	$ -	$ -	$ 323,862
19	Direct labor cost, total	$ 590,660	$ 446,552	$ 393,105	$ 430,543	$ 355,666	$ 280,789	$ 4,781,720
20	Material cost, total	$ 1,628,698	$ 1,318,200	$ 1,211,668	$ 1,330,383	$ 1,101,759	$ 871,984	$ 14,660,195
21	**Total manufacturing cost**	$ 2,219,358	$ 1,764,751	$ 1,604,772	$ 1,760,926	$ 1,457,425	$ 1,152,773	$ 19,441,915
22	**INVENTORY LEVEL**							
23	Start of month, units	384	352	288	630	1,538	2,274	
24	End of month, units	352	288	630	1,538	2,274	2,838	
25	Average, units	368	320	459	1,084	1,906	2,556	
26	**INVENTORY VALUE, AT COST**							
27	Start of month	$ 236,976	$ 223,303	$ 180,732	$ 391,924	$ 957,457	$ 1,417,487	
28	Added	$ 2,219,358	$ 1,764,751	$ 1,604,772	$ 1,760,926	$ 1,457,425	$ 1,152,773	
29	Total before sales	$ 2,456,335	$ 1,988,054	$ 1,785,505	$ 2,152,850	$ 2,414,882	$ 2,570,260	
30	Average unit cost of those sold	$634.38	$627.54	$622.13	$622.60	$623.37	$624.13	
31	End of month (total after sales)	$ 223,303	$ 180,732	$ 391,924	$ 957,457	$ 1,417,487	$ 1,771,377	
32	Average value of inventory	$ 230,140	$ 202,018	$ 286,328	$ 674,691	$ 1,187,472	$ 1,594,432	
33	**CASH INFLOWS FROM SALES**							
34	Cash from sales last month	$ 2,457,600	$ 2,252,800	$ 1,843,200	$ 1,433,600	$ 1,228,800	$ 1,024,000	$ 20,004,267
35	Cash from sales this month	$ 1,126,400	$ 921,600	$ 716,800	$ 614,400	$ 512,000	$ 409,600	$ 10,043,733
36	**Total sales receipts (cash inflow)**	$ 3,584,000	$ 3,174,400	$ 2,560,000	$ 2,048,000	$ 1,740,800	$ 1,433,600	$ 30,048,000
37	**MISCELLANEOUS EXPENSES**							
38	Salaries *increase in August*	$ 80,000	$ 84,000	$ 84,000	$ 84,000	$ 84,000	$ 84,000	$ 980,000
39	Advertising *pct of preceding sales*	$ 92,160	$ 84,480	$ 69,120	$ 53,760	$ 46,080	$ 38,400	$ 750,160
40	Commissions *pct of sales*	$ 135,168	$ 110,592	$ 86,016	$ 73,728	$ 61,440	$ 49,152	$ 1,205,248
41	Fringe benefits *pct of wages and salaries*	$ 201,648	$ 195,613	$ 195,613	$ 210,963	$ 180,263	$ 149,563	$ 2,229,522
42	Interest on long-term notes	$ 12,000	$ 12,000	$ 12,000	$ 12,000	$ 12,000	$ 12,000	$ 144,000
43	Inventory holding cost *pct of avg inventory*	$ 4,603	$ 4,040	$ 5,727	$ 13,494	$ 23,749	$ 31,889	$ 307,213
44	Long-term leases	$ 85,000	$ 85,000	$ 85,000	$ 100,000	$ 100,000	$ 100,000	$ 1,065,000
45	Income tax			$ 120,000			$ 130,000	$ 470,000
46	Dividends to shareholders	$ 50,000			$ 50,000			$ 200,000
47	**Total miscellaneous expenses**	$ 660,579	$ 575,725	$ 657,475	$ 597,944	$ 507,532	$ 595,004	$ 7,351,143
48	Cost of manufacturing labor and materials	$ 2,219,358	$ 1,764,751	$ 1,604,772	$ 1,760,926	$ 1,457,425	$ 1,152,773	$ 19,441,915
49	**CASH OUTFLOW FROM OPERATIONS**	$ 2,879,937	$ 2,340,476	$ 2,262,248	$ 2,358,870	$ 1,964,958	$ 1,747,777	$ 26,793,058
50	**NET CASH FLOW FROM OPERATIONS**	$ 704,063	$ 833,924	$ 297,752	$ (310,870)	$ (224,158)	$ (314,177)	$ 3,254,942
51	**CASH FLOWS FOR FINANCIAL ACTIVITIES**							
52	Opening cash balance	$ 50,000	$ 50,000	$ 50,000	$ 50,000	$ 50,000	$ 50,000	
53	Return of previous invested principal	$ 2,249,233	$ 2,962,668	$ 3,808,936	$ 4,122,559	$ 3,828,866	$ 3,620,662	
54	Interest inflow from previous investing	$ 9,372	$ 12,344	$ 15,871	$ 17,177	$ 15,954	$ 15,086	$ 89,459
55	Payoff of previous borrowed principal	$ -	$ -	$ -	$ -	$ -	$ -	
56	Interest outflow for previous borrowing	$ -	$ -	$ -	$ -	$ -	$ -	$ (17,830)
57	Cash balance before new short-term investing or borrowing	$ 3,012,668	$ 3,858,936	$ 4,172,559	$ 3,878,866	$ 3,670,662	$ 3,371,571	
58	New short-term investing	$ 2,962,668	$ 3,808,936	$ 4,122,559	$ 3,828,866	$ 3,620,662	$ 3,321,571	
59	New short-term borrowing	$ -	$ -	$ -	$ -	$ -	$ -	
60	**Ending cash balance**	$ 50,000	$ 50,000	$ 50,000	$ 50,000	$ 50,000	$ 50,000	

(Continued)

Figure 8-17
_____

Cash Flow Reconciliation and Other Information for Ashley Manufacturing

	A	B	C	D	E	F	G
66	ASHLEY MANUFACTURING: Strategy #3						
67	Cash Inflow-Outflow Reconciliation for the Year						
68	Inflows			Outflows			
69	Starting cash balance	$ 45,000		Manufacturing labor and material			$ 19,441,915
70	Sales receipts	$ 30,048,000		Other operating expenses			$ 7,351,143
71	Interest earned on short-term investing	$ 89,459		Interest paid on short-term borrowing			$ 17,830
72	Total	$ 30,182,459		End-of-year short-term investments			$ 3,321,571
73				Ending cash balance			$ 50,000
74						Total	$ 30,182,459
75	Other Information for Comparison of Strategies						
76	Inventory holding cost for the year	$ 307,213		End-of-year numbers			
77	Net cash flow from operations for the year	$ 3,254,942		Inventory, units			2,838
78				Inventory, value at cost			$ 1,771,377
79				Inventory + short-term investments			$ 5,092,948

(Annual capacity is 30,000 units and overtime is worked to satisfy demand and provide 10% safety stock.)

Change the label for Row 12 to "Units produced on regular time." Insert new rows for Rows 13 and 14, and label them "Units produced on overtime" and "Total units produced." The units produced on overtime must make up for any shortfall between the forecast demand plus the safety stock (i.e., 110 percent of forecast demand) and the units available before working any overtime (i.e., the units from inventory at the beginning of the month and the units produced on regular time). To calculate the number of units produced on overtime, use an IF statement that first checks on whether or not there is a shortfall and then either calculates the number of units if there is a shortfall or enters zero if there is no shortfall. To do this, enter =IF(C23+C12<(1+$B$11)*C5,(1+$B$11)*C5-C23-C12,0) in Cell C13 and copy to D13:N13. For the total units produced, enter =C12+C13 in Cell C14 and copy to D14:N14.

Change the label for the entries in Row 17 to "Direct labor cost, regular time" and insert two new rows between Rows 17 and 18. Label the entries in the new Row 18 "Direct labor cost, overtime," and label the entries in the new Row 19 "Direct labor cost, total." Enter =1.5*C13*C15 in Cell C18 and copy to D18:N18. The multiplier 1.5 is used because there is a 50 percent premium for working overtime. For the total cost of direct labor, enter =C17+C18 in Cell C19 and copy to D19:N19.

Edit the total material cost values by entering =C14*C16 in Cell C20 and copying to D20:N20. Change the entry in Cell C21 for the total manufacturing cost to =C19+C20 and copy to D21:N21.

For the month-end units in inventory, change the entry in Cell C24 to =C23+C14-C6 and copy to D24:N14. If this is done correctly, the number of units in inventory at the ends of June, July, and August will equal 10 percent of the forecast demands for those three months. (Note that these were the three months for which there were lost sales for Strategy 2.)

Edit the average unit cost of those sold by entering =C29/(C14+C23) in Cell C30 and copying to D30:N320.

Note that the entries below Row 30 remain unchanged. This includes the entry for fringe benefits, which is linked to the salaries and direct labor cost on regular time but does **not** include direct labor cost for overtime. Workers do not get extra days of vacation and other benefits for working overtime; their reward is the 50 percent overtime premium pay.

Figure 8-17 is a reconciliation of the cash inflow and outflow and other information. Compare the results in this figure with those in Figure 8-9. Note the improvements by working overtime when necessary to satisfy demand. The net operating income for the year is the highest, and all customer demands are satisfied. The end-of-year short term investments is higher than for either of the other two situations, the number of units held in

(Continued)

inventory is less than when capacity equals demand, and the total value of inventory and short-term investments is higher. Working overtime provides flexibility for meeting peak seasonal demands without having too much capacity at other times. But it has its limits. Asking workers to work too much overtime ultimately causes their efficiency to drop and invites quality problems. It may also delay maintenance of equipment, cause excessive wear, and hasten breakdowns. Spreadsheets can, of course, be modified to include a limit on the amount of overtime allowed in any period.

Sensitivity Analysis

Figure 8-18 is a one-variable input table that shows the sensitivity of selected results to the policy for setting safety stock.

Figure 8-18

Sensitivity of Selected Results to the Policy for Setting Safety Stock (Strategy #3)

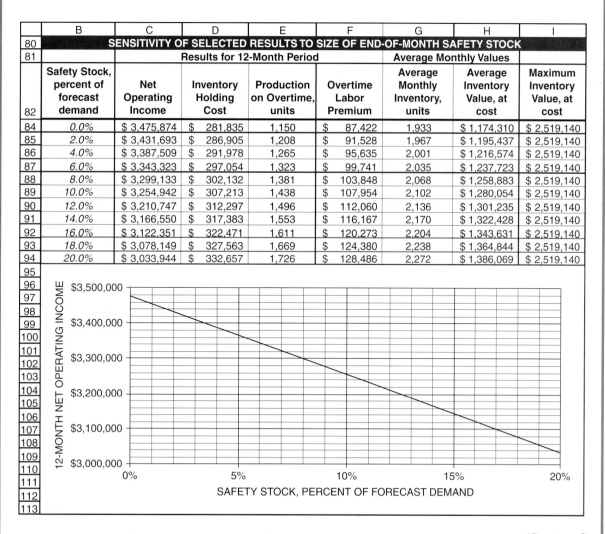

	B	C	D	E	F	G	H	I
80	SENSITIVITY OF SELECTED RESULTS TO SIZE OF END-OF-MONTH SAFETY STOCK							
81		Results for 12-Month Period				Average Monthly Values		
82	Safety Stock, percent of forecast demand	Net Operating Income	Inventory Holding Cost	Production on Overtime, units	Overtime Labor Premium	Average Monthly Inventory, units	Average Inventory Value, at cost	Maximum Inventory Value, at cost
84	0.0%	$ 3,475,874	$ 281,835	1,150	$ 87,422	1,933	$ 1,174,310	$ 2,519,140
85	2.0%	$ 3,431,693	$ 286,905	1,208	$ 91,528	1,967	$ 1,195,437	$ 2,519,140
86	4.0%	$ 3,387,509	$ 291,978	1,265	$ 95,635	2,001	$ 1,216,574	$ 2,519,140
87	6.0%	$ 3,343,323	$ 297,054	1,323	$ 99,741	2,035	$ 1,237,723	$ 2,519,140
88	8.0%	$ 3,299,133	$ 302,132	1,381	$ 103,848	2,068	$ 1,258,883	$ 2,519,140
89	10.0%	$ 3,254,942	$ 307,213	1,438	$ 107,954	2,102	$ 1,280,054	$ 2,519,140
90	12.0%	$ 3,210,747	$ 312,297	1,496	$ 112,060	2,136	$ 1,301,235	$ 2,519,140
91	14.0%	$ 3,166,550	$ 317,383	1,553	$ 116,167	2,170	$ 1,322,428	$ 2,519,140
92	16.0%	$ 3,122,351	$ 322,471	1,611	$ 120,273	2,204	$ 1,343,631	$ 2,519,140
93	18.0%	$ 3,078,149	$ 327,563	1,669	$ 124,380	2,238	$ 1,364,844	$ 2,519,140
94	20.0%	$ 3,033,944	$ 332,657	1,726	$ 128,486	2,272	$ 1,386,069	$ 2,519,140

(Continued)

Row 83, **which has been hidden** in Figure 8-18, carries the following entries for transferring values from the main body of the spreadsheet:

Cell B83 =B11	Cell E83 =O13	Cell G83 =AVERAGE(C25:N25)
Cell C83 =O50	Cell F83 =O18/3	Cell H83 =AVERAGE(C32:N32)
Cell D83 =O43		Cell I83: =MAX(C32:N32)

To complete the table, drag the mouse cursor over the range B83:I94, open the Table dialog box from the Data drop-down menu, and enter B11 for the column input cell, as shown in Figure 8-19.

Figure 8-19

Table Dialog Box with Entry for Completing the Sensitivity Analysis

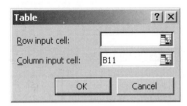

Reducing the size of the safety stock, and reaping the benefits from doing so, depends on how accurately future demands can be forecast. The more accurate the forecasts, the less safety stock is needed to ensure being able to satisfy customers' demands promptly, and the higher is the net operating income.

Case Study: Ashley Manufacturing (continued)

Strategy 4: Overtime, Reduced Capacity, and Backordering

When a product cannot be delivered immediately upon receipt of a customer's order, the customer is often willing to wait several weeks. The order is placed on "backorder" and delivered as soon as the product is available. This reduces the manufacturer's need to carry a safety stock and its attendant carrying costs. At the same time, backordering eliminates the penalty of losing a sale.

We now analyze the situation of Ashley Manufacturing if, instead of providing a safety stock (as in the second strategy), the company adds any unfilled orders one month to the forecast demand for the following month and then fills the orders on backorder first, before satisfying any new demand. That is, the total demand for any month is the sum of the demand forecast for the month plus any backorders carried over from the preceding month.

As before, the company's annual capacity is 30,000 units on regular time and the number of units on hand at the end of December 1996 is 3,400 units. The company expects that its new strategy of using backordering will reduce its year-end inventory for 1997.

Assume also that the company's policy is not to use overtime in a given month unless the number of units of unsatisfied demand at the end of a month would otherwise exceed 20 percent of the forecast demand for the month. As a result of this policy, enough overtime must be worked so that the number of units on backorder at the end of any month does not exceed 20 percent of the forecast demand for the month.

Figures 8-20, 8-21, and 8-22 show the results for the fourth strategy. To perform the analysis, copy the spreadsheet for the third strategy to a new spreadsheet and insert rows and labels as indicated in Figure 8-20 and discussed below.

(Continued)

Figure 8-20

First Six Months of Cash Budget with Overtime and Backordering (Strategy #4)

	A	B	C	D	E	F	G	H
1		ASHLEY MANUFACTURING: Strategy #4						
2		Dec-96	Jan-97	Feb-97	Mar-97	Apr-97	May-97	Jun-97
3	**SALES**							
4	Percent of annual		5%	7%	9%	11%	14%	12%
5	Forecast demand, units	1,200	1,600	2,240	2,880	3,520	4,480	3,840
6	Backorders from preceding month, units		0	0	0	0	0	0
7	Total demand, units		1,600	2,240	2,880	3,520	4,480	3,840
8	Sales completed, units	1,200	1,600	2,240	2,880	3,520	4,480	3,803
9	Backorders to following month, units		0	0	0	0	0	37
10	Unit selling price	$920.00	$920.00	$920.00	$920.00	$920.00	$920.00	$960.00
11	Sales completed, dollars	$ 1,104,000	$ 1,472,000	$ 2,060,800	$ 2,649,600	$ 3,238,400	$ 4,121,600	$ 3,650,833
12	**MANUFACTURING**							
13	Workdays		19	19	21	22	21	21
14	Maximum backorders, pct of forecast demand	20%						
15	Units produced on regular time		2,336	2,336	2,582	2,705	2,582	2,582
16	Units produced on overtime		0	0	0	0	0	0
17	Total units produced		2,336	2,336	2,582	2,705	2,582	2,582
18	Direct labor cost, $/unit *increase in July*	5.0%	$145.00	$145.00	$145.00	$145.00	$145.00	$145.00
19	Material cost, $/unit *annual increase*	3.0%	$460.00	$461.15	$462.30	$463.46	$464.62	$465.78
20	Direct labor cost, regular time		$ 338,730	$ 338,730	$ 374,385	$ 392,213	$ 374,385	$ 374,385
21	Direct labor cost, overtime		$ -	$ -	$ -	$ -	$ -	$ -
22	Direct labor cost, total		$ 338,730	$ 338,730	$ 374,385	$ 392,213	$ 374,385	$ 374,385
23	Material cost, total		$ 1,074,590	$ 1,077,277	$ 1,193,651	$ 1,253,618	$ 1,199,627	$ 1,202,626
24	**Total manufacturing cost**		$ 1,413,320	$ 1,416,006	$ 1,568,036	$ 1,645,831	$ 1,574,012	$ 1,577,011
25	**INVENTORY LEVEL**							
26	Start of month, units		3,400	4,136	4,232	3,934	3,119	1,221
27	End of month, units	3,400	4,136	4,232	3,934	3,119	1,221	0
28	Average, units		3,768	4,184	4,083	3,527	2,170	610
29	**INVENTORY VALUE, AT COST**							
30	Start of month		$ 2,035,000	$ 2,486,456	$ 2,551,823	$ 2,378,588	$ 1,890,676	$ 742,035
31	Added		$ 1,413,320	$ 1,416,006	$ 1,568,036	$ 1,645,831	$ 1,574,012	$ 1,577,011
32	Total before sales		$ 3,448,320	$ 3,902,462	$ 4,119,859	$ 4,024,418	$ 3,464,688	$ 2,319,045
33	Average unit cost of those sold		$601.16	$602.96	$604.61	$606.18	$607.74	$609.80
34	End of month (total after sales)	$2,035,000	$ 2,486,456	$ 2,551,823	$ 2,378,588	$ 1,890,676	$ 742,035	$ -
35	Average value of inventory		$ 2,260,728	$ 2,519,140	$ 2,465,205	$ 2,134,632	$ 1,316,355	$ 371,017
36	**CASH INFLOWS FROM SALES**							
37	Cash from sales last month	66.67%	$ 736,000	$ 981,333	$ 1,373,867	$ 1,766,400	$ 2,158,933	$ 2,747,733
38	Cash from sales this month	33.33%	$ 490,667	$ 686,933	$ 883,200	$ 1,079,467	$ 1,373,867	$ 1,216,944
39	**Total sales receipts (cash inflow)**		$ 1,226,667	$ 1,668,267	$ 2,257,067	$ 2,845,867	$ 3,532,800	$ 3,964,678
40	**MISCELLANEOUS EXPENSES**							
41	Salaries *increase in August*	5.0%	$ 80,000	$ 80,000	$ 80,000	$ 80,000	$ 80,000	$ 80,000
42	Advertising *pct of preceding sales*	2.5%	$ 27,600	$ 36,800	$ 51,520	$ 66,240	$ 80,960	$ 103,040
43	Commissions *pct of sales*	4.0%	$ 58,880	$ 82,432	$ 105,984	$ 129,536	$ 164,864	$ 146,033
44	Fringe benefits *pct of wages and salaries*	41.0%	$ 171,679	$ 171,679	$ 186,298	$ 193,607	$ 186,298	$ 186,298
45	Interest on long-term notes		$ 12,000	$ 12,000	$ 12,000	$ 12,000	$ 12,000	$ 12,000
46	Inventory holding cost *pct of avg inventory*	2.0%	$ 45,215	$ 50,383	$ 49,304	$ 42,693	$ 26,327	$ 7,420
47	Long-term leases		$ 85,000	$ 85,000	$ 85,000	$ 85,000	$ 85,000	$ 85,000
48	Income tax				$ 100,000			$ 120,000
49	Dividends to shareholders		$ 50,000			$ 50,000		
50	**Total miscellaneous expenses**		$ 530,374	$ 518,294	$ 670,106	$ 659,076	$ 635,449	$ 739,792
51	Cost of manufacturing labor and materials		$ 1,413,320	$ 1,416,006	$ 1,568,036	$ 1,645,831	$ 1,574,012	$ 1,577,011
52	**CASH OUTFLOW FROM OPERATIONS**		$ 1,943,693	$ 1,934,300	$ 2,238,142	$ 2,304,907	$ 2,209,461	$ 2,316,803
53	**NET CASH FLOW FROM OPERATIONS**		$ (717,027)	$ (266,033)	$ 18,924	$ 540,960	$ 1,323,339	$ 1,647,875
54	**CASH FLOWS FOR FINANCIAL ACTIVITIES**							
55	Opening cash balance		$ 45,000	$ 30,000	$ 30,000	$ 30,000	$ 30,000	$ 50,000
56	Return of previous invested principal		$ -	$ -	$ -	$ -	$ -	$ 877,333
57	Interest inflow from previous investing		$ -	$ -	$ -	$ -	$ -	$ 3,656
58	Payoff of previous borrowed principal		$ -	$ (702,027)	$ (972,155)	$ (958,902)	$ (423,535)	$ -
59	Interest outflow for previous borrowing		$ -	$ (4,095)	$ (5,671)	$ (5,594)	$ (2,471)	$ -
60	Cash balance before new short-term investing or borrowing		$ (672,027)	$ (942,155)	$ (928,902)	$ (393,535)	$ 927,333	$ 2,578,864
61	New short-term investing		$ -	$ -	$ -	$ -	$ 877,333	$ 2,528,864
62	New short-term borrowing		$ 702,027	$ 972,155	$ 958,902	$ 423,535	$ -	$ -
63	**Ending cash balance**	$ 45,000	$ 30,000	$ 30,000	$ 30,000	$ 30,000	$ 50,000	$ 50,000
64			Cash balance policy					
65			Minimum month-end balance		$30,000			
66			Maximum month-end balance		$50,000			
67			Annual interest rate for borrowing		7.0%			
68			Annual interest rate for investing		5.0%			

(Continued)

Figure 8-21

Last Six Months of Cash Budget with Overtime and Backordering (Strategy #4)

	A	I	J	K	L	M	N	O
1		ASHLEY MANUFACTURING: Strategy #4						
2		Jul-97	Aug-97	Sep-97	Oct-97	Nov-97	Dec-97	All 1997
3	**SALES**							
4	Percent of annual	11%	9%	7%	6%	5%	4%	
5	Forecast demand, units	3,520	2,880	2,240	1,920	1,600	1,280	32,000
6	Backorders from preceding month, units	37	704	576	234	0	0	
7	Total demand, units	3,557	3,584	2,816	2,154	1,600	1,280	
8	Sales completed, units	2,853	3,008	2,582	2,154	1,600	1,280	32,000
9	Backorders to following month, units	704	576	234	0	0	0	
10	Unit selling price	$960.00	$960.00	$960.00	$960.00	$960.00	$960.00	
11	Sales completed, dollars	$ 2,738,927	$ 2,887,680	$ 2,478,689	$ 2,067,871	$ 1,536,000	$ 1,228,800	$ 30,131,200
12	**MANUFACTURING**							
13	Workdays	22	21	21	23	19	15	244
14	Maximum backorders, pct of forecast demand							
15	Units produced on regular time	2,705	2,582	2,582	2,828	2,336	1,844	30,000
16	Units produced on overtime	148	426	0	0	0	0	574
17	Total units produced	2,853	3,008	2,582	2,828	2,336	1,844	30,574
18	Direct labor cost, $/unit *increase in July*	$152.25	$152.25	$152.25	$152.25	$152.25	$152.25	
19	Material cost, $/unit *annual increase*	$466.94	$468.11	$469.28	$470.45	$471.63	$472.81	
20	Direct labor cost, regular time	$ 411,824	$ 393,105	$ 393,105	$ 430,543	$ 355,666	$ 280,789	$ 4,457,859
21	Direct labor cost, overtime	$ 33,829	$ 97,295	$ -	$ -	$ -	$ -	$ 131,125
22	Direct labor cost, total	$ 445,653	$ 490,400	$ 393,105	$ 430,543	$ 355,666	$ 280,789	$ 4,588,983
23	Material cost, total	$ 1,332,212	$ 1,408,077	$ 1,211,668	$ 1,330,383	$ 1,101,759	$ 871,984	$ 14,257,470
24	**Total manufacturing cost**	$ 1,777,865	$ 1,898,477	$ 1,604,772	$ 1,760,926	$ 1,457,425	$ 1,152,773	$ 18,846,454
25	**INVENTORY LEVEL**							
26	Start of month, units	0	0	0	0	674	1,410	
27	End of month, units	0	0	0	674	1,410	1,974	
28	Average, units	0	0	0	337	1,042	1,692	
29	**INVENTORY VALUE, AT COST**							
30	Start of month	$ -	$ -	$ -	$ -	$ 419,600	$ 879,239	
31	Added	$ 1,777,865	$ 1,898,477	$ 1,604,772	$ 1,760,926	$ 1,457,425	$ 1,152,773	
32	Total before sales	$ 1,777,865	$ 1,898,477	$ 1,604,772	$ 1,760,926	$ 1,877,026	$ 2,032,012	
33	Average unit cost of those sold	$623.15	$631.14	$621.53	$622.70	$623.62	$624.43	
34	End of month (total after sales)	$ -	$ -	$ -	$ 419,600	$ 879,239	$ 1,232,736	
35	Average value of inventory	$ -	$ -	$ -	$ 209,800	$ 649,420	$ 1,055,987	
36	**CASH INFLOWS FROM SALES**							
37	Cash from sales last month	$ 2,433,889	$ 1,825,951	$ 1,925,120	$ 1,652,459	$ 1,378,581	$ 1,024,000	$ 20,004,267
38	Cash from sales this month	$ 912,976	$ 962,560	$ 826,230	$ 689,290	$ 512,000	$ 409,600	$ 10,043,733
39	**Total sales receipts (cash inflow)**	$ 3,346,864	$ 2,788,511	$ 2,751,350	$ 2,341,750	$ 1,890,581	$ 1,433,600	$ 30,048,000
40	**MISCELLANEOUS EXPENSES**							
41	Salaries *increase in August*	$ 80,000	$ 84,000	$ 84,000	$ 84,000	$ 84,000	$ 84,000	$ 980,000
42	Advertising *pct of preceding sales*	$ 91,271	$ 68,473	$ 72,192	$ 61,967	$ 51,697	$ 38,400	$ 750,160
43	Commissions *pct of sales*	$ 109,557	$ 115,507	$ 99,148	$ 82,715	$ 61,440	$ 49,152	$ 1,205,248
44	Fringe benefits *pct of wages and salaries*	$ 201,648	$ 195,613	$ 195,613	$ 210,963	$ 180,263	$ 149,563	$ 2,229,522
45	Interest on long-term notes	$ 12,000	$ 12,000	$ 12,000	$ 12,000	$ 12,000	$ 12,000	$ 144,000
46	Inventory holding cost *pct of avg inventory*	$ -	$ -	$ -	$ 4,196	$ 12,988	$ 21,120	$ 259,646
47	Long-term leases	$ 85,000	$ 85,000	$ 85,000	$ 100,000	$ 100,000	$ 100,000	$ 1,065,000
48	Income tax			$ 120,000			$ 130,000	$ 470,000
49	Dividends to shareholders	$ 50,000			$ 50,000			$ 200,000
50	**Total miscellaneous expenses**	$ 629,476	$ 560,593	$ 667,952	$ 605,841	$ 502,388	$ 584,235	$ 7,303,576
51	Cost of manufacturing labor and materials	$ 1,777,865	$ 1,898,477	$ 1,604,772	$ 1,760,926	$ 1,457,425	$ 1,152,773	$ 18,846,454
52	**CASH OUTFLOW FROM OPERATIONS**	$ 2,407,341	$ 2,459,070	$ 2,272,725	$ 2,366,766	$ 1,959,813	$ 1,737,009	$ 26,150,029
53	**NET CASH FLOW FROM OPERATIONS**	$ 939,523	$ 329,442	$ 478,625	$ (25,017)	$ (69,232)	$ (303,409)	$ 3,897,971
54	**CASH FLOWS FOR FINANCIAL ACTIVITIES**							
55	Opening cash balance	$ 50,000	$ 50,000	$ 50,000	$ 50,000	$ 50,000	$ 50,000	
56	Return of previous invested principal	$ 2,528,864	$ 3,478,924	$ 3,822,861	$ 4,317,415	$ 4,310,387	$ 4,259,115	
57	Interest inflow from previous investing	$ 10,537	$ 14,496	$ 15,929	$ 17,989	$ 17,960	$ 17,746	$ 98,312
58	Payoff of previous borrowed principal	$ -	$ -	$ -	$ -	$ -	$ -	
59	Interest outflow for previous borrowing	$ -	$ -	$ -	$ -	$ -	$ -	$ (17,830)
60	Cash balance before new short-term investing or borrowing	$ 3,528,924	$ 3,872,861	$ 4,367,415	$ 4,360,387	$ 4,309,115	$ 4,023,452	
61	New short-term investing	$ 3,478,924	$ 3,822,861	$ 4,317,415	$ 4,310,387	$ 4,259,115	$ 3,973,452	
62	New short-term borrowing	$ -	$ -	$ -	$ -	$ -	$ -	
63	**Ending cash balance**	$ 50,000	$ 50,000	$ 50,000	$ 50,000	$ 50,000	$ 50,000	

(Continued)

Figure 8-22

Cash Flow Reconciliation for Overtime and Backordering (Strategy #4)

	A	B	C	D	E	F	G
69	ASHLEY MANUFACTURING: Strategy #4						
70	Cash Inflow-Outflow Reconciliation for the Year						
71	Inflows			Outflows			
72	Starting cash balance	$ 45,000		Manufacturing labor and material			$ 18,846,454
73	Sales receipts	$ 30,048,000		Other operating expenses			$ 7,303,576
74	Interest earned on short-term investing	$ 98,312		Interest paid on short-term borrowing			$ 17,830
75	Total	$ 30,191,312		End-of-year short-term investments			$ 3,973,452
76				Ending cash balance			$ 50,000
77						Total	$ 30,191,312
78	Other Information for Comparison of Strategies						
79	Inventory holding cost for the year	$ 259,646		End-of-year numbers			
80	Net cash flow from operations for the year	$ 3,897,971		Inventory, units			1,974
81				Inventory, value at cost			$ 1,232,736
82				Inventory + short-term investments			$ 5,206,188

Sales section: Ashley's sales organization will want to keep track of how well their customers' demands are satisfied. To do this, add two new rows after Row 5 of the "Sales" section to keep track of the backorders from the preceding month and the total demand (i.e., the sum of the forecast demand plus backorders from the preceding month). Label new Row 6 "Backorders from preceding month, units" and label new Row 7 "Forecast demand plus backorders, units" or "Total demand, units." Then make the following entries in the new rows:

- For the backorders from the preceding month: Enter =B9 in Cell C6 and copy to Cells D6:N6.
- For the total demand (i.e., the forecast demand plus backorders from preceding month): Enter =C5+C6 in Cell C7 and copy to Cells D7:N7.
- For the sales completed: Change the entry in Cell C8 to =IF(C17+C26>C7,C7,C17+C26) and copy to Cells D8:N8.
- For the backorders to the following month: Add another row after Row 8 to create a new Row 9 and label the new row "Backorders to following month, units." Then enter =IF(C7>C8,C7-C8,0) in Cell C9 and copy the entry to Cells D9:N9.
- For the dollar value of the sales completed: Change the entry in Cell C11 to =C6*B10+(C8-C6)*C10 and copy to D11:N11. This entry is the sum of the backorders completed at the selling price in effect the preceding month (i.e., when the backorders were placed) plus new orders completed at the current price. (Actually, omitting this change does not affect the results for the conditions of this particular problem because the first month in which backorders occur (i.e., June) is the first month for the price increase to $960/unit from $920/unit.)

Manufacturing: Manufacturing needs to respond to the new rules for overtime. Change the label in Cell A14 to "Maximum backorders, percent of forecast demand," and change the value in Cell B14 to 20%.

If the difference (or "shortfall") between the total demand and what is available from regular time production and beginning inventory is greater than 20 percent of the forecast demand, overtime must be worked. The number of units produced on overtime must then equal the shortfall minus 20 percent of the forecast demand. Otherwise, no overtime is needed. To calculate the number of units produced on overtime, change the entry in Cell C16 to =IF(C7-(C26+C15)>$B$14*C5,C7-(C26+C15)-$B$14*C5,0) and copy to Cells D16:N16. (Study this entry carefully and note how it corresponds to the statements of the first three sentences of this paragraph.)

(Continued)

Because of the linkages already established for the second strategy, no further editing should be required to produce the results shown in Figures 8-20, 8-21, and 8-22.

Sensitivity Analysis

We will use a one-variable input table to show the impact of the maximum percentage of forecast monthly demand permitted on backorder on (1) the net cash flow from operations for the year, (2) the average number of units in inventory during the year, (3) the average value of inventory during the year, (4) the inventory holding cost for the year, (5) the number of units produced on overtime during the year, and (6) the labor cost for working overtime during the year. Figure 8-23 shows the results in tabular format, and Figure 8-24 plots the result from the first two columns to show the impact of the backorder policy on the net cash flow from operations for the year.

Figure 8-23

Sensitivity of Net Operating Cash Flow and Other Variables to the Backordering Policy, Expressed as the Maximum Percent of Monthly Demand Allowed on Backorder

	B	C	D	E	F	G	H
89	SENSITIVITY TO BACKORDER POLICY, AS EXPRESSED BY THE MAXIMUM PERCENT OF FORECAST DEMAND PERMITTED ON BACKORDER						
90	Maximum Percent of Forecast Demand on Backorder	Net Cash Flow from Operations for the Year	Average Number of Units in Inventory	Average Value of Inventory	Inventory Holding Cost for the Year	Number of Units Produced on Overtime during the Year	Labor Cost for Working Overtime during the Year
92	0%	$ 3,475,874	1,933	$ 1,174,310	$ 281,835	1,150	$ 262,266
93	10%	$ 3,688,151	1,849	$ 1,122,033	$ 269,288	862	$ 196,897
94	20%	$ 3,897,971	1,784	$ 1,081,857	$ 259,646	574	$ 131,125
95	30%	$ 4,107,359	1,724	$ 1,044,469	$ 250,673	286	$ 65,353
96	40%	$ 4,315,585	1,665	$ 1,007,315	$ 241,756	0	$ -
97	50%	$ 4,315,585	1,665	$ 1,007,315	$ 241,756	0	$ -
98	60%	$ 4,315,585	1,665	$ 1,007,315	$ 241,756	0	$ -
99	70%	$ 4,315,585	1,665	$ 1,007,315	$ 241,756	0	$ -
100	80%	$ 4,315,585	1,665	$ 1,007,315	$ 241,756	0	$ -
101	90%	$ 4,315,585	1,665	$ 1,007,315	$ 241,756	0	$ -
102	100%	$ 4,315,585	1,665	$ 1,007,315	$ 241,756	0	$ -

Key Cell Entries in Row 85 for Transferring Values
B91: =B14   C91: =O53   D91: =AVERAGE(C28:N28)
E91: =AVERAGE(C35:N35)
F91: =O46   G91: =O16   H91: =O21

(Row 91 has been hidden.)

(Continued)

Figure 8-24

Sensitivity of Net Operating Cash Flow and Other Variables to the Backordering Policy, Expressed as the Maximum Percent of Monthly Demand Allowed on Backorder

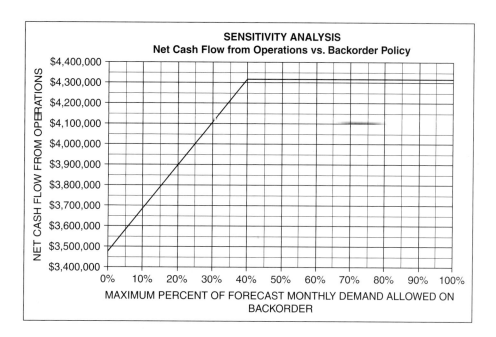

The preparation of the table and chart follows the same procedure as for the earlier sensitivity analyses. Be sure that the results are **not** plotted as a smooth curve but as a pair of straight-line segments that meet at the common point, as in Figure 8-24. (To do this, delete the check in the "Smoothed line" box on the "Patterns" tab of the "Format Data Series" dialog box.)

Lines of Credit

Operating Lines of Credit are the most common type of borrowing to provide a firm's working capital. They are designed to meet the short-term working capital needs for purchasing inventories of goods and supplies and for paying salaries and other operating expenses. They provide liquidity during the operating cycles of businesses, and they are therefore important components of cash budgets. Many businesses could not survive without them. (For long-term [i.e., over one year] borrowing to purchase capital assets, for example, a term loan, or a term loan plus the issuance of stock, would be most typically used for financing.)

A **Line of Credit** ("Line") allows a borrower to take advances (up to a preset limiting amount) during a defined period and repay the advances at the borrower's discretion at any time. A Line has a preset limit on the amount that may be borrowed and a maturity date on which the outstanding balance on the loan plus accrued interest is due and can be called by the lender. Each Line is negotiated separately between a company and a bank. Generally, collateral and loan guaranty are not required for approval, unless the applicant's basic credit criteria are not met.

A bank will usually require certified business and personal tax returns for the past three years, personal statements, and other supplemental information to qualify for this type of financing. The preset or authorized limit on the amount that can be borrowed will depend on a firm's historical and/or projected annual income. A positive cash flow will be required; that is, the firm must be profitable and able to demonstrate that the debt can be repaid on a regular basis. After issuance, the firm may borrow up to the preset limit, either in one lump sum or incrementally, during the lifetime of the Line. It may repay any amount borrowed and re-draw funds as needed up to the preset limit.

The level of control exercised by the bank will depend on the perceived credit risk and the Line limit. For smaller lines to companies with good credit, there may be no active controls on line of credit usage. That is, the customer can take advances and repay them at will, and the bank may analyze Line usage only annually or at renewal. If the Line did not properly "revolve" during the year, the line of credit would generally be converted to a fully amortizing term loan and the line of credit closed out. For large lines of credit and companies with a high credit risk, a bank will monitor and control a Line closely and as often as daily.

Other Short-Term Financial Instruments

Short-term financial instruments (such as "commercial paper") include unsecured promissory notes, drafts, and bills of exchange that have original maturities up to as long as nine months (270 days), excluding days of grace or renewal. In practice, most commercial paper (CP) is issued for periods shorter than nine months. Corporations use short-term debt instruments when they need cash to finance such short-term needs as accounts receivable, inventories, and meeting short-term liabilities. On the other hand, when a company wishes to earn interest on excess funds that are available for a limited time, it issues commercial paper that is purchased by banks, institutional investors, or other companies that have a short-term need for funds. CP is exempt from registration with the U.S. Securities and Exchange Commission because its maturities do not exceed nine months and its proceeds are typically used only for short-term transactions. The proceeds are not allowed to be used for fixed assets, such as new plants and facilities, without SEC approval.

CP is unsecured; that is, it is usually not backed up by any form of collateral. Therefore, only firms with high-quality debt ratings can find buyers for their CP without having to offer a substantial discount to the buyer. CP is usually less liquid than bonds, as there is no real secondary market for it.

The interest rate of CP is generally a lower cost alternative to borrowing from banks or other institutions. However, the savings from issuing it are so small in comparison to raising funds by simpler means, such as borrowing from a bank, that the use of CP is usually limited to corporations borrowing large amounts.

An issuer of CP can either sell it directly to a buyer or have a dealer sell it on its behalf. Direct selling avoids dealer fees and provides greater flexibility for adjusting the amounts, interest rates, and maturities. Dealers of CP are large security firms and the subsidiaries of bank holding companies; they usually issue CP on a discount basis only.

Concluding Remarks

A cash budget is a plan. It is a primary tool for short-term financial planning. It identifies a firm's short-term financial needs and opportunities. That is, cash budgets tell CFOs how much they will need to borrow, and how much they will have to invest in short-term securities. This provides time for them to meet with their bankers and other lenders to ensure that their needs to borrow or invest money can be satisfied promptly and efficiently.

Is that really the **only** use a CFO might have for a cash budget? We think not. In addition to their stated primary purpose, cash budgets provide an excellent opportunity for a CFO to look into the details of how different parts of a firm are operating. Cash budgets can help integrate and coordinate an organization's functions so that the sales department does not try to sell more than manufacturing can produce, for example, or so that inventory safety stocks are sufficient to meet sales needs without becoming unnecessarily large and chewing up profits, or so that executives know when capacity should be increased to avoid excessive amounts of overtime to satisfy sales demands.

Much as a spreadsheet model links cells, a good cash budget links organizations. The systematic approach of spreadsheets helps illuminate essential linkages between organizations. It helps pull the organizational pieces together and create a team effort.

Feedback from Students

This was a brand new topic for me to study. I had never been exposed to cash budgeting procedures before. This [chapter] will deepen my understanding of various types of companies (such as manufacturing and retail), how they operate, and the likely impacts on their profits from making operational changes in inventory management and overtime policies.

* * *

I had to put together a daily and weekly cash forecast in a banking function in the late 1980s just to manage daily cash balances. This was critical, as we did not like having idle cash balances. We wanted to put it to work, even if it meant only earning interest overnight. However, the daily and weekly cash forecasts were not at the level of detail of this chapter. I can see now that it is very important to exercise the rigor of this chapter's cash budgeting process so as to optimally manage working capital.

* * *

I have seen this time and time again: Some members of the sales force only cared about booking a sale and not about collecting on the sale. "It ain't over" until the cash is collected. The different parts of the corporation are definitely interconnected, and it is incumbent upon all of us to think "beyond the scope of your desk." Thinking this way has helped me in my career tremendously.

* * *

The production line balancing challenge really stood out to me in Strategy #4, where the largest inventory is held when it is needed the least. This gave me a better understanding of why "on-demand" supply chains strategies are becoming increasingly popular and why CFO's are so willing to sport the cash for integrated ERP systems. Refining manufacturing strategies to make them on-demand takes a lot of cross-organization coordination and I don't think it would be possible to accomplish this successfully without the right systems in place.

* * *

(Continued)

I find that cash budgeting is no less important than capital budgeting or any other financial decisions made by a firm. The cash budget is a critical link between many divisions of a firm. I also see that cash budgeting is not a passive activity or mere information gathering, but it is an influential driver for production, marketing, finance, and sales people to plan their resources and activities.

* * *

I wish to share with you all about my trip to Vietnam on July 14, 2008 and how this class is related. Recently, the Vietnam economy is overheated. As a result, the bank is reducing credit; so many investors are running out of cash flow, so the real estate is dirt cheap over there because the investors or the companies did not anticipate the cash flow crisis. The point is that cash flow is like the blood circulating in the body. As soon as the flow is stuck or blood is short, the body will experience crisis. Always watch out for the cash flow. [*This comment was actually posted by a student in my online class just two months ahead of the beginning of the 2008 financial crisis. How prescient! F.J.Clauss*]

Because cash budgets link financial results to data from a firm's marketing, sales, and production divisions, they provide an opportunity to look at how different parts of a firm **are** operating compared to how they were **planned** to operate. By comparing *actual* against forecast or *planned* values, problems can be identified early in their development and corrected before they adversely impact profitability. The key to controlling a firm's operations is to have a good plan for the future and a good system for monitoring how well operations are matching the plan.

Profits can clearly be increased in several ways: (1) an increase in revenues without a proportionate change in costs, (2) a decrease in costs without a proportionate change in revenues, or (3) a combination of increased revenues and decreased costs. During periods of an expanding economy and the absence of competition, the emphasis has largely been on the first method. During the periods of a stagnant or contracting economy and the presence of fierce global competition in more recent times, emphasis has shifted to the second method.

Cash Budgeting and Cost Accounting

To minimize and control costs, one needs to know what the costs are for specific items and times. Financial managers have found that traditional methods of cost accounting do not provide the detailed information needed to do this. Traditional cost-accounting methods failed because they could not identify where significant costs were being incurred. Instead, they allocated many operating and indirect costs as a percentage or "fair share" of the direct costs for producing goods or providing services. They hid the causes of many costs and gave clouded pictures of where costs were being incurred.

Inventory holding costs are a notable example of costs that are often hidden. They have typically been grouped with other costs that comprise a company's "indirect costs." The result is they are "out of sight," not understood, and poorly managed. Remember the old management adage: "Out of sight is out of mind." The purpose of any cost-accounting system is, as the term implies, to account for any costs.

So-called "Just-in-Time" policies have focused management attention on inventory costs and resulted in very significant savings. The success of companies such as Wal-Mart Stores and Dell Computers over their competitors is related to their excellent inventory management. The case studies in this chapter that analyze Ashley Manufacturing's strategies demonstrate how production capacity and inventory management affect cash flows and net income.

Traditional cost-accounting systems simply fail to do an important part of their job. They fail to show where costs are being incurred and where management action is needed to preserve profits. They can lead to cutting costs in the wrong places and worsen a condition instead of correcting it. To remedy the shortcomings of traditional methods, "activity-based costing," or ABC accounting has been introduced. ABC systems assign costs to each activity. They trace the cost of each activity and identify specific organizational resources that are being consumed to support a firm's activities. They differ from traditional systems by focusing on the consumption of resources and capturing costs as they occur rather than simply allocating what has already been spent. When done properly, ABC accounting is a dedicated tattletale that provides details on the trail of money through the organization. CFOs will find it useful to follow the money trail to identify what organizations are spending how much and why.

ABC accounting systems are more complex and costly than traditional systems. On the other hand, modern information technology reduces costs and expedites the collection and storage of data to a much finer level of detail than possible with traditional systems. They make it possible to create, revise, and update reports at frequent intervals. With data that are more complete, accurate, and timely, CFOs are better able to control costs and improve a company's ability to compete.

The amount of detailed information that can be gleaned from a cash budget depends on the amount of detailed information put into it and how well the information is organized. This has been the guiding principle behind the cash budgets presented in this chapter, and the spreadsheets presented throughout the text. Spreadsheets have been designed to exploit the potential offered by spreadsheets for assembling data, analyzing it, and presenting information as a basis for action. Computer-based ABC accounting systems have become the source for much of the data used in cash budgets.

Garbage In, Garbage Out

It costs good money to get good data. The alternative, bad data, can be even more expensive. That is the bottom line. And the bottom line is what GIGO is really all about.

Cash Budgeting and Management Information Systems

Cash budgets are part of the forecast-plan-implement-control loop of management information systems shown in Figure 8-25. At the top of the loop are the monthly or quarterly sales forecasts that are the basis for financial and other plans, including the cash budgets presented in this chapter. No plan for the future can be any better than the assessment of what the future will bring. A CFO can examine the cash budgets for successive periods and compare forecast sales with actual sales for the same period. If there is serious disagreement or systematic bias, the forecasting models and procedures need correcting.

Figure 8-25

The Forecast-Plan-Implement-Control Loop of Management Information Systems

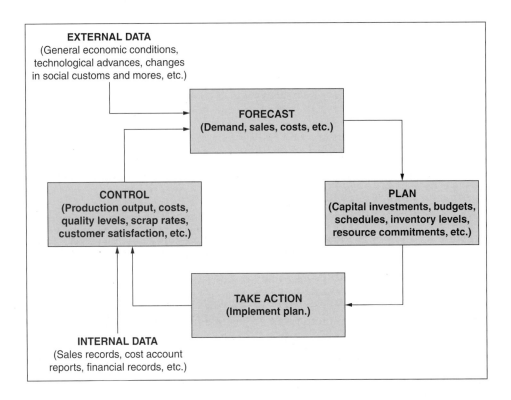

Much of a cash budget is taken up with such matters as (1) the collection of accounts receivable for goods or services sold; (2) payments for labor, materials, and supplies for producing the company's products; (3) scheduled output of products; and (4) various other expenses. The accounts receivable, accounts payable, cost accounting, production records, and other parts of management information systems track the actual amounts of these items. When actual values differ significantly from planned values, a CFO should insist that the offending organizations take corrective action—and the sooner, the better.

Enterprise Resource Planning

Enterprise resource planning (ERP) systems are large computer-based software systems used to manage and coordinate the resources and functions of corporations based on information from shared data stores.

ERP systems evolved in stages from the systems for material requirements planning (MRP) that were used during the 1960s and early 1970s to calculate material requirements for manufacturing; through the later systems for MRP to schedule the use of materials, factory tools, and personnel; and, finally, culminating in the overall concept and implementation of today's ERP systems.

(Continued)

ERP systems are cross-functional. They coordinate such financial functions as the general ledger (i.e., the main accounting record of a business, which keeps account of such items as current assets, fixed assets, liabilities, revenues, and expenses), cash budgeting and management, accounts receivable, accounts payable, and fixed assets.

Besides financial functions, ERP systems include managing and procurement of goods and services; manufacturing and service operations; inventories of materials, supplies, and finished goods; quality control of incoming goods and finished products and services; human resources; and customer relations.

The elements of an ERP system include (1) a data warehouse that has self-service interfaces for customers, suppliers, and employees for inputting and accessing data; (2) an access control system that limits users to those with proper authorization; and (3) customization to extend or change the functions covered and the flow of information to fit a corporation's special needs.

ERP systems are basically large-scale linked systems that combine the basic functions of data access, analysis, and reporting that can be done with Microsoft Excel.

Cash Budgets and Operations

Besides being a financial plan, a cash budget is an operating plan and an operating budget. The elements of cash budget spreadsheets can be organized in modules according to organizations and their functions. One module covers such marketing information as sales forecasts of customer demands. Another module covers a firm's production or operations organization and indicates the units of output each period and the flow of units into and out of warehouses or other holding areas. A third covers financial management and reports on cash inflows and outflows. A cash budget spreadsheet integrates the operations and links results in one area with those in others.

When several strategies are available for coping with problems or capitalizing on opportunities, spreadsheets serve as digital laboratories for experimenting with each and identifying which is best. Start your analysis with a spreadsheet for the base conditions. Then modify the spreadsheet (or a copy of it) for each strategy to determine revenues, costs, and other marketing, operating, and financial information.

Revising and Updating

How often should a cash budget be updated? Many students look at a cash budget as a one-year plan that should be updated annually. The smarter ones recognize that it should be updated at least monthly, which matches the 30-day period for short-term commercial paper. Some companies update their plans weekly.

Information technology (IT) is what makes frequent updating practical. IT has revolutionized the way many companies do business. It transfers information quickly and accurately in the form of bytes of data rather than bits of paper. It has helped integrate plans and coordinate actions across corporate divisions and supplier networks. It works between offices in the same building, and it works between firms on opposite sides of the world.

Information technology has improved companies' productivity for manufacturing goods and raised their efficiency for serving customers. The development of various types of programmed models for financial, marketing, and operations management, and the shift to computer-based networks for sharing information have become permanent parts of doing business.

> ### Putting Out Fires before They Start
>
> Frequent updating and quick reaction are among the keys of good management. Periodic updating takes advantage of the most recent data on actual sales and operating efficiencies. Frequent updating puts a premium on having a management information system that links results from different parts of the company so that updating is done automatically as new data are entered. The payoff is closer management control and higher profits. Cisco Systems, the networking giant, is an example of how information technology is being used to stay on top of operations. Cisco uses a proprietary Internet-based financial reporting system that allows it to close its books and produce a complete income statement and balance sheet, along with after-tax income, on a daily basis something most companies don't do more often than monthly or quarterly. The company can get hourly reports on its revenues, orders, gross margins, and operating expenses. Cisco gives its account managers a daily sales goal and monitors their performance every day.
>
> Good managers stay on top of things and take corrective action before problems become catastrophes. As an old adage teaches, "An ounce of prevention is worth a pound of cure." Cash budgets enable managers to recognize when an "ounce of prevention" is needed.

Rates of Interest

What is a reasonable rate of interest a corporation should pay for a loan, or receive for lending its unused funds? A good place to start is with the federal funds rate, which is what big banks pay for their funds. The Federal Reserve Board releases this information daily on the Internet, along with the prime rate and the rates for short-term commercial paper, CDs, treasury bills, etc. You can access this information at the Web sites or either the Federal Reserve Board (www.federalreserve.gov/releases/cp/) or the Federal Reserve Bank of New York (www.ny.frb.org/pihome/mktrates/dlyrates).

The rate that banks charge for small commercial loans of $100,000 or less averages about 4.22 percentage points higher than the rate for federal funds. For example, if the current rate for federal funds is 6.50 percent, the rate for small commercial loans would be about 10.72 percent. Depending on the economy and competition among banks, the spread varies but rarely strays more than half a point in either direction from the average of 4.22 percent. The lowest spread in recent years was 3.5 percent in 1989, when loan rates were at an all-time high of 13.39 percent, and the highest spread was 5.06 percent in 1992. (*Business Week*, March 29, 1999) The spread for a specific loan would, of course, vary with other conditions. If a company was in poor financial health, for example, a bank would increase the spread and adjust the interest rate upwards.

Firms generally negotiate revolving lines of credit with banks. These are understandings, either formal or informal, that specify the maximum loan balance the bank will allow at any time.

Chapter 9

Cost of Capital

CHAPTER OBJECTIVES

Management Skills

- Understand what is meant by the cost of capital and how it is calculated.
- Identify sources of capital and their costs.
- Understand the components of capital and how they appear in a corporation's capital structure.
- Understand what is meant by flotation costs.
- Recognize the relationship of WACC to the discount rate used in capital budgeting (Chapters 12 to 14).

Spreadsheet Skills

- Calculate the weighted average cost of capital (WACC) from its components.
- Use Excel's Goal Seek and Solver tools to determine the value of an independent variable that's needed to satisfy a related goal.
- Distinguish between WACC based on book value and WACC based on market value, and show how to calculate them.
- Include flotation costs in the calculation of WACC.
- Calculate the WACC for different amounts of total capital raised and create a chart that shows WACC as a function of the total capital raised.

Overview

In this chapter we consider the cost of the capital a firm must pay in order to raise funds for large-scale ventures it wishes to undertake. Examples of such ventures include:

- Acquiring new plant facilities and equipment
- Upgrading existing facilities and equipment
- Expanding distribution networks
- Developing new products
- Improving the safety or efficiency of operations
- Reducing pollution from operations
- Installing computer networks and management information systems

Such ventures have long-time impacts on a company's future. Therefore, they are carefully planned by a firm's financial, marketing, production or operations, and other functional organization.

Large-scale ventures are very expensive and completing them can take years. When retained earnings are insufficient to pay their entire cost, additional capital is raised through borrowing (i.e., debt) and issuing stock (i.e., equity). These cash inflows are related to values on the right side of the balance sheet, under the headings long-term debt and shareholders' equity (i.e., preferred and common stock). The associated cash outflows affect the left side of the balance sheet, under the heading fixed or long-term assets.

The cost of capital is the cost of financing. It is expressed as an annual rate of return that an investment must achieve in order to return the cost of financing and begin to be profitable. The cost of raising capital is important in determining whether or not a venture will be profitable. As discussed in later chapters on capital budgeting, the cost of capital sets the discount rate used to determine an investment's payoff in terms of its net present value, rate of return, and years to break even.

Long-time capital investments are wagers on a company's future. They carry no guarantees of success. Risks and potential losses accompany expectations of profit. To compensate for the risks, the potential payoffs should exceed the cost of capital by a margin that increases with the riskiness of the venture.

This chapter shows how to determine the cost of capital that a firm raises to pay for large-scale ventures. At the very least, the projected rate of return on a proposed project should not be less than the cost of the capital for the project—that is, the interest rate a firm must pay for the money it raises to fund the venture. It would be unwise, for example, to finance a new factory with a projected rate of return of only 10 percent if the firm had to pay 12 percent to borrow money to pay for the new factory. For an investment to be profitable, its return must be larger than its cost of capital.

A Firm's Value and Its Capital Structure

The amounts of debt and equity on a firm's balance sheet determine its capital structure. This is often shown graphically in the form of a pie chart, such as Figure 9-1. The firm's equity is the sum of the values

Figure 9-1

Capital Structure of the ABC Company at the End of 20X2

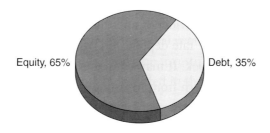

for preferred stock, common stock, and retained earnings. For the ABC Company whose balance sheet was shown in Figure 1-8, this is the sum of Cells B31:B34, which is $3,545.0 million at the end of 20X2. The debt of the ABC Company is the value in Cell B23, which is $1,900.0 million at the end of 20X2. These values give the percentage distribution shown in Figure 9-1.

The total value of the firm is the sum of the values for its equity and long-term debt. One of a CFO's jobs is to find the value for the debt-to-equity ratio that maximizes the firm's value. In an ideal world with no risks or taxes, a firm's value is independent of its debt-to-equity ratio.[1] In the real world with risks and taxes, however, a firm's value can be increased by increasing the ratio of debt to equity. A firm's debt-to-equity ratio is limited, however, by the risk that lenders are willing to assume in lending their money. We shall return to this matter in the discussion of leverage in Chapter 10.

Sources of Capital

Corporations can raise outside capital for major projects from three general sources: (1) borrowing from banks or other lenders, usually in the form of long-term bonds; (2) issuing preferred stock; and (3) issuing common stock. The current amounts from these sources appear on a firm's balance sheet as long-term debt, preferred stock, and common stock, respectively.

The obligation to repay is different for each source. Debt is a contractual obligation to repay a loan. Amounts borrowed must be repaid to creditors at the rates specified by the loan agreements or the coupon rate of any bonds issued.

Debt is more risky than equity from a corporation's standpoint, but is less risky for a lender or investor. Interest on debt must be paid out before dividends, and if a company goes into liquidation, lenders are first in line to be repaid before shareholders. From a company's standpoint, debt is less expensive and interest on debt is a tax-deductible expense. On the other hand, a company is not liable for repaying shareholders for their purchases of stock.

[1] This is known as the MM Proposition 1 of F. Modigliani and E. Miller, which appeared in their article "The Cost of Capital, Corporation Finance, and the Theory of Investment," *American Economic Review*.

The Weighted Average Cost of Capital

Firms must pay interest and other expenses to obtain additional capital. The cost is expressed by an annual percentage rate, which is different for each source.

A firm's **weighted average cost of capital** (WACC) is, as the term implies, a composite of the costs for raising capital from all sources. It is also expressed as an annual percentage rate.

A firm's WACC is used in capital budgeting for determining the discount rate of money—that is, for the rate that is used to discount future cash flows to their present values. It is important for measuring the success or failure of an investment. (This use of a firm's WACC is discussed in later chapters.)

Calculating the Weighted Average Cost of Capital

A firm's WACC varies with the relative amounts of debt, preferred stock, and common stock in the capital raised. It is computed by adding together the products obtained from multiplying the percentage return for each source by its percentage of the total capital raised.

WACC Based on Book Value

Values for the percentage returns for each source can be determined from their book or market values. The following example illustrates the calculation of the WACC based on book value.

Example 9.1:   The Turnbull Corporation's capital structure is composed of 40 percent debt, 5 percent preferred stock, and 55 percent common equity. ABC needs to raise $1 million to buy a small office building.

The effective or after-tax rate of interest ABC pays on its long-term debt is 8 percent, and its preferred stockholders receive a rate of return of 10 percent. Alternate investments that are available to shareholders with equal risks have rates of return of 13 percent. What would be ABC's cost of capital if it wishes to retain the same relative amounts of debt, preferred stock, and common stock in its capital structure?

Solution: Figure 9-3 is a spreadsheet solution. Key cell entries are shown at the bottom of the spreadsheet.

The values entered in Cells B4:B6 are the relative amounts in the firm's capital structure that the firm wishes to maintain. The total amount of capital to be raised is entered as data in Cell C7. The amounts to be raised from each source are calculated by entering =B4*$C$7 in Cell C4 and copying it to Cells C5:C6.

The rates of interest to be paid are entered as data in Cells D4:D6. The after-tax costs for the various sources are calculated by entering =C4*D4 in Cells E4 and copying the entry to Cells E5:E6. The total after-tax cost for all sources is calculated in Cell E7 by the entry =SUM(E4:E6).

The value 10.6 percent for the WACC is calculated in Cell D7 by the entry =E7/C7. The investment must earn a rate of return of at least 10.6 percent in order to provide each source of funds with its required rate of return. If the investment earns less than 10.6 percent, the common stockholders will receive less than 13 percent. On the other hand, if the investment earns more than 10.6 percent, the sum available to common equity (i.e., dividends on common stock plus retained earnings) will be more than 13 percent. In other words, the WACC of 10.6 percent is the minimum acceptable rate of return that satisfies the requirements of three fund sources.

(Continued)

Figure 9-3

Weighted Average Cost of Capital Based on Book Value

	A	B	C	D	E
1	**Example 9.1: TURNBULL CORP., COST OF CAPITAL BASED ON BOOK VALUE**				
2				Cost of Financing	
3	Source of Funds	Capital Structure	Amount to be Obtained	Required Rate to Pay	After-Tax Cost
4	Debt (i.e, Borrowing)	45.0%	$ 450,000	8.0%	$ 36,000
5	Preferred Stock	5.0%	$ 50,000	10.0%	$ 5,000
6	Common Stock	50.0%	$ 500,000	13.0%	$ 65,000
7	Total	100.0%	$ 1,000,000	10.6%	$ 106,000
8					
9				Book-Value WACC	
10					

Key cell entries:
C4: =B4*$C$7, copy to C4:C5
E4: =C4*D4, copy to E5:E6
E7: =SUM(E4:E6)
D7: =E7/C7

The same result is obtained if the weighted average cost of capital is calculated by the following equation:

$$WACC = w_{debt}k_{debt} + w_{preferred}k_{preferred} + w_{common}k_{common} \qquad (9.1)$$

where the ws are the weights or relative amounts of each source of capital and the ks are the rates of return for each source of capital. Thus, using the values for Example 9.1,

$$WACC = (0.45 \times 0.08) + (0.05 \times 0.10) + (0.50 \times 0.13) = 0.106 = 10.6\%$$

If the required rate for common stock equity is raised to 16 percent to compensate for increased risk, the minimum acceptable rate of return for the investment is calculated as

$$WACC = (0.45 \times 0.08) + (0.05 \times 0.10) + (0.50 \times 0.16) = 0.121 = 12.1\%$$

Example 9.2: Given an 8 percent cost of borrowing and a return of 10 percent on preferred stock, as in Example 9.1, what would be the return on common stock for a WACC of 10 percent?

Solution: Figure 9-4 is a spreadsheet solution obtained with Excel's Goal Seek tool. The spreadsheet setup is the same as in Example 9.3. Begin by saving the spreadsheet of Figure 9-3 and copying it to a new worksheet. Then, use Excel's Goal Seek tool with the settings shown in Figure 9-5. Figure 9-5 shows that Cell D5 is to be changed to whatever value is needed to achieve a value of 10 percent for the WACC in Cell D6. The result in Figure 9-4 shows that the return on common stock would be 11.8 percent.

(Continued)

Figure 9-4

Return on Common Stock for a WACC of 10%

	A	B	C	D	E
1	Example 9.2: ABC CORPORATION, COST OF CAPITAL BASED ON BOOK VALUE				
2	Source of Funds	Capital Structure	Amount to be Obtained	Required Rate to Pay	After-Tax Cost
3	Debt (i.e., Borrowing)	45.0%	$ 450,000	8.0%	$ 36,000
4	Preferred Stock	5.0%	$ 50,000	10.0%	$ 5,000
5	Common Stock	50.0%	$ 500,000	11.8%	$ 59,000
6	Total	100.0%	$ 1,000,000	10.0%	$ 100,000
7	**Goal Seek Settings:** Target cell is D6, to be set equal to 10%.				
8	Changing cell is D5.			Return on Common Stock	
9				for a WACC of 10.0%	
10					

Figure 9-5

"Goal Seek" Dialog Box with Settings for Example 9.2

Excel provides another tool called Solver that can be used to solve Example 9.2. It is shown in Figure 9-6 with the settings to solve Example 9.2. The result with Solver is the same as with Goal Seek for this problem.

Figure 9-6

"Solver Parameters" Dialog Box with Settings for Example 9.2

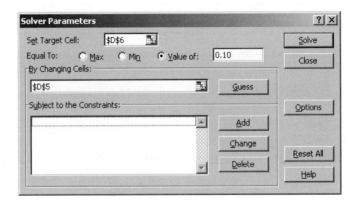

(Continued)

The same result is obtained inserting known values in equation 9.1, rearranging to the following form, and solving:

$$k_{common} = \frac{10\% - (0.45 \times 8\%) - (0.05 \times 10\%)}{0.50} = \frac{10\% - 3.6\% - 0.5\%}{0.50} = \frac{5.9\%}{0.50} = 11.8\%$$

Should You Choose Goal Seek or Solver?

The Goal Seek and Solver tools can be used interchangeably to solve many problems that involve setting a target cell equal to a specified value by changing the value of one other cell. The advantage of Goal Seek is that it is simpler to explain and use. Solver, however, is a much more powerful and versatile tool. We will demonstrate some of Solver's uses in later chapters.

Both tools use an iterative procedure of successive approximations. The first iteration of Goal Seek uses a trial value for the changing cell to calculate the value of the target cell. The calculated value of the target cell is compared with its targeted value. If the difference is greater than a specified amount (i.e., the default precision), Goal Seek adjusts the trial value and makes a new calculation of the target cell. A second comparison and adjustment are made, and this is repeated until the calculated and targeted values of the target cell agree within the specified amount. In most cases, the result with Goal Seek is sufficiently precise for the purpose of a problem.

The default level for Solver is tighter than for Goal Seek. Solver's results can therefore be more accurate for problems that are more complex than Example 9.2. In addition, Solver can find the conditions for maximizing or minimizing the value of a target cell as well as setting it to a specified value. Solver also makes it possible to have more than one changing cell and to add constraints that limit the values that the changing cells can take. These features of Solver will be demonstrated in later chapters.

In comparison to Solver, Goal Seek is a limited tool. Solver can do everything Goal Seek can, as well as do more, and do it better. Once you understand how to use Solver, it should become your tool of preference.

Example 9.3: Given the starting conditions of Example 9.1, prepare a table and chart that show how the WACC varies with borrowing rates from 6 to 8 percent (in increments of 0.5%) and required rates of return for common stockholders from 10 to 16 percent (in increments of 2%).

Solution: Figure 9-7 provides a two-variable input table and a chart that show how the value of WACC varies with different combinations of borrowing rates and rates of return on common stock.

Figure 9-7 can be created as an addition to the spreadsheet of Figure 9-3 or a copy of it. Enter values for the required rates of return to common stockholders in Cells B11:E11 and values for the borrowing rates in Cells A12:A16. Next, enter =D7 in Cell A11. In order to avoid confusion, hide the entry in Cell A11 by custom formatting Cell A11 as ;;;. (Click on Cell A11, select Format/Cells/ Number/Custom and type three semicolons in the format box.)

Drag the mouse to select the Range A11:E16. Click on Data/Table to expose the dialog box shown in Figure 9-8, and enter D6 for the row input cell and D4 for the column input cell. Click on the OK button or press Enter. The result will be the values shown in Cells B12:E16.

(Continued)

Figure 9-7

Effects of Borrowing Rate and Rate of Return for Common Stockholders on the Weighted Average Cost of Capital

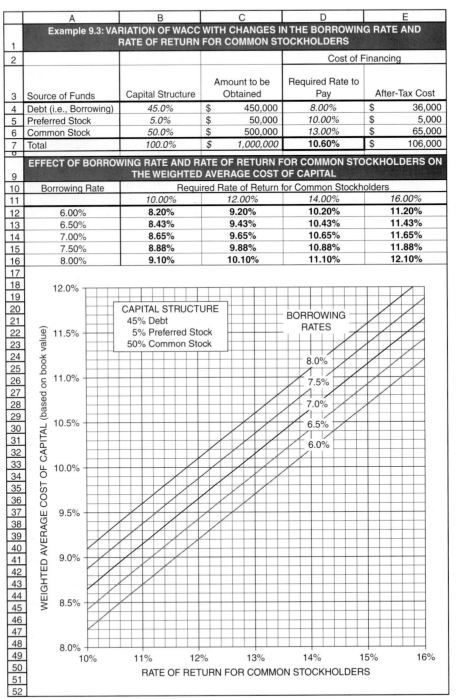

	A	B	C	D	E
1	Example 9.3: VARIATION OF WACC WITH CHANGES IN THE BORROWING RATE AND RATE OF RETURN FOR COMMON STOCKHOLDERS				
2				Cost of Financing	
3	Source of Funds	Capital Structure	Amount to be Obtained	Required Rate to Pay	After-Tax Cost
4	Debt (i.e., Borrowing)	45.0%	$ 450,000	8.00%	$ 36,000
5	Preferred Stock	5.0%	$ 50,000	10.00%	$ 5,000
6	Common Stock	50.0%	$ 500,000	13.00%	$ 65,000
7	Total	100.0%	$ 1,000,000	10.60%	$ 106,000
9	EFFECT OF BORROWING RATE AND RATE OF RETURN FOR COMMON STOCKHOLDERS ON THE WEIGHTED AVERAGE COST OF CAPITAL				
10	Borrowing Rate	Required Rate of Return for Common Stockholders			
11		10.00%	12.00%	14.00%	16.00%
12	6.00%	8.20%	9.20%	10.20%	11.20%
13	6.50%	8.43%	9.43%	10.43%	11.43%
14	7.00%	8.65%	9.65%	10.65%	11.65%
15	7.50%	8.88%	9.88%	10.88%	11.88%
16	8.00%	9.10%	10.10%	11.10%	12.10%

(Continued)

Figure 9-8

Dialog Box with Entries for Creating a Two-Variable Input Table

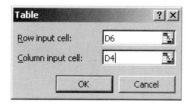

To create the chart shown in Figure 9-7, drag the mouse cursor to select Cells B11:E16. Select the XY-scatter type chart and identify the data as being in rows rather than columns, as shown in Figure 9-9.

Figure 9-9

Step 2 with Series in Rows Selected

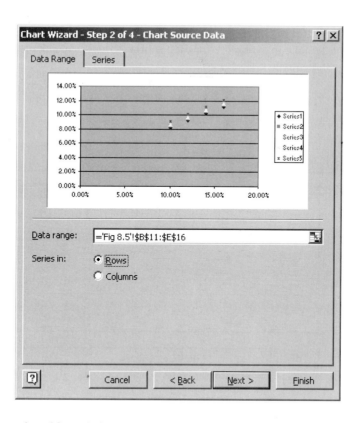

Note that the values in the table and chart of Figure 9-7 are valid only for the capital structure and rate for preferred stockholders shown in Cells B4:B6 and D5. Changing the values in these cells causes the values in the table and chart to change also. (Try it!)

WACC Based on Market Value

In Example 9.1, we used the book-value weights of the long-term debt and preferred equity to calculate WACC. Accordingly, the result is defined as the **book-value** WACC, or the WACC based on past historical values. However, because the market constantly re-values a firm's securities, the book-value weights probably do not represent true *present* weights. To get the present weights, the total market value of each type of capital source needs to be determined.

To determine the relative weights for the **market-value** WACC, we begin by determining the total market value of each type of security. Once that is done, the relative weight of each source of capital is determined by dividing its market value by the total market value of the firm's capital structure.

Example 9.4: Suppose that the total value of debt carried by the ABC Corporation (see Example 9.1) is $3,850,000, there are 500,000 shares of preferred stock at a market value of $1/share, and there are 1,000,000 shares of common stock outstanding with a market value of $5.50/share. Suppose also that the returns are to be the same as given in Example 9.1—that is, an 8 percent return on borrowing, a 10 percent return on preferred stock, and a 13 percent return on common stock. For these conditions, what would be the value for the WACC based on the market value of the capital structure?

Solution: Figure 9-10 is a spreadsheet solution. The total market values for preferred and common stocks are calculated by entering =B4*C4 in Cell D4 and copying the entry to Cell D5.

The percentages of the total market value for each source of funds are calculated by entering =D3/$D$6 in Cell E3 and copying the entry to Cells E4:E5.

Figure 9-10

WACC Based on Market Value

	A	B	C	D	E	F	G	H
1	Example 9.4: TURNBULL CORP., COST OF CAPITAL BASED ON MARKET VALUE							
2	Source of Funds	Number of Shares	Market Value, per Share	Total Market Value	Percentage of Total Market Value	Amount of Capital to be Raised	Rate of Return	After-Tax Cost
3	Debt (i.e., Borrowing)			$ 3,850,000	39.1%	$ 390,863	8.0%	$ 31,269
4	Preferred Stock	500,000	$ 1.00	$ 500,000	5.1%	$ 50,761	10.0%	$ 5,076
5	Common Stock	1,000,000	$ 5.50	$ 5,500,000	55.8%	$ 558,376	13.0%	$ 72,589
6	Total			$ 9,850,000	100.0%	$ 1,000,000	10.89%	$ 108,934
7								
8						Market-Value WACC		
9								

Key Cell Entries

D4: =B4*C4, copy to D5
D6: =SUM(D3:D5)
E3: =D3/$D$6, copy to E4:E5
E6: =SUM(E3:E5)
F3: =E3*$F$6, copy to F4:F5
G6: =SUMPRODUCT(F3:F5,G3:G5)/F6 or H6/F6
H3: =F3*G3, copy to H4:H5
H6: =SUM(H3:H5)

(Continued)

The amounts of capital to be raised from each source are calculated by entering =E3*$F$6 in Cell F3 and copying the entry to F4:F5.

The after-tax costs of funds from each source are calculated by entering =F3*G3 in Cell H3 and copying the entry to H4:H5. The total after-tax cost is calculated by entering =SUM(H3:H5) in Cell H6.

The market-value WACC is calculated in by entering =SUMPRODUCT(F3:F5,G3:G5)/F6 or H6/F6 in Cell G6. The result is a WACC equal to 10.89%.

Note that the market-value WACC (10.89%) is higher than the book-value WACC (10.60%) computed in Example 9.1. This is because ABC's market-based capital structure has a higher percentage of common equity (55.8% vs. 50%), which has the highest expected rate of return, and a lower percentage of debt (39.1% vs. 45%), which has the lowest expected rate of return.

Component Costs

The previous discussion has assumed that the component costs of capital are given. This is not the real-life case. We discuss in this section how to calculate the costs of the components, which change from day-to-day. In fact, the component costs change continuously as the equity markets change.

Cost of Debt

The **pre-tax** cost of debt is the rate of return on the bonds issued to raise capital. It appears as the value k_d in the following equation for the value of a bond:

$$V_B = Pmt \left[\frac{1 - \frac{1}{(1+k_d)^N}}{k_d} \right] + \frac{FV}{(1+k_d)^N} \tag{9.2}$$

where V_B = the value of a bond issued in return for borrowing
  N = the life of the bond
  Pmt = the periodic bond payment
  FV = the future value of the bond ($1,000)

Equation 9.2 cannot be rewritten as an explicit function for k_d. It can only be solved by an iterative technique that uses known values for V_D, Pmt, N, and FV and assumes different values for k_d until the calculated value of the right side of equation 9.2 equals the known value of the bond on the left. Fortunately, this task can be either performed by using Excel's Solver tool or avoided by using Excel's RATE function. The syntax for Excel's RATE function is

RATE(*number of periods, periodic payment, present value, future value, type, guess*)

Adjustment for Income Tax

The payments to interest on a corporation's debts are tax-deductible expenses. Therefore, the *after-tax* interest payments are less than the full amount of their *pre-tax* values. To calculate the after-tax value, multiply the pre-tax value by 1 minus the tax rate. Thus, if the pre-tax cost of debt is $80 on a $1000 bond and the tax rate is 40 percent, the dollar after-tax cost of debt would be only $48 (computed as $80X(1-0.40)) and the percentage after-tax cost of debt would be 4.8 percent (computed as $48/$1000). (Note that there is no tax adjustment for preferred or common equity because dividends are not tax-deductible expenses for the company.)

Under present tax law, the costs related to the issuance of debt or equity securities are not tax deductible. As such, the before-tax and after-tax costs of equity (preferred and common) securities are the same. If some of the flotation costs were to become tax deductible, then the after-tax costs of equity would be less than the before-tax costs.

Example 9.5: The chief financial officer of the Monarch Investment Corporation is interested in buying bonds as an investment of surplus cash. Some bonds that are available provide semiannual payments with an annual coupon rate of 8 percent. Their redemption value is $1000, and they reach maturity in 15 years. The bonds are available at a price of $560. What would be Monarch's after-tax rate of return on the bonds if they were purchased at the current offering price? You may assume that Monarch's tax rate is 40 percent.

Solution: Figure 9-11 is a spreadsheet showing two methods for determining the rate. The upper method uses the RATE function, and the lower method uses the formula given by the right side of equation 9.2 and Solver. Solver changes the trial value entered in Cell B16 to the correct value to give the desired after-tax rate of return. Both methods give a pre-tax rate of return of 7.86 percent, which is converted to an after-tax rate of return of 4.71 percent.

Figure 9-11

Cost of Debt Borrowing

	A	B
1	**Example 9.5: RATE OF RETURN**	
2	**Solution with RATE Function**	
3	Current Price of Bond	$560.00
4	Coupon Rate	8%
5	Redemption Value	$1,000
6	Maturity, years	15
7	Frequency, payments/year	2
8	Before-Tax Rate of Return	7.86%
9	Tax Rate	40%
10	After-Tax Rate of Return	4.71%
11	**Key Cell Entries**	
12	B8: =RATE(B6*B7,B4*B5/B7,−B3,B5)	
13	B10: =B8*(1−B9)	
14	**Alternate Solution with Formula 8.2 and Solver**	
15	Value	$560.00
16	Before-Tax Rate of Return	7.86%
17	After-Tax Rate of Return	4.71%
18	**Key Cell Entries**	
19	B15: =(B4*B5/2)*(1−1/((1+B16)^(B6*B7)))/B16	
20	+B5/((1+B16)^(B6*B7))	
21	B16: Enter a trial value, which will be changed by Solver.	
22	B17: =B16*(1−B9)	
23	**Solver Settings**	
24	Target Cell is B15, to be set equal to $560.	
25	Change arbitrary value entered in Cell B16.	

Cost of Preferred Equity

The value of a share of preferred stock, V_p, is given by the equation

$$V_P = \frac{D}{k_P} \tag{9.3}$$

where D = the dollar dividend per share and
and k_P = the rate of return on the preferred stock

Equation 9.3 can be rearranged to the following form for calculating the rate of return from known values for V_P and D:

$$k_P = \frac{D}{V_P} \tag{9.4}$$

Cost of Common Equity

A company's cost of common equity can be determined by either the dividend discount model or the CAPM.

The Dividend Discount Model for Common Equity

This model uses the following equation to discount a stream of dividends (D) from common stock with a constant rate of growth (g) and rate of return (k_{CS}) to the stock's present value (V_{CS}):

$$V_{CS} = \frac{D_0(1+g)}{k_{CS} - g} = \frac{D_1}{k_{CS} - g} \tag{9.5}$$

Rearrangement of equation 9.5 gives the rate of return for shareholders of common stock in terms of current market price of the stock, its current dividends, and its rate of growth; thus

$$k_{CS} = \frac{D_0(1+g)}{V_{CS}} + g = \frac{D_1}{V_{CS}} + g \tag{9.6}$$

In other words, the required rate of return on common stock equals the sum of the dividend yield plus the rate of growth of the dividends.

Example 9.6: The common stock of the Argus Corporation sells for $50/share and provides quarterly dividends of $1.00. It is anticipated that the stock's dividends will increase by an average of 10 percent per year for the next five years. What is the stock's value in terms of a rate of return?

Solution: Substituting values into equation 9.6 gives

$$k_{CS} = \frac{\$4.00}{\$50.00} + 0.10 = 0.08 + 0.10 = 0.18 = 18\%$$

The CAPM Model for Common Equity

The CAPM model uses the following equation to give the expected rate of return for a security ($E(R_i)$) in terms of the risk-free rate of interest (R_f), the market risk premium ($(R_m - R_f)$), and the risk of the security relative to a market portfolio (β_i):

$$E(R_i) = R_f + \beta_i(R_m - R_f) \tag{9.7}$$

Example 9.7: Use the CAPM model to calculate the expected rate of return for the security described in Example 9.5. You may assume that the risk-free rate of return is 4 percent, the return on a market portfolio is 12.5 percent, and the beta value of the security is 1.10.

Solution: Inserting values into equation 9.7 gives

$$E(R_i) = 0.04 + 1.10(0.125 - 0.04) = 0.04 + 0.0935 = 0.1335 = 13.35\%$$

Flotation Costs

The process of selling new issues of securities (e.g., bonds, preferred stock, and common stock) to raise capital is commonly referred to as *floating* a new issue, and its costs are referred to as flotation costs.

Selling securities is a complicated process that generally involves a great deal of the time of corporate officers and the services of an outside investment banker. Investment bankers serve as intermediaries between firms issuing securities and the public and other buyers, and they are paid handsome fees for their services. Their services generally include:

- Forming the underwriting syndicate to sell the securities
- Preparing the registration statement for the Securities and Exchange Commission (SEC)
- Acting as a consultant to the issuing firm, with advice on the pricing of the issue and its timing.

Flotation costs must be added to the component cost of capital to give a correct value for the cost of capital. The most common method for adding flotation costs is termed the **cost of capital adjustment technique**. This method calculates the net amount the company receives from the sale of the securities by *decreasing* the market price for the new securities by their floatation costs.

When flotation costs are included, equations 9.2, 9.4, and 9.6 are revised to the following, where f is the flotation cost and the other variables are as defined before:

For the pre-tax cost of new debt with the flotation cost f included,

$$V_B - f = Pmt \left[\frac{1 - \frac{1}{(1+k_d)^N}}{k_d} \right] + \frac{FV}{(1+k_d)^N} \tag{9.8}$$

For the cost of new preferred equity with the flotation cost *f* included,

$$k_P = \frac{D}{V_P - f}$$ (9.9)

For the cost of new common equity with the flotation cost *f* included,

$$k_{CF} = \frac{D_0(1+g)}{V_{CS} - f} + g = \frac{D_1}{V_{CS} - f} + g$$ (9.10)

Example 9.8: The Holdberg Corporation must raise $1 million to finance the remodeling of its corporate headquarters. It plans to do this by increasing the number of shares of preferred and common stock and by issuing 15-year corporate bonds with a face value of $1000 and annual payments at a coupon rate of 9.0 percent.

The corporation's long-term debt currently amounts to 20,000 corporate bonds with a current market value of $910.00/bond. The corporation has 50,000 shares of preferred stock outstanding with a market value of $125.00/share. The corporation also has 1,500,000 outstanding shares of common stock with a current market value of $45.00/share.

Holders of preferred stock receive annual dividends of $10/share, and holders of common stock receive annual dividends of $4.00/share. The annual growth rate of common stock is 5 percent.

Flotation costs are 1 percent for bonds, 2 percent for preferred stock, and 4.5 percent for common stock. Holdberg's tax rate is 40 percent.

What is the weighted average cost of capital?

Solution: Figure 9-12 is a spreadsheet solution. Total market value is calculated as before—that is, by multiplying the number of bonds or shares by their current market values. The percentage of the total market value for each component and the amount of capital to be raised by each component are also calculated as before.

Figure 9-12

WACC with Flotation Costs

	A	B	C	D	E	F	G
1	\multicolumn{7}{c|}{Example 9.8: HOLDBERG CORPORATION, COST OF CAPITAL BASED ON MARKET VALUE WITH FLOTATION COSTS ADDED}						
2	Source of Funds	Number of Bonds or Shares	Current Market Value, per Bond or Share	Total Market Value	Percentage of Total Market Value	Amount of Capital to be Raised	After-Tax Cost
3	Bonds (i.e., Borrowing)	20,000	$910.00	$ 18,200,000	19.79%	$ 197,934	6.20%
4	Preferred Stock	50,000	$125.00	$ 6,250,000	6.80%	$ 67,972	8.16%
5	Common Equity	1,500,000	$45.00	$ 67,500,000	73.41%	$ 734,095	14.77%
6	Total			$ 91,950,000	100.00%	$ 1,000,000	12.63%
7	\multicolumn{2}{c}{Additional Bond Data}						
8	Tax Rate	40%				WACC	
9	Coupon Rate	9.0%					
10	Face Value	$1,000		\multicolumn{4}{c|}{Key Cell Entries}			
11	Years to Maturity	15		D3:	=B3*C3, copy to D4:D5		
12	Flotation Cost	1.0%		D6:	=SUM(D3:D5)		
13	\multicolumn{2}{c}{Additional Preferred Stock Data}		E3:	=D3/$D$6, copy to E4:E5			
14	Dividend, $/share	$10.00		E6:	=SUM(E3:E5)		
15	Flotation Cost	2.0%		F3:	=$F$6*E3, copy to F4:F5		
16	\multicolumn{2}{c}{Additional Common Equity Data}		G3:	=RATE(B11,B9*B10,−C3*(1−B12),B10)*(1−B8)			
17	Dividend, $/share	$4.00		G4:	=B14/(C4*(1−B15))		
18	Annual Growth Rate	5.0%		G5:	=(B17*(1+B18))/(C5*(1−B19))+B18		
19	Flotation Cost	4.5%		G6:	=SUMPRODUCT(E3:E5,G3:G5)		

(Continued)

The after-tax cost of the bonds is calculated by using Excel's RATE function to calculate the pre-tax cost and then multiplying the pre-tax cost by 1 minus the tax rate. This is done by the following entry in Cell G3: =RATE(B11,B9*B10,-C3*(1-B12),B10)*(1-B8).

The after-tax cost of preferred and common equity is closely approximated by their pre-tax values. These are calculated by the entry =B14/(C4*(1-B15)) in Cell G4 for the cost of preferred equity and by the entry (B17*(1+B18))/(C5*(1-B19))+B18 in Cell G5 for the cost of common equity.

The WACC is calculated in Cell G6 by the entry =SUMPRODUCT(E3:E5,G3:G5). The result is the value 12.63 percent.

Cost of Retained Earnings

A corporation's retained earnings can be either (1) returned to the stockholders in the form of dividends or share buybacks or (2) reinvested in profitable ventures. Profitable ventures are those that earn at least the common shareholder's required rate of return.

If retained earnings are used for funding new projects, there are no flotation costs. Therefore, the cost of using retained earnings (V_{RE}) is the same as the cost of using new common equity without flotation costs, as given by equation 9.6.

The Marginal Wacc Curve

The supply of available new capital is not without limit. Therefore, as firms raise more and more new money, the incremental cost of additional amounts increases. In addition, total flotation costs may increase as more capital is raised. This section interprets these increases in terms of a marginal WACC curve, which is simply a chart on which the cost of capital is plotted as the ordinate against the amount of capital to be raised. The following example illustrates the construction of a marginal WACC curve.

Example 9.9: Assume that the Holdberg Corporation's (see previous example) after-tax cost of raising capital varies as follows for the amounts raised from the various sources:

Source of Capital	Amount Sold or Borrowed	Marginal After-Tax Cost
Debt Borrowing	Up to $200,000	7.0%
	$200,001 to $400,000	8.0%
	More than $400,000	8.5%
Preferred Stock	Up to $50,000	10.0%
	$50,001 to $100,000	12.0%
	More than $100,000	13.0%
Common Stock	Up to $250,000	12.5%
	$250,000 to $500,000	14.0%
	$500,001 to $1,000,000	16.0%
	More than $1,000,000	16.5%

Prepare a chart that shows how the weighted average cost of capital varies with the amount of capital raised, from zero to $2 million. If Holdberg must borrow $1 million, what will its WACC be? If Holdberg must borrow $2 million, what will its WACC be?

(Continued)

Solution: Figure 9-13 is a spreadsheet solution.

Figure 9-13

Marginal WACC Curve

	A	B	C	D	E
1	Example 9.9: MARGINAL WEIGHTED AVERAGE COST OF CAPITAL CURVE FOR HOLDBERG CORPORATION BASED ON MARKET VALUE WITH FLOTATION COSTS ADDED				
2	**Source**	**% of total**	**Level**	**After-Tax cost**	**Break-Points**
3	Debt	19.79%	*Up to $200,000*	*7.00%*	$1,010,440
4			*$200,001 to $400,000*	*8.00%*	$2,020,879
5			*More than $400,000*	*8.50%*	$2,020,879
6	Preferred	6.80%	*Up to $50,000*	*10.00%*	$735,600
7			*$50,001 to $100,000*	*12.00%*	$1,471,200
8			*More than $100,000*	*13.00%*	$1,471,200
9	Common	73.41%	*Up to $250,000*	*12.50%*	$340,556
10			*$250,001 to $500,000*	*14.00%*	$681,111
11			*$500,001 to $1,000,000*	*16.00%*	$1,362,222
12			*More than $1,000,000*	*16.50%*	$1,362,222
13	**Total Capital**	**Cost of Debt**	**Cost of Preferred**	**Cost of Equity**	**WACC**
14	$0	7.00%	10.00%	12.50%	11.24%
15	$340,556	7.00%	10.00%	12.50%	11.24%
16	$340,556	7.00%	10.00%	14.00%	12.34%
17	$681,111	7.00%	10.00%	14.00%	12.34%
18	$681,111	7.00%	10.00%	16.00%	13.81%
19	$735,600	7.00%	10.00%	16.00%	13.81%
20	$735,600	7.00%	12.00%	16.00%	13.95%
21	$1,010,440	7.00%	12.00%	16.00%	13.95%
22	$1,010,440	8.00%	12.00%	16.00%	14.14%
23	$1,362,222	8.00%	12.00%	16.00%	14.14%
24	$1,362,222	8.00%	12.00%	16.50%	14.51%
25	$1,471,200	8.00%	12.00%	16.50%	14.51%
26	$1,471,200	8.00%	13.00%	16.50%	14.58%
27	$2,020,879	8.00%	13.00%	16.50%	14.58%
28	$2,020,879	8.50%	13.00%	16.50%	14.68%
29	$3,000,000	8.50%	13.00%	16.50%	14.68%

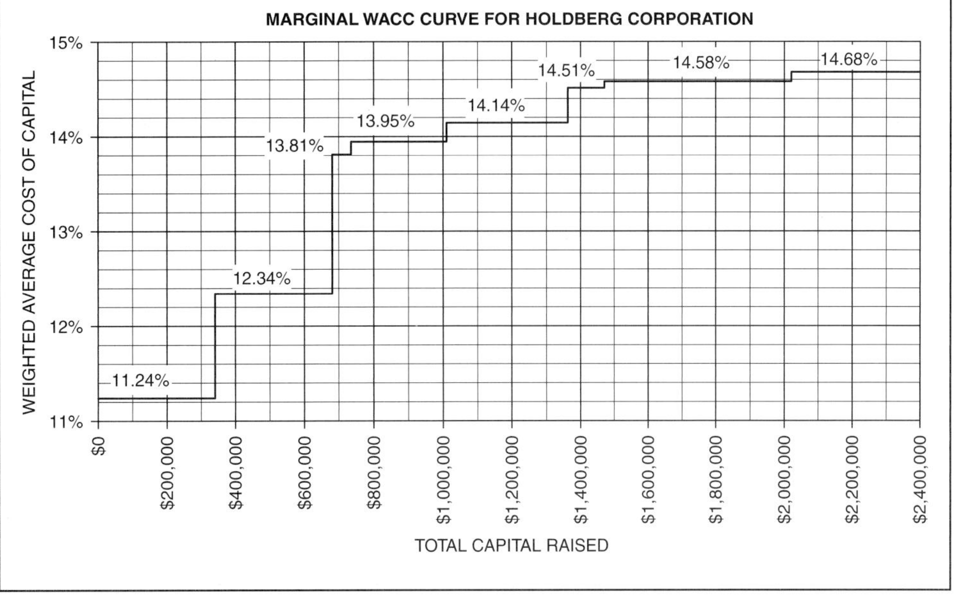

MARGINAL WACC CURVE FOR HOLDBERG CORPORATION

(Continued)

To transfer the percentages of total market value that were calculated in Cells E3:E5 of Example 9.8, make the following entries in Figure 9-13:

Cell	Entry
B3	='Figure 9-12'!E3
B6	='Figure 9-12'!E4
B9	='Figure 9-12'!E5

To make these entries on Figure 9-13, click on Cell B3 on Figure 9-13, enter =, click on the Sheet tab for Figure 9-12, click on Cell E3 on Figure 9-12, and press Enter. Repeat to transfer values for Cells B6 and B9 of Figure 9-13 from Cells E4 and E5 of Figure 9-12.

The data values for the amounts sold or borrowed are entered in Cells C3:C12. For example, enter 200000 in Cell C3, enter 400000 in Cell C4, etc. Custom format the cells to hide the data values and display the text shown in Figure 9-13. For example, the custom formats for the entries in Cells C9:C12 are as follows:

Cell	Custom Format
C9	"Up to "$#,###
C10	"$250,001 to "$#,###
C11	"$500,001 to "$#,###
C12	"More than "$#,###

In place of the "$#,### parts of the custom formats, Excel inserts the data values entered in the cells.

The break-even points—the amount of capital raised that causes after-tax cost to shift to the next higher percentage—are calculated by entering =C3/B$3 in Cell E3 and copying the entry to E4:E5, by entering =C6/B$6 in Cell E6 and copying the entry to E7:E8, and by entering =C9/B$9 in Cell E9 and copying the entry to E10:E12.

The table of values in Rows 13 to 27 is used to create the marginal WACC chart at the bottom of Figure 9-13. The table begins with the total capital equal to zero Cell A14. At this point the after-tax costs for the three sources are at their minimum values (Cells B14:D14), and the value of WACC (Cell E14) is calculated by the entry =$B$3*B14+$B$6*C14+$B$9*D14.

The values in Cells A15:A28 are the break-points in Cells E3:E12 sorted by increasing values. The final value in Cell A29 is set at a value greater than the last break-point. The value should be at least as large as the last value on the chart to be plotted.

The costs for raising capital from each of the sources are discontinuous rather than continuous. They change from one value to a higher value as the amount of capital raised passes through each break-point. Up to a break-point, they have one value. As a break-point is reached and exceeded (theoretically, by one penny), they take on a higher value. Therefore, there are two values for the WACC at each break-point: one for capital raised up to and including the break-point and another for capital raised that exceeds the break-point. The WACC then continues unchanged until the next break-point is reached.

The first break-point is $340,556 (Cell E9), at which the after-tax cost of common equity changes from 12.50 percent (Cell D9) to 14.00 percent (Cell D10). Copy the value in Cell E9 to Cells A15:A16 by entering =E$9 in Cell A15 and copying the entry to Cell A16. Repeat this step to enter each successively higher break-point in Cells E3:E12 twice in Cells A17:A28. In Cell A29, enter an arbitrary value larger than the highest break-point for which values of WACC might be of interest.

(Continued)

To transfer the percentages for the after-tax costs, enter the following set of three IF statements in Cells B14, C14, and D14 and copy them to the ranges B15:B28, C15:C28, and D15:D28, respectively:

Cell B14	=IF(A15*$B$3<=$C$3,$D$3,IF(A15*$B$3<=$C$4,$D$4,$D$5))
Cell C14	=IF(A15*$B$6<=$C$6,$D$6,IF(A15*$B$6<=$C$7,$D$7,$D$8))
Cell D14:	IF(A15*$B$9<=$C$9,$D$9,IF(A15*$B$9<=$C$10,$D$10,IF(A15*$B$9<=$C$11,$D$11,$D$12)))

Note in these entries that the row for values in the A column (e.g., Cell A15) is the row immediately below the row in which the entry is made. (If you find it difficult to understand the logic of the IF statements, try verbalizing them; try translating the expressions into words, using the meanings of the cells and terms in place of the column and row identities.)

In Cell B29, enter =D5; in Cell C29, enter =D8; and in Cell D29, enter D12.

To compute the WACCs, enter =$B$3*B14+$B$6*C14+$B$9*D14 in Cell E14 and copy the entry to the Range E15:E29.

To create the chart shown at the bottom of Figure 9-13, select the Ranges A14:A29 and E14:E29 and plot with a scatter type chart. Be sure to delete the check in the "Smoothed line" box on the "Patterns" tab of the "Format Data Series" dialog box, as shown in Figure 9-14.

If Holdberg must borrow $1 million, its WACC will be 13.95 percent. If Holdberg must borrow $2 million, its WACC will be 14.58 percent.

Figure 9-14

Settings on "Patterns Tab" of the "Format Data Series" Dialog Box

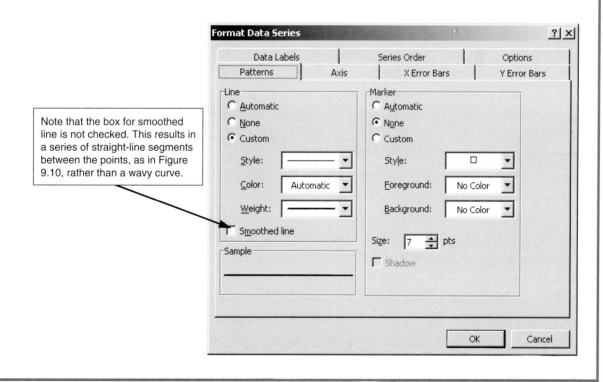

Concluding Remarks

Debt and equity are the most common sources of capital that firms use to raise funds. Debt is usually bonds, and equity is preferred and common stock. Table 9-1 provides a quick comparison of the important characteristics of these sources.

Table 9-1

Comparison of Debt and Equity Capital

Characteristic	Debt	Preferred Stock	Common Stock
Voting rights	None, unless a firm violates its contractual obligations to the lender.	None, unless a firm violates its contractual obligations to the stockholders.	Stockholders have a right to vote on selecting a firm's directors and on special issues brought before them.
Claims on income and assets	Senior; that is, first in line to have their claims satisfied, including both interest and scheduled principal payments.	Second in line. Dividends and other claims cannot be paid until those of the debt creditors are satisfied.	Last in line. Dividends and other claims cannot be paid until those of the debt creditors and holders of preferred stock are satisfied.
Tax treatment	Interest paid to creditors is a tax-deductible expense for the firm.	Dividends paid to stockholders are not deductible expenses for the firm.	Dividends paid to stockholders are not deductible expenses for the firm.

The weighted average cost of capital (WACC) is expressed as an annual percentage rate. It is calculated by multiplying the cost of each type of capital by its percent of the total capital raised.

As the amount of capital raised by a firm increases, the WACC increases. This behavior can be expressed by the marginal WACC curve, which is a plot of WACC against the total capital raised.

The WACC is the basis for the discount rate used to discount a project's future cash flows in capital budgeting, as discussed in later chapters. If the project has the normal uncertainty of doing business, there is no adjustment for risk and the WACC is used as the discount rate. If the risk is higher, however, the discount rate is adjusted upward from the WACC. For risky projects, greater emphasis is placed on short-term results and less emphasis on long-term results. For example, as risk increases, the break-even point should be reached in shorter times.

Various terms are used for the value of the WACC after adjusting for risk. Among them are *discount rate, hurdle rate, cutoff rate,* and *minimum acceptable rate of return*. We prefer the term *minimum acceptable rate of return*, abbreviated MARR, because it best describes the concept. MARR is the minimum rate of return that a project should provide in order to induce a firm to invest in the project.

Struggling firms with an inadequate supply of capital cannot afford to invest in anything but the most critical projects with low risk and high projected rates of return. Furthermore, if the firms are in a volatile, strongly competitive industry, they may limit their investments to those with break-even periods as short as one or two years. On the other hand, large firms with excess capital can afford to invest in long-term, high-risk projects with potentially large rates of return if they succeed.

Students' Feedback on WACC

After developing a proposal for a capital project, I can attest to just how important the cost of capital can be when used to calculate a go/no-go decision on funding a project. With the standard cost of capital given by the corporate annual report, my proposal returned a go decision. However, upper management increased the WACC by 3 percentage points because the project was deemed risky. Needless to say, these extra points turned the NPV negative and the project was rejected. So, making sure you have the right WACC can make a huge difference during the capital budget decision process.

* * *

The cost of capital is absolutely critical for public utilities in California because it is the essential component for the return on rate base that generates profits for the company. Utilities make profits in a different manner than other companies and the WACC is the crucial component. This return on rate base will be determined through rate cases done through the California Public Utilities Commission (CPUC).

There is really no argument about the WACC calculation itself. The real battle involves the component costs, especially the return on common equity. There are usually three groups who are involved: a group from the CPUC (usually a group of economists), the utility itself, and a group called interveners. The utility would like to maximize the ROCE for the sake of its shareholders, while the interveners would like to minimize it to keep rates low. These battles can be ferocious.

* * *

This chapter really helped me understand how to calculate a correct value for WACC for making decisions. I can tell you for a fact that in my former workplace, where we had to perform replacement analysis and project selection on a regular basis for the plant and equipment in our manufacturing factory, the common perception was that calculating WACC was a waste of time. Instead, the CFO directed a WACC number to use. His estimate was based on a WACC he had calculated five years earlier, which he tweaked up or down depending on the target capital structure.

* * *

Finding WACC with Excel is so much easier and faster than calculating by hand, which was what I learned to do in [an earlier class in financial management]. And the model provides flexibility when changes happen.

Interest Rate for Borrowing

What is a reasonable rate of interest a corporation should pay for a loan? A good place to start is with the federal funds rate, which is what big banks pay for their funds. The Federal Reserve Board releases this information daily on the Internet, along with the prime rate and the rates for short-term commercial paper, CDs, treasury bills, and so forth. You can access the information at the Web sites of either the Federal Reserve Board (http://www.bog.frb.fed.us/releases/h15/Current/) or the Federal Reserve Bank of New York (http://www.ny.frb.org/pihome/mktrates/dlyrates).

The rate that banks charge for small commercial loans of $100,000 or less averages about 4.22 percentage points higher than the rate for federal funds. (For a rate of 6.50 percent for federal funds, that would be 10.72 percent for a small commercial loan.) Depending on the economy and competition among banks, the spread varies but rarely strays more than half a point in either direction from the average of 4.22 percent. According to a report in *Business Week*, the lowest spread in recent years was 3.5 percent in 1989, when loan rates were at an all-time high of 13.39 percent, and as high as 5.06 percent in 1992. (*Business Week*, March 29, 1999) The rates banks charge would vary with other conditions. For example, a bank would adjust the interest rate for a loan upward for a company in poor financial health.

Restructuring a Firm's Capital Structure to Reduce Debt

Continued borrowing of money may require a firm to sell additional stock to maintain an acceptable ratio between owners' equity and debt. Firms having trouble meeting current obligations or in the process of recovering from bankruptcy may reduce their debt by increasing their equity. For example: "Winterland Productions, the entertainment merchandising company founded by rock 'n' roll impressario Bill Graham, announced [on January 14, 1998] that it has emerged from Chapter 11 bankruptcy after only five months. Chief Executive Don Tice said Winterland has cut its $2 million plus annual interest payments in half by converting $24 million in short-term debt to equity and longer term debt." (Business Digest column of *SF Chronicle* for Jan. 14, 1998)

Capital Markets

Capital markets for issues of debt and equity that are publicly traded are divided between primary and secondary markets. Primary markets handle the initial sales of government and corporate securities. Corporate sales of debt and equity are through public offerings and private placements. Public offerings are generally through syndicates of investment banking firms that underwrite the offerings. Underwriting syndicates buy a firm's securities for their own account and then offer them to the public and others at a higher price. Private placements avoid the high legal and accounting costs with registering publicly issued debt and equity with the Securities and Exchange Commission. In this case, corporate securities are sold to large financial institutions, such as insurance companies and mutual funds, on the basis of private negotiations.

Secondary markets trade financial securities after they have been sold in the primary markets. There are two kinds of secondary markets: auction markets and dealer markets. The most important auction market for equity is the New York Stock Exchange (NYSE), which handles between 80 and 90 percent of all shares of stock traded in the auction markets. Other auction markets for equity include the American Stock Exchange, the National Association of Securities Dealers Automated Quotation (NASDAQ) system, and regional exchanges such as the Midwest Stock Exchange. Some stock is traded in dealer markets referred to as over-the-counter (OTC) markets. Most debt securities are traded in the dealer markets. Investors contact bond dealers when they want to buy or sell and negotiate the sale.

Better Communicating with Custom Formatting

Custom formatting, as illustrated in this and other chapters, can help improve communications and avoid errors. Here are a couple of comments from students who have found it valuable.

Students' Feedback on Custom Formatting

Custom formatting is a topic we learned in the very first chapter, and I have been using it since. But I didn't recognize its true beauty up until this chapter. The ultimate power of custom formatting is to display text descriptions about data values while Excel still sees the whole text as entered values so they can be used for calculating other values.

I have come to the full appreciation about how spreadsheets are not only for analyzing data but also for communicating results. This tool just better serves the communication purpose. Think about it: How could you type in text descriptions which you need terribly and at the same time use them as values for calculating? Well, Excel has a way to do it. It is magical and fascinating. I give this technique a full score.

* * *

The most interesting and useful take-away for me on this chapter is the custom formatting of the levels in the table. I recently spent a lot of time at work trying to figure out why various amounts were being booked incorrectly to one of my projects. It turned out that someone in Corporate Accounting had created a table with rates for charging hours to projects. The table had both text fields and numerical fields (with the numerical fields hidden). The two fields were not linked and people selected a rate based upon the text field. But the underlying numerical field was not the same as what was displayed in the text field. If they had used this custom formatting technique, then the text fields in the table would have shown the appropriate numerical value that the formula was using in the calculation of the rate.

Chapter 10

Profit, Break-Even, and Leverage

CHAPTER OBJECTIVES

Management Skills
- Understand what is meant by profit, break-even, and leverage.
- Understand the difference between fixed and variable costs.

Spreadsheet Skills
- Create a model to evaluate the profit from making and selling a product.
- Compare algebraic and spreadsheet methods for determining break-even points (i.e., the sales volumes needed to recoup costs).
- Use Excel's Solver tool to determine the sales volume needed to break even or achieve other financial goals.
- Relate sales volume to selling price and use Excel's Solver tool to identify an optimum selling price for greatest profit.
- Create one-variable input tables to perform sensitivity analysis for the effects of selling price on the number of units sold, sales revenue, net income, and other items on a firm's income statement.
- Create charts to show graphically the impact of selling price on the number of units sold, sales revenue, net income, and other items on a firm's income statement.

Overview

Simply put, **profit** is what is left from a firm's income after it pays its costs. There are, however, various types of profits. First is a firm's gross profit, which was defined in Chapter 1 as the difference between sales revenues and the cost of goods sold. Other measures of profit defined in Chapter 1 include the net operating income (i.e., gross profit less operating expenses), the earnings before interest and taxes (EBIT), pre-tax earnings (EBT), and after-tax earnings (EAT).

The **break-even point** is usually defined as the number of units at which a firm's earnings before interest and taxes (EBIT) is zero, although other definitions are also used. Companies use this number to determine the level of sales needed to recoup their fixed costs.

Leverage is an important measure of a firm's sensitivity to the ups and downs of business cycles. There are three types of leverage. **Operating leverage ratio** (OLR) is the ratio of the percentage change in EBIT to the percentage change in sales. Firms with high operating leverages are "risky." Although they are in favorable positions to profit from increased sales during an expanding economy, they are susceptible to heavy losses during economic downturns.

Financial leverage ratio (FLR) measures the extent to which a firm relies on debt. (Recall that debt and equity are the two ways of financing a firm. A firm with debt, which is the usual situation, is termed a *levered firm*.) Financial leverage is akin to operating leverage. However, whereas operating leverage is sensitive to the amount of a firm's *fixed costs of operation*, financial leverage is sensitive to the amount of a firm's *fixed costs of financing*. A levered firm (i.e., one with debt) must make interest payments on its debt regardless of the firm's sales. In a manner similar to that for operating leverage, a firm with high financial leverage is in a favorable position to profit from an expanding economy, when sales are growing, and is in an unfavorable or dangerous position in a contracting economy. Most firms use both operating and financial leverage in establishing their capital structure. The combined effect of the two is given by the **combined leverage** (CL) or **combined leverage ratio** (CLR), which is defined as the product of the first two.

Profit and Break-Even

We begin with the basics. Later in this chapter, we will use an income statement to illustrate the calculations.

Revenues, Costs, and Profit

The basic relationship for profit is expressed by the well-known equation:

$$\text{Profit} = \text{Revenues} - \text{Costs} \tag{10.1}$$

Revenues, or income, depend on both the unit selling price of a company's products and the number of units sold. Costs include both the fixed and variable costs of producing goods or providing services.

Examples of **variable costs** are: (1) the cost of raw materials used in factory production; (2) the cost of parts and components that a firm assembles into finished products; (3) the hourly wages paid to workers; (4) the cost of fuel to operate planes and other transportation equipment; and, (5) sales commissions for selling a firm's products. Variable costs are directly related to a firm's level of sales; that is, they are expected to increase or decrease in proportion to any increase or decrease in the number of units of product sold.

Examples of **fixed costs** are: (1) rent and lease payments; (2) the salaries of supervisors, managers, executives, and other administrators; and (3) the depreciation of equipment. Fixed costs are constant, regardless of the level of production or sales.

In a strict sense, variable costs may not be exactly proportional to the level of production or sales. Nor are fixed costs precisely constant, regardless of the level of production or sales. However, treating variable costs as proportional to production or sales and fixed costs as fixed provides satisfactory approximations for computing profit over some relevant range of operation.

Accordingly, the model of equation 10.1 can be rewritten in the following form, which identifies the effects of fixed and variable cost on the earnings before interest and taxes:

$$EBIT = N \times SP - (FC + N \times VC) \qquad (10.2)$$

where $EBIT$ = Earnings before interest and taxes (EBIT is a measure of what we can call net operating income before considering taxes and the interest paid or received from short-term borrowing and lending.)

N = Number of units produced and sold (As a simplification, all units produced are assumed to be sold.)

SP = Unit selling price, or the selling price per unit

FC = Fixed operating cost

VC = Unit variable cost, or the variable cost per unit produced and sold (e.g., the cost of the direct labor and materials to make and sell one unit of the product)

Equation 10.2 expresses very succinctly the dependence of *EBIT* on unit selling price, number of units made and sold, fixed cost, and unit variable cost. In this form, *EBIT* is said to be the *dependent variable*. Its value depends on the values of the variables on the right side of the equal sign, which are called the *independent variables*.

When values are assigned to the independent variables on the right side of equation 10.2, the value of the dependent variable on the left side can be calculated. For example, if *FC* is $100,000, *VC* is $8/unit, *SP* is $12/unit, and N is 50,000 units,

$$\begin{aligned} EBIT &= (50{,}000 \text{ units})(\$12/\text{unit}) - [\$100{,}000 + (50{,}000 \text{ units})(\$7/\text{unit})] \\ &= \$600{,}000 - \$100{,}000 - \$350{,}000 \\ &= \$150{,}000 \end{aligned}$$

Figure 10-1 shows a spreadsheet solution. Data values have been inserted into cells B2, B3, B4, and B5. The calculation of profit has been programmed in cell B6 by the entry =B5*B4-(B2+B5*B3).

An important assumption made in this profit model is that the company can sell 50,000 units at a selling price of $12/unit. Later we will examine the effect of selling price on the number of units that can be sold and on the resulting costs and profit.

Figure 10-1

Profit as a Function of Fixed Cost, Unit Variable Cost, Unit Selling Price, and Number of Units Sold

	A	B	C
1	PROFIT MODEL: Profit for Producing and Selling 50,000 Units		
2	Fixed cost	$100,000	Entry in B2 is data value.
3	Unit variable cost	$7.00	Entry in B3 is data value.
4	Unit selling price	$12.00	Entry in B4 is data value.
5	Units sold	50,000	Entry in B5 is data value.
6	Profit	$150,000	Entry in B6 is =B5*B4–(B2+B5*B3).

Break-Even Point

The **break-even point** of the profit model is the number of units at which EBIT is zero. Companies use this number to determine the level of sales needed to recoup their fixed costs.

Equation 10.2 can be used in several ways to determine the break-even point. The algebraic method would be to set the right side of equation 10.2 equal to zero and solve for N. The result is

$$N_0 = \frac{FC}{SP - VC} \tag{10.3}$$

N is written with a subscript zero in equation 10.3 to indicate it is the special value for which *EBIT* is zero. Equation 10.3 treats the break-even point as the dependent variable and defines its dependence on the fixed cost, selling price, and unit variable cost. The break-even point defined by equation 10.3 is sometimes referred to as the **operating break-even point**.

For the same values of *FC*, *SP* and *VC* as before, the break-even point can be calculated as

$$N_0 = \frac{\$100,000}{\$12/\text{unit} - \$7/\text{unit}} = \frac{\$100,000}{\$5/\text{unit}} = 20,000 \text{ units}$$

The expression in the denominator (i.e., the difference between the unit selling price and the unit variable cost) is known as the **marginal profitability** or the **marginal contribution to profit**. The company must make and sell 20,000 units, each with a marginal profitability of $5, to recover an investment of $100,000 in facilities, equipment, and any other fixed costs.

With a spreadsheet, the break-even point can be determined without performing the algebraic manipulations to rearrange equation 10.2 into the form of equation 9.3. Figure 10-2 shows the results by using Excel's Solver tool with the spreadsheet shown as Figure 10-1. As with the algebraic solution, the break-even point is found to be 20,000 units.

Figure 10-3 shows the dialog box for using Excel's Solver tool. To access the tool, pull down the Tools menu and click on the Solver box. Cell B6 (the value of profit) is designated as the target cell and its target value is set equal to zero. Cell B5 is allowed to change from the value on the spreadsheet to whatever value will make B6 equal to its target value. To execute Solver, click on Solve or press Enter.

Figure 10-2

Determining the Break-Even Point with Excel's Solver Tool

	A	B	C
1	PROFIT MODEL: Break-Even Analysis with Solver Tool		
2	Fixed cost	$100,000	
3	Unit variable cost	$7.00	
4	Unit selling price	$12.00	
5	**Units sold**	**20,000**	Cell B5 gives break-even point for zero profit.
6	Profit	$0	Entry in B6 is =B5*B4–(B2+B5*B3).
7			B6 is the target cell, with a target value of zero.
8			Value of B5 is allowed to vary to hit target (i.e., B6 = 0).

Figure 10-3

"Solver Parameters" Dialog Box with Settings for Break-Even Point

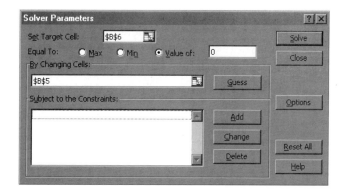

The break-even point in dollars (BEP) equals the break-even point in units multiplied by the unit selling price; that is,

$$\$BEP = N_0 \times SP \tag{10.4}$$

For a break-even point of 20,000 units and a selling price of $12/unit, the break-even point in dollars of sales is calculated by equation 9.4 as

$$\$BEP = 20,000 \text{ units} \times \$12/\text{unit} = \$240,000$$

Substituting equation 10.3 into equation 10.4 gives

$$\$BEP = \left(\frac{FC}{SP - VC}\right) \times SP \tag{10.5}$$

which can be rearranged in the form

$$\$BEP = \frac{FC}{(SP - VC)/SP} \tag{10.6}$$

The ratio $(SP - VC)/SP$ is the ratio of the marginal profitability to the selling price—that is, it measures marginal profitability as a fraction or percentage of the price. For a price of $12/unit and a variable cost of $7/unit, the marginal profitability is 41.67 percent (calculated as $(12 - 7)/12 = 5/12 = 0.4167 = 41.67\%$). For a fixed cost of $100,000, the break-even point in dollars is calculated by equation 10.6 as

$$\$BEP = \frac{\$100,000}{5/12} = \$240,000$$

which is the same value, by multiplying the number of units at the break-even point by the selling price.

Graphic Models

Figure 10-4 shows how costs, receipts, and profits vary with changes in the number of units made and sold *so long as the fixed cost, selling price, and unit variable cost remain fixed at the values specified earlier.* Because the fixed cost does not change with the number of units, it appears as a horizontal straight line in the upper chart of Figure 10-4. The total variable cost, total cost, and sales receipts are also straight lines but slope upward, indicating that their values are proportional to the number of units; that is, they are *linear functions* of the number of units.

Graphs are often an effective means of presenting results at meetings. Financial officers might use them to make presentations to corporate executives or boards of directors, or to bankers with whom they are negotiating loans. Charts make it possible to show results for either a particular set of conditions or a range of conditions. They help show the sensitivity of results to changes in conditions that might occur in real life. They help demonstrate the risks involved with investments.

The break-even point of 20,000 units appears in the upper chart at the intersection of the straight lines for sales receipts and total costs. When the number of units is greater than the break-even value (i.e., when sales are to the right of the break-even point of Figure 10-4), receipts exceed costs and the operation is profitable. When the number of units is less than the break-even value, costs exceed receipts and the operation loses money. The lower chart shows how profitability varies with sales volume—from losses when the number of units is less than the break-even value to profits when it is greater.

For a break-even point to exist, the slope of the receipt line ($12/unit) must be greater than the slope of the cost line ($7/unit). The difference between the two ($5/unit) is the slope of the profit line. This may be clearer if we rewrite equation 10.2 in the following equivalent form:

$$P = (SP - VC) \times N - FC \tag{10.7}$$

Using the Income Statement

In this section we show how to use Excel's Solver tool to calculate the break-even point and other values on an income statement. We will use the income statement developed in Chapter 1 for the ABC Corporation for the year 20X2.

Figure 10-4

Effect of Number of Units Made and Sold on Sales Revenues, Costs, and Profits

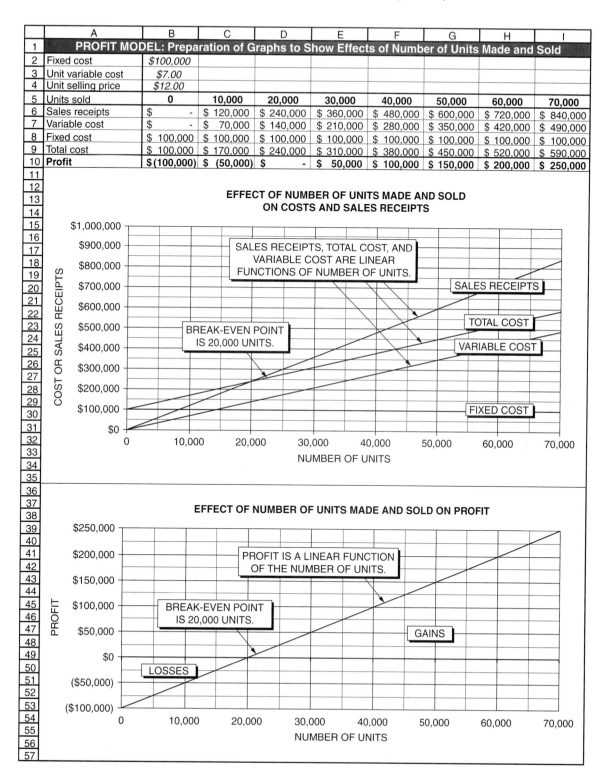

	A	B	C	D	E	F	G	H	I
1	PROFIT MODEL: Preparation of Graphs to Show Effects of Number of Units Made and Sold								
2	Fixed cost	$100,000							
3	Unit variable cost	$7.00							
4	Unit selling price	$12.00							
5	Units sold	0	10,000	20,000	30,000	40,000	50,000	60,000	70,000
6	Sales receipts	$ -	$ 120,000	$ 240,000	$ 360,000	$ 480,000	$ 600,000	$ 720,000	$ 840,000
7	Variable cost	$ -	$ 70,000	$ 140,000	$ 210,000	$ 280,000	$ 350,000	$ 420,000	$ 490,000
8	Fixed cost	$ 100,000	$ 100,000	$ 100,000	$ 100,000	$ 100,000	$ 100,000	$ 100,000	$ 100,000
9	Total cost	$ 100,000	$ 170,000	$ 240,000	$ 310,000	$ 380,000	$ 450,000	$ 520,000	$ 590,000
10	Profit	$(100,000)	$ (50,000)	$ -	$ 50,000	$ 100,000	$ 150,000	$ 200,000	$ 250,000

Calculating the Break-Even Point

Rows 1 to 30 of Figure 10-5 are a copy of the income statement for the ABC Corporation from Chapter 1 (Figure 1-1). Additional information we will need has been added in Rows 31 to 36.

Figure 10-5

Copy of Income Statement from Chapter 1 with Additions in Rows 31 to 36

	A	B
1	**ABC COMPANY**	
2	**Income Statement for the Year Ended December 31, 20X2**	
3	Dollar values are in $ thousand except for per share and per unit values.	
4	Total Operating Revenues (or Total Sales Revenues)	$2,575.0
5	Less: Cost of Goods Sold (COGS)	$1,150.0
6	**Gross Profits**	**$1,425.0**
7	Less: Operating Expenses	
8	Selling Expenses	$275.0
9	General and Administrative Expenses (G&A)	$225.0
10	Depreciation Expense	$100.0
11	Fixed Expenses	$75.0
12	**Total Operating Expenses**	**$675.0**
13	**Net Operating Income**	**$750.0**
14	Other Income	$20.0
15	**Earnings before Interest and Taxes (EBIT)**	**$770.0**
16	Less: Interest Expense	
17	Interest on Short-Term Notes	$10.0
18	Interest on Long-Term Borrowing	$50.0
19	**Total Interest Expense**	$60.0
20	**Earnings before Taxes (EBT)**	**$710.0**
21	Less: Taxes	
22	Current	$160.0
23	Deferred	$124.0
24	Total Taxes (rate = 40%)	$284.0
25	**Earnings after Taxes (EAT)**	**$426.0**
26	Less: Preferred Stock Dividends	$95.0
27	**Net Earnings Available for Common Stockholders**	**$331.0**
28	Earnings per Share (EPS), 100,000 shares outstanding	$3.31
29	Retained Earnings	$220.0
30	Dividends Paid to Holders of Common Stock	$111.0
31	**Added Information**	
32	**Unit Selling Price**	$25.75
33	**Number of Units Sold**	100,000
34	**COGS, as percent of Sales**	44.66%
35	**Break-Even Point, units (algebraic method)**	45,965
36	**Break-Even Point, sales in $ thousand**	$1,183.6

Key Cell Entries

B4: =B32*B33
B5: =B4*B34
B35: =(B12−B14)/(B32*(1−B34))
B36: =B35*B32

As defined in the present chapter, the break-even point is the number of units at which the EBIT is zero. To provide the information needed on the income statement, add the entries shown in Rows 31 to 36 of Figure 10-5. Enter the row headings in Cells A32:A36. Enter $25.75 and 100,000 as data values for the unit selling price and number of units sold in Cells B32 and B33. For later use, calculate COGS as a percent of sales revenues by entering =B5/B4 in Cell B34. The result of this calculation, shown to two decimal places, is 44.66 percent. We will assume that COGS remains at 44.66 percent of sales, regardless of the sales level. To fix the value in Cell B34 so that it does not change with later changes in Cells B5 or B4, press the Ctrl and C keys to copy the entry, access the Paste Special dialog box on the Edit drop-down menu, and paste the value back into the cell by checking "Values" on the Paste Special dialog box.

In Cell B4, replace the data value of $2,575,000 by the formula =B32*B33. This entry links the unit selling price and number of units sold to the total operating revenues, and, therefore, to all other calculations in the income statement.

In Cell B5, replace the data value of $1,150,000 by the formula =B4*B34. This entry calculates COGS as the product of sales revenue (Cell B4) multiplied by 44.66 percent (the value of the ratio of cost of units sold to sales revenue that you pasted in Cell B34).

Algebraic Method for Break-Even Point

For the EBIT to equal zero, the sum of the sales revenues (Cell B4, which equals B32*B33) and other income (Cell B14) must equal the sum of COGS (Cell B5, which equals B4*B34, or B32*B33*B34) and the total operating expenses (Cell B12). Note that the value of other income is a data value, the total operating expenses is the sum of data values, and COGS is a fixed percent of sales (Cell B34). Therefore, at the break-even point,

$$B32*B33 + B14 = B32*B33*B34+B12$$

That is,

$$\text{Sales Revenues} + \text{Other Income} = \text{Cost of Goods Sold} + \text{Total Operating Expense}$$

Rearranging to place all terms with the variable B33 on the left side of the equation,

$$B32*B33-B32*B33*B34 = B12-B14$$

Therefore, at the break-even point,

$$B33 = (B12-B14)/(B32-B32*B34) = (B12-B14)/(B32*(1-B34))$$

We will reserve Cell B35 for the break-even value of B33. That is, the number of units for the ABC Corporation to break even (i.e., for EBIT = 0) is calculated by the entry =(B12-B14)/(B32*(1-B34)) in Cell B35. The sales revenue to break even is calculated by the entry =B35*B32 in Cell B36. The results are 45,965 units and $1,183,600.

Solver Method for Break-Even Point

The linkage established in Figure 10-5 between the total operating revenues (Cell B4) and the unit selling price and number of units sold (Cells B32 and B33) can now be exploited to determine the break-even point and its effects on other values on the income statement **without resorting to an algebraic solution**.

Begin by copying Figure 10-5 to a new worksheet and delete Rows 35 and 36 for the algebraic method. Label the new worksheet Figure 10-6. Access the Solver tool by clicking on Solver on the Tools menu. Figure 10-7 shows the Solver dialog box with the settings. The target cell is B15 (which is the EBIT) and is to be set equal to zero by changing Cell B33 (the number of units that must be sold for breaking even). When these settings are executed, Solver returns the results shown in Figure 10-6.

Figure 10-6

Income Statement at the Break-Even Point (Value of Break-Even Point Determined with Excel's Goal Seek Tool)

	A	B
1	ABC COMPANY	
2	Income Statement at the Break-Even Point for the Year Ended December 31, 20X2	
3	Dollar values are in $ thousand except for per share and per unit values.	
4	Total Operating Revenues (or Total Sales Revenues)	$1,183.6
5	Less: Cost of Goods Sold (COGS)	$528.6
6	Gross Profits	$655.0
7	Less: Operating Expenses	
8	Selling Expenses	$275.0
9	General and Administrative Expenses (G&A)	$225.0
10	Depreciation Expense	$100.0
11	Fixed Expenses	$75.0
12	Total Operating Expenses	$675.0
13	Net Operating Income	−$20.0
14	Other Income	$20.0
15	Earnings before Interest and Taxes (EBIT)	$0.0
16	Less: Interest Expense	
17	Interest on Short-Term Notes	$10.0
18	Interest on Long-Term Borrowing	$50.0
19	Total Interest Expense	$60.0
20	Earnings before Taxes (EBT)	−$60.0
21	Less: Taxes (rate = 40%)	
22	Current	$160.0
23	Deferred	−$184.0
24	Total Taxes (rate = 40%)	−$24.0
25	Earnings after Taxes (EAT)	−$36.0
26	Less: Preferred Stock Dividends	$95.0
27	Net Earnings Available for Common Stockholders	−$131.0
28	Earnings per Share (EPS), 100,000 shares outstanding	−$1.31
29	Retained Earnings	$220.0
30	Dividends Paid to Holders of Common Stock	−$351.0
31	Added Information	
32	Unit Selling Price	$25.75
33	Number of Units Sold	45,965
34	COGS, as Percent of Sales	44.66%

EBIT = 0 at the break-even point.

Solver solution for the break-even point

Solver Settings

Target Cell is B15, to be set equal to zero by changing Cell B33.

Figure 10-7

"Solver Parameters" Dialog Box with Settings for Determining the Number of Units to Break Even (i.e., EBIT = 0)

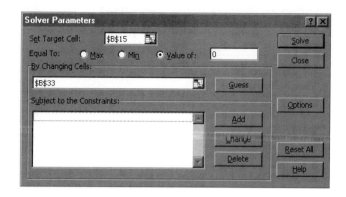

The break-even point is 45,965 units (Cell B33, Figure 10-6), the same as with the algebraic solution (Cell B35, Figure 10-5). Note, however, that other values on the spreadsheet have changed to correspond to their values at the break-even point. For example, the sales revenues for breaking even is $1,183,600 (Cell B4, Figure 10-6), the same as with the algebraic solution (Cell B36, Figure 10-5).

The Solver solution of Figure 10-6 gives additional information on the Income Statement at the break-even point, such as the cost of goods sold (Cell B5), net operating income (Cell B13), and earnings before taxes (Cell B20). Although EBIT equals zero, interest expenses result in a loss for the company, as shown by the negative value for EBT in Cell B20.

Clearly, simply "breaking even" is not a satisfactory goal for the company. In fact, if breaking even is equated to setting the EBIT equal to zero, the ABC Corporation actually loses money at the break-even point. And if the company maintains its policy for retaining $220,000 of earnings, there are no funds available for distribution to holders of common stock, as indicated by the negative value in Cell B30.

Setting Other Goals

In this section, we will use our spreadsheet model of ABC's income statement to examine other goals the company might set.

One goal might be to provide stockholders with a specified amount of earnings per share. We can ask, for example, for the number of units ABC must sell for the earnings per share to equal $3.00. To answer this question, copy Figure 10-6 and label it Figure 10-8. Then execute Solver with Cell B28 in Figure 10-6 set equal to 3 by changing Cell B33. The results are shown in Figure 10-8.

Experiment yourself with other goals. For example, use a target of $300,000 for the EAT, or a target of $75,000 for the dividends to common stockholders. Each time the Solver tool is executed with a new

Figure 10-8

Income Statement with Number of Units Sold for Earnings of $3.00 per Share

	A	B
1	**ABC COMPANY**	
2	**Income Statement for the Year Ended Dec. 31, 20X2**	
3	**Dollar values are in $ thousand, except for per share and unit selling price.**	
4	Total Operating Revenues (or Total Sales Revenues)	$2,481.6
5	Less: Cost of Goods Sold (COGS)	$1,108.3
6	**Gross Profits**	**$1,373.3**
7	Less: Operating Expenses	
8	Selling Expenses	*$275.0*
9	General and Administrative Expenses (G&A)	*$225.0*
10	Depreciation Expense	*$100.0*
11	Fixed Expenses	*$75.0*
12	**Total Operating Expenses**	**$675.0**
13	**Net Operating Income**	**$698.3**
14	Other Income	$20.0
15	**Earnings before Interest and Taxes (EBIT)**	**$718.3**
16	Less: Interest Expense	
17	Interest on Short-Term Notes	*$10.0*
18	Interest on Long-Term Borrowing	*$50.0*
19	**Total Interest Expense**	$60.0
20	**Earnings before Taxes (EBT)**	**$658.3**
21	Less: Taxes	
22	Current	*$160.0*
23	Deferred	$103.3
24	Total Taxes (rate = 40%)	$263.3
25	**Earnings after Taxes (EAT)**	**$395.0**
26	Less: Preferred Stock Dividends	$95.0
27	**Net Earnings Available for Common Stockholders**	**$300.0**
28	Earnings per Share (EPS), 100,000 shares outstanding	$3.00
29	Retained Earnings	*$220.0*
30	Dividends Paid to Holders of Common Stock	$80.0
31	**Information added for determining break-even point**	
32	**Unit Selling Price**	$25.75
33	**Number of Units Sold**	96,374
34	COGS, as percent of Sales	44.66%

EPS = $3.00/share

Number of units sold for EPS = $3.00/share

Solver Settings
Target Cell is B28, to be set equal to 3 by changing Cell B33.

target, the results will be a new value for the number of units that must be sold and a new set of values for its impact on other items on the income statement.

Because of the linkage of cells in the spreadsheet, all of these "What if"? experiments can be done without resorting to algebraic manipulations!

Selling Price and Income Statement for Maximum Profit

In the preceding discussions, we assumed that the number of units ABC can sell is not affected by the selling price—that is, ABC can sell any number of units at any price it chooses to charge. Actually, in the absence of a monopoly, the number of units a company can sell depends very much on the selling price. The higher the price, the fewer the units that can be sold, and the more customers will buy from competitors who offer similar products at lower prices. Setting a product's selling price involves inputs from both a firm's sales and marketing division and either its purchasing department or its operations or production division. The selling price needs to consider the effect of selling price on the number of units that can be sold and their cost to produce or acquire.

To explore the effect of selling price on the maximum profit and values in a company's income statement, copy Figure 10-8 to a new worksheet. Label the new worksheet Figure 10-9. Let us assume that the firm's marketing division has done some customer research and, as a result, has concluded that the effect of selling price on the number of units that can be sold is as given in Table 10-1.

Figure 10-9 shows the new worksheet with values from Table 10-1 entered in Cells B41:B46 and D41:D46. We need to use this information to link the number of units sold (Cell B33) to the selling price (Cell B32). We will do this by creating a regression equation that expresses the number of units sold as a function of the selling price. The technique for creating the regression equation is the same as we used to create forecasting models in Chapters 3. However, instead of forecasting annual revenues as a function of the year, our units-sold/price model will forecast the number of units sold as a function of the selling price.

The first step in developing the regression model for forecasting the number of units sold as a function of the selling price is to decide whether to use a linear, quadratic, exponential or other type of model. As in Chapter 3, we can create a scatter diagram of the data and insert different types of trend lines until we get a satisfactory match between the inserted trend line and the data.

At the left of the data in Figure 10-9 is a scatter diagram of the values, with a quadratic (or second-order polynomial) trend line inserted, along with the regression equation and its coefficient of determination. The match looks good.

Table 10-1

Effect of Selling Price on the Number of Units That Can be Sold

Unit Selling Price	Number of Units That Can be Sold
$20.00	120,000
$22.00	115,000
$24.00	108,000
$25.75	100,000
$28.00	84,000
$30.00	60,000

Figure 10-9

Income Statement at Optimum Selling Price

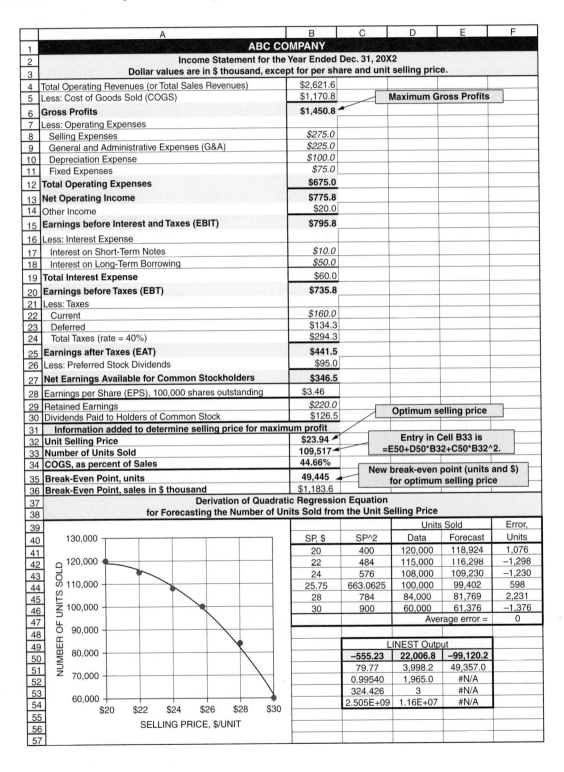

	A	B	C	D	E	F
1		ABC COMPANY				
2		Income Statement for the Year Ended Dec. 31, 20X2				
3		Dollar values are in $ thousand, except for per share and unit selling price.				
4	Total Operating Revenues (or Total Sales Revenues)	$2,621.6				
5	Less: Cost of Goods Sold (COGS)	$1,170.8		Maximum Gross Profits		
6	**Gross Profits**	**$1,450.8**				
7	Less: Operating Expenses					
8	Selling Expenses	$275.0				
9	General and Administrative Expenses (G&A)	$225.0				
10	Depreciation Expense	$100.0				
11	Fixed Expenses	$75.0				
12	**Total Operating Expenses**	**$675.0**				
13	**Net Operating Income**	**$775.8**				
14	Other Income	$20.0				
15	**Earnings before Interest and Taxes (EBIT)**	**$795.8**				
16	Less: Interest Expense					
17	Interest on Short-Term Notes	$10.0				
18	Interest on Long-Term Borrowing	$50.0				
19	**Total Interest Expense**	**$60.0**				
20	**Earnings before Taxes (EBT)**	**$735.8**				
21	Less: Taxes					
22	Current	$160.0				
23	Deferred	$134.3				
24	Total Taxes (rate = 40%)	$294.3				
25	**Earnings after Taxes (EAT)**	**$441.5**				
26	Less: Preferred Stock Dividends	$95.0				
27	**Net Earnings Available for Common Stockholders**	**$346.5**				
28	Earnings per Share (EPS), 100,000 shares outstanding	$3.46				
29	Retained Earnings	$220.0				
30	Dividends Paid to Holders of Common Stock	$126.5		Optimum selling price		
31	**Information added to determine selling price for maximum profit**					
32	**Unit Selling Price**	**$23.94**		Entry in Cell B33 is		
33	**Number of Units Sold**	**109,517**		=E50+D50*B32+C50*B32^2.		
34	**COGS, as percent of Sales**	**44.66%**		New break-even point (units and $)		
35	**Break-Even Point, units**	**49,445**		for optimum selling price		
36	**Break-Even Point, sales in $ thousand**	**$1,183.6**				
37		Derivation of Quadratic Regression Equation				
38		for Forecasting the Number of Units Sold from the Unit Selling Price				
39				Units Sold		Error,
40		SP, $	SP^2	Data	Forecast	Units
41		20	400	120,000	118,924	1,076
42		22	484	115,000	116,298	−1,298
43		24	576	108,000	109,230	−1,230
44		25.75	663.0625	100,000	99,402	598
45		28	784	84,000	81,769	2,231
46		30	900	60,000	61,376	−1,376
47					Average error =	0
48						
49				LINEST Output		
50				−555.23	22,006.8	−99,120.2
51				79.77	3,998.2	49,357.0
52				0.99540	1,965.0	#N/A
53				324.426	3	#N/A
54				2.505E+09	1.16E+07	#N/A
55						
56						
57						

Chart (rows 40–55): NUMBER OF UNITS SOLD vs SELLING PRICE, $/UNIT

To use Excel's LINEST command to determine the parameters for the quadratic model, we first need to add values for the squares of the selling prices in Cells C41:C46. To do this, enter =B41^2 in Cell C41 and copy it to C42:C46. Then use Excel's LINEST command to evaluate the parameters for the quadratic equation. To do this, drag the mouse to select Cells C50:E54 and type =LINEST(D41:D46, B41:C46,1,1). Press the Control/Shift/Enter keys to enter LINEST. Our "forecasting" model is now expressed by the equation

$$Y = -99,120.2 + 22,006.80X - 555.23X^2$$

where Y = number of units sold, X = selling price (in dollars), and the values of the three coefficients are in Cells E50, D50, and C50.

Validate this model in the same way as any other forecasting models—that is, by showing that the average forecast error is zero and the errors scatter randomly. To forecast units sold, enter =$E$50+$D$50*B41+$C$50*B41^2 in Cell E41 and copy the entry to E42:E46. To calculate errors, enter =D41-E41 in Cell F41 and copy the entry to F42:F46. To calculate the average error, enter =AVERAGE(F41:F46) in Cell F47. By examining the sequence of errors in Cells F41 to F46, you should be able to recognize that their scatter is random. (If you need a picture to recognize this, prepare a chart with the values in Cells F41:F46 plotted on the Y-axis against those in Cells B41:B46 on the X-axis.)

The agreement between forecast values for the units sold and the estimates from the marketing division for the number of units that can be sold at different selling prices appears satisfactory; it is within the errors we might expect for the estimates from the marketing division.

The next step is to link our model to the income statement. To do this, enter a **trial** value for selling price in Cell B32. The trial value will be changed later, so don't hesitate to enter a value. (The value 24 would be a good choice, but other values would be satisfactory.) To calculate the number of units that can be sold at the selling price in Cell B32, enter =E50+D50*B32+C50*B32^2 in Cell B33. (Recall that the operating revenues in Cell B4 is the product of the values in Cells B32 and B33.)

We now use Excel's Solver tool to change the *trial* value in Cell B32 to the value that will maximize the Gross Profits in Cell B6. Figure 10-10 shows the settings. Executing Solver produces the results shown in Figure 10-9.

The results in Figure 10-9 show that the optimum selling price is $23.94/unit (Cell B32). At this selling price, sales will be an estimated 109,517 units (Cell B33). The combination of this selling price and number of units sold gives total operating revenues of $2,621,600 (Cell B4) and maximum gross profits of $1,450,800 (Cell B6). The break-even point at this selling price is 49,445 units (Cell B35), which is well below the 109,517 we can expect to sell. Figure 10-9 also shows, for example, that at this selling price the EBIT is $795,800 dollars and the earnings per share is $3.46.

Sensitivity Analysis

In this section, we use a one-variable input table to explore the sensitivity of profits and other financial measures to the selling price. The results are shown in Figure 10-11.

Figure 10-10

"Solver Parameters" Dialog Box with Settings to Determine Selling Price for Maximum Profit

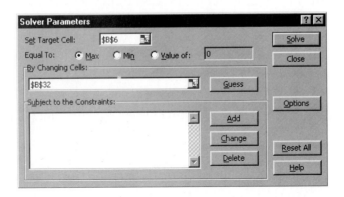

Figure 10-11 has been created in a convenient spot on the spreadsheet of Figure 10-9. A series of unit selling prices, running from $20 to $30 in $1 increments, is entered in Cells B62:B72. The key entries for transferring values from the main section of the spreadsheet are made in Row 61 as follows: Cell B61: =B32; Cell C61: =B33; Cell D61: =B4; Cell E61: =B6; Cell F61: =B13; Cell G61: =B15; Cell H61: =B20; Cell I61: =B25; Cell J61: =B35; and Cell K61: =B36. To prevent confusion, these entries have been hidden by formatting them with the custom format ;;; (i.e., three semicolons).

Excel's Table tool is used to fill in the values. To do this, first drag the mouse to select the Range B61:K72. Next, access the dialog box shown in Figure 10-12 by selecting Table from the Data pull-down menu. Enter B32 for the column input values and click the OK button or press Enter. The result, after formatting, is the table of values in the upper portion of Figure 10-11. The chart below the table shows graphically the effect of selling price on gross profit.

The results show how sensitive gross profit, net profit, and other financial measures are to the unit selling price. For example, gross profit remains above $1,400,000 for unit selling prices from approximately $21.60 to $26.10. This compares to a maximum gross profit of $1,450,800 at a unit selling price of $23.94. In other words, the company can set the selling price anywhere within a fairly wide range without substantially reducing the gross profit below its maximum. For example, the company could set the selling price at a low value, such as $22.00 per unit, in order to increase market share without sacrificing much in the way of profit.

Leverage

Leverage is a measure of how well a firm can operate when its sales revenues are cyclical. High leverage is associated with high risk. Although firms with high operating and financial leverage do well during

Figure 10-11

Sensitivity of Gross Profit and Other Items to the Unit Selling Price

	B	C	D	E	F	G	H	I	J	K
58					ABC COMPANY					
59		Sensitivity Analysis ($ values are in thousands of dollars except for unit selling price.)								
60	Unit Selling Price	Number of Units Sold	Total Sales Revenue	Gross Profit	Net Operating Income	Earnings before Interest and Taxes (EBIT)	Earnings before Taxes (EBT)	Earnings after Taxes	Units to Break Even	Dollar Sales to Break Even
61										
62	$20.00	118,924	$2,378.5	$1,316.2	$641.2	$661.2	$601.2	$300.7	50,180	$1,183.6
63	$21.00	118,166	$2,481.5	$1,373.2	$698.2	$718.2	$658.2	$394.9	56,362	$1,183.6
64	$22.00	116,298	$2,558.6	$1,415.9	$740.9	$760.9	$700.9	$420.5	53,800	$1,183.6
65	$23.00	113,319	$2,606.3	$1,442.3	$767.3	$787.3	$727.3	$436.4	51,461	$1,183.6
66	$24.00	109,230	$2,621.5	$1,450.7	$775.7	$795.7	$735.7	$441.4	49,317	$1,183.6
67	$25.00	104,031	$2,600.8	$1,439.3	$764.3	$784.3	$724.3	$434.6	47,344	$1,183.6
68	$26.00	97,721	$2,540.7	$1,406.0	$731.0	$751.0	$691.0	$414.6	45,523	$1,183.6
69	$27.00	90,300	$2,438.1	$1,349.2	$674.2	$694.2	$634.2	$380.5	43,837	$1,183.6
70	$28.00	81,769	$2,289.5	$1,267.0	$592.0	$612.0	$552.0	$331.2	42,271	$1,183.6
71	$29.00	72,128	$2,091.7	$1,157.6	$482.6	$502.6	$442.6	$265.5	40,814	$1,183.6
72	$30.00	61,376	$1,841.3	$1,019.0	$344.0	$364.0	$304.0	$182.4	39,453	$1,183.6

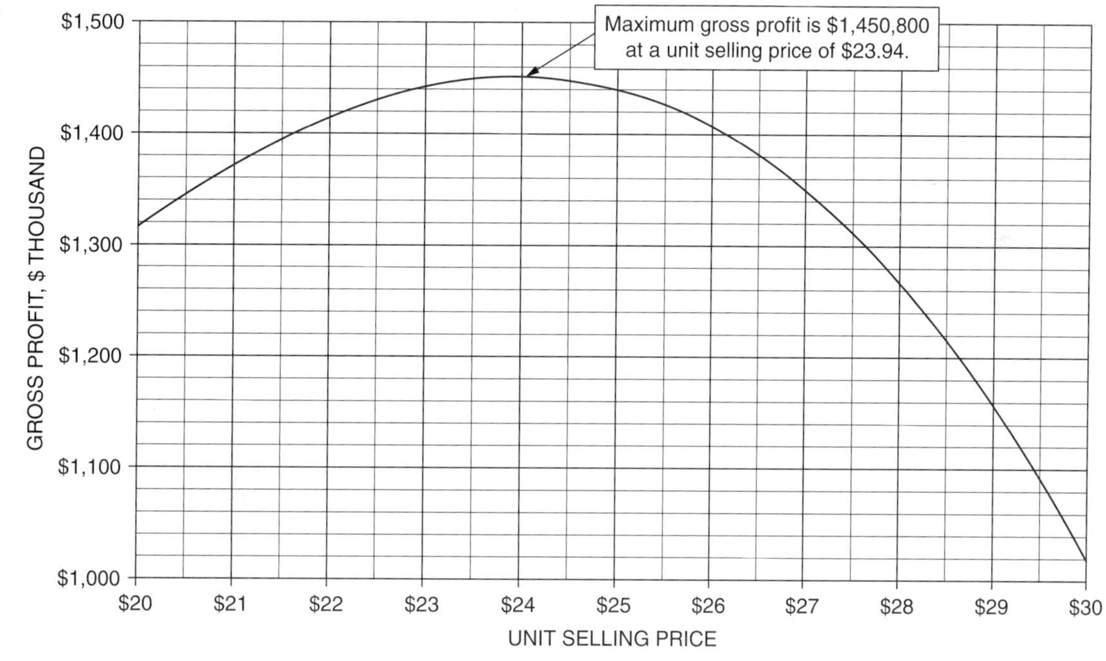

Maximum gross profit is $1,450,800 at a unit selling price of $23.94.

Key Cell Entries for Transferring Values from Main Spreadsheet Section

B61: =B32   C61: =B33   D61: =B4   E61: =B6   F61: =B13   G61: =IB15   H61: =B20   I61: =B25   J61: =B35   K61: =B36

Figure 10-12

Table Dialog Box with Unit Selling Price Designated for Column Input Cell

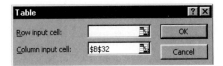

expansion phases of business cycles, they do poorly during contraction phases. Conversely, although not as profitable during periods of economic expansion, firms with low leverage survive better during the downside of business cycles.

Information for computing a firm's leverage ratios is obtained from the firm's income statement.

Operating Leverage

The degree of operating leverage (DOL) is the ratio of the percentage change in EBIT to the percentage change in sales. It can be defined by the following equation, which gives three equivalent forms of the right side:

$$DOL = \frac{\%\Delta EBIT}{\%\Delta Sales} = \frac{\frac{\Delta EBIT}{EBIT}}{\frac{\Delta Sales}{Sales}} = \frac{\Delta EBIT}{EBIT} \times \frac{Sales}{\Delta Sales} \qquad (10.8)$$

A more direct way for calculating the degree of operating leverage is

$$DOL = \frac{Sales - Variable\ Cost}{EBIT} \qquad (10.9)$$

A firm's operating leverage is sensitive to the relative amounts of its fixed and variable costs. If a firm's costs are all variable (i.e., if there are no fixed costs), and if the variable costs are a constant percentage of the sales, the percentage change in EBIT will exactly equal the percentage change in sales. However, if a firm has fixed costs as well as variable, the percentage change in EBIT will be greater than the percentage change in sales.

The degree of operating leverage for the ABC Company can be computed by substituting values from Figure 10-5 in equation 10.9. Thus,

$$DOL = \frac{\$2,575,000 - \$1,150,000}{\$770,000} = \frac{\$1,425,000}{\$770,000} = 1.85$$

The following example considers the choice between two processes—a labor-intensive one and a capital intensive one—that a company is considering for manufacturing a product.

Example 10.1:   The Hancock Corporation is considering two processes to manufacture a product. Process A is a labor-intensive process with relatively low fixed cost and high variable cost. Process B is a capital-intensive process with relatively high fixed cost and low variable cost. Values are as follows:

Process A (Labor-Intensive)	Process B (Capital-Intensive)
Fixed cost = $10,000/year	Fixed cost = $20,000/year
Variable cost = $7/unit	Variable cost = $5/unit

Hancock expects to sell 5,000 units a year at a selling price of $10/unit. (Since the product is the same for both processes, the selling price of the product is the also the same for both processes.)

a. What is the firm's operating leverage for each process at the expected number of units sold?
b. What is the firm's operating leverage for each process if the number of units sold is 10 percent greater than expected?
c. What is the firm's operating leverage for each process if the number of units sold is 10 percent less than expected?
d. What are the percentage changes in DOL and EBIT for a 10 percent increase and a 10 percent decrease in the number of units sold?
e. Interpret the results in terms of their impact on a firm's strategy.

Solution: Figure 10-13 is a spreadsheet solution. The operating leverage at the base condition is calculated by two different methods.

a. *Method 1*: The operating leverages at the base conditions can be evaluated by comparing the results when the sales volume is changed with the results at the base conditions. The results in Rows 4 to 24 show the comparison at the base conditions and for a 10 percent increase and a 10 percent decrease in the number of units sold. Key cell entries are shown at the bottom of the spreadsheet. The operating leverages at the base conditions are 3.00 for Process A (Cells C18 and D18) and 5.00 for Process B (Cells F18 and G18).
   Method 2: Substituting in equation 10.9 gives the same results; thus,

$$DOL_A = \frac{(5,000 \text{ units})(\$10/\text{unit}) - (5,000 \text{ units})(\$7/\text{unit})}{\$5,000} = \frac{\$15,000}{\$5,000} = 3.00$$

$$DOL_B = \frac{(5,000 \text{ units})(\$10/\text{unit}) - (5,000 \text{ units})(\$5/\text{unit})}{\$5,000} = \frac{\$25,000}{\$5,000} = 5.00$$

b. For a 10 percent increase in the number of units sold, Process B enjoys a greater increase in EBIT ($2500, Cell F14) than Process A ($1500, Cell C14). At the new sales level, the operating leverages are lowered to 2.54 for Process A and 3.67 for Process B.
c. For a 10 percent decrease in the number of units sold, Process B suffers a greater decrease in EBIT (-$2500, Cell G14) than Process A (-$1500, Cell D14). At the new sales level, the operating leverages are raised to 3.86 for Process A and 9.00 for Process B.
d. The percentage changes in DOL and EBIT from the base conditions are shown in Rows 23 and 24 of Figure 10-13. Note that the swings in these values are much higher for Process B than for Process A.

(Continued)

e. We might reasonably conclude from this analysis that if there is a high probability that demand for the product will be low and Hancock is in such financial shape that it would be difficult to cope with a large reduction in its expected EBIT, the CFO should prefer Process A. On the other hand, if the company is in good financial shape and it is likely that demand for the product will be strong, the CFO should choose Process B.

Figure 10-13

Operating Leverage at Base Conditions and for 10% Increases and Reductions in Sales Volume

	A	B	C	D	E	F	G
1		HANCOCK CORPORATION					
2		Process A			Process B		
3		Base Sales	10% Increase in Sales	10% Decrease in Sales	Base Sales	10% Increase in Sales	10% Decrease in Sales
4	Fixed cost	$ 10,000	$ 10,000	$ 10,000	$ 20,000	$ 20,000	$ 20,000
5	Unit variable cost	$7.00	$7.00	$7.00	$5.00	$5.00	$5.00
6	Selling price	$10.00	$10.00	$10.00	$10.00	$10.00	$10.00
7	Units sold per year	5,000	5,500	4,500	5,000	5,500	4,500
8	Break-even point, units	3,333	3,333	3,333	4,000	4,000	4,000
9	Sales revenue	$ 50,000	$ 55,000	$ 45,000	$ 50,000	$ 55,000	$ 45,000
10	Less variable costs	$ 35,000	$ 38,500	$ 31,500	$ 25,000	$ 27,500	$ 22,500
11	Less fixed costs	$ 10,000	$ 10,000	$ 10,000	$ 20,000	$ 20,000	$ 20,000
12	EBIT	$ 5,000	$ 6,500	$ 3,500	$ 5,000	$ 7,500	$ 2,500
13		Changes from Base					
14	Change in EBIT		$ 1,500	$ (1,500)		$ 2,500	$ (2,500)
15	Relative change in EBIT		30.0%	−30.0%		50.0%	−50.0%
16	Change in sales revenue		$ 5,000	$ (5,000)		$ 5,000	$ (5,000)
17	Relative change in sales revenue		10.0%	−10.0%		10.0%	−10.0%
18	Operating leverage at base		3.00	3.00		5.00	5.00
19		Operating Leverage at Conditions in Row 3					
20	Sales less variable costs, SLVC	$ 15,000	$ 16,500	$ 13,500	$ 25,000	$ 27,500	$ 22,500
21	Degree of operating leverage, DOL	3.00	2.54	3.86	5.00	3.67	9.00
22		Percent Changes from Base Conditions					
23	Percent change in DOL	Base	−15.4%	28.6%	Base	−26.7%	80.0%
24	Percent change in EBIT	Base	30.0%	−30.0%	Base	50.0%	−50.0%

Key Cell Entries

B8: =–D4/(B6–B5), copy to C8:G8
B9: =B7*B6, copy to C9:G9
B10: =B7*B5, copy to C10:G10
B12: =B9–B10–B11, copy to C12:G12
C14: =C12–$B12, copy to D14
C15: =C14/$B12, copy to D15
C16: =C9–$B9, copy to D16
C17: =C16/$B9, copy to D17
C18: =C15/C17, copy to D18 and to F18:G18

B20: =B9–B10, copy to C20:G20
B21: =B20/B12, copy to C21:G21
F14: =F12–$E12, copy to G14
F15: =F14/$E12, copy to G15
F16: =F9–$E9, copy to G16
F17: =F16/$E9, copy to G17
C23: =(C21–$B$21)/$B$21, copy to D23
F23: =(F21–$E$21)/$E$21, copy to G23
C24: =C14/$B$12, copy to D24
F24: =F14/$E$12, copy to G24

Incorporating the Effect of Number of Units on the Unit Cost of Goods Sold on Profits and Leverage

As production and sales volume increase, a product's unit cost generally decreases. The cost of goods sold may be lowered, for example, by taking advantage of volume discounts for purchasing raw materials and supplies in larger quantities, by training workers to work more efficiently, by better management of inventories, or from other payoffs for operating on a larger scale.

The following example analyzes the effect of scale on values in the income statement and a firm's operating leverage.

Example 10.2. For purposes of illustration, suppose we start with the conditions shown in Figure 10-9 for the maximum profit for the ABC Company. The unit cost under these conditions is $10.69, which can be determined by dividing the value for COGS in Cell B5 ($1,170,800) by the number of units in Cell B33 (109,517). Call these values the base values. Now suppose that each increase of 1000 units above the base value of 109,517 units reduces the unit cost by $0.25 below the base value of $10.69.

What will be the optimum selling price if the company takes advantage of the reduction in cost by increasing the number of goods it produces? How does this affect the value of COGS and other items on the income statement? Assume there is no change in fixed costs.

Solution: Figure 10-14 is a spreadsheet solution. To create this spreadsheet (while saving Figure 10-9), copy Figure 10-9 to a new worksheet. Insert new Rows 37 and 38. Compute the unit costs in Cell B37 by the entry =B5/B33. Compute the operating leverage in Cell B39 by the entry =(B4-B5)/B15. Then copy all entries in Column B to Column C.

As in Figure 10-9, the number of units sold (Cell C33) is determined by the selling price (C32) and is calculated from the values of the parameters in Cells C52:E52 of the LINEST output. (If the parameters of the quadratic equation that relates the number of units sold to the selling price was not entered in Cell B33 as absolute references with $ signs, you will need to correct these entries after copying to Cell C33 so that the value 109,517 appears in Cell C33. This value will change when Column C is edited.)

We are now ready to edit Column C to take into account the reduction in cost due to volume discounts. To evaluate the effect of the number of units sold in Cell C33 on the unit cost, enter $0.25 in Cell C38 and change the entry in Cell C37 to =B37-C38*(C33-B33)/1000. To link the number of units sold and the unit cost to the total cost of goods sold (i.e., to COGS), change the entry in Cell C5 to =C33*C37. To calculate COGS as a percent of sales, change the entry in Cell C34 to =C5/C4.

To find the selling price that maximizes the profit, use Solver with a target of maximizing Cell C6 by changing Cell C32. The result is a selling price of $22.30/unit, which gives a sales volume of 115,534 units (Cell C33), a unit cost of $9.19 (Cell C37).

Note that the number of units has increased by 6,017 units (or approximately 6,000 units) and the unit cost has decreased by $1.50, which is a decrease of $0.25 per 1000 units. This confirms the correctness of our entry in Cell C37.

Also, note that, although the sales revenue (Cell C4) decreases from the base value as a result of decreasing the selling price, the cost of goods sold (Cell C5) is less, the number of units sold (C33) is more, and the financial payoffs (C6, C15, C20, C24, C27, and C36) are greater. The operating leverage drops to 1.76 (Cell C39), a reduction of 3.35 percent from the base optimum. All of these are favorable results from reducing the selling price. The break-even point (Cell C35) is slightly greater.

The percentage changes are evaluated in Column D by entering =(C4-B4)/B4 in Cell D4 and copying to the cells below. Note that unit cost is reduced by 14.07 percent (Cell D37) as a result of the increased number of units sold.

(Continued)

Figure 10-14

Income Statement with the Addition of the Effect of Number of Units Sold on the Cost of Goods Sold

	A	B	C	D	E	F
1	ABC COMPANY					
2	Income Statement for the Year Ended December 31, 20X2					
3	Dollar values are in $ thousand except for per share and per unit values.	Base Optimum	New Optimum	Percent Change		
4	Total Operating Revenues (or Total Sales Revenues)	$2,621.6	$2,575.9	−1.74%		
5	Less: Cost of Goods Sold (COGS)	$1,170.8	$1,061.4	−9.35%		
6	**Gross Profits**	$1,450.8	$1,514.5	4.39%		
7	Less: Operating Expenses					
8	Selling Expenses	$275.0	$275.0	0.00%		
9	General and Administrative Expenses (G&A)	$225.0	$225.0	0.00%		
10	Depreciation Expense	$100.0	$100.0	0.00%		
11	Fixed Expenses	$75.0	$75.0	0.00%		
12	**Total Operating Expenses**	$675.0	$675.0	0.00%		
13	**Net Operating Income**	$775.8	$839.5	8.21%		
14	Other Income	$20.0	$20.0	0.00%		
15	**Earnings before Interest and Taxes (EBIT)**	$795.8	$859.5	8.01%		
16	Less: Interest Expense					
17	Interest on Short-Term Notes	$10.0	$10.0	0.00%		
18	Interest on Long-Term Borrowing	$50.0	$50.0	0.00%		
19	**Total Interest Expense**	$60.0	$60.0	0.00%		
20	**Earnings before Taxes (EBT)**	$735.8	$799.5	8.66%		
21	Less: Taxes					
22	Current	$160.0	$160.0	0.00%		
23	Deferred	$134.3	$159.8	18.98%		
24	Total Taxes (rate = 40%)	$294.3	$319.8	8.66%		
25	**Earnings after Taxes (EAT)**	$441.5	$479.7	8.66%		
26	Less: Preferred Stock Dividends	$95.0	$95.0	0.00%		
27	**Net Earnings Available for Common Stockholders**	$346.5	$384.7	11.04%		
28	Earnings per Share (EPS), 100,000 Shares Outstanding	$3.46	$3.85	11.04%		
29	Retained Earnings	$220.0	$220.0	0.00%		
30	Dividends Paid to Holders of Common Stock	$126.5	$164.7	30.23%		
31	Information Added to Determine Selling Price for Maximum Profit.					
32	Unit Selling Price for Maximum EBIT	$23.94	$22.30	−6.86%		
33	Number of Units Sold	109,517	115,534	5.49%		
34	COGS, as Percent of Sales	44.66%	41.20%	−7.74%		
35	Break-Even Point (EBIT = 0), Units	49,445	49,966	1.05%		
36	Break-Even Point (EBIT = 0), Sales in $ Thousands	$1,183.6	$1,114.0	−5.88%		
37	Unit Cost	$10.69	$9.19	−14.07%		
38	Reduction in Unit Cost per 1,000 Units	na	$0.25			
39	Degree of Operating Leverage	1.82	1.76	−3.35%		
40	Derivation of Quadratic Regression Equation					
41	for Forecasting the Number of Units Sold from the Unit Selling Price (SP)					

	A (chart)	SP, $	SP^2	Units Sold Data	Units Sold Forecast	Error, units
42						
43		$20.00	400	120,000	118,924	1,076
44		$22.00	484	115,000	116,298	−1,298
45		$24.00	576	108,000	109,230	−1,230
46		$25.75	663	100,000	99,402	598
47		$28.00	784	84,000	81,769	2,231
48		$30.00	900	60,000	61,376	−1,376
49					Average error =	0
50						
51				LINEST Output		
52			−555.231	22006.803	−99120.18	
53			79.7717	3998.19	49356.98	
54			0.99540	1964.96	#N/A	
55			324.426	3	#N/A	
56			2.51E+09	11583168	#N/A	
57						

Chart (rows 42–56, columns A): NUMBER OF UNITS SOLD vs UNIT SELLING PRICE, y-axis 60,000–130,000, x-axis $20–$30.

$$Y = -99{,}120 + 22{,}007X - 555.2X^2$$
$$R^2 = 0.9954$$

Financial Leverage Ratio

Degree of financial leverage ratio (DFL) measures the extent to which a firm relies on debt. Recall that debt and equity are the two ways for financing a firm. A firm with debt, which is the usual situation, is termed a financially **leveraged firm**.

Financial leverage is akin to operating leverage. However, whereas operating leverage is sensitive to the amount of a firm's **fixed costs of operation**, financial leverage is sensitive to the amount of a firm's **fixed costs of financing**. Interest payments on debt must be paid regardless of sales level. Therefore, in a manner similar to that for operating leverage, a firm with high financial leverage is in a favorable position to profit from an expanding economy, when sales are growing, and is in an unfavorable or dangerous position in a contracting economy.

The degree of financial leverage (DFL) is the ratio of the percentage change in earnings per share (EPS) to the percentage change in earnings before interest and taxes (EBIT). It can be defined by the following equation, which gives three equivalent forms of the right side:

$$DFL = \frac{\%\Delta EPS}{\%\Delta EBIT} = \frac{\frac{\Delta EPS}{EPS}}{\frac{\Delta EBIT}{EBIT}} = \frac{\Delta EPS}{EPS} \times \frac{EBIT}{\Delta EBIT} \qquad (10.10)$$

A more direct way for calculating the operating leverage is

$$DFL = \frac{EBIT}{EBT - \frac{PD}{(1 - Tax\ Rate)}} \qquad (10.11)$$

where EBT is earnings before taxes and PD is the preferred dividends paid to holders of preferred stock.

Whenever the percentage change in EPS is greater than the percentage change in EBIT, DFL is greater than one and the firm is said to be financially leveraged.

Note that preferred stock is treated as part of a firm's debt in calculating financial leverage. (Although in one sense preferred stock is part of a firm's equity—that is, the owners' investment in the firm. In another sense preferred stock is part of a firm's debt, because dividends on preferred stock are fixed and must be paid before dividends to holders of common stock). Investors who hold preferred stock are guaranteed to receive their dividends before holders of common stock. Payments to preferred stockholders therefore reduce the earnings per share (EPS) available to common stockholders. Because preferred dividends are paid with *after*-tax dollars, the second term of the denominator of equation 10.11 is needed to reduce the EBT— the earnings *before* taxes—by the *before*-tax dollars needed to pay preferred dividends.

Substituting values from the income statement for the ABC Company into equation 10.11 gives

$$DFL = \frac{\$770,000}{\$710,000 - \frac{\$95,000}{(1 - 0.40)}} = \frac{\$770,000}{\$551,667} = 1.40$$

Degree of Combined or Total Leverage

Most firms use both operating and financial leverage in establishing their capital structure. The combined effect of the two is given by the degree of combined or total leverage (DCL), which is defined as the product of the first two; that is,

$$DCL = DOL \times DFL = \frac{\%\Delta EBIT}{\%\Delta Sales} \times \frac{\%\Delta EPS}{\%\Delta EBIT} = \frac{\%\Delta EPS}{\%\Delta Sales} \qquad (10.12)$$

Equation 10.12 can also be written in the following form:

$$DCL = \frac{Q \times (P - VC)}{Q \times (P - VC) - FC - I - \left(PD \times \dfrac{1}{1-T}\right)} \qquad (10.13)$$

where I equals the amount of interest, T is the tax rate, and the other symbols are as defined previously.

The combined leverage for the ABC Company is calculated as follows from the values of OLR and FLR calculated earlier:

$$DCL = 1.85 \times 1.40 = 2.59$$

Leverage, Risk, and Rate of Return

The rate of return required to justify making an investment varies with the level of risk associated with the investment and with its potential gains and losses. The greater the risk, the greater should be the projected rate of return to justify taking the risk. In this section we discuss the minimum acceptable rate of return and its relationship to the leverage ratios and the degree of risk.

The risks for a firm's debit and equity are measured by their beta values, and the total risk is the weighted average of the betas of the debt and equity; that is,

$$\beta_{Asset} = \frac{Debt}{Debt + Equity} \times \beta_{Debt} + \frac{Equity}{Debt + Equity} \times \beta_{Equity} \qquad (10.14)$$

Equation 10.14 indicates that the beta of a company's fiancial structure, or its **asset beta**, is the sum of the beta for debt multiplied by the fraction (or percent) of debt in the firm's financial structure plus the beta for equity multiplied by the fraction (or percent) of equity in the firm's financial structure. Because the beta for debt is very low in practice, we can assume that it is zero and simplify equation 10.14 to

$$\beta_{Asset} = \frac{Equity}{Debt + Equity} \times \beta_{Equity} \qquad (10.15)$$

Furthermore, the fraction $Equity/(Debt + Equity)$ is less than one for a levered company, so that $\beta_{Asset} < \beta_{Equity}$ and, by rearrangement of equation 10.15,

$$\beta_{Equity} = \beta_{Asset}\left(1 + \frac{Debt}{Equity}\right) \qquad (10.16)$$

If corporate taxes are included, the relationship between a firm's asset beta and its equity beta is given by the relationship

$$\beta_{Equity} = \beta_{Asset}\left(1 + (1-T) \times \frac{Debt}{Equity}\right) \tag{10.17}$$

Concluding Remarks

What happens in a firm's marketing and operating divisions goes directly to the values on the firm's income statement. Excel's tools for regression analysis, sensitivity analysis, and optimization help make spreadsheets useful tools for analyzing the impacts of different management strategies and tactics on a firm's profits, break-even points, and leverage—and then for choosing the best strategy for implementing.

Leverage ratios measure how well firms are using their resources. Operating leverage reflects the degree to which fixed assets and their associated fixed costs are utilized relative to variable operating costs. Financial leverage reflects the degree to which debt is utilized relative to a firm's equity—that is, to its debt-to-equity ratio.

Students' Feedback on Leverage

The aspect on this lesson I appreciated the most was the discussion of leverage. Financial and operating leverage is a crucial determinant of profitability and a strong indication of the riskiness of a firm's stock. For example, one hears financial commentators currently talking about owning "deep cyclicals" and companies that are "leveraged" to an economic recovery. What this really means is that these types of companies usually carry more debt (financial leverage) than other companies on average. They also tend to be companies that have high fixed costs relative to variable costs in their operations. Their fortunes are tied closely to the state of the economy. Therefore, with a significant amount of leverage (financial and operational), when the economy improves, not only do these types of firms experience revenue growth, but the profitability growth can be 100 to 200% greater, because of the leverage. As the economy moves through other phases of the cycle, different companies with different leverage characteristics become more attractive investments, relatively speaking.

※ ※ ※

My company relies heavily on the leverage ratios for analysis. These leverage ratios are the "elasticities" we learned in our microeconomics course and they are used for managerial decision making. … The leverage ratios are used as risk management tools. A standard forecast error is the most accurate measure of risk but does not indicate the source of risk. The CAPM uses a company-specific beta to determine a risk-adjusted rate of return. Leverage ratios fall somewhere in between the standard forecast error and the risk-adjusted rate of return. The leverage ratios measure risk and identify two specific sources of risk: fixed operating expenses and financing charges (interest expense and lease payments). I think this is an important chapter because it teaches us how to model the leverage ratios, an important risk mitigation tool. This gives us a clearer picture of the uncertainties we are dealing with.

※ ※ ※

I like this chapter. It points out the value of a company with low debt. Since I'm a value-oriented investor with long holding periods in mind for investments, it makes sense to look for companies with low leverage. That way they don't go under in tough economic times.

※ ※ ※

(Continued)

Is debt a bad thing? It all depends. You have to look at whether a company can service its debt, what its prospects are, etc. Just because a company has low debt doesn't mean it is a good investment option.

Companies unwilling to take on debt are also often very conservative in aggressively attacking their marketplace. They have their place in a portfolio, but I wouldn't make up an entire portfolio with safe companies.

* * *

Companies that are visibly fearful of using debt to take advantage of its benefits will get mowed down in this market. Being conservative is nice, but it doesn't allow the risk you need to take to gain the reward part of investments.

High leverage ratios increase profitability during times of increasing sales and lowering costs. This will be reflected in increases in a firm's return on assets (ROA) and return on equity (ROE). The reverse is also true when sales decrease or costs increase.

Leverage is a two-edged sword; it magnifies the potential for both gain and loss. Thus, borrowing to finance the acquisition of fixed assets amplifies the potential gain but also increases the potential loss. Gain occurs when earnings increase at a greater rate than the cost of the amount borrowed. Loss occurs when the interest and principal payments on the amount borrowed (which are known at the time of borrowing) are higher than the amount earned by the investment (which is not known until afterward). The level of risk depends on how well future earnings can be forecast—both their magnitude and their probability. We will use Monte Carlo simulation and the probability distributions for future revenues and costs to develop risk curves for capital investments in Chapter 15.

Chapter 11

Depreciation and Taxes

CHAPTER OBJECTIVES

Management Skills

- Understand the concept of depreciation and the various types of depreciation schedules used in business.
- Understand the difference between income tax on regular income and income tax on capital gains and be able to calculate them.

Spreadsheet Skills

- Use Excel's function commands to calculate depreciation schedules for capital assests.

Overview

Depreciation and taxes are essential elements of the financial statements covered in Chapter 1. They are also essential elements of capital budget plans, which are discussed in the four chapters that follow.

Government is a silent (and sometimes not so silent) partner of business. Federal, state, and local governments share in the profits and losses of firms through their powers to set rates for depreciation and taxes.

Both depreciation and taxes are large and complex topics, with many modifications of the general rules for exceptional situations. Although the general concepts remain, details change from year to year. Contact the Internal Revenue Service, *www.irs.gov*, for the latest federal rules, and contact state and local governments for others that apply.

Depreciation

Depreciation is an accounting technique that systematically reduces the book value of a capital asset over the asset's lifetime. It is an important item in the financial statements discussed in earlier chapters. Depreciation is an allowable business expense and has an important effect on reducing a firm's tax liability for earned income. For the latest rules on depreciation, consult the current edition of *IRS Publication 534: Depreciation*.

The Concept of Depreciation

Assume that a company spends $1 million to support its operations. Can it then deduct the entire $1 million from its earnings to determine its profits for the same year?

The answer depends on what the $1 million was spent for. If, for example, it was paid as wages to workers or to purchase goods that were sold the same year, the entire $1 million is an allowable operating expense. As an allowable expense, it can be deducted from earnings in order to determine the company's taxable income, its income tax, and the income left after paying taxes.

If, however, the $1 million was spent to construct a factory or to purchase a major item of equipment that remains at the end of the year, only a portion of the $1 million is an allowable expense. Only a portion can be deducted from earnings in order to determine the company's tax liability. The Internal Revenue Service (IRS) regards the $1 million as being spent on a capital asset that remains rather than being consumed in the company's operations. The money is still there, the IRS reasons, but in a different form than dollars.

How, then, can a company recover its costs for capital investments? The answer is through depreciation. Depreciation is the process of spreading the cost of an asset against earned income over a period of time. Analysts describe the bookkeeping entries as "writing off" the cost of an asset. Depreciation allows companies to reduce the book values of their investments year by year over the asset's lifetime. The depreciation is an allowable operating expense that can be deducted from earnings to determine taxable income and profit.

Federal laws governing depreciation change from time to time. The 1981 Economic Recovery Act radically revised depreciation rules by replacing traditional depreciation methods by the Accelerated Cost Recovery System (ACRS). ACRS was modified by the Tax Reform Act that became effective January 1, 1987 and replaced it with the Modified Accelerated Cost Recovery System (MACRS). ACRS and MACRS cover the depreciation of most assets placed into service after 1981. Situations remain, however, when other methods are still appropriate.

Depreciable Property

Depreciable property includes tangible goods, such as business buildings and equipment, as well as certain intangible goods, such as patents, copyrights, and franchises. (Depreciation of intangible goods is called amortization, which is usually done by the straight-line method described below.) To be depreciable, property must meet all three of the following requirements:

1. It must be used in business or held for the production of income.
2. It must have a determinable life longer than one year or one business cycle.
3. It must be something that wears out, decays, gets used up, becomes obsolete, or loses value from natural causes.

Although a building is depreciable, the land on which it is erected is **not**. Land is not considered a depreciable asset because it has an infinite life. (Depletion allowances rather than depreciation are used for the exhaustion of mineral and petroleum deposits or the cutting of standing timber.)

Only the owner of depreciable property can depreciate it. One who merely rents or leases property cannot depreciate it. (For tax purposes, a business tenant recovers any costs of renting or leasing as an operating expense.)

Depreciable Life

The shorter an asset's depreciable life, the more quickly after-tax cash flow is created by the depreciation write-off.

Table 11-1 lists the depreciable lifetimes or recovery periods allowed by the IRS for eight classes of common assets. The 3-, 5-, 7-, and 10-year classes are the ones used most routinely by business. For assets not listed in the Table 11-1, consult *IRS Publication 534: Depreciation* or a tax adviser. If an asset does not match one of the descriptions in the publication, it means the IRS has not assigned a lifetime to it. In that case, use a lifetime of seven years.

Table 11-1

Class Lives of Some Common Assets (Reference: *IRS Publication 534: Depreciation*)

Class Life, years	Asset
3	Research and experimental equipment, certain special tools, over-the-road tractors, and racehorses
5	Computers, word-processing systems, typewriters, copiers, duplicating equipment, calculators, cars, light-duty trucks, airplanes, and qualified technological equipment
7	Office furniture and fixtures, most manufacturing equipment, and printing and typesetting equipment
10	Equipment used in petroleum refining or in the manufacture of tobacco and certain food products, barges, and tugs
15	Land improvements
20	Farm buildings
27.5	Residential real estate
39	Nonresidential real estate placed into service after 5-12-93 (31.5 years for nonresidential real estate placed into service after 12-31-86 and before 5-13-93)

Traditional or Classical Depreciation Methods

Before ACRS and MACRS were created, other methods were used to calculate depreciation. These methods are still used for property placed into service before 1981 and for intangible and other property that does not qualify for ACRS or MACRS.

Firms may use different methods for the same asset depending on whether they are preparing income tax statements or corporate financial statements. For tax purposes, the depreciation of corporate assets is regulated by the Internal Revenue Code. Compared to the straight-line method described below, ACRS and MACRS provide accelerated rates of depreciation that increase deductions, lower taxable income, and reduce income tax during the early periods of an asset's life. This means a firm recovers the cost of its capital investments more quickly and, because money has a time value, provides a higher net present value and rate of return than the straight-line method. When allowed, straight-line depreciation is used if a firm expects to have offsetting losses during an asset's early years and wishes to defer the depreciation deduction to offset large incomes in later years.

Straight-Line Depreciation

The total amount to be depreciated (TD) is the difference between an asset's cost or price (P) and its salvage value (S) at the end of its life. That is,

$$TD = P - S \tag{11.1}$$

From one point of view, salvage value is an estimate of what the capital asset can be sold for at the end of its life. It equals the original cost of the equipment less the dollar equivalent of the wear and tear the asset suffers during its use. It is also subject to technical obsolescence, which may reduce its value even further. On the other hand, inflation may increase an asset's market value over its original cost, as in the case of hotels and office buildings. For these reasons, salvage value should not be confused with market value. An asset's salvage value and its market value at the end of its life are entirely different concepts and may have no real relationships to each other.

For straight-line depreciation, the total depreciation is written off at a constant rate. The annual depreciation (AD) is therefore the total depreciation divided by the number of years (N) in the asset's lifetime. That is,

$$AD = \frac{TD}{N} = \frac{P-S}{N} \tag{11.2}$$

The Excel command for straight-line depreciation is

$$\text{SLN}(cost, \, salvage, \, life)$$

where *cost* is the initial cost of the asset, *salvage* is the asset's value at the end of its life, and *life* is the number of years over which the asset is being depreciated.

The book value (BV) of a capital asset at any time is its original cost less the accumulated depreciation. For an asset having a lifetime of N years that is depreciated by the straight-line method for n years (where $n<=N$), the book value at the end of the nth year (BV_n) can be calculated as

$$BV_n = P - TD\left(\frac{n}{N}\right) \tag{11.3}$$

Example 11.1: A company purchases special equipment for \$75,000. The equipment will be subjected to wear and will need to be replaced in five years. Its salvage value at the end of five years is estimated to be \$10,000. What are the total and annual depreciation, and what is the equipment's book value at the end of each year if it is depreciated by the straight-line method?

Solution: Figure 11-1 is a spreadsheet solution. Note that the book value has been depreciated to the salvage value at the end of the fifth year.

Sum-of-the-Years-Digits Depreciation

The **sum-of-the-years-digits** (SYD) method provides faster depreciation than the straight-line method. Since money has a time value, it is generally advantageous to write off the cost of capital assets as rapidly as possible.

The sum of the year's digits (SYD) over a lifetime of N years is simply

$$SYD = 1 + 2 + 3 + ... + (N-1) + N \tag{11.4}$$

For example, the sum of the years digits for a lifetime of five years is 15 (i.e., $1 + 2 + 3 + 4 + 5$).

Figure 11-1

Straight-Line Depreciation

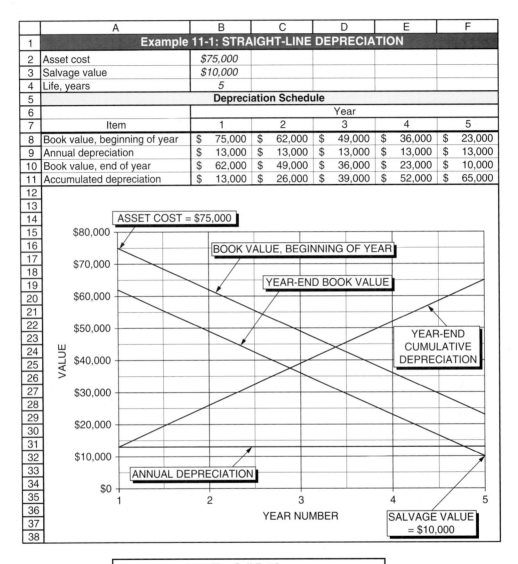

	A	B	C	D	E	F
1	Example 11-1: STRAIGHT-LINE DEPRECIATION					
2	Asset cost	$75,000				
3	Salvage value	$10,000				
4	Life, years	5				
5	Depreciation Schedule					
6		Year				
7	Item	1	2	3	4	5
8	Book value, beginning of year	$ 75,000	$ 62,000	$ 49,000	$ 36,000	$ 23,000
9	Annual depreciation	$ 13,000	$ 13,000	$ 13,000	$ 13,000	$ 13,000
10	Book value, end of year	$ 62,000	$ 49,000	$ 36,000	$ 23,000	$ 10,000
11	Accumulated depreciation	$ 13,000	$ 26,000	$ 39,000	$ 52,000	$ 65,000

Key Cell Entries

B8: =B2
C8: =B10, copy to D8:F8
B9: =SLN($B2,$B3,$B4), copy to C8:F8
B10: =B8–B9, copy to C10:F10
B11: =SUM($B$9:B9), copy to C11:F11

In using the sum-of-the-years-digits method of depreciation, the first year's depreciation (AD_1) is calculated as

$$AD_1 = \frac{N}{SYD}TD \qquad (11.5)$$

and the second year's depreciation (AD_2) is calculated as

$$AD_2 = \frac{N-1}{SYD} TD \tag{11.6}$$

This procedure is continued, with the numerator above SYD decreasing by 1 each year from its initial value to 1 for the last year of the asset's lifetime. Thus, the last year's depreciation is

$$AD_N = \frac{1}{SYD} TD \tag{11.7}$$

In general, the equation for calculating the annual depreciation in any year n from 1 to N is

$$AD_n = \frac{N+1-n}{SYD} TD \tag{11.8}$$

Excel's command for calculating the depreciation during any period is

SYD(*cost, salvage, life, period*)

where cost is the initial cost of the asset, salvage is the asset's value at the end of its life, life is the number of periods over which the asset is depreciated, and period is the number of the period (e.g., the year if life is measured in years, or the quarter if life is measured in quarters) for which depreciation is to be calculated.

Example 11.2: Solve Example 11.1 with sum-of-the-years-digits depreciation rather than straight-line.

Solution: Figure 11-2 is a spreadsheet solution. Note that the book value has been depreciated to the salvage value at the end of the fifth year.

Declining-Balance Depreciation

Since the fair market value of a capital asset is generally highest in the year of its purchase and declines continuously thereafter, it seems reasonable that the amount of annual depreciation should be adjusted yearly to make it proportional to the asset's changing value. This gives rise to **declining-balance** (DB) methods of depreciation. Like the SYD method, DB methods write down an asset's value faster than the STL method and are a means for accelerating depreciation.

With DB methods, the annual depreciation is calculated by multiplying the asset's book value at the beginning of the period by a rate that is different for different types of assets. When depreciating by the **double-declining-balance** method, the rate of depreciation is twice that for STL depreciation. For example, an asset with a five-year life would have an annual rate of depreciation of 20 percent for STL depreciation and 40 percent for double-declining-balance (DDB) depreciation. For some assets depreciated by the DB method, the rate is 1.5 times the straight-line rate.

Figure 11-2

Sum-of-the-Years-Digits Depreciation

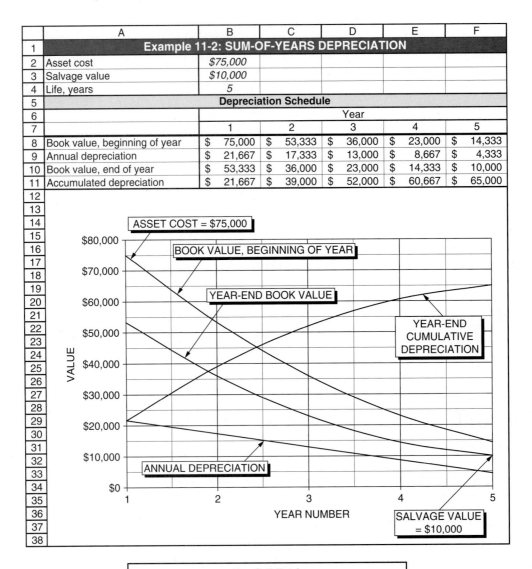

	A	B	C	D	E	F
1	Example 11-2: SUM-OF-YEARS DEPRECIATION					
2	Asset cost	$75,000				
3	Salvage value	$10,000				
4	Life, years	5				
5	Depreciation Schedule					
6		Year				
7		1	2	3	4	5
8	Book value, beginning of year	$ 75,000	$ 53,333	$ 36,000	$ 23,000	$ 14,333
9	Annual depreciation	$ 21,667	$ 17,333	$ 13,000	$ 8,667	$ 4,333
10	Book value, end of year	$ 53,333	$ 36,000	$ 23,000	$ 14,333	$ 10,000
11	Accumulated depreciation	$ 21,667	$ 39,000	$ 52,000	$ 60,667	$ 65,000

Key Cell Entries

B8: =B2
C8: =B10, copy to D11:F11
B9: =SYD($B$2,$B$3,$B$4,B7), copy to C9:F9
B10: =B8–B9, copy to C10:F10
B11: =SUM($B$9:B9), copy to C11:F11

Salvage value is not included in calculations based on traditional DB depreciation, except that the total depreciation cannot exceed the difference between the cost of an asset and its salvage value. When the salvage value is low in relation to original cost, the total depreciation calculated by the DB method may be less than the difference between cost and salvage value. In such cases, a firm will switch to either the straight-line or SYD method to make the final book value equal to the salvage value. Usually a firm will defer this choice as long as it is to its advantage. In practice, this means not making the conversion to STL or SYD so long as DB provides more depreciation. Once the switch is made, however, IRS rules do not allow a change back to the declining-balance method.

Excel's command for declining-balance depreciation is

$$DDB(cost, salvage, life, period, factor)$$

where *cost* is the initial cost of the asset, *salvage* is the asset's value at the end of the depreciation, *life* is the number of *periods* over which the asset is being depreciated, *period* is the number of the period (e.g., the year if *life* is measured in years, or the quarter if *life* is measured in quarters) for which the depreciation is to be calculated, and *factor* is the rate at which the balance declines. The value of *factor* is 2 for double-declining balance and 1.5 for 150%-declining balance. If a value is omitted for factor in the command, it is assumed to be 2.

Example 11.3: Solve Example 11.1 with double-declining balance depreciation rather than straight-line.

Solution: Figure 11-3 is a spreadsheet solution obtained by using the DDB command. Note that the book value has been depreciated to the salvage value at the end of the fourth year and there has been no further depreciation during the fifth year. This is because 40 percent of the book value of $16,200 at the end of three years equals $6480, which would have resulted in a book value of $9700 at the end of the fourth year, which is less than the salvage value of $10,000.

Figure 11-3

Double-Declining Balance Depreciation (without adjustment for salvage value)

	A	B	C	D	E	F
1	Example 11-3: DOUBLE-DECLINING BALANCE DEPRECIATION					
2	Asset cost	$75,000				
3	Salvage value	$10,000				
4	Life, years	5				
5	Depreciation Schedule					
6		Year				
7		1	2	3	4	5
8	Book value, beginning of year	$ 75,000	$ 45,000	$ 27,000	$ 16,200	$ 10,000
9	Annual depreciation	$ 30,000	$ 18,000	$ 10,800	$ 6,200	$ -
10	Book value, end of year	$ 45,000	$ 27,000	$ 16,200	$ 10,000	$ 10,000
11	Accumulated depreciation	$ 30,000	$ 48,000	$ 58,800	$ 65,000	$ 65,000

Key Cell Entries
B8: =B2
C8: =B10, copy to D8:F8
B9: =DDB($B2,$B3,$B4,B7,2), copy to C9:F9
B10: =B8–B9, copy to C10:F10
B11: =SUM($B9:B9), copy to C11:F11

(Continued)

Figure 11-4 shows an adjusted DDB solution. The correction is made by using the straight-line method to calculate depreciation for the last two years. Because the total depreciation during the last two years is $6200 (calculated as the difference between the book value at the beginning of the fourth year and the salvage value), the SLN method during years four and five is $3100, or one-half the total.

The SYD method can be used instead of the SLN method for the last two years. In that case, the depreciation for the fourth year would have been $4133 (i.e., 2/3 of $6200), and for the fifth year it would have been $2067 (1/3 of $6200).

Figure 11-4

Double-Declining Balance Depreciation with Adjustment

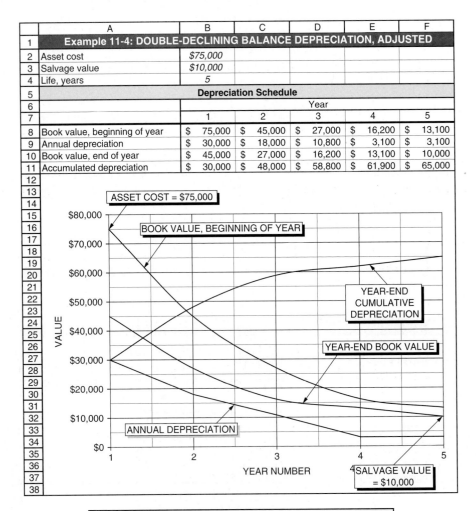

	A	B	C	D	E	F
1	Example 11-4: DOUBLE-DECLINING BALANCE DEPRECIATION, ADJUSTED					
2	Asset cost	$75,000				
3	Salvage value	$10,000				
4	Life, years	5				
5	Depreciation Schedule					
6		Year				
7		1	2	3	4	5
8	Book value, beginning of year	$ 75,000	$ 45,000	$ 27,000	$ 16,200	$ 13,100
9	Annual depreciation	$ 30,000	$ 18,000	$ 10,800	$ 3,100	$ 3,100
10	Book value, end of year	$ 45,000	$ 27,000	$ 16,200	$ 13,100	$ 10,000
11	Accumulated depreciation	$ 30,000	$ 48,000	$ 58,800	$ 61,900	$ 65,000

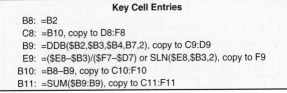

Key Cell Entries
B8: =B2
C8: =B10, copy to D8:F8
B9: =DDB($B2,$B3,$B4,B7,2), copy to C9:D9
E9: =($E8–$B3)/($F7–$D7) or SLN($E8,$B3,2), copy to F9
B10: =B8–B9, copy to C10:F10
B11: =SUM($B9:B9), copy to C11:F11

Modified Accelerated Cost Recovery System (MACRS)

Prior to January 1, 1981, the traditional methods of depreciation described earlier were used for tax purposes. The Tax Reform Act of 1980 established new rules for declining balance depreciation called the **Accelerated Cost Recovery System (ACRS)**. ACRS was subsequently changed to the **Modified Accelerated Cost Recovery System (MACRS)**. In brief, ACRS applies to assets placed in service after December 31, 1980 and before January 1, 1987, and MACRS applies to property placed in service after December 31, 1986.

MACRS generally provides faster write-offs than the depreciation methods it replaces. Under MACRS, a taxpayer does not have to anticipate the useful life of an asset or its salvage value, nor decide the method of depreciation. These are automatically fixed by law according to the type of asset. Over an asset's depreciable life, its entire original cost is recovered. It is important to recognize that the yearly depreciation is calculated on the basis of the **original cost**, without subtracting an expected salvage value.

Table 11-2 lists MACRS depreciation allowances for properties with different class lives. Depreciation begins when an asset is **"ready and available"** for use in a trade or business, regardless of when the asset was purchased or when its *actual* use began. Mid-quarter or half-year conventions are used depending on when depreciation begins—either in the first, second, third, or fourth quarter, or in the first or second half of the year.

Each property class has two recovery periods. The **General Depreciation System (GDS)**, referred to as "regular MACRS," is usually of shorter length and provides a more rapid write-off. The other recovery period is the **Alternative Depreciation System (ADS)**, referred to as "Alternate MACRS," which applies straight-line depreciation over the recovery period. ADS or straight-line depreciation has a slower rate of write-off and **may** be elected for most property; it is **mandatory**, however, in some situations (e.g., for imported property, foreign-use property, tax-exempt use property, and automobiles used 50 percent or less for business). The election is irrevocable and must be made by the due date (including extensions) of the return for the year in which the property is placed in service.

Example 11.5: Use MACRS to solve Example 11.1. Assume that the asset was placed into service during April, May, or June. Show the annual depreciation and end-of-year book values for six years.

Solution: Figure 11-5 is a spreadsheet solution. Note that depreciation rates in Cells B8:G8 are those listed in Table 11-2 for the mid-quarter convention based on acquiring the asset in the second quarter. The final amount of depreciation (4.26%, or $3,195l) does not occur until the sixth year.

Income Tax

Taxes are of various types, such as sales taxes, gasoline taxes, property taxes, and income taxes. In this chapter we focus on the income taxes imposed on the earnings of private, for-profit companies. These include taxes on both ordinary income and on capital gains. Our coverage here examines only the fundamental concepts of income tax laws that apply to most businesses.

Table 11-2

MACRS Depreciation (For property placed in service after December 31, 1986)

3-Year Property

(Tractor units for use over the road, race horses over two years old, and any other horses over 12 years old)

Year	Half-Year Convention	Mid-Quarter Convention			
		Quarter in which acquired			
		1st	2nd	3rd	4th
1	33.33%	58.33%	41.67%	25.00%	8.33%
2	44.45	27.78	38.89	50.00	61.11
3	14.81	12.35	14.14	16.67	20.37
4	7.41	1.54	5.30	8.33	10.19

5-Year Property

(Taxis, buses, automobiles, light trucks, computers, typewriters, calculators, and copiers)

	MACRS Depreciation					Optional Straight-Line Depreciation				
	Half-Year	Mid-Quarter Convention				Half-Year	Mid-Quarter Convention			
		Quarter in which acquired					Quarter in which acquired			
Year	Convention	1st	2nd	3rd	4th	Convention	1st	2nd	3rd	4th
1	20.00%	35.00%	25.00%	15.00%	5.00%	10%	17.5%	12.5%	7.5%	2.5%
2	32.00	26.00	30.00	34.00	38.00	20	20.0	20.0	20.0	20.0
3	19.20	15.60	18.00	20.40	22.80	20	20.0	20.0	20.0	20.0
4	11.52	11.01	11.37	12.24	13.68	20	20.0	20.0	20.0	20.0
5	11.52	11.01	11.37	11.30	10.94	20	20.0	20.0	20.0	20.0
6	5.76	1.38	4.26	7.06	9.58	10	2.5	7.5	12.5	17.5

7-Year Property

(Office furniture fixtures, equipment, and any property that does not have a class life and that is not, by aw, in any other class)

MACRS Depreciation / Optional Straight-Line Depreciation

Year	Half-Year Convention	Mid-Quarter Convention — Quarter in which acquired				Half-Year Convention	Mid-Quarter Convention — Quarter in which acquired			
		1st	2nd	3rd	4th		1st	2nd	3rd	4th
1	14.29%	25.00%	17.85%	10.71%	3.57%	7.14%	12.50%	8.93%	5.36%	1.79%
2	24.49	21.43	23.47	25.51	27.55	14.29	14.29	14.29	14.29	14.29
3	17.49	15.31	16.76	18.22	19.68	14.29	14.28	14.28	14.28	14.28
4	12.49	10.93	11.97	13.02	14.06	14.28	14.29	14.29	14.29	14.29
5	8.93	8.75	8.87	9.30	10.04	14.29	14.28	14.28	14.23	14.28
6	8.92	8.74	8.87	8.85	8.73	14.28	14.29	14.29	14.23	14.29
7	8.93	8.75	8.87	8.86	8.73	14.29	14.28	14.28	14.23	14.28
8	4.46	1.09	3.33	5.53	7.64	7.14	1.79	5.36	8.93	12.50

MACRS—RESIDENTIAL RENTAL PROPERTY, 27.5-YEAR DEPRECIABLE LIFE

(Residential houses and apartments)

Straight-Line, Mid-Month Convention

Year	Month Placed in Service											
	1	2	3	4	5	6	7	8	9	10	11	12
1	3.485%	3.182%	2.879%	2.576%	2.273%	1.970%	1.667%	1.364%	1.061%	0.758%	0.455%	0.152%
2–9	3.636	3.636	3.636	3.636	3.636	3.636	3.636	3.636	3.636	3.636	3.636	3.636
10	3.637	3.637	3.637	3.637	3.637	3.637	3.636	3.636	3.636	3.636	3.636	3.636
11	3.636	3.636	3.636	3.636	3.636	3.636	3.637	3.637	3.637	3.637	3.637	3.636
12	3.637	3.637	3.637	3.637	3.637	3.636	3.636	3.636	3.636	3.636	3.636	3.637
13	3.636	3.636	3.636	3.636	3.636	3.637	3.637	3.637	3.637	3.637	3.636	3.636
14	3.637	3.637	3.637	3.637	3.637	3.636	3.636	3.636	3.636	3.636	3.637	3.637
15	3.636	3.636	3.636	3.636	3.636	3.637	3.637	3.637	3.636	3.636	3.636	3.636
16	3.637	3.637	3.637	3.637	3.637	3.636	3.636	3.636	3.637	3.637	3.637	3.637
17	3.636	3.636	3.636	3.636	3.636	3.636	3.637	3.637	3.637	3.636	3.636	3.636

(Continued)

Table 11-2

MACRS Depreciation (For property placed in service after December 31, 1986) (Continued)

MACRS—NONRESIDENTIAL REAL PROPERTY, 39-YEAR DEPRECIABLE LIFE

(Nonresidential rental property such as office buildings, warehouses, and qualified home offices that were placed into service after May 12, 1993)

Straight-Line, Mid-Month Convention

Year	Month Placed in Service											
	1	2	3	4	5	6	7	8	9	10	11	12
1	2.461%	2.247%	2.033%	1.819%	1.605%	1.391%	1.177%	0.963%	0.749%	0.535%	0.321%	0.107%
2–39	2.564	2.564	2.564	2.564	2.564	2.564	2.564	2.564	2.564	2.564	2.564	2.564
40	0.107	0.321	0.535	0.749	0.963	1.177	1.391	1.605	1.819	2.033	2.247	2.461

MACRS—NONRESIDENTIAL REAL PROPERTY, 31.5-YEAR DEPRECIABLE LIFE

(Nonresidential rental property such as office buildings, warehouses, and qualified home offices that were placed into service after December 31, 1986 and before May 12, 1993)

Straight-Line, Mid-Month Convention

Year	Month Placed in Service											
	1	2	3	4	5	6	7	8	9	10	11	12
1	3.042%	2.778%	2.513%	2.249%	1.984%	1.720%	1.455%	1.190%	0.926%	0.661%	0.397%	0.132%
2–7	3.175	3.175	3.175	3.175	3.175	3.175	3.175	3.175	3.175	3.175	3.175	3.175
8	3.175	3.174	3.175	3.174	3.175	3.174	3.175	3.175	3.175	3.175	3.175	3.175
9	3.174	3.175	3.174	3.175	3.174	3.175	3.174	3.175	3.174	3.175	3.174	3.175
10	3.175	3.174	3.175	3.175	3.175	3.174	3.175	3.175	3.175	3.175	3.175	3.175

Figure 11-5

MACRS Depreciation

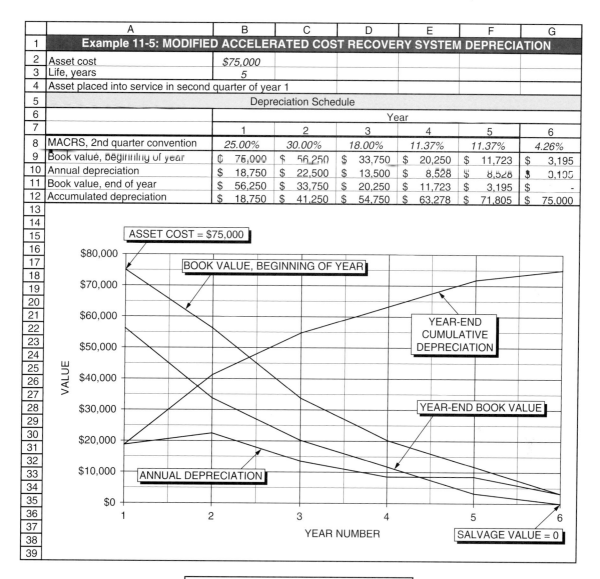

	A	B	C	D	E	F	G
1	Example 11-5: MODIFIED ACCELERATED COST RECOVERY SYSTEM DEPRECIATION						
2	Asset cost	$75,000					
3	Life, years	5					
4	Asset placed into service in second quarter of year 1						
5	Depreciation Schedule						
6		Year					
7		1	2	3	4	5	6
8	MACRS, 2nd quarter convention	25.00%	30.00%	18.00%	11.37%	11.37%	4.26%
9	Book value, beginning of year	$ 75,000	$ 56,250	$ 33,750	$ 20,250	$ 11,723	$ 3,195
10	Annual depreciation	$ 18,750	$ 22,500	$ 13,500	$ 8,528	$ 8,528	$ 3,195
11	Book value, end of year	$ 56,250	$ 33,750	$ 20,250	$ 11,723	$ 3,195	$ -
12	Accumulated depreciation	$ 18,750	$ 41,250	$ 54,750	$ 63,278	$ 71,805	$ 75,000

Key Cell Entries

B9: =B2
C9: =B11, copy to D9:G89
B10: =$B2*B8, copy to C10:G10
B11: =B9–B10, copy to C11:G11
B12: =SUM($B10:B10), copy to C12:G12

Table 11-3 summarizes the steps in moving from a company's income to its after-tax cash flow.

Table 11-3

From Sales Revenues to Net Income after Taxes

Sales Revenues (i.e., income from sale of goods or services)

− Cost of Goods Sold (COGS)

Gross Profit

− General and Administrative Expenses

Net Operating Income

+ Other Income (e.g., capital gains, interest income, and insurance proceeds)

− Other Expenses (e.g., capital losses and dividends)

Net Income before Taxes (or, Before-Tax Cash Flow)

− Depreciation

Taxable Income

− Federal Income Tax

− State Income Tax

− Local Income Tax

Net Income after Taxes (or, After-Tax Cash Flow)

Taxable Regular Income

The amount of a firm's taxes depends on its **taxable income** and the applicable **tax rate**. To calculate a firm's taxable income, we start with its total or *gross receipts or sales*, less any returns and allowances. From this we subtract the *cost of goods sold* (COGS) to determine the *gross profit*. In general, COGS is the price of buying or the cost of making an item that is sold. For retail firms, COGS is the purchase price of the items sold. For manufacturers, COGS is the sum of the direct material (i.e., raw materials, parts, and components), labor, and factory overhead expenses incurred in producing the finished products that are sold. Under the Uniform Capitalization Rules, a business may also be required to include an allocated portion of most indirect costs in computing COGS.

The **net operating income** is next calculated by deducting the *normal operating expenses* from the gross profit. Normal operating expenses are all ordinary and necessary expenses to conduct the business, *other than capital expenditures*. Examples include the compensation paid to corporate officers, employee salaries and wages, certain repair and maintenance expenses, rents, license fees, employee benefits, and so forth. These are classified as General and Administrative Expenses (G&A).

Except for land, the cost of any capital expenditure is recovered through depreciation, amortization, or depletion charges. (*Depletion charges* are similar to depreciation but apply to the exhaustion of natural resources such as mineral properties, oil and gas wells, and standing timber as a result of their removal.)

When an asset is sold, there is usually a *capital gain or loss*. Net capital gain income (or loss) is added to (or subtracted from) other income to determine the firm's taxable income. (There are specific rules for calculating net capital gain or loss that must be followed.)

Finally, the *taxable income* is calculated by subtracting other deductible expenses, such as the interest on loans or mortgages and depreciation from the sum of the net operating income and net capital-gain income.

Types of Business

The most common types of business are Corporations (or C Corporations), S Corporations, Partnerships, Sole Proprietorships, and Limited Liability Companies (LLC). Each type has different legal and tax considerations. The following information is quoted from the IRS Web site, www.irs.gov/businesses, which can be accessed for detailed information on taxes and instructions for filling out the tax forms.

Corporations (also know as C Corporations): In forming a corporation, prospective shareholders exchange money, property, or both, for the corporation's capital stock. A corporation generally takes the same deductions as a sole proprietorship to figure its taxable income. A corporation can also take special deductions. For federal income tax purposes, a C corporation is recognized as a separate taxpaying entity. A corporation conducts business, realizes net income or loss, pays taxes, and distributes profits to shareholders. The profit of a corporation is taxed to the corporation when earned, and then is taxed to the shareholders when distributed as dividends. This creates a double tax. The corporation does not get a tax deduction when it distributes dividends to shareholders. Shareholders cannot deduct any loss of the corporation.

S Corporations: An eligible domestic corporation can avoid double taxation (once to the shareholders and again to the corporation) by electing to be treated as an S corporation. Generally, an S corporation is exempt from federal income tax other than tax on certain capital gains and passive income. On their tax returns, the S corporation's shareholders include their share of the corporation's separately stated items of income, deduction, loss, and credit, and their share of nonseparately stated income or loss.

Partnerships: A partnership is the relationship existing between two or more persons who join to carry on a trade or business. Each person contributes money, property, labor or skill, and expects to share in the profits and losses of the business. A partnership must file an annual information return to report the income, deductions, gains, losses, etc. from its operations, but it does not pay income tax. Instead, it "passes through" any profits or losses to its partners. Each partner includes his or her share of the partnership's income or loss on his or her tax return.

Sole Proprietorships: A sole proprietor is someone who owns an unincorporated business by himself or herself. However, if you are the sole member of a domestic limited liability company (LLC), you are not a sole proprietor if you elect to treat the LLC as a corporation.

Limited Liability Companies (LLC): A Limited Liability Company (LLC) is a relatively new business structure allowed by state statute. LLCs are popular because, similar to a corporation, owners have limited personal liability for the debts and actions of the LLC. Other features of LLCs are more like a partnership, providing management flexibility and the benefit of pass-through taxation.

Owners of an LLC are called members. Since most states do not restrict ownership, members may include individuals, corporations, other LLCs, and foreign entities. There is no maximum number of members. Most states also permit "single member" LLCs: those having only one owner.

A few types of businesses generally cannot be LLCs, such as banks and insurance companies. Check your state's requirements and the federal tax regulations for further information. There are special rules for foreign LLCs.

Capital Expenditures and Capital-Gain Income

A firm's capital assets include items that are purchased for use in manufacturing products or providing services over long periods of time rather than products that are purchased for near-term wholesaling or retailing. The primary examples of capital assets are buildings, machinery, equipment, furniture, vehicles, etc. with a useful life of more than one year.

Capital expenditures are not treated as deductible operating expenses. Instead, the costs are recovered through depreciation, amortization, or depletion. This cost-recovery treatment extends to the costs for improvements that add value to an asset, that appreciably lengthen its useful life, or that adapt it to a different use.

When a capital asset is sold or exchanged, there is generally a **capital gain or loss**. For tax purposes, the amount of taxable capital gain or loss is the amount realized from the sale (i.e., the selling price less selling expenses) minus the asset's **adjusted tax basis**. An asset's adjusted tax basis is its original acquisition cost, including purchase expenses, plus the cost of any capital improvements less the cumulative depreciation at the time of sale. A taxpayer has the burden of proof to provide evidence for the adjusted tax basis.

When evaluating an investment's payoff, the focus is on the capital gain or loss for only the investment rather than on a company's total capital gain or loss.

The treatment of capital gains tax varies for individuals and for different types of corporations and partnerships. Tax treatments are subject to a number of qualifications, exceptions, and year-to-year changes that work to keep tax specialists employed. Therefore, the following are only general guidelines.

Individuals

If the asset is held more than 12 months before being sold, the capital gain or loss is treated as a **long-term gain or loss**; whereas if it is sold in less than 12 months from its purchase, the gain or loss is treated as a **short-term gain or loss**. For most types of capital assets, the maximum tax rate on long-term capital gains is currently 20 percent. However, for certain types of properties, the tax rate may be as high as 28 percent, and for qualified assets that have been held more than five years it drops to 18 percent. The maximum tax rate on short-term gains is the same as for ordinary income.

Corporations and Partnerships

For C corporations, capital losses can only be deducted to the extent of capital gains. If there are no capital gains to offset the losses, the losses can be carried back as far as three years and forward for up to 15 years from the loss year. For an S corporation or partnership, capital gains or losses are usually passed through to the shareholders or partners and are usually subject to the special tax treatment afforded individuals relative to capital gains and losses (assuming that the partner is an individual).

Tax Rates

Corporations and individuals may pay a combination of federal, state, and local taxes on their taxable income. Table 11-4 shows the federal tax rates for corporations. For example, the federal income tax for a corporation with taxable income of $80,000 would be $15,450, which is calculated as follows:

$$\$80,000 \times 34\% - \$11,750 = \$27,200 - \$11,750 = \$15,450$$

The tax rates for individuals apply to firms that are partnerships or sole proprietorships.

Table 11-4

Schedule of Federal Tax Rates for Corporations (for Tax Years beginning after December 31, 1992)

TAXABLE INCOME			×	%	MINUS	$	=	TAX
$0	to	$50,000	×	15%	minus	$0	=	Tax
$50,001	to	$75,000	×	25%	minus	$5,000	=	Tax
$75,001	to	$100,000	×	34%	minus	$11,750	=	Tax
$100,001	to	$335,000	×	39%	minus	$16,750	=	Tax
$335,001	to	$10,000,000	×	34%	minus	$0	=	Tax
$10,000 001	to	$15,000,000	×	35%	minus	$100,000	=	Tax
$15,000,001	to	$18,333,333	×	38%	minus	$550,000	=	Tax
$18,333,334	and over		×	35%	minus	$0	=	Tax

State and city taxes on the income of corporations doing business within their jurisdictions vary widely. The combined federal, state, and local tax rate on the regular income of large corporations is usually close to 40 percent.

For C corporations, the tax rate for capital gain is currently the same as the tax rate for ordinary corporate income. (At times in the past, however, **the rates for ordinary income and long-term capital gains or losses have been different**. We have allowed for this difference in some of the examples and spreadsheets in later chapters by specifying the rates for each in separate cells.)

Tax

Basically, as shown above, tax is the product obtained by multiplying the taxable income by the applicable tax rate. That is,

$$\text{Tax} = \text{Taxable Income} \times \text{Tax Rate} \tag{11.9}$$

where the taxable income is the difference between the firm's income or revenues and its deductible expenses; therefore,

$$\text{Taxable Income} = \text{Total Income or Revenues} - \text{Deductible Expenses} \tag{11.10}$$

where deductible expenses includes, for example, operating expenses (e.g., the costs for materials and labor, managers' salaries, building leases, and maintenance), depreciation, and mortgage interest. Note that depreciation is not a cash flow item, whereas all other items are.

After-Tax Cash Flow

The after-tax cash flow (ATCF) generated by an investment should be used as the basis for calculating an investment's net present value, rate of return, and break-even point. These are important criteria for evaluating investments and are discussed in the next chapter, which focuses on capital budgeting. The ATCF can be calculated for many situations (**but not all**) from the before-tax cash flow (BTCF), depreciation (DEP), and tax rate (TR) by the equation

$$\text{ATCF} = (\text{BTCF} - \text{DEP}) \times (1 - \text{TR}) + \text{DEP} \qquad (11.11)$$

Equation 11.11 can be derived from the basic relationship by the following steps:

$$
\begin{aligned}
\text{ATCF} &= \text{BTCF} - \text{Tax} \\
&= \text{BTCF} - \text{Taxable Income} \times \text{TR} \\
&= \text{BTCF} - (\text{BTCF} - \text{DEP}) \times \text{TR} \\
&= \text{BTCF} \times (1 - \text{TR}) + \text{DEP} \times \text{TR} \\
&= (\text{BTCF} - \text{DEP}) \times ((1 - \text{TR}) + \text{DEP} \times \text{TR} + \text{DEP} \times (1 - \text{TR})) \\
&= (\text{BTCF} - \text{DEP}) \times (1 - \text{TR}) + \text{DEP}
\end{aligned}
$$

To use equation 11.11 for calculating ATCF, depreciation is first subtracted from the BTCF, the difference is multiplied by 1 minus the tax rate, and the depreciation is then added back.

An important situation where Equation 11.11 is **not** correct is when there are mortgage payments. Although the *entire* amounts of mortgage payments are included in a firm's before-tax cash flow, **only the interest portion of mortgage payments is a deductible expense for computing taxable income and tax.**

Chapter 12

Capital Budgeting: The Basics

CHAPTER OBJECTIVES

Management Skills

- Identify the cash flows associated with capital budgeting and their timing.
- Understand the difference between an internal rate of return (IRR) and a modified internal rate of return (MIRR), and why using IRR can lead to errors.
- Use the correct financial criteria (e.g., net present value, modified internal rate of return, and years to break even) for evaluating investments in capital assets.
- Understand the importance of judgment, experience, and nonfinancial criteria to the proper selection of investments in capital assets.

Spreadsheet Skills

- Create worksheets that show the steps in moving from sales revenues to after-tax cash flow (or net income), including the places of depreciation and taxes in the process.
- Use Excel's financial commands to calculate financial measures of success, such as an investment's net present value (NPV), internal rate of return (IRR), modified internal rate of return (MIRR), and payback period (or years to break even).
- Formulate a nested IF statement to calculate the payback period (or years to break even).
- Create a two-variable input table that shows the sensitivity of financial measures of success to variations in real-world conditions, such as tax rates and the discount rate of money.
- Use Excel's Goal Seek and Solver tools to determine changes that must be made in order to achieve financial goals, such as achieving a given net present value, modified internal rate of return, or breaking even in a given time.
- Create a spreadsheet protocol for including judgment, experience, and nonfinancial criteria in the evaluation of alternate investments in capital assets.
- Use binary variables with Excel's Solver tool to identify the optimum choices from a list of potential projects that are competing for limited funds.

Introduction

Chief financial officers (CFOs) and other corporate executives are accountable for the safekeeping of the assets entrusted to them and for their efficient and profitable use. But that is not all! On top of managing existing assets, CFOs agree that one of their most important responsibilities is figuring out the best way to increase shareholders' equity. This can be done, for example, by investing in projects to produce and market new products, improve existing products, or reduce costs. Such projects may involve large expenditures for acquiring buildings, equipment, and land; for conducting research and development; or for improving distribution networks.

Investments in capital projects are long-term decisions that involve large sums of money, most of which must be raised from sources described in Chapter 9. Whatever investments are selected, they usually lock a company into a future mode of operation for years.

The goal of capital budgeting is simple: Increase shareholders' equity by investing capital in projects that make more money than they cost. The difficult part is choosing where to invest—that is, determining those projects with the highest rewards and the least risk. Companies that are most successful are continually involved in capital budgeting. They have ongoing programs for identifying, evaluating, and selecting long-term investments in projects that are vital to their financial well-being.

Capital budgeting involves the analysis and selection of long-term investments that satisfy company goals and are within the company's financial resources. The most common long-term investments are for the acquisition of *fixed assets*, such as land, factories, buildings, and equipment. Such assets are often referred to as *earning assets* because they are the means for a company's earning profits. Other examples of long-term investments include research and development of new products, redesigning existing products, and acquiring other companies. The end result of the capital budgeting process is the allocation of a company's capital resources in a way that appears to offer the best opportunities to increase shareholder wealth.

A **capital expenditure** is an outlay of funds that is expected to produce benefits over a period of time greater than one year, such as an investment in facilities or equipment. A **current expenditure**, on the other hand, is one that is expected to produce benefits within a year, such as a purchase of raw materials, goods for resale, or operating supplies.

The capital budgeting process begins with the generation of proposals. Ideas for new products, for example, may come from the suggestions of customers or the results of research and development. Ideas for reducing costs may come from employee suggestions or from technological advances in the equipment for manufacturing goods, providing services, or distributing products.

The costs and benefits (e.g., future cash flows) of the proposals are next determined and reviewed. For promising proposals, the financial manager selects the best financing method, which might be, for example, using funds from accumulated profits, borrowing from a bank or other lender, issuing bonds or additional shares of stock, or a combination of these.

For expensive proposals that cost more than a certain amount, an executive committee selects those that will be approved and funded. Approved proposals become projects. Small projects may be directed and controlled as part of a company's normal chain of command. Special project management teams are usually created for projects that are large, complex, and cut across a company's functional divisions or involve outside subcontractors. (Project management is a discipline that requires special leadership skills and uses formalized tools and methods that are described in the abundant literature on the subject.)

Executives periodically review the status of projects as they progress through the stages from conception to completion. A project may be continued, changed, accelerated, decelerated, or terminated at any stage.

The dilemma CFOs face in making investments is to balance aggressive measures to maximize profits through growth and greater efficiency on the one hand with the need to minimize risk on the other. This chapter and the next evaluate options in a deterministic manner that shows financial payoffs based on given conditions. This includes sensitivity analysis to understand how changes in conditions affect the payoffs. Unfortunately, conditions are not always certain. This leads to Chapter 15, which evaluates options in a probabilistic manner that determines the probabilities and risks associated with the payoffs that are caused by uncertainties in the conditions.

Cash Flows

Capital budgeting is concerned with cash flows. This focus on cash flows distinguishes capital budgeting from cost accounting, which treats profits and losses. For example, a purchase of equipment for $1 million cash is a **current cash outflow** of $1 million. However, if the equipment is depreciated by the straight line method over a period of 10 years to zero salvage value, its **current cost** is only $100,000. The balance of $900,000 shows up on the company's annual income statements for the next nine years as a depreciation cost of $100,000. Accumulated depreciation is shown on the balance sheet.

The cash flows associated with a project's capital budgeting analysis must be **the incremental cash flows** associated with the project. In other words, the relevant cash flows are those that occur *in addition to* those that the firm already has, or would continue to have if the project were not undertaken. For example, if introducing a new product reduces the sales revenues from an existing product, the relevant cash flow is only the increase in sales revenues—that is, the incremental cash flow is the sales revenue generated by the new product minus its impact on decreasing sales for an old product.

Cash flows should, of course, include the effects of depreciation and taxes, which are discussed in the preceding chapter. Calculations of an investment's net present value, rate of return, and payback period must be based on *after*-tax rather than *before*-tax cash flows. Determining the before-tax and after-tax cash flows is the key to capital budgeting.

Sunk costs should not be included in a project's cash flow analysis. Sunk costs are those that have been incurred in the past and cannot be recovered. Financing costs should also not be included in the cash flow analysis. Though important, financing costs are implicitly included in the discount rate that is used to evaluate a project's net present value and rate of return.

Cash flow streams have three phases: (1) an initial outlay, (2) future cash flows, and (3) a terminal cash flow. These are discussed in the sections that follow.

Initial Outlay

The initial outlay is the cash outflow that occurs at time zero (i.e., the beginning of the project). Initial outlays include all costs to get a project up and running. For example, the initial outlay for new equipment includes not only the price paid for it but also any shipping and installation expenses, plus the cost of training employees to operate the equipment. As another example, the initial outlay for a building includes not only the price paid to the seller but also any fees paid to a broker and any costs for remodeling to make the building suitable for its intended use. The sum of these costs is the depreciable base for the project. It is the amount that will be depreciated over the life of the project.

When new equipment is purchased to replace existing equipment, the amount received from selling the old equipment must be considered in calculating the initial outlay. This may involve tax considerations. When the market value or selling price of the old equipment exceeds its book value (i.e., its tax base minus accumulated depreciation), taxes must be paid on the difference, which represents a capital gain. On the other hand, when the selling price of the old equipment is less than its book value, there is a capital loss that reduces the firm's taxable income.

Prepaid expenses associated with the new capital asset (e.g., "up-front" payments on contracts for maintenance and other services) may also be included in the initial cash outflow.

Future Cash Flows

The projected future cash flows generated by the project include (1) **additional revenues**, (2) **cost savings**, (3) **additional expenses**, and (4) **taxes**. Additional revenues are typically the *incremental* sales revenues from new products, either new services or new manufactured goods. Cost savings may result from the use of new equipment that reduces the cost of labor (e.g., replacing manually operated machinery with automatic machinery), improvements in production efficiency, or lower costs for maintenance and repair. Additional expenses might include the costs of labor and materials associated with using the new equipment, hiring consultants or outside services to program computers or automatic equipment, or higher costs to maintain larger inventories of raw materials or finished goods. In addition, the initial investment may be followed by major maintenance and repair costs or subsequent capital investments to increase capacity or productivity. Major equipment overhauls and building expansions can qualify as capital expenditures rather than as additional operating expenses. Taxes are the income tax paid on the cash flows.

Depreciation, although it is a bookkeeping adjustment rather than an actual cash flow, has an important effect on after-tax cash flow. Depreciation reduces a firm's taxable income, and that, in turn, reduces a firm's tax. The net result of depreciation is therefore to increase a firm's after-tax cash flow.

Terminal Cash Flow

The terminal cash flow includes, in addition to the projected annual cash flow for the last period, certain cash flows that occur only in the final time period of the project. These include the cash flow from the sale of capital assets and its effect on taxes, the recovery of any investment in net working capital (e.g., the reduction in inventory costs), the payoff of any outstanding loans for acquiring the capital asset, and any shut-down expenses.

Financial Criteria

Among the criteria for evaluating capital budgets are (1) net present value (NPV), (2) internal rates of return (IRR), (3) modified internal rates of return (MIRR), and (4) payback or break-even periods. The calculations of these criteria are based on the after-tax cash flows projected for the investment.

Net Present Value

An investment's **net present value** (NPV) is the present value of all incremental cash flows associated with the investment. This includes the initial cash outflow for the investment (which is usually taken as a present value) and the values of future cash flows discounted back to their *present* values. The discount rate for discounting future values back to their present equivalents should not be less than the firm's cost of capital and should be adjusted for the investment's risk. If an investment's NPV is greater than zero, the investment will be profitable; conversely, if an investment's NPV is negative, it will lose money and be unprofitable.

Excel's NPV function calculates the net present value of a series of future cash flows. It has the following syntax:

$$\text{NPV}(\textit{rate,value1,value2,...})$$

where *rate* is the rate of discount over the length of one period and *value1,value2,...* is the series of future cash flows (up to a maximum of 29). The rate is based on the weighted annual cost of capital for making the investment. The series of cash flows must be equally spaced in time and occur at the end of each period. This means that value 1 occurs at the end of period 1, *value 2* at the end of period 2, and so forth.

Internal Rate of Return

The **internal rate of return** (IRR) is the discount rate that makes the present value of future benefits equal to the present value of any costs, thereby causing NPV to equal zero. If the rate of return for an investment with a five-year life is 10 percent, it means that the investment under consideration brings in enough revenue in five years to pay for itself and provide a return of 10 percent on the invested capital. Another way to say this is that if the firm finances its operation by borrowing money at an annual rate of 10 percent, the cash generated by the investment will be exactly the amount needed to repay the principal and interest charges for the loan in five years. Therefore, if the firm can borrow capital to finance the project at a lower rate of interest than the investment's rate of return, the investment will be profitable. On the other hand, if the rate paid to borrow money is higher than the investment's rate of return, the investment will lose money and be unprofitable.

Excel's IRR function calculates the internal rate of return of a series of cash flows. It has the following syntax:

$$IRR(value0,value1,value2,...,guess)$$

where rate is the rate of discount over the length of one period and value0,value1,value2,... is the series of cash flows occurring at the ends of equally space periods.

Note that the series of cash flows for the IRR function is slightly different from that for the NPV function. At least one of the values must be negative and at least one must be positive. The first value in the IRR function, value0, is at time zero, which may be interpreted as either the **end** of period zero or the **beginning** of the first period. Its value is the initial cash outflow for the investment. The second value, value1, and all subsequent values are at the ends of the future periods—the same as in the NPV function.

The argument guess is the number that you estimate is close to the value of IRR. (Excel is very tolerant and can use even wild guesses that are fairly wide of the mark.) In most cases, you do not need to provide a guess for the IRR calculation. If guess is omitted, Excel uses the default value of 0.10 (i.e., 10%). Excel starts with the guess or default value and uses an iterative technique to find a value for IRR that is accurate within 0.00001 percent. If IRR cannot find a result after 20 tries, it returns the #NUM! error value. If IRR gives the #NUM! error value, or if the result is not close to what you expected, try again with a different value for guess.

Although widely used, IRR suffers from several problems. To begin with, IRR assumes that any future cash flows have the same time value as IRR. That is, if the IRR of an investment equals 13 percent, it assumes that any future cash inflows are reinvested at the same rate of 13 percent. This assumption is satisfactory so long as reinvestment rates are close to the IRR. However, it is misleading when the calculated IRR is much higher or lower than current rates of interest charged by lenders or paid by borrowers. In such a situation, the modified internal rate of return is a more realistic value for the rate of return on an investment. Another problem with IRR is the possibility of several different solutions when initial cash outflows are followed by future cash outflows as well as inflows during a project's lifetime.

Modified Internal Rate of Return (MIRR)

The **modified internal rate of return** (MIRR) is based on both the cost of capital (i.e., the discount rate used for evaluating an investment's NPV) and the rate of interest received on the reinvestment of future cash flows. Its syntax is

$$MIRR(values,finance\_rate,reinvest\_rate)$$

where values is the series of cash flows (value0,value1,value2,...) occurring at the ends of equally space periods, finance_rate is the discount rate paid to finance the investment, and reinvest_rate is the rate of interest earned by reinvesting future cash flows.

As with the IRR function, at least one of the values in the MIRR function must be negative and at least one must be positive. The first value in the MIRR function, *value0*, is at time zero, which may be interpreted as either the **end** of period zero or the **beginning** of the first period. Its value is the initial cash outflow for the investment. The second value, *value1*, and all subsequent values are at the ends of the future periods—the *same* as in the NPV and IRR functions.

Comparison of IRR and MIRR

The evaluation of an investment's IRR assumes that any future cash flows are reinvested at the same rate as the IRR at the end of the analysis period. This can result in reinvestment rates that are unrealistically high.

Assume, for example, the situation shown in the spreadsheet of Figure 12-1. An investment of $100,000 (Cell B5) generates after-tax cash flows of $35,000 at the ends of years 1 to 4 and $50,000 at the end of year 5. If the discount rate is 10 percent (Cell B2), the IRR at the end of year 5 is 24.55% (Cell G7, computed by the entry = IRR(B5:G5,*guess*)). This result assumes that the $35,000 cash inflows at the ends of years 1 to 4 are reinvested at the calculated IRR rate of 24.55 percent and are allowed to accumulate to the end of year 5, when the accumulated values would be added to the $50,000 inflow at the end of year 5.

Figure 12-1

Comparison of IRR and MIRR

	A	B	C	D	E	F	G
1	COMPARISON OF IRR AND MIRR						
2	Discount Rate	10.00%					
3	Reinvest Rate	12.00%					
4	**Year**	0	1	2	3	4	5
5	Year-End Cash Flow	−$100,000	$35,000	$35,000	$35,000	$35,000	$50,000
6	NPV		−$68,182	−$39,256	−$12,960	$10,945	$41,991
7	IRR		−65.00%	−20.81%	2.48%	14.96%	24.55%
8	MIRR		−65.00%	−13.86%	5.70%	13.73%	18.87%
9	Analysis of value at end of year 5 of the year-end cash flows reinvested at 24.55%						
10	Year-5 Value of Year-1 Cash Flow		$35,000				$84,231
11	Year-5 Value of Year-2 Cash Flow			$35,000			$67,627
12	Year-5 Value of Year-3 Cash Flow				$35,000		$54,296
13	Year-5 Value of Year-4 Cash Flow					$35,000	$43,593
14	Year-5 Value of Year-5 Cash Flow						$50,000
15						Total =	$299,748
16					Fifth root of $299,748/$100,000 − 1 =		**24.55%**
17	Analysis of value at end of year 5 of the year-end cash flows reinvested at 12.00%						
18	Year-5 Value of Year-1 Cash Flow		$35,000				$55,073
19	Year-5 Value of Year-2 Cash Flow			$35,000			$49,172
20	Year-5 Value of Year-3 Cash Flow				$35,000		$43,904
21	Year-5 Value of Year-4 Cash Flow					$35,000	$39,200
22	Year-5 Value of Year-5 Cash Flow						$50,000
23						Total =	$237,350
24					Fifth root of $237,350/$100,000 − 1 =		**18.87%**

The total at the end of year 5 would be $299,748, as shown by the calculations in Rows 10 to 15. Thus, for example, the $35,000 received at the end of year 1 would be reinvested for four years at 24.55 percent, which would provide a total of

$$\$35,000 \times (1 + 0.2455)^4 = \$84,231$$

The result of this calculation is shown in Cell G10. Similar calculations are made for reinvesting the cash inflows for years 2, 3, and 4, with the results at the end of 5 years shown in Cells G11:G13. Their sum is then added to the year-end $50,000 inflow for year 5 (Cell G14) to give a total of $299,748 at the end of year 5 (Cell G15). The rate of return would then be calculated as

$$\sqrt[5]{\frac{\$299,748}{\$100,000}} - 1 = 1.2455 - 1 = 0.2455 = 24.55\%$$

A reinvestment rate of 24.55 percent is probably too high to be realistic. We might assume a more reasonable rate of 12 percent, as indicated in Cell B3. In this case, the value of the modified rate of return, or the rate of return adjusted for the reinvestment rate, as calculated in Cell G8 by the entry =MIRR(B5:G5,B2,B3), is only 18.87 percent.

Rows 18 to 24 show the analysis for reinvesting the cash flows for years 1 to 4 at a rate of 12 percent. In this case, the $35,000 received at the end of year 1 would be reinvested for four years at 12 percent, which would provide a total at year 5

$$\$35,000 \times (1 + 0.12)^4 = \$55,073$$

as indicated in Cell G18. Repeating this calculation for the other years (Cells G19:G21) and adding the cash flow for year 5 (Cell G22) gives a total of $237,350 at the end of year 5 (Cell G23). The rate of return would then be

$$\sqrt[5]{\frac{\$237,350}{\$100,000}} - 1 = 1.1887 - 1 = 0.1887 = 18.87\%$$

In other words, if the discount rate is 10 percent and the reinvest rate is 12 percent, the investment's actual rate of return is 18.87 percent rather than 24.55 percent.

The bottom line of this comparison is that the *modified* internal rate of return generally provides a more realistic assessment of an investment's financial merit than the internal rate of return.

Break-Even Point

When time is money, speed is profit! The race today is to reach pay dirt before the competition. Companies must recoup their investments for developing new products and installing production facilities while there is still a market for their output. Beyond reaching a break-even point quickly, companies hope to earn a positive amount on their investments so long as the products continue to sell well.

The time for an investment to pay back its cost has become critical in high-technology industries. Break-through products encounter competition sooner than ever before, and commercial lifetimes can be as short as one or two years. Patents no longer provide long-term market protection for many types of new products. The knowledge base for products in telecommunications and other information technology industries, as well as in pharmaceuticals and biotechnology firms, can become obsolete in 18 months, or less. (For example, Monsanto's Celebrex, a medicine for treating arthritis, faced competition from a similar product from Merck within five months of its introduction.) The profit race is won by those who move new products from their research laboratories to markets quickly and reach the break-even point first.

Breaking-even means achieving a net present value of zero—that is, when the present value of the future cash inflows equals the value of the investment. Because money has a time value, the future cash inflows should be discounted back to the same time as making the investment. Some analysts emphasize this need by referring to it as the **discounted** payback period or break-even point. Failure to discount future cash flows to their present value results in shorter payback periods that are misleading because they fail to recognize the time value of money.

Figure 12-2 shows the change in NPV from a negative value at the end of period n to a positive value at the end of the following period, period $n+1$. The break-even point, when the NPV is zero, is at an intermediate point between n and $n+1$. Using linear interpolation between the two known points gives the following formula for the number of periods to break even:

$$\text{Periods to break even} = n + \frac{-NPV_n}{NPV_{n+1} - NPV_n} \tag{12.1}$$

Figure 12-2
————————

Interpolation of the Break-Even Point between a Negative and a Positive Net Present Value

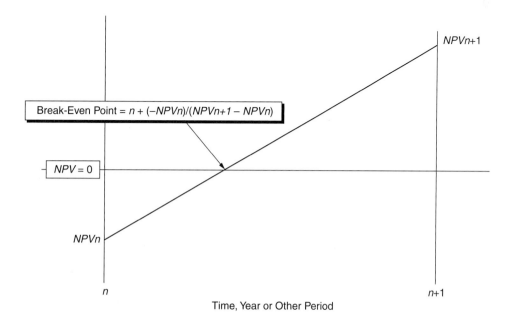

Equation 12.1 simply indicates that the number of periods to break even is the **last** period at which the NPV is **negative** plus a fraction of the next period, where the fractional part of the next period is calculated by the second term on the right side of the equation.

An Example

The following example shows how to create a spreadsheet for evaluating the various financial measures of success for given cash flows, discount rates, and depreciation conditions.

Example 12.1: Consolidated Enterprises is a large manufacturing firm. It plans to invest $100,000 in new factory equipment to increase the production efficiency for one of its many products. The equipment will be depreciated by the straight-line method, and its salvage value at the end of five years is expected to be $10,000.

The firm's industrial engineers and market analysts estimate that the increases in the firm's annual net operating income before depreciation and taxes due to the equipment will vary as follows:

Years after Investment	Year-End Annual Benefit
1	$40,000
2	$55,000
3	$60,000
4	$45,000
5	$30,000

Considering the risks involved and the other investment opportunities, Consolidated's chief financial officer decides on using a discount rate of 14 percent for evaluating the investment. The value of 14 percent will also be used for the rate at which future cash inflows can be reinvested.

Consolidated's income tax rate is 40 percent.

What is the net present value of the investment, its internal rate of return, its modified internal rate of return, and its break-even point?

Solution: Figure 12-3 shows a spreadsheet solution. Data values are entered in Rows 1 to 9, and calculated or transferred values are in Rows 10 to 18.

The before-tax cash flow (BTCF) for Year 0 in Cell B10 is the negative value of the investment in Cell B2. The year-end BTCFs for the following years, except the last, are the same as the year-end annual benefits; that is, the entry in C10 is =C9 and is copied to D9:F9. The year-end BTCF for the fifth (final) year is the sum of the year-end annual benefit plus the salvage value; that is, the entry in G10 is =G9+B3.

The annual depreciation is calculated by entering =SLN($B2,$B3,$B4) in Cell C11 and copying the entry to D11:G11.

Except for the final year, taxable income is calculated as the difference between the BTCF and the depreciation; that is, enter =C10-C11 in Cell C12 and copy the entry to D12:F12. The taxable income for the **final** year requires an adjustment for salvage value, since the salvage value income is not taxable when the income equals the projected salvage value. The entry for taxable income for the final year is =G10-G11-B3 in Cell G12.

(Continued)

Figure 12-3

Capital Budgeting Analysis for Consolidated Enterprises

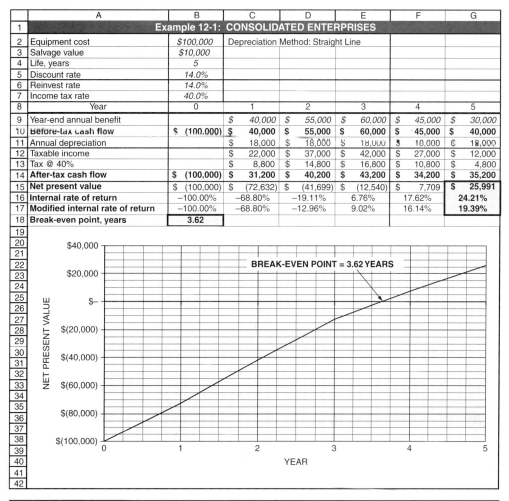

	A	B	C	D	E	F	G
1		Example 12-1: CONSOLIDATED ENTERPRISES					
2	Equipment cost	$100,000	Depreciation Method: Straight Line				
3	Salvage value	$10,000					
4	Life, years	5					
5	Discount rate	14.0%					
6	Reinvest rate	14.0%					
7	Income tax rate	40.0%					
8	Year	0	1	2	3	4	5
9	Year-end annual benefit		$ 40,000	$ 55,000	$ 60,000	$ 45,000	$ 30,000
10	Before-tax cash flow	$ (100,000)	$ 40,000	$ 55,000	$ 60,000	$ 45,000	$ 40,000
11	Annual depreciation		$ 18,000	$ 18,000	$ 18,000	$ 18,000	$ 18,000
12	Taxable income		$ 22,000	$ 37,000	$ 42,000	$ 27,000	$ 12,000
13	Tax @ 40%		$ 8,800	$ 14,800	$ 16,800	$ 10,800	$ 4,800
14	After-tax cash flow	$ (100,000)	$ 31,200	$ 40,200	$ 43,200	$ 34,200	$ 35,200
15	Net present value	$ (100,000)	$ (72,632)	$ (41,699)	$ (12,540)	$ 7,709	$ 25,991
16	Internal rate of return	−100.00%	−68.80%	−19.11%	6.76%	17.62%	24.21%
17	Modified internal rate of return	−100.00%	−68.80%	−12.96%	9.02%	16.14%	19.39%
18	Break-even point, years	3.62					

Key Cell Entries

B10 =−B2 (Investment at Year 0 is a cash outflow.)
C10 = C9, copy to D10:F10 (Year-end cash flows for years 1 to 4 are the annual benefits.)
G10 =G9+B3 (Year-end cash flow year 5 is the annual benefit plus salvage value.)
C11 =SLN($B2,$B3,$B4), copy to D11:G11 (Computes annual depreciation by straight-line method.)
C12 = C10−C11, copy to D12:F12 (Taxable income for years 1 to 4 is before-tax cash flow less depreciation.)
G12 = G10−G11−B3 (Taxable income for year 5 is before-tax cash flow less depreciation and salvage value.)
C13 =C12*$B7, copy to D13:G13 (Tax is taxable income multiplied by tax rate.)
B14 =B10−B13, copy to C14:G14 (After-tax cash flow is before-tax cash flow less tax.)
B15 =B14 (Net present value at time zero is the cash outflow for the investment.)
C15 =NPV($B5,$C14:C14)+$B14, copy to D15:G15 (Computes net present value at ends of years 1 to 5.)
B16 =−100%
C16 =IRR($B$14:C14,guess), copy to D16:G16 (Computes internal rate of return at ends of years 1 to 5.)
B17 =−100%
C17 =MIRR($B$14:C14,$B5,$B6), copy to D16:G16 (Computes modified internal rate of return at ends of years 1 to 5.)
B18 =IF(C15>0,B8−B15/(C15−B15), IF(D15>0,C8−C15/(D15−C15), IF(E15>0,D8−D15/(E15−D15),
    IF(F15>0,E8−E15/(F15−E15), IF(G15>0,F8−F15/(G15−F15), "failed"))))) (Computes years to break even.)

(Continued)

Tax is calculated as the product of the taxable income multiplied by the tax rate; that is, the entry in Cell C13 is C12*$B7 and is copied to D13:G13.

After-tax cash flows (ATCFs) are calculated as what is left of the BTCFs after paying taxes; that is, the entry in cell B14 is =B10-B13 and is copied to C14:G14. (An alternate method for calculating the ATCFs is discussed later.)

Enter =B14 in Cell B15 for the net present value of the investment at year 0. To calculate the investment's net present value at the ends of other years, enter =NPV($B5,$C14:C14)+$B14 in Cell C15 and copy it to D15:G15. **Note that because the value in Cell B14 is already a present value, it is not included in the range for the NPV function.** The NPV function discounts only *future* values to their present equivalents at the given discount rate.

Enter =-100% in Cell B16 for the investment's internal rate of return at year 0. To calculate the investment's internal rate of return at the ends of other years, enter =IRR($B14:C14,-0.40) in Cell C16 and copy it to D16:G16. The guess of -0.40 is close enough for the result in Cell C16. In whatever cells the guess of -0.40 (or any other guess) is not close enough for the IRR function to converge in 20 iterations to a value, the result will be the error message #NUM!. If this occurs, simply change the *guess* to a value that is closer to the expected result.

Enter =-100% in Cell B17 for the investment's modified internal rate of return at year 0. To calculate the investment's modified internal rate of return at the ends of other years, enter =MIRR($B14:C14,$B5,$B6) in Cell C17 and copy it to D17:G17.

Figure 12-4

Capital Budgeting Analysis for Consolidated Enterprises (Alternate Calculation of After-Tax Cash Flow)

	A	B	C	D	E	F	G
1	Example 12-1: CONSOLIDATED ENTERPRISES (ALTERNATE CALCULATION OF ATCF)						
2	Equipment cost	$100,000	Depreciation Method: Straight Line				
3	Salvage value	$10,000					
4	Life, years	5					
5	Discount rate	14.0%					
6	Reinvest rate	14.0%					
7	Income tax rate	40.0%					
8	Year	0	1	2	3	4	5
9	Year-end annual benefit		$ 40,000	$ 55,000	$ 60,000	$ 45,000	$ 30,000
10	Before-tax cash flow	$ (100,000)	$ 40,000	$ 55,000	$ 60,000	$ 45,000	$ 40,000
11	Annual depreciation		$ 18,000	$ 18,000	$ 18,000	$ 18,000	$ 18,000
12	After-tax cash flow	$ (100,000)	$ 31,200	$ 40,200	$ 43,200	$ 34,200	$ 35,200
13	Net present value	$ (100,000)	$ (72,632)	$ (41,699)	$ (12,540)	$ 7,709	$ 25,991
14	Internal rate of return	−100.00%	−68.80%	−19.11%	6.76%	17.62%	24.21%
15	Modified internal rate of return	−100.00%	−68.80%	−12.96%	9.02%	16.14%	19.39%
16	Break-even point, years	3.62					

Change in Key Cell Entries from Figure 12-3
B12 =B10
C12 =(C9−C11)*(1−$B7)+C11, copy to D12:F12
G12 =(G9−G11)*(1−B7)+G11+B3

(Continued)

To calculate the number of years for the investment to break even, we need an entry that instructs the computer to move across the values for NPV in Row 15 and, when it encounters the first positive value, to back up one year and add a fraction of the next year, as shown in Figure 12-2. The entry to do this is a succession of IFs that check successive cells in the Range C15:G15 to see if the NPV is positive (i.e., the NPV>0). When the first Cell with a positive NPV is found, the cell value of the preceding year in the range C8:G8 is identified and the fractional part of a year is added to it. The entry in Cell B18 to do this is the following:

=IF(C15>0,B8-B15/(C15-B15),IF(D15>0,C8-C15/(D15-C15),IF(E15>0,D8-D15/(E15-D15),
IF(F15>0,E8-E15/(F15-E15),IF(G15>0,F8-F15/(G15-F15),"failed")))))

Note that if none of the NPVs is greater than 0, the investment fails to break even during the analysis horizon.

The results give the investment's NPV at the end of 5 years as $25,991, its IRR as 24.21 percent, its MIRR as 19.39 percent, and its break-even point as 3.62 years. The chart in the center of Figure 12-3 shows how the NPV increases from the negative value of -$100,000 at the time of the investment, reaches zero NPV after 3.62 years, and increases further to a positive value of $25,991 at the end of 5 years. (To make the Y-axis line at zero heavy, as shown in Figure 12-3, double-click on the axis to open the Format Axis dialog box, select the Patterns tab, and scroll down the Weight box to the second entry from the bottom.)

Figure 12-4 shows a solution with the ATCFs calculated by an alternate method. This method omits the calculations of taxable income and tax in Rows 12 and 13 of Figure 12-3. The after-tax cash flows at the ends of years 1 and 4 are calculated by the entry =(C9-C11)*(1-$B7)+C11 in Cell C12 and copying the entry to D12:F12. The entry in G12 for year 5 is =(G9-G11)*(1-B7)+G11+B3, where B3 is the salvage value.

Changing Input Values to Achieve Financial Goals

A manager's job is not simply to accept whatever is handed to him or her. If financial goals cannot be achieved under a given set of input conditions, a CFO needs to examine what can be done about it. Developing a spreadsheet to calculate results for a given set of conditions is only the start of its usefulness. Using a spreadsheet to examine alternatives is one of the chief reasons for spending the time to develop it. Spreadsheets are low-cost test platforms for analyzing what it takes to do better, or what might happen if things get worse.

The following sections illustrate how a spreadsheet might be used to evaluate the changes needed for reaching specific financial goals.

Changes in Input Conditions for Breaking Even in a Given Time

As markets fluctuate more widely and as the product lifetimes become shorter, financial officers become more concerned with their investments' breaking even in shorter times. They may therefore limit investments to values that will be returned in a reasonably short time. The following example shows how to use Excel's Goal Seek or Solver tool to determine the maximum investment that will be returned in a given time.

Example 12.2: Given the year-end annual benefits and other conditions in Example 12.1, determine the maximum investment in equipment that Consolidated can afford to make that will paid back in three years.

Solution: Figure 12-5 shows that for the given values of projected cash flows, discount rate, reinvestment rate, and depreciation conditions, the investment must be limited to not more than $84,599 in order to break even in three years.

Figure 12-5

Maximum Equipment Cost for Breaking Even in Three Years

	A	B	C	D	E	F	G
1	Example 12-2: CONSOLIDATED ENTERPRISES						
2	Equipment cost	$84,599	Depreciation Method: Straight Line				
3	Salvage value	$10,000					
4	Life, years	5		Maximum equipment cost			
5	Discount rate	14.0%		for breaking even in 3 years			
6	Reinvest rate	14.0%					
7	Income tax rate	40.0%					
8	Year	0	1	2	3	4	5
9	Year-end annual benefit		$ 40,000	$ 55,000	$ 60,000	$ 45,000	$ 30,000
10	**Before-tax cash flow**	$ (84,599)	$ 40,000	$ 55,000	$ 60,000	$ 45,000	$ 40,000
11	Annual depreciation		$ 14,920	$ 14,920	$ 14,920	$ 14,920	$ 14,920
12	Taxable income		$ 25,080	$ 40,080	$ 45,080	$ 30,080	$ 15,080
13	Tax @ 40%		$ 10,032	$ 16,032	$ 18,032	$ 12,032	$ 6,032
14	**After-tax cash flow**	$ (84,599)	$ 29,968	$ 38,968	$ 41,968	$ 32,968	$ 33,968
15	**Net present value**	$ (84,599)	$ (58,312)	$ (28,327)	$ -	$ 19,520	$ 37,162
16	**Internal rate of return**	−100.00%	−64.58%	−12.15%	14.00%	24.55%	**30.79%**
17	**Modified internal rate of return**	−100.00%	−64.58%	−7.02%	14.00%	20.07%	**22.61%**
18	**Break-even point, years**	3.00					

To create this spreadsheet, copy the spreadsheet of Figure 12-3. Select Goal Seek from the Tools menu to open the dialog box shown in Figure 12-6. Enter Cell E15 (the NPV at the end of three years) and a target value of 0. Enter Cell B2 (the equipment cost) as the changing cell. Click on the OK button or press Enter. The result is Figure 12-5. (The break-even chart at the bottom has been omitted.)

Figure 12-6

Goal Seek Dialog Box with Entries for Solving Example 12.2

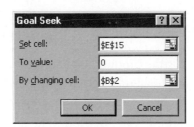

(Continued)

You can also solve this example with Excel's Solver tool. Figure 12-7 shows the Solver settings with an alternate target of setting Cell B18 (the break-even point in years) equal to 3. The result is the same, because the break-even point is the time for the NPV to equal zero. However, the goal of setting the NPV equal to zero requires fewer calculations and is computationally more efficient and faster.

Figure 12-7

Solver Settings to Solve Example 12.3

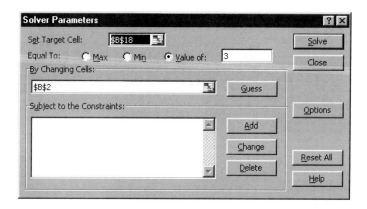

Satisfying Financial Goals by Increasing Sales

There are countless variations of Example 12.3 that might be of interest. For example, a CFO might want to know the sales level needed to satisfy his or her goal for a specified net present value or rate of return at the end of a given number of years.

Increasing sales is an alternative to reducing investment costs that might be tried in order to reach higher financial goals than possible under the given conditions. The following example shows how to evaluate the increase needed to attain a specific goal.

Example 12.3:   Consolidated's CFO (see preceding example) is concerned about a $100,000 investment's taking more than three years to break even. If the investment cannot be reduced below $100,000, she wants to know how much the annual benefits would have to increase in order to break even at the end of three years. She plans to use this information to discuss strategies for accomplishing her goal with the company's marketing division.

Solution: Figure 12-8 is a spreadsheet solution. To create this spreadsheet, copy the previous spreadsheet and insert two new rows, Rows 9 and 10, in Figure 12-8. This will move everything below Row 8 in the previous spreadsheet down two rows.

Copy the values for the projected annual benefits, which will now be in Cells C11:G11, to Cells C9:G9 and label these the **projected** year-end annual benefits. Use Paste Special/Values to paste the values from Cells C11:G11 rather than paste the entries. Enter a trial value, such as 0.10 (i.e., 10%) in Cell B10 for the

(Continued)

Figure 12-8

Increase in Projected Year-End Annual Benefits for Breaking Even by the End of Three Years

	A	B	C	D	E	F	G
1	Example 12-3: CONSOLIDATED ENTERPRISES						
2	Equipment cost	$100,000	Depreciation Method: Straight Line				
3	Salvage value	$10,000					
4	Life, years	5	Increase in year-end annual benefits to break even in 3 years				
5	Discount rate	14.0%					
6	Reinvest rate	14.0%					
7	Income tax rate	40.0%					
8	Year	0	1	2	3	4	5
9	Projected year-end annual benefits		$ 40,000	$ 55,000	$ 60,000	$ 45,000	$ 30,000
10	Yearly increase	17.73%					
11	Year-end annual benefit		$ 47,090	$ 64,749	$ 70,636	$ 52,977	$ 35,318
12	Before-tax cash flow	$ (100,000)	$ 47,090	$ 64,749	$ 70,636	$ 52,977	$ 45,318
13	Annual depreciation		$ 18,000	$ 18,000	$ 18,000	$ 18,000	$ 18,000
14	Taxable income		$ 29,090	$ 46,749	$ 52,636	$ 34,977	$ 17,318
15	Tax @ 40%		$ 11,636	$ 18,700	$ 21,054	$ 13,991	$ 6,927
16	After-tax cash flow	$ (100,000)	$ 35,454	$ 46,050	$ 49,581	$ 38,986	$ 38,391
17	Net present value	$ (100,000)	$ (68,900)	$ (33,466)	$ -	$ 23,083	$ 43,022
18	Internal rate of return	-100.00%	-64.55%	-12.14%	14.00%	24.56%	30.55%
19	Modified internal rate of return	-100.00%	-64.55%	-7.01%	14.00%	20.08%	22.46%
20	Break-even point, years	3.00					

> **Key Cell Entry:** Cell C11: =C9*(1+$B10), copy to D11:G11
> **Goal Seek or Solver Settings:** Target Cell is E17, to be set equal to 0 by changing Cell B10.

benefit increase. Enter =C9*(1+$B10) in Cell C11 and copy it to D11:G11. Label these the year-end annual benefit. They are the original projected values in Cells C9:G9 increased by the percentage in Cell B10.

Use Excel's Solver (or Goal Seek) tool with a target of setting Cell E17 (i.e., the NPV at the end of year 3), equal to 0 by changing the percentage value in Cell B10 (i.e., the increase needed in the projected annual benefits).

The results show that the annual benefits must be increased 17.73 percent from their projected values in order for the investment to break even by the end of the third year.

Should You Use Goal Seek or Solver?

Although either the Goal Seek or Solver tool can be used interchangeably to solve the examples in this chapter, Solver is a better choice because it provides a higher degree of precision. For example, Goal Seek gives the value 42.46 percent for Cell B10 of Example 12.5 (Figure 12-9), while Solver gives the value 42.48 percent. The relative difference between the two values is only 0.05 percent and either result suffices for the purpose of the example. However, the result provided by Solver and other values that depend on it is more accurate.

Both tools use an iterative procedure that refines a starting value for the changing cell until successive results agree within a prescribed level of accuracy. The default level for Solver is more precise than for Goal Seek. Solver also provides an option for increasing the precision further.

Goal Seek is a simpler tool to use and explain. However, Solver is more powerful, versatile, and accurate. Solver can do everything Goal Seek can—and more, and better.

Rather than setting a goal for the years to break even, a CFO's goals might be to reach a given net present value or rate of return by a specified time, as illustrated by the following example.

Example 12.4: Not satisfied with the results from Example 12.3, Consolidated's CFO now wants to know how much the annual benefits would have to increase in order to provide an MIRR of 25 percent by the end of the fourth year.

Solution: Figure 12-9 is a spreadsheet solution. The spreadsheet is produced by copying the spreadsheet of Figure 12-8 to a new spreadsheet and changing the Solver setting of the Solver tool to a goal of 0.25 (i.e., 25%) in Cell F19 by changing the value in Cell B10. The results show that the annual benefits must increase by 42.48 percent from their projected values in order for the investment's MIRR to equal 25 percent by the end of the fourth year.

Note that the time to break even has been reduced to 2.56 years, and the investment's NPV has increased to $66,804.

Figure 12-9

Increase in Projected Year-End Annual Benefits to Achieve a 25% Modified Internal Rate of Return at the End of Four Years

	A	B	C	D	E	F	G
1	Example 12-4: CONSOLIDATED ENTERPRISES						
2	Equipment cost	$100,000	Depreciation Method: Straight Line				
3	Salvage value	$10,000					
4	Life, years	5	Increase in year-end annual benefits to				
5	Discount rate	14.0%	achieve a 25% MIRR at the end of 4 years				
6	Reinvest rate	14.0%					
7	Income tax rate	40.0%					
8	Year	0	1	2	3	4	5
9	Projected year-end annual benefits		$ 40,000	$ 55,000	$ 60,000	$ 45,000	$ 30,000
10	Increase in projected benefits	42.48%					
11	Year-end annual benefit		$ 56,992	$ 78,363	$ 85,487	$ 64,116	$ 42,744
12	Before-tax cash flow	$ (100,000)	$ 56,992	$ 78,363	$ 85,487	$ 64,116	$ 52,744
13	Annual depreciation		$ 18,000	$ 18,000	$ 18,000	$ 18,000	$ 18,000
14	Taxable income		$ 38,992	$ 60,363	$ 67,487	$ 46,116	$ 24,744
15	Tax @ 40%		$ 15,597	$ 24,145	$ 26,995	$ 18,446	$ 9,897
16	After-tax cash flow	$ (100,000)	$ 41,395	$ 54,218	$ 58,492	$ 45,669	$ 42,846
17	Net present value	$ (100,000)	$ (63,689)	$ (21,970)	$ 17,511	$ 44,551	$ 66,804
18	Internal rate of return	−100.00%	−58.61%	−2.82%	23.57%	33.73%	39.07%
19	Modified internal rate of return	−100.00%	−58.61%	0.70%	20.30%	25.00%	26.28%
20	Break-even point, years	2.56					

Key Cell Entry: Cell C11: =C9*(1+$B10), copy to D11:G11
Goal Seek or Solver Settings: Target Cell is F19, to be set equal to 25% by changing Cell B10.

Sensitivity to Input Conditions

Because it deals with the future, capital budgeting is based on many assumptions or expectations that may prove wrong. Analysts should therefore ask themselves what might possibly go wrong—and then perform a sensitivity analysis to evaluate its impacts on the expected payoffs.

A great advantage of spreadsheets is that once they have been created, the effects of variations in input variables can be studied by editing the spreadsheet or by creating auxiliary tables. The examples that follow illustrate how to perform sensitivity analysis with one- and two-variable input tables.

Effect of Changes in the Year-End Benefits on Financial Payoffs

The year-end benefits are forecasts, and even the best forecasts are wrong. The following example examines the sensitivity of the financial payoffs to changes in the year-end benefits.

Example 12.5:   Use the spreadsheet of Figure 12-9 to evaluate the impacts of changes in the annual year-end benefits from –20% to +20%. Show the results as a one-variable input table with values for the NPV, IRR, and MIRR at the end of five years and the years to break even for the changes in annual benefits.

Solution: Figure 12-10 shows the solution. Charts have been added that show how the changes in annual benefits affect the net present value and years to break even.

The one-variable input table in Figure 12-10 is created by the following entries in Row 23. (The height of Row 23 has been reduced, and the entries hidden by custom formatting them with three semicolons.)

Cell B23: =B10   Cell C23: =G17   Cell D23: =G18   Cell E23: =G19   Cell F23: =B20

These entries link the table in Rows 21 to 32 with the spreadsheet model above. The next step is to highlight the Range B23:F32 and access the Table dialog box shown in Figure 12-11 from the Data drop-down menu. After making the entries shown in Figure 12-11, click OK or press Enter to create the table of results. Format the values as shown in Figure 12-10.

Example 12.6:   Use the spreadsheet of Figure 12-9 to create two-variable input tables for showing sensitivity of the NPV at the end of five years and the years to break even to changes in the annual benefits from –20% to +20% and values for the discount rate from 10 percent to 18 percent.

Solution: Figure 12-12 shows the solution.

The entry in Cell B23 is =G17, and the entry in Cell B31 is =B20. These entries link the first table to the NPV at the end of five years and to the years to break even in the body of the spreadsheet. To create the first table, highlight the Range B23:G28 and make the entries shown in Figure 12-13 in the "Table" dialog box. Repeat the procedure to create the second table.

(Continued)

Figure 12-10

Impacts of Changes in Annual Year-End Benefits on Financial Measures of Success

	A	B	C	D	E	F	G
1		Example 12-5: CONSOLIDATED ENTERPRISES					
2	Equipment cost	$100,000	Depreciation Method: Straight Line				
3	Salvage value	*$10,000*					
4	Life, years	*5*					
5	Discount rate	*14.0%*					
6	Reinvest rate	*14.0%*					
7	Income tax rate	*40.0%*					
8	Year	0	1	2	3	4	5
9	Projected year-end annual benefits		$ 40,000	$ 55,000	$ 60,000	$ 45,000	$ 30,000
10	Increase in projected benefits	10.00%					
11	Year-end annual benefit		$ 44,000	$ 60,500	$ 66,000	$ 49,500	$ 33,000
12	**Before-tax cash flow**	$ (100,000)	$ 44,000	$ 60,500	$ 66,000	$ 49,500	$ 43,000
13	Annual depreciation		$ 18,000	$ 18,000	$ 18,000	$ 18,000	$ 18,000
14	Taxable income		$ 26,000	$ 42,500	$ 48,000	$ 31,500	$ 15,000
15	Tax @ 40%		$ 10,400	$ 17,000	$ 19,200	$ 12,600	$ 6,000
16	**After-tax cash flow**	$ (100,000)	$ 33,600	$ 43,500	$ 46,800	$ 36,900	$ 37,000
17	**Net present value**	$ (100,000)	$ (70,526)	$ (37,054)	$ (5,466)	$ 16,382	$ 35,599
18	**Internal rate of return**	−100.00%	−66.40%	−15.14%	10.89%	21.58%	27.82%
19	**Modified internal rate of return**	−100.00%	−66.40%	−9.55%	11.88%	18.41%	21.16%
20	**Break-even point, years**	3.25					
21		SENSITIVITY OF FINANCIAL PAYOFFS TO CHANGE IN THE YEAR-END ANNUAL BENEFITS					
22		Change in Annual Benefits	NPV at End of Five Years	IRR at End of Five Years	MIRR at End of Five Years	Years to Break Even	
24		−20.0%	$6,775	16.73%	15.50%	4.59	
25		−15.0%	$11,579	18.63%	16.53%	4.31	
26		−10.0%	$16,383	20.51%	17.51%	4.06	
27		−5.0%	$21,187	22.37%	18.47%	3.83	
28		0.0%	$25,991	24.21%	19.39%	3.62	
29		5.0%	$30,795	26.02%	20.29%	3.43	
30		10.0%	$35,599	27.82%	21.16%	3.25	
31		15.0%	$40,403	29.59%	22.01%	3.09	
32		20.0%	$45,206	31.35%	22.83%	2.95	

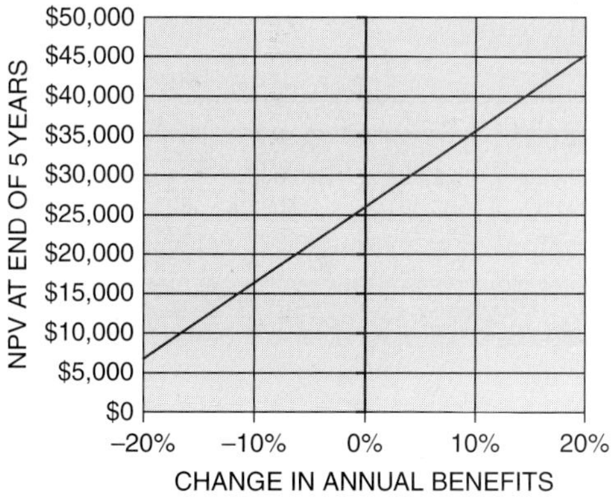

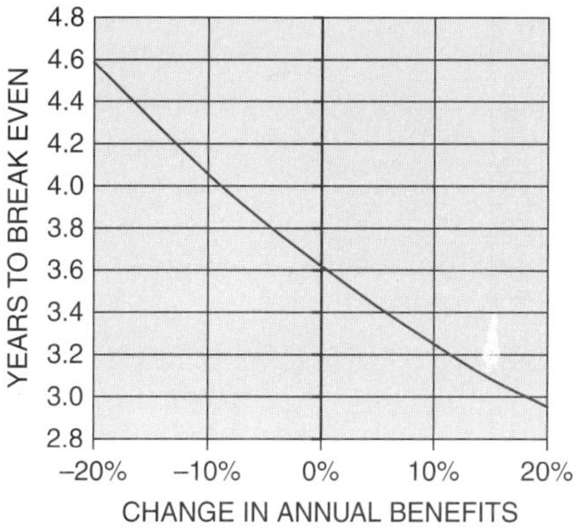

(Continued)

Figure 12-11

"Table" Dialog Box with Entry for the One-Variable Input Table of Figure 12-10

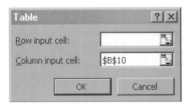

Figure 12-12

Sensitivity of NPV and Years to Break Even to Changes in Annual Benefits and the Discount Rate

	A	B	C	D	E	F	G
1	Example 12-6: CONSOLIDATED ENTERPRISES						
2	Equipment cost	$100,000	Depreciation Method: Straight Line				
3	Salvage value	$10,000					
4	Life, years	5					
5	Discount rate	14.0%					
6	Reinvest rate	14.0%					
7	Income tax rate	40.0%					
8	Year	0	1	2	3	4	5
9	Projected year-end annual benefits		$ 40,000	$ 55,000	$ 60,000	$ 45,000	$ 30,000
10	Increase in projected benefits	0.00%					
11	Year-end annual benefit		$ 40,000	$ 55,000	$ 60,000	$ 45,000	$ 30,000
12	Before-tax cash flow	$ (100,000)	$ 40,000	$ 55,000	$ 60,000	$ 45,000	$ 40,000
13	Annual depreciation		$ 18,000	$ 18,000	$ 18,000	$ 18,000	$ 18,000
14	Taxable income		$ 22,000	$ 37,000	$ 42,000	$ 27,000	$ 12,000
15	Tax @ 40%		$ 8,800	$ 14,800	$ 16,800	$ 10,800	$ 4,800
16	After-tax cash flow	$ (100,000)	$ 31,200	$ 40,200	$ 43,200	$ 34,200	$ 35,200
17	Net present value	$ (100,000)	$ (72,632)	$ (41,699)	$ (12,540)	$ 7,709	$ 25,991
18	Internal rate of return	−100.00%	−68.80%	−19.11%	6.76%	17.62%	24.21%
19	Modified internal rate of return	−100.00%	−68.80%	−12.96%	9.02%	16.14%	19.39%
20	Break-even point, years	3.62					
21		SENSITIVITY OF NET PRESENT VALUE AT END OF 5 YEARS TO CHANGES IN THE YEAR-END ANNUAL BENEFITS AND DISCOUNT RATE					
22		Change in Annual Benefits			Discount Rate		
23			10.0%	12.0%	14.0%	16.0%	18.0%
24		−20.0%	$18,108	$12,215	$6,775	$1,744	−$2,918
25		−10.0%	$28,683	$22,288	$16,383	$10,920	$5,856
26		0.0%	$39,259	$32,361	$25,991	$20,096	$14,631
27		10.0%	$49,835	$42,435	$35,599	$29,272	$23,405
28		20.0%	$60,410	$52,508	$45,206	$38,448	$32,180
29		SENSITIVITY OF THE NUMBER OF YEARS TO BREAK EVEN TO CHANGES IN THE YEAR-END ANNUAL BENEFITS AND DISCOUNT RATE					
30		Change in Annual Benefits			Discount Rate		
31			10.0%	12.0%	14.0%	16.0%	18.0%
32		−20.0%	4.08	4.32	4.59	4.88	Failed
33		−10.0%	3.63	3.83	4.06	4.31	4.60
34		0.0%	3.25	3.43	3.62	3.82	4.05
35		10.0%	2.95	3.09	3.25	3.43	3.62
36		20.0%	2.76	2.85	2.95	3.09	3.25

(Continued)

Figure 12-13

"Table" Dialog Box with Entries for Creating the First of the Two-Variable Input Tables of Figure 12-12

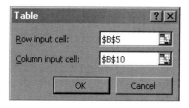

Capital Gains or Losses When Equipment Is Sold for a Different Amount Than Its Book Value

In the preceding examples, the equipment's salvage value and its book value at the time of sale were the same, so that there was no capital gain or loss on its sale. The following example illustrates the calculations when the sale price and book value at the time of sale are different.

Example 12.7: Start with the conditions for Example 12.1. Assume that at the end of four years, technological advances have made more efficient equipment available and the company decides to sell the original equipment. Assume also that the equipment's market value has dropped to only $7,500 at the time of sale and that the tax rate for long-term capital gains or losses is 30 percent (whereas the tax rate for regular income continues to be 40 percent). How would this change the payoffs from what had been planned under the original conditions?

Solution: Figure 12-14 shows the solution.

In Figure 12-14, the cash flows from operations and from the sale of the equipment have been separated. Note that the cash flows from normal operation are the same for years 0 to 4 as for the original conditions. To compute the book value at the time of sale, enter =B2-SUM(C11:F11) in Cell F16. Since the book value is more than obtained from selling the equipment, there is a capital loss, which is computed in Cell F17 by the entry =F15-F16. This loss generates a tax benefit (i.e., a reduction in the tax the company must pay), which is calculated in Cell F18 by the entry =–F17*F6. (Note the use of the tax rate for capital gains or losses, which is different in this example from the tax rate for ordinary income.) The after-tax cash flow from the sale of the equipment is computed in Cell F19 by the entry =F15l+F18. The net tax cash flow is computed in Row 20 by entering =B14+B19 in Cell B20 and copying the entry to Cells C20:F20. This changes the payoffs in Rows 21:24 to the values shown in Figure 12-14.

Using the Correct Financial Criteria to Select Investments

The preceding discussions have used four measures of an investment's financial success: (1) the net present value, (2) the internal rate of return, (3) the modified internal rate of return, and (4) the time to break even. Different financial criteria can lead to different choices among alternate investments. The best criterion is not always obvious.

Figure 12-14

Early Sale, with Sale Price Less Than Book Value

	A	B	C	D	E	F
1	Example 12-7: CONSOLIDATED ENTERPRISES					
2	Equipment cost	$100,000	Depreciation Method: Straight Line			
3	Salvage value	$10,000	Selling price of equipment at end			
4	Life, years	5			of year 4	$7,500
5	Discount rate	14.0%	Tax rate for long-term capital gains			
6	Reinvest rate	14.0%			or losses	30.0%
7	Tax rate on regular income	40.0%				
8	Year	0	1	2	3	4
9	Year-end annual benefit		$ 40,000	$ 55,000	$ 60,000	$ 45,000
10	Before-tax cash flow from operations	$ (100,000)	$ 40,000	$ 55,000	$ 60,000	$ 45,000
11	Annual depreciation		$ 18,000	$ 18,000	$ 18,000	$ 18,000
12	Taxable income		$ 22,000	$ 37,000	$ 42,000	$ 27,000
13	Tax @ 40%		$ 8,800	$ 14,800	$ 16,800	$ 10,800
14	After-tax cash flow from operations	$ (100,000)	$ 31,200	$ 40,200	$ 43,200	$ 34,200
15	Before-tax cash flow from sale of equipment					$7,500
16	Book value of equipment					$28,000
17	Capital gain (loss) on sale of equipment					($20,500)
18	Tax benefit from sale of equipment					$6,150
19	After-tax cash flow from sale of equipment					$13,650
20	Net after-tax cash flow	$ (100,000)	$ 31,200	$ 40,200	$ 43,200	$ 47,850
21	Net present value	$ (100,000)	$ (72,632)	$ (41,699)	$ (12,540)	$ 15,791
22	Internal rate of return	−100.00%	−68.80%	−19.11%	6.76%	20.98%
23	Modified internal rate of return	−100.00%	−68.80%	−12.96%	9.02%	18.26%
24	Break-even point, years	3.44				

Given two options with large positive NPVs, for example, should an investor select the one with the higher NPV, the higher IRR, the higher MIRR, or the shorter time to break even? The choice depends on the amounts invested, the cost of capital, the timing of the future cash flows, and the volatility of market demand for a product. It is important to recognize when one choice is correct, and the others are wrong.

Check the Amount Invested

The correct choice may depend on the amount invested. Would you choose an investment of $100,000 with an NPV of $10,000 at the end of one year over an investment of $20,000 with an NPV of $5,000 at the end of one year? If you selected the first alternative because it provides a higher NPV, you would be making a costly mistake. You should recognize that the first investment has a rate of return of only 10 percent on the investment, whereas the second has an return of 25 percent, which is more than twice the first. The difference of $80,000 in the first investment has added only $5,000 to the NPV. This is a return of only 6.25 percent on the **incremental** investment, which may be less than the discount rate of money. Wouldn't you prefer to spend $20,000 to make the smaller investment of the two and then try to find a better investment for the other $80,000?

Now consider two *equal* investments. The following example illustrates why, when choosing between two investments that are **equal and mutually exclusive**, it is correct to choose the investment that provides the higher NPV rather than the one that provides the higher IRR. In addition, the example shows that the investment with the higher NPV also has the higher MIRR. Finally, the example shows that the investment with the higher NPV and MIRR depends on the discount rate or cost of capital.

Example 12.8: Mayberry Investments is considering two mutually exclusive investments of $500,000. The future year-end cash flows over the five-year lives of the investments are as follows:

	Year 1	Year 2	Year 3	Year 4	Year 5
Alternative A	$100,000	$150,000	$200,000	$250,000	$300,000
Alternative B	$250,000	$300,000	$150,000	$100,000	$50,000

The cost of capital (or discount rate) is 11.5 percent for both investments, and the future cash flows will be reinvested at 11.5 percent.

    a. What are the NPV, IRR, MIRR, and years to break even for each alternative?
    b. Which investment should Mayberry choose? Give a justification for your response.
    c. At what cost of capital (or discount rate) are the NPVs and MIRRs of the two investments equal?

Solution: Figure 12-15 is a spreadsheet solution. The upper section of the spreadsheet shows results for both alternatives as well as for the difference between the two alternatives (i.e., for Alternative A minus Alternative B).

    a. The results in Rows 14 to 17 show that A has a higher NPV and MIRR than B, but B has a higher IRR and breaks even sooner. The higher IRR and shorter break-even period of B is due to the timing of the cash flows, with B providing larger cash inflows for the first two years and A providing larger cash inflows for the last three years.
    b. The choice between the two alternatives depends on the results for the difference between them. If we accept A and reject B, the results for the difference should be favorable. As the spreadsheet results show, the difference A – B provides a positive NPV, and A should therefore be accepted. If we had chosen B in preference to A, we would have rejected the positive NPV for the difference, which would be a bad decision. (You should be able to show choosing B in preference to A results in a negative NPV for the difference B – A and B should therefore not be accepted.)
    c. The analysis in Rows 18 to 34 of Figure 12-15 shows that the choice between alternatives varies with the cost of capital (or discount rate) and reinvestment rate (**which are set equal to one another in this analysis**). For discount and reinvestment rates of 14.5 percent or less (Rows 20 to 31), Alternative A has higher NPVs and MIRRs and should be chosen, whereas for discount and reinvestment rates of 15.0 percent of more (Rows 32 to 34), Alternative B has higher NPVs and MIRRs and should be chosen. Note that the NPV of the difference A – B changes from a positive to a negative value as we pass through the range 14.5 percent to 15.0 percent.

To find the cost of capital at which the two alternatives are equal, we can use Excel's Solver or Goal Seek tool to find the value of the cost of capital that makes the NPV of the difference A – B equal to zero. The results in Row 36 show that at a cost of capital of 14.85 percent, both Alternatives A and B have an NPV of $126,619 and an MIRR of 20.15 percent. At the same time, the difference A – B has an MIRR of 14.85 percent, which is the same as the cost of capital.

The conclusion to be drawn from this example is that IRR should **not** be used as a basis for choosing between two *equal* and mutually exclusive investments. As between the usual financial criteria (i.e., NPV, IRR, and MIRR), the proper choice is the investment with the higher NPV.

(Continued)

Figure 12-15

Analysis of Alternative Investments of Equal Amounts

	A	B	C	D	E	F	G
1		Example 12-8: MAYBERRY INVESTMENTS					
2		Alternative					
3		A		B		A - B	
4	Amount of investment	$500,000		$500,000		$0	
5	Cost of capital	11.5%		11.5%		11.5%	
6	Reinvest rate	11.5%		11.5%		11.5%	
7	Year	After-tax cash flows	NPV	After-tax cash flows	NPV	After-tax cash flows	NPV
8	0	$ (500,000)	$ (500,000)	$ (500,000)	$ (500,000)	$ -	$ -
9	1	$ 100,000	$ (410,314)	$ 250,000	$ (275,785)	$ (150,000)	$ (134,529)
10	2	$ 150,000	$ (289,660)	$ 300,000	$ (34,477)	$ (150,000)	$ (255,183)
11	3	$ 200,000	$ (145,380)	$ 150,000	$ 73,733	$ 50,000	$ (219,113)
12	4	$ 250,000	$ 16,368	$ 100,000	$ 138,432	$ 150,000	$ (122,064)
13	5	$ 300,000	$ 190,448	$ 50,000	$ 167,446	$ 250,000	$ 23,002
14	NPV	$190,448		$167,446		$23,002	
15	IRR	23.29%		28.22%		14.85%	
16	MIRR	18.93%		18.13%		13.44%	
17	Years to break even	3.90		2.32		4.84	
18	Analysis of Effect of Cost of Capital and Reinvestment Rate on NPV and MIRR						
19	Cost of Capital and Reinvestment Rate	NPV	MIRR	NPV	MIRR	NPV	MIRR
20	9.00%	$ 244,518	18.03%	$ 201,028	16.62%	$ 43,489	12.38%
21	9.50%	$ 233,218	18.21%	$ 194,081	16.92%	$ 39,138	12.59%
22	10.00%	$ 222,169	18.39%	$ 187,251	17.23%	$ 34,918	12.80%
23	10.50%	$ 211,361	18.57%	$ 180,537	17.53%	$ 30,824	13.02%
24	11.00%	$ 200,790	18.75%	$ 173,936	17.83%	$ 26,854	13.23%
25	11.50%	$ 190,448	18.93%	$ 167,446	18.13%	$ 23,002	13.44%
26	12.00%	$ 180,328	19.12%	$ 161,063	18.43%	$ 19,266	13.65%
27	12.50%	$ 170,426	19.30%	$ 154,785	18.73%	$ 15,641	13.86%
28	13.00%	$ 160,735	19.48%	$ 148,610	19.04%	$ 12,125	14.07%
29	13.50%	$ 151,250	19.66%	$ 142,536	19.34%	$ 8,714	14.28%
30	14.00%	$ 141,964	19.84%	$ 136,561	19.64%	$ 5,404	14.49%
31	14.50%	$ 132,874	20.03%	$ 130,681	19.94%	$ 2,192	14.70%
32	15.00%	$ 123,973	20.21%	$ 124,896	20.24%	$ (923)	14.91%
33	15.50%	$ 115,256	20.39%	$ 119,203	20.55%	$ (3,947)	15.12%
34	16.00%	$ 106,720	20.58%	$ 113,600	20.85%	$ (6,880)	15.33%
35	Conditions for Alternatives A and B equally attractive						
36	14.85%	$ 126,619	20.15%	$ 126,619	20.15%	$ (0)	14.85%

Do not generalize beyond the choice of NPV as the correct choice between two equal and mutually exclusive investments. If the investments are not equal or if the discount and reinvestment rates vary independently of each other, you should make an analysis based on the specific conditions.

Before leaving this example, we might want to reconsider the basis for our choice. The time to break even is 3.90 years for Alternative A and 2.32 years for Alternative B. Suppose that the investments are risky and that future cash flows after three years might be substantially less than those projected or that the investments' lifetimes might be shorter than five years. Alternative B might then be a better choice. In a later chapter we will include an analysis of the risks due to uncertainties in projected cash flows in the selection process.

Optimizing the Choice of Multiyear Projects

The funds available in a company's capital budgets for the next few years limit the selection and number of choices. The following example uses binary programming with Excel's Solver tool to identify the set of choices that best satisfy the financial criterion of maximizing the set's net present value when there are budgetary constraints over a number of years.

Binary programming restricts the values of specified cells to 0 or 1. These correspond to answers of "no" or "yes" (or "no, don't do it" versus "yes, do it") for identifying which choices are best.

Example 12.9: The executives of Goliath Industries are reviewing their capital budgets for the next three years. Table 12-1 lists the options before them and the CFO's estimates of their net present values (NPVs) and their annual costs to complete. Note that the initial costs can extend over several years. The table also shows how much money the CFO expects will be available for capital expenditures during the next three years. (Note that the NPVs of all options are positive. Therefore, all are worthwhile investments.)

If Goliath chooses to build a new plant, it will **not** modernize the existing one. On the other hand, if the company decides not to build a new plant, it **will** modernize the existing one.

   a. What options should Goliath choose, and why?
   b. What will be the net present values of the chosen options, how much of the available funds will be committed each year, and how much of the available funds will be left uncommitted?

Table 12-1

Proposals for Capital Expenditures

		Annual Costs		
Option	NPV	Year 1	Year 2	Year 3
Modernize existing plant	$250,000	$150,000	0	0
Build new plant	$650,000	$100,000	$300,000	0
Expand distribution network	$150,000	$80,000	$20,000	0
Redesign existing Product A	$175,000	$75,000	0	0
Redesign existing Product B	$225,000	$100,000	$45,000	0
R&D on new Product X	$400,000	$50,000	$200,000	$75,000
R&D on new Product Y	$600,000	$60,000	$250,000	$200,000
Available funds		$350,000	$300,000	$300,000

Solution: Figure 12-16 is a spreadsheet solution. Excel's Solver tool was used to select the options that gave the maximum NPV for the choices, consistent with their costs and the budgets available for the next three years and the requirement either to build a new plant or modernize the existing one, but not both.

(Continued)

Figure 12-16

Optimum Solution for Goliath Industries

	A	B	C	D	E	F
1	Example 12-9: GOLIATH INDUSTRIES					
2	Input Data		Present	Annual Costs		
3	Option		Value	Year 1	Year 2	Year 3
4	Modernize existing plant		$ 250,000	$ 150,000		
5	Build new plant		$ 650,000	$ 100,000	$ 300,000	
6	Expand distribution network		$ 150,000	$ 80,000	$ 20,000	
7	Redesign existing product A		$ 175,000	$ 75,000		
8	Redesign existing product B		$ 225,000	$ 100,000	$ 45,000	
9	Develop new product X		$ 400,000	$ 50,000	$ 200,000	$ 75,000
10	Develop new product Y		$ 600,000	$ 60,000	$ 250,000	$ 200,000
11	Available funds			$ 350,000	$ 300,000	$ 300,000
12	Decisions	Choices				
13		(1 = Yes,	Present	Annual Costs		
14	Option	0 = No)	Value	Year 1	Year 2	Year 3
15	Modernize existing plant	1	$ 250,000	$ 150,000	$ -	$ -
16	Build new plant	0	$ -	$ -	$ -	$ -
17	Expand distribution network	0	$ -	$ -	$ -	$ -
18	Redesign existing product A	0	$ -	$ -	$ -	$ -
19	Redesign existing product B	1	$ 225,000	$ 100,000	$ 45,000	$ -
20	Develop new product X	0	$ -	$ -	$ -	$ -
21	Develop new product Y	1	$ 600,000	$ 60,000	$ 250,000	$ 200,000
22	Present value and annual costs		$ 1,075,000	$ 310,000	$ 295,000	$ 200,000
23	Uncommitted funds			$ 40,000	$ 5,000	$ 100,000
24	Build OR modernize plant constraint	1				
25	Sum of uncommitted funds	$ 145,000				

```
Key cell entries:   B24: =B15+B16
                    B25: =SUM(D23:F23)
                    C15: =$B15*C4, copy to C15:F21
                    C22: =SUM(C15:C21), copy to D22:F22
                    D23: =D11–D22, copy to E23:F23
Solver settings:    Target cell is C22, to be maximized.
                    Cells to vary are B15:B21.
                    Constraints: B15:B21 = binary
                                 D22:F22 <= D11:F11
                                 B24 = 1 (Either modernize or build new plant.)
                    Options: Assume linear model
```

The decision variables are the binary values in cells B15:B21. These are 1 for an option that **is** selected and 0 for an option that is **not** selected. Enter trial values of 1 in these seven cells. By multiplying the decision variables in B15:B21 by the present values and annual costs for the options in C4:F10, the present values and annual costs for the **selected** options are calculated in C15:F21. The calculations are made by entering =$B15*C4 in Cell C15 and copying the entry to C15:F21. Options that are chosen have values of 1 in Cells B15:B21. Those that are not chosen have zero values in Cells B15:B21.

Note the logic of the entry =B15+B16 in Cell B24. When the Solver tool is executed, the value of this cell must equal one. This requires that either B15 or B16 must equal one, but not both: Either the existing plant must be modernized or a new one must be built.

The sums of the present values and annual costs for the selected options are calculated by entering =SUM(C15:C21) in Cell C22 and copying the entry to D22:F22. The uncommitted funds each year are

(Continued)

calculated by entering =D11-D22 in Cell D23 and copying the entry to E23:F23. The sum of the uncommitted funds is calculated in Cell B25 by the entry =SUM(D23:F23).

The Solver tool is executed with a goal of maximizing the total present value in C22. The trial values of the decision variables entered in Cells B15:B21 are allowed to vary to achieve this goal, subject to the constraint that they are binary values of 1 and 0 (i.e., B15:B21=binary). (For some reason, it seems to work best to scroll down to bin, for binary, before entering the cell identities. An alternative is to enter the constraints B15:B21>=0, B15:B21<=1, and B15:B21=integer.) Additional constraints are imposed by requiring that capital expenditures each year are not more than the funds available (D22:F22<=D11:F11) and that **either** the existing plant *must* be modernized **or** a new plant *must* be built (B24=1). Figure 12-17 shows the settings for these items.

Figure 12-17

Solver Settings for Optimizing the Choices for Capital Budgeting

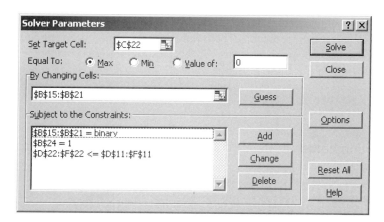

Click the Options button on the Solver Parameters dialog box and select "Assume Linear Model," as shown in Figure 12-18. Linear models can be solved faster than nonlinear ones. The linear model can be used here

Figure 12-18

Solver Options Dialog Box with Assume Linear Model Selected

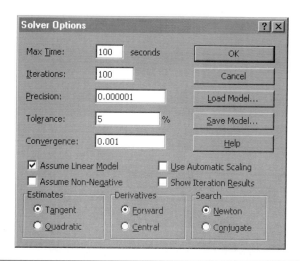

(Continued)

because the entries in Cells C15:F23 are **all linear** functions of the decision variables in Cells B15:B21. (In other situations where Solver is used and the "Assume Linear Model" option has been chosen, an error message is given when the entries are **not** linear models of the decision variables and a solution is attempted. In such cases, go back and click off the choice.)

The solution shows that the best choices are to modernize the existing plant, redesign existing product B, and develop new product Y. These give a total present value of $1,075,000. There are uncommitted funds in each of the three years, with a total of $145,000 for all three years.

Example 12.10: How would the results for Example 12.9 change if the available funds were increased to $500,000 for year 1 and $600,000 for year 2?

Solution: A solution is obtained by copying Figure 12-17 to a new worksheet, editing Cells D11 and E11 with the new values $500,000 and $600,000, and executing Solver again. In fact, *depending on the starting values in Cells B15:B21*, **two** solutions can be obtained, both providing the same maximum present value of $1,650,000 in Cell C22. The first of these is shown in Figure 12-19. This solution was obtained with the starting values for the decision variables the same as those in Figure 12-17.

Figure 12-19

Solution A: Starting Values in Cells B15:B21 Are Those Shown in Figure 12-17

	A	B	C	D	E	F
1	Example 12-10 GOLIATH INDUSTRIES (First solution with increase in available funds)					
2	**Input Data**		Present	Annual Costs		
3	Option		Value	Year 1	Year 2	Year 3
4	Modernize existing plant		$250,000	$150,000		
5	Build new plant		$650,000	$100,000	$300,000	
6	Expand distribution network		$150,000	$80,000	$20,000	
7	Redesign existing product A		$175,000	$75,000		
8	Redesign existing product B		$225,000	$100,000	$45,000	
9	Develop new product X		$400,000	$50,000	$200,000	$75,000
10	Develop new product Y		$600,000	$60,000	$250,000	$200,000
11	`			$500,000	$600,000	$300,000
12	**Decisions**	Choices				
13		(1 = Yes,	Present	Annual Costs		
14	Option	0 = No)	Value	Year 1	Year 2	Year 3
15	Modernize existing plant	1	$250,000	$150,000	$0	$0
16	Build new plant	0	$0	$0	$0	$0
17	Expand distribution network	0	$0	$0	$0	$0
18	Redesign existing product A	1	$175,000	$75,000	$0	$0
19	Redesign existing product B	1	$225,000	$100,000	$45,000	$0
20	Develop new product X	1	$400,000	$50,000	$200,000	$75,000
21	Develop new product Y	1	$600,000	$60,000	$250,000	$200,000
22	Present value and annual costs		$1,650,000	$435,000	$495,000	$275,000
23	Uncommitted funds			$65,000	$105,000	$25,000
24	Build OR modernize plant constraint	1				
25	Sum of uncommitted funds	$ 195,000				

(Continued)

An alert CFO might also seek a second goal of minimizing the annual costs—or, in other words, maximizing the sum of the uncommitted funds in Cell B25—while, at the same time, still achieving the first goal of maximizing the present value of the investments. To achieve this second goal while still achieving the first, we need to solve the example again with new Solver settings. The new target is Cell B25, which contains the sum of the uncommitted funds. The objective is to maximize this. A new constraint is added that requires the total present value in Cell C22 to equal $1,650,000, which is the value that satisfies the first goal. Figure 12-20 shows the new Solver settings.

Figure 12-20

Solver Settings for Maximizing Uncommitted Funds with Same Total Present Value

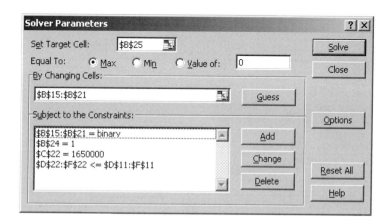

Figure 12-21 shows the results when the spreadsheet is executed a second time with the new Solver settings. Note that the present value of the investments in Cell C22 equals $1,650,000, as before, and the sum of the uncommitted funds has been increased to $270,000. This is an increase of $75,000 over the earlier value of $195,000, a saving of $75,000 in cost over the earlier solution.

The best decision is to build the new plant, redesign existing products A and B, and develop new product Y. This provides a present value of $1,650,000 for the decisions and leaves $270,000 of uncommitted funds.

The existence of alternate solutions that satisfy an objective is not unusual. Rather than an annoyance, it is an opportunity. Two or more optimum solutions mean that CFOs have a choice of options—and an opportunity to invoke a second objective in addition to the first. It is sort of like having your cake and eating it too!

Risk and Non-Financial Criteria

A warning! Note the caveat in the chapter introduction: "The difficult part is choosing where to invest—that is, determining those projects with the highest rewards *and the least risk*" (italics added).

As a practical matter, many criteria that should be included are difficult to translate into a net present value, modified internal rate of return, or years to break even. They involve uncertain information and risks. They include not knowing exactly what the future will bring, how competitors will act, the technical

Figure 12-21

Solution with Maximum Present Value and Maximum Sum of Uncommitted Funds

	A	B	C	D	E	F
1	Example 12-10: GOLIATH INDUSTRIES (Increase in available funds + 2nd goal)					
2	Input Data		Present	Annual Costs		
3	Option		Value	Year 1	Year 2	Year 3
4	Modernize existing plant		$ 250,000	$ 150,000		
5	Build new plant		$ 650,000	$ 100,000	$ 300,000	
6	Expand distribution network		$ 150,000	$ 80,000	$ 20,000	
7	Redesign existing product A		$ 175,000	$ 75,000		
8	Redesign existing product B		$ 225,000	$ 100,000	$ 45,000	
9	Develop new product X		$ 400,000	$ 50,000	$ 200,000	$ 75,000
10	Develop new product Y		$ 600,000	$ 60,000	$ 250,000	$ 200,000
11	Available funds			$ 500,000	$ 600,000	$ 300,000
12	Decisions	Choices				
13		(1 = Yes,	Present	Annual Costs		
14	Option	0 = No)	Value	Year 1	Year 2	Year 3
15	Modernize existing plant	0	$ -	$ -	$ -	$ -
16	Build new plant	1	$ 650,000	$ 100,000	$ 300,000	$ -
17	Expand distribution network	0	$ 0	$ 0	$ 0	$ -
18	Redesign existing product A	1	$ 175,000	$ 75,000	$ -	$ -
19	Redesign existing product B	1	$ 225,000	$ 100,000	$ 45,000	$ -
20	Develop new product X	0	$ -	$ -	$ -	$ -
21	Develop new product Y	1	$ 600,000	$ 60,000	$ 250,000	$ 200,000
22	Present value and annual costs		$ 1,650,000	$ 335,000	$ 595,000	$ 200,000
23	Uncommitted funds	First goal		$ 165,000	$ 5,000	$ 100,000
24	Build OR modernize plant constraint	1	Second goal			
25	Sum of uncommitted funds	$ 270,000				

Key cell entries:	B24	=B15+B16
	C15	=$B15*C4, copy to C15:F21
	C22	=SUM(C15:C21), copy to D22:F22
	D23	=D11–D22, copy to E23:F23

Solver settings: **Target cell is B25, to be maximized.**
Cells to vary are B15:B21
Constraints: B15:B21=binary
D22:F22<=D11:F11

Achieving the first goal is a constraint on achieving the second goal.

B24=1 (Either modernize or build new plant.)
C22=1650000
Options: Assume linear model

feasibility of new products or production methods, energy costs, environmental hazards and constraints, political stability of foreign countries in which facilities might be located, the volatility of currency exchange rates, the length of time for completing construction of new facilities or remodeling existing ones, and so forth. Such criteria are difficult to quantify fully. Each will have different levels of importance. How well an investment satisfies them may be a subjective judgment rather than a hard number.

When decisions involve criteria that are subjective, "Rating and Ranking" scorecards can be used to help make the decisions more objective. Figure 12-22 illustrates the method.

Figure 12-22

Scorecard with Ratings for a Particular Investment or Project

	A	B	C	D	E	F	G	H
1	"RATING AND RANKING" SCORECARD FOR AN INVESTMENT OR PROJECT							
2		Relative	Rating of Potential Investment					
3		Importance	Excellent	Good	Fair	Poor	Terrible	Weighted
4	Criterion	or Weight	100	75	50	25	0	Score
5	Net present value	40%		1				30.00
6	Technical feasibility	15%	1					15.00
7	Political feasibility	20%				1		5.00
8	Market competition	15%					1	0.00
9	Time to complete	10%			1			5.00
10		100%				Total weighted score		**55.00**

Key Cell Entry: H5: =B5*SUMPRODUCT($C$4:$G$4,C5:G5), copy to H6:H9

Figure 12-22 lists five criteria (Column A) and their relative importance (Column B). The degree to which a project satisfies the criteria is judged excellent, good, fair, poor, or terrible—with a numerical value attached (Columns C to G). In Figure 12-22, the ratings for a particular project against each of the criteria are indicated by entering the number 1 in the appropriate cells. For example, the investment in Figure 12-22 is rated good for its net present value, excellent for its technical feasibility, and so on to a rating of fair for the time to complete. Multiplying a criterion's relative importance by a project's rating for the criterion gives the weighted score for the criterion (Column H). Thus, the weighted criterion score for satisfying the net present value criterion is 30.00 (calculated as 40 percent of 75). Adding the weighted scores for all criteria gives the investment's total weighted score, which is 55.00 (Cell H10).

Each investment is rated in the same manner, and the investments are ranked in the order of their total weighted scores.

The scorecard technique can be used to solicit the ratings of several judges and minimize personal biases. Each judge uses the scorecard approach to rate each investment in a consistent manner. The priorities for the different investments are then ranked according to the judges' average total weighted score for each project. Projects with higher values for their average total weighted scores are given higher priority than those with lower values. The scorecard helps ensure completeness and consistency among the judges in ranking alternative.

The choice of the scale for project rating is arbitrary and not important. Instead of a scale from 0 to 100, as in Figure 12-22, a scale from 0 to 10 might be used. The important thing is that the scale be applied consistently among judges and among the competing investments.

Admittedly, ranking isn't completely objective. The list of desirable criteria, their relative importance (or "weight"), and the ratings of how well an investment satisfies the criteria depends on the knowledge and experience of those judging the alternatives. The chief values of this approach are that it evaluates projects in a consistent manner and it helps avoid overlooking things that should be considered.

The technique is certainly not new. Most executives and lower-level managers already use it, although often subconsciously and superficially. Its value is enhanced by formalizing it into a well-defined procedure. This helps accomplish the following:

1. It motivates decision-makers. A formal procedure forces them to clarify their thinking and evaluations, and to develop clear concepts of worth and value relevant to the project and its cost.
2. It improves objectivity. A formal procedure helps limit prejudices and personal biases that might otherwise influence decisions.
3. It provides a systematic and consistent basis for evaluating projects. This is especially important when evaluations are sought from a number of judges who represent different points of view or biases.

Figure 12-23 summarizes the steps in assessing alternatives by ranking. Note that developing the procedure and using it to evaluate specific alternatives are separate steps. After the procedure has been developed, judges use it to rate each investment or project and use their total weighted scores to rank them.

Identify Assessment Criteria

The basis for deciding what is best should be well defined if choices are to be objective. The assessment procedure therefore begins with a list of criteria that describes what is wanted. Start with the objectives in very general terms, then translate or break them down into specific elements appropriate to the alternatives to be assessed. For example, a business goal of profitability might be subdivided into short-term and long-term profitability. A further breakdown might be the profitability contributed directly by a new product and that contributed indirectly by supporting the balance of a company's product line. For a company producing seasonal items, the potential for a new product to smooth out seasonal highs and lows in consumer demands may be important.

The list of criteria should be specific and complete. They represent a project's potential benefits against which its total value will be judged. The scope of criteria is wide. For company-sponsored projects, they should include all parts of the firm that will be affected by the decision—marketing, finance, operations, quality control, procurement, distribution, personnel, etc.—as well as the firm's suppliers, its customers, and the community. Do not overlook any factor that might affect whether or not a project should be done. The list should contain all criteria that are important in assessing the relative merits of the alternatives.

Foreign investments have special criteria and risks to be considered, such as available labor skills, expropriation (i.e., official government seizure of private property), ethnic strife, political instability, corruption, and currency fluctuation.

The criteria should be mutually exclusive, or at least relatively independent, so that judges can trade off satisfying one criterion at the expense of another. They should be significant in making the assessment. Don't waste time with criteria that are insignificant in reaching the project's objectives or that are satisfied equally by all alternatives.

Figure 12-23

Steps in Formalizing the Rating and Ranking Procedure

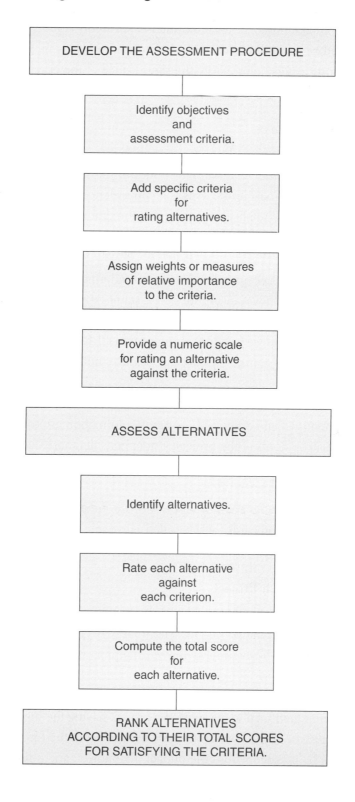

Add Criteria Measures

Identify how criteria can be measured. For example, the objective of compatibility with existing facilities and equipment might be measured by the dollars that would have to be invested in new facilities. As another example, the compatibility of a new computer-based information system with the existing workforce might be measured by the number of new job categories or skills that would be needed to operate and maintain it. Adding measures helps clarify the significance of the criteria, even though it is not possible to assign exact values to all the measures for the various alternatives at the time of evaluating.

Assign Measures of Importance

Each criterion should be assigned a weighting factor that expresses its relative importance to a company's overall objectives compared to other criteria. The values of the weighting factors in Figure 12-24 have been chosen so that their sum equals unity. This is a convenience, but not a necessity. Other scales can be used so long as they reflect the relative importance of the different criteria.

Provide a Scale for Assessing How Well Criteria Are Satisfied

Assign relative numerical values to express how well each alternative satisfies the criteria. Several rating systems can be used. In the one shown in Figure 12-22, point ratings from 0 to 100 (in increments of 25 points) have been used, so that a "perfect" score for a project would be 100. Other systems use values from −1 to +1, with −1 for complete failure to satisfy a criterion to +1 for complete success. Still other systems use values from 0 to 10. In any systems, the scales are relative, not absolute.

Identify Alternatives

Each project must be identified and described. As much information as possible should be included that might help assess the relative merits of the projects under consideration.

Assess Each Project against All Criteria

Judge how well each project satisfies each criterion. For the procedure illustrated by Figure 12-24, this is done by preparing separate scorecards for each alternative and checking the appropriate columns, as indicated by the number 1s in Figure 12-24.

Compute Total Scores for Each Project

A project's score for each criterion is obtained by multiplying how well the project satisfies the criterion by the criterion's importance or relative weight. The total score for a project is the sum of its weighted scores for each criterion. Spreadsheets simplify the scoring process.

Ranking Alternative

List projects in the order of their total scores, with the project having the highest total score at the top and one with the lowest total score at the bottom. Choose the project at the top and as many more in succession from the top as can be pursued within the budget, manpower, and other constraints.

Figure 12-24

Solution of Example 12.10 with Total Weighted Scores from Rating Used in Place of Net Present Values for the Investments or Projects

	A	B	C	D	E	F	G
1	Example 12-10: GOLIATH INDUSTRIES (With investments rated)						
2	**Input Data**		Present	Rating	Annual Costs		
3	Option		Value	Score	Year 1	Year 2	Year 3
4	Modernize existing plant		$250,000	65.00	$ 150,000		
5	Build new plant		$650,000	55.00	$ 100,000	$ 300,000	
6	Expand distribution network		$150,000	50.00	$ 80,000	$ 20,000	
7	Redesign existing product A		$175,000	52.50	$ 75,000		
8	Redesign existing product B		$225,000	40.00	$ 100,000	$ 45,000	
9	Develop new product X		$400,000	55.00	$ 50,000	$ 200,000	$ 75,000
10	Develop new product Y		$600,000	35.00	$ 60,000	$ 250,000	$ 200,000
11	Available funds				$ 350,000	$ 300,000	$ 300,000
12	**Decisions**	Choices					
13		(1 = Yes,	Present	Rating	Annual Costs		
14	Option	0 = No)	Value	Score	Year 1	Year 2	Year 3
15	Modernize existing plant	1	$250,000	65.00	$ 150,000	$ -	$ -
16	Build new plant	0	$0	0.00	$ -	$ -	$ -
17	Expand distribution network	0	$0	0.00	$ -	$ -	$ -
18	Redesign existing product A	1	$175,000	52.50	$ 75,000	$ -	$ -
19	Redesign existing product B	0	$0	0.00	$ -	$ -	$ -
20	Develop new product X	1	$400,000	55.00	$ 50,000	$ 200,000	$ 75,000
21	Develop new product Y	0	$0	0.00	$ -	$ -	$ -
22	**Total rating score and allocated funds**		$825,000	172.50	$ 275,000	$ 200,000	$ 75,000
23	Uncommitted funds				$ 75,000	$ 100,000	$ 225,000
24	Build OR modernize plant constraint	1					
25	**Sum of uncommitted funds**	$ 400,000					

```
Key cell entries:  C15:  =$B15*C4, copy to C15:G21
                   C22:  =SUM(C15:C21), copy to D22:G22
                   B24:  =B15+B16
                   B25:  =SUM(D23:F23)
                   E23:  =E11–E22, copy to F23:G23
Solver settings:   Target cell is D22, to be maximized.
                   Cells to vary are B15:B21.
                   Constraints: B15:B21 = binary
                                E22:G22 <= E11:G11
                                B24 = 1 (Either modernize or build new plant.)
```

Ratings can be substituted for net present values for selecting investments with funding over several years. Figure 12-24, for example, illustrates how Example 12.10 can be solved based on maximizing the total rating scores of the chosen investments or projects rather than on their net present values.

To create Figure 12-24, copy Figure 12-19 and insert a column for a set of rating scores (Column D in Figure 12-24). Enter values that have been determined for the rating scores in Cells D4:D10. Copy the entries in Cell C15:C21 to D15:D21.

Figure 12-24 shows that incorporating "nonfinancial considerations" into management decisions can provide markedly different results and decisions based solely on financial values.

There are many variations on the simple rating and ranking technique for selecting investments or projects. One of the most sophisticated of these is the Analytic Hierarchy Process (AHP), which is being used for many complex decisions in industry and government. AHP is based on a pairwise comparison of all possible combinations of criteria and investments or projects. Although relatively easy to apply when the number of investments or projects and criteria is small, the number of comparisons and calculations when there are more than three investments and four criteria requires the use of special software to make the technique practical. For more details, see the reference by Saaty in the bibliography.

Students' Feedback on Rating and Ranking

I found the Rating and Ranking scorecard in the section on nonfinancial criteria most interesting because it is an objective and organized way of arriving at critical decisions in complex situations—personal or professional. I have probably used this process before, albeit subconsciously, and so it is nice to learn how to do it in an organized way as it will make subsequent decisions more manageable.

* * *

I could have used the example of Goliath Industry earlier this year. I was working on an optimization problem that had decisions akin to the binary choices made in the examples. This is a very useful optimization technique, which I will use in the future.

* * *

Including nonfinancial criteria is an important consideration for my company. We use two categories: risk and quality. In addition to presenting financial criteria for a project, we provide an assessment of how the project would either reduce risk for the organization or provide improved quality in our products or services.

* * *

International businesses must consider political risks when deciding whether or not to invest in projects in foreign countries. Projects in countries with frequent leader changes are very vulnerable to failure because the new government that comes into power may be unfavorable to them.

* * *

The most useful thing I found in this chapter was the use of Solver to optimize a set of goals. It allowed us to maximize a goal and, at the same time, while still achieving the first goal, proceed to other goals with lower priorities. Also, with the scenario analysis, we can measure the sensitivity of the outputs to variations in the input variables, which allows us to see the effects of changes more clearly on the outcomes.

* * *

This session couldn't have come at a better time for me. We had one of the divisional controllers come into our staff meeting last week to talk about the capital budgeting process. Among other things, she was showing spreadsheets similar to the ones we've been creating in this class.

Concluding Remarks

Capital budgeting is the making and managing of expenditures in long-lived assets such as plants, equipment, real estate, and new product development. Such expenditures involve large sums of money and can determine a large part of a company's operations in the future and how profitable it will be.

Companies generally have a number of potential projects competing for capital funds. Capital budgets for the alternatives are therefore analyzed closely to determine their costs and payoffs before selecting those for funding.

Be sure to use the correct criterion for financial payoffs. The most commonly used criterion is net present value (NPV function). If the rate of return is used as a criterion, be sure to use the modified internal rate of return (MIRR function) rather than the internal rate of return (IRR function). For investments in new products that may have short lives, the years to break even can be a more important criterion than the net present value.

This chapter shows how to create spreadsheets to evaluate the financial payoffs from capital investments. It also shows how to measure the sensitivity of payoffs to variations in the input variables (so-called What if? or scenario analysis), and how to determine what a good CFO must do to improve results (Goal Seek and optimization with Solver). It shows how to optimize a single goal or a succession of goals—satisfying the most important goal first, and then proceeding to other goals with progressively lower priorities.

Nonfinancial criteria are also important. A positive NPV is only a signal for evaluating other factors, such as risks, competition, and technical feasibility. As globalization and the "flattening" of the world continues, considerations such as political stability, government assistance and restrictions, low-cost labor, availability of required labor skills, and others become increasingly important.

This chapter also demonstrates the use of binary variables for making dichotomous decisions. These can be yes/no decisions that identify which capital projects should be selected to optimize their aggregate net present worth and that are within the constraints of funds available for the next few years. They help plan multiyear capital asset programs.

Finally, the chapter discussed a common technique ("Rating and Ranking" scorecards) for including subjective or nonfinancial criteria in the selection of projects for investing capital funds. Many times a project with the highest net present value is not selected for political or other reasons that cannot be directly included in calculating the net present value.

Capital budgets, such as those developed in this chapter, are related to cash budgets, such as those developed in Chapter 8, as well as to income statements, balance sheets, and cash flow statements, such as those developed in Chapter 1 and forecast in Chapter 5. All of these documents are integrated in "Enterprise Resource Planning" (ERP) systems. As plans, they are the basis for creating systems for measuring actual performance, such as cost accounting structures, customer satisfaction surveys, and quality control reports. Differences between planned and actual performance, in turn, become the basis for management actions, including corrective action when actual performance falls short of what was planned.

Chapter 13

Capital Budgeting: Applications

CHAPTER OBJECTIVES

Management Skills

- Understand how to evaluate the financial payoffs for various types of capital budgeting alternatives.
- Understand the importance of product quality in making decisions.

Spreadsheet Skills

- Apply Excel's NPV, IRR, and MIRR commands to calculate the net present value, internal rate of return, and modified internal rate of return from various types of capital investments.
- Formulate nested IF statements to calculate the payback periods (or years to break even) for various types of capital investments.
- Use one- and two-variable input tables to analyze the sensitivity of financial payoffs to changes in the cash inflows, interest rates, and other conditions with which managers must cope.
- Create downside risk curves that display the probabilities for achieving financial goals.
- Use Solver to identify the changes needed to satisfy new goals.
- Create a "spider plot" to compare the impacts of changes in input variables on an investment's payoff.

Overview

The preceding chapter covered the basic principles of capital budgeting. In this chapter, we apply the principles to create spreadsheets for analyzing several types of capital budgeting problems, such as the following:

- New facilities
- Nonresidential real estate
- Replacing equipment
- Improving processes of production

- Research and development of new products
- Redesigning existing products
- Leasing equipment or facilities
- Creating new distribution systems

New Facilities

New facilities such as factories for manufacturing goods, office buildings, equipment for serving customers, and management information systems are major investments. They involve large expenditures of capital with major impacts on cash flows and profit.

Case Study: Albertus Enterprises, Inc.

Albertus Enterprises, Inc. is a large manufacturing firm. It plans to invest $800,000 in buying and installing new factory equipment that will increase its production capacity. The company expects that the new equipment will increase its net annual income, after subtracting operating costs and other expenses from its revenues, by $350,000.

    Albertus expects to pay for and have the equipment installed and operating during the first quarter of the year. As a result, the equipment will qualify for a full year's depreciation for each year of its use. The company expects that the equipment will remain in use for five years, at the end of which time the company expects to sell the equipment for one-tenth of its original value. The company will pay tax on its capital gain if the equipment is sold at more than its book value at the time of sale, and the company will receive a reduction in its corporate tax if the equipment is sold at less than its book value at the time of sale.

    Under IRS rules, new factory equipment has a class life of seven years. **For tax purposes**, the annual depreciation must be computed according to the Modified Accelerated Cost Recovery System (MACRS). (*IRS Publication 534: Depreciation*) Use the appropriate schedule in Figure 11-2 in Chapter 11 for the percentages of the capital investment to be depreciated each year. Note that because the equipment will be acquired in the first quarter of the year, Albertus will use values in the first column for the mid-quarter convention in the table.

    The company will use a discount rate (i.e., cost of capital or "hurdle rate") of 12.5 percent to evaluate the investment. It expects that any reinvestment of future cash flows would be at the same rate. Albertus pays a combined federal-state-local tax rate of 40 percent, based on its taxable income.

    1. What is the investment's net present value (NPV), internal rate of return (IRR), and modified internal rate of return (MIRR) at the end of five years?

    2. What is the discounted payback period (or break-even point) for the capital investment?

    3. Prepare a chart that shows how the net present value (NPV) of the capital investment changes with time, from the time of the investment to the end of five years. Identify the break-even point on the chart.

(Continued)

4. Prepare a second chart that shows how the IRR and MIRR change with time, from the time of the investment to the end of five years. Identify the break-even point on the chart.
5. If the CFO of Albertus wishes to break even by the end of 3.5 years, how much would the annual year-end benefits from the investment have to be?
6. Examine the sensitivity of the investment's NPV, IRR, and MIRR at the end of five years and the payback period to the annual benefits from the equipment. Use annual benefits from $200,000 to $500,000 in increments of $50,000. Prepare charts that show how the NPV, MIRR, and payback period vary with the annual benefits.
7. Would you recommend that Albertus invest in the new equipment? Justify your recommendation.

Solution: 1 and 2: Figure 13-1 is a spreadsheet solution for parts 1 and 2.

Figure 13-1

Capital Budgeting Analysis for Albertus Enterprises, Inc.

	A	B	C	D	E	F	G
1	ALBERTUS ENTERPRISES, INC.						
2	Equipment cost, including installation	$800,000					
3	Salvage value, as percent of cost	10.0%					
4	Market value, end of Year 5	$80,000					
5	Discount and reinvest rates	12.5%					
6	Tax rate	40.0%					
7	Year	0	1	2	3	4	5
8	Depreciation and Book Value Schedule						
9	Depreciation base	$ 800,000					
10	Annual depreciation, per MACRS		25.00%	21.43%	15.31%	10.93%	8.75%
11	Annual depreciation, dollars		$ 200,000	$ 171,440	$ 122,480	$ 87,440	$ 70,000
12	Year-end book value		$ 600,000	$ 428,560	$ 306,080	$ 218,640	$ 148,640
13	Year-End Cash Flow Analysis						
14	**Regular income**						
15	Annual year-end benefit		$ 350,000	$ 350,000	$ 350,000	$ 350,000	$ 350,000
16	Taxable regular income		$ 150,000	$ 178,560	$ 227,520	$ 262,560	$ 280,000
17	Tax on regular income		$ 60,000	$ 71,424	$ 91,008	$ 105,024	$ 112,000
18	ATCF for regular income		$ 290,000	$ 278,576	$ 258,992	$ 244,976	$ 238,000
19	**Sale of equipment**						
20	Income from sale of equipment						$ 80,000
21	Capital gain(loss)						$ (68,640)
22	Capital gain tax (benefit)						$ (27,456)
23	ATCF from sale of equipment						$ 107,456
24	After-Tax Cash Flow Analysis						
25	After-tax cash flow (ACTF)	$ (800,000)	$ 290,000	$ 278,576	$ 258,992	$ 244,976	$ 345,456
26	Net present value	$ (800,000)	$ (542,222)	$ (322,113)	$ (140,214)	$ 12,723	$ 204,426
27	Internal rate of return (IRR)	–100.00%	–63.75%	–20.14%	1.75%	13.28%	22.34%
28	Modified internal rate of return (MIRR)	–100.00%	–63.75%	–13.05%	5.50%	12.94%	17.74%
29	Discounted break-even point, years	3.92					

Key Cell Entries

B29: =IF(D26>=0,C7–C26/(D26–C26),IF(E26>=0,D7–D26/(E26–D26),IF(F26>=0,E7–E26/(F26–E26),
IF(G26>=0,F7–F26/(G26–F26),"Failed"))))

C11: =$B$9*C10, copy to D11:G11
C12: =B9–C11
D12: =C12–D11, copy to E12:G12
C16: =C15–C11, copy to D16:G16
C17: =C16*$B$6, copy to D17:G17
C18: =C15–C17, copy to D18:G18

G21: =B4–G12
G22: =G21*B6
G23: =G20–G22
C25: =C18+C23, copy to D25:G25
C26: =NPV($B$5,$C$25:C25)+$B$25, copy to D26:G26
C27: =IRR($B$25:C25,–0.5), copy to D27:G27
C28: =MIRR($B$25:C25,$B$5,$B$5), copy to D28:G28

(Continued)

Data values are shown in italics in the upper left corner of Figure 13-1. The market value of the equipment at the end of five years is calculated by the entry =B2*B3 in Cell B4.

Annual depreciation and book value are calculated in rows 9 to 12. Values for the annual percentage depreciation for MACRS are entered as data in Cell C10:G10. Annual depreciation is calculated by entering =C10*$B$9 in Cell C11 and copying to D11:G11. Year-end book values are calculated by entering =B9-C11 in Cell C12, entering =C12-D11 in Cell D12, and copying the last entry to E12:G12.

Year-end after-tax cash flows from the regular income are calculated in Rows 15 to 18. In this example, the annual year-end benefits are the same each year, and we will examine the sensitivity of the results to the value. Therefore, enter the data value 350,000 in Cell C15, enter =$C$15 in Cell D15, and copy the entry in D15 to E15:G15. When a new value is entered in C15, this will result in the same value in all cells in the Range C15:G15.

The taxable regular income is calculated by entering =C15-C11 in Cell C16 and copying to D16:G16. The tax on the regular income is calculated by entering =C16*$B$6 in Cell C17 and copying to D17:G17. The after-tax cash flow for the regular income is calculated by entering =C15-C17 in Cell C18 and copying to D18:G18.

The series of calculations for the after-tax cash flow from the sale of the equipment at the end of year 5 is in Rows 20 to 23. The income from the sale of the equipment is calculated by entering =B4 in Cell G20. The capital gain(loss), which equals the difference between the book value at the time of sale minus the sale price, is calculated by entering =G20-G12 or =B4-G12 in Cell G21. Note that this is a loss because the book value is greater than the sale price. This creates a tax benefit, which is calculated by entering =G21*B6 in Cell G22. The after-tax cash flow from the sale of the equipment is calculated by entering =G20-G22 in Cell G23.

The series of calculations for the payoffs of the investment is in Rows 25 to 29. The after-tax cash flows from the investment are calculated by entering =-B9 in Cell B25, =C18 in Cell C25, copying the entry in C25 to D25:F25, and entering =G18+G23 in Cell G25.

The net present value at year 0 is entered as =B25 in Cell B26. The net present values for years 1 to 5 are calculated by entering =NPV($B$5,$C$25:C25)+$B$25 in Cell C26 and copying to D26:G26.

The internal rate of return at year 0 is entered as =-1 in Cell B27 and formatted as a percent. The internal rates of return for years 1 to 5 are calculated by entering =IRR($B$25:C25,-0.5) in Cell C27 and copying to D27:G27. (Note that the value -0.5 is a *guess* value. The guess should be changed to a better guess whenever the IRR command fails to converge to a value and returns an error message.)

The modified internal rate of return at year 0 is entered as =-1 in Cell B28 and formatted as a percent. The modified internal rates of return for years 1 to 5 are calculated by entering =MIRR($B$25:C25,$B$5,$B$5) in Cell C28 and copying to D28:G28.

The discounted break-even or payback period is calculated in Cell B29 by the entry

=IF(D26>=0,C7-C26/(D26-C26),IF(E26>=0,D7-D26/(E26-D26),
IF(F26>=0,E7-E26/(F26-E26),IF(G26>=0,F7-F26/(G26-F26),"Failed"))))

The results show that the investment's net present value at the end of five years is $204,426, its internal rate of return is 22.34 percent, its modified internal rate of return is 17.74 percent, and its discounted break-even or payback period is 3.92 years.

3 and 4. The upper chart of Figure 13-2 shows that the curve for the net present value crosses the line for NPV = 0 at 3.92 years. The lower chart of Figure 13-2 shows that the curves for the internal rate of return and the modified internal rate of return reach a value of 12.5 percent, which is the cost of capital and the reinvestment rate, at 3.92 years. (Recall that breaking even requires the rate of return to equal the discount rate of money, which is equivalent to requiring the NPV to equal zero.)

(Continued)

Figure 13-5

Sensitivity of the NPV, MIRR, and Break-Even Point to Annual Year-End Benefits

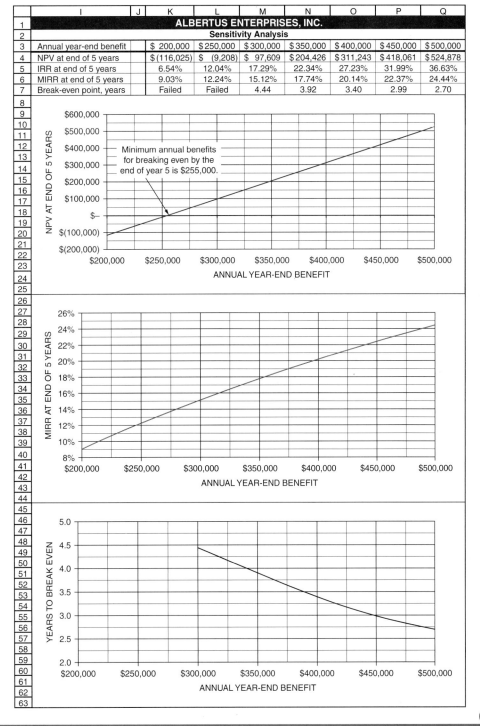

	I	J	K	L	M	N	O	P	Q
1			ALBERTUS ENTERPRISES, INC.						
2			Sensitivity Analysis						
3	Annual year-end benefit		$200,000	$250,000	$300,000	$350,000	$400,000	$450,000	$500,000
4	NPV at end of 5 years		$(116,025)	$(9,208)	$97,609	$204,426	$311,243	$418,061	$524,878
5	IRR at end of 5 years		6.54%	12.04%	17.29%	22.34%	27.23%	31.99%	36.63%
6	MIRR at end of 5 years		9.03%	12.24%	15.12%	17.74%	20.14%	22.37%	24.44%
7	Break-even point, years		Failed	Failed	4.44	3.92	3.40	2.99	2.70

(Continued)

You can use a one-variable input table to create the table at the top of Figure 13-5. To do this, enter the labels in Cells I3:I7. Make the following entries in Cells J3:J7 to connect cells in the main program with the sensitivity analysis portion of the spreadsheet shown at the top of Figure 13-5:

Cell J3: =C15 (This transfers the annual year-end benefit in Cell C15 to J3. Be sure the entries in Cells D15:G15 will vary when the value in Cell C15 is changed. One way to do this is to enter =C15 in Cell D15 and copy the entry to E15:G15.)
Cell J4: =G26   Cell J5: =G27   Cell J6: =G28   Cell J7: =B29

As these entries are made in Cells J3:J7, the cells will show the current values in C15, G26, G27, G28, and B29. To hide these values so they won't be confusing with the rest of the table, use the ;;; custom format (i.e., three semicolons). Figure 13-5 also shows the width of column J decreased. (You can also avoid showing the values in Cells J3:J7 by hiding column J.)

Enter the series of annual benefits in Cells K3:Q3. One convenient way to do this is to enter 200,000 and 250,000 in Cells K3:L3, center and format them as currency, select Cells K3:L3 with the mouse, grab the dark "move" box at the lower right corner of Cell L3, and drag to M3:Q3.

Highlight the range J3:Q7 and click on Table on the Data menu to access the Table dialog box shown in Figure 13-6. Enter C15 as the Row input cell and click OK or press Enter. The result is the set of values in Cells K4:Q7 of Figure 13-5. Format these to complete the table.

Figure 13-6

Entries in the Table Dialog Box for Sensitivity Analysis

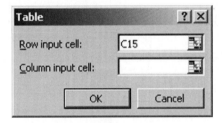

Plot the results to create the charts shown below the table in Figure 13-5. Note that the curve for years to break even does not extend to annual benefits less than $300,000, which is the lowest value for which the investment breaks even within the five-year analysis period. (If you really want to project the curve to lower values, you will have to generate additional values to do so. Or, you can recognize from the chart for NPV vs. Annual Benefit that the curve of the bottom chart would project to five years at annual benefits of approximately $255,000.)

7. Albertus should invest in the new equipment because its net present value is greater than zero and its rate of return is greater than the discount rate (or cost of capital). The equipment's payback period is 3.92 years. The investment will more than break even unless the annual year-end benefits drop below approximately $255,000 from the expected value of $350,000.

Case Study: The Dreyfuss Insurance Company

The Dreyfuss Insurance Company is considering the installation of a local area network (LAN) that will serve 15 employees at its Seattle headquarters.

Initial (startup) costs are as follows:

$60,000	Hardware acquisition	Computers, network routers, servers, and wiring
20,000	Software acquisition	Programming, licenses, and antivirus protection
10,000	Delivery and installation	Four-day project
5,000	Training	Week of on-site training and computer tutorials
15,000	Support and maintenance	Initial payment for the first year of a four-year maintenance contract

Continuing year-end annual costs are as follows:

$12,000	Support and maintenance	Three annual payments for the four-year maintenance contract, made at the ends of the first, second, and third years

Year-end annual benefits are as follows:

$50,000	Direct labor	Elimination of one worker
20,000	Support labor	Savings from reducing secretarial and clerical support
5,000	Materials	Reduced cost of paper and photocopies

Depreciation: MACRS, 5-years life, first-quarter convention. IRS regulations provide that software included in the purchase price of a computer system can be added to the basis of the computer system and depreciated. (The depreciable base of the company's investment is the sum of the costs of hardware, software, delivery, installation, and training.)

The company expects the system's useful life will be four years, at which point the market value of the hardware and software will be zero and will be discarded.

The risk-adjusted cost of capital is 12 percent, and the reinvest rate is 13 percent.

Tax rate is 40 percent for regular income and 30 percent for capital gain or loss.

※ ※ ※

In your answers to the following, format dollar values to the nearest whole dollar, format percentages for IRR and MIRR with two decimal places, and format the number of years to break even with two decimal places.

1. Calculate the values for NPV, IRR, and MIRR at the ends of years 1, 2, 3, and 4.
2. Calculate the number of years to break even.
3. The company's CFO is concerned with the effects of changes in the risk-adjusted cost of capital on the net present value of the investment at the end of four years and the years to break even. Prepare a one-variable input table that shows the effect of risk-adjusted costs of capital from 10 to 15 percent on the net present value at the end of four years and the years to break even.
4. Use your results from part 3 to prepare charts showing the effect of the risk-adjusted cost of capital on the net present value at the end of four years and the years to break even. Values on the X-axis of the charts should range from 10 to 15 percent with major increments of 1 percent and minor increments of 0.5 percent. Values on the Y-axis of the NPV chart should have major increments of $5,000 and minor increments of $2,500. Values on Y-axis of the Years to Break Even chart should have major increments of 0.10 year and minor increments of 0.05 year.

(Continued)

Solution: Figures 13-7 and 13-8 show the solution for this case study. Note that the annual payments for the maintenance and support contract are operating costs. These are incremental cash outflows that are tax deductible expenses. The initial "up-front" payment of $15,000 is part of the company's incremental cash outflow at time zero, and the other three payments of $12,000 each are part of the company's incremental cash outflow at the ends of years 1, 2, and 3.

Figure 13-7

Spreadsheet Solution for Dreyfuss Insurance Company Case Study

	A	B	C	D	E	F
1	DREYFUSS INSURANCE COMPANY					
2	**Initial costs**					
3	Hardware acquisition	$ 60,000				
4	Software acquisition	$ 20,000				
5	Delivery and installation	$ 10,000				
6	Training	$ 5,000				
7	Total cost (depreciable base)	$ 95,000				
8	Support and maintenance	$ 15,000	Initial "up-front" payment			
9	Initial cash outflow	$ 110,000				
10	**Depreciation of hardware and software**					
11	MACRS, 5-year life, 1st quarter					
12	Salvage value at end of third year	$ -				
13	**Continuing costs of operation**					
14	Support and maintenance	$ 12,000	Paid at ends of 1st, 2nd, and 3rd years.\			
15	**Year-end benefits**					
16	Eliminate one worker	$ 50,000				
17	Reduce secretarial and clerical support	$ 20,000				
18	Reduce cost of paper and photocopies	$ 5,000				
19	Total	$ 75,000				
20	**Financial rates**					
21	Risk-adjusted cost of capital	12.0%				
22	Reinvest rate	13.0%				
23	Tax rate on regular income	40.0%				
24	Tax rate for capital gains or losses	30.0%				
25	**Analysis (3-year period)**					
26	Year	0	1	2	3	4
27	Investment	$ (95,000)				
28	Year-end benefits		$ 75,000	$ 75,000	$ 75,000	$ 75,000
29	Support and maintenance	$ (15,000)	$ (12,000)	$ (12,000)	$ (12,000)	
30	**Before-tax cash flow**	$ (110,000)	$ 63,000	$ 63,000	$ 63,000	$ 75,000
31	MACRS depreciation rate		35.00%	26.00%	15.60%	11.01%
32	Annual depreciation		$ 33,250	$ 24,700	$ 14,820	$ 10,460
33	Taxable regular income	$ (15,000)	$ 29,750	$ 38,300	$ 48,180	$ 64,541
34	Tax on regular income	$ (6,000)	$ 11,900	$ 15,320	$ 19,272	$ 25,816
35	Capital loss (equals BV of investment)					$ 11,771
36	Tax benefit of capital loss					$ 3,531
37	**After-tax cash flow**	$ (104,000)	$ 51,100	$ 47,680	$ 43,728	$ 52,715
38	Net present value	$ (104,000)	$ (58,375)	$ (20,365)	$ 10,760	$ 44,261
39	Internal rate of return	-100.0%	-50.9%	-3.4%	18.1%	31.08%
40	Modified internal rate of return	-100.0%	-50.9%	0.7%	16.1%	22.83%
41	Year to break even (i.e., for NPV = 0)	2.65				

(Continued)

Figure 13-8

Sensitivity Analysis for Dreyfuss Insurance Company Case Study

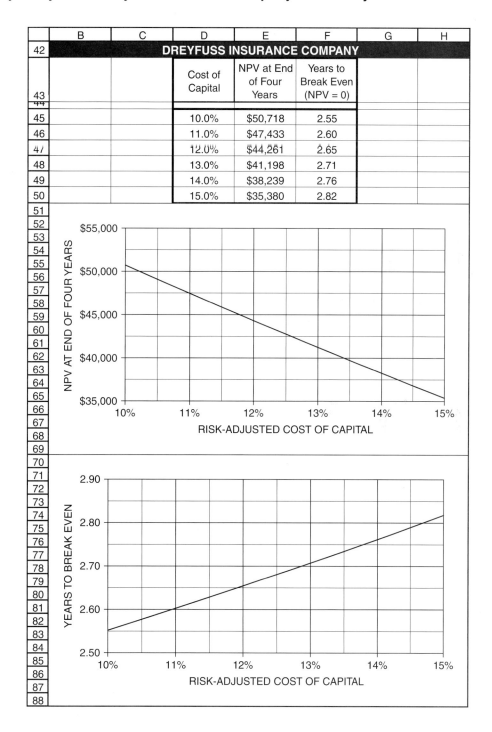

	B	C	D	E	F	G	H
42			DREYFUSS INSURANCE COMPANY				
43			Cost of Capital	NPV at End of Four Years	Years to Break Even (NPV = 0)		
44							
45			10.0%	$50,718	2.55		
46			11.0%	$47,433	2.60		
47			12.0%	$44,261	2.65		
48			13.0%	$41,198	2.71		
49			14.0%	$38,239	2.76		
50			15.0%	$35,380	2.82		

Nonresidential Real Estate

The real estate investments considered in this section are investments in income-producing properties, such as office buildings, warehouses, and homes that are leased or rented. This type of property is normally purchased by making a down payment and taking out a mortgage on the remainder of the purchase price.

Investing in income-producing property has many risks. It also yields handsome profits to those who can manage the risks successfully.

The appreciation of property has been a major attraction to investors. Although market and rental rates have increased over the long run, there have been periods when they have dropped. Investors hope for positive cash flows—that is, that rental income will be enough to cover mortgage payments and other expenses—until they sell a property, when they expect to reap a handsome profit. Sometimes, however, cash flows are negative and investors must reach into their own pockets to make up the balance.

Determining the net present values and rates of return for investments in nonresidential real estate requires handling a number of factors discussed in earlier chapters, such as property depreciation, taxes on regular income, and capital gains and losses. However, the Internal Revenue Service has special rules for these that must be followed.

IRS rules require nonresidential real property to be depreciated by the straight-line method with a life of 39 years and zero salvage value. The MACRS depreciation schedule (Table 11-2 in Chapter 11) shows percentage values depending on the month the property is placed in service. Depreciation is limited to buildings and installed equipment. *No depreciation is allowed for land.*

In general, a taxpayer will realize either a capital gain or loss when real estate investment property is sold. In recent years, real property has generally appreciated in value between the time of its purchase and sale, so that there is usually a capital gain when it is sold. The taxable capital gain is the amount realized from the sale (i.e., the selling price less selling expenses) minus the property's "adjusted tax basis." The property's "adjusted tax basis" is its original acquisition cost, including purchase expenses, plus the cost of any capital improvements less the cumulative depreciation at the time of sale. A taxpayer bears the burden of proof to provide evidence for the "adjusted tax basis."

The interest paid on mortgage loans is a deductible expense for figuring taxable income. Note that although the entire amounts of mortgage payments affect cash flows, *only the interest portion is a deductible expense.*

Property insurance, management cost, and the cost of routine maintenance are operating expenses that affect net income. Capital improvements (e.g., building additions and major remodeling of interiors or exteriors) are depreciable expenses.

Case Study: Armstrong Properties

Armstrong Properties is a large corporation that owns and manages many business properties. It is currently considering the purchase of an office building in downtown Central City. The purchase price of the building and the land on which it is built is $5 million. Armstrong would make a down payment of $1 million and take a 30-year first mortgage for the balance. The annual rate of interest on the mortgage would be 9.25 percent, and mortgage payments would be made monthly, beginning at the end of the first month. Expenses incurred by Armstrong for purchasing the building and land will be $50,000.

The market value of the property is expected to increase at an annual rate of 4 percent. Armstrong would sell the property at the end of five years at its market value at the time. The company estimates its expenses for selling the property will be $250,000.

The building has a rentable floor area of 20,000 square feet. Armstrong would rent space the first two years at a monthly rate $5/square foot, and the rate would increase by 4 percent each year after the first two. Occupancy is expected to average 85 percent for the first year, 92 percent for the second year, 95 percent for the third year, and 98 percent thereafter. The sum of annual expenses for maintenance, management, and property taxes is expected to be $500,000 for the first year and to increase at a rate of 3.5 percent each year thereafter.

The building will be depreciated by straight-line depreciation, based on zero salvage value and a life of 39 years. *Because land is not depreciable*, the property's depreciation is based on the initial cost of only the building, which is 80 percent of the property's purchase price. Assume that the property is placed in service in the first month of the first year. Depreciation, mortgage **interest**, and annual expenses for maintenance, management, and property taxes are deductible expenses for computing taxable normal income. Use 40 percent for the tax rate on the taxable normal income.

Because of the property's appreciation, there will be a substantial taxable capital gain when it is sold. The taxable capital gain is the amount realized from the sale (i.e., the price at which Armstrong sells the property less its selling expenses) minus the property's "tax basis." The property's "tax basis" is its original $5 million purchase price plus any purchase expenses and capital improvement costs less the cumulative depreciation at the time of sale. Use a value of 25 percent for the tax rate on taxable capital gain. Armstrong uses a risk-adjusted rate of return of 13 percent to evaluate the net present value of this type of investment. You may assume that the rate of return for reinvesting any cash inflow from the investment will also be 13 percent.

Do a year-end financial analysis for the five years to determine the after-tax net present value, internal rate of return, and modified rate of return for the investment.

Solution: Figure 13-9 is a spreadsheet solution. A problem such as this has many related parts. To simplify the logic, it is helpful to divide the spreadsheet into segments, as shown in Figure 13-9. Data values are at the top of the spreadsheet, and key cell entries are indicated at the bottom.

The end-of-the-month mortgage payments are calculated in Cell F6 by the entry =PMT(F4/12,F5*12,F3). Because the rate of interest is given in Cell F4 as the nominal annual rate, it is necessary to divide by 12 to convert to the actual monthly rate. Also, because the term is expressed in Cell F5 in years, it is necessary to multiply by 12 to convert to the number of months.

Rental rates and occupancy are shown in Rows 14 to 16. Note that the initial values change with time according to the percentages in Rows 15 and 16. The annual rental income is calculated by entering =$B$8*C14*12*C16 in C21 and copying to D21:G21.

Annual operating expenses in Row 17 change with time according to the percentages in Row 18. The values in Row 18 are repeated as cash outflows in Row 22. The annual mortgage payments are calculated by entering =12*$F$6 in Cell C23 and copying to D23:G23.

When the property is sold at the end of five years, there is a cash inflow equal to the selling price; this is calculated by the entry =B3*(1+B6)^G13 in Cell G24. You should recognize this entry as the right side of the equation for calculating a future value—vis-à-vis, F = P*(1+i)^n. There are also cash outflows for paying the selling expenses and for paying off the principal remaining on the mortgage. The latter is calculated by entering =-F3-CUMPRINC(F4/12,F5*12,F3,1,G13*12,0) in Cell G26. Be careful to get the signs correct in this entry.

(Continued)

Figure 13-9

Solution for Real Estate Investment

	A	B	C	D	E	F	G
1	Case Study: ARMSTRONG PROPERTIES (Sell at end of fifth year)						
2	Property Information				Mortgage Information		
3	Purchase price	$5,000,000		Principal		$4,000,000	
4	Down payment	$1,000,000		Annual rate		9.25%	
5	Purchase expenses	$50,000		Term, years		30	
6	Annual appreciation in market value	4.0%		End-of-month payment		($32,907)	
7	Selling expenses at sale	$250,000		Tax Rates			
8	Rentable area, sq.ft.	20,000		Taxable regular income		40.0%	
9	Building value, as % of price	80%		Taxable capital gains		25.0%	
10	Depreciable life, year	39					
11	Salvage value	$0					
12	Risk-adjusted rate of return or discount rate	13.0%					
13	Year	0	1	2	3	4	5
14	Rent rate, $/sq.ft/month		$5.00	$5.00	$5.200	$5.408	$5.624
15	Rental rate increase, %				4.0%	4.0%	4.0%
16	Occupancy		85.0%	92.0%	95.0%	98.0%	98.0%
17	Annual operating expenses		$500,000	$517,500	$535,613	$554,359	$573,762
18	Operating expenses increase, %			3.50%	3.50%	3.50%	3.50%
19	Year-end before-tax cash flows						
20	Property purchase	$ (1,050,000)					
21	Annual rental income		$ 1,020,000	$ 1,104,000	$ 1,185,600	$ 1,271,962	$ 1,322,840
22	Annual operating expenses		$ (500,000)	$ (517,500)	$ (535,613)	$ (554,359)	$ (573,762)
23	Annual mortgage payment		$ (394,884)	$ (394,884)	$ (394,884)	$ (394,884)	$ (394,884)
24	Receipts from sale of property (i.e., selling price)						$ 6,083,265
25	Selling expenses						$ (250,000)
26	Pay unpaid balance of mortgage						$ (3,842,564)
27	Total before-tax cash flow	$ (1,050,000)	$ 125,116	$ 191,616	$ 255,103	$ 322,718	$ 2,344,895
28	Tax calculation for regular income						
29	Regular income (rental income)		$ 1,020,000	$ 1,104,000	$ 1,185,600	$ 1,271,962	$ 1,322,840
30	Deductible Expenses						
31	Operating Expenses		$ 500,000	$ 517,500	$ 535,613	$ 554,359	$ 573,762
32	Depreciation (80% of purchase price/39 years)		$ 103,590	$ 103,590	$ 103,590	$ 103,590	$ 103,590
33	Mortgage interest		$ 368,917	$ 366,411	$ 363,663	$ 360,649	$ 357,345
34	Total deductible expenses		$ 972,507	$ 987,501	$ 1,002,865	$ 1,018,598	$ 1,034,696
35	Taxable regular income		$ 47,493	$ 116,499	$ 182,735	$ 253,364	$ 288,144
36	Tax on regular income		$ 18,997	$ 46,600	$ 73,094	$ 101,346	$ 115,258
37	Tax calculation for capital gain						
38	Amount realized from sale						$ 5,833,265
39	Tax basis						$ 4,532,051
40	Taxable capital gain						$ 1,301,213
41	Tax on capital gain (@ 25%)						325,303
42	Total tax		$ 18,997	$ 46,600	$ 73,094	$ 101,346	$ 440,561
43	After-tax results						
44	After-tax income or cash flow	$ (1,050,000)	$ 106,119	$ 145,016	$ 182,009	$ 221,373	$ 1,904,334
45	Net present value	$ (1,050,000)	$ (956,090)	$ (842,521)	$ (716,379)	$ (580,607)	$ 452,989
46	Internal rate of return	−100.00%	−89.89%	−57.44%	−32.04%	−15.11%	23.09%
47	Modified internal rate of return	−100.00%	−89.89%	−49.77%	−22.89%	−7.60%	21.40%

Cell entries for tax on regular income	Cell entries for cash flow from sale of property
C29: =C21, copy to D29:G29	G24: =B3*(1+B6)^G13
C31: =−C22, copy to D31:G31	G26: =−F3−CUMPRINC(F4/12,F5*12,F3,1,G13*12,0)
C32: =$B$9*($B$3+$B$5)/$B$10, copy to D32:G32	Cell enries for tax on capital gain
C33: =−CUMIPMT($F$4/12,$F$5*12,$F3,12*C13−11,12*C13,0), copy to D33:G33	G38: =G24+G25
C34: =SUM(C31:C33), copy to D34:G34	G39: =B3+B5−SUM(C32:G32)
C35: =C29−C34, copy to D35:G35	G40: =G38−G39
C36: =$F$8*C35, copy to D36:G36	G41: =G40*F9

Cell entries for total tax and after-tax income or cash flow
C42: =C36+C41, copy to D42:G42 (Total tax. Note that values in C41:F41 are zero.)
B44: =B27−B42, copy to C44:G44 (After-tax income or cash)
Other cell entries
E14: =D14*(1+E15), copy to F14:G14 (Rental rate, $/sq.ft/month)
C21: =$B$8*C14*12*C16, copy to D21:G21 (Annual rental income)
F6: =PMT(F4/12,F5*12,F3), (Monthly mortgage payment)
D17: =C17*(1+D18), copy to E17:G17 (Annual operating expenses)
C23: =12*$F$6, copy to D23:G23 (Annual mortgage payment)

(Continued)

The regular income from rents is transferred from Row 21 by entering =C21 in Cell C29 and copying to D29:G29. The tax on the regular income is based on the taxable regular income, which is calculated in Row 35 as the difference between the rental income in Row 29 and the sum of the deductible expenses in Rows 31 to 33. Although the total mortgage payments are part of the cash flow, only the interest portion is a deductible expense. This is calculated by entering =CUMIPMT($F$4/12,$F$5*12, $F$3,12*C13-11,12*C13,0) in Cell C33 and copying the entry to D33:G33. Note that the initial month each year is calculated by the term 12*C13-11, and the final month of each year by the term 12*C13. (For example, for year 2, the first month is 12*2 - 11 = 13, and the last month is 12*2 = 24; and so on.)

Annual depreciation is based on 80 percent of the sum of the purchase price and purchase expenses. The entry in Cell C32 is =$B$9*($B$3+$B$5)/$B$10 and is copied to D32:G32.

The calculations of the capital gain tax for selling the property at the end of year 5 are given in Rows 38 to 41. The amount realized from the sale is the selling price minus the selling expenses; this is calculated by the entry =G24-B7 or =G24+G25 in Cell G38. The tax basis is calculated by the entry =B3+B5-SUM(C32:G32) in Cell G39. The taxable capital gain is calculated by the entry =G38-G39 in Cell G40, and the tax on the capital gain is calculated by the entry =G40*F9 in Cell G41.

The total tax in Row 42 is the sum of the tax on regular income in Row 36 and the tax on the capital gain in Row 41. (The tax on capital gain is zero for all but year 5.) To calculate total tax, enter =C36+C41 in Cell C42 and copy to D42:G42.

The after-tax cash flow is the difference between the before-tax cash flow in Row 27 and the tax in Row 42. Enter =B27-B42 in Cell B44 and copy to C44:G44.

Once the after-tax cash flow is obtained, the net present value, internal rate of return, and modified internal rate of return are calculated as before, with Excel's NPV, IRR, and MIRR functions.

Note that the net present value is less than zero until the property is sold in year 5. After the initial investment in the property, the annual after-tax cash flow is positive throughout the balance of the analysis period—that is, the investment generates enough income to cover its costs. The investment pays off when the property is sold because of the appreciation in the property's value and the amount of leverage obtained by the down payment of only 20 percent of the property's cost. The gamble the investors have taken in making the investment is their expectation that property values will rise. If property values go down instead of up, there would be a substantial loss.

Case Study: Armstrong Properties Revisited

The CFO of Armstrong Properties is concerned about what might happen if the annual rate of appreciation of the property's value is different from the anticipated value of 4 percent. After some study, Armstrong's management staff reports that the annual rate of appreciation over the five-year period might go as low as a negative 4 percent to as high as a positive 10 percent. The staff also reports that their best estimates for the probabilities of the different rates are as shown in Table 13-1.

Table 13-1

Probabilities for Different Rates of Appreciation of Property Value

Rate of Appreciation	−4%	−2%	0	+2%	4%	6%	8%	10%
Probability	2%	5%	10%	25%	30%	20%	6%	2%

(Continued)

The values in Table 13-1 are given in increments of 2 percent for the rate of appreciation. They show that there is 30 percent probability that the most probable rate of appreciation will be 4 percent. However, there is a 2 percent chance it might go as low as –4 percent and a 1 percent chance it might go as high as 10 percent. And there is a 10 percent chance the property's value won't change at all.

1. Evaluate the sensitivity of Armstrong's earlier results (Figure 13-7) to variations in the annual rate of appreciation of the property's value from –4% to +10% in increments of 2% (i.e., rates of –4%, –2%, 0, 2%, 4%, 6%. 8%, and 10%).
2. Use the probabilities for the different rates of appreciation to determine the expected value of the investment and the probabilities for the investment earning various levels of net present value at the end of the fifth year, or less.

Solution: Figure 13-10 shows the results.

1. A one-variable input table has been used to perform the sensitivity analysis. Values for the rate of appreciation are entered in Cells I5:I12. The entries for transferring values back and forth between the main body of the spreadsheet and the table are as follows:

Cell I4:	=B6	This transfers values from Cells I5:I12 to B6.
Cell J4:	=G45	This transfers values from Cell G45 to J5:J12.
Cell K4:	=G46	This transfers values from Cell G46 to K5:K12.
Cell L4:	=G47	This transfers values from Cell G47 to L5:L12.

When these entries are made, the values in Cells I4:L4 will be 4.0%, $452,989, 23.09%, and 21.40%. To hide these values, custom format the cells with the text entries shown. To do this for Cell I4, select the cell, click on Custom on the Format menu, type "Apprcn" in the dialog box, and enter. Cells J4:L4 are formatted the same way.

Drag the mouse over the Range I4:L12, access the Table dialog box from the Data menu, and enter B6 as the column input cell, as shown in Figure 13-11. Click on OK or press Enter to create the set of values shown in Cells J5:L12 in Figure 13-10.

The analysis shows that the investment will barely break even if there is no appreciation in the property's value. It can lose as much as an NPV of $363,756 if the rate of appreciation drops to a negative 4 percent, which has only a 2 percent chance of happening. It can make as much as an NPV of $1,254,626 if the rate of appreciation is 10 percent, which has only a 2 percent chance of happening.

The middle portion of Figure 13-10 is a chart on which the net present value of the investment at the end of five years is plotted against the rate of appreciation. At a zero percent rate of appreciation, the investment does slightly better than breaking even (NPV equals $11,278, Cell J7).

2. An expected value analysis examines the payoffs and probabilities for all possible outcomes and discounts the payoffs by their probabilities. The analysis for Armstrong Properties has simplified this by classifying all possible outcomes to the eight rates of appreciation. The probabilities of these are entered in Cells M5:M12. The entry in Cell O5 is =$M5*J5 and is copied to O5:Q12. This multiplies each of the values in Cells J5:L12 by the probabilities in the same rows in M5:M12. The results in Cells O5:Q12 are called "weighted values"—that is, the payoffs are weighted by their probabilities of happening. The entry in Cell O13 is =SUM(O5:O12) and is copied to P13:Q13. The values in Cells O13:Q13 are known as the investment's "expected values" for NPV, IRR, and MIRR.

If a company uses this strategy on a number of similar investments, the total payoff for all investments should be approximately equal to the sum of the expected values of the payoffs for the individual investments. That is, some investments will do better than expected, and others will do worse. Those that do better will be balanced by those that do worse, so the total result should be as expected.

(Continued)

Figure 13-10

Effect of Annual Rate of Appreciation of Property Value on Financial Payoff

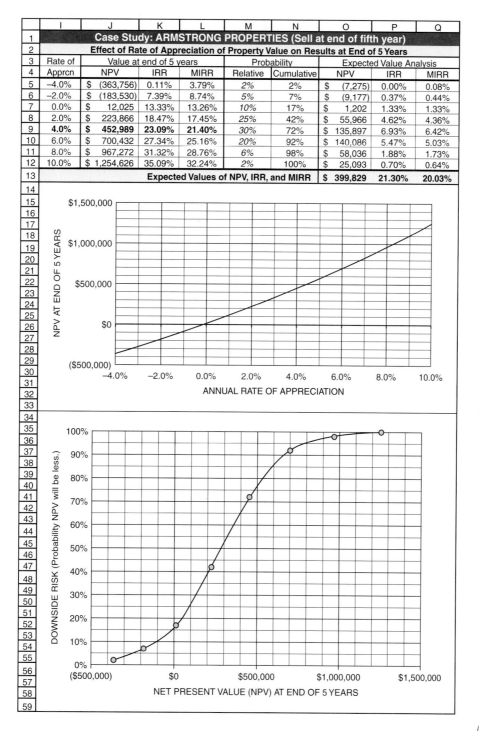

	I	J	K	L	M	N	O	P	Q
1		Case Study: ARMSTRONG PROPERTIES (Sell at end of fifth year)							
2		Effect of Rate of Appreciation of Property Value on Results at End of 5 Years							
3	Rate of	Value at end of 5 years			Probability		Expected Value Analysis		
4	Apprcn	NPV	IRR	MIRR	Relative	Cumulative	NPV	IRR	MIRR
5	–4.0%	$ (363,756)	0.11%	3.79%	2%	2%	$ (7,275)	0.00%	0.08%
6	–2.0%	$ (183,530)	7.39%	8.74%	5%	7%	$ (9,177)	0.37%	0.44%
7	0.0%	$ 12,025	13.33%	13.26%	10%	17%	$ 1,202	1.33%	1.33%
8	2.0%	$ 223,866	18.47%	17.45%	25%	42%	$ 55,966	4.62%	4.36%
9	**4.0%**	**$ 452,989**	**23.09%**	**21.40%**	**30%**	**72%**	**$ 135,897**	**6.93%**	**6.42%**
10	6.0%	$ 700,432	27.34%	25.16%	20%	92%	$ 140,086	5.47%	5.03%
11	8.0%	$ 967,272	31.32%	28.76%	6%	98%	$ 58,036	1.88%	1.73%
12	10.0%	$ 1,254,626	35.09%	32.24%	2%	100%	$ 25,093	0.70%	0.64%
13		Expected Values of NPV, IRR, and MIRR					$ 399,829	21.30%	20.03%

(Continued)

Figure 13-11

Table Dialog Box for One-Variable Input Table

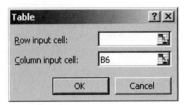

Expected values are a less than satisfactory means for evaluating one-time investments. Better techniques will be demonstrated in Chapters 14 and 15. However, expected values are very useful to identify optimum operating tactics. A good example is the practice of airlines to overbook seats. Airlines use the probabilities of no-shows and standbys to determine the optimum number of seats to overbook on a flight in order to minimize losses due to flying empty seats because of no-shows and the losses due to paying penalties when they cannot seat a ticketed customer. The optimum overbooking strategy is the one that minimizes the expected value of the loss on a flight. In the long run, over many flights, the **average** loss per flight for the optimum strategy equals the expected value. Investors can use expected values as part of their investment tactics for multi-stock portfolios.

3. Cumulative probabilities for the different levels of appreciation are calculated by entering =SUM($M$5:M5) in Cell N5 and copying the entry to N6:N12. The results show, for example, there is a probability of 72 percent (Cell N9) that the net present value will be $452,989 (Cell J9), or less. The lower chart in Figure 13-10 is a plot of the cumulative probabilities (Cells N5:N12) against the NPVs (Cells J5:J12). Such a chart is called a downside risk chart because it shows the probabilities that the NPV will be less than the values on the X-axis. We shall see more of this type of chart in later chapters.

Equipment Replacement

Factories and service facilities often find it profitable to replace equipment before it has worn out or reached the end of its useful life. The reasons are many, but technological obsolescence has been one of the primary reasons in recent years. New equipment that incorporates advances made possible by information technology is replacing old equipment in order to improve productivity, lower costs, and provide better service to customers. Whether or not to replace the old equipment with new equipment depends on the incremental costs and benefits—that is, the differences in the costs and benefits for investing in new equipment and those for continuing to operate with the old.

The initial cost of the new equipment replacement should include the cost of new equipment itself, any costs for delivering and installing the equipment, and any costs for training workers to operate it. In other words, the initial cost of the new equipment is the total of all expenses to make the equipment available for its intended use.

The initial cost for equipment replacement also includes the financial impacts of discarding the old equipment. Discarding the old equipment can involve capital gains or losses and the accompanying tax expenses or benefits, depending on whether or not the equipment's book value is more or less than the sale price.

The financial analysis should be based on the incremental annual benefits from the new equipment. For example, if the new equipment will reduce production costs, the incremental benefit is the difference between operating costs with the old and new equipment. Besides any savings in direct costs for labor, materials, and supplies, the total cost reduction should include any reductions in scrap losses for defective output and any savings in maintenance costs.

The financial analysis should also be based on the incremental value of depreciation between that for the new equipment and the depreciation deduction given up by discarding the old equipment, in other words, the depreciation deduction for the replacement.

Case Study: Zollner Electroplating Company

One of the pieces of equipment used in electroplating products at the Zollner Electroplating Company has been in use for five years and is being considered for replacement. The new equipment being considered to replace it would save $28,000 a year in production and related costs.

When the old equipment was purchased five years ago, it cost $40,000 for the equipment itself. There was also a charge of $500 to deliver the equipment to the factory and another $3,000 to install it. No operator training was necessary. At the time of purchase, it was thought that the equipment would last 10 years and have a salvage value of $5,000. Its current market value is $10,000. The company is using the straight-line method to depreciate the equipment.

The new equipment the company contemplates buying would cost $65,000. It would cost $1,000 to deliver it to the factory and $6,500 to install it in place of the old. It would also cost Zollner $500 to send a worker to the equipment manufacturer's plant for training in operating the equipment.

The new equipment would be put into operation in the first quarter of Zollner's financial year. MACRS would be used to depreciate the new equipment. MACRS uses a life of seven years for this type of manufacturing equipment and a salvage value of zero. However, Zollner's industrial engineer estimates that they would get rid of the new equipment at the end of five years, at which time they could sell it for $6,000.

Zollner's cost of capital for buying the equipment would be 13 percent. They expect that any future annual benefits from the new equipment could be invested at 13 percent.

Zollner's tax rate is 40 percent.

1. Calculate the net present value, internal rate of return, modified internal rate of return, and break-even point in years for replacing the old equipment with the new equipment.
2. Prepare a chart showing the change in the replacement's net present value with time over the five-year analysis period. Include grid lines for both the X and Y axes of the chart. Label both axes. Indicate the break-even point on the chart.

(Continued)

Figure 13-12

Equipment Replacement for Zollner Electroplating

	A	B	C	D	E	F	G
1	ZOLLNER ELECTROPLATING COMPANY						
2	Equipment Replacement Analysis						
3	Equipment Information	Old Machine	New Machine		Company Information		
4	Machine price	$40,000	$65,000		Marginal Tax Rate		40%
5	Expected life, years	10	5		Required Rate of Return		13%
6	Expected end-of-life salvage value	$5,000	$6,000				
7	Depreciation method	St. Line	MACRS				
8	Delivery to factory	$500	$1,000				
9	Installation	$3,000	$6,500				
10	Operator training	$0	$500				
11	"Ready-to-go" cost of equipment	$43,500	$73,000				
12	Years of use to date	5	0				
13	Current market value	$10,000	na				
14	Annual saving in operating costs	na	$28,000				
15	**Year**	**0**	**1**	**2**	**3**	**4**	**5**
16	Cash flows and calculations associated with replacing old equipment with new						
17	"Ready-to-go" cost of new equipment (cash outflow)	$ (73,000)					
18	Sale of old equipment	$ 10,000					
19	Accumulated depreciation for old equipment	$ 19,250					
20	Book value of old equipment	$ 24,250					
21	Taxable gain(loss) from sale of old equipment	$ (14,250)					
22	Capital gain tax on sale of old equipment	$ 5,700					
23	After-tax cash flow from sale of old equipment	$ 15,700					
24	**Net cash flow for replacing old equipment with new**	**$ (57,300)**					
25	**Annual saving in operating costs**		$ 28,000	$ 28,000	$ 28,000	$ 28,000	$ 28,000
26	Calculations of depreciation and taxes for replacement option						
27	Depreciation foregone on old equipment		$3,850	$3,850	$3,850	$3,850	$3,850
28	MACRS depreciation for new equipment		25.00%	21.43%	15.31%	10.93%	8.75%
29	Depreciation allowed on new equipment		$ 18,250	$ 15,644	$ 11,176	$ 7,979	$ 6,388
30	Net depreciation allowance for replacement option		$ 14,400	$ 11,794	$ 7,326	$ 4,129	$ 2,538
31	Taxable operating income		$ 13,600	$ 16,206	$ 20,674	$ 23,871	$ 25,463
32	Income tax on operating income		$ 5,440	$ 6,482	$ 8,269	$ 9,548	$ 10,185
33	**Net after-tax cash flow from operating income**		**$ 22,560**	**$ 21,518**	**$ 19,731**	**$ 18,452**	**$ 17,815**
34	**Adjustment for sale of new equipment at end of year 5**						
35	Cash inflow from sale (i.e., selling price)						$ 6,000
36	Book value						$ 13,563
37	Capital loss from selling new equipment						$ 7,563
38	Capital loss tax benefit						$ 3,025
39	**After-tax cash flow from sale of new equipment**						**$ 9,025**
40	**Total after-tax cash flow for replacement option**	**$ (57,300)**	**$ 22,560**	**$ 21,518**	**$ 19,731**	**$ 18,452**	**$ 26,840**
41	NPV	$ (57,300)	$ (37,335)	$ (20,484)	$ (6,810)	$ 4,507	**$ 19,075**
42	IRR	−100.00%	−60.63%	−15.95%	5.71%	16.88%	**25.82%**
43	MIRR	−100.00%	−60.63%	−9.42%	8.33%	15.16%	**19.68%**
44	Break-even point, years	**3.60**					

(Continued)

Solution: Figure 13-12 is a spreadsheet solution.

1. The spreadsheet of Figure 13-12 is divided into five modules. From top to bottom, they are
   (1) Input data and calculations
   (2) Analysis of the replacement cost at year 0
   (3) Analysis of the replacement's year-end benefits on operating income for years 1 to 4
   (4) Analysis of the sale of the new equipment at the end of year 5
   (5) Determination of the total after-tax cash flows and their effects on NPV, IRR, MIRR, and break-even point.

   You can, of course, combine entries and shorten the spreadsheet. There is no harm in doing that if the programmer has the ability to do so. However, many students (even good ones, in the author's experience) lose their way in the details and the tax consequences of selling and buying, depreciating the new and losing the depreciation of the old, and so forth. Showing all the steps better exposes the logic and avoids omissions and mistakes. From a management standpoint, the type of organization shown in Figure 13-12 provides a better understanding of how money is flowing in and out, and why.

   The "ready-to-go" cash outflows for the old and new equipment are calculated by entering =B4+SUM(B8:B10) in Cell B11 and copying the entry to C11. The cash outflow for paying for the "ready-to-go" cost of the new equipment is entered as -C11 in Cell B17. The cash inflow from the sale of the old equipment is entered as =B13 in Cell B18. The five years of accumulated straight-line depreciation for the old equipment is calculated as =(B5-B12)*(B11-B6)/B5 in Cell B19. The book value of the old equipment is calculated as =B11-B19 in Cell B20. The taxable capital gain or loss on the sale of the old equipment is calculated as =B18-B20 in Cell B21. Because the selling price of $10,000 is less than the book value of $24,250, there is a capital loss of $14,250. This generates a tax saving or cash inflow of $5,700, which is calculated in Cell B22 by the entry =-G4*B21. The after-tax cash flow from the sale of the old equipment is calculated by the entry =B18+B22 in Cell B23, which is the sum of the selling price plus the tax saving due to the capital loss. The net cash flow for replacing the old equipment with the new is calculated by the entry =B17+B23 in Cell B24. This value is repeated in Cell B25 as the total after-tax cash flow at year 0.

   The annual savings in operating costs for years 1 to 5 are entered in Row 25 by copying the entry =$C$14 in Cell C25 to D25:G25. To calculate the net allowance for depreciation, we need to subtract the depreciation that has been given up for selling the old equipment from the depreciation for the new equipment. This is accomplished by the following steps: The straight-line depreciation foregone on the old equipment is calculated by entering =($B$11-$B$6)/$B$5 in Cell C27 and copying it to D27:G27. The MACRS depreciation allowance for the new equipment is calculated by entering the appropriate percentage values from Table 11-2 in Chapter 11 into Cells C28:G28, entering =C28*$C$11 in C29, and copying the entry in C29 to D29:G29. The net depreciation allowance is calculated by entering =C29-C27 in C30 and copying to D30:G30. The taxable operating income is calculated by entering =C25-C30 in Cell C31 and copying to D31:G31. The tax on the operating income is calculated by entering =$G$4*C31 in C32 and copying to D32:G32. The net after-tax cash flow from operating income is calculated by entering =C25-C32 in Cell C33 and copying to D33:G33.

   The entry in Cell G35 for the cash inflow from selling the new equipment at the end of year 5 is =C6. The book value of the new equipment at the time of sale is calculated in Cell G36 by the entry =C11-SUM(C29:G29). Because the book value is more than the selling price, there is a capital loss that is calculated in Cell G37 by the entry =G36-G35. This results in a capital loss tax benefit calculated in Cell G38 by entry =G4*G37. The after-tax cash from the sale of the new equipment is calculated by the entry G35+G38 in Cell G39.

(Continued)

Values for the total after-tax cash flow for the replacement option are calculated by entering =B24+B33+B39 in Cell B40 and copying the entry to C40:G40. Values for the net present value, internal rate of return, modified internal rate of return, and break-even point are calculated from the total after-tax cash flow in the same manner as before.

2. Figure 13-13 shows the net present value of the replacement option as a function of the number of years from the time of the investment. The break-even point is 3.60 years.

Figure 13-13

Net Present Value vs. Time for Equipment Replacement Proposal

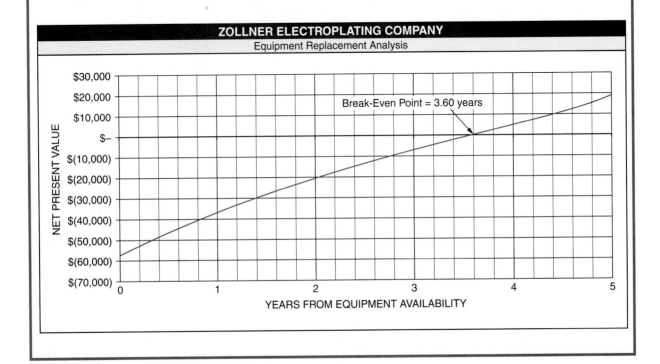

Process Improvement

Improving productivity is a never-ending goal in factories and service facilities. Corporations spend millions each year to cash in on savings made possible by advances in information, production, and distribution technologies. They spend additional millions to educate and train their workforces, including tuition reimbursement programs to send employees to universities to learn better management techniques. They also spend millions to convert to processes that reduce the adverse effects of toxic wastes on the environment.

Case Study: Bracken Manufacturing

For the past two years, Bracken Manufacturing has produced a major component for one of the automobile models built by the Redford Motor Company. The two companies recently signed a long-term contract for the procurement of 800,000 units each year for the next three, beginning at the end of the current year. The contract provides that Bracken will upgrade its manufacturing processes with the twin goals of (1) reducing the unit variable cost of production, and (2) improving quality so that fewer units fail to satisfy performance specifications and end up as scrap.

Bracken is considering two process improvements, designated A and B, to improve the output from the final assembly area of its plant. Table 13-2 gives information for the current process and the two options.

Table 13-2

Investment Cost and Unit Variable Cost for Final Assembly

Process	Investment	Unit Variable Cost
Current Process	NA	$325
Process A	$1,000,000	$340
Process B	$5,000,000	$340

Units from final assembly are inspected 100 percent. Those that pass inspection are shipped to Redford Motors, whereas those that fail to pass inspection are either reworked or scrapped, depending on the cause for failing to pass inspection. Reworked units are sent back for a second inspection and are either accepted, sent back for being reworked a second time, or scrapped. The cycle is repeated for a maximum of three reworkings. Any units that fail to pass inspection after the third reworking are scrapped. It costs $25/unit for inspection and an average of $95 to rework a unit that has failed to pass inspection. Because of toxic materials used in the units, scrapping costs $5/unit.

Table 13-3 gives the probabilities for being accepted and shipped to the customer after inspection, for being sent to rework after inspection, and for being scrapped after inspection. For example, for the current production process, there is a 75 percent probability that units will pass inspection after final assembly or after rework. There is a 20 percent probability that a unit will be sent for reworking after inspection, and a 5 percent probability that a unit will be scrapped after inspection. (In other words, for every 100 units that go to inspection, 75 units are accepted, 20 units are reworked, and 5 units are scrapped.) After the third rework, all 25 percent that fail to pass inspection are scrapped.

Table 13-3

Transition Probabilities from Inspection

From Inspection	Current Process			Process A			Process B		
	To Customer	To Rework	To Scrap	To Customer	To Rework	To Scrap	To Customer	To Rework	To Scrap
1 to 3	75%	20%	5%	80%	17%	3%	85%	13%	2%
4	75%	0%	25%	80%	0%	20%	85%	0%	15%

(Continued)

The three-year contact helps Bracken raise capital to buy the new equipment to improve its production facility; for example, it can borrow at a lower rate of interest from banks because of the assurance their loan will be repaid. As part of the incentive for process improvement, the contract provides that savings will be shared. Bracken will retain 75 percent of the amount by which it is able to reduce the variable cost of production and pay back the other 25 percent to Redford.

1. Determine the after-tax rates of return for the two new processes. Use a three-year period for financial analysis. Use the MACRS method with a seven-year lifetime for the equipment, and assume that the equipment will be put into operation during the first quarter of Bracken's fiscal year. You may also assume that the market value of the equipment will be the same as its book value at the end of three years. Use a cost of capital of 13 percent and a tax rate of 40 percent for the incremental income that Bracken will earn from the investment.
2. Prepare a chart that provides separate curves for the change in the net present values of the investments in Process A and Process B over the three-year lifetime of the contract.
3. Which process should Bracken choose? Why?

Solution: Figure 13-14 shows the flow of units from final assembly through the cycles of inspection, rework, delivery to customers, and scrap cycles of the current process. It traces the flow from final assembly to inspection and then to (1) good products that can be shipped to customers, (2) defective products that are reworked and sent back to be inspected again, and (3) defective products that are scrapped.

Figure 13-14

Flow of Products from Final Assembly, with Transition Probabilities for the First Three Inspection Rounds with the Current Process

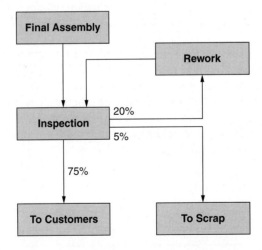

Figure 13-15 is a spreadsheet solution for part 1 of the problem. The challenge in solving this case study is to determine the financial benefits from the process improvements being considered. Part of this challenge is handling the costs of inspecting, reworking, and scrapping units.

1. The first step calculates the variable costs of producing good units with the current assembly process. This analysis is shown in the top of Figure 13-15.

(Continued)

Figure 13-15

Total Annual Costs and Unit Variable Costs

	A	B	C	D	E	F	G	H	I
1					BRACKEN MANUFACTURING				
2			Old assembly process with 800,000 good units/year to customer						
3				Transition Probabilities					
4				from Inspection					
5			To	To	To				
6			Customer	Rework	Scrap				
7	Rounds 1 to 3		75%	20%	5%				
8	After 3rd rework		75%	0%	25%				
9		Assemble-Inspect-Rework-Scrap Cycle Analysis							
10			Number of Units						
11		From	To	To	To		Variable Cost Analysis		
12	Round	Inspection	Customer	Rework	Scrap		Units	Unit Cost	Cost
13	1	854,701	641,026	170,940	42,735	Assemblies	854,701	$325	$ 277,777,778
14	2	170,940	128,205	34,188	8,547	Inspections	1,066,667	$25	$ 26,666,667
15	3	34,188	25,641	6,838	1,709	Reworks	211,966	$95	$ 20,136,752
16	4	6,838	5,128	0	1,709	Scrap	54,701	$5	$ 273,504
17	Totals	1,066,667	800,000	211,966	54,701	Total annual variable cost =			$ 324,854,701
18						Variable cost of a good unit =			$406.07
19		New assembly process A with 800,000 good units/year to customer ($1,000,000 investment)							
20				Transition Probabilities					
21				from Inspection					
22			To	To	To				
23			Customer	Rework	Scrap				
24	Rounds 1 to 3		80%	17%	3%				
25	After 3rd rework		80%	0%	20%				
26		Assemble-Inspect-Rework-Scrap Cycle Analysis							
27			Number of Units						
28		From	To	To	To		Variable Cost Analysis		
29	Round	Inspection	Customer	Rework	Scrap		Units	Unit Cost	Cost
30	1	830,694	664,555	141,218	24,921	Assemblies	830,694	$340	$ 282,435,893
31	2	141,218	112,974	24,007	4,237	Inspections	1,000,000	$25	$ 25,000,000
32	3	24,007	19,206	4,081	720	Reworks	169,306	$95	$ 16,084,089
33	4	4,081	3,265	0	816	Scrap	30,694	$5	$ 153,469
34	Totals	1,000,000	800,000	169,306	30,694	Total annual variable cost =			$ 323,673,451
35						Annual saving in variable cost from new assembly process A =			$ 1,181,250
36						Annual payback to customer (25% of annual saving) =			$ 295,312
37						Total annual cost =			$ 323,968,763
38						Variable cost of a good unit =			$404.96
39		New assembly process B with 800,000 good units/year to customer ($5,000,000 investment)							
40				Transition Probabilities					
41				from Inspection					
42			To	To	To				
43			Customer	Rework	Scrap				
44	Rounds 1 to 3		85%	13%	2%				
45	After 3rd rework		85%	0%	15%				
46		Assemble-Inspect-Rework-Scrap Cycle Analysis							
47			Number of Units						
48		From	To	To	To		Variable Cost Analysis		
49	Round	Inspection	Customer	Rework	Scrap		Units	Unit Cost	Cost
50	1	819,057	696,199	106,477	16,381	Assemblies	819,057	$340	$ 278,479,537
51	2	106,477	90,506	13,842	2,130	Inspections	941,176	$25	$ 23,529,412
52	3	13,842	11,766	1,799	277	Reworks	122,119	$95	$ 11,601,306
53	4	1,799	1,530	0	270	Scrap	19,057	$5	$ 95,287
54	Totals	941,176	800,000	122,119	19,057	Total annual variable cost =			$ 313,705,542
55						Annual saving in variable cost from new assembly process B =			$ 11,149,159
56						Annual payback to customer (25% of annual saving) =			$ 2,787,290
57						Total annual cost =			$ 316,492,831
58						Variable cost of a good unit =			$395.62

(Continued)

Figure 13-15 is divided into three modules. Each calculates the variable costs for producing 800,000 good units of product. The top module calculates the costs for the current assembly process, the middle module calculates the costs for Process A, and the bottom module calculates the costs for Process B. Each module is organized in the same manner. In each module, the number of good units supplied to the customer is 800,000 (Cells C17, C34, and C54), as required by Bracken's contract with Redford.

Enter a trial value (e.g., 100,000) in Cell B13 for the number of units that move from final assembly to the first round of inspection. To calculate the number of units that move from the first, second, and third rounds of inspection to customers, rework, and scrap, enter =$B13*C$7 in Cell C13 and copy to C13:E15. Change this entry to =$B16*C8 in Cell C16 and copy to D16:E16. The number of units that move from rework to inspection on each round is entered as =D13 in B14 and copied to B15:B16. Calculate the totals by entering =SUM(B13:B16) in Cell B17 and copying to C17:E17.

The next step is to use Excel's Goal Seek tool to determine the number of units from final assembly (i.e., the number of units from inspection on the first round in Cell B13) needed to end with 800,000 units of good products to customers (the value in Cell C17). Figure 13-16 shows the Goal Seek dialog box with the settings. The result in Cell B13 is 854,701 units. (Excel's Solver tool can be used as an alternative to the Goal Seek tool.)

Figure 13-16

Goal Seek Dialog Box with Settings to Determine the Number of Units from Final Assembly to Produce 800,000 Units of Good Product with Bracken's Current Assembly Process

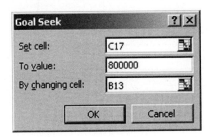

The annual variable cost for producing 800,000 units of good product with Process A, and the resulting unit cost, are computed in Cells G13:I18. The total cost includes the cost of assembling 854,701 units, inspecting 1,066,667 units, reworking 211,966 units, and scrapping 54,701 units. These values are calculated in Cells B13, B17, D17, and E17 and transferred to Cells G13:G16. Cells H13:H16 have data values for the unit costs for assembling with Process A, inspecting, reworking, and scrapping. Multiplying the number of units by the unit costs gives the total costs; that is, the entry in I13 is =G13*H13 and the entry is copied to I14:I16. The total cost is calculated in Cell I17 by the entry =SUM(I13:I16). The variable cost of a good unit is calculated by the entry =I17/C17 in Cell I18.

The analysis for Process A is made in the same manner. Cells A2:I18 are copied to the lower portions of the spreadsheet and edited with the new transition probabilities and unit costs. Excel's Goal Seek tool is used to determine the number of units to inspection from final assembly that must be made to produce 800,000 good units. Three rows are added for calculating the annual saving with the new assembly process, the annual payback to Bracken's customer, and Bracken's total annual cost for producing 800,000 good units. To compute the first of these for Process A, enter =I17-I34 in Cell I35. To compute the second, enter =0.25*I35 in Cell I36. To compute the third, enter =I34+I36 in Cell I37. The variable cost of a good unit for Process A is then calculated in Cell I38 by the entry =I37/C34. The analysis for Process B is made in the same manner.

(Continued)

2. Figure 13-17 calculates the net present value, internal rate of return, and modified internal rate of return at the end of three years for investing in the process improvements. The chart at the bottom shows changes in the net present values of the two processes with years from the investment, then one year, as compared to almost two years for Process A.

Figure 13-17

Capital Budgeting Analysis for Process Improvement at Bracken Manufacturing

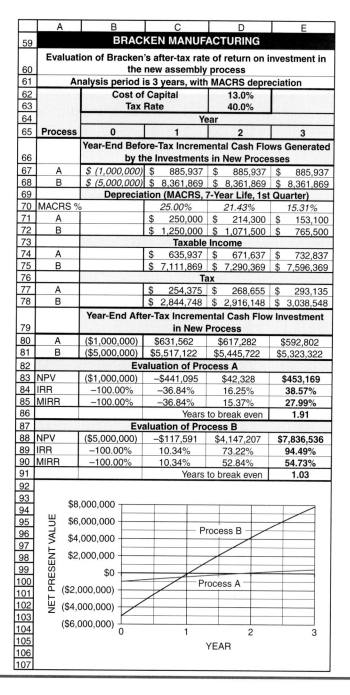

	A	B	C	D	E
59	**BRACKEN MANUFACTURING**				
60	Evaluation of Bracken's after-tax rate of return on investment in the new assembly process				
61	Analysis period is 3 years, with MACRS depreciation				
62		Cost of Capital		13.0%	
63		Tax Rate		40.0%	
64		Year			
65	**Process**	0	1	2	3
66		Year-End Before-Tax Incremental Cash Flows Generated by the Investments in New Processes			
67	A	$ (1,000,000)	$ 885,937	$ 885,937	$ 885,937
68	B	$ (5,000,000)	$ 8,361,869	$ 8,361,869	$ 8,361,869
69		Depreciation (MACRS, 7-Year Life, 1st Quarter)			
70	MACRS %		25.00%	21.43%	15.31%
71	A		$ 250,000	$ 214,300	$ 153,100
72	B		$ 1,250,000	$ 1,071,500	$ 765,500
73		Taxable Income			
74	A		$ 635,937	$ 671,637	$ 732,837
75	B		$ 7,111,869	$ 7,290,369	$ 7,596,369
76		Tax			
77	A		$ 254,375	$ 268,655	$ 293,135
78	B		$ 2,844,748	$ 2,916,148	$ 3,038,548
79		Year-End After-Tax Incremental Cash Flow Investment in New Process			
80	A	($1,000,000)	$631,562	$617,282	$592,802
81	B	($5,000,000)	$5,517,122	$5,445,722	$5,323,322
82		Evaluation of Process A			
83	NPV	($1,000,000)	–$441,095	$42,328	**$453,169**
84	IRR	–100.00%	–36.84%	16.25%	**38.57%**
85	MIRR	–100.00%	–36.84%	15.37%	**27.99%**
86				Years to break even	**1.91**
87		Evaluation of Process B			
88	NPV	($5,000,000)	–$117,591	$4,147,207	**$7,836,536**
89	IRR	–100.00%	10.34%	73.22%	**94.49%**
90	MIRR	–100.00%	10.34%	52.84%	**54.73%**
91				Years to break even	**1.03**

(Continued)

The first step in this series of calculations is to enter the year-end before-tax incremental cash flows generated by the investments in the new processes. The entries in Cells B67 and B68 are the negative values of the investments. The incremental savings are calculated by entering =$I$35-$I$36 in Cell C67 and copying the entry to D67:E67, and by entering =$I$55-$I$56 in Cell C68 and copying the entry to D68:E68.

Depreciation is calculated by using the MACRS schedule for seven-year property and the mid-quarter convention for putting the equipment into service in the first quarter (Table 11-2). Taxable income, tax, and after-tax cash flows are calculated in the same manner as before.

Once the after-tax cash flows have been determined, the NPV, IRR, and MIRR functions are used to calculate the net present value, internal rate of return, and modified internal rate of return. The reinvestment rate for calculating the modified internal rates of return is assumed to be the same as the cost of capital. The years to break even item is determined by interpolating between the NPV values at the ends of years 1 and 2 (which are the last year for a negative NPV and the first year for a positive NPV for both processes).

3. Bracken should choose Process B because of its higher NPV and MIRR. The return on the investment of $5 million in Process B at the end of 3 years is an MIRR of 54.73 percent. Process B breaks even in just slightly more.

Improving quality requires management attention and often involves costs. Yet it is a truism that "Quality doesn't cost. It pays!" Increased profits can far outweigh the cost of investing in quality. Nevertheless, quality can be a "hard sell" to executives focused on short-time profits.

A firm's industrial engineers make analyses such as those for the Bracken case to justify recommendations to do what is needed to improve quality. This type of analysis encourages financial managers to recognize rather than overlook the benefits from improving production processes and the savings possible from quality control—*despite an increase in manufacturing costs.*

The Bracken case study illustrates several points that astute executives have learned in implementing the "Just-in-Time" (JIT) philosophy correctly. By giving its supplier a three-year contract, rather than doling out short-term purchase orders, Redford Motors has made it possible for Bracken to go to its lenders and borrow money to make the large investment needed to improve its production process. The arrangement provides incentives to both buyer and supplier. Both share the cost savings.

Note also the impact of quality control. Although the investment for Process B is five times as much as for Process A and has the same unit cost for final assembly ($340/unit) as Process A, it reduces the number of units that must be produced, inspected, reworked, and scrapped in order to end up with same 800,000 units per year to Redford Motors. **Doing it right the first time has a huge payoff!**

A note in *Business Week* points out: "Because most top managers were weaned on finance or marketing, manufacturing often gets short shrift when capital budgets are drawn up. Consultants find that manufacturers routinely funnel millions into reducing costs, yet pinch pennies when it comes to the factory, where investment can bring big gains in productivity and profits." (*Business Week*, November 23, 1998, p. 137)

Business Week's comments apply as much to service facilities as to factories. I daresay none of us is without examples we can cite from our experience of the costs of shoddy service. In fact, as the example illustrates, the benefits from quality control can far outweigh the costs for having to repeat and repair—and often losing customers. *Quality costs and benefits are an important part of financial analysis for capital budgeting.*

Leasing

Leasing is a common method for financing property, facilities, and equipment. Leases are contracts between an asset's owner (called the lessor) and the user (the lessee). A lease gives the lessee the right to use the asset in exchange for periodic payments to the lessor.

For defining operating leases of equipment, the lessor is often a manufacturer that leases its own products to the lessee (**sales-type leases**). Sometimes the lessor is an independent leasing company that buys from the manufacturer and leases it to the lessee (**direct leases**). In this case, the lessor may borrow funds from creditors in order to buy the equipment from the manufacturer (**leveraged leases**). At other times, the owner of an asset sells it to another firm and immediately leases it back (**sale and lease-back leases**). This allows the original owner to raise cash for immediate needs and still retain the use of the asset while the lease is paid off.

Lease terms vary. **Operating leases** are generally for shorter durations than the useful life of the asset leased and, for this reason, they are not fully amortized; the lessor does not recover the asset's full cost. The lessor reacquires possession of the asset at the expiration of the operating lease and can lease it again for further use. **Financial leases**, on the other hand, are fully amortized. A lessee can cancel an operating lease before its expiration date. However, a lessee cannot cancel a financial lease and must make all payments or face bankruptcy. Leases also differ in requirements for the lessee to insure and maintain the leased asset and the right of the lessee to renew on the expiration of the lease.

Leasing a car for a day or week during a vacation trip is an example of a short-term lease. Leasing trucks, factory machinery, computers, or airplanes for a number of years are examples of long-term financial leases that are involved in capital budgeting. Such leases are the most common method of financing equipment.

For the lessee, the choices are to buy or to lease. For the lessor, the problem is to identify the highest rental rate that would be acceptable to a lessee.

The following case study is for a long-term financial lease of operating equipment from the standpoint of the lessee. It shows how to identify whether it is better for a company to lease or buy operating equipment. Note the treatment of depreciation, the firm's cost of capital or discount rate, the lessor's rental rate, and taxes. As the owner of the asset leased, the lessor gets a tax shield for the asset's depreciation. The lessee can claim the lease payments as an operating expense. The benefits generated by the equipment and such expenses as maintenance, repair, and insurance are assumed to be the same regardless of whether the equipment is leased or purchased.

Case Study: Epplewhite Corporation

The executives of Epplewhite Corporation must decide whether to purchase or lease equipment with an installed cost of $100,000. The equipment will be used for seven years and sold by the owner for 10 percent of the cost. Other details of the two options are given at the top of Figure 13-18, which also provides the solution.

(Continued)

Figure 13-18

Evaluation of Lease and Buy Options for Epplewhite Corporation

	A	B	C	D	E	F	G	H	I
1					**EPPLEWHITE CORPORATION**				
2					**Evalution of Lease-vs-Buy Options**				
3	**Purchase Option**		**Lease Option**				**Comparison of Options**		
4	Equipment Cost	$100,000	Lease Principal			$100,000	NPV for Lease Option		$ (62,862)
5	Discount Rate (WACC)	10.00%	Annual Interest Rate			12.00%	NPV for Buy Option		$ (66,992)
6	Corporate Tax Rate	40%	Life of Loan, Years			7	NPV for (Lease - Buy)		$ 4,130
7	MACRS depreciation, first-quarter convention		Annual Payment			$19,564	Which option is better?		**Lease**
8	Life, years	7							
9	Salvage value, pct of cost	10%							
10					**Year**				
11			0	1	2	3	4	5	6	7
12	**MACRS factor**		25.00%	21.43%	15.31%	10.93%	8.75%	8.74%	8.75%
13			**Lease Option**						
14	Lease payments	$ (19,564)	$ (19,564)	$ (19,564)	$ (19,564)	$ (19,564)	$ (19,564)	$ (19,564)	$ -
15	Tax benefit from lease payments	$ 7,826	$ 7,826	$ 7,826	$ 7,826	$ 7,826	$ 7,826	$ 7,826	$ -
16	Incremental After-Tax Cash Flow	$ (11,738)	$ (11,738)	$ (11,738)	$ (11,738)	$ (11,738)	$ (11,738)	$ (11,738)	$ -
17	NPV of Lease Option								$ (62,862)
18			**Buy Option**						
19	Purchase equipment	$ (100,000)							
20	Depreciation		$ 25,000	$ 21,430	$ 15,310	$ 10,930	$ 8,750	$ 8,740	$ 8,750
21	Tax benefit from depreciation		$ 10,000	$ 8,572	$ 6,124	$ 4,372	$ 3,500	$ 3,496	$ 3,500
22	Cash inflow from sale of equipment								$ 10,000
23	Book value at time of sale								$ 1,090
24	Taxable capital gain								$ 8,910
25	Tax on capital gain @ 40%								$ 3,564
26	Cash inflow from sale of equipment								$ 6,436
27	Incremental After-Tax Cash Flow	$ (100,000)	$ 10,000	$ 8,572	$ 6,124	$ 4,372	$ 3,500	$ 3,496	$ 9,936
28	NPV of Buy Option								$ (66,992)
29			**After-Tax Cash Flow, Lease Option - Buy Option**						
30	Lease - Buy After-Tax Cash Flow	$ 88,262	$ (21,738)	$ (20,310)	$ (17,862)	$ (16,110)	$ (15,238)	$ (15,234)	$ (9,936)
31	NPV of Lease instead of Buy								$ 4,130
32				**Sensitivity of Lease-or-Buy Decision**					
33				**to Interest Rates for Leasing and Buying**					
34			Buy Rate			Lease Rate			
35				9.0%	10.0%	11.0%	12.0%	13.0%
36			7.0%	Lease	Buy	Buy	Buy	Buy
37			8.0%	Lease	Lease	Lease	Buy	Buy
38			9.0%	Lease	Lease	Lease	Lease	Lease
39			10.0%	Lease	Lease	Lease	Lease	Lease
40			11.0%	Lease	Lease	Lease	Lease	Lease
41			12.0%	Lease	Lease	Lease	Lease	Lease

Key Cell Entries

F7: =–PMT(F5,F6,F4,0,1)
B14: =–$F$7, copy to C14:H14
B15: =$B$6*B14, copy to C15:H15
B16: =B14–B15, copy to C16:H16
B19: =–B4
C20: =$B$4*C12, copy to D20:I20
C21: =$B$6*C20, copy to D21:I21
B27: =B19
C27: =C21, copy to D27:H27
B30: =B16–B27, copy to C30:I30

I22: =B9*B4
I23: =B4–SUM(C20:I20)
I24: =I22–I23
I25: =B6*I24
I26: =I22–I25
I27: =I21+I26
I17: =NPV($B$5,C16:H16)+B16, copy to I28 and I31
I4: =I17
I5: =I28
I6: =I4–I5
I7: =IF(I6>0.1,"Lease",IF(I6<–0.1,"Buy","Neutral"))

(Continued)

Solution: The annual payment for the lease option is calculated by the entry =-PMT(F5,F6,F4,0,1) in Cell F7. Note that the value of the final argument is 1 because the payments are made at the beginning of each period rather than the end.

The lease payments calculated in Cell F7 are transferred to Cells B14:H14. These payments are operating expenses for Epplewhite and are therefore deductible for tax purposes. The annual values of the tax benefit they generate are calculated by entering =$B$6*B14 in Cell B15 and copying it to Cells C15:H15. The incremental after-tax cash flows are calculated by entering =B14-B15 in Cell B16 and copying to Cells C16:H16. The net present value of the lease to Epplewhite at the end of seven years is calculated in Cell I17 by the entry =NPV(B5,C16:H16)+B16 in Cell I17.

The initial cash outflow for the buy option is entered in Cell B19 by the entry =-B4. The annual depreciation is calculated by entering =C12*$B$4 in Cell C20 and copying it to Cells D20:I20. The annual values of the tax benefit by depreciation are calculated by entering =$B$6*C20 in Cell C21 and copying to Cells D21:I21.

The terminal cash flow from the sale of the equipment at the end of seven years is calculated in Cell I22 by the entry =B4*B9. The equipment's book value at the time of sale is calculated in Cell I23 by the entry =B4-SUM(C20:I20). The taxable capital gain is calculated in Cell I24 by the entry I22-I23, and the tax is calculated in Cell I25 by the entry =B6*I24. The after-tax cash flow from the sale of the equipment is calculated in Cell I26 by the entry =I22-I25.

The incremental after-tax cash flows for the purchase option are calculated in by entering =B19 in Cell B27, by entering =C21 in Cell C27 and copying to Cells D27:H27, and by entering =I21+I26 in Cell I27. The net present value of the purchase option is calculated by entering =NPV(B5,C27:I27)+B27 in Cell I28.

As a check, the after-tax cash flows for the differences between the lease and purchase options are calculated by entering =B16-B27 in Cell B30 and copying to Cells C30:I30. The net present value of these after-tax cash flows is calculated in Cell I31 by the entry =NPV(B5,C30:I30)+B30.

For convenience, the net present values are copied to Cells I4, I5, and I6. To determine the better choice, enter =IF(I6>0,"Lease",IF(I6<0,"Buy","Neutral")). For the conditions of the problem, the lease option is the better choice.

Sensitivity Analysis: The two-variable input table in Rows 32:41 of Figure 13-18 is prepared by entering a range of values for lease rates in Cells E35:I35 and a range of values for the discount rate (i.e., the firm's WACC) in Cells D36:D41. The entry in Cell D35 is =I7, which links the table values to the choice of option. To create the table, choose "Table" from the "Data" drop-down menu and enter F5 for the row entries and B5 for the column entries, as shown in Figure 13-19. Then click "OK" or press Enter. The results indicate that the buy option is preferred when the firm's cost of borrowing is low and the cost of leasing is high.

Figure 13-19

"Table" Dialog Box with Entries

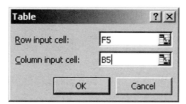

(Continued)

The Lessor's Problems: The lessor's first problem is to determine the maximum lease rate that would be acceptable to the lessee. We can define this as the rate at which the net present values of the two options are equal. To determine this value, use Solver with the settings shown in Figure 13-20. Figure 13-21 shows the results in the upper portion of the spreadsheet.

Figure 13-20
_____

"Solver Parameters" Dialog Box with Entries for Determining the Maximum Lease Rate Acceptable to the Lessee

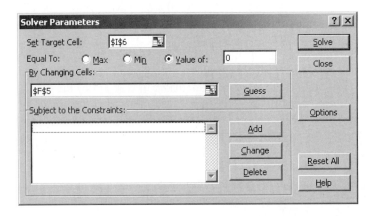

Figure 13-21
_____

Determination of Maximum Lease Rate Acceptable to the Lessee

	A	B	C	D	E	F	G	H	I
1	EPPLEWHITE CORPORATION								
2	Evalution of Lease-vs-Buy Options								
3	**Purchase Option**		**Lease Option**				**Comparison of Options**		
4	Equipment Cost	$100,000	Lease Principal			$100,000	NPV for Lease Option		$ (66,992)
5	Discount Rate (WACC)	10.00%	Annual Interest Rate			**14.88%**	NPV for Buy Option		$ (66,992)
6	Corporate Tax Rate	40%	Life of Loan, Years			7	NPV for (Lease - Buy)		$ (0)
7	MACRS depreciation, first-quarter convention		Annual Payment			$20,849	Which option is better?		**Neutral**
8	Life, years	7	**Maximum Rate Acceptable to Lessee**						
9	Salvage value, pct of cost	10%							

Note that the entry in Cell I7 is =IF(I6>0.1,"Lease",IF(I6<−0.1,"Buy","Neutral"))). This avoids round-off errors with the entry =IF(I6>0,"Lease",IF(I6<0,"Buy","Neutral"))).

In practice, the lessor's next problem is to obtain the equipment so that it can be leased to the lessee at a rate that earns a profit for the lessor and is acceptable to the lessee. This usually involves creating a partnership that involves six parties: the equity partners in the lease, the lessee, an owner trustee, an indenture trustee, the equipment's manufacturer, and a broker or leasing company responsible for packaging the lease. This involves a complex of accounting considerations for the partnership members.

(Continued)

Spider Plots: Figure 13-22 shows an alternate way to present the results of sensitivity analysis known as a "spider plot." This type of plot (and the table on which it is based) compares the **relative** impacts of changes in input variables on an output. It is called a "spider plot" because the lines for the results radiate out from the center, like the strands of a spider's web.

Figure 13-22
___

"Spider Plot" to Compare Impacts of Changes in Selected Input Variables on the Net Present Value for Example 13-1

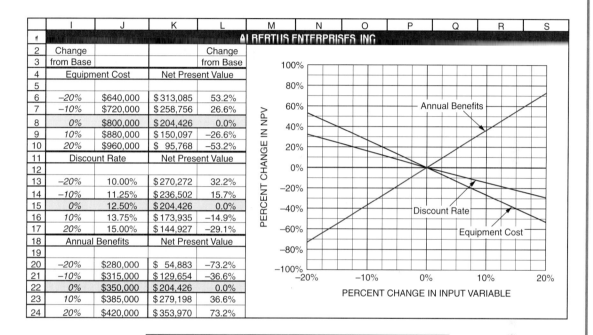

	I	J	K	L
1			ALBERTUS ENTERPRISES, INC	
2	Change			Change
3	from Base			from Base
4	Equipment Cost		Net Present Value	
5				
6	–20%	$640,000	$313,085	53.2%
7	–10%	$720,000	$258,756	26.6%
8	0%	$800,000	$204,426	0.0%
9	10%	$880,000	$150,097	–26.6%
10	20%	$960,000	$ 95,768	–53.2%
11	Discount Rate		Net Present Value	
12				
13	–20%	10.00%	$270,272	32.2%
14	–10%	11.25%	$236,502	15.7%
15	0%	12.50%	$204,426	0.0%
16	10%	13.75%	$173,935	–14.9%
17	20%	15.00%	$144,927	–29.1%
18	Annual Benefits		Net Present Value	
19				
20	–20%	$280,000	$ 54,883	–73.2%
21	–10%	$315,000	$129,654	–36.6%
22	0%	$350,000	$204,426	0.0%
23	10%	$385,000	$279,198	36.6%
24	20%	$420,000	$353,970	73.2%

Key Cell Entries

J5: =B2 (Hide by custom formatting as ";;;.")
J6: =(1+I6)*800,000, copy to J7:J10
J12: =B5 (Hide by custom formatting as ";;;.")
J13: =(1+I13)*0.125, copy to J14:J17
J19: =C15 (Hide by custom formatting as ";;;.")
J20: =(1+I20)*350,000, copy to J21:J24
K5: =$G$26, copy to K12 and K19 (Hide by custom formatting as ";;;.")
L6: =(K6–$K$5)/$K$5, copy to L7:L10, L13:L17, and L20:L24

   Figure 13-22 shows how reducing or increasing the values of the equipment cost, discount rate, and annual benefits from –20 to +20 percent of their base values (i.e., their values for 0 percent change) impacts the net present value of the capital investment described in Example 13-1. By using relative or percentage changes in the values of the three input variables, it is possible to compare their effects on the same chart, even though the units for discount rate (percent) are different from those for equipment cost and annual benefits (dollars). For example, the NPV of the investment can be increased by 20 percent by reducing the discount rate by 12.5 percent, reducing the equipment cost by 7.5 percent, or increasing the annual benefits by 5.5 percent.

(Continued)

To prepare Figure 13-22, copy the setup shown in Columns A to G of Figure 13-1 to a new worksheet. Enter the values in Column I as data, and calculate the values in Column J by the cell entries shown at the bottom of the figure. Create the three one-variable input tables shown in Columns J and K of Figure 13-22. For example, to create the first one, drag the mouse to highlight Cells J5:K10, select Table from the Data drop-down menu, and enter B2 for the Column Input variable (see Figure 13-23). Repeat for the other two one-variable input tables. Calculate the percentage changes in Column L by the entries shown at the bottom of the figure. Plot the values in Cells I6:I10, L6:L10, L13:L17, and L20:L24. (Alternatively, if the dollar values of NPV are to be plotted on the charts ordinate instead of the percentage changes from the base, plot the values in Cells I6:I10, K6:K10, K13:K17, and K20:K24.)

Figure 13-23

Entry for First One-Variable Input Table

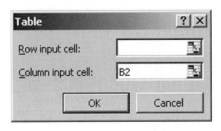

Concluding Remarks

Capital budgeting situations come in a variety of types and sizes. This chapter provides examples of the more important ones. Understand the financial principles and spreadsheet tools illustrated in the examples—and be prepared to adapt and extend the examples to whatever situations you face.

The Three Steps of Capital Budgeting

1. Develop proposals. Determine their costs and incremental cash flows.
2. Evaluate proposals. Determine their net present values, rates of return, and years to break even. Use sensitivity analysis to identify risks and their impacts.
3. Decide which proposals to accept and which to reject.

Focus on the incremental cash inflows and outflows generated by the investment. Determine the before-tax cash flows over the investment's lifetime. Add considerations of depreciation and capital gains or losses to determine taxable incomes. Use the taxable income to calculate tax. Subtract tax from before-tax income to get after-tax income.

Once you have the after-tax income, the rest should be easy. Use Excel's NPV, IRR, and MIRR functions and enter an expression for the number of years to break even.

Use Excel's Goal Seek and Solver tools to determine values needed to achieve specific goals. Use one- and two-variable input tables to analyze the sensitivity of payoffs to changes in conditions. Create charts and downside risk curves to help present results in formats that are easy to understand and convincing.

Chapter 14

Capital Budgeting: Risk Analysis with Scenarios

CHAPTER OBJECTIVES

Management Skills

- Understand the concept of risks and the use of probability distributions to evaluate them.

Spreadsheet Skills

- Use probability distributions to calculate the risks for achieving success or suffering failure.
- Apply Excel's Scenario Manager tool to analyze the effects of various combinations of conditions (e.g., best-on-best, worst-on-worst, and most probable) on future payoffs.
- Create "downside risk charts" to express risks in a graphical format that can be easily understood and used to make decisions that involve risks.

Overview

Corporate executives and boards are moving beyond their traditional roles of strategic and tactical planning and taking on the additional responsibility for managing risk. For many risks, buying liability, property, or casualty insurance is a standard procedure. For other types of risks, such as capital investments in new products or processes, insurance is not a practical answer, and decisions must be made in the face of potentially suffering large losses. In this chapter, we look at the use of scenarios to analyze the risks with capital budgeting with which managers must cope.

In the discussions of capital budgeting in Chapters 12 and 13, future cash flows and other input variables were treated as though they were known with certainty. This is never the case. Realistically, cash flows can be expected to vary above and below the forecast values. Investments themselves may not be known with 100 percent accuracy at the time of deciding whether to invest or not. Future operating costs may be higher or lower than anticipated, causing net operating incomes to be lower or higher. The lack of certainty creates risks that a CFO may wish to avoid.

This chapter begins a two-chapter discussion of the risks associated with capital budgeting. In this chapter we will show how to measure risk in terms of probability for a simple situation, and we will use scenarios for more complex situations to define the upper and lower bounds of the range of possible outcomes as well as the most probable outcome. In the next chapter, we will extend our discussion to use the Monte Carlo simulation to define risk in more complex situations in terms of their probabilities.

Knowing the worst that can happen helps corporations prepare for what they may be powerless to dodge. Knowing the best helps define goals and shows where reducing risks has the highest payoffs.

Using Probabilities to Define Risks

Of all the future values that are uncertain in capital budgeting, the least certain are usually future sales. These directly affect year-end benefits and the calculations of an investment's profitability.

As we learned in Chapter 3, statistical projections of past sales have margins of error. In addition, changes from past trends occur because of changes in the general economy, demographics, and other factors that are largely outside the control of a company. These all translate into risks.

Our goal in this section is to create a downside risk chart, such as the one shown in Figure 14-1. This figure shows the risk level for the investment's payoff in terms of the probability for failing to achieve different net present values. The chart is based on the variability of a single factor—the annual year-end benefits. In the next chapter, we will extend the discussion to the variability of more than a single factor.

We have used the Albertus Enterprises case study in Chapter 13 to prepare Figure 14-1. To use the results from Chapter 13 to prepare the downside risk chart, copy Figure 13-1 and clear the information on

Figure 14-1

Downside Risk Curve for Net Present Value (Albertus Enterprises Case Study from Chapter 13)

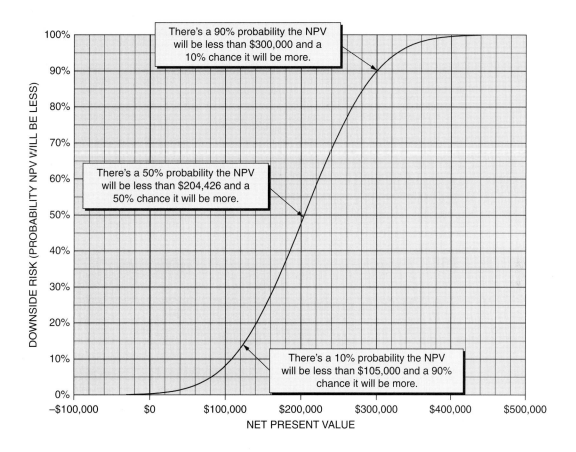

key cell entries and the charts below Row 29. To provide for entries that will be made later, insert a new column B and change the widths of Columns A and B. This provides the upper portion of Figure 14-2.

To create the downside risk chart shown as Figure 14-1, we need to plot a series of probabilities on the Y-axis against the series of net present values (NPV) on the X-axis. The range of X-values should cover a range from the lowermost value, at which there is very little probability of doing worse, to the highest value, at which there is very little probability for doing better. These correspond to the smallest annual demand that we might expect to the highest.

The expected annual year-end benefit is the forecast of $350,000 in Cell F31 of Figure 14-2. The forecast has a standard error of forecast of 10 percent, or $35,000. Enter the series of values from $240,000 to $460,000 in increments of $10,000 in Cells A36:A58 for the annual year-end benefits. This range covers slightly more than three standard forecast errors above and below the forecast annual values; that is, there is less than a 0.3 percent chance that the future year-end benefits will be outside the range from $240,000 to $460,000. That pretty well covers all likely values.

Figure 14-2

Risk Analysis Based on Forecast Annual Benefits and Their Standard Forecast Error

	A	B	C	D	E	F	G	H
1	ALBERTUS, INC. — CAPITAL BUDGETING SPREADSHEET							
2	Equipment cost, including installation		$800,000					
3	Salvage value, as percent of cost		10%					
4	Market value, end of Year 5		$80,000					
5	Discount and reinvestment rate		12.5%					
6	Tax rate		40.0%					
7	Year		0	1	2	3	4	5
8	Depreciation and Book Value Schedule							
9	Depreciation base		$ 800,000					
10	Annual depreciation, per MACRS			25.00%	21.43%	15.31%	10.93%	8.75%
11	Annual depreciation, dollars			$ 200,000	$ 171,440	$ 122,480	$ 87,440	$ 70,000
12	Year-end book value			$ 600,000	$ 428,560	$ 306,080	$ 218,640	$ 148,640
13	Year-End Cash Flow Analysis							
14	Regular income							
15	Annual year-end benefit			$ 350,000	$ 350,000	$ 350,000	$ 350,000	$ 350,000
16	Taxable regular income			$ 150,000	$ 178,560	$ 227,520	$ 262,560	$ 280,000
17	Tax on regular income			$ 60,000	$ 71,424	$ 91,008	$ 105,024	$ 112,000
18	ATCF for regular income			$ 290,000	$ 278,576	$ 258,992	$ 244,976	$ 238,000
19	Sale of equipment							
20	Income from sale of equipment							$ 80,000
21	Capital gain(loss)							$ (68,640)
22	Capital gain tax (benefit)							$ (27,456)
23	ATCF from sale of equipment							$ 107,456
24	After-Tax Cash Flow Analysis							
25	After-tax cash flow (ACTF)		$ (800,000)	$ 290,000	$ 278,576	$ 258,992	$ 244,976	$ 345,456
26	Net present value		$ (800,000)	$ (542,222)	$ (322,113)	$ (140,214)	$ 12,723	$ 204,426
27	Internal rate of return (IRR)		−100.00%	−63.75%	−20.14%	1.75%	13.28%	22.34%
28	Modified internal rate of return (MIRR)		−100.00%	−63.75%	−13.05%	5.50%	12.94%	17.74%
29	Discounted break-even point, years		3.92					
30	ALBERTUS,INC - DOWNSIDE PROBABILITY (RISK) ANALYSIS							
31				Forecast annual year-end benefits		$350,000	Risks are based on the	
32				Standard error of forecast, percent		10.00%	forecast annual year-end	
33				Standard error of forecast, dollars		$35,000	benefits (Cell F31) and	
34	Annual year-end benefits	NPV at end of 5 years	IRR at end of 5 years	MIRR at end of 5 years	Years to break even	Downside risk	the standard error of forecast (Cell F32 or F33).	
35								
36	$240,000	−$30,571	10.96%	11.63%	Failed	0.08%		
37	$250,000	−$9,208	12.04%	12.24%	Failed	0.21%		
38	$260,000	$12,156	13.11%	12.84%	4.92	0.51%		
39	$270,000	$33,519	14.17%	13.43%	4.80	1.11%		
40	$280,000	$54,883	15.22%	14.00%	4.67	2.28%		
41	$290,000	$76,246	16.26%	14.57%	4.56	4.32%		
42	$300,000	$97,609	17.29%	15.12%	4.44	7.66%		
43	$310,000	$118,973	18.31%	15.66%	4.33	12.65%		
44	$320,000	$140,336	19.33%	16.20%	4.23	19.57%		
45	$330,000	$161,700	20.34%	16.72%	4.13	28.39%		
46	$340,000	$183,063	21.34%	17.23%	4.03	38.75%		
47	$350,000	$204,426	22.34%	17.74%	3.92	50.00%		
48	$360,000	$225,790	23.33%	18.24%	3.80	61.25%		
49	$370,000	$247,153	24.31%	18.72%	3.70	71.61%		
50	$380,000	$268,517	25.29%	19.20%	3.59	80.43%		
51	$390,000	$289,880	26.26%	19.68%	3.49	87.35%		
52	$400,000	$311,243	27.23%	20.14%	3.40	92.34%		
53	$410,000	$332,607	28.19%	20.60%	3.31	95.68%		
54	$420,000	$353,970	29.15%	21.05%	3.22	97.72%		
55	$430,000	$375,334	30.10%	21.50%	3.14	98.89%		
56	$440,000	$396,697	31.04%	21.94%	3.06	99.49%		
57	$450,000	$418,061	31.99%	22.37%	2.99	99.79%		
58	$460,000	$439,424	32.92%	22.79%	2.93	99.92%		
59	Key Cell Entries							
60	A35: =D15	B35: =H26	C35: =H27	D35: =H28	E35: =C29			
61	F36: =NORMDIST(A36,F$31,F$31*F$32,TRUE), copy to F37:F58							

For each value of annual year-end benefits in Cells A36:A58, we next calculate the investment's NPV, IRR, and MIRR at the end of five years and the number of years to break even. We will use a one-variable input table to do this. Make the following entries in Row 35:

In Cell A35, enter =D15 (This connects the table to the annual benefits in the main program.)
In Cell B35, enter =H26 (This connects the table to the NPV in the main program.)
In Cell C35, enter =H27 (This connects the table to the IRR in the main program.)
In Cell D35, enter =H28 (This connects the table to the MIRR in the main program.)
In Cell E35, enter =C29 (This connects the table to the years to break even in the main program.)

As each of the above entries is made, the value in the referenced cell will appear. For example, the value $350,000 will appear in Cell A35 when =D15 is entered there. To hide these values, format the cells with the custom format ;;; (i.e., three semicolons).

(N.B. Make sure the values in Cells E15:H15 depend on and are the same as the value in Cell D15. You should set up your spreadsheet with the value 350,000 entered in Cell D15, and with the entry =$D$15 in Cells E15:H15. Alternatively, you can enter =D15 in Cell E15 and copy it to F15:H15.)

Drag the mouse to select the Range A35:E58. From the Data menu on the toolbar, click on Table to open the dialog box shown in Figure 14-3. Enter D15 as the column input cell and click OK or press Enter.

Format the results in Cells B36:E58 as shown in Figure 14-2. We now have values that tell us what the NPV, IRR, MIRR, and payback period will be for each of the assumed values for the year-end annual benefits. For example, if we ask, "What happens if the annual benefits are $300,000?" we can read the resulting values for the NPV, IRR, MIRR, and years to break even in Cells B42:E42.

Our next step is to express the probabilities associated with each of the assumed values for annual year-end benefits. To do this, we use the forecast of $350,000, the standard forecast error of 10 percent (or $35,000), and Excel's NORMDIST function. The syntax for the NORMDIST function is

$$NORMDIST(x, mean, standard\_dev, cumulative)$$

where $\quad x$ = the value for which you want the distribution (in this case, the values in Cells A36:A58)

$\quad mean$ = the arithmetic mean of the distribution (here, the forecast of $350,000 in Cell F30)

Figure 14-3

Table Dialog Box with Entry for One-Variable Input Table

>   *standard_dev* = the standard deviation of the distribution (here, the standard forecast error of $35,000, which can be entered either as the product of F31*F32 or the value in Cell F33)
>
> and *cumulative* = *true* if the cumulative value of the distribution is wanted, *false* if the probability mass function is wanted (here, we want the cumulative function, so enter *true*)

Therefore, to calculate the downside risks, enter =NORMDIST($A36,F$31,F$31*F$32,TRUE) in Cell F36 and copy the entry to F37:F58. (Note the $ signs. We will copy this entry later to columns G and H.) Format the results as percentages with two decimal places. The result is as shown in Figure 14-2.

To plot a downside risk curve for the investment's NPV, select the Ranges B36:B58 and F36:F58 and use a scatter diagram. Figure 14-1 shows the result, after formatting and adding text boxes to explain the chart's use.

Similar charts can be created for the downside risks for IRR, MIRR, and payback period.

Reduced Risk: The Payoff from Forecast Accuracy

Before leaving this case study, let's examine how the accuracy of the forecast annual benefits affects risk. Repeat the forecast annual sales in Cells G31:H31 of Figure 14-4, and enter the new percentage errors in Cells G32:H32. We have arbitrarily chosen new errors of 5 percent and 15 percent. Copy the entry in Cell F33 to G33:H33 to compute the new standard forecast errors in dollars. Then copy the entry in Cell F36 to G36:H58. Figure 14-4 is the resulting spreadsheet, and Figure 14-5 adds downside risk curves for NPV for forecast errors of 5 percent and 15 percent to the curve already obtained at 10 percent.

Take a good look at Figure 14-5. It has an important message about forecasting. Note how improving the forecast accuracy has reduced the downside risk! Whereas there was a 10 percent probability that the NPV would be less than $105,000 for a standard forecast error of 10 percent, the minimum NPV at the same 10 percent level of risk is about $157,000 for a standard forecast error of 5 percent.

To compare the risks another way, an NPV of $100,000 is virtually certain for a standard forecast error of 5 percent; there is about an 8 percent chance it will be less for a standard forecast error of 10 percent, and there is about 17.5 percent chance it will be less for a standard forecast error of 15 percent.

Good forecasts of future revenues help minimize downside risks. By carefully projecting the past and adjusting any trends for how the world is changing, CFOs can reduce their investment risks—and sleep a little better.

Scenario Analysis

One- and two-variable input tables, although convenient for the above sensitivity analysis, are not powerful enough for more complex conditions. Instead, to evaluate the impacts of a number of independent variable on one or more dependent variables, we can use Excel's Scenario Manager tool. In the following case study, for example, we will use the Scenario Manager tool to evaluate the impacts of changes in the annual market, investment, and variable cost on the NPV, IRR, MIRR, and years to break even for

Figure 14-4

Probability Analysis with Standard Forecast Errors of 5%, 10%, and 15%

	A	B	C	D	E	F	G	H
1	ALBERTUS, INC. — CAPITAL BUDGETING SPREADSHEET							
2	Equipment cost, including installation		$800,000					
3	Salvage value, as percent of cost		10%					
4	Market value, end of Year 5		$80,000					
5	Discount and reinvestment rate		12.5%					
6	Tax rate		40.0%					
7	Year		0	1	2	3	4	5
8	Depreciation and Book Value Schedule							
9	Depreciation base		$ 800,000					
10	Annual depreciation, per MACRS			25.00%	21.43%	15.31%	10.93%	8.75%
11	Annual depreciation, dollars			$ 200,000	$ 171,440	$ 122,480	$ 87,440	$ 70,000
12	Year-end book value			$ 600,000	$ 428,560	$ 306,080	$ 218,640	$ 148,640
13	Year-End Cash Flow Analysis							
14	Regular income							
15	Annual year-end benefit			$ 350,000	$ 350,000	$ 350,000	$ 350,000	$ 350,000
16	Taxable regular income income			$ 150,000	$ 178,560	$ 227,520	$ 262,560	$ 280,000
17	Tax on regular income			$ 60,000	$ 71,424	$ 91,008	$ 105,024	$ 112,000
18	ATCF for regular income			$ 290,000	$ 278,576	$ 258,992	$ 244,976	$ 238,000
19	Sale of equipment							
20	Income from sale of equipment							$ 80,000
21	Capital gain(loss)							$ (68,640)
22	Capital gain tax (benefit)							$ (27,456)
23	ATCF from sale of equipment							$ 107,456
24	After-Tax Cash Flow Analysis							
25	After-tax cash flow (ACTF)		$ (800,000)	$ 290,000	$ 278,576	$ 258,992	$ 244,976	$ 345,456
26	Net present value		$ (800,000)	$ (542,222)	$ (322,113)	$ (140,214)	$ 12,723	$ 204,426
27	Internal rate of return (IRR)		−100.00%	−63.75%	−20.14%	1.75%	13.28%	22.34%
28	Modified internal rate of return (MIRR)		−100.00%	−63.75%	−13.05%	5.50%	12.94%	17.74%
29	Discounted break-even point, years		3.92					
30	ALBERTUS, INC — DOWNSIDE PROBABILITY (RISK) ANALYSIS							
31				Forecast annual year-end benefits		$350,000	$350,000	$350,000
32				Standard error of forecast, percent		10.00%	5.00%	15.00%
33				Standard error of forecast, dollars		$35,000	$17,500	$52,500
34	Annual year-end benefits	NPV at end of 5 years	IRR at end of 5 years	MIRR at end of 5 years	Years to break even	Downside risk	Downside risk	Downside risk
35								
36	$240,000	−$30,571	10.96%	11.63%	Failed	0.08%	0.00%	1.81%
37	$250,000	−$9,208	12.04%	12.24%	Failed	0.21%	0.00%	2.84%
38	$260,000	$12,156	13.11%	12.84%	4.92	0.51%	0.00%	4.32%
39	$270,000	$33,519	14.17%	13.43%	4.80	1.11%	0.00%	6.38%
40	$280,000	$54,883	15.22%	14.00%	4.67	2.28%	0.00%	9.12%
41	$290,000	$76,246	16.26%	14.57%	4.56	4.32%	0.03%	12.65%
42	$300,000	$97,609	17.29%	15.12%	4.44	7.66%	0.21%	17.05%
43	$310,000	$118,973	18.31%	15.66%	4.33	12.65%	1.11%	22.31%
44	$320,000	$140,336	19.33%	16.20%	4.23	19.57%	4.32%	28.39%
45	$330,000	$161,700	20.34%	16.72%	4.13	28.39%	12.65%	35.16%
46	$340,000	$183,063	21.34%	17.23%	4.03	38.75%	28.39%	42.45%
47	$350,000	$204,426	22.34%	17.74%	3.92	50.00%	50.00%	50.00%
48	$360,000	$225,790	23.33%	18.24%	3.80	61.25%	71.61%	57.55%
49	$370,000	$247,153	24.31%	18.72%	3.70	71.61%	87.35%	64.84%
50	$380,000	$268,517	25.29%	19.20%	3.59	80.43%	95.68%	71.61%
51	$390,000	$289,880	26.26%	19.68%	3.49	87.35%	98.89%	77.69%
52	$400,000	$311,243	27.23%	20.14%	3.40	92.34%	99.79%	82.95%
53	$410,000	$332,607	28.19%	20.60%	3.31	95.68%	99.97%	87.35%
54	$420,000	$353,970	29.15%	21.05%	3.22	97.72%	100.00%	90.88%
55	$430,000	$375,334	30.10%	21.50%	3.14	98.89%	100.00%	93.62%
56	$440,000	$396,697	31.04%	21.94%	3.06	99.49%	100.00%	95.68%
57	$450,000	$418,061	31.99%	22.37%	2.99	99.79%	100.00%	97.16%
58	$460,000	$439,424	32.92%	22.79%	2.93	99.92%	100.00%	98.19%

Figure 14-5

Downside Risk Curves for Net Present Value with Standard Forecast Errors of 5%, 10%, and 15%

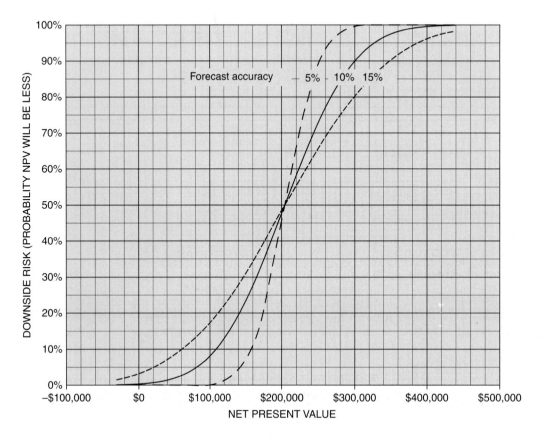

a capital investment. Three scenarios, or sets of independent variables of particular interest, are the worst combination of input conditions, the best, and the most probable.

Case Study: Aladdin Games

Problem Statement: Ted Heinlen, Chairman and Chief Executive Officer of Aladdin Games, Inc., has convened his weekly staff meeting to hear more about a new board game that the company's creative staff has developed. At their last meeting, the executives heard details of the game itself, called "Wall Street Invaders," from its originators. The game excited their interest. Mr. Heinlen said then that, in his modest opinion, "'Wall Street Invaders" has a perfect combination of office politics, insider trading, personal ambitions, back-stabbing, and greed. It has the kind of real-life nonviolence that should appeal to everyone. I just don't see how it can possibly miss."

Everyone at the prior meeting agreed with the boss' assessment. They now meet again, a week later, to begin analyzing the financial aspects of producing and marketing the game.

Sam Yamoto, vice president of sales, asks Igor Vukonovich, his marketing specialist, to present the results of their marketing research. Igor presents the following: "The total annual market for board games of the type

(Continued)

of 'Invaders' varies somewhat from year to year about a mean value of 180,000 sets—that is for our competitors as well as for us. The statistical data on which this value is based also indicate that the actual demand can be treated as normally distributed about the mean value with a standard deviation of 18,000 sets/year. In other words, our forecasts have a standard deviation of plus-or-minus 10 percent."

"Okay," says Ted. "So what would be our share of the market with 'Invaders'?"

Igor continues, "The share of the total market that 'Invaders' might be expected to capture for us depends very much on its price. The less we charge our distributors, the less they have to charge the retailers, so that the less the retailers in turn have to charge their customers, the more sets we can sell."

"Sounds reasonable," Ted interjects. "So what are the numbers?"

Igor resumes, "Well, we're not really sure yet what our wholesale price must be to recoup our costs. Our marketing research indicates that we should sell 'Invaders' to our wholesalers for between $4.25 and $5.25 a set. Based on prices within this range, we expect that our share of the total market will vary with price as shown by Chart A."

Chart A. Effect of Wholesale Price of "Wall Street Invaders" on Aladdin's Share of the Total Market for This Type of Board Game

Wholesale Price, $/set	$4.25	$4.50	$4.75	$5.00	$5.25
Market Share	18%	17%	15%	11%	6%

"Okay, that gives us some numbers for market share we can work with." Ted says. "We'll need to figure out what's the best wholesale price to give us the maximum profit. But at least that's one variable we have under our own control and don't have to leave for fate to decide."

Turning to Geraldine Murray, the company's vice president for manufacturing, Ted then asks, "How does the cost picture look to you, Gerri?"

Ms. Murray reports, "Our production specialists have gone over the equipment needs and the processes we expect to use. We don't have final figures yet, but at this point in time we're guessing. Sorry, I mean we're estimating that our variable costs for producing 'Invaders' would most likely be about $2.15 a set. However, they could go as low as $1.60 a set or as high as $2.35. We just can't say exactly until we resolve some quality issues with Sam's marketing people and have a better idea of volume."

"And what about the fixed costs for production?" asks Mr. Heinlen.

"Again, we don't know for sure yet," Ms. Murray responds. "But we can say with reasonable certainty that fixed costs won't be any less than $86,000 or more than $98,000. That should cover our initial, one-time investment in equipment for getting 'Invaders' into production and putting it into the hands of our wholesalers. In between those numbers? I'd say any number in between is equally likely."

"Okay," says Ted. "I think that gives us some figures to work with. Let's come back next week with a financial analysis based on the numbers that Sam and Gerri have thrown out. Can we do that, Ralph?" Ted asks, turning to Ralph Zimmerman, his vice president for finance. "What sort of basis do you think would be right for doing a financial analysis?"

Ralph responds, "Well, I would say that our experience has been that board games of the type of 'Invaders' will be popular with the public and will sell well for a limited time—something, I would say, on the order of five years. I would say that we ought to use a five-year period for evaluating the dollar return we might make on whatever Gerri says it will cost and whatever Sam says we might get from our sales. We can depreciate the initial investment by straight-line depreciation to a salvage value of zero at the end of five years. I would say whatever special equipment we buy to produce 'Invaders' will be worthless by the end of five years."

"What about taxes and our cost of capital?" Ted asks.

Ralph responds, "Our incremental tax rate for whatever profits we might make on 'Invaders' will be 40 percent. And I would certainly add, in view of the other possibilities we have for investing our limited capital, that we ought to earn a return on whatever we spend on 'Invaders' of at least 13 percent or we shouldn't invest

(Continued)

in it. I mean by that that our cost of capital to invest in 'Invaders' will be about 13 percent. I would say that we shouldn't accept anything less than that. And, frankly, with all the other financial commitments we have on the table, I would say we shouldn't run too high a risk for making anything less than 13 percent after taxes."

"What about selling and other nonproduction costs?" Ted asks.

Ralph notes, "These are currently running about 30 percent of our sales revenues. I don't see any reason they should be different for 'Wall Street Invaders'."

"Okay, that says it for now," says Ted. "Let's wrap a report around this and see what comes out. See you all again—same time, next week—and we'll decide then whether or not to go ahead with this one."

Solution: Figures 14-6 and 14-7 show the spreadsheet solution for Aladdin's most probable outcome. The data values are entered in Rows 2 to 15.

Figure 14-6

Spreadsheet Solution for Most Probable Scenario and Optimum Wholesale Price

	A	B	C	D	E	F	G
1	ALADDIN GAMES						
2	Total annual market forecast, sets	180,000		Selling price/Market share information			
3	Standard forecast error, sets	18,000		Price,		Market Share	
4	Minimum facility investment	$86,000		$/set	Price^2	Data	Forecast
5	Maximum facility investment	$98,000		$4.25	18.063	18%	17.97%
6	Equipment life, years	5		$4.50	20.250	17%	17.11%
7	Salvage value	0		$4.75	22.563	15%	14.83%
8	Depreciation method	St. Line		$5.00	25.000	11%	11.11%
9	Minimum variable cost, $/set	$1.60		$5.25	27.563	6%	5.97%
10	Most probable variable cost, $/set	$2.15		LINEST OUTPUT			Average =
11	Maximum variable cost, $/set	$2.35		−0.11429	0.96571	−1.86029	
12				0.00723	0.06870	0.16250	
13	Non-production costs, % of sales	30%		0.99941	0.169%	#N/A	
14	Cost of capital and reinvest rate	13%		1700	2	#N/A	
15	Tax rate	40%		0.00971	0.00001	#N/A	
16	**Most probable scenario**	Year					
17		0	1	2	3	4	5
18	Total annual market, sets		180,000	180,000	180,000	180,000	180,000
19	Wholesale price, sets		$4.66	$4.66	$4.66	$4.66	$4.66
20	Market share, percent		15.81%	15.81%	15.81%	15.81%	15.81%
21	Sets sold		28,462	28,462	28,462	28,462	28,462
22	Sales receipts, $		$132,644	$132,644	$132,644	$132,644	$132,644
23	Investment, $	$92,000					
24	Unit variable cost, $/set		$2.15	$2.15	$2.15	$2.15	$2.15
25	Total variable cost, $		$61,193	$61,193	$61,193	$61,193	$61,193
26	Gross profit		$71,451	$71,451	$71,451	$71,451	$71,451
27	Nonproduction expenses, 30% of sales		$39,793	$39,793	$39,793	$39,793	$39,793
28	Before-tax cash flow	($92,000)	$31,657	$31,657	$31,657	$31,657	$31,657
29	Annual depreciation		$18,400	$18,400	$18,400	$18,400	$18,400
30	Taxable income		$13,257	$13,257	$13,257	$13,257	$13,257
31	Tax, @ 40%		$5,303	$5,303	$5,303	$5,303	$5,303
32	After-tax cash flow	($92,000)	$26,354	$26,354	$26,354	$26,354	$26,354
33	**Net present value, NPV**	($92,000)	($68,678)	($48,038)	($29,773)	($13,610)	$694
34	**Internal rate of return, IRR**	−100.00%	−71.35%	−30.27%	−7.21%	5.68%	13.31%
35	**Modified internal rate of return, MIRR**	−100.00%	−71.35%	−21.89%	−0.81%	8.57%	13.17%
36	**Break-even point, years**	4.95					

(Continued)

Figure 14-7

Output of LINEST Command and Forecast Values

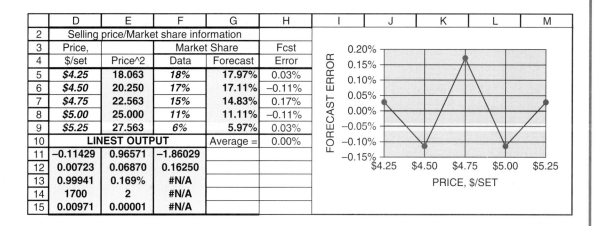

	D	E	F	G	H	I	J	K	L	M
2	Selling price/Market share information									
3	Price,		Market Share		Fcst					
4	$/set	Price^2	Data	Forecast	Error					
5	*$4.25*	18.063	*18%*	17.97%	0.03%					
6	*$4.50*	20.250	*17%*	17.11%	−0.11%					
7	*$4.75*	22.563	*15%*	14.83%	0.17%					
8	*$5.00*	25.000	*11%*	11.11%	−0.11%					
9	*$5.25*	27.563	*6%*	5.97%	0.03%					
10	LINEST OUTPUT			Average =	0.00%					
11	−0.11429	0.96571	−1.86029							
12	0.00723	0.06870	0.16250							
13	0.99941	0.169%	#N/A							
14	1700	2	#N/A							
15	0.00971	0.00001	#N/A							

Most Probable Scenario: Under the most probable conditions, the total market is 180,000 sets each year (i.e., the mean value entered in Cell B2), and the unit variable cost of production is $2.15/set (i.e., the most probable value in Cell B10).

For the facility investment, there is no most probable value because the possible values vary on a uniform distribution between the minimum and maximum values of $86,000 and $98,000. Any value in that range is equally likely. Therefore, as a proxy for the most probable value, we use the average of $92,000, since it is equally likely that the value is more than or less than the mean of a uniform distribution.

We will proceed by the following steps to complete the most probable scenario.

Total Annual Market, sets: In Cell C18, enter =B2. In Cell D18, enter =C18 and copy to E18:G18.
Wholesale Price, per set: In Cell C19, enter 4.5 and format it as currency with two decimal places to give $4.50. **This is a trial value. We will change it later** to find the value that maximizes the net present value at the end of five years. In cell D19, enter =C19 and copy it to Cells E19:G19.
Market Share: The market share will depend on the wholesale price. Therefore, we must link the value in Cell C20 for market share to the value in Cell C19 for wholesale price. To satisfy this need, we will use the market research results to develop a regression equation that relates the values for market share in Cells F5:F9 to the wholesale prices in Cells D5:D9.

We must first select an appropriate regression equation to relate market share to wholesale price. You should be able to do this by using the procedure covered in Chapter 3 to select an appropriate regression equation to relate annual sales to the year. You should be able to show that a linear regression equation does not provide a valid model, and that a quadratic regression equation is the most suitable type for relating Aladdin's market share to wholesale price.

Return now to the spreadsheet of Figure 14-6 where Excel's LINEST command has been used to determine the parameters of the quadratic equation. Supply values for the squares of the wholesale price by entering =D5^2 in Cell E5 and copy the entry to Cells E5:E9. Next, drag the mouse to highlight Cells D11:F15 and type =LINEST(F5:F9,D5:E9,1,1). Enter the command by pressing the Control, Shift, and Enter keys. This gives the results shown in Cells D11:F15 of Figure 14-6. To demonstrate the model's validity, you can calculate the errors and create the chart shown in Columns H to M of Figure 14-7. (Columns H to M are not shown in Figure 14-6.)

(Continued)

The important cells of Figure 14-6 for this problem are the coefficients of the quadratic equation in Cells D11:F11. They indicate that the equation relating market share to wholesale price is

$$Y = -1.86029 + 0.96571X - 0.11429X^2$$

where Y is the market share and X is the wholesale price in $/set.

We will now use our quadratic equation to link the market share in Cell C20 to the wholesale price in C19. To do this, enter =F11+E11*C19+D11*C19^2 in Cell C20, then enter =C20 in D20 and copy it to Cells E20:G20 to repeat the values calculated in Cell C20.

Sets Sold: The number of sets sold each year is the product of the total annual market times the company's market share. In Cell C21, enter =C18*C20 and copy it to D21:G21.

Sales Receipts: The sales receipts each year is the product of the number of set sold times the selling price. In Cell C22, enter =C21*C19 and copy it to D22:G22.

Investment: Because any value between the minimum and maximum values in Cells B4 and B5 is equally likely, their average is used as a proxy for the most probable investment. (Note the term "proxy." The average is used for a uniform distribution because the probabilities are equal that the future value will be greater or less than the average, and no value in the range is more probable than any other.) Therefore, in Cell B23 enter =AVERAGE(B4:B5).

Unit Variable Cost: The most probable unit variable cost is the value $2.15 in Cell B10. Therefore, in cell C24 enter =B10, then enter =C24 in D24 and copy to E24:G24.

Total Variable Cost: The total variable cost is the product of the number of units sold times the unit variable cost. Enter =C21*C24 in Cell C25 and copy the entry to Cells D25:G25. (When we do scenario analysis later, we will want the change in Cell C25 to be reproduced in Cells D25:G25.)

Gross Profit: Gross profit is the difference between sales revenues and the cost of goods sold (COGS). Enter =C22-C25 in Cell C26 and copy the entry to Cells D26:G26.

Nonproduction Expenses: Nonproduction costs are given as 30 percent of sales in Cell B13. Therefore, to calculate nonproduction expenses, enter =$B$13*C22 in Cell C27 and copy the entry to Cells D27:G27.

Before-Tax Cash Flow: For Year 0, the before-tax cash flow is the outflow for the investment. Therefore, enter =-B23 in Cell B28. For other years, the before-tax cash flow is calculated by subtracting the nonproductive expenses from the gross profit. Therefore, enter =C26-C27 in Cell C28 and copy the entry to Cells D28:G28.

Depreciation: The investment is depreciated by the straight-line method over a period of five years to zero salvage value. You can calculate annual depreciation by entering =$B$23/$B$6 in Cell C29 and copying it to Cells D29:G29. Or use Excel's function for straight-line depreciation. The syntax for Excel's function for straight-line depreciation is =SLN(*cost,salvage value,life*). To use the SLN function, enter =SLN($B$23,$B$7,$B$6) in Cell C29 and copy the entry to Cells D29:G29.

It is worth noting that Excel also provides function commands for calculating depreciation by declining balance and sum of the years methods. Or it might be appropriate to use MACRS.

Taxable Income: The taxable income is calculated as the income (i.e., sales revenues) minus deductible expenses (i.e., total variable cost, nonproductive expenses, and depreciation). To include depreciation in what has already been calculated, enter =C28-C29 in Cell C30 and copy the entry to Cells D30:G30.

Tax: Tax equals the taxable income multiplied by the tax rate, which is given as 40 percent in Cell B15. Enter =C30*$B$15 in Cell C31 and copy the entry to Cells D31:G31.

After-Tax Cash Flow: The after-tax cash flow for Year 0 is the outflow for the investment. Enter =B28 or =-B23 in Cell B32. For Years 1 to 5, the **after**-tax cash flow equals the **before**-tax cash flow minus the tax. Enter =C28-C31 in Cell C32 and copy the entry to Cells D32:G32.

(Continued)

Net Present Value: Use Excel's function command NPV to calculate the net present values of the investment at the ends of Years 1 to 5. The syntax for this command is NPV(*rate,range of values*).

Enter =NPV($B$14,$C$32:C32)+$B$32 in Cell C33 and copy the entry to Cells D33:G33. When this entry is executed in Cell C33, it discounts the after-tax cash flow in Cell C32 back to the present at the rate given in Cell B14 (13%) and adds the value in Cell B32. Note that the value in Cell B32 (i.e., the cash outflow for the investment) is not included in the range of values to be discounted to the present because it is already a present value.

When the entry in Cell C33 is copied to Cells D33:G33, the range of values discounted back to the present increases by one year for each column. The entry in Cell G33 will be = NPV($B$14, $C$32:G32)+$B$32 and evaluates the investment's net present value at the end of the fifth year.

Internal Rate of Return: Use Excel's function command IRR to calculate the internal rate of return at the ends of Years 1 to 5. The IRR function returns the internal rate of return for a series of periodic cash flows, at least one of which is negative (here, the initial investment) and one or more are positive (here, the year end cash inflows). The syntax for this command is IRR(*range of values,guess*). If the *guess* value is omitted, Excel provides the default value of 0.10 (i.e., 10%). Excel uses the guess value as the starting point from which to do a series of calculations that ends when the calculated value of IRR converges to a solution with an accuracy of 0.00001 percent. The number of iterations is limited to 20. The calculations may fail to converge if the guess value is too far away from the solution. In this case, Excel returns the error message #NUM!. If this happens, try again with a different guess value that is closer to the solution.

Enter =IRR($B$32:C32) in Cell C34 and copy the entry to Cells D34:G34. If the error message #NUM! occurs, edit the cell entry by changing the guess value.

Recall that in the calculation of an investment's IRR, future cash inflows are assumed to be reinvested for the life of the project at the same rate as the IRR. This assumption is not likely to be satisfied for projects with very high or very low IRRs. If future cash inflows are reinvested at some other rate, the actual average rate of return will be different from the calculated value of IRR. Because of this problem, the IRR for an investment can be misleading. (See the discussion in Chapter 2 for details.)

Modified Internal Rate of Return: Use Excel's MIRR function to return the modified internal rate of return for a series of periodic cash flows. MIRR differs from IRR in that it considers both the cost of capital for the investment and the interest received on any reinvestment of cash generated by the investment. The syntax for Excel's MIRR function is MIRR(*range of values,finance rate (or cost of capital),reinvest rate*). Unless there is reason to use another value, the reinvest rate is assumed to equal the finance rate (i.e., the cost of capital for the investment).

Enter =MIRR($B$32:C32,$B$14,$B$14) in Cell C35 and copy the entry to Cells D35:G35.

Break-Even Point: By definition, the break-even point is the time for an investment's net present value to equal zero. To develop an expression for calculating the break-even point in Cell C36, note that the net present value is initially less than zero (because the investment in Year 0 is a cash outflow) and increases each year thereafter because the after-tax cash flows are positive.

To detect when the break-even point has been reached, we need to recognize when the net present value first becomes positive. If, for example, the net present value is negative at the ends of Years 1 and 2 and positive at the end of Year 3, we know that the break-even point is somewhere between the ends of Years 2 and 3. We can use linear interpolation between the NPVs at the ends of Years 2 and 3 to determine how far beyond the second year the net present value is zero. The development of an expression for identifying the years to break even was given in Chapter 12.

The following entry in Cell B36 is used to determine the break-even point for Aladdin's investment:

=IF(D33>=0,C17-C33/(D33-C33),IF(E33>=0,D17-D33/(E33-D33),

IF(F33>=0,E17-E33/(F33-E33),IF(G33>=0,F17-F33/(G33-F33),"Failed")))).

(Continued)

This expression checks across the row of NPV values until it reaches a positive NPV at a year n. It then backs up one year to year n-1 and adds a fraction of a year equal to the quotient: $-NPV_{n-1}/(NPV_{n-1}-NPV_n)$. (Note that the value of NPV_{n-1} is negative, so that using the minus sign before the quotient makes it positive.) If the value of NPV in the last column is still negative, the investment fails to break even over the duration of the analysis period.

Optimizing the Wholesale Selling Price: Recall that the value of $4.50/set we entered in Cell B19 was a **trial** value. We now want to determine the **optimum** value—that is, we want to find the value for the wholesale price that will give the greatest net present value. We will use Excel's Solver tool to do this. The Solver tool is accessed by clicking the Solver button on the Tools menu on the standard toolbar. Figure 14-8 shows the dialog box for the Solver tool with the entries for finding the optimum wholesale price—the wholesale price the company should select for maximizing the investment's net present value at the end of the five-year analysis period. Cell G33, the net present value at the end of five years, is therefore the target cell. We want to maximize its value by changing Cell C19, the wholesale price.

Solver identifies the optimum wholesale price as $4.66/set, which is slightly more than the trial value of $4.50/set. Under the most probable conditions, with the wholesale price set at $4.66/set, the net present value of the investment at the end of five years is $694, its internal rate of return is 13.31 percent, its modified internal rate of return is 13.17 percent, and its break-even point is 4.95 years. Although the analysis shows that the project is profitable under the most probable conditions, there should be some concern that the future might be less favorable and the project would fail.

Figure 14-8

Solver Parameters Dialog Box with Entries for Finding Optimum Wholesale Price

Other Scenarios

In this section, we use Excel's Scenario tool to perform "What If?" analysis and evaluate the net present values, rates of return, and break-even points under conditions other than the most probable. Specifically, we might ask what the financial payoffs might be under the worst combination of conditions that might reasonably occur, or under the best combination of conditions that might reasonably occur. The answers to such queries can provide additional help for a company's financial officers to decide whether or not to proceed with a project.

Table 14-1

Scenario Conditions

Scenario	Total Annual Market, sets	Investment	Unit Variable Cost, $/set
Best-on-Best	216,000	$86,000	$1.60
Most Probable	180,000	$92,000	$2.15
Worst-on-Worst	144,000	$98,000	$2.35

Table 14-1 shows values for the total annual market, the facility investment, and the unit variable cost under what we describe as the best-on-best, most probable, and worst-on-worst conditions. For the best-on-best conditions, we assume that (1) the total annual market is the forecast value of 180,000 units **plus** twice the standard forecast error of 18,000, which gives a total of 216,000 units; (2) the investment is the lowest value of $86,000; and (3) the unit variable cost is the lowest value of $1.60/set.

The most probable conditions in Table 14-1 are those we have already analyzed. For the best-on-best conditions, we assume that (1) the total annual market is the forecast value of 180,000 units **plus** twice the standard forecast error of 18,000, which gives a total of 216,000 units; (2) the investment is the lowest value of $86,000; and (3) the unit variable cost is the lowest value of $1.60/set. For the worst-on-worst conditions, we assume that (1) the total annual market is the forecast value of 180,000 units **minus** twice the standard forecast error of 18,000, which gives a total of 144,000 units; (2) the investment is the highest value of $98,000; and (3) the unit variable cost is the highest value of $2.35/set. It is highly unlikely that all three factors would simultaneously be at the best or worst values, so the results should bracket the range of possible outcomes the company might face.

Before using Excel's Scenario Manager tool, test the worksheet to see that all output cells are linked to the cells that will be allowed to vary. To do this, change the value in an input cell and check to see that other cells that should be linked to the input cell change as expected. Excel's auditing tool (described in Chapter 1) can also be used to verify cell linkages. **Failure to ensure that all cells are correctly linked is the most common cause for errors in using Excel's Scenario tool**.

To use Excel's Scenario tool, be sure the spreadsheet solution for the most probable scenario is open. Next, click on the Tools menu and select Scenario. This will display the Scenario Manager dialog box shown in Figure 14-9.

Click the Add button to display the dialog box shown in Figure 14-10.

In the "Add Scenario" dialog box of Figure 14-10, enter "Best-on-Best" for the name of the scenario and enter C18,B23,C24 for the cells that are to change. (These cells have the current values for total annual market, investment, and unit variable cost.) Click on the OK button or press Enter to go to the "Scenario Values" dialog box of Figure 14-11. Enter the values for the best total annual market (216,000 in Cell C18), best investment ($86,000 in Cell B23), and best unit variable cost ($1.60/set in Cell C24).

Click the OK button to return to the "Add Scenario" dialog box (Figure 14-10) and add the second scenario (Most Probable). Note that the changing cells will be the same as for the best-on-best scenario,

Figure 14-9

Scenario Manager Dialog Box

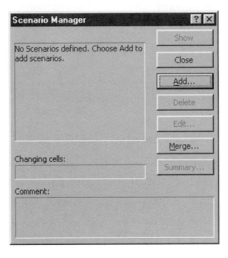

Figure 14-10

Dialog Box for Adding the Best-on-Best Scenario

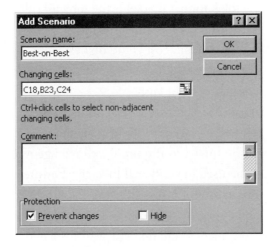

Figure 14-11

"Scenario Values" Dialog Box with Values for the Changing Cells for the Best-on-Best Scenario

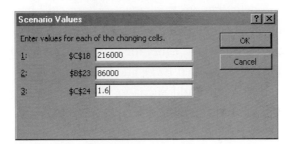

although their values will be different (i.e., 180,000, $92,000, and $2.15). Click the OK button or press Enter to return to the "Scenario Values" dialog box. The values for the changing cells will be the same as on the current worksheet, which will be the most probable values unless they have been changed. (You can, if you wish, omit adding the Most Probable scenario from the scenario analysis because it simply reproduces the current values.)

Repeat the steps to add the worst-on-worst scenario. Enter the conditions from Table 14-1 for the worst-on-worst scenario in the same manner. After all three scenarios have been entered, return to the "Scenario Manager" dialog box, which will appear as Figure 14-12.

Click the "Summary" button to obtain the "Scenario Summary" dialog box, Figure 14-13.

Enter the cell identities for the result cells (G33:G35 for the NPV, IRR, and MIRR values at the end of five years and B36 for the break-even point). Click the OK button or press Enter to obtain the scenario summary shown in Figure 14-14. This will appear on a new worksheet titled "Scenario Summary."

Edit the scenario summary of Figure 14-14 to provide the finished scenario summary shown in Figure 14-15. Replace the column and row numbers for the variables in Cells C6:C8 and C10:C14 of

Figure 14-12
_____

"Scenario Manager" Dialog Box with All Three Scenarios Entered

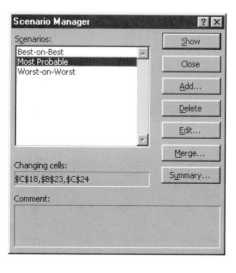

Figure 14-13
_____

Scenario Summary Dialog Box with Result Cells Identified

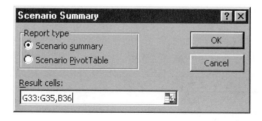

Figure 14-14

Scenario Summary with Results (Unedited)

	A	B	C	D	E	F	G
1								
2		**Scenario Summary**						
3				Current Values:	Best-on-Best	Most Probable	Worst-on-Worst
5		**Changing Cells:**					
6			$C$18	180000	216000	180000	144000
7			$B$23	92000	86000	92000	98000
8			$C$24	2.15	1.6	2.15	2.35
9		**Result Cells:**					
10			$G$33	$694	$58,010	$694	($26,589)
11			$G$34	13.31%	38.15%	13.31%	1.19%
12			$G$35	13.17%	25.27%	13.17%	6.07%
13			$B$36	4.95	2.62	4.95	Failed
14		Notes: Current Values column represents values of changing cells at					
15		time Scenario Summary Report was created. Changing cells for each					
16		scenario are highlighted in gray.					

Figure 14-14 with the names of the variables, as in Figure 14-15. You can make other changes, such as deleting the note, editing the titles and centering them, centering column titles and values, and so forth, to produce a finished scenario summary, as shown in Figure 14-15. The goal is to provide the results of the scenario analysis in a management-oriented presentation. Make sure that what is essential is included, and delete what is not needed.

Note that under the worst-on-worst conditions, the investment will fail to break even at the end of five years.

Figure 14-15

Scenario Summary after Editing and Formatting

	A	B	C	D
1	**SCENARIO SUMMARY FOR ALADDIN GAMES**			
2	**Wholesale Price = $4.66/set and Market Share = 15.81%**			
3		**Best-on-Best**	**Most Probable**	**Worst-on-Worst**
5	**Changing Variables**			
6	Total Annual Market, sets	216,000	180,000	144,000
7	Investment, dollars	$86,000	$92,000	$98,000
8	Unit Variable Cost, $/set	$1.60	$2.15	$2.35
9	**Results at End of 5 Years**			
10	Net Present Value	$58,010	$694	($26,589)
11	Internal Rate of Return	38.15%	13.31%	1.19%
12	Modified Internal Rate of Return	25.27%	13.17%	6.07%
13	**Time for Investment's Breaking Even during the 5-Year Analysis Period**			
14	Break-Even Point, years	2.62	4.95	Failed

One should also recognize that the results shown in Figure 14-15 are for a selling price of $4.66/set and a market share of 15.81 percent. These are the optimum values for the most probable conditions. Because the company does not know the future actual conditions beforehand, it is reasonable for the purpose of the analysis to set the selling price for the most probable conditions. The decision to be made at the point of analysis is whether or not to make and market the new product. Once that decision is implemented and as better cost and market data become available, the price can be adjusted to what is best for whatever conditions prevail.

Locking a Scenario

The output of the Scenario Manager can be locked to prevent output values from changing. To lock (or unlock) the Scenario Manager tool, go to the Scenario Manager dialog box, click on the "Edit" box to open the "Edit Scenario" dialog box, and then check (or uncheck) the "Prevent Changes" box.

Students' Comments on Excel's Scenario Manager

One of my jobs is long-term financial planning ... and we do a lot of risk analysis based on certain scenarios. ... It is too bad our [corporate] software doesn't have the scenario analysis capabilities that Excel does because it would make our lives much easier. Many times we have to "put the hammer" to our [corporate] software to try to model an unusual situation.

* * *

The Scenario Manager tool is a handy one to help organize a range of scenarios or "What if?" cases. For my job, it would be cases of portfolio position (long, short) against very high or very low commodity prices.

* * *

Scenario analysis is a very handy tool. In the home finance industry, it could be most useful in comparing the potential downside with the most probable to see if the risks are manageable and if they are outweighed by the likely reward. For example, a decision to refinance using an adjustable-rate mortgage vs. a fixed-rate mortgage could be weighed by looking at the worst case future rate scenario compared to the most likely scenario.

* * *

The scenario manager provides a really efficient way to change different variables and to see the results. ... I could see using this in real estate financing and other investment decisions. ... I think this tool can make an investment decision much easier to understand and I can see how useful it could be in presentations.

* * *

Learning about the scenario manager tool for the first time was kind of like obtaining a new secret weapon for battling your enemies. Once armed with this knowledge, one can easily perform scenarios for all types of business situations from rolling out a new product to making a new capital investment. Providing this information will give both the optimists and conservatives a certain level of comfort in knowing what direction the project can take from one end to the other.

Concluding Remarks

Risks are part of life. Death is the only cure for avoiding them completely. In the meantime, prudent people live by choosing actions that limit their risks to acceptable levels. These vary with the rewards if things turn out well and the penalties if they do not, as well as the probabilities associated with each.

Attitudes toward risk are often summarized in such statements as "No pain, no gain," or the question "Do you wish to eat well or sleep well?"

Making intelligent decisions in the face of risk requires knowing the values of the gains, along with the values of the pains that go with them. Scenario analysis is a management tool for evaluating these outcomes. It provides an opportunity to examine the results for whatever the future might hold—or at least those combinations of future conditions that an analyst can identify and believes are within the realm of concern.

Although it is more work to use, Excel's Scenario Manager is a much more versatile tool than one- or two-variable input tables. Scenario Manager allows an analyst to vary a large number of input variables and evaluate the impacts on a large number of output variables. Any number of scenarios can be examined in addition to the most probable, best-on-best, and worst-on-worst cases.

Cell linkage is critical! In order for the Scenario Manager to work, there must be an unbroken linkage between the input cells that vary and the output cells with results. Any break in the link will make it impossible for an output variable to respond properly to a change in an input variable and will invalidate the results. Before using the Scenario Manager, test a worksheet to see that all parts respond properly to changes in the input variables.

In this chapter we have used scenario analysis to examine the impacts of various combinations of conditions that we cannot know exactly. We have also examined the risks or probabilities of the outcomes when the probability of one of the conditions is known. In the next chapter, we extend our discussion of risk to outcomes that depend on the probabilities of more than one condition.

Chapter 15

Capital Budgeting: Risk Analysis
with Monte Carlo Simulation

CHAPTER OBJECTIVES

Management Skills

- Understand the concept of Monte Carlo simulation and its use to evaluate the risks for achieving success or suffering failure in capital budgeting decisions.

Spreadsheet Skills

- Use Monte Carlo simulation to determine the possible payoffs for capital investments with several input variables that have different types of probability distributions.
- Generate random numbers with several types of distributions.
- Use random numbers to simulate random values or events.
- Execute a large number of iterations to ensure that the simulation results are not compromised by "the luck of the draw," which can occur with only a small number of iterations.
- Use Excel's FREQUENCY and NORMDIST commands to convert the results from a large number of iterations into probability distributions for possible outcomes or payoffs.
- Create "downside risk curves" that express the probability distributions in a graphical format that can be easily understood and used for making decisions.

Overview

Monte Carlo simulation is a powerful tool that overcomes the limitations of scenario analysis, which was discussed in the preceding chapter. Scenario analysis is limited to showing only what will happen **IF** certain conditions occur. It is very helpful in alerting CFOs to potential misfortunes **IF** things don't turn out as well as expected—or to future windfalls **IF** things turn out better than expected.

Unfortunately, although "What if?" analyses can evaluate an investment's payoffs under various combinations of assumed conditions, they cannot evaluate all possible combinations of the future that will affect results. Nor can they evaluate how probable the conditions are. In a word, they are too "iffy."

The concept of risk introduced at the beginning of the preceding chapter took scenario analysis one step further. It showed how to use a forecast's standard error and the properties of the normal curve to evaluate the risks that an investment's NPV or other measure of success would be less than given values. It also showed how to present the results in the form of a downside risk curve. This technique can be applied when there is only one uncertain outcome, and all others are fixed—or assumed to be fixed.

In real life, there are many variables and their combinations that affect the outcome of investments and vary independent of each other. We need a technique that can assess risks when there is more than one input variable whose values vary over a range of possible values. Monte Carlo simulation is a technique for doing this. It is being widely used by sophisticated CFOs to define the financial risks of capital ventures.

The essence of Monte Carlo simulation is the use of random numbers to simulate random values or events. Spreadsheets have become powerful enough to apply Monte Carlo simulation to many problems of practical interest. In this chapter, we will apply the technique to the Aladdin Games case study in the preceding chapter, where we evaluated the investment's outcome based on best-on-best, worst-on-worst, and most probable "What if" scenarios. However, we will not limit ourselves to these three scenarios. We will use Monte Carlo simulation to develop a downside risk curve that reacts to **all possible combinations** of the three input variables—that is, to the total annual markets in each of the five years, the unit variable cost, and the investment. We will allow the values of these variables to occur with the frequencies and over the ranges defined by their probability distributions.

Case Study: Aladdin Games

We return to the case study analyzed in the preceding chapter. The random values to be simulated are the total annual markets in each of the five years, the unit variable cost, and the investment. Each of these is a probability distribution rather than a single, fixed value. We need to know something about the probability distributions in order to simulate them. What we know about each is as follows:

1. *Total annual market in each of the five years*: These are normally distributed (i.e., lie along a "bell-shaped curve") with a mean of 180,000 sets and a standard deviation or forecast error of 18,000 sets.
2. *Unit variable cost*: This has a triangular distribution with a minimum of $1.60, a most probable value of $2.15, and a maximum of $2.35.
3. *Investment*: This has a uniform distribution between a minimum of $86,000 and a maximum of $98,000.

Solution: Enter the column headings and row labels shown in Figure 15-1. (Note that because of the size of the spreadsheet, this figure appears in two sections—the first for Rows 1 to 58 and the second for Rows 59 to 82.)

(Continued)

Figure 15-1

Spreadsheet Setup for Alladin Games (Rows 1 to 58 only)

	A	B	C	D	E	F	G	H
1	ALADDIN GAMES: MONTE CARLO SIMULATION							
2	Total annual market forecast, sets	180,000						
3	Standard forecast error, sets	18,000						
4	Minimum facility investment	$86,000						
5	Maximum facility investment	$98,000						
6	Equipment life, years	5						
7	Salvage value	0						
8	Depreciation method	St. Line						
9	Minimum variable cost, $/set	$1.60						
10	Most probable variable cost, $/set	$2.15						
11	Maximum variable cost, $/set	$2.35						
12	(MP-MIN)/(MAX-MIN)							
13	Nonproduction costs, % of sales	30%						
14	Cost of capital	13%						
15	Tax rate	40%						
16	Monte Carlo Simulation with Wholesale Price and Market Share from Most Probable Scenario							
17	Wholesale price, $/set							
18	Market share at wholesale price							
19	**Iteration number**	1	2	3	4	5	6	7
20	Total annual market, sets in year 1							
21	Total annual market, sets in year 2							
22	Total annual market, sets in year 3							
23	Total annual market, sets in year 4							
24	Total annual market, sets in year 5							
25	Sales receipts, year 1							
26	Sales receipts, year 2							
27	Sales receipts, year 3							
28	Sales receipts, year 4							
29	Sales receipts, year 5							
30	Random number to simulate variable cost							
31	Unit variable cost, $/set							
32	Total variable cost, year 1							
33	Total variable cost, year 2							
34	Total variable cost, year 3							
35	Total variable cost, year 4							
36	Total variable cost, year 5							
37	Nonproduction costs, year 1							
38	Nonproduction costs, year 2							
39	Nonproduction costs, year 3							
40	Nonproduction costs, year 4							
41	Nonproduction costs, year 5							
42	Before-tax cash flow, year 1							
43	Before-tax cash flow, year 2							
44	Before-tax cash flow, year 3							
45	Before-tax cash flow, year 4							
46	Before-tax cash flow, year 5							
47	Investment, $							
48	Annual depreciation							
49	Taxable income, year 1							
50	Taxable income, year 2							
51	Taxable income, year 3							
52	Taxable income, year 4							
53	Taxable income, year 5							
54	Tax, year 1							
55	Tax, year 2							
56	Tax, year 3							
57	Tax, year 4							
58	Tax, year 5							

(Continued)

Figure 15-1
_____

Spreadsheet Setup for Alladin Games (Rows 59 to 82 only) (*continued*)

	A	B	C	D	E	F	G	H
59	After-tax cash flow, year 0							
60	After-tax cash flow, year 1							
61	After-tax cash flow, year 2							
62	After-tax cash flow, year 3							
63	After-tax cash flow, year 4							
64	After-tax cash flow, year 5							
65	Net present value, end of year 0							
66	Net present value, end of year 1							
67	Net present value, end of year 2							
68	Net present value, end of year 3							
69	Net present value, end of year 4							
70	**Net present value, end of year 5**							
71	**Internal rate of return (IRR)**							
72	**Modified internal rate of return (MIRR)**							
73	**Years to break even**							
74	**Summary of Results for 200 Iterations**							
75		**NPV**	**IRR**	**MIRR**	**Years to Break Even**			
76	**Minimum**							
77	**Average**							
78	**Maximum**							
79	**Standard deviation**							
80	**Skewness**							
81	**Kurtosis**							
82	**Probability for failing to break even by the end of 5 years**							

Figure 15-1 shows the shell, with column headings and row labels, which will be used to organize the calculations. The steps that follow will lead you through the series of cell entries for completing the spreadsheet. We will use the Monte Carlo technique to simulate 200 random combinations of values for the total market demands, unit variable cost, and investment. We will use the results to evaluate the same financial measures of success that were evaluated in the preceding chapter with scenario analysis. Beyond that, Monte Carlo simulation will provide the probabilities for the values and help understand investment risks.

Ratio in Cell B12: Calculate the value in Cell B12 by entering =(B10-B9)/(B11-B9). You should get the value 0.733. We will explain this value later when we use it to simulate the unit variable cost.

Wholesale Price and Market Share: Insert a trial value in Cell B17 for the wholesale price. A good value is $4.66/set, which was the value that we found to be optimum for the most probable set of conditions in the preceding chapter. Enter the formula =F11+E11*B17+D11*B17^2 in Cell B18 for the market share at the wholesale price in Cell B17. (The formula was derived in the preceding chapter.)

Total Annual Market: We will use normally distributed numbers with a mean of 180,000 and a standard deviation of 18,000 to simulate the total market demand. We will use 200 iterations for each of the five years. The results will be spread over the Range B20:GS24 (i.e., five rows of 200 numbers each). To create the values, we will use Excel's Random Number Generator. To access the generator, first make sure it has been added to your system.

If Data Analysis cannot be found on your Tools menu, you need to add it in. To do that, click on Add-Ins on the Tools menu to open the Add-Ins dialog box shown in Figure 15-2. Click on Analysis ToolPak at the top of the list of add-ins and then either click OK or press Enter.

(Continued)

Figure 15-2

Add-In Dialog Box with Options Selected

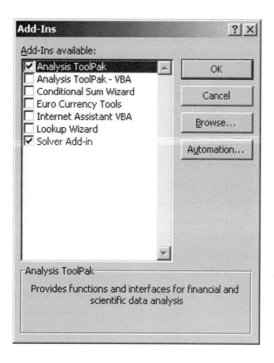

Once the Analysis TookPak has been added in, clicking on the Data Analysis option at the bottom of the Tools pull-down menu will open the Data Analysis dialog box shown in Figure 15-3. Scroll down and select Random Number Generation. Then click OK or press Enter to open the Random Number Generator dialog box shown in Figure 15-4.

Figure 15-3

Data Analysis Dialog Box with Random Number Generation Selected

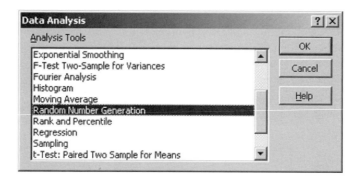

(Continued)

Figure 15-4

Random Number Generation Dialog Box with Entries
(The normal distribution has been selected.)

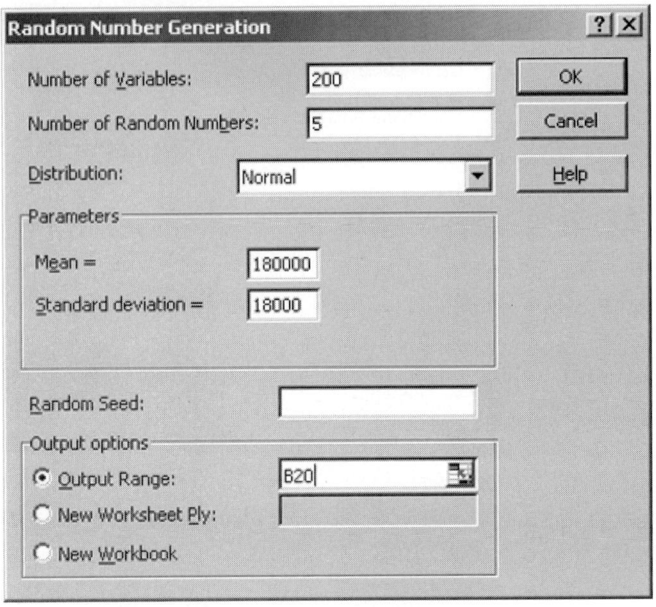

Scroll down on the Distribution box and select Normal. Enter the values shown in Figure 15-4 and click the OK button or press Enter. This will generate a series of 1,000 random numbers (i.e., five rows of 200 numbers each) that are normally distributed about a mean of 180,000 with a standard deviation of 18,000 and place their values in Cells B20:GS24. Because of "the luck of the draw" in generating random numbers, your values will be somewhat different from those shown later in the solution spreadsheet. However, the general behavior will be similar.

Sales Receipts: Sales receipts are the product of the total market, market share, and selling price. Enter =B20*$B$18*$B$17 in Cell B25 and copy to B25:GS29.

Unit Variable Cost: For Aladdin Games, the unit variable cost for "Wall Street Invaders" has a minimum value of $1.60, a most probable value of $2.15, and a maximum value of $2.35. This type of distribution is called a triangular distribution and is shown in Figure 15-5.

Excel does not provide a built-in random number generator for the triangular distribution. We will substitute uniformly distributed random numbers (RN) between 0 and 1 into the following two equations to generate a series of random numbers with a triangular distribution.

$$X = X_{min} + \sqrt{RN(X_{mp} - X_{min})(X_{max} - X_{min})} \quad \text{for} \quad RN \le \frac{(X_{mp} - X_{min})}{(X_{max} - X_{min})} \tag{15.1}$$

and

$$X = X_{max} - \sqrt{(1-RN)(X_{max} - X_{mp})(X_{max} - X_{min})} \quad \text{for} \quad RN \ge \frac{(X_{mp} - X_{min})}{(X_{max} - X_{min})} \tag{15.2}$$

(Continued)

Figure 15-5

Triangular Distribution with Most Probable Value (X_{Mp}) between Minimum and Maximum Values (X_{Min} and X_{Max})

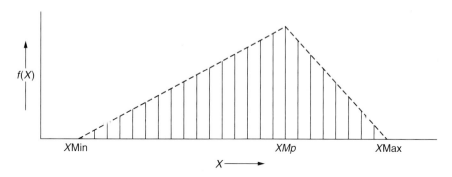

The ratio that determines which of the above two equations to use is the ratio evaluated in Cell B12. It has a value of 0.733, which means that the most probable value is 73.3 percent of the increment from the minimum to the maximum value. When we draw a random number less than or equal to 0.733, we use equation 15.1; otherwise, we use equation 15.2.

Figure 15-6 shows the Random Number Generation box with the settings for generating a uniform series of 200 random numbers between 0 and 1 and placing the results in Cells B30:GS30. (Note that because we have entered 200 for the number of variables, it is not necessary to include GS30 in the range.)

Figure 15-6

Random Number Generation Dialog Box (Entries for Simulating 200 Values of Uniformly Distributed Random Numbers between 0 and 1 for Use in Creating a Triangular Distribution of Unit Variable Costs)

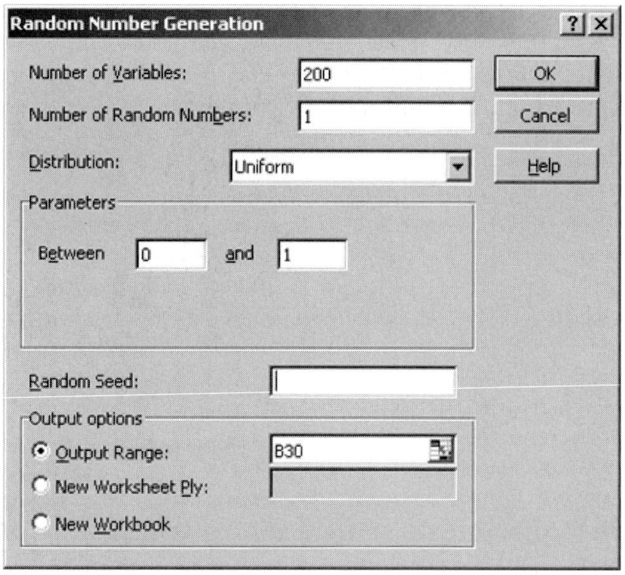

Random Number Generation	? X
Number of Variables:	200	OK
Number of Random Numbers:	1	Cancel
Distribution:	Uniform ▼	Help
Parameters		
Between 0 and 1		
Random Seed:		
Output options		
● Output Range:	B30	
○ New Worksheet Ply:		
○ New Workbook		

(Continued)

To convert the **uniformly** distributed random numbers in B30:GS30 into a **triangular** distribution of unit variable costs in B31:GS31, enter the following IF statement in Cell B31 and copy it to Cells C31:GS31:

=IF(B30<$B$12,$B$9+SQRT(B30*($B$10-$B$9)*($B$11-$B$9)),

$B$11-SQRT((1-B30)*($B$11-$B$10)*($B$11-$B$9)))

Note the $ signs to fix the entries for B9, B10, and B11 when the expression is copied across Row 31 to Cell GS31. B30, the random number, will change to C30, D30, …, GS30.

Test to see that the IF statement responds properly to the random numbers in Row 30. Change the value in Cell B30 to zero to see that the response in Cell B31 is the minimum value of the distribution. Repeat by inserting values of one and the ratio in Cell B12 into Cell B30. Correct the IF statement if the correct results do not appear in Cell B31. When finished checking, return the random number to Cell B30.

Total Variable Cost: We will assume that the number of units made is the same as the number of units sold. The total variable cost is therefore the product of the total market times the market share times the unit variable cost. Enter =B20*$B$18*B$31 in Cell B32 and copy to Cells B32:GS36.

Nonproduction Costs: Nonproduction costs are 30 percent of sales revenues (the value in Cell B13). Enter =$B$13*B25 in Cell B37 and copy the entry to B37:GS41.

Before-Tax Cash Flow: The before-tax cash flows for Years 1 to 5 are the cash inflows of sales revenues minus the cash outflows of total variable cost and nonproduction costs. Enter =B25-B32-B37 in Cell B42 and copy the entry to B42:GS46.

Investment: The investment is a uniformly distributed value between 86,000 and 98,000. Figure 15-7 shows the dialog box with the entries for generating these values and placing them in Cells B47:GS47. (The average of Cells B47:GS47 should be close to 92,000. Ideally, it should be exactly 92,000, but there will be a difference because of "the luck of the draw.")

Figure 15-7

Random Number Generation Dialog Box (Entries for Simulating 200 Values of Uniformly Distributed Random Numbers between 86,000 and 98,000 for Simulating 200 Iterations of the Capital Investment)

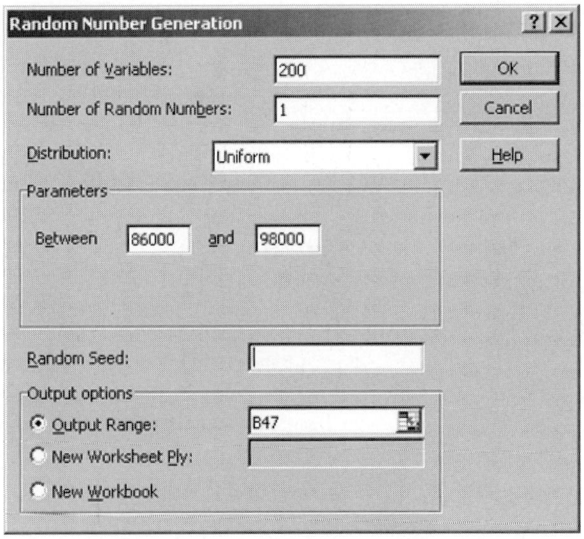

(Continued)

Annual Depreciation: The investment is depreciated by straight-line method over a period of five years (the value in Cell B6) to zero salvage value. Enter =B47/$B$6 in Cell B48 and copy the entry to C48:GS48.

Taxable Income: Taxable income equals income less deductible expenses. Deductible expenses in this problem include the total variable costs and the nonproduction costs, which have already been used to calculate the before-tax cash flow, plus the annual depreciation. Enter =B42-B$48 in Cell B49 and copy the entry to B49:GS53. Note the placement of the dollar sign in the entry B$48; when this entry is copied across and down, the column changes but the row remains Row 48.

Tax: Tax equals taxable income multiplied by the tax rate (the value in Cell B15). Enter =B49*$B$15 in Cell B54 and copy the entry to B54:GS58.

After-Tax Cash Flow: The after-tax cash flow for Year 0 is the cash outflow for the investment. Enter =-B47 in Cell B59 and copy the entry to C59:GS59. For Years 1 to 5, the after-tax cash flow equals the before-tax cash flow minus tax. Enter =B42-B54 in Cell B60 and copy the entry to B60:GS64.

Net Present Values: The net present values of the investment at the ends of years 0 to 5 are evaluated in Rows 65 to 70. For Year 0, enter either =B59 or =-B47 in Cell B65 and copy to C65:GS65. For Years 1 to 5, enter =NPV($B$14,B$60:B60)+B$65 in Cell B66 and copy to B66:GS70.

Internal Rate of Return at End of 5 Years: Enter =IRR(B59:B64,0.10) in Cell B71 and copy the entry to C71:GS71. (If you omit the discount rate in this entry, Excel will use the default value of 0.10.)

Modified Internal Rate of Return at End of 5 Years: Enter =MIRR(B59:B64,$B$14,$B$14) in Cell B72 and copy the entry to C72:GS72.

Years to Break Even: Enter =IF(B67>0,1-B66/(B67-B66),IF(B68>0,2-B67/(B68-B67),IF(B69>0,3-B68/(B69-B68),IF(B70>0,4-B69/(B70-B69),"failed")))) in Cell B73 and copy to C73:GS73.

Figure 15-8 shows the results to this point in Row 1 to 73 and Columns B to H—that is, the results for the first 7 of 200 iterations. (Values for the last 173 iterations will be in Columns I to GS, which would have extended beyond the right side of the printed page and not have been printed. You should be able to find them by scrolling to the right of your computer screen.)

Summary of Results for 200 Iterations: Rows 74 to 82 of Figure 15-8 show a summary of the results of the 200 iterations. The summary includes the values of six statistical functions for the investment's NPV, IRR, and MIRR. The minimum, average, maximum, and standard deviation should require no explanation. Explanations for skewness and kurtosis will be given later.

Calculate values for the investment's NPV at the end of five years as follows:

Statistical Function	Entry and Cell
Minimum:	Enter =MIN(B70:GS70) in Cell B76
Average:	Enter =AVERAGE(B70:GS70) in Cell B77
Maximum:	Enter =MAX(B70:GS70) in Cell B78
Standard deviation:	Enter =STDEV(B70:GS70) in Cell B79
Skewness:	Enter =SKEW(B70:GS70) in Cell B80
Kurtosis:	Enter =KURT(B70:GS70) in Cell B81

Repeat this set of six statistical functions for IRR, and MIRR in Cells C76:D81.

For the minimum years to break even, enter =MIN(B73:GS73) in Cell E76. Note that we cannot calculate an average, maximum, or other statistical measures for the years to break even because the investment fails to break even on some of the iterations.

For the probability to break even by the end of five years, we need to use Excel's COUNT function to count the number of entries in the Range B73:GS73 that have numerical values (i.e., that are not "failed").

(Continued)

Figure 15-8

Results for the First Seven of 200 Iterations of Monte Carlo Simulation (The value in Cell B17 has been optimized by using Excel's Solver tool.)

	A	B	C	D	E	F	G	H
1	ALADDIN GAMES: MONTE CARLO SIMULATION							
2	Total annual market forecast, sets	180,000		Selling price/Market share information				
3	Standard forecast error, sets	18,000		Price,		Market Share		Fcst.
4	Minimum facility investment	$86,000		$/set	Price^2	Data	Forecast	Error
5	Maximum facility investment	$98,000		$4.25	18.063	18%	17.97%	0.03%
6	Equipment life, years	5		$4.50	20.250	17%	17.11%	−0.11%
7	Salvage value	0		$4.75	22.563	15%	14.83%	0.17%
8	Depreciation method	St. Line		$5.00	25.000	11%	11.11%	−0.11%
9	Minimum variable cost, $/set	$1.60		$5.25	27.563	6%	5.97%	0.03%
10	Most probable variable cost, $/set	$2.15		LINEST OUTPUT			Avg. Error	0.00%
11	Maximum variable cost, $/set	$2.35		−0.11429	0.96571	−1.86029		
12	(MP-MIN)/(MAX-MIN)	0.733		0.00723	0.06870	0.16250		
13	Nonproduction costs, % of sales	30%		0.99941	0.169%	#N/A		
14	Cost of capital and reinvestment rate	13%		1700	2	#N/A		
15	Tax rate	40%		0.00971	0.00001	#N/A		
16	Monte Carlo Simulation							
17	Wholesale price, $/set	$4.63						
18	Market share at wholesale price	16.10%						
19	Iteration number	1	2	3	4	5	6	7
20	Total annual market, sets in year 1	174,596	157,002	184,397	202,977	201,570	211,196	140,695
21	Total annual market, sets in year 2	184,085	183,861	179,866	157,971	184,237	182,668	193,544
22	Total annual market, sets in year 3	175,345	191,510	157,067	189,345	197,577	164,450	186,686
23	Total annual market, sets in year 4	166,004	161,987	159,219	134,697	158,441	192,025	194,447
24	Total annual market, sets in year 5	192,438	188,888	162,046	199,920	156,661	191,987	153,380
25	Sales receipts, year 1	$130,159	$117,043	$137,465	$151,316	$150,268	$157,444	$104,887
26	Sales receipts, year 2	$137,233	$137,066	$134,088	$117,765	$137,346	$136,177	$144,284
27	Sales receipts, year 3	$130,717	$142,768	$117,091	$141,154	$147,291	$122,595	$139,172
28	Sales receipts, year 4	$123,754	$120,759	$118,696	$100,415	$118,116	$143,152	$144,958
29	Sales receipts, year 5	$143,460	$140,813	$120,803	$149,038	$116,789	$143,124	$114,343
30	Random number to simulate variable cost	0.4386	0.1782	0.6286	0.9883	0.1220	0.5470	0.8998
31	Unit variable cost, $/set	$2.03	$1.87	$2.11	$2.31	$1.82	$2.08	$2.23
32	Total variable cost, year 1	$56,931	$47,296	$62,617	$75,422	$59,204	$70,554	$50,454
33	Total variable cost, year 2	$60,025	$55,387	$61,078	$58,699	$54,112	$61,024	$69,405
34	Total variable cost, year 3	$57,175	$57,691	$53,336	$70,357	$58,031	$54,938	$66,946
35	Total variable cost, year 4	$54,130	$48,797	$54,067	$50,051	$46,536	$64,150	$69,729
36	Total variable cost, year 5	$62,749	$56,901	$55,027	$74,287	$46,013	$64,137	$55,002
37	Nonproduction costs, year 1	$39,048	$35,113	$41,240	$45,395	$45,080	$47,233	$31,466
38	Nonproduction costs, year 2	$41,170	$41,120	$40,226	$35,330	$41,204	$40,853	$43,285
39	Nonproduction costs, year 3	$39,215	$42,830	$35,127	$42,346	$44,187	$36,779	$41,752
40	Nonproduction costs, year 4	$37,126	$36,228	$35,609	$30,125	$35,435	$42,946	$43,487
41	Nonproduction costs, year 5	$43,038	$42,244	$36,241	$44,711	$35,037	$42,937	$34,303
42	Before-tax cash flow, year 1	$34,180	$34,634	$33,609	$30,499	$45,984	$39,657	$22,967
43	Before-tax cash flow, year 2	$36,038	$40,559	$32,783	$23,737	$42,030	$34,300	$31,594
44	Before-tax cash flow, year 3	$34,327	$42,247	$28,628	$28,451	$45,073	$30,879	$30,474
45	Before-tax cash flow, year 4	$32,498	$35,734	$29,020	$20,240	$36,145	$36,057	$31,741
46	Before-tax cash flow, year 5	$37,673	$41,668	$29,535	$30,040	$35,739	$36,050	$25,037
47	Investment, $	$92,662	$96,568	$89,718	$88,927	$97,519	$88,499	$97,070
48	Annual depreciation	$18,532	$19,314	$17,944	$17,785	$19,504	$17,700	$19,414
49	Taxable income, year 1	$15,648	$15,321	$15,665	$12,714	$26,480	$21,957	$3,553
50	Taxable income, year 2	$17,505	$21,246	$14,840	$5,951	$22,526	$16,600	$12,180
51	Taxable income, year 3	$15,794	$22,933	$10,684	$10,665	$25,569	$13,179	$11,060
52	Taxable income, year 4	$13,966	$16,420	$11,076	$2,454	$16,641	$18,357	$12,327
53	Taxable income, year 5	$19,141	$22,355	$11,592	$12,254	$16,235	$18,350	$5,623
54	Tax, year 1	$6,259	$6,128	$6,266	$5,086	$10,592	$8,783	$1,421
55	Tax, year 2	$7,002	$8,498	$5,936	$2,381	$9,010	$6,640	$4,872
56	Tax, year 3	$6,318	$9,173	$4,274	$4,266	$10,228	$5,272	$4,424
57	Tax, year 4	$5,586	$6,568	$4,431	$982	$6,656	$7,343	$4,931
58	Tax, year 5	$7,656	$8,942	$4,637	$4,902	$6,494	$7,340	$2,249

(Continued)

Figure 15-8

Results for the First Seven of 200 Iterations of Monte Carlo Simulation (*Continued*)

	A	B	C	D	E	F	G	H
59	After-tax cash flow, year 0	–$92,662	–$96,568	–$89,718	–$88,927	–$97,519	–$88,499	–$97,070
60	After-tax cash flow, year 1	$27,921	$28,506	$27,343	$25,415	$35,391	$30,874	$21,546
61	After-tax cash flow, year 2	$29,036	$32,061	$26,848	$21,357	$33,019	$27,660	$26,722
62	After-tax cash flow, year 3	$28,009	$33,073	$24,354	$24,186	$34,845	$25,607	$26,051
63	After-tax cash flow, year 4	$26,912	$29,166	$24,590	$19,259	$29,488	$28,714	$26,811
64	After-tax cash flow, year 5	$30,017	$32,726	$24,899	$25,139	$29,244	$28,710	$22,789
65	Net present value, end of year 0	–$92,662	–$96,568	–$89,718	–$88,927	–$97,519	–$88,499	–$97,070
66	Net present value, end of year 1	–$67,953	–$71,342	–$65,521	–$66,436	–$66,199	–$61,177	–$78,003
67	Net present value, end of year 2	–$45,214	–$46,234	–$44,495	–$49,711	–$40,341	–$39,515	–$57,075
68	Net present value, end of year 3	–$25,802	–$23,313	$27,616	$32,040	$10,100	$21,707	–$39,021
69	Net present value, end of year 4	–$9,297	–$5,425	–$12,535	–$21,137	$1,894	–$4,157	–$22,577
70	Net present value, end of year 5	$6,995	$12,337	$979	–$7,493	$17,767	$11,426	–$10,208
71	Internal rate of return (IRR)	16.04%	18.04%	13.46%	9.45%	20.50%	18.24%	8.65%
72	Modified internal rate of return (MIRR)	14.66%	15.75%	13.25%	11.03%	16.85%	15.78%	10.52%
73	Years to break even	4.57	4.31	4.93	failed	3.90	4.27	failed

	Summary of Results for 200 Iterations							
74								
75		NPV	IRR	MIRR	Years to Break Even			
76	Minimum	–$11,944	7.75%	10.00%	3.25			
77	Average	$8,577	16.73%	14.95%				
78	Maximum	$36,064	28.62%	21.08%				
79	Standard deviation	$10,822	4.70%	2.48%				
80	Skewness	0.37	0.33	0.23				
81	Kurtosis	–0.45	–0.47	–0.53				
82	Probability for failing to break even by the end of 5 years				20.50%			

Since there are 200 cells in the range, the number of iterations for which the investment failed to break even equals 200 minus the number that did not fail, that is, 200-COUNT(B73:GS73). The percent of the iterations for which the investment failed to break even is therefore calculated by entering =(200-COUNT(B73:GS73))/200 in Cell E82 and formatting the result as a percent. (You can also enter the expression =(200-COUNTIF(B73:GS73,">0"))/200 in Cell E82 to count the number of values greater than zero in the range B73:GS73 and convert the results to the percent of iterations that failed to break even.)

Your exact values will differ from those shown because of differences in the random numbers drawn. However, the minimum values for NPV, IRR, and MIRR should not be less than those for the worst-on-worst scenario in Chapter 14, and the maximum values should not be more than those for the best-on-best scenario.

Skewness is a measure of the degree of asymmetry of a distribution about its mean. A normal distribution is symmetric about the mean; that is, the skewness of a normal distribution is zero. Positive skewness indicates a distribution with an asymmetric tail extending toward more positive values, and negative skewness indicates a distribution with an asymmetric tail extending toward more negative values. The values of skewness in Row 80 indicate that the NPV, IRR, and MIRR distributions are slightly skewed to positive values. The values, however, are close to zero; that is, the 200 values of NPV, IRR, and MIRR are very close to being normally distributed.

Kurtosis is a measure of the relative peakedness or flatness of a distribution compared with the normal distribution. The kurtosis of a normal distribution calculated with Excel's KURT function is zero. Positive kurtosis indicates a relatively peaked distribution. Negative kurtosis indicates a relatively flat distribution. The values of kurtosis in Cells CP1:E81 indicate the distributions of the 200 NPV, IRR, and MIRR values are slightly flatter than a normal distribution, but not markedly so.

(Continued)

Downside Risk Charts

Downside Risk Chart for Net Present Value: Set up a series of NPV values that range from slightly less than the minimum in Cell B76 to slightly more than the maximum in Cell B78. Because of differences in the random numbers, your values for the minimum and maximum NPV values will differ somewhat from those shown in Cells B85 and B107 of Figure 15-9.

For the values shown in Figure 15-9, the set of bin values should start at less than the minimum of –$11,944 and end at more than the maximum of $36,064. Cells D85:D107 in Figure 15-9 show a set of bin values running from –$15,000 to +$40,000 in increments of $2,500. (Since the results will be plotted in a downside risk chart, the bin values and increments should be chosen so that one of the bin values is zero, which is the investment's break-even point.)

Figure 15-9

Downside Risk Curve for Net Present Value at End of Five Years

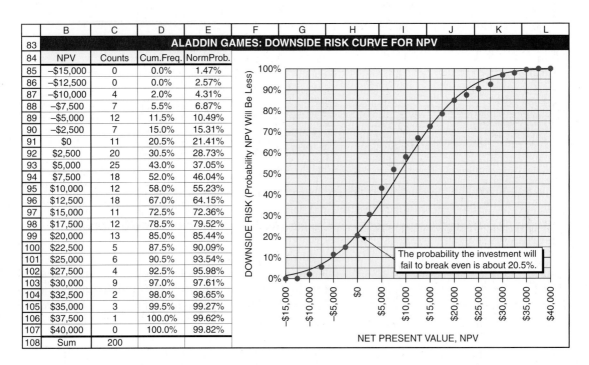

	B	C	D	E
83	ALADDIN GAMES: DOWNSIDE RISK CURVE FOR NPV			
84	NPV	Counts	Cum.Freq.	NormProb.
85	–$15,000	0	0.0%	1.47%
86	–$12,500	0	0.0%	2.57%
87	–$10,000	4	2.0%	4.31%
88	–$7,500	7	5.5%	6.87%
89	–$5,000	12	11.5%	10.49%
90	–$2,500	7	15.0%	15.31%
91	$0	11	20.5%	21.41%
92	$2,500	20	30.5%	28.73%
93	$5,000	25	43.0%	37.05%
94	$7,500	18	52.0%	46.04%
95	$10,000	12	58.0%	55.23%
96	$12,500	18	67.0%	64.15%
97	$15,000	11	72.5%	72.36%
98	$17,500	12	78.5%	79.52%
99	$20,000	13	85.0%	85.44%
100	$22,500	5	87.5%	90.09%
101	$25,000	6	90.5%	93.54%
102	$27,500	4	92.5%	95.98%
103	$30,000	9	97.0%	97.61%
104	$32,500	2	98.0%	98.65%
105	$35,000	3	99.5%	99.27%
106	$37,500	1	100.0%	99.62%
107	$40,000	0	100.0%	99.82%
108	Sum	200		

The next step is to count the number of NPV values in Row 70 that are in each bin—that is, within a bin that is less than a bin value in one of the Cells B85:D107 but greater than the bin value immediately preceding it. (For example, an NPV of $6,995 would be counted opposite bin value $10,000.) We will use Excel's FREQUENCY function to count the NPVs in each bin. The syntax for this function is

FREQUENCY(*range of values, range of bins*)

Use the mouse to select Cells C85:C107, type =FREQUENCY(B70:GS70,B85:B107), and press Ctrl/Shift/Enter. To be sure that all 200 NPVs have been counted, enter =SUM(C85:C107) in Cell C108. The result should be 200 in Cell C108.

To calculate the cumulative percent of values for the NPVs, enter =SUM($C$85:C85)/200 in Cell D85, copy the entry to D86:D107, and format the values as percents. The values for cumulative frequency should

(Continued)

run from 0% in D85 to 100% in D107. One way to create the downside risk curve is to plot the cumulative frequencies in Cells D85:D107 against the NPV bin values in Cells B85:B107.

Recall that the analysis of the skewness and kurtosis indicated the 200 values of NPV closely followed a normal distribution. We will test this in our downside risk curve for NPV by including a plot of the line for the cumulative percentages of a normal distribution with the average value and standard deviation shown in Cells B77 and B79 for the 200 NPV values. To calculate the values on this curve for the bin values, enter =NORMDIST(B85,$B$77,$B$79,TRUE) in Cell E85 and copy to E86:E107.

To create the downside risk chart for NPV shown at the right of Figure 15-9, highlight the range B85:B107, press and hold down the Ctrl key, highlight the range D85:E107, and release the Ctrl key. Click on the Chart Wizard button, select XY Scatter chart, and proceed as before in the Scenario section. The result is the downside risk chart at the right of Figure 15-9. Values in Cells D85:D107 are shown as solid points, and values in Cells E85:E107 have been plotted as a smooth curve. The downside risk curves and the values calculated indicate that there's a probability of 20.5 percent that the investment will fail to break even by the end of five years.

Notice that the points in Figure 15-9 follow the curve closely. This, of course, is because our analysis of the skewness and kurtosis showed that the NPV values closely follow a normal distribution. **This is not always the case**. When the results of the iterations are highly skewed or are significantly more peaked or flatter than a normal curve, the downside risk curve should be plotted from the values for the iterations. But it does not hurt to test a normal distribution and satisfy yourself whether or not a normal distribution is justified. In many cases, as here, the values do follow a normal distribution fairly closely.

Downside Risk Chart for Modified Internal Rates of Return: Figure 15-10 shows a downside risk curve for the investment's modified internal rate of return at the end of five years. The chart is prepared in the same manner as the downside risk chart for NPV.

Figure 15-10

Downside Risk Curve for Modified Internal Rate of Return at End of Five Years

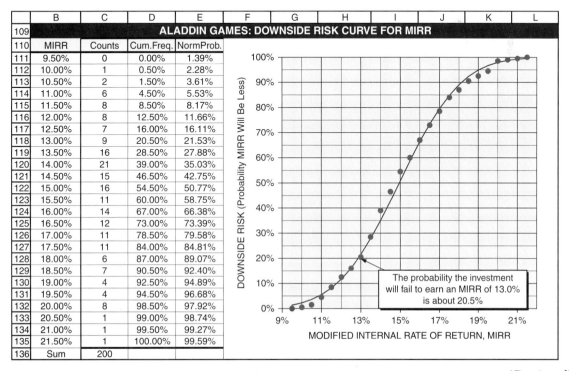

	B	C	D	E
109	ALADDIN GAMES: DOWNSIDE RISK CURVE FOR MIRR			
110	MIRR	Counts	Cum.Freq.	NormProb.
111	9.50%	0	0.00%	1.39%
112	10.00%	1	0.50%	2.28%
113	10.50%	2	1.50%	3.61%
114	11.00%	6	4.50%	5.53%
115	11.50%	8	8.50%	8.17%
116	12.00%	8	12.50%	11.66%
117	12.50%	7	16.00%	16.11%
118	13.00%	9	20.50%	21.53%
119	13.50%	16	28.50%	27.88%
120	14.00%	21	39.00%	35.03%
121	14.50%	15	46.50%	42.75%
122	15.00%	16	54.50%	50.77%
123	15.50%	11	60.00%	58.75%
124	16.00%	14	67.00%	66.38%
125	16.50%	12	73.00%	73.39%
126	17.00%	11	78.50%	79.58%
127	17.50%	11	84.00%	84.81%
128	18.00%	6	87.00%	89.07%
129	18.50%	7	90.50%	92.40%
130	19.00%	4	92.50%	94.89%
131	19.50%	4	94.50%	96.68%
132	20.00%	8	98.50%	97.92%
133	20.50%	1	99.00%	98.74%
134	21.00%	1	99.50%	99.27%
135	21.50%	1	100.00%	99.59%
136	Sum	200		

(Continued)

Risk Curve for Years to Break Even: Figure 15-11 shows a risk curve for the probability that the investment will take more than a specified number of years to break even. Note the differences between this curve and those for NPV and MIRR (Figures 15-9 and 15-10). The "downside" is that the years to break even will be **more** than the specified number of years to break even rather than less, as with the values of NPV and MIRR. Therefore, the cumulative frequency percentages in Cells D139:D159 have been converted to downside risks in Cells E139:E159 by subtracting their values from 100 percent. The curve ends to 20.5 percent for five years rather than zero percent because there's a 20.5 percent chance the investment will fail to break even in five years, which is the duration of the analysis of the financial investment. It is not possible to determine a normal curve for the years to break even because, lacking values beyond five years, we do not know the average or standard deviation of the distribution of years to break even. Instead, we have inserted a second-order trend line through the points we do have. Reading from the chart or interpolating between values in the table gives a value of 4.53 years for the point at which there is a 50 percent chance the years to break even will be more or will be less.

Figure 15-11

Risk Curve for Years to Break Even

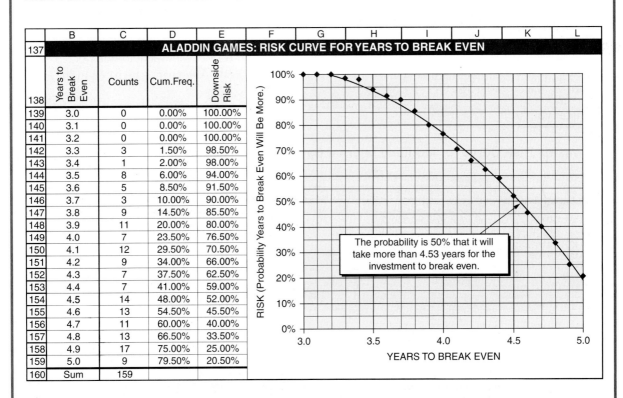

Optimization of Wholesale Selling Price

Although values for the product's total market, the cost of the investment, and the unit variable cost are beyond the ability of the company to determine exactly at the time the investment is to be made, the wholesale selling price is a variable the company can control. The goal is to select a selling price that maximizes the value of the investment. To determine the optimum selling price, use Excel's Solver tool with the settings shown in Figure 15-12. The result, $4.65/set, is almost the same as determined for the optimum selling price for the most probable scenario in Chapter 14.

(Continued)

Figure 15-12

Excel's Solver Tool with Settings to Find Selling Price for Maximum NPV

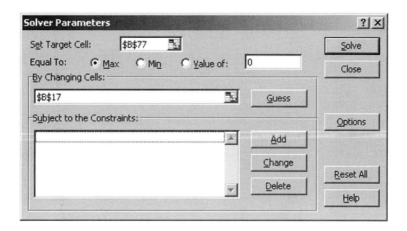

Sensitivity Analysis

Figure 15-13 is a one-variable input table for analyzing the sensitivity of NPV and other payoffs to the wholesale selling price.

Figure 15-13

One-Variable Input Table to Analyze the Sensitivity of Average Net Present Value and Other Financial Measures to the Unit Selling Price
(N.B. The value 0.00 in Cell G149 for the minimum years to break even at a selling price of $5.25/unit is an unfortunate result of a spreadsheet limitation. To change the entry in Cell G149 to na, copy the Range B140:H149 and paste it back with Paste Special/Values. Then change the entry in Cell G149 to "na.")

	B	C	D	E	F	G	H
161	ALADDIN GAMES: SENSITIVITY TO UNIT WHOLESALE PRICE						
162	Unit Wholesale Price	Market Share	Average NPV	Average IRR	Average MIRR	Minimum Years to Break Even	Probabililty for Failing to Break Even
163							
164	$4.25	17.97%	−$999	12.46%	12.62%	3.50	57.50%
165	$4.50	17.11%	$7,317	16.17%	14.65%	3.25	27.50%
166	$4.55	16.77%	$8,086	16.51%	14.83%	3.24	23.50%
167	$4.60	16.37%	$8,504	16.69%	14.93%	3.24	21.00%
168	$4.65	15.91%	$8,548	16.72%	14.95%	3.26	20.00%
169	$4.70	15.40%	$8,194	16.57%	14.87%	3.30	20.50%
170	$4.75	14.83%	$7,421	16.23%	14.70%	3.36	21.50%
171	$4.80	14.20%	$6,205	15.71%	14.42%	3.42	25.50%
172	$5.00	11.11%	−$3,545	11.38%	12.06%	3.95	69.50%
173	$5.25	5.97%	−$28,438	−0.66%	4.90%	0.00	100.00%

(Continued)

To create the table shown in Figure 15-13, enter a series of selling prices in Cells B164:B173. Make the following entries in Row 163 to transfer values from the main body of the spreadsheet:

Cell B163 =B17	Transfers values from Cells B164:B1173
Cell C163 =B18	Transfers values for market share
Cell D163 =B77	Transfers values for average NPV at end of 5 years
Cell E163 =C77	Transfers values for average IRR at end of 5 years
Cell F163 =D77	Transfers values for average MIRR at end of 5 years
Cell G163 =E76	Transfers values for minimum years to break even
Cell H163 =E82	Transfers values for probability for failing to break even

To avoid confusion, the entries in Row 143 have been hidden by using ";;;" (i.e, three semicolons) to custom format them. To complete the table, drag the mouse to select the Range B163:H173. Use Data/Table to access the Table dialog box and enter B17 for the column input value, as shown in Figure 15-14.

Figure 15-14

Table Dialog Box with Entry for One-Variable Input Table

The tabular results in Figure 15-13 are used to create the charts shown in Figures 15-15 and 15-16. These show the sensitivity of the average net present value and the probability for breaking even in five years to whole-sale prices in the range from $4.25 to $5.00/unit.

Figure 15-15

Sensitivity of Average NPV to Unit Wholesale Price

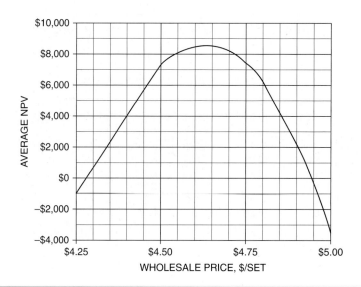

(Continued)

Figure 15-16

Sensitivity of Average Net Present Value and the Probability for Failing to Break Even in Five Years to the Whole Price

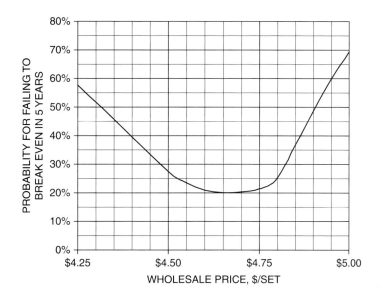

Figure 15-15 shows that the NPV is reasonably close to its maximum so long as the selling price is within the range $4.50 to $4.75/unit, but that it drops off rather sharply below $4.50 and above $4.75/unit.

Figure 15-16 shows similar behavior for the probability of breaking even within five years. In other words, choosing the best wholesale price is a critical decision. This type of curve is sometimes referred to as a "bath tub curve." It has a relatively flat bottom with steep sides. So long as one sits near the bottom, there is not much change from the low point. But sitting on one of the steep sides exposes one to the danger of falling overboard.

An advantage of Monte Carlo simulation is that models of great complexity can be created. In the following case study, for example, the total market increases at first, reaches a maximum, and then falls off in the manner followed by many high-tech products with short lifetimes. The example also includes decreases in unit variable cost and selling price from the product's initial values. Such reductions are typical as production costs decline with the learning curve effect and as selling prices are dropped to maintain market share in the face of competition and consumer preference for newer products.

Case Study: Allegro Products

The chief financial officer (CFO) of Allegro Products has been asked to analyze the returns and risks on an investment to manufacture a new product. The CFO will use four years for the financial analysis period, 12 percent for the discount and reinvestment rates, and 38 percent for the income tax rate. The total of selling costs and general and administrative (G&A) expenses are estimated to be 20 percent of sales revenue.

As a result of its market research, the firm's marketing division has forecast the total, industry-wide demand for the type of product being considered will be 400,000 units during the first year of the product's introduction and will increase to 600,000 units during the second year; following that, the total market will drop to 500,000 units during the third year and 250,000 units during the fourth. The standard errors for the forecasts, as percentages of the total market, are 10, 11, 13, and 15 percent for the first, second, third, and fourth years, respectively.

Allegro's share of the total market will depend on how much the company charges for its product. The marketing division estimates that at a selling price of $30.00/unit, the company's share of the total market would be 25 percent. They also estimate that increasing the selling price would reduce the market share according to the relation

$$MS = 25\% - 1\% X(SP - 30)^2$$

where MS = market share (percent) and SP = selling price ($/unit). Thus, at a selling price of $31/unit, the predicted market share would be 24 percent; at a selling price of $32/unit, the predicted market share would be 21 percent, and so forth. Actual market share would be normally distributed above the value predicted, with a standard deviation of 2 percent; that is, for a predicted market share of 24 percent, the range for one standard deviation about the predicted value would be from 22 to 26 percent.

In order to retain the same percentage market share in the second, third, and fourth years as achieved in the first year, marketing analysts estimate that each year they will have to drop the selling price by 10 percent of the average selling price for the preceding year.

The firm's industrial engineers estimate the required capital investment in equipment will most probably be $3.3 million, with a minimum of $2.5 million and a maximum of $4.5 million. The equipment will be depreciated to zero salvage value by straight-line depreciation over four years.

Allegro's industrial engineers also estimate that the variable cost of producing the product will be between $6.80/unit and $8.00/unit, with any value in that range equally likely. As a result of the "learning curve" effect, they expect that the average unit cost will decrease 10 percent each year.

Would you recommend Allegro to make the investment? Justify your recommendation.

Solution: Figure 15-17 is the upper and lower portions of the spreadsheet solution for a selling price of $30.58/unit, which is the optimum value for maximizing the average NPV.

Data values are shown in the upper portion of Figure 15-17 and are italicized. Detailed results for the first 6 of 200 iterations are shown below the data section in Rows 19 to 82. For convenience, a summary of important results from 200 iterations is shown in the upper-right corner of Figure 15-17.

Total Market: The total market (in units) for each of the four years is simulated by using Excel's random number generator for a normal distribution. For Year 1, the mean value is the data value for the forecast total market (in units) in Cell C12 and the standard deviation is the value calculated in Cell C14 by the entry =C12*C13. Two hundred values are inserted into Cells C20:GT20 by executing the random number generator for the normal distribution with a mean of 400,000 and a standard deviation of 40,000 (the values in Cells C12 and C14). Note: To use the random number generator, it is necessary to specify the values (400,000 and 40,000) rather than the cell identities (C12 and C14).

For Years 2, 3, and 4, the random number generator is used with the mean values in Cells D12, E12, and F12 and the standard deviations in Cells D14, E14, and F14. The outputs are placed in Cells C21:GT21, C22:GT22, and C23:GT23.

(Continued)

Figure 15-17

Rows 1 to 61 of Spreadsheet Solution for Allegro Products

	A	B	C	D	E	F	G	H
1	Case Study: ALLEGRO PRODUCTS							
2	Capital investment: Minimum (MIN)		$2,500,000		Summary of Results for 200 Iterations			
3	Most probable (MP)		$3,300,000			Minimum	Average	Maximum
4	Maximum (MAX)		$4,500,000		NPV	($656,979)	$666,843	$1,852,437
5	Ratio, (MP-MIN)/(MAX-MIN)		0.4000		MIRR	7.33%	17.29%	27.22%
6	Unit variable cost, year 1	Minimum	$6.80		Period for analysis, years	4	Simulation Averages	
7		Maximum	$8.00		Depreciation method	Straight line	Market, units	
8	Annual cost decrease, pct		10%		Salvage value	0	Year 1	400,032
9	Selling & G&A expenses, pct of sales		20%		Income tax rate	38%	Year 2	599,501
10	Discount and reinvestment rates		13.0%				Year 3	500,872
11	Year		Year 1	Year 2	Year 3	Year 4	Year 4	251,971
12	Total market forecast, units		400,000	600,000	500,000	250,000	Market Share	24.80%
13	Standard forecast error		10%	11%	13%	15%	Unit Var Cost	$7.447
14	Standard forecast error, units		40,000	66,000	65,000	37,500	Investmt RN	0.5088
15	Unit selling price, years 1 to 4		$30.58	$27.52	$24.77	$22.29	Investment	$3,448,541
16	Expected market share, pct		24.66%		Selling price has been optimized.			
17	Std. deviation of market share, pct		2.00%					
18	Annual price decrease, pct		10%		Note how well simulation averages meet expectations.			
19	**Iteration Number**		1	2	3	4	5	6
20	Total market, units	Year 1	477,186	389,506	347,039	398,340	371,492	410,149
21		Year 2	544,493	764,259	587,133	647,365	541,622	506,495
22		Year 3	482,468	579,026	597,455	554,115	610,003	497,302
23		Year 4	234,064	254,799	274,364	268,655	267,055	253,947
24	Random number for market share		−0.3002	−1.2777	0.2443	1.2765	1.1984	1.7331
25	Market share		24.06%	22.11%	25.15%	27.21%	27.06%	28.13%
26	Units sold	Year 1	114,811	86,101	87,277	108,402	100,516	115,362
27		Year 2	131,006	168,941	147,658	176,171	146,548	142,461
28		Year 3	116,082	127,995	150,255	150,794	165,050	139,875
29		Year 4	56,316	56,324	69,000	73,111	72,258	71,427
30	Sales receipts	Year 1	$ 3,511,230	$ 2,633,197	$ 2,669,159	$ 3,315,222	$ 3,074,027	$ 3,528,069
31		Year 2	$ 3,605,846	$ 4,649,993	$ 4,064,203	$ 4,848,983	$ 4,033,639	$ 3,921,149
32		Year 3	$ 2,875,583	$ 3,170,678	$ 3,722,092	$ 3,735,462	$ 4,088,607	$ 3,464,977
33		Year 4	$ 1,255,548	$ 1,255,727	$ 1,538,336	$ 1,629,980	$ 1,610,968	$ 1,592,453
34	Unit variable cost	Year 1	$7.650	$6.821	$7.997	$7.335	$7.166	$7.162
35	Cost of goods sold	Year 1	$ 878,322	$ 587,319	$ 697,993	$ 795,174	$ 720,262	$ 826,202
36		Year 2	$ 901,990	$ 1,037,153	$ 1,062,801	$ 1,163,055	$ 945,104	$ 918,254
37		Year 3	$ 719,317	$ 707,201	$ 973,338	$ 895,971	$ 957,984	$ 811,428
38		Year 4	$ 314,071	$ 280,082	$ 402,279	$ 390,959	$ 377,459	$ 372,920
39	Gross profit	Year 1	$ 2,632,908	$ 2,045,878	$ 1,971,166	$ 2,520,048	$ 2,353,765	$ 2,701,867
40		Year 2	$ 2,703,855	$ 3,612,840	$ 3,001,402	$ 3,685,928	$ 3,088,535	$ 3,002,895
41		Year 3	$ 2,156,266	$ 2,463,477	$ 2,748,754	$ 2,839,491	$ 3,130,623	$ 2,653,550
42		Year 4	$ 941,477	$ 975,644	$ 1,136,056	$ 1,239,020	$ 1,233,509	$ 1,219,533
43	Selling & G&A expenses	Year 1	$ 702,246	$ 526,639	$ 533,832	$ 663,044	$ 614,805	$ 705,614
44		Year 2	$ 721,169	$ 929,999	$ 812,841	$ 969,797	$ 806,728	$ 784,230
45		Year 3	$ 575,117	$ 634,136	$ 744,418	$ 747,092	$ 817,721	$ 692,995
46		Year 4	$ 251,110	$ 251,145	$ 307,667	$ 325,996	$ 322,194	$ 318,491
47	Gross profit less selling	Year 1	$ 1,930,662	$ 1,519,239	$ 1,437,334	$ 1,857,004	$ 1,738,960	$ 1,996,253
48	and G&A expenses	Year 2	$ 1,982,686	$ 2,682,841	$ 2,188,561	$ 2,716,132	$ 2,281,807	$ 2,218,665
49		Year 3	$ 1,581,149	$ 1,829,342	$ 2,004,335	$ 2,092,399	$ 2,312,902	$ 1,960,554
50		Year 4	$ 690,367	$ 724,499	$ 828,389	$ 913,024	$ 911,316	$ 901,042
51	Investment random number		0.9805	0.9783	0.9888	0.5155	0.0509	0.2265
52	Investment	Year 0	$ 4,283,660	$ 4,271,636	$ 4,336,047	$ 3,421,655	$ 2,785,305	$ 3,102,048
53	Annual depreciation		$ 1,070,915	$1,067,909	$ 1,084,012	$ 855,414	$ 696,326	$ 775,512
54	Taxable income	Year 1	$ 859,747	$ 451,330	$ 353,322	$ 1,001,590	$ 1,042,634	$ 1,220,741
55		Year 2	$ 911,771	$ 1,614,932	$ 1,104,550	$ 1,860,718	$ 1,585,481	$ 1,443,153
56		Year 3	$ 510,234	$ 761,433	$ 920,324	$ 1,236,985	$ 1,616,576	$ 1,185,042
57		Year 4	$ (380,547)	$ (343,410)	$ (255,623)	$ 57,611	$ 214,989	$ 125,530
58	Income tax, @ 38%	Year 1	$ 326,704	$ 171,505	$ 134,263	$ 380,604	$ 396,201	$ 463,882
59		Year 2	$ 346,473	$ 613,674	$ 419,729	$ 707,073	$ 602,483	$ 548,398
60		Year 3	$ 193,889	$ 289,344	$ 349,723	$ 470,054	$ 614,299	$ 450,316
61		Year 4	$ (144,608)	$ (130,496)	$ (97,137)	$ 21,892	$ 81,696	$ 47,702

(Continued)

Figure 15-17

Rows 62 to 82 of Spreadsheet Solution for Allegro Products (*Continued*)

	A	B	C	D	E	F	G	H
62	After-tax cash flow	Year 0	$ (4,283,660)	$ (4,271,636)	$ (4,336,047)	$ (3,421,655)	$ (2,785,305)	$ (3,102,048)
63		Year 1	$ 1,603,958	$ 1,347,733	$ 1,303,072	$ 1,476,400	$ 1,342,759	$ 1,532,371
64		Year 2	$ 1,636,213	$ 2,069,167	$ 1,768,832	$ 2,009,059	$ 1,679,324	$ 1,670,267
65		Year 3	$ 1,387,260	$ 1,539,997	$ 1,654,612	$ 1,622,345	$ 1,698,603	$ 1,510,238
66		Year 4	$ 834,976	$ 854,995	$ 925,526	$ 891,132	$ 829,620	$ 853,341
67	Net present value	Year 1	($2,851,554)	($3,068,303)	($3,172,590)	($2,103,441)	($1,586,413)	($1,733,860)
68		Year 2	($1,547,175)	($1,418,775)	($1,762,488)	($501,831)	($247,666)	($402,333)
69		Year 3	($559,751)	($322,636)	($584,767)	$652,921	$961,366	$672,625
70		**Year 4**	**($29,109)**	**$220,729**	**$3,421**	**$1,219,252**	**$1,488,605**	**$1,214,938**
71	Internal rate of return		11.64%	14.59%	12.04%	29.14%	36.66%	31.05%
72	Modified internal rate of return		11.81%	13.42%	12.02%	20.87%	24.65%	21.65%
73	Break-even point, years		failed	3.59	3.99	2.43	2.20	2.37
74		Summary of Results for 200 Iterations						
75			NPV	IRR	MIRR	Years to Break Even		
76		Minimum	($656,979)	3.73%	7.33%	1.80		
77		Average	$666,843	22.29%	17.29%			
78		Maximum	$1,852,437	44.86%	27.22%			
79		Std. Dev.	$469,350	7.78%	3.89%			
80		Skewness	(0.082)	0.302	0.134			
81		Kurtosis	(0.324)	(0.229)	(0.345)			
82		Probability for failing to break even in 4 years				9.00%		

Unit Selling Price: Start with an arbitrary value, such as $31.00/unit, for the Year 1 selling price in Cell C15. After completing the spreadsheet with the selected arbitrary value, we will use a one-variable input table to evaluate results for a range of selling prices, and we will use Solver to locate the optimum value. (To provide the results shown in Figures 15-17 and 15-18, the trial selling price for the first year has been replaced by the optimum value of $30.58/unit.)

In order to hold the expected market share constant for four years, Allegro plans to drop the selling price by 10 percent each year from the preceding year's selling price (Cell C18). Selling prices for Years 2, 3, and 4 are calculated by entering =C15*(1-$C$18) in Cell D15 and copying it to E15:F15.

Expected Market Share: The **expected** market share is a function of the selling price selected, as defined by the equation given in the problem statement. Its value in Year 1 is calculated by entering =0.25-0.01*(C15-30)^2 in Cell C16. Note that the market share will remain the same for all four years as a result of the reduction in selling price from its original value.

Actual Market Share: Values for the actual market shares are simulated in Cells C25:GT25. Because the marketing division does not know the relationship between selling price and market share exactly, the equation that forecasts market share as a function of price is subject to error.

The **actual** market share each year is expected to follow a normal distribution with a mean equal to the **expected** market share (Cell C16) and a **standard deviation** equal to 2 percent of the expected market share (Cell C17). To simulate the actual market share, we will add the product of the standard deviation multiplied by a random number that is normally distributed about a mean of zero and a standard deviation of one to the expected market share. The series of normally distributed random numbers is generated in Cells C24:GT24 by using the random number generator for a normal distribution with a mean of 0 and a standard deviation of 1. The actual market shares are then simulated in Row 25 by entering =$C$16+C24*$C$17 in Cell C25 and copying the entry to D25:GT25.

(Continued)

Units Sold: The number of units sold is the product of the total market for the product (Row 20 to 23) and Allegro's share of the market (Row 25). The **total** market changes from year to year, whereas Allegro believes that by dropping its prices each year, it can maintain a constant market share equal to its first-year value. The units sold in each of the four years is simulated by entering =C20*C$25 in Cell C26 and copying the entry to C26:GT29. (Note the placement of the dollar sign in the entry.)

Sales Receipts: Sales receipts are the products of the units sold (Rows 26 to 29) and selling price (Cells C15 to F15). They are calculated by the following entries:

Cell	Entry	Copy to
C30	=C26*$C15	D30:GT30
C31	=C27*$D15	D31:GT31
C32	=C28*$E15	D32:GT32
C33	=C29*$F15	D33:GT33

Unit Variable Cost: Values for the unit variable cost of units sold **during the first year** can be simulated by using the random number generator for a uniform distribution between the values of $6.80 and $8.00 in Cells C6 and C7. The values are placed in Cells C34:GT34.

Cost of Goods Sold: The total cost of goods sold in any year equals the product of the number of units sold (Rows 25 to 28) and the unit variable cost. Recall that as a result of the "learning curve" effect, the unit variable cost drops each year by 10 percent of the cost the year before. Values for the four years are calculated by the following entries:

Cell	Entry	Copy to
C35	C26*C34	D35:GT35
C36	C27*C34*(1-$C$18)	D36:GT36
C37	C28*C34*(1-$C$18)^2	D37:GT37
C38	C29*C34*(1-$C$18)^3	D38:GT38

Gross Profit: Gross profit is the difference between sales receipts and the cost of goods sold. It is calculated in Rows 39 to 42 by entering =C30-C35 in Cell C39 and copying it to C39:GT42.

Selling and G&A Expenses: These expenses are estimated as 20 percent of the sales receipts (Cell C9). They are calculated in Rows 43 to 44 by entering =$C$9*C30 in Cell C43 and copying it to C43:GT46.

Gross Profit Less Selling and G&A Expenses: These are the difference between gross profit (Rows 39 to 42) and selling and G&A expenses (Rows 43 to 46). They are calculated by entering =C39-C43 in Cell C47 and copying it to C47:GT50.

Investment: Allegro's capital investment to produce the new product has a most probable value (C3) and a range from a minimum to a maximum value (Cells C2 and C4). The general form of a triangular distribution is shown in Figure 15-5.

Using equations 15.1 and 15.2 on a spreadsheet can be implemented by the following steps: (1) Enter values for MIN, MP, and MAX in Cells C2, C3, and C4; (2) compute the ratio (MP-MIN)/(MAX-MIN) by the entry =(C3-C2)/(C4-C2) in Cell C5; (3) use Excel's Random Number generator to generate a uniform series of random numbers between zero and one in Cells C51:GT51; and (4) enter the following expression in Cell C52 and copy it to D52:GT52:

=IF(C51<$C$5,$C$2+SQRT(C51*($C$3-$C$2)*($C$4-$C$2)),
$C$4-SQRT((1-C51)*($C$4-$C$3)*($C$4-$C$2))

(Continued)

Annual Depreciation: The capital investment is depreciated by the straight-line method to zero salvage value over a four-year life (Cells F8 and F6). Annual depreciation (Row 53) is therefore the same each year and equals one-fourth the capital investment (Row 52). To calculate annual depreciation, enter =(C52-$F$8)/$F$6 or =SLN(C52,$F$8,$F$6) in Cell 53 and copy it to D53:GT53.

Taxable Income: Depreciation is a deductible expense that reduces a firm's taxable income. Taxable income is calculated by subtracting annual depreciation (Row 53) from the difference "gross profits less selling and G&A expenses" (Rows 47 to 50). To calculate taxable incomes, enter =C47-C$53 in Cell C54 and copy it to C54:GT57.

Income Tax: Income tax is the product of taxable income times tax rate. Allegro's tax rate is given as 38 percent (Cell F9). To calculate income tax, enter =$F$9*C54 in Cell C58 and copy it to C58:GT61.

After-Tax Cash Flow: The capital investment creates an after-tax cash outflow at time zero (Row 62). To calculate this, enter =-C52 in Cell C62 and copy it to D62:GT62.

After-tax cash inflows for Years 1 to 4 are what is left of the "gross profit less selling and G&A expenses" (Rows 47 to 50) after paying income taxes (Rows 58 to 61). To calculate these, enter =C47-C58 in Cell C63 and copy it to C63:GT66.

Net Present Value: The net present value (NPV) of the investment is the future cash flows generated by it (Rows 63 to 66) discounted back to their present value less the capital investment. The future values are discounted at the given discount rate of money (Cell C10).

Use Excel's NPV function to calculate the net present values of the investment at the end of each year. To do this, enter =NPV($C$10,C$63:C63)+C$62 in Cell C67 and copy it to D67:GT70.

Internal Rate of Return at End of Four Years: Use Excel's IRR function to calculate the internal rate of return (ROR). To do this, enter =IRR(C62:C66,0.1) in Cell C71 and copy it to D71:GT71.

Modified Internal Rate of Return at End of Four Years: Use Excels MIRR function to calculate the modified internal rate of return (MIRR). To do this, enter MIRR(C62:C66,$C$10,$C$10) in Cell C72 and copy it to D72:GT72.

Note that this calculation assumes that the rate of interest for reinvesting future cash flows is the same as the discount rate in Cell C10. Enter the correct rate if it is different.

Break-Even Point, Years: To calculate the break-even point, enter the following in Cell C73 and copy it to D73:GT73: =IF(C68>0,1-C67/(C68-C67),IF(C69>0,2-C68/(C69-C68),IF(C70>0,3-C69/(C70-C69),"failed"))).

Note that the investment fails to break even for the first iteration (Cell C73).

Summary of Results for 200 Iterations: Use Excel's MIN, AVERAGE, and MAX functions to calculate the minimum, average, and maximum values of the NPV, IRR, and MIRR for the 200 iterations. The entries for NPV are =MIN(C70:GT70) in Cell C76, =AVERAGE(C70:GT70) in Cell C77, and =MAX(C70:GT70) in Cell C78. Similar entries are made for IRR and MIRR and for the minimum value of the number of years to break even. Note that we cannot calculate average or maximum values for the number of years to break even because the investment fails to break even on some of the iterations.

For convenience, the minimum, average, and maximum values of NPV and MIRR are transferred to Cells F4:H5 at the top of Figure 15-17.

Rows 79, 80, and 81 show the values for several statistical measures of the distributions of NPV, IRR, and MIRR values. For NPV, the standard deviation is calculated entering =STDEV(C70:GT70) in Cell C79, the skewness is calculated by entering =SKEW(C70:GT70) in Cell C80, and the kurtosis is calculated by entering =KURT(C70:GT70) in Cell C81. Similar calculations are made for the distributions of IRR and MIRR values.

The probability for the investment's failing to break even in four years is calculated by entering =(200-COUNT(C73:GT73))/200 in Cell F82.

Downside Risk Analysis: Figure 15-18 shows the results of the downside risk analysis. Frequency distributions for the NPV and MIRR values have been determined in the same manner as before—that is, by setting up bins that cover the range from slightly below the minimum values to slightly above the maximum values, using Excel's FREQUENCY command to count the values in each bin, and converting the cumulative frequencies to the downside percentages. The downside percentages are shown as solid points on the charts at the bottom of Figure 15-18.

(Continued)

Figure 15-18

Downside Risk Analysis for Net Present Value and Modified Internal Rate of Return

	A	B	C	D	E	F	G	H
83				Downside Risk Analysis				
84		Frequency Distribution, NPV				Frequency Distribution, MIRR		
85		NPV Bin	Frequency	Percent	Normal Dist.	MIRR Bin	Frequency	Percent	Normal Dist.
86		−$800,000	0	0.00%	0.09%	6.00%	0	0.00%	0.18%
87		−$600,000	1	0.50%	0.35%	7.00%	0	0.00%	0.41%
88		−$400,000	0	0.50%	1.15%	8.00%	1	0.50%	0.85%
89		−$200,000	4	2.50%	3.24%	9.00%	2	1.50%	1.65%
90		$0	13	9.00%	7.77%	10.00%	1	2.00%	3.05%
91		$200,000	15	16.50%	16.00%	11.00%	7	5.50%	5.30%
92		$400,000	21	27.00%	28.48%	12.00%	7	9.00%	8.70%
93		$600,000	34	44.00%	44.34%	13.00%	11	14.50%	13.52%
94		$800,000	33	60.50%	61.17%	14.00%	12	20.50%	19.90%
95		$1,000,000	28	74.50%	76.11%	15.00%	14	27.50%	27.83%
96		$1,200,000	25	87.00%	87.20%	16.00%	23	39.00%	37.04%
97		$1,400,000	14	94.00%	94.09%	17.00%	17	47.50%	47.07%
98		$1,600,000	9	98.50%	97.66%	18.00%	22	58.50%	57.28%
99		$1,800,000	2	99.50%	99.21%	19.00%	19	68.00%	67.03%
100		$2,000,000	1	100.00%	99.77%	20.00%	15	75.50%	75.74%
101			200			21.00%	12	81.50%	83.03%
102						22.00%	14	88.50%	88.73%
103						23.00%	7	92.00%	92.92%
104						24.00%	5	94.50%	95.79%
105						25.00%	5	97.00%	97.64%
106						26.00%	3	98.50%	98.75%
107						27.00%	2	99.50%	99.38%
108						28.00%	1	100.00%	99.71%
109							200		

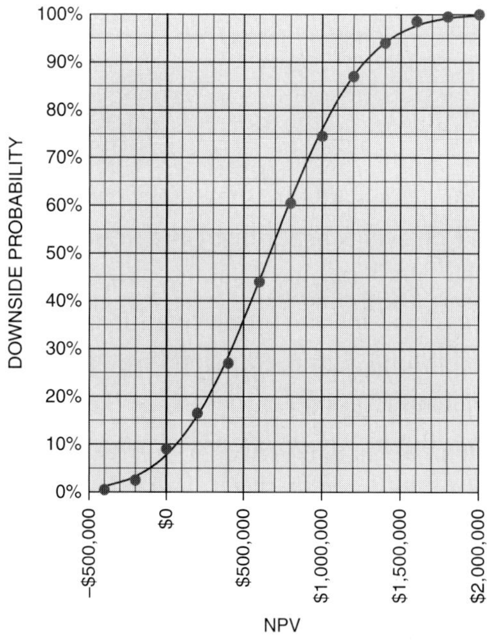

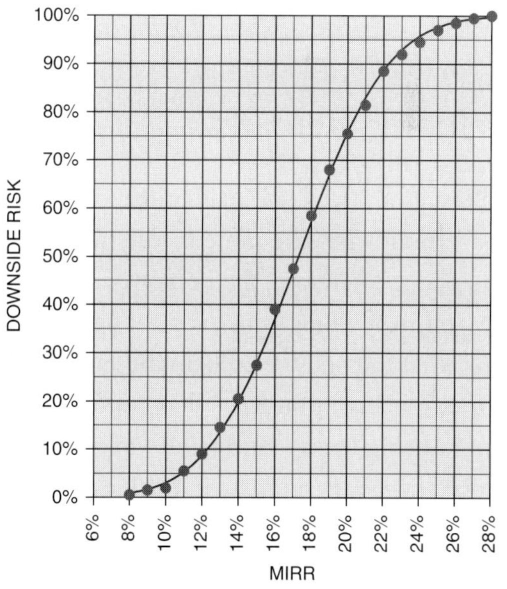

(Continued)

478 ⋙ Corporate Financial Analysis with Microsoft Excel®

The normal distribution curves are created by using Excel's NORMDIST function and the values for the averages and standard deviations of the 200 values of NPV and MIRR to calculate the cumulative probabilities for the bin values. These calculations are made with the following entries:

Cell	Entry	Copy
D86	=NORMDIST(A86,$C$77,$C$79,TRUE)	D87:D100
H86	=NORMDIST(E86,$E$77,$E$79,TRUE)	H87:H108

Note that the normal distribution curve is a close approximation to the trend of the calculated values (plotted as points). This is because the distributions of the values are close to being normally distributed, as indicated by the values calculated earlier for skewness and kurtosis. **This is not always the case**. The values for the normal distribution are plotted as curves without points on the charts at the bottom of Figure 15-18.

Sensitivity Analysis: Figure 15-19 shows the impact of first-year selling prices on the expected market share, average NPV, average MIRR, minimum number of years to break even, and the probability that the investment will fail to break even by the end of four years. The table of results was created by using a one-variable input table with the following entries in Row 141:

Cell	B141	C141	D141	E141	F141	G141
Entry	C15	C16	C77	E77	F76	F82

Conclusions and Recommendation: The results show that the optimum selling price is located at about $30.58/unit. At the optimum selling price, the probability for failing to break even is about 9 percent, and there is a 50:50 chance for doing better or worse than a net present value of approximately $680,000 and a modified internal rate of return of approximately 17.2 percent. Allegro Products should make the investment.

Concluding Remarks

Regardless of how well you play bridge or other card games, the cards are sometimes stacked against you and you cannot win. The same is true in business. Random events occur that cause losses with even the best laid plans. Therefore, the best one can do is "play the odds." Playing the odds is a strategy that generally pays off in the long run, even though there are occasional losses. But playing the odds depends on knowing what the odds or probabilities are. This is where Monte Carlo simulation can be most helpful.

Does success in business depend on being lucky? Unquestionably, success can and does result at times from being lucky—and failure from being unlucky. But being prepared is an important part of getting lucky and being successful. Luck can be most helpful in the early stages of developing and providing new consumer goods or services. But more often, success depends (1) on recognizing and exploiting opportunities early, before others develop competitive products (as in the old saying, "The early bird gets the worm"), and (2) on recognizing and taking prompt corrective action when adverse conditions develop that would otherwise cause severe losses.

Spreadsheets and Monte Carlo simulation are a powerful combination for showing both the upside and downside risks of financial investments—and the impacts of company strategies thereon.

Figure 15-19

One-Variable Input Table and Chart for Sensitivity Analysis

	B	C	D	E	F	G
139	Case Study: ALLEGRO PRODUCTS					
140	First-Year Unit Selling Price	Market Share	Average NPV	Average MIRR	Minimum Years to Break Even	Probability for Failing to Break Even in 4 Years
141						
142	$30.00	25.00%	$622,949	16.97%	1.83	11.00%
143	$30.10	24.99%	$636,586	17.07%	1.82	11.00%
144	$30.20	24.96%	$647,740	17.15%	1.81	10.50%
145	$30.30	24.91%	$656,374	17.21%	1.81	10.00%
146	$30.40	24.84%	$662,452	17.26%	1.80	9.50%
147	$30.50	24.75%	$665,941	17.28%	1.80	9.00%
148	$30.60	24.64%	$666,803	17.29%	1.80	9.00%
149	$30.70	24.51%	$665,004	17.27%	1.80	9.00%
150	$30.80	24.36%	$660,508	17.24%	1.80	10.50%
151	$30.90	24.19%	$653,279	17.19%	1.80	10.50%
152	$31.00	24.00%	$643,283	17.12%	1.80	10.50%
153	$31.10	23.79%	$630,483	17.02%	1.81	11.00%
154	$31.20	23.56%	$614,844	16.91%	1.81	11.50%
155	$31.30	23.31%	$596,331	16.78%	1.82	12.00%
156	$31.40	23.04%	$574,907	16.62%	1.83	13.50%
157	$31.50	22.75%	$550,539	16.44%	1.84	14.50%
158	$31.60	22.44%	$523,189	16.24%	1.85	15.00%
159	$31.70	22.11%	$492,823	16.02%	1.86	15.50%
160	$31.80	21.76%	$459,405	15.77%	1.87	17.50%
161	$31.90	21.39%	$422,899	15.50%	1.88	18.00%
162	$32.00	21.00%	$383,271	15.20%	1.90	21.00%
163						
164			**Optimum selling price is $30.58/unit.**			

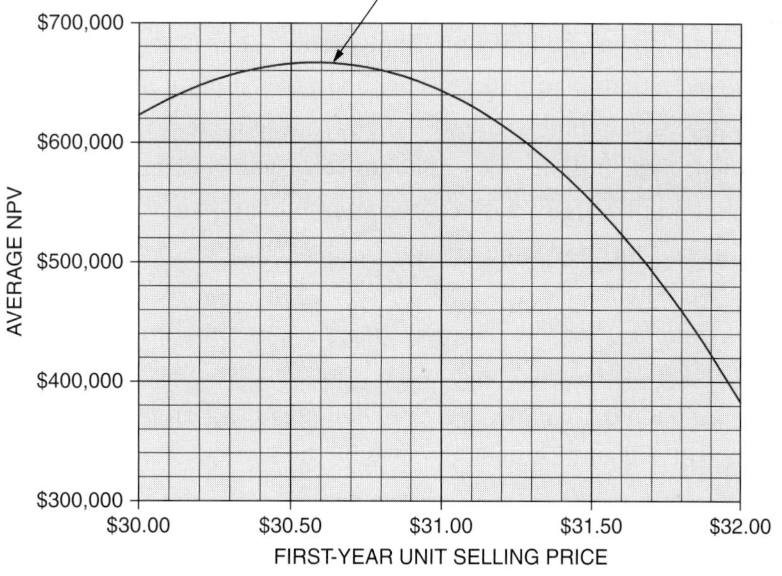

Marketing Strategies

Today's markets are customer driven, and marketing strategies are vital elements of corporate strategies. As the Aladdin case study illustrates, a company's sales depends on the total market for the product, the company's share of the total market, and the price it will charge. The total market will depend on many factors associated with personal incomes and the general economy. These are essentially *outside* the company's control. On the other hand, a company's share of the total market is influenced by many factors that are *within* the company's control. These include the performance and quality characteristics of the product and the price at which the company sells the product, with a lower price favoring a larger share. Market share will also depend on the company's expenditures to advertise and promote its product against similar products by competitors.

Selling Prices and Market Share

Lower selling prices favor larger market shares. One of the responsibilities of a company's marketing division is to define the relationship between price and market share. This might be in the form of an equation or a table, with the values either estimated from experience or established by market research. Because the relationship between price and market share is not exact, it should include most probable values for market share as a function of price and a measure of the variability of the market share at a given price. The variability of market share about a most probable value can be simulated by using random numbers in a Monte Carlo simulation study, as the case study demonstrates.

"Learning Curve" Effects of Product Cost

Through its effects on market share, selling prices also affect the cost of goods sold. With a larger sales volume, a company can afford to invest in more efficient equipment and deliver its products at a lower cost. Also, as a result of a company's learning from experience, as shown by a "learning curve," costs should continually come down as a company implements better procedures for producing and delivering its products. The reduction in cost allows a company to maintain its profit margins while selling at a lower price. At the same time, selling at a lower price tends to increase market share, which provides still more learning experience and further cost reductions. The synergetic effect of the learning experience on costs, selling price, and profit margins has become an important part of aggressive marketing strategies in highly competitive markets for short-lived consumer products, such as computer software, hardware, and many other electronic products.

In today's environment, short development times are essential for getting new products to market ahead of competitors. Companies can create markets for new products by selling initially at prices below their costs, in the expectation that as sales increase, their costs will drop as they gain experience. "Getting down on the learning curve before competitors" can be the key to successful marketing of new products.

Forecasts

Forecasts are a basis for planning. New products generally experience an incubation period with slow demands following their introduction. Demand grows with product acceptance, followed by a dropping off as new products supersede the old. Spreadsheets make it easy to program forecasts and to use random numbers to simulate variable demand rates about the expected values. They can help demonstrate the value of good forecasts, with low standard forecast errors, in reducing the downside investment risks.

Realism

Realistic conditions are generally more complex than the case study presented in this chapter. They can have a large number of variables that are probability distributions rather than specific known values. Spreadsheets allow many more probability distributions to be included in the analysis than the three variables considered in the Aladdin Games case study. As with other financial models, making analyses more realistic is a matter of additional programming. Ultimately, the spreadsheet software and the computer's memory limit the size of the program and the number of iterations.

Accuracy

The accuracy of results from Monte Carlo simulation, as with any analysis, depends on the quality of the inputs as well as the number of iterations used for simulating the operation. Spreadsheets offer an ability to incorporate information from various parts of a business to reach decisions that are in the best interests of the entire organization.

Although 200 iterations are sufficient to demonstrate the principles of Monte Carlo simulation, in practice a thousand or more may be needed to obtain statistically valid results. Because of the great number of repetitive calculations involved, Monte Carlo simulation was not practical until the advent of computers. Even very large-scale simulations can be run on today's personal computers, with the size limited to the capacities of the spreadsheet and computer system. So-called "supercomputers" have been used to perform very large and complex Monte Carlo simulations.

Excel 2003 spreadsheets can have as many as 65,536 rows but only 256 columns. Therefore, if one wants more than 255 iterations, successive iterations can be programmed on successive rows rather than successive columns, as in the example in this chapter. An alternative is to rerun a program with only 200 or so iterations a number of times, save the results from each run, and use statistics to provide a better estimate of the mean value and standard deviation. Or you can change the spreadsheet format and interchange the information on columns and rows instead of rows and columns. (Excel 2007 is another alternative. It provides 1,048,576 rows and up to 65,536 columns.)

Type of Distribution

It is essential that the correct types of distributions be used. A normal distribution is specified by a mean value and standard deviation. A triangular distribution is specified by minimum, maximum, and most probable value. A uniform distribution is specified by a minimum and maximum value. Because any number in the range from the minimum to the maximum of a uniform distribution is equally likely, the uniform distribution does not have a most probable value. The mean value can be used as a proxy for the most probable value of a uniform distribution since numbers greater than or less than the mean are equally likely.

When All Else Fails

Monte Carlo simulation is a "brute force" method. There is nothing elegant about it. All it takes is setting up a program that links inputs and results in a real-life environment, and then running enough iterations to allow the laws of chance an opportunity to exert themselves. It is an analytical tool that works when nothing else does. The technique is a game of chance, and its name refers to the gambling casino of Monte Carlo.

The name Monte Carlo for this type of simulation model was given by scientists who developed the first atomic bomb. They used the technique to determine the thickness of shielding material required to absorb thermal neutrons released in an atomic pile. Scientists could not make this calculation at the time in a straightforward manner. They therefore invented a game in which random numbers were used to simulate a "random walk" of neutrons as they were deflected and bounced off the nuclei of the shielding material. At each bounce, some of their energy was lost until what remained was low enough to render them harmless. The game of chance calculated how thick to make the shield to ensure enough collisions and bounces. Monte Carlo was the code name given at the time.

Living with Life's Uncertainties

Monte Carlo simulation does not give a single correct answer. Instead, it gives a probability distribution. That disturbs anyone who likes to have everything "black or white." Unfortunately, most things in life are not that way. There are shades of grey between white and black. Uncertainty is what you have to face in life. Monte Carlo simulation helps managers understand the risks of doing business.

Because Monte Carlo simulation is a game of chance, it is necessary to run a large number of iterations to obtain accurate results. The 200 iterations used to illustrate the principles in this chapter are not enough to define results precisely. With a small number of iterations, results depend "on the luck of the draw" of the random numbers. In practice, many thousands of iterations are needed for an accurate simulation.

Students' Feedback on Monte Carlo Simulation

The major advantages of using Monte Carlo simulation include "getting your arms around" the possibilities of a potential project—the downside risks and the possible upsides—as well as the ability to study a model of great complexity. It expands greatly upon the simple best-on-best/most probable/worst-on-worse type of scenario analysis.

The future is certainly uncertain, and the best strategy we have to handle that uncertainty is to use the tools we have available (mathematics, statistics, commonsense, and intuition) to understand the possibilities and, more importantly, the probabilities of potential outcomes. Monte Carlo serves this purpose.

* * *

The major advantage of using Monte Carlo simulation to make better management decisions is the ability to understand the range of probable output based on range of probable inputs. The best-on-best, most probable, and worst-on-worst scenarios from the last chapter are useful as quick summary indicators, while the Monte Carlo approach adds a significantly increased amount of depth to the analysis. I can see using the quicker scenario approach as a first filter, and then using Monte Carlo to perform more detailed analysis if a project looks like it has potential.

* * *

Given the recent turmoil in the mortgage industry, I can see the huge advantages to using Monte Carlo simulation. It can give you a range of possible outcomes even when the inputs aren't known for certain. In particular, companies that service large portfolios of outstanding loans would be able to use the simulation to get a range of possible losses from loan defaults and foreclosures.

Putting Up with Nonsense

There is a great deal of published and spoken nonsense about Monte Carlo simulation, much of which appears to come from critics who have never used it or are biased against it. Like any analysis, the accuracy of its outputs is no better than the accuracy of its inputs. The future is uncertain, and it is precisely when the uncertainties are greatest that Monte Carlo is most useful. It is risky to base an analysis on a single set of uncertain values that are essentially an analyst's best guesses or are considered most probable. The risks are better recognized by doing scenario analyses, using worst-on-worst and best-on-best conditions in addition to whatever else is thought likely or possible.

Monte Carlo simulation adds an analysis of probabilities to scenario analyses. In the absence of knowing the type of distribution for input variables, triangular distributions can be used as approximations. Though less than exact, they are better than basing an analysis on the single value regarded as most probable. Presenting the results in the form of downside risk charts and doing sensitivity analyses provides a better understanding of the probabilities and magnitudes of the risks involved, and potential losses as well as potential gains.

Don't let the number of iterations scare anyone. With today's computers, thousands of iterations are easily provided, even on laptops. Monte Carlo simulation is not new. It is being widely used in industry—and has been widely used for more than 50 years.

Excel has proven capable of large, complex Monte Carlo simulation models. The author has used Excel to create a successful multiyear, multiproduct financial plan for a corporation that included 35 input variables, each of which was modeled with most probable, minimum, and maximum estimates. The model's file consisted of 17 worksheets and included statistical summaries, downside risk charts, and column charts for the overall plan and each of five product areas. Input values were entered on a separate worksheet, with the input cells linked to cells on the other worksheets in the file. Each random variable was simulated with 2,000 iterations to provide satisfactory accuracy, with a total of 288,000 random numbers generated. The file used no techniques that are not covered in this chapter. No add-on software was used. Contrary to what some would have you believe, Monte Carlo simulation is not terribly difficult, and you should not be discouraged by their ill-formed misgivings.

Finally

Yes, there are random events that occur outside the scope of even the best analysis. Wars, fires, terrorist attacks, hurricanes, deaths, bankruptcies, and other disasters are a fact of life. After doing the best possible, you still need to cope with these things in your business as well as your personal life. That is why one buys life insurance to protect one's family against the death of the breadwinner, looks in both directions before crossing a street to avoid being hit by an oncoming car, builds one's home on ground that is not likely to be flooded or torn apart in an earthquake, avoids dangerous situations, prepares as best as possible for disasters, and so forth. With luck, you and your business will survive. You can base your decisions on probabilities and risk analysis, but you still need to be prepared for the unknown random events that might hit you.

Epilogue

The worldwide economic meltdown that officially began in December 2007 raises serious issues with the use—and, more especially, with the MISuse—of quantitative analysis.

Let's recap the book's message: Information technology is a tool for business management. Spreadsheets and databases are the "nuts and bolts" of information technology used by managers. The role of spreadsheets is to access the data in databases, analyze it, convert it to useful information, and present the results in a manner that is easily understood and convincing. The justification for all of this is to identify, recommend, and justify profitable courses of action.

With the massive databases of information collected in the last decades, it is ironic that business often appears hobbled in processing data into useful information. Instead of solving problems, we have created them. Instead of minimizing risks, we have increased them and their consequences. What went wrong?

The outputs of numerical analysis depend on the input data and assumptions. When these are fixed, the outputs are valid only for the given set of input data values and assumptions. However, input conditions are seldom known with certainty, and they change with time. One-time solutions may be useful for teaching the principles of financial management, but they have limited value in real life. Financial managers need information on the possible ranges of output values and their probabilities. Without such information, factories and service facilities cannot be properly designed and operated with the flexibility needed to serve uncertain and changing demands, investors cannot incorporate risk into their decisions, and executives cannot frame effective long-term strategies. Models, such as those shown in the examples and case studies in the preceding chapters, are needed rather than one-time solutions.

Excel is a superb tool for creating mathematical models. The models can be used to do sensitivity or "What if?" analysis to help managers and investors cope with life's uncertainties. With Excel's Solver tool, these models identify conditions for optimizing payoffs. With Monte Carlo simulation, models can identify risks and payoffs as conditions change.

Still, you need to do more.

The admonitions, suggestions, and thoughts that follow are offered to help you avoid going wrong in creating and using spreadsheet models.

Verify Input Data

The number one cause of bad quantitative models is bad data. Bad data are any data that is incomplete, inaccurate, not timely, or misleadingly labeled.

The result of bad data is expressed pointedly as "Garbage in, garbage out," abbreviated as the well-known acronym GIGO. This acronym has become so overused that many are insensitive to its meaning. Others who understand GIGO's meaning act as though they are immune to its consequences. They are not immune. Nor are you!

A principal source of a company's financial information is its cost accounting system. Other sources are its marketing and sales records, its service and manufacturing records, and its quality control records. These should provide income and cost values to a level of detail sufficient for close management.

Good data can be expensive to obtain. But if you think good data are expensive, consider the cost of bad data. Bad data lead to bad decisions that can be orders of magnitude more costly than the cost of good data.

Take a hard look at the numbers you work with.

Understand the Principles of Financial Management

You cannot be a good programmer unless you understand what you are doing. You need to know the principles of financial management. You need to know how the components of a firm's finance organization interact with each other and with the production, services, marketing, quality control, and other functional organizations. You need to understand what is needed in the way of outputs and what is needed in the way of inputs.

Spend Time Organizing a Spreadsheet

Organizing a spreadsheet begins with setting up a matrix of rows and columns.

All rows and columns should be labeled with names that are precise and unambiguous, and with the units in which values are expressed or measured. Remember Murphy's Law: "If anything can go wrong, it will." The corollary to Murphy's Law as applied to written documents, including spreadsheets, is: "If something I say can be misunderstood, it will be." Therefore, it's **not** sufficient to write and label clearly enough to be understood. You must organize and label your spreadsheets so clearly that they can**not** be **mis**understood.

The revenge of the language lurks behind misleading labels. Remember the Biblical parable of the tower of Babel, and how a "confusion of tongues" thwarted a sky-high project. When all else fails, it **is** permissible to say exactly what you mean.

Don't expect that your first attempt at organizing a spreadsheet will be perfect. You may need to reorganize the rows and columns once or twice before being satisfied.

Show All Input Data

Don't hide input data. That may sound obvious, but real life teaches it is not. You might be surprised at how often business meetings are stopped when someone asks: "Where did that number come from?" or "How did we get to those results?"

The upper left corner of a spreadsheet is often the best place to put input data, although some programmers like to put input data at the end. Find out where your boss prefers.

Show Assumptions

Don't hide assumptions. They are as important as input data to understanding results and how you arrived at those results.

Verify the Model

Check cell linkages. Use the formula auditing tool. Change input values one by one and note whether cells that are supposed to be connected to them change in an appropriate manner.

Program checks wherever possible. It is easy to include a simple expression on a balance sheet to see that a firm's assets match the sum of its liabilities and net worth. (Don't think you are immune from making mistakes. I actually had an MBA graduate from another school in my class who submitted not one but two balance sheets that did not balance. There is no excuse for that sort of thing, and it only makes you look foolish and amateurish.) Reconcile the cash inflows and outflows on cash budget plans. Be inventive in devising ways to verify your spreadsheet models.

Make Good Use of Excel's Tools

Mirosoft Excel is powerful! It provides a well-stocked tool kit for business professionals. It has proven its worth for accessing information in databases, analyzing numbers, and preparing reports. It is an essential tool for all serious professionals, whether they work in logistics, personnel, marketing, manufacturing and service operations, quality control, or just about any other business function as well as financial management.

Excel can do many things that special software can do—and do it just as well. Special software can be costly and difficult to learn. Some people pay its price when they could use Excel to do the same thing. Before you invest in special software, check to see if you can do the same thing with Excel.

Understand Any Assumptions

Understand the assumptions on which a model is based. The well-publicized failure of Long-Term Capital Management (LTCM) was due to not understanding the limits of the assumptions of the Black-Scholes model for pricing options; specifically, the model was based on data for a relatively short term that understated long-term volatility. It is wrong to assume that a given set of conditions will persist indefinitely. Be prepared if they don't.

Look Ahead as Well as Behind

Managing is a forward-looking job. Much of a manager's job is planning for the future, monitoring to see that what actually happens follows the plan, and taking corrective action when what happens deviates from the plan. Management information systems include the four steps of forecasting, planning, monitoring, and triggering corrective action. They are tools for good management.

Forecasting is a two-step process. Spreadsheets are useful tools for projecting past trends forward. Spreadsheets are also useful tools for consolidating knowledge of how past trends may change and adjusting projections of past trends for anticipated changes. The output of the forecasting process is best given as a probability distribution rather than a single value. Downside risk curves are a useful tool for showing the probabilities for different outcomes or payoffs.

Understand the Randomness in Your Models

As a recent book makes clear, randomness rules our lives. (Mlodinow, *The Drunkard's Walk: How Randomness Rules Our Lives*, Pantheon Books, 2008) Turbulent times may suggest there is no way to prepare for an uncertain future.

Don't despair. If the future is not completely certain, neither is it completely chaotic. It is somewhere in between. There are trends, and there is scatter around the trends. Some scatter around a trend is random, and some is seasonal or periodic. Both are normal conditions. But when new data scatters outside the confidence limits of the trend established by the old data, it trend indicates the trend itself has changed and new conditions must be faced. When that happens, take corrective action promptly—and the sooner, the better.

Include the teachings of statistics and probability theory in your analytical models. This can help you operate more efficiently and provide enough flexibility to cope with changes in customer demands and cash flows. It can show the downside risks for investing in capital assets. Use sensitivity or "What if?" analysis to take into account what could or might happen or go wrong.

Prepare for Disasters You Cannot Avoid

Some random events are unavoidable and invite disaster. On a personal level, breadwinners buy life insurance to provide for their families in case they die or are killed. Corporations also buy insurance. Redundant systems, similar to a "belt-and-suspenders" combination, provide backups in case one part of the system fails. Do all that you can to prepare for disasters you cannot avoid.

Index

Note: Boldface numbers indicate illustrations; italic *t* indicates a table.